TEACHER AS STRANGER

EDUCATIONAL PHILOSOPHY FOR THE MODERN AGE

TEACHER AS STRANGER

EDUCATIONAL PHILOSOPHY FOR THE MODERN AGE

Maxine Greene

Teachers College, Columbia University

Wadsworth Publishing Company, Inc.
Belmont, California

Designer: Gary Head

Editor: Sandra Mangurian

Cover and text illustrator: Barbara Ravizza

ISBN: 0-534-00205-6

L. C. Cat. Card No.: 72-87809

Printed in the United States of America

1 2 3 4 5 6 7 8 9 10—77 76 75 74 73

This book is printed on recycled paper.

Beacon Press: for the excerpt from *The Trial of the Catonsville Nine* by Daniel Berrigan.
Reprinted by permission of Beacon Press.

Joan Daves: for the excerpt from "Letter from a Birmingham Jail" in *Why We Can't Wait* by
Martin Luther King, Jr. Copyright © 1963 by Martin Luther King, Jr. Reprinted by permission
of Joan Daves.

Faber and Faber Ltd.: for the excerpt from "Little Gidding" in *Collected Poems 1909–1962* by
T. S. Eliot and for the excerpt from "For the Union Dead" in *For the Union Dead* by Robert
Lowell. Reprinted by permission of Faber and Faber Ltd.

Farrar, Straus & Giroux, Inc.: for the excerpt from "For the Union Dead" in *For the Union Dead*
by Robert Lowell, copyright © 1960 by Robert Lowell. Reprinted by permission of Farrar, Straus
& Giroux, Inc.

Harcourt Brace Jovanovich, Inc.: for the excerpt from "Little Gidding" in *Four Quartets,* by T.
S. Eliot, copyright, 1942, 1943 by T. S. Eliot, renewed, 1970 by Esme Valerie Eliot. Reprinted
by permission of Harcourt Brace Jovanovich, Inc.

Harper & Row, Publishers: for the excerpt from "Letter from a Birmingham Jail" in *Why We
Can't Wait* by Martin Luther King, Jr., and for the excerpt from "The Doctrine of the Point of
View" in *The Modern Theme* by José Ortega y Gasset. Reprinted by permission of Harper & Row,
Publishers.

Houghton Mifflin Company: for the excerpt from "American Letter" in *New Found Land* by
Archibald MacLeish. Copyright 1930, 1952, Archibald MacLeish. Reprinted by permission
of Houghton Mifflin Company.

Alfred A. Knopf, Inc.: for the excerpt from "Six Significant Landscapes" in *The Collected Poems of Wallace Stevens*. Reprinted by permission of Alfred A. Knopf, Inc.

The Macmillan Company: for "Gratitude to the Unknown Instructors" in *The Collected Poems of W. B. Yeats*. Copyright 1933 by The Macmillan Company, renewed 1961 by Bertha Georgia Yeats. Reprinted by permission of The Macmillan Company.

The New Yorker: for the excerpt from *The New Yorker,* December 20, 1969. Reprinted by permission.

Laurence Pollinger Limited: for "Non-Existence" in *The Complete Poems of D. H. Lawrence*. Reprinted by permission of Laurence Pollinger Limited and the Estate of the late Mrs. Frieda Lawrence.

Random House, Inc.: for the excerpt from "The Unknown Citizen" in *Collected Shorter Poems 1927–1957* by W. H. Auden. Reprinted by permission of Random House, Inc.

University of California Press: for "Initiation" and "Torso of an Archaic Apollo" by Rainer Maria Rilke in *Rilke Selected Poems* trans. by C. F. MacIntyre. Originally published by the University of California. Reprinted by permission of The Regents of the University of California.

The Viking Press, Inc.: for "Non-Existence" in *The Complete Poems of D. H. Lawrence* ed. by Vivian de Sola Pinto and F. Warren Roberts. Copyright © 1964, 1971 by Angelo Ravagli and C. M. Weekley. All rights reserved. Reprinted by permission of The Viking Press, Inc.

A. P. Watt & Son: for "Gratitude to the Unknown Instructors" in *The Collected Poems of W. B. Yeats*. Reprinted by permission of Mr. M. B. Yeats, Macmillan & Co. Ltd., and the Macmillan Company of Canada Ltd.

A Note of Acknowledgment

I wish to thank my first and most memorable philosophy of education professor, George E. Axtelle, without whom none of this would have been possible. Also, I wish to express my appreciation to Richard Greenberg, who kept prodding and encouraging and sustaining until (against all expectations) this book was finally completed. He is gifted; he is generous; he is a very good friend. Lastly, I wish to say how grateful I am for the rigorous, elegant, and loving work done on my manuscript by Sandra Mangurian. She was not only an editor; she was a teacher. I am in her debt.

Maxine Greene

Preface

This book is specifically addressed to the teacher or teacher-to-be who is in the process of choosing as his "fundamental project" the activity of teaching in a classroom. The vantage point of the reader is conceived to be that of a person who is involved and responsible, someone who looks out on the educational landscape from inside a specifiable "form of life."

The reader is challenged to do philosophy, to take the risk of thinking about what he is doing when he teaches, what he means when he talks of enabling others to learn. He is asked to become progressively more self-conscious about the choices he makes and the commitments he defines in the several dimensions of his professional life. He is asked to look, if he can, at his presuppositions, to examine critically the principles underlying what he thinks and what he says. The assumption is made that he is, at some level, aware of the uncertainties afflicting American culture—of the attacks on existing institutions, the erosion of old authorities, the restless questioning of values. The widely reported "crisis" of belief has affected ways of thinking about human nature, knowledge getting and knowledge claims, moral decisions and moral standards; and no teacher can avoid the problems this crisis creates.

After the two initial chapters, the main body of the book is divided according to philosophic problem areas having to do with man, knowledge, and values. The philosophic treatment of each problem is prefaced by an overview of the contemporary dialogue with respect to the issue. The overviews are, quite naturally, devised by a writer who cannot escape her own biographical situation, her own location in the modern world. (The point is made throughout the book that "reality" is always mediated, that there is always a selective process at work when individuals attempt to point to what is "there.") The standpoint of the author is that of a person who was reared and educated in an urban environment, who has taught primarily in cities (in public as well as private institutions), and who derives at least part of her world picture from such publications as *The New York Times, Saturday Review, The Nation, The New Republic, The New Yorker, Harper's, Commentary, The New York Review of Books, Encounter,* as well as a great variety of academic journals. This is said to make clear the type of urban consciousness behind these pages, a consciousness which must be taken into account by readers trying to define their own, perhaps different, selves. In fact, this book will have been a failure if, after having read it, those with different backgrounds and orientations simply adopt or appropriate the selective vision they find presented here.

The objective of this book is to stimulate the reader to heightened self-consciousness and greater clarity. This is the reason why various points of view are discussed in each section. It is the reason why a certain disquietude is deliberately provoked, what John Dewey thought of as a sense of problem, what Albert Camus described as "rebellion" against the blankness of the sky. Only if the reader is moved to prove his own uncertainties, to ask his own painful (and perhaps unanswerable) questions, will he be moved to do philosophy. There is a sense in which this book ought to function as art functions: to confront the individual with himself; to stimulate a personal search for patterning and meaning; to open perspectives beyond the everyday—most particularly where teaching is concerned.

The overall orientation of this book is that of a phenomenological existentialist with considerable sympathy for aspects of pragmatism. No apology is offered for this. An attempt has been made to do justice to other ways of sense making, especially the ways associated with analytic philosophy. The author has defended against the temptation to slant, to argue, to debate; but she is entirely aware that total objectivity is impossible, that she cannot function as does James Joyce's "indifferent God . . . paring his nails." The tension so frequently identified in the chapters has been experienced—is still being experienced, now that the book is done. How *can* one act on one's commitment and at once set others free to be? This seems to us to be one of the crucial questions confronting the self-conscious teacher; it is the crucial question confronting the writer. Perhaps the responsibility, after all, belongs to the reader. He must launch himself on his own journey; he must choose to see through his own eyes.

Contents

TEACHER AS STRANGER

EDUCATIONAL PHILOSOPHY FOR THE MODERN AGE

Chapter One

Doing Philosophy and Building a World

> For a thought to change the world, it must first change the
> life of the man who carries it. It must become an example.
>
> Albert Camus
> *Notebook V, September 1945–April 1948*

> Philosophy is a battle against the bewitchment of our
> intelligence by means of language.
>
> Ludwig Wittgenstein
> *The Blue Book*

> Philosophy is thinking what the known demands of us—what
> responsive attitude it exacts. It is an idea of what is possible, not
> a record of accomplished fact.
>
> John Dewey
> *Democracy and Education*

Education, in one perspective, is a process of initiating young people
into the ways of thinking and behaving characteristic of the culture into
which they were born. In another perspective, it is the development of a
person from innocence to experience, from the confines of childish
immediacies to the open plains of conceptual thought. In still another, it is
the effort of a community to recreate itself with the rise of each new
generation and to perpetuate itself in historic time.

At first glance, the enterprise appears to be unquestionably valuable.
Enlightenment and growth, after all, are supremely worthwhile, as is the
preservation of a viable community's life. But education does not occur in
a vacuum; and the value of what educators intend or achieve is to some
degree a function of the contexts in which their work is done. If a given
culture is thought by many people to be deficient in fulfillments, is it truly

valuable to guide all the youth into membership? If the experiences associated with adulthood in the society are widely considered to be restrictive or meaningless, might it not be preferable to sustain innocence, to permit the flowering of "natural" and childish men? If the community is clearly unjust and inequitable, should not the educator be concerned primarily with social change? Why transmit a heritage conceived to be sterile or "sick"? Why keep a declining culture alive?

These are extreme questions, but they are not unrelated to the preoccupations of a teacher who is aware of and disturbed by current criticisms of American society.[1] If he takes those criticisms seriously, the teacher will perceive contradictions and ambiguities in conventional justifications of the work he does. Committed though he may be to the nurture of cognitive development, the encouragement of self-realization, or the promotion of citizenship, for example, he cannot help being affected by the doubts and uncertainties below the familiar surfaces of classroom and school. On the one hand, more is being asked of education than ever before in history; on the other hand, institutionalized education is being ·attacked for its inefficacy and is losing both legitimacy and support. Held accountable for failures in his classes, asked to come forth with a better product, to individualize, to become more immediately concerned, the teacher suddenly finds himself pulled in many directions. To whom is he responsible—the community, the administrators of the school, his students, his profession? And for what is he responsible?

Only through education, he is told, can people be equipped to deal with the contemporary environment, to contribute to the general welfare, to achieve good lives for themselves. Only through education can individuals be liberated for independent and critical thinking, to create meanings for themselves. Only through education can vocations be chosen and careers developed. Only through education can injustices be alleviated, national security protected, social progress guaranteed. If he permits it to do so, the rhetoric will bombard him wherever he goes. He will read it in the newspapers, hear it in the meeting rooms, even on the streets. Taxpayers complain; poor people protest; industry demands improved performance; students call for a voice in planning; government representatives impose norms.

Teachers react in a variety of ways. At times they screen out the scapegoating and the incessant challenges to what they are doing. Like beleaguered Hemingway heroes, they bite down hard and say, "It is better not to think about it." They concentrate on the daily routines, trying to be cool and disengaged, as functional and impersonal as machines. At other times the gap between what is asked for and what seems possible becomes so wide that they experience outrage or despair. They may then project their frustrations outward to the children or the young people in their classrooms by inventing self-fulfilling prophecies and resigning themselves to the likelihood that they and their students will fail. Most commonly, they behave like clerks, subjects of a remote authority that issues orders, supervises, and asks little more than conformity to custom, to the prevailing "law." They are powerless and they accede.

There are, clearly, manifold ways of adjusting—and manifold ways of refusing. Too many of them involve denials, evasions of confrontation. In self-protection, a teacher develops techniques for avoiding full consciousness; he postpones "real life" until the hours after school. After all, when one becomes self-conscious, one is present as a person in any situation; the mechanisms of denial and detachment do not work. One is compelled to put oneself and one's commitments on the line. New possibilities may be terrifying in the vistas they disclose. It is not easy to take one's authentic stance, to choose oneself as personally responsible. It is never easy to act upon what one—for good, defensible reasons—truly believes.

In education, one is easily tempted to accept slogans or precepts as truths. Teachers are continually bemused by metaphors linking children to flowers, the process of learning to blooming in the light of the sun. Or they are assuaged by the language of piety and righteousness, often having little to do with the way they feel. In Jonathan Kozol's *Death at an Early Age,* for example, there are instances of such language. In the inhumane ghetto schools Kozol describes, it is used to gloss over hopelessness and hatred. Consider the introduction to a Course of Study prepared by some teachers of children who are desperate, alienated, and poor:

> The classroom is the child's home for many hours each day. It is also his place of work. Therefore, the classroom should reflect the happiness, the protection, the loving guidance of the home, as well as the efficiency of the workshop. ... In addition to consideration for the physical welfare and intellectual advancement of the child, an atmosphere of culture must permeate the teaching scene.[2]

For all its familiarity to teachers in the urban slums, this extreme instance is not really remote from the ceremonial language customarily used to describe what is desired for the "average" child. The detached or discouraged teacher is in danger of being lulled to a kind of intellectual sleep by such language. He is likely to "go stupid," as do some of the children John Holt describes in *How Children Fail.* He is likely, in other

words, not to "get it" when a student says something tentatively or
obliquely; he is likely to miss the signs that indicate vague explorations or
incoherent beginnings of inquiry. The consequence can only be a kind of
boredom with what he is doing. Nothing is less rewarding for the person
eager to feel alive.

In her prologue to *The Human Condition,* Hannah Arendt points out
that one of the distinctive traits of our time is a "heedless recklessness or
hopeless confusion or complacent repetition of 'truths' which have become
trivial and empty. . . . "[3] This is well known to those who teach in
American schools. Most of the time the sources are perplexity and lack of
confidence rather than ignorance; but along with the denials that are so
prevalent, they are indications that reconsiderations are needed. They
might well be reconsiderations of the educational process from (as Arendt
puts it) "the vantage point of our newest experience and our most recent
fears." She makes what she calls a simple proposal, worth attending to by
the teacher who wants to be himself and to achieve something meaningful
in the world. The proposal "is nothing more than to think what we are
doing."

Obviously, the teacher thinks what he is doing a good deal of the
time; but Arendt has something distinctive in mind, something that relates
directly to "our newest experience and our most recent fears." She is
talking *philosophically* about what we are doing. And, indeed, this is our
focal concern in the following chapters. The "we" refers to individuals
engaged or planning to be engaged in some educational activity, within or
outside the schools. (The "he," we would add, refers to the teacher as
person, man *or* woman, in the absence of a pronoun referring to both.)
The interest dominating this book is in the possibility of arousing
individuals to wide-awakeness, to "thinking" in Arendt's sense about their
own commitments and actions wherever they work and make their lives.
In other words, we shall attempt to do philosophy with respect to
teaching, learning, the aims and policies of education, the choices to be
made in classrooms, the goods to be pursued.

Many philosophers now agree that the term *philosophy* does not refer
to a distinctive structure of knowledge, as *history* or *biology* does. Indeed,
it is difficult for philosophers to claim that they offer substantive
knowledge of any sort. The student, of course, can come to know a good
deal about what philosophers have thought in the past and what they are
writing now. He can become acquainted with the ways in which
philosophic subject matter has been divided and categorized; and he can
become informed about the types of problems with which philosophers of
diverse schools dealt. But this is quite different from saying that
philosophic thinking will enable a teacher finally to know what is best and

most desirable in teaching situations or that it will lead him to some sort of truth about education or the ways in which certain kinds of teaching equip the young to learn how to learn.

Philosophy may be regarded as a way of approaching (or looking at or taking a stance with respect to) the knowledge gained by the natural and human sciences, the awarenesses made possible by the arts, and the personal insights into existence each human being accumulates as he lives. Philosophy is a way of framing distinctive sorts of questions having to do with what is presupposed, perceived, intuited, believed, and known. It is a way of contemplating, examining, or thinking about what is taken to be significant, valuable, beautiful, worthy of commitment. It is a way of becoming self-aware, of constituting meanings in one's life-world. Critical thinking is demanded, as are deliberate attempts to make things clear. Efforts to explore background consciousness may be involved, as may explorations of boundaries and the creation of unifying perspectives. There may be normative thinking as well: the probing of what might be, what should be; the forging of ideals. To do philosophy, then, is to become highly conscious of the phenomena and events in the world as it presents itself to consciousness. To do philosophy, as Jean-Paul Sartre says, is to develop a fundamental project, to go beyond the situations one confronts and refuse reality as given in the name of a reality to be produced.

Educational philosophy is a matter of doing philosophy with respect to the educational enterprise as it engages the educator—doing it from his vantage point as actor and from the vantage point of his newest experience and his most recent fears. To do educational philosophy is to become critically conscious of what is involved in the complex business of teaching and learning. It is to clarify the meanings of education (and training, instructing, conditioning, and teaching), of such terms and phrases as *behavioral objectives, acculturation, citizenship, nurturing growth, stimulating conceptual development.* It is to become clear as well about the preferences with respect to "good" and "right" which motivate pressure groups, bureaucrats, community representatives, and parents when they make demands of the schools. What teacher today can ignore the contesting notions of relevancy, appropriateness, value? What teacher can escape the challenges and complexities of decision making in the midst of a not-always-friendly world? If he can learn to do philosophy, he may liberate himself for understanding and for choosing. He may liberate himself for reflective action as someone who knows who he is as a historical being, acting on his freedom, trying each day to *be.*

This can be a tonic and fulfilling enterprise for the individual daring to perceive himself in the midst of things. The person with the courage to undertake it is no longer content to be a mere cipher, a functionary, a clerk.

No matter what his relation to power, he desires to be the kind of person who trusts his perceptions, who ponders and takes a stand. Like Ralph Ellison's narrator in *Invisible Man,* he wants to "condemn and affirm, say no and say yes, say yes and say no." He wants to conceive a plan of living for himself which does not "lose sight of the chaos against which that pattern was conceived." We take the term *chaos* to signify not only the remembered inchoateness of what has seemed incomprehensible in earlier days, not only the teacher's uncertainty respecting who he is and what he can do. We take it also to mean the huge disorder of our day where values, beliefs, aspirations, and ideals are concerned. The teacher can no longer simply accept what is transmitted by "experts" and feel he is properly equipped to interpret the world. He cannot even rely on the authority of accumulated knowledge or the conventional wisdom on which so many people depend. He must make decisions of principle, which may make necessary a definition of *new* principles, more relevant norms and rules. Therefore, he must become accustomed to unconventional presentations of situations around him, to ways of talking with which textbooks cannot deal. Only if he breaks with fixed, customary modes of seeing can he remove the blinders of complacency. Only then can he take responsibility for his pursuits of norms and meanings. Naturally, he is a function of a culture—a member of various social groups, participating in their orientations. But he is also a unique person with his own biographical standpoint. He must become aware of this uniqueness and of his capacity to unify what constitutes the "sub-universes of meaning" in his life; he must take action to pattern his world.

Why not accommodate to the patterns that exist? Why can he not simply observe and catalog what takes place? Only an infant can look on the world with anything approximating receptive or "innocent" eyes. Even before he begins speaking, the infant begins ordering what he perceives. Once he is old enough to use a language and to symbolize reality, the child cannot help imposing several kinds of order on the buzzing, booming confusion of things. The configurations *he* has created as well as those he has appropriated though learning are bound to mediate everything he perceives from then on. As long as he continues to learn, he categorizes objects and events under more and more diverse rubrics. The more he expands and varies the perspectives through which he looks on his world, the more rational he becomes; the more he "knows." The subject matters he studies, the art experiences he enjoys, the "recipes" provided by the culture all supplement his commonsense discoveries, his perceptual awareness, his personal knowledge. If he is fortunate, he will build a many-faceted stock of knowledge, a multiplicity of constructs he can use to order his experience. To the degree he does this, his perspectives will diversify; and he will find himself living in a progressively more meaningful world.

When he reaches out to question what surrounds him, therefore, the teacher must look (and try to become aware of looking) from many vantage points. He should not limit himself to the technological view and should not be content with a predominantly noncognitive or intuitive view. He is not required to choose himself as a predominantly rational man *or* a sensuous man; an objectivist *or* a subjectivist; an activist *or* a quietist. In a multifarious culture, no single schema or category can be sufficient for organizing the flux of reality. Abstractions—racist, blue-collar, capitalist, dissenter, politician—inevitably obscure the existence of particular persons with their ambivalences, their hopes, their fears. Relying totally on the concrete and specific, the participant or the observer will be unable to effect connections, see resemblances, generalize, explain. To take a statistical view only leads to depersonalization. To deal emotively with occurrences makes judgment next to impossible. In any case, to identify oneself with a one-dimensional view is always to deny a part of one's humanity. It takes at least what the poet William Blake once described as a fourfold vision—derived from feeling, sensation, and intuition as well as mind—to encompass one's experience adequately and humanly.

Looking at the pluralist society within the United States and then looking outward to the innumerable distinctive ways of life in the world, we cannot help being reminded of the necessity for a type of cultural relativism, of the importance of realizing that multiple ways of seeing the world exist. More than any other students of human existence, anthropologists make this need clear. Their studies of different cultures throughout the world have shown the multiplex ways in which men codify their reality and the ways in which perceived reality depends in each case on the codification involved. Few teachers are unfamiliar with the work reported in Ruth Benedict's *Patterns of Culture* or with the diverse cultural forms among the Pueblo Indians, the Dobu Islanders, the Dionysian tribes along the Northwest Coast. Most teachers are acquainted with Margaret Mead's *Coming of Age in Samoa* and her later, openhearted introductions to such people as the Arapesh with their sense of timelessness and all-prevailing custom, the New Guineans who manage to maintain a sense of changeless identity within a framework of continuous interchange, and the Scandinavians who came to Minnesota and continued their familiar way of life in a totally strange land. Each culture has its recognizable identity; and each is ordered by particular constructs—myths, fictions, patterns of belief. The *meaning* of each culture is a function of the way its members think about reality, symbolize it, describe it; and people exist within and by means of the codifications that develop over time. Dorothy Lee, for instance, describes the Trobriand Islanders' apprehension of reality and shows how their language makes it impossible to speak of lineal connections between events or objects. Where "valued activity is concerned, the Trobrianders do not act on an assumption of lineality at any level. There is organization or rather coherence in their acts because Trobriand activity is patterned activity. One act within this pattern brings into existence a pre-ordained cluster of acts."[4] Their lives have no climaxes; past and future both exist in the present. They do not follow *lines* of thought; they do not *bridge* gaps nor *draw* conclusions. Because reality depends on the way one mediates or codifies the world, Trobriand reality is nonlineal. The implication is not that the Trobrianders (or the Papuans or the Hopi or the Arapesh) are in some manner retarded, "primitive" in the old pejorative sense. In *The Savage Mind,* Claude Lévi-Strauss says that "the thought we call primitive" is, like the sciences, founded on "a demand for order." In fact, as he sees it, savage thought must be thought of "as a system of concepts embedded in images."

The point is that reality does not exist for anyone as given, as independently *there.* It is encountered by means of the patterns of thinking, feeling, imaging, which distinguish particular languages and cultures. To do philosophy, the teacher who wishes to be fully conscious must confront this contingency of the real. He must become aware of how his consciousness intends—or *grasps*—the world he inhabits. He must become equally sensitive to the process of patterning and to the methods or protocols each kind of structure demands of him. The difference between his thought and "primitive" thought is largely the relative one-dimensionality of primitive orders. Unlike an islander or a tribesman in the bush, sealed from the contemporary world, the teacher has access to a great range of perspectives, which he is unlikely to confuse (if he thinks about them) with "reality-in-itself." Unlike the individual in a more ritualized, closed culture, the teacher is free to stand off and look at orthodoxies and sacred writs, just as he is free to see how the conventions of his language limit and enclose his world. Most important, the teacher can become self-conscious about his role in the sense-making process. If he recognizes this role, he will have intensely personal reasons for clearing up ambiguities and for raising questions about what "reality" means, what "truth" means, what "the good" implies. Then, of course, the teacher is primed to do philosophy.

As we have said, we do not philosophize to answer factual questions, establish guidelines for our behavior, or enhance our aesthetic awareness. We philosophize when, for some reason, we are aroused to wonder about how events and experiences are interpreted and should be interpreted. We philosophize when we can no longer tolerate the splits and fragmentations in our pictures of the world, when we desire some kind of wholeness and integration, some coherence which is our own.

To be stirred thus, we need wide-awake involvements with the surrounding world, with other human beings, with the community at large. To be closed away because of snobbery, ignorance, or fear is to be deprived of the content that makes concepts meaningful. It is, as well, to be deprived of the very ground of questioning. For this reason, the teacher who dares to do philosophy must be open to such a multiplicity of realities. He cannot do so if he cannot perceive himself, in both his freedom and his limitations, as someone who must constitute his *own* meanings with the aid of what his culture provides. Nor can he do so if he is incapable of "bracketing," or setting aside, on occasion the presuppositions that fix his vision of the world.

The teacher must probe, therefore, and try to understand what impinges on him in the everyday: the messages of the media; the impact of the crowded streets; the atmosphere of shopping centers, government bureaus, schools; the privacy of his home. If he can write down some of what he perceives each day, so much the better. If not, he can still look closely at his responses to what Marshall McLuhan has called the simultaneity of events, the bombardment of information which makes it so hard to distinguish foreground from background, fantasy from fact. He can try to deal directly with the protective numbness shielding him from the images of suffering on his television set and from the instances of suffering on the street. Like his students, the teacher cannot help living much of the time in a world others prefabricate for what they consider to be the public. On occasion, he must be critically attentive; he must consciously choose what to appropriate and what to discard. Reliance on the natural attitude—a commonsense taking for granted of the everyday—will not suffice. In some fashion, the everyday must be rendered problematic so that questions may be posed.

Of course, numerous patterns are alternative to and in tension with those imposed by common sense or by the media. As we touch on some of them to suggest the range of potential vantage points, we do not intend to project a hierarchical arrangement of constructs or realms of meaning. Because we start off with references to art forms, we do not necessarily consider the arts either "higher" or "lower" than the sciences, practical undertakings, or philosophy. We are concerned with the teacher as a human being who generates a variety of symbolic structures so that he (as he expects his students to do) can look from different angles on his life-world. *Within* each domain or discipline, there may well be a development from fundamental principles to concepts of increasing

complexity; but we do not choose to arrange our subject matters according
to any scale of value or profundity. We are not, as we will make clear,
thinking of analogues to some great chain of being or to any of the
pyramidal designs of time past.

We turn, then, somewhat arbitrarily to modern artists—painters,
sculptors, film makers, literary men. Graphic artists today frequently
render experience through the use of collage or machinelike construction.
Or they communicate by means of pop images, selections from the banal
surfaces of a commercialized society—abstracted, magnified, sometimes
repeated ad infinitum until significance drains away (like Andy Warhol's
soup can or electric chair). Or they render what they perceive to be reality
by tensely applying daubs of color, drawing spare, minimal bars in empty
space, letting paint explode in whorls. They create surreal or "magic"
images, suggesting ambiguous, private feelings or the by-products of
haunted dreams. Or they present no images at all but only words *about*
art, ditches opened up in desert places, sheets thrown over cliffs. Where
realism (or inhumanism) exists, it is often posterlike, depersonalized, cold.
Rarely do we find the photographic representations of familiar landscapes
and composed faces we used to admire years ago, or the communal
symbolism that made the visual arts a unifying force in earlier times.[5]
Because the symbolisms now being devised strike so many people as
esoteric or ugly or "sick," mass audiences tend to reject the "avant-garde."
Yet the new works, technically daring as many are, anxious and
indefinable as they are felt to be, are important indicators of how great
numbers of skilled, sensitive human beings form their feelings about the
universe today. Whether their presentations are harbingers of the future or
strange messages from some nether world, they demand noticing,
especially by those struggling to find their idiom and make their authentic
sense. By tampering with inherited conventions, questioning the very idea
of art, painters and sculptors are forcing us to examine our own
preconceptions and expectations. Deliberately shocking the straitlaced and
closeminded, these modern artists are at least as important to the meaning
of our culture as are the ones they alienate. The beholder who knows how
to absorb, how to move with new materials and forms, is bound to
discover something new about his encounters with reality.

Imaginative writers are wont to disturb in the same manner, although
the medium of language is more resistant to experiment than the multiple
media presently used by graphic artists, "destructivists," "funk artists,"
"minimalists," "earth artists," and the rest. Yet writers too are
demonstrating that the traditional styles and techniques are sterile and
dysfunctional in the altered modern world. Many have become painfully
aware of the discrepancies between scientific descriptions and human

perceptions. They are conscious of how the shape, tone, and import of reality depend not only on the imagination of the beholder but on his technical means. At the same time, they are conscious of the insufficiency of language when it comes to describing their perception of reality. How are silence and pure contingency to be communicated? In *End of the Road,* for example, John Barth talks of "the raggedness of things," the unexpected accidents in life which no advance "script" can encompass or explain. In that novel, Jake Horner tries to cope with the "weatherlessness" of his life by assigning roles to himself and to others, by treating what happens around him as a drama with a predefined plot. The trouble is that human beings will not do what their assigned roles demand: the rational man will, on occasion, behave like a sensualist and a fool; the man who cannot feel or choose will find himself loving and hating another man's wife. When Rennie, the wife, becomes pregnant, it seems a simple thing to arrange an abortion. Who could predict that because she ate too large a lunch, she would choke to death in the Treatment Room? "Lord," muses the narrator, "the raggedness of it; the incompleteness!" The novel form, even language itself can only falsify; writing about life, talking about it are a "betrayal of experience." Like Jake Horner, the modern artist realizes this and at the same time knows that only when he *does* articulate what happens can he deal with life; only then does he feel (like Jake Horner) "alive and kicking."

How is innerness to be presented now that we are aware of the masks we wear, the roles we play? Like the painters and sculptors who explore inner and outer boundaries, the writers experiment as much as they can with their medium. Because the meanings of literary works emerge from an interplay between language and design, the content of contemporary writing often suggests that the time-honored modes of sense making are no longer sufficient for those committed to express their feelings in words.

What is this age as they present it? For numerous writers it is one dominated by a version of what Joseph Heller calls "Catch-22." (" 'Catch-22', the old woman repeated, rocking her head up and down. 'Catch-22. Catch-22 says they have a right to do anything we can't stop them from doing.' "[6]) Depersonalization, powerlessness, indifference, and hierarchical systems of control afflict writer after writer. Society is experienced as "a slick, streamlined setup," quite devoid of any "place for erratic behavior."[7] In rejecting slickness and sterility, authors create fictional characters who cultivate the erratic, the perverse, the wildly sensual. Sometimes such characters plunge into subterranean realms of nightmare, addiction, or fearful crime, all to the end of feeling alive, feeling their singularity in a nonhuman, overly organized world. At other times, as in Edward Albee's play *Who's Afraid of Virginia Woolf?,* they accede to living by illusion and treating social life as if it were a round of brutal children's games. Many are invisible in Ellison's sense; many are brutalized; some take precarious refuge in withdrawals, drug experiences, mysticism, flight. A few writers, like Bernard Malamud in *The Fixer* and Saul Bellow in *Herzog,* strive to invent new embodiments of dignity and self-transcendence. They, too, as the fictional Moses Herzog puts it, recognize "the obsessions, the compulsions of collectivity." But they are moved to affirm, in whatever way they can: "We must get it out of our heads that this is a doomed time, that we are waiting for the end, and the rest of it."[8]

We might have difficulty agreeing with such an affirmation, however, if we contemplate the powerlessness and discouragement in our society, the sporadic violence, the dreary injustices that persist. If we realize the degree of intersubjective agreement among expressive artists who ponder the human plight today, we may experience a feeling of absurdity, as more and more writers break with conventions like the well-made plot and the sense of an ending. Thomas Pynchon's *V,* the strange account of an odyssey through an automated world, insists on the absurdity of most of our human orderings—heroism, myth, and history. Donald Barthelme's novels and short stories stem from a sense of the provisional character of our lives and play games with time, space, fact, and probability. Kurt Vonnegut, Richard Brautigan, Ken Kesey, John Updike, John Hawkes, Joan Didion, Norman Mailer, John Barth, and numerous others stress, in their idiosyncratic ways, that our traditional standards have been shattered irreparably. The darkness bears down, they are saying, with the ice and the filing cabinets and the abstractness of what Albert Camus calls the "plague." And the response? Not heroic resistance; not a stunning revelation of man's fate. Survival in asylums, in bars, or in outer space; escape to the woods or to Mexico; role playing, encounter groups, intoxication, terrorism—and, occasionally, whispered assertions of rebellion and love.

Not surprisingly, the films most popular with young people create similar imaginary worlds. Some years ago, *Bonnie and Clyde* imaged a land so sterile and uncaring that the violent crimes committed by Bonnie Parker and Clyde Barrow took on an appealing glamour for young audiences. Moral judgments were transvalued; most people condemned the local sheriff for finally murdering the runaway pair. *The Graduate,* which many hailed as the first youth culture film, renders the brittle surfaces of middle-class existence, where the sounds of silence drown out communication, the world of work is summed up as plastic, and the young are either objects or victims—unless they can ride off (purposelessly, mockingly) down the empty road. Since, there has been *Easy Rider,* with its rendering of the American Dream gone rotten and corrupt. In an exemplary American journey, "Billy the Kid" and "Wyatt Earp" (financed by a sale of cocaine at the Mexican border), ride fabulous motorcycles toward a latter-day Heavenly City, New Orleans at Mardi Gras. The film evokes Huckleberry Finn's journey to "the territory ahead" and Huck's entrapments in evil little towns. The landscape is still grand and spacious; but, in addition to open ranches and hippie communes, there are places where passing riders are jailed and given haircuts with rusty shears. The journey ends in an LSD trip in an Indian graveyard and, soon afterward, in death. Few people who saw the movie can forget Wyatt's flat "we blew it. . . ." just before they are so pointlessly murdered on the road. They "blew" the historical search, the experiment with freedom, their effort to realize the Dream. The young who crowded in to see the film recognized the implication. They were no more shocked by the statement than they were by the fact that the two antiheroes financed their trip by selling drugs to the Mafia. Such a reaction says something about the consciousness of young people, which no teacher can afford to ignore. Obviously, we do not mean all American students in all age groups. Neither do we mean that *Easy Rider* is unquestionably a work of art. However, aware that such films have become the most significant art forms for the new generation, aware of the number of film makers who have made movies to appeal explicitly to youth, we cannot underestimate the clues.

We might also recall *Five Easy Pieces,* with its appalling rendition of an alienated "stranger" against the majestic West Coast landscape, as well as the perverse sentimentality of *Midnight Cowboy,* with its rendering of the underside of urban life. There was *Woodstock,* too, with its premature annunciation of Charles Reich's "greening"; and there was *Gimme Shelter* not long afterward, presenting a rock festival in Altamont, California, where drugs and violence together once again bury the dream of sweet communion. The so-called "cult pictures," such as *2001: A Space Odyssey, El Topo,* and *A Clockwork Orange,* may well reveal how certain young people perceive breakthroughs of consciousness and technology, how they tune in to Gothic visions, how (more seriously) they think of the future— which, for them, is more dehumanizing than any time in the past. Indeed, *Love Story, The Last Picture Show,* and other more reassuring cinema fictions may have a greater appeal. The proliferation of pornographic and violent films may be of no consequence. But we should not ignore the melancholy excitement that the more disturbing movies cause, the lines that form and form again outside the "art" theaters. The films suggest something of how young people interpret the age in which they live. They are also modes of patterning, of codifying; and individuals who have grown up with them cannot help encompassing the visions they provide in efforts to make sense of the world.

The teacher should at least be acquainted with the movies of his day.

No matter what his estimate of them, he must understand (and try to help his students understand) that they are not instances of photographed reality; they are not empirically "true." For all their immediacy and impact, the individual must not confuse them with documents or see them as keys to the nature of things. Like novels, poems, paintings, they tap realms of *imaginative* possibility; if they are works of art, they embody their makers' visions of the world. They offer alternative ways of structuring experience, as dreams and other kinds of imaging do. Engaging with them, the individual gains no factual information. If he is fortunate and knows what stance to take and how to look, he may well see facets of his own experience afresh; he may even reevaluate some of his knowledge. He may be moved to ask the kinds of questions about his condition basic to self-consciousness: questions relating to certain themes in his biography and therefore stimulating more far-reaching questions, such as those involved in philosophy.

If he is willing to open himself to works of art as a subjectively aware human being, the teacher can do much to help young people articulate what works of art have made them think and feel. Much can be done, in discussions of art, to help young people appreciate the importance of style and technique in the expressive process. The function of art, as Joseph Conrad once said, is to make people *see.* What they see and how they see are greatly dependent on the way the materials of a given work are formed. Under the guidance of form, those who read or look or listen attentively can create new orders within themselves. Doing so, they are likely to discover new meanings, unsuspected angles of vision; they may discover original perceptions of what it is like to be alive, "themes of relevance" against which students can pose worthwhile questions.

Such discoveries cannot substitute for intelligent understanding of phenomena, however, although they may provide a grounding for it. The same must be said about "noncognitive" and "affective" awareness in general, which some educators today have made equivalent or even superior to conceptual knowing. Nondiscursive insights are clearly valuable. They may heighten motivation because of the way they order the inner world. But they are not sufficient to equip human beings for effective functioning in today's society or for transforming what is given "in the name of a reality to be produced."

The teacher ought to realize this profoundly enough to treat his cognitive learnings as existentially significant, just as he treats his encounters with the works of art he cherishes and the personal knowledge he gains. Only if he succeeds in treating his subject matter as a potential means of expanding his vision of things will he be able to communicate what it means for other persons to launch cognitive quests. To generate, on one's initiative, the structure of a discipline such as history (or physics or sociology) is to achieve a type of liberation because one transcends one's limits in doing so; one breaches boundaries, breaks through walls. Just as a creative artist provides new perspectives by the way he forms and embodies his experience, so does a historian or a physicist enable a learner to see differently by appropriating the norms of a particular discipline.

In later chapters, we shall discuss how philosophers look at the question of mastery. At this point, we wish mainly to draw attention to the teacher's opportunity to engage with the world by means of the variety of cognitive structures available to him. If he can treat these structures as resources for personal sense making, as potential perspectives to be brought into reciprocal relationship, the teacher will become far more sensitive to the connections between conceptual learning and the individual's progressive patterning of the world. At the same time, he may become more critically aware of the paradigms he uses to pattern his existence and give it meaning and worth.

A paradigm is a standard, or some exemplary device, for giving significance to life. In the language we have already used, the function of this symbolic structure is to organize experience in various domains. But paradigms also play a part in the history of thought and the development of particular disciplines; and the teacher attempting to diversify his perspectives should be clear about the standards or guides *he* chooses to use. Without such an awareness, he will have difficulty achieving the wholeness he presumably desires, to bring his disparate vantage points into relationship, to develop a standpoint which is authentically his.

Thomas Kuhn, writing about "scientific revolution" and the emergence of new scientific theories, sees scientific paradigms as "accepted examples of actual scientific practice—examples which include law, theory, application, and instrumentation together—[which] provide models from which spring particular coherent traditions of scientific research."[9] For instance, the practice long associated with "classical" or Newtonian physics provided generations of scientists with a language, a methodology, and a set of standards or norms. In the 1920s, a number of physicists, realizing that Newtonian accounts of the structure of the atom no longer applied to their discoveries, had to reject the familiar paradigm and search for a new language and a new conceptual apparatus. "We are in much the same position," suggested Niels Bohr at the time, "as a sailor, marooned on a remote island where conditions differ radically from anything he has known and where, to make things worse, the natives speak a completely alien tongue."[10] They could only keep experimenting in the hope that "in due course, new concepts will emerge which may somehow help us to grasp these inexpressible processes in the atom."

Surely analogues exist for the individual learner, as he gradually comes to grasp the previously inexpressible processes in the various domains of his life. Concerning his knowledge of the natural world, for example, he undoubtedly grew up with certain paradigms, which permitted him to make sense of the earth and the planets in relation to the sun. More than likely, he imagined man's universe to exist in absolute space and time. When, later on, he heard about an expanding universe or the beginnings of space travel or, say, the electron microscope, he had no way of understanding because he had in mind the orderly, balanced universe of "normal science." Because of the paradigm he still used, he expected that he could visualize cosmic reality; he probably thought of the world within the electron to be a microcosm of the planetary world, which he could easily describe in words. So, too, he might have felt like a marooned sailor with respect to atomic physics and the mathematical notations now used to interpret physical reality; he, too, would find what was happening "inexpressible." Engaging himself in the study of modern physics, he would become cognizant of the need to break with the familiar paradigm, reassuring as it was; and he would gradually begin to master and make use of the concepts Bohr, Werner Heisenberg, and Albert Einstein once had to invent, to extend and revise *his* notions of reality. Likewise, in his study of history, the learner would learn to give up his "normal" ideas respecting the determinate role of statesmen and generals, or his ideas respecting design. In the study of economics, he might find the incidence of poverty or inflation incompatible with a "market mechanism" paradigm. The point is that the learning enterprise also engages an individual with multiple realities; and if teacher and student are aware of this and of the paradigms that make it possible to see differently, both may recognize the central role of the patterning process in orienting the self in the world.

To move from one reality to another is to experience a jolt, which reminds the individual of his *presence* as a perceiving consciousness. The teacher today must confront not only paradigms that alter over time but also contesting, yet coexisting, paradigms in certain subject matter areas. In history, for example, some individuals believe that they can write objective accounts of past occurrences and, simultaneously, "contribute directly to the understanding and explanation of current affairs."[11] Others find that this approach lacks rigor, and they choose to concentrate on disclosing the complexity in motives, interest, and behavior at specific moments in history. Not concerned with promoting liberal and democratic reforms, as are the pragmatic historians, they have been called consensus historians, appealing primarily to conservatives. There are scientific historians, historians concerned to apply the concepts of political science or economic or ecology, historians who believe "that the fundamental thing is the dialogue between the historian and his material leading to the establishment of narrative accounts within a time dimension of the major human experiences of the past."[12] There are individuals who demand a "New History . . . [a] radical re-creation of the forms of human culture,"[13] and those who want to concentrate on the lives of ordinary people and minority groups—to do history "from the ground up."[14] Each approach has developed a characteristic methodology; each works according to a particular set of norms.

The same is true of economics, which the teacher must inevitably engage in if he is to clarify his thinking about "the system," "the technological society," "the growth mania," or "the New Industrial State." As in the case of constructs in general, economists' pictures of reality vary with the methods they use. Certain economists use purely analytic techniques to study problems of maximizing resources; they pay little, if any, attention to priorities and goals. Others are concerned with policy making and use their expertise to promote economic growth. Still others concentrate on the consequences of military domination in American life or on taxation or on the role of corporate structures. Some radical economists talk of the need to disperse economic power and alter the institutional frameworks in such a way as to remedy poverty, halt pollution, resolve urban conflicts. They demand a "reconstruction of economics—a new synthesis and a new paradigm," which moves toward "greater concern for humane values, toward a humane economy on a worldwide scale."[15]

Kindred things are happening in sociology. Diverse constructs are used in the study of cultures and institutions: some speak of systems, others of classes, others of structures; a few stress the social construction of reality. Here, too, radical challenges exist. For example, Alvin Gouldner, objecting to academic sociologists' denial of any responsibility to make a better world, says that a value-free conception of the social sciences is a way of accommodating to an insufficient society: "within such a value-free conception, sociologists are allowed to say that it is not their task to restore the equilibrium between power and goodness, thus permitting them to accommodate to a power that they themselves may deem of dubious morality."[16] Like other behavioral scientists today, Gouldner would have the sociologist take his standpoint into account. He calls on his colleagues to become self-aware and reminds his readers that what they are taught to conceive as real is contingent upon a way of knowing, a way of seeing, a location in historical time.

In later chapters, we shall explore similar crucial disagreements among psychologists, ethnologists, and others concerning paradigms and methods of inquiry. Throughout, we shall keep in mind the many differing models of the educational process, which underlie so much of educational controversy. With respect to all the fields of study, including education, we shall be concerned with the possibility of looking from many vantage points, checking conceptual formulations against personal visions and perspectives opened up by the disciplines. We shall be concerned with the teacher's becoming more and more self-conscious about the manifold schemata he needs to interpret modern life, more responsible in the choices he makes among the available paradigms—that is, in deciding how to see.

There is a loss of anchorage in our society. Even in the academic world, there are few enduring norms. The teacher can only try to find out how to think about what is happening around him and, after that, how to think what he is doing in the crisis-ridden world. How is he to make reasonable sense of the hydra-headed culture into which he is asked to initiate the young? How is he to move his students from spontaneity to systematic thinking, without forcing them to lose touch with their existential reality, their feeling of being *present* in the world? How is he to avoid manipulations, to deal with strategies of control? How is he to launch the slow and the apathetic into a search for meaning? How is he to liberate the outraged and the gifted to transform what they cannot endure? How is he to justify intervening in so many lives? How is he to justify his own project—his efforts to involve himself, to *be?*

At one time, the teacher might have been told to turn to the educational philosopher for answers to such questions. The philosopher considered himself in a position to speak prescriptively, to tell uncertain practitioners what they ought to do and what the aims of education ought to be. As we will see in the next chapter, the view that philosophy was a superior type of science once justified "telling" in this manner. Philosophers were thought to possess a privileged awareness of Truth and Goodness, of what the human being ought to do and be. Moreover, they were thought capable of constructing great systems of thought, inclusive world pictures that transcended individual perceptions and personal responses to being alive. Educational philosophers were understandably inclined to draw implications for education from such bodies of thought. In the implications of Idealism implied (or Realism or Materialism or Pragmatism), they discovered guides for the practicing teacher or for those assigned to determine educational aims.

Today there are no guides; there is no higher wisdom to be tapped. Yet there are clues to be found by the individual eager to clarify educational concepts and issues. There are vantage points to be taken by the person concerned to gain insight into his situation as an educator in the midst of a problematic world. Of course, it is useful to find out what philosophers of different orientations have said and how they have thought about such problems as the nature of man, knowledge, truth, reality, value, and all the other perplexities the sciences can never resolve. But the point of finding out is to learn how to engage in philosophic activity oneself. The point of finding out is to learn how to confront educational contexts with a sense of responsibility—with a capacity to clarify, to order, to disclose. But it begins in wonder; philosophy always begins in wonder. The individual must be moved to ask questions about the universe, to engage in dialogue with himself about the world as it impinges on him and about the explanations others provide. He must stand, if he dares, in "the wind of thought," examining doctrines and opinions and preconceptions. He must realize his thinking in judgments, in *praxis,* particularly if he is a teacher concerned with discovering what the known demands.

In philosophic questioning, we continually ask what the known demands of the teacher. What follows—for *action*—from a consideration of competing images of man? What is entailed by current understanding of thinking, knowing, believing, abiding by norms and rules? What is demanded of the teacher who confronts the disintegration of cultural norms, the arbitrariness of value claims, the doubts respecting free will? The individual must continually struggle to clarify, to pattern (without losing sight of "the chaos against which that pattern was conceived"). And he must recognize the multiplicity of options to be confronted, the difficult choices constantly to be made.

In *Confessions of a Disloyal European,* Jan Myrdal talks of the necessity for the individual to develop insight into his situation and writes of the dangers of "brainwashing," which every teacher and teacher-to-be knows well. But then he reminds his reader that "no brainwashing can ever be complete" and that a person must "see himself from the outside just for a moment." After that, "maybe his consciousness can take over and make a human being out of him before the insane normality of our Western culture once more mechanizes him."[17] And, indeed, one of the objectives of this book is to enable the reader to let his consciousness take over, to enable him—in the face of mechanization and controls—to create himself as a human being, as a teacher capable of freeing other human beings to choose themselves.

Notes and References

1. As examples, see the following:
   General: William Braden, *The Age of Aquarius* (Chicago: Quadrangle Books, 1970); Charles Reich, *The Greening of America* (New York: Random House,

1970); Philip Slater, *The Pursuit of Loneliness* (Boston: Beacon Press, 1970); Alvin Toffler, *Future Shock* (New York: Random House, 1970).

Youth Problems, Value Change, and Dissent: Daniel Berrigan and Robert Coles, *The Geography of Faith* (Boston: Beacon Press, 1971); Noam Chomsky, *American Power and the New Mandarins* (New York: Pantheon Books, 1969); Erik H. Erikson, *Identity: Youth and Crisis* (New York: W. W. Norton & Company, 1968); Erving Goffman, *Relations in Public* (New York: Basic Books, 1972); Paul Goodman, *Growing Up Absurd* (New York: Vintage Books, 1962); Francine Gray, *Divine Disobedience* (New York: Vintage Books, 1971); Jules Henry, *Culture Against Man* (New York: Random House, 1963); Kenneth Keniston, *Young Radicals* (New York: Harcourt Brace Jovanovich, 1968); Margaret Mead, *Culture and Commitment* (Garden City, N.Y.: Natural History Press, Doubleday & Company, 1970); Jack Newfield, *A Prophetic Minority* (New York: New American Library, 1966); Theodore Roszak, ed., *The Dissenting Academy* (New York: Pantheon Books, 1968); Roszak, *The Making of a Counter Culture* (Garden City, N.Y.: Doubleday Anchor Books, 1969).

Race Problems and Disorder: James Baldwin, *The Fire Next Time* (New York: Dell Publishing Company, 1964); Kenneth Clark, *Dark Ghetto* (New York: Harper & Row, Publishers, 1965); Robert Coles, *Children of Crisis* (Boston: Atlantic Monthly Press, Little, Brown & Company, 1967), vols. 2 and 3, 1972; William H. Grier and Price M. Cobbs, *Black Rage* (New York: Basic Books, 1968); *Report of the National Advisory Commission on Civil Disorders* (New York: E. P. Dutton & Company, 1968); Charles E. Silberman, *Crisis in Black and White* (New York: Random House, 1964); Robert Penn Warren, *Who Speaks for the Negro?* (New York: Vintage Books, 1966).

2. Jonathan Kozol, *Death at an Early Age* (Boston: Houghton Mifflin Company, 1967), p. 170.

3. Hannah Arendt, *The Human Condition* (Garden City, N.Y.: Doubleday Anchor Books, 1959), p. 6.

4. Dorothy Lee, *Freedom and Culture* (Englewood Cliffs, N.J.: Prentice-Hall, 1959), p. 113.

5. For views of modern painting, see Gregory Battcock, ed., *The New Art* (New York: E. P. Dutton & Company, 1966); Nicolas Calas, *Art in the Age of Risk* (New York: E. P. Dutton & Company, 1968); Michael Kirby, *The Art of Time* (New York: E. P. Dutton & Company, 1969); Harold Rosenberg, *The Tradition of the New* (New York: McGraw-Hill Book Company, 1965). Also consult *Art in America,* 1968–1972.

6. Joseph Heller, *Catch-22* (New York: Simon & Schuster, 1961), p. 398.

7. Kurt Vonnegut, Jr., *Player Piano* (New York: Avon Books, 1952), p. 25.

8. Saul Bellow, *Herzog* (New York: Viking Press, 1964), p. 289.

9. Thomas S. Kuhn, *The Structure of Scientific Revolutions,* 2nd ed. (Chicago: University of Chicago Press, International Encyclopedia of Unified Science, vol. 2, no. 2, 1970), p. 10.

10. Werner Heisenberg, *Physics and Beyond* (New York: Harper & Row, Publishers, 1971), p. 40.

11. Morton White, *Social Thought in America: The Revolt Against Formalism* (Boston: Beacon Press, 1957), p. 49.

12. Max Beloff, "On Thinking About the Past," *Encounter,* October 1969, p. 49.
13. Robert Jay Lifton, "Notes on a New History: The Young and the Old," *The Atlantic,* September 1969, p. 47.
14. See Jesse Lemisch, "The American Revolution Seen From the Bottom Up," in *Towards a New Past: Dissenting Essays in American History,* ed. Barton J. Bernstein (New York: Pantheon Books, 1968), pp. 3–45.
15. Daniel R. Fusfeld, "Post-Post-Keynes: The Shattered Synthesis," *Saturday Review,* January 22, 1972.
16. Alvin W. Gouldner, *The Coming Crisis of Western Sociology* (New York: Basic Books, 1970), p. 487.
17. Jan Myrdal, *Confessions of a Disloyal European* (New York: Pantheon Books, 1968), p. 133.

Further Reading

Philosophy and Philosophy of Education

Hannah Arendt, "Thinking and Moral Considerations," *Social Research,* vol. 38, no. 3, Autumn 1971.

Albert Camus, *The Myth of Sisyphus and Other Essays,* tr. Justin O'Brien (New York: Alfred A. Knopf, 1955).

Paulo Freire, *Pedagogy of the Oppressed* (New York: Herder and Herder, 1970).

Aron Gurwitsch, "The Approach to Consciousness," in *Essays in Phenomenology,* ed. Maurice Natanson (The Hague: Martinus Nijhoff, 1966).

Richard M. Hare, *The Language of Morals* (New York: Oxford University Press, 1964).

Nelson B. Henry, ed., *Modern Philosophies and Education,* The Fifty-fourth Yearbook of the National Society for the Study of Education, pt. 1 (Chicago: University of Chicago Press, 1955).

William James, *Principles of Psychology,* vol. 2 (New York: Dover Publications, 1950).

B. Paul Komisar and James E. McClellan, "The Logic of Slogans," in *Language and Concepts in Education,* ed. B. Othanel Smith and Robert H. Ennis (Chicago: Rand McNally & Company, 1961).

Herbert Marcuse, *One Dimensional Man* (Boston: Beacon Press, 1964).

Maurice Merleau-Ponty, *Phenomenology of Perception* (London: Routledge and Kegan Paul, 1962).

Philip H. Phenix, *Realms of Meaning* (New York: McGraw-Hill Book Company, 1964).

Michael Polanyi, *Personal Knowledge* (New York: Harper & Row, Publishers, 1964).

Jean-Paul Sartre, *Being and Nothingness,* tr. Hazel E. Barnes (New York: Philosophical Library, 1959).

————, *Search for a Method*, tr. Hazel E. Barnes (New York: Alfred A. Knopf, 1963).

Israel Scheffler, *The Language of Education* (Springfield, Ill.: Charles C Thomas, Publisher, 1960).

Alfred Schutz, "The Life-World," in *Collected Papers* III, ed. Maurice Natanson (The Hague: Martinus Nijhoff, 1967).

Social Sciences and Education

Ruth Benedict, *Patterns of Culture* (Boston: Houghton Mifflin Company, 1947).

Peter L. Berger and Thomas Luckmann, *The Social Construction of Reality* (Garden City, N.Y.: Doubleday Anchor Books, 1967).

Daniel J. Boorstin, *The Genius of American Politics* (Chicago: University of Chicago Press, 1953).

John Holt, *How Children Fail* (New York: Pitman Publishing Corporation, 1964).

Claude Lévi-Strauss, *The Savage Mind* (Chicago: University of Chicago Press, 1966).

Arthur O. Lovejoy, *The Great Chain of Being* (New York: Harper & Row, Publishers, 1960).

Marshall McLuhan, *Understanding Media: The Extensions of Man* (New York: McGraw-Hill Book Company, 1964).

Margaret Mead, *Coming of Age in Samoa* (New York: New American Library, 1949).

Autobiography, Criticism, and Imaginative Literature

Edward Albee, *Who's Afraid of Virginia Woolf?*, in *Best American Plays,* 5th ser., 1957–1963, ed. John Gassner (New York: Crown Publishers, 1963).

John Barth, *End of the Road* (New York: Avon Books, 1964).

Donald Barthelme, *Snow White* (New York: Atheneum, 1967).

————, *City Life* (New York: Farrar, Straus & Giroux, 1970).

Richard Brautigan, *Trout Fishing in America* (New York: Dell Publishing Company, 1967).

Joan Didion, *Play It As It Lays* (New York: Bantam Books, 1971).

Ralph Ellison, *Invisible Man* (New York: Random House, 1952).

John Hawkes, *The Lime Twig* (New York: New Directions Publishing Corporation, 1961).

Frank Kermode, *The Sense of an Ending* (New York: Oxford University Press, 1967).

Ken Kesey, *One Flew Over the Cuckoo's Nest* (New York: Viking Press, 1962).

Norman Mailer, *An American Dream* (New York: Dial Press, 1965).

————, *The Armies of the Night* (New York: New American Library, 1968).

————, *Why Are We in Vietnam?* (New York: G. P. Putnam's Sons, 1967).

Bernard Malamud, *The Fixer* (New York: Farrar, Straus & Giroux, 1966).

Thomas Pynchon, *V* (Philadelphia: J. B. Lippincott Company, 1963).

Harold Rosenberg, *The Anxious Object: Art Today and Its Audience* (New York: New American Library, 1969).

John Updike, *Rabbit Run* (New York: Alfred A. Knopf, 1960).

——, *Rabbit Redux* (New York: Alfred A. Knopf, 1971).

Chapter Two

Choosing a Past

> We shall not cease from exploration
> And the end of all our exploring
> Will be to arrive where we started
> And know the place for the first time.
>
> T. S. Eliot
> "Little Gidding," *Four Quartets*

We have talked of freedom, self-consciousness, and the achievement of perspectives; and we have linked these to doing philosophy. Now we shall look at philosophy in a wider context, moving back in history for a moment to highlight the questions asked over the years. Historical understanding, writes Maurice Merleau-Ponty, "only presupposes the possibility that we have a past which is ours and that we can recapture in our freedom the work of so many other freedoms. It assumes that we can clarify the choices of others through our own and ours through theirs, that we adjust one by the other and finally arrive at the truth."[1] Making the same assumption, we search for continuities and discontinuities, instances of insight, persisting paradigms. We, too, have choices to make; we, too, are attempting to arrive at truth.

We begin not with a philosopher but with the mythical character Prometheus, the tortured hero of Aeschylus's play *Prometheus Bound.* In many senses, Prometheus is and has been the exemplary figure for those concerned to liberate by helping people become knowledgeable and aware. He speaks, describing the condition of men before he stole the fire from heaven:

> For men at first had eyes but saw to no purpose; they had
> ears but did not hear. Like the shapes of dreams they dragged
> through their long lives and handled all things in bewilderment
> and confusion. They did not know of building houses with
> bricks to face the sun; they did not know how to work in wood.
> They lived like swarming ants in holes in the ground, in the
> sunless caves of the earth.[2]

Rebelling on man's behalf against Zeus's brutal, mindless rule, he taught men how to use tools, to study the stars, to organize their experiences. Most significantly, he enabled men to become rational creatures; he stirred them into consciousness and gave them hope. And in his stubborn resistance to the dominance of force, he prefigured the philosophers to come. His very imagery holds intimations of the future: Plato, too, would write of releasing human beings from "sunless caves."

Indeed, this notion was the major thrust of philosophy in its early days. To philosophize was to search for the light—the rational insight that exemplified the highest self-realization, the veritable perfection of man. The "Myth of the Cave" in *The Republic* illustrates something of this idea. As Socrates tells it (in an attempt to show "in a figure how far our nature is enlightened or unenlightened"), certain human beings live underground, with their legs and necks chained in such a way that they can only look at the wall in front of them. A fire is behind them; and all they can see on the wall are their shadows and the shadows of various objects being carried by men who pass along a raised way at the prisoners' backs. The shadows represent the only "truth," the only "reality" they know.

Now and then a prisoner is liberated. When he turns toward the fire and then toward the light at the mouth of the cave, the prisoner is momentarily blinded and suffers pain. An instructor may explain to him that what he previously thought was real was merely a shadow, an illusion. When he is dragged up the steep incline, out of the cave and into the sunlight, the prisoner is dazzled at first; but, at last, "he will be able to see the sun, and not mere reflections of him in the water . . . he will contemplate him as he is." The sun represents perfect Truth, the Good, pure and abstract Form. To contemplate it is to be wholly fulfilled as a human being, to have achieved the highest degree of education. To contemplate it (as only a privileged few can do) is to be wise—to be a philosopher.

The root meaning of the term *philosophy* is "love of wisdom." And to the Greeks, wisdom meant apprehension of an absolute and ultimate truth which only the wonderstruck eyes of the mind could contemplate. To pursue wisdom, to "love" it was to break with earthly things and time and change, to yearn upward, toward the unearthly Ideal. In Plato's *Symposium,* there is another rendering of that ascent. In explaining his conception of the nature of love, Socrates repeats a tale he once heard from a wise woman named Diotima: ". . . wisdom is a most beautiful thing, and Love is of the beautiful; and therefore Love is also a philosopher or lover of wisdom, and being a lover of wisdom is a mean between the wise and the ignorant." Loving, she meant, implies desiring. We can only yearn for wisdom if we are conscious of our ignorance. And then we must move from the approximations of beauty surrounding us on earth toward the fundamental idea, the essential form. Diotima, too, had spoken of philosophy as an ascent:

> And the true order of going, or being led by another, to the things of love, is to begin from the beauties of earth and mount upwards for the sake of that other beauty, using these as steps only, and from one going on to two, and from two to all fair forms, and from fair forms to fair practices, and from fair practices to fair notions, until from fair notions he arrives at the notion of absolute beauty, and at last knows what the essence of beauty is.[3]

For Plato, philosophizing was an activity reserved for those endowed at birth with the ability to ascend by means of dialectical reason. It meant turning one's face from the world of ordinary experiences and sensations toward the timeless realm of Ideas. For Aristotle, philosophy meant an awareness of a storied, purposeful universe in which all things were "caused" to seek their own perfection. No longer existing prior to the natural world and beyond it, form was now conceived to be immanent in material phenomena; form represented, in fact, the actuality of each particular thing. For example, form gave the acorn the potentiality to become an oak tree and moved it to seek fulfillment through growth. The essence—the form—of the human being was rationality. Man actualized his potential, therefore, to the extent he could engage in contemplative activity in accordance with virtue. All things, seeking fulfillment, aspired toward the absolute, the Unmoved Mover—pure, untrammeled Form. The universe as a whole was like a vast, palpitating pyramid, characterized by an upward movement from inchoate matter through the stages of evolution —to God.

The orientation toward essences and hierarchies affected philosophic thinking for centuries. Even today it connotes a picture of reality that seems to be somehow "right." In spite of (and sometimes in defiance of) what scientists tell them about the universe, many men and women refuse to give up their belief in an orderly, "human" cosmos, which they can visualize as a totality and describe harmoniously in words. Like the ancient Greeks, they are convinced that "reality" must be susceptible to explanation in terms of language—and that it has a special relationship to logic and "clarity."

Many people, too, cling to the conviction that something in the universe is "higher" and more valuable than the human drama with all its ambiguities and pettiness. They are convinced (sometimes unconsciously) that an ultimate Reality exists, which a perfected rational faculty as well as religious faith can grasp. For this reason, many literary works dealing with journeys and ascents have great appeal. The beginning of Dante's *Inferno* is an example, dealing with a lost and confused man looking for the light:

> Midway this way of life we're bound upon,
> I woke to find myself in a dark wood,
> Where the right road was wholly lost and gone.[4]

Where is he to find the light? By looking *upward,* to the top of a steep hill to see "the morning rays/ Mantle its shoulder from that planet bright/ Which guides men's feet aright on all their ways." Readers can recognize immediately the implication here: Dante, although he may have to go downward into the darkness at first, will inevitably ascend. Human beings seem to recognize, almost universally, the necessity to move out of darkness. Metaphors of darkness (and inchoate matter) are used to describe ignorance, confusion, and sinfulness. Wisdom and redemption are associated with the light (and pure, unalloyed form). This notion may be why so many people are still inclined to conceive abstract studies— mathematics, logic, physics—to be "higher" than concrete undertakings (applied engineering, nursing, automobile repair). It may be why the liberal arts scholar has so often been ranked more highly than the scholar of the practical or the technical arts. It is certainly why philosophy is expected to deal with disembodied things, to disclose only what the sun makes manifest: the Good, the Beautiful, the True.

But why is this the case, even in a scientific age? Surely most people know better than to believe in the existence of hierarchies or Ideal Forms. Why does the classical view haunt men so? Why do they feel, as so many existentialists say, "homesick" for the perfectly ordered cosmos of the past? Indeed, deep within themselves, many modern men resemble the speaker in John Keats' "Ode on a Grecian Urn." Like that speaker, they yearn after unheard melodies; they might well say (if they had the words): "Pipe to the spirit ditties of no tone. . . ."

This is another instance, perhaps the exemplary instance, of what we have called a paradigm. This one has dominated the thinking of Western men for centuries. Somehow the notion of an ordered, unchanging universe (even if known only "to the spirit") helped people feel at home in the world. Moreover, it enabled some persons to transcend imaginatively; it gratified, and so it persisted. And it may well persist even today; like all such symbolic constructs, it can never be proved empirically false. But the teacher should recognize this notion as a perfectly adequate way of making sense in classic times but purely fictive now. Writing about various kinds of fictions (such as "the Heavenly City" and "the Apocalypse" or the end of the world), Frank Kermode talks of the need to distinguish fictions from myths. "Fictions can degenerate into myths whenever they are not consciously held to be fictive. . . . Fictions are for finding things out, and they change as the needs of sense-making change. Myths are the agents of stability, fictions the agents of change. Myths call for absolute, fictions for conditional assent."[5]

We must remember that our modern scientific understanding came centuries later; and the paradigm—or fiction—of dark and light, lower and higher, matter and form, was (for ancient Greeks and those who followed them) a fruitful way of structuring and "finding things out." At least until the seventeenth century, philosophy was considered "the queen of the sciences," therefore, the source and resource of all significant knowledge about the universe and man. Only on rare occasions, in those days, did philosophy threaten religion. When a group of church scholars in the Middle Ages rediscovered Aristotle's ideas, these scholars were soon absorbed in the great Medieval Synthesis. This structure of theological and philosophical ideas was created by Thomas Aquinas, who integrated the thinking of early Christianity with the "pagan" notions of classical Greece into what we know as Scholasticism. Hence, the traditional paradigm, already almost two thousand years old, was not crucially challenged until the efflorescence of science and mathematics in the eighteenth century, and even then not in the minds of most men.

The challenge developed slowly, levied mainly against an ancient conception of reason as a "natural light" and of a truth that reason alone could disclose. The great seventeenth century pioneers of the scientific method, René Descartes and Francis Bacon, still clung to a notion of preexisting truth that could become manifest in sufficiently pure minds. If prejudice and ignorance were eradicated, they believed, men would inevitably come to know truth. They further believed that because every person carried within him the sources of knowledge, he needed only a proper education that could sweep away the cobwebs of superstition and whatever else obscured clear and distinct ideas. They could always rely on the truth of such ideas because God would never have made any false idea seem clear and distinct.

Descartes, of course, went to extremes; and no ordinary person could be expected to go so far. He withdrew completely and concentrated all his energies on ridding himself "of all the opinions [he] had held previously" and on destroying his prejudices in the heroic effort to achieve a "naked mind."[6] We have already spoken of the teacher's need to set aside his preconceptions or bracket out what he takes for granted; but it would be unreasonable to ask anyone to go as far as Descartes in trying to begin again at the beginning. He came eventually to a single certainty: "Cogito, ergo sum"—"I think, therefore I am"—which became the foundation for his later thinking. The lesson was inescapable for anyone who could understand what Descartes had done: the mind was prior and supreme; the "eyes" of the mind were equipped to see.

Francis Bacon, known for his discovery of the inductive method of inquiry, wrote eloquently about the various idols that kept people in darkness. If they could break, he said, through the prejudice, wishfulness, and conventionality, they would be able to pursue the certainties they were inherently capable of knowing. Yet, despite the many changes in perspective and the growing concern with facts and particulars in the seventeenth century, the greatest minds could not break with the old paradigm. They were "liberal" men in the most literal sense: they wanted to liberate the intellect and in that manner "save" mankind. But the old hope and the old images still remained. The light was preexistent; to be free meant to know the Absolute, the Word, the purity of Form.

Challenges accumulated with the rise of Newtonian science; by the end of the seventeenth century, John Locke was questioning the doctrine that human beings were born with innate ideas about truth and reality. The mind, he asserted, was a "tabula rasa," a wax tablet; it was experience which inscribed what was eventually known. Each mind was a discrete mental substance, with the power to transmute sensations into perceptions, to link perceptions so as to form ideas. Seeking to understand how the world as sensed became the world as known, Locke speculated about the "signs" men used to symbolize their experiences and about the strange human habit of confusing words with things. The foundations were being laid for the modern view that the great metaphysical visions of reality were only verbal fictions.

In the eighteenth century, Bishop George Berkeley said that many persons who had written so confidently of the Good and True had simply assumed that the words they used inevitably referred to preexistent ideas or to something actually present in the world. He thought that philosophers should be concerned with the confusions language, even the language of morals, creates. He had, of course, a professional interest in man's spiritual and ethical life; but he could also perceive that the Good did not necessarily refer to something fixed. Rather, he wrote, it referred to certain rules of conduct or to attitudes or to commitments men had formulated for themselves.

Finally, a skeptic named David Hume carried the argument to its conclusion. Not only was the faculty of reason, he pointed out, quite incapable of providing insights into any absolute Good; it could not provide certain knowledge of cause and effect, necessity, justice, or universal harmony. No such thing as manifest truth existed; there were only sensations, habits, customary ways of taking things for granted. The presumed certainties on which so many had relied were merely sophistries and delusions, and Hume relegated these to the flames. Doing so, he destroyed the familiar foundations of knowledge. No wonder he gave up philosophy; no anchorage was left.

The German philosopher, Immanuel Kant, recast the whole problem; and most historians agree that he completed the revolution in thought. Probing the meaning of science and ethics, Kant demonstrated that nothing can be called factual or real beyond what human understanding defines. The principles of human reason, he said, were the principles of understanding; but their function was not to disclose or create truth. Rather, their purpose was to enable human beings to organize and categorize the phenomena of sense experience, to effect relationships, to move from premises to conclusions. Whatever order man perceives—in other words, whatever harmony or design—depends on the categories of his understanding. No objective realm of pure Form or Idea exists; no "great chain of being" for men to contemplate. We cannot say anything about reality in itself. We can only speak meaningfully about that to which our minds give meaning; and the order we impose is contingent on the categories of our minds.

When we talk of factual knowledge, we are referring to orders effected by our minds. Kant drew a sharp distinction, however, between factual knowledge and moral principles—the determined universe described by science and the domain of free will. Moral principles were not equated with some preexisting Good; but Kant suggested that being a rational being *entailed* being aware of free will, of the existence of God, and of one's duty in life. Moral principles were known in some a priori manner; they did not stem from the experiences of life. Rather, they took the form of imperatives. Logically, they guided a man of goodwill much as rules of procedure guide the inquiries of a scientist. They did not *require* an individual to behave virtuously or dutifully; he was free to do or not do what he knew was right. If he did his duty and performed a virtuous act, he could be judged good only in terms of his motives: a good act was performed because it was good and because the actor chose to do his duty.

If he did something good for any other reason—out of benevolence, pity, the wish to be loved—he would not be called righteous for doing it. For Kant, duty was much like William Wordsworth's description in his "Ode to Duty":

> Stern Daughter of the Voice of God!
> O Duty! If that name thou love
> Who art a light to guide, a rod
> To check the erring, and reprove;
> Thou who art victory and law
> When empty terrors overawe;
> From vain temptations dost set free,
> And calm'st the weary strife of frail humanity![7]

The point is that duty was an internal light, illuminating the way for a rational being. He remained free, however, to follow an alternate road, a shadowy road. He could not be rational without *knowing* the moral law or the "categorical imperative"; but he was an autonomous being capable of making choices.

Other philosophers, particularly the German idealists G. W. F. Hegel and Arthur Schopenhauer, went on to build great metaphysical systems and ideologies. Hegel, especially, satisfied a need on the part of thinkers seeking some foothold in the universe, some mode of maintaining their faith in the midst of continuing change. The cosmos, as Hegel presented it, was "God thinking"—a spiritual and developing organism, progressively realizing the "World Spirit," which unfolded in an orderly, dialectical movement toward the Absolute, the One. History moved forward and upward, toward an eventual consummation; every person, every idea, every action had a part to play and a contribution to make in the vast totality. This idea offered temporary solace to many men. It offered inspiration and new beginnings to others. But it never involved a return to the ancient paradigm of unchanging Truth existing like a perfect urn in the sun.

Many restless spirits began to challenge the notion of a totality. Søren Kierkegaard wrote of the "Single One" whose subjective existence could not be encompassed by an abstraction. Systems submerged the living person and extinguished his individual consciousness, said Fyodor Dostoevsky, raging against the threat of making men "piano keys" manipulated from without. Friedrich Nietzsche wrote of the need for lives of risk and intensity; he defied those who talked of individual fulfillments as the general welfare. One after another, they objected to the anonymity of membership in a crowd, or the public, or the masses. In Martin Buber's words, there remained (after all the metaphysical systems were built, after the great collectivities appeared) "the mystery of your own comprehension of the world and the mystery of your own being." Or as Edmund Husserl was to say, there remained the consciousness of the living being and the life-world constituted by each subjectivity. So the existential and phenomenological revolts against systems and absolutes took shape; so the rebels on behalf of subjectivity and existence prepared for the modern world.

But these people, mainly Europeans, were not alone in challenging the "superscience" of metaphysics. Philosophers in England, Austria, and America were carrying on the Humean and Kantian revolution and focusing on the narrow contexts of ordinary, humdrum experience and on the language men actually used for ordering and interpreting their worlds. Ultimates did not concern them; cosmic notions seemed to be only verbal fictions; the object was to be clear. Some men concentrated, therefore, on the problem of the relationship between language and facts; others, on approaches to examination of the uses of particular terms; still others, on the ways categories or constructs organized particulars and became the means for viewing the world. Early in the twentieth century, George E. Moore in England and William James in the United States were both, in their distinctive ways, rebelling against idealism—Moore in the name of a commonsense realism, James in the name of a radical empiricism. Moore directed attention to the realm of solid fact and the physical objects that existed in everyone's daily life. James affirmed the concreteness of experience and railed against "abstraction and insufficiency . . . fixed principles, closed systems, and pretended absolutes. . . ."

No longer interested in metaphysical speculation, more and more thinkers began pondering the sciences instead and the kinds of explanations they provided of the natural world. This led some of them to studies of scientific description, of logical formulas and mathematics in the contexts where they were used. While Bertrand Russell and Ludwig Wittgenstein were refining methods of logical and language analysis in Cambridge, a Vienna Circle (composed of Moritz Schlick, Rudolph Carnap, and others) were using the tools of analysis on scientific reports on the physical world. Were these reports on what existed objectively and independently, or were they reports on mere sense data? What was the relationship between the laws of logic and natural laws? Was it possible to develop a language pure enough and comprehensive enough to mirror the real world?

Bertrand Russell studied the logic of sentences and other linguistic constructions. Ludwig Wittgenstein, a student of Russell's (and later the inspiration of the Vienna Circle) talked of the fabric of the world as composed of facts rather than things. Facts, however, were thought to be atoms of logic, existing in a logical space pictured by the propositions of language. The work of the philosopher was to discover a purified language, properly to picture the real world. After World War II, Wittgenstein began emphasizing the dynamic character and multiple functions of language. The problem now seemed to him to be one of determining *how* language is used in the manifold contexts of life itself. Men had to realize that they could not see the world that lay beyond their linguistic conventions (what they had learned how to say). The primary task of philosophy, then, was not to unveil some encompassing or hidden reality; it was to clarify the ways in which human beings thought about the world, to counter the "bewitchment of intelligence." This entailed a necessity to explicate the conventions used in the several realms of discourse, to shed light on human "language games."

The analysts, the students of ordinary language, and the positivist inquirers into the problem of meaning differed markedly from the existentialists. Both groups, however, helped to create—and are still creating—the situation in which we do philosophy today. The great pragmatists, William James and Charles Sanders Peirce, also had a profound effect on present-day philosophy through their emphasis on human experience in an indeterminate world; on knowing as a kind of participant action; on truths tested by their efficacy in settling uncertainties, by their consequences for thinking and for life. John Dewey, like them a rebel against absolutes and the "closed universe," saw philosophy as a response to the conflicts in social life. Many of these conflicts were a result of anachronistic quests for certainty, he thought; many were a result of the tendency to use outmoded intellectual tools to solve the problems of an industrialized world. Assenting to the rise of experimental sciences, accepting the beginnings of technology, he talked about finding ways to direct the changes wrought by the new knowledge to humane and life-sustaining ends. To Dewey, one of the chief functions of philosophy was to make clear what scientific thinking involved—and what shaping (in the light of such thinking) a better, more desirable world involved.

Concerned as he was with the uses of intelligence and the possibilities of extending human controls, Dewey turned understandably to education, which he called the vantage ground from which to penetrate the human significance of philosophic inquiry. Education, he said, was the means for developing the kinds of dispositions appropriate to the new and changing world. Like many of his contemporaries, Dewey treated philosophy as an activity, a way of thinking about what was known and valued rather than as a body of doctrines or truths. Philosophy was to be carried on in the situations of an open, challenging, perplexing world in which human hopes could never be finally realized. It was linked to the cause of growth and the cause of progress, both of which were to be pursued amid continuities and change.

Looking about us now, we find the old questions still open; we find that we have to choose in our freedom. We live and do our teaching at a moment when rationality is being challenged, when the sciences offer neither safety nor solace, when autonomy and self-determination are being questioned. All over the world, men and women are demanding liberation from what burdens and inhibits them: racial and sexual discrimination, alien or foreign domination, credential systems, conditioning mechanisms, overpopulation, poverty, environmental pollution, and exclusion from decision-making. Confronting their powerlessness, people are refusing to live passively any longer, refusing simply to endure. And, more and more, they are insisting on a sense of meaningfulness, of purpose in life. If ever there was a desire to be released from "sunless caves," the desire is apparent now. If ever there was a need for sunlit mountaintops, the need exists today.

As we have seen, to yearn after knowledge of some higher realm is no longer viable or sensible. For almost two centuries, philosophers have been trying to learn to live without certainties, without the conviction of privileged awareness. Today they stake out diverse fields to cultivate, most of which are this-worldly fields, coextensive with human experience, human logics, languages, consciousness. And the workers in those fields no longer justify by pointing to scrolls and tablets they have unearthed from ancient tombs. They define their undertakings by distinctive sorts of questions—queer questions, some have called them—which demand distinctive sorts of performances in response.

The performance varies with the philosopher. But few performances involve acting as a guru or a sage, prescribing for others what is excellent and good. And so it is with educational philosophy, done from the vantage point of the person involved. Nevertheless, worlds remain to be explored.

There is the chance of increasing clarity: the ability to say what one means and can defend, to provide good reasons for what one believes. There is the chance of intensified commitment to values. There is the chance of combating the sense of meaninglessness and nihilism which afflicts so many—indeed, of transforming the world.

Albert Camus, writing in his Notebooks, expressed deep concern for the confusion of modern intelligence at a moment of proliferating knowledge, when the mind has lost its resting place—its "point d'appui." It is a fact, he wrote, "that we are suffering from nihilism." Who does not recognize the suffering he had in mind? The confusion, the emptiness, the void? Who does not know that there is no point in calling for a return to the old solutions, to old dreams of caves and firelight? We must adjust to the new knowledge somehow—even the knowledge of what we cannot know. We must confront our human situation in a universe lacking guarantees:

> To be cured, we must come to terms with this lucidity, this clear-sightedness. We must take into consideration the awareness of our exile which we have suddenly acquired. The intelligence is not in confusion because knowledge has turned the world upside down. It is in confusion because it cannot come to terms with this upheaval. It has not "got used to the idea." Let it once get used to it and the confusion will disappear. There will remain only the upheaval and the lucid knowledge that the mind has of it. There is a whole civilization to be remade.[8]

This chapter has dealt mainly with the "upheaval," where man and knowledge and value are concerned. Philosophy, for the teacher, may be a coming to terms, a getting used to the upheaval and a consideration of its consequences for teaching and enabling others to learn. It may become a way of understanding old paradigms and the lure of them, a way of revealing the presuppositions that lead so many into confusion, complacency, or despair. It may be an activity that leads the individual to a discovery of what lucidity can mean for his existence—and his commitment to making a humane civilization. If philosophy turns out to be these things, each of us will have learned "to think what we are doing." Each of us will have advanced the process of shaping a decent future and the struggle to identify ourselves.

Notes and References

1. Maurice Merleau-Ponty, *The Primacy of Perception* (Evanston, Ill.: Northwestern University Press, 1964), p. 204.

2. Aeschylus, *Prometheus Bound,* tr. David Grene, in *The Complete Greek Trage-dies,* vol. 1, ed. David Grene and Richmond Lattimore (Chicago: University of Chicago Press, 1959), p. 327.

3. Plato, "The Symposium," tr. B. Jowett, in *The Works of Plato* (New York: Tudor Publishing Company, n.d.), pp. 340–341.

4. Dante, Cantica I, *Hell (L'Inferno),* in *The Comedy of Dante Alighieri the Floren-tine,* tr. Dorothy L. Sayers (Baltimore: Penguin Books, 1954), p. 71.

5. Frank Kermode, *The Sense of an Ending* (New York: Oxford University Press, 1967), p. 39.

6. George Poulet, "The Dream of Descartes," in *Studies in Human Time,* tr. Elliott Coleman (New York: Harper & Row, Publishers, 1959), p. 53.

7. William Wordsworth, "Ode to Duty," in *The Prelude, Selected Poems and Son-nets,* ed. Carlos Baker (New York: Holt, Rinehart & Winston, 1962), p. 144.

8. Albert Camus, *Notebooks* 1942–1951 (New York: The Modern Library, 1965), p. 17.

Further Reading

Aristotle, *The Nicomachean Ethics of Aristotle,* tr. D. P. Chase (New York: E. P. Dutton & Company, 1920), bk. 1, sects. 2, 3; bk. 7.

John L. Austin, *How to Do Things with Words,* ed. J. O. Urmson and G. J. Warnock (London: Oxford University Press, 1965).

Alfred J. Ayer, *Language, Truth and Logic* (London: Victor Gollancz, 1950).

Francis Bacon, *Novum Organum,* in *The English Philosophers from Bacon to Mill,* ed. Edwiñ A. Burtt (New York: The Modern Library, 1939), pp. 14–123.

George Berkeley, "Three Dialogues between Hylas and Philonous," in *The Works of George Berkeley,* vol. 1, ed. A. C. Fraser (Oxford, Eng.: Clarendon Press, 1901).

Isaiah Berlin, "The Subject Matter of Philosophy," *The London Times Sunday Maga-zine,* November 4, 1962.

Max Black, ed., *The Importance of Language* (Englewood Cliffs, N.J.: Prentice-Hall, 1962).

René Descartes, "Discourse 4," in *Discourses on Method and Other Writings,* tr. E. F. Sutcliffe (Baltimore: Penguin Books, 1968).

John Dewey, *Democracy and Education* (New York: The Macmillan Company, 1916).

———, "The School and Society," in *Dewey on Education,* ed. Martin S. Dworkin (New York: Bureau of Publications, Teachers College, Columbia University, 1959).

Fyodor Dostoevsky, "Notes from Underground," in *The Short Novels of Dostoevsky* (New York: Dial Press, 1945).

Georg W. F. Hegel, *Philosophy of History,* tr. J. Sibree (New York: P. F. Collier, 1902).

Martin Heidegger, *What Is Philosophy?,* tr. William Kluback and Jean T. Wilde (New York: Twayne Publishers, 1958).

David Hume, "An Enquiry Concerning Human Understanding," in *Enquiries Concerning the Human Understanding and Concerning the Principles of Morals,* 2nd ed., ed. L. A. Selby-Bigge (Oxford: Clarendon Press, 1951).

Edmund Husserl, *Ideas,* tr. W. R. Boyce Gibson (New York: Collier Books, 1962).

William James, *Talks to Teachers on Psychology and to Students on Some of Life's Ideals* (New York: W. W. Norton & Company, 1958).

Immanuel Kant, "Critique of Pure Reason," in *Kant Selections,* ed. Theodore Meyer Greene (New York: Charles Scribner's Sons, 1929).

———, "Theory of Ethics," in *Kant Selections,* ed. Theodore Meyer Greene (New York: Charles Scribner's Sons, 1929).

Søren Kierkegaard, "Concluding Unscientific Postscript to the 'Philosophical Fragments'," in *A Kierkegaard Anthology,* ed. Robert Bretall (Princeton, N.J.: Princeton University Press, 1947).

———, " 'The Individual'," in *The Point of View for My Work as an Author,* ed. Benjamin Nelson (New York: Harper & Row, Publishers, 1962).

John Locke, "Of Ideas," *An Essay Concerning Human Understanding,* bk. 2 (New York: E. P. Dutton & Company, 1947).

Friedrich Nietzsche, "Twilight of the Idols," in *The Portable Nietzsche,* ed. Walter Kaufmann (New York: Viking Press, 1954).

———, *The Genealogy of Morals,* First Essay, tr. Francis Golffing (Garden City, N.Y.: Doubleday Anchor Books, 1956).

José Ortega y Gasset, *Man and People,* tr. Willard R. Trask (New York: W. W. Norton & Company, 1963).

———, *The Revolt of the Masses* (New York: W. W. Norton & Company, 1957).

Charles Sanders Peirce, "The Fixation of Belief" and "How to Make Our Ideas Clear," in *Philosophical Writings of Peirce,* ed. Justus Buchler (New York: Dover Publications, 1955).

Plato, "The Republic," tr. B. Jowett, in *The Works of Plato* (New York: Tudor Publishing Company, n.d.).

Josiah Royce, *The Spirit of Modern Philosophy* (New York: George Braziller, 1955).

Bertrand Russell, *Human Knowledge: Its Scope and Limits* (New York: Simon & Schuster, 1948).

———, *An Inquiry into Meaning and Truth* (New York: W. W. Norton & Company, 1940).

———, "The Philosophy of Logical Atomism" (1918), in *Logic and Knowledge,* ed. R. C. Marsh (London: Macmillan and Company, 1956).

Benedict D. Spinoza, "On the Improvement of the Understanding," in *Works of Spinoza,* vol. II, tr. R. H. M. Elwes (New York: Dover Publications, 1955).

Alfred North Whitehead, *Science and the Modern World* (New York: New American Library, 1948).

Ludwig Wittgenstein, *Philosophical Investigations,* 3rd ed. (New York: The Macmillan Company, 1968).

————, *Tractatus Logico-Philosophicus* (London: Routledge and Kegan Paul, 1961).

Chapter Three

Man: The Contemporary Dialogue

Men may seem detestable as joint stock-companies and
nations; knaves, fools, and murderers there may be; men may
have mean and meagre faces; but man, in the ideal, is so noble
and so sparkling, such a grand and glowing creature, that over
every ignominious blemish in him all his fellows should run to
throw their costliest robes.

Herman Melville
Moby Dick

Our researchers into Public Opinion are content
That he held the proper opinions for the time of
  year;
When there was peace, he was for peace; when there
  was war, he went.
He was married and added five children to the
  population,
Which our Eugenist says was the right number for
  a parent of his generation,
And our teachers report that he never interfered with
  their education.
Was he free? Was he happy? The question is absurd:
Had anything been wrong, we should certainly have
  heard.

W. H. Auden
"The Citizen"

"What is man?" This is one of the oldest philosophical questions,
asked with varying degrees of confidence over the years. The traditional
answer refers to some definable "essence," an abstract quality possessed by
every human being. For the ancient Greeks, it was rationality, or a
rational soul, evident in the ability to speak logically and to function as a
free man in a public sphere. For the Christians, the distinguishing quality
was inward and spiritual: the immortal soul, the sacred spark, glowing in

the breasts of slaves as well as in the breasts of the powerful and free. For the Renaissance thinkers, a combination of intellect and virtue defined Man in his glory and excellence. He was, according to Shakespeare's Hamlet, "the paragon of animals"; he was also a "quintessence of dust." For some, as the years went on, man's animality seemed dominant; his life was "nasty, brutish and short."[1] Conflicts arose between those who saw the natural as good and those who saw it as Yahoo-like and bad. Whether "man" has been defined as animal or angel, sentient or rational, tool-using or symbol-using, solitary or gregarious, the tendency has been to focus on "Man" in the abstract rather than on individual men.

Today this abstraction is no longer sufficient because at this moment in history the status, the dignity, and the "nature" of man have all become problematic. Pondering the known universe, which scientists generally described in mathematical symbols, an individual can no longer assert—as Giovanni Pico della Mirandola did in 1486—that "man is rightly called and considered a great miracle and a truly marvelous creature." Pico could rejoice, as we cannot, in the knowledge that the Great Artisan had placed man in the middle of the universe and permitted him to define his nature according to his free will:

> Whatever seeds each man cultivates will grow and bear fruit in him. If these seeds are vegetative, he will be like a plant; if they are sensitive, he will become like beasts; if they are rational, he will become like a heavenly creature; if intellectual, he will be an angel and a son of God. And if, content with the lot of no created being, he withdraws into the centre of his own oneness, his spirit, made one with God in the solitary darkness of the Father, which is above all things, will surpass all things.[2]

This was the triumph of the Promethean vision. Man, "this chameleon of ours," was seen to be the center of reality, the favored child of God. Even now, knowing better, we feel that this is the way man *ought* to be viewed. And we are nostalgic for the old certainties.

There is no solace today in being told that man is a rational being or the son of God, for the person lashing out against invisibility, for the person suffering from feelings of powerlessness, for the person feeling obliterated by institutions or city crowds. Such a person must ask, "Who am *I*? What am *I*? What can I make of myself?" If he grants the existence of the free will Pico spoke of, he may find it as much a burden as a blessing because he knows that *his* world has no encompassing design, no Plan, no guarantees. He cannot even be sure that each man possesses "seeds" to cultivate or that—if he does—he will know which ones to choose.

Groping, uncertain, he has to cope with other people's views of his personality; he has to resist (if he can) the pressure of official classifications and definitions. He may find, no matter what he knows himself to be, that the role he plays, the clothes he wears, the class he belongs to, the color of his skin, all identify him. Most of the time, he avoids ultimate questions about his status in the universe; but when he suspects that he is invisible to others, made into a statistic by others, or manipulated by others, he may well begin wondering what being human means.

It does not matter if such wondering and questioning make empirical sense. It does not matter if the person struggling with such feelings is called unhealthy for having them. In the modern corporate society, many individuals feel this way. Many seriously believe that their lives are objectively meaningless, that they do not matter in the flow of things. Martin Luther King, Jr., once wrote of the feelings of "nobodyness" suffered by the black man in America. There may be more Americans than even he knew who feel "nobodyness" to be an entirely reasonable reaction to the society in which they live.

More and more people write of the "malaise of powerlessness." Marcus Raskin writes on middle-class people who find they are losing their sense of personal value in the mazes of corporate finance, among government and business bureaucracies. Even executives and engineers begin to feel expendable, nothing more than statistical averages to the companies for which they work. Americans in general, Raskin says, exist in colonizer—colonized relationships in a series of overlapping colonies: the Violence Colony, where the military dominates; the Plantation Colony, where commerce and industry lock people into meaningless jobs; the Channeling Colony, which, by means of education, breaks people down into specialized servants of the great pyramidal authority; and the media-created Dream Colony, which cultivates a taste for what is happening in the Violence and Plantation realms.[3] In his essay "The Limits of Duty," Charles Reich asserts that "personal responsibility and personal awareness have been obliterated by a system deliberately designed to do just that—eliminate or minimize the human element and insure the supremacy of the system."[4] Bertram M. Gross writes in *The New York Times* that we live in "a managed society ruled by a faceless and widely dispersed complex of warfare–welfare–industry–community–police bureaucracies caught up in developing a new style emphatically based on a technological ideology, a culture of alienation, multiple scapegoats, and competing control networks."[5]

The important thing is the prevalence of another paradigm having to do with a monolithic system and individuals who are totally controlled. If we heed these statements, we are likely to conclude that people around us hold a defensible belief in the *objective* diminution of man. Philip Slater warns against the "monolithic pretense" and reminds us that every person is "a motley collection of ambivalent feelings, contradictory needs and values, and antithetical ideas."[6] Nevertheless, the belief that the person is a monolithic totality and *can* be subordinated to the system or the colony remains operative. It affects behavior and expectation; it shapes many judgments people make. It must, therefore, be granted significance. We must try to understand its implications for our educational projects; therefore, our philosophical questions about the human being must in some manner be concerned with it. This does not mean that we anticipate being able to provide absolute or even comforting reassurances about the status and dignity of man. But if we pay sufficient heed, we will be able to clarify what is involved and define some viable responses. Hopefully, we will then be better equipped to think what we are doing when we encounter other human beings in our schools and in the other places where we spend our lives.

There are bound to be implications for education when so many individuals find their lives so inconsequential, if only because people who feel anonymous and unimportant are unable to assume responsibility for effecting change. They are like Samuel Beckett's two derelicts in *Waiting for Godot*, Vladimir and Estragon, who believe they have lost their rights:

> *Vladimir*: Nothing you can do about it.
> *Estragon*: No use struggling.
> *Vladimir*: One is what one is.
> *Estragon*: No use wriggling.
> *Vladimir*: The essential doesn't change.[7]

In a sad, resigned—perhaps even comic—way, such people are convinced that they do not, objectively speaking, count. They can only wait helplessly on the road, hoping against hope that "Godot" will finally come. Beckett's play concludes:

> *Vladimir*: Well? Shall we go?
> *Estragon*: Yes, let's go.
>   (They do not move.)[8]

There are young people—and children—who feel this way. They are the students who are not what public school people call "motivated"; they appear to their teachers to be apathetic, disinterested, dull. Because we have traditionally thought of the public school as a place where *all* children were provided equal opportunities for pursuing success, little sympathy has been given to the child who did not take advantage of his opportunity. Only recently have we admitted that the school has actually been providing unequal opportunities. The child who has been motivated to succeed has almost always been the child whose belief in himself and his future has been sustained and reinforced by his family and by society. To be motivated is to take responsibility for one's learning; but to do so, one must have confidence in oneself.

In *Children of Crisis,* psychiatrist Robert Coles presents some appalling evidence of the way our culture can teach a child that he or she is worthless, perhaps even subhuman. Coles describes and reproduces pictures drawn by black children in the South during the school desegregation crises. A little girl named Ruby, for instance, took several months before she dared to use the colors brown and black.

> She did, however, distinguish between white and Negro people. She drew white people larger and more lifelike. Negroes were smaller, their bodies less intact. A white girl we both knew to be her own size appeared several times taller. While Ruby's own face . . . lacked an eye in one drawing, an ear in another, the white girl never lacked any features. . . . Moreover, Ruby drew the white girl's hands and legs carefully, always making sure that they had the proper number of fingers and toes. Not so with her own limbs, or those of any other Negro children she chose (or was asked) to picture. A thumb or a forefinger might be missing, or a whole set of toes. The arms were shorter, even absent or truncated.[9]

On a nonverbal level, Ruby *knew* that she was not human in the way white children were human. She was expressing through her pictures what for too many people today is a "fact": if they are to be ranked as human, they are nobodies; they possess no value. Ruby had to be helped and supported before she developed enough confidence to nourish any hope for her future. She was—and is—a tragic exemplar for those convinced (even if they cannot articulate it) that they are nothing, mere incidents, grotesques, specks of dust. What would be the significance of telling Ruby she is a "rational animal," a "chameleon" free to be as she willed, the favored child of God? And if someone were to reassure her in such language, would he be speaking the truth?

Not all persons who feel diminished, of course, react in apathy and self-depreciation. Some people reach desperately outside themselves for stimuli. Needing urgently to feel alive, they search for sharp sensations to counteract the boredom and reduce the emptiness. They may yearn for the "expansion of consciousness" that drugs purportedly make possible; they may find relief in hitchhiking across the country, in ceaseless movement "hugging the white line." In school, such people act out their restlessness and frustrations in delinquency, truancy, various kinds of disruption, various escapes to where the action is. If they cared—or knew how—to say why, they too would tell us they were convinced that they were expendable, that they were of no consequence in the world. They might be the "children who hate"; they might be the looters and the petty thieves. But they would justify their actions, as the black writer Claude Brown did, by saying that only "the white man's law" forbade them. Excluded from the white man's world (perhaps even from the human domain), they have no need to feel guilt for breaking his law. Brown tells how he was sent to court from a training school and how his father "acted so goddam scarey." On the way home, he looked his father in the eye and said, "I guess we ain't nothing or nobody, huh, Dad?"

> He went on talking like he didn't even hear me, and I wasn't listening to what he was saying either. I just wanted to get back to Wiltwyck and steal something and get into a lot of trouble. . . . I wanted to be around K. B. and Horse and Tito and other cats like me. We could all get together up at Wiltwyck, raise a lot of hell, and show people that we weren't pigs.[10]

We do not know whether, at that age, Brown thought the "cats" he knew were human as respectable people were human. Chances are he was creating an alternative world where the highest achievement was showing "that we weren't pigs."

There is an irony in the insistence on the appellation "Man" in such a world. Warren Miller's novel *The Cool World* provides another example:

> Hurst live in a cellar an don't know whut the world all about. He dont know the world run by crooks pushers an hood from the top to the bottom. In the White Houses an in the vegetable stores on the corners all of them got big hands in the pie. Its no world to be nice in. If you want the littlest crumb from the pie you got to fight you way to it. Evry body runnin an screamin for they little bit. Once you get you hand in the pie Man you got it made. Whut Mister Hurst got? He got a room that keep him warm in the cold that whut he got. I dont want none of

> that. . . . We dyin all the time but when you get you hand in the
> pie you get to be old like them white hair women on Park
> Avenue they walk with canes but they still alive. Unless some
> body cut you down while he tryen to get his. Well Man that the
> chance you take. You dont want to take the chance why you
> live in the cellar.[11]

This, of course, is fiction; but we may assume that Miller is presenting
something like a ghetto boy's philosophy of his own existence. The
discourse is based on firm convictions about the nature of the world and
its inhabitants, similar to the convictions on which slum children build
their images of life. In answer to the ancient question, "What is man?", a
slum child might well answer, "Crooks pushers an hood. . . ." (And what
is "Man"? The one who gets his hand in the pie and refuses to be a pig.)

The person who counts himself as nothing in his culture cannot rejoice
in the thought today. Medieval saints might have rejoiced in their
humility, as might some of the early Puritans who abased themselves
before the Lord. In our own times there is a nagging sense that things
ought not to be this way. There is a belief that to be human is to be
visible, potent, free. It may be that this belief, too, cannot be justified. To
think in such a way may be to confuse fiction with reality. The old fictions
and paradigms may still be exerting an influence: the heroes of *The Iliad;*
the princes and kings in Shakespeare's plays; the explorers and conquerors
of time past. Is it indeed the case that the man proud enough and strong
enough to defy even the gods was more truly "human" than the
domesticated little man who stayed behind? Did the victims of the Nazi or
Stalinist terror become less "human" because they did not or could not
take revenge? Does the collaborator lose his manhood to the resistance
fighter? The pacifist to the warrior—or the hawk to the dove? How, after
all, are we to conceive the human being?

Today, more than ever before, individuals rebel against what
dehumanizes and exploits them; and they do so in the light of some
"image of man." The modes of rebellion are multiple; the degrees of
articulateness vary; but a common theme is evident: the refusal to submit
to powerlessness and insignificance, however perceived. Whether the rebels
are college-aged youth, black militants, slum dwellers, outraged women,
war resisters, or defiant professors, they all demand a voice in decision
making; they demand a share in determining the shape of their lives, their
studies, their jobs. They are less likely to argue for this in terms of historic
precedents than in terms of "human" rights.

Radical leader Thomas Hayden, a founder of the Students for a
Democratic Society, said in a 1962 speech at the University of Michigan:

> ... A sense of powerlessness evolves, powerlessness with regard
> to changing the state of affairs evoked by the ideology of
> "complexity," a powerlessness that is often hidden beneath
> joviality and complacency. To the student things seem to happen
> because of a mixture of graft and manipulation by an unseen
> "them," the modern equivalent of "fate." To the extent that
> these powerless participate in public affairs, they participate with
> impotency, adapting themselves to the myriad of rules, initiated
> and imposed from without, that constitute the university game.
> ... They seek to conform their actions to what the Top People
> like, they just try and get by, feeling pretty content most of the
> time, enjoying the university's benevolent laxity about drinking
> regulations, building up their exam files, "playing it cool."[12]

At the end of the address, he said meaningfully to his audience: *"Do not wish to be a student in contrast to being a man.* Do not study as a student, but as a man who is alive and who cares." Aware of the sincerity of this demand, we ask what it means to study as a man rather than as a student. Do we define "man" in terms of his ability to care? Does the individual who wishes to be a student sacrifice some of his humanity? Is the student *objectively* powerless? In what sense is "power" fundamental to a viable contemporary image of man?

Kenneth Keniston's *Young Radicals* presents images of postadolescent rebels who do not make lasting commitments to adult occupations or to relationships. They refuse integration with established society, remaining ambivalent outsiders. They conceive social roles as entanglements, as threats to their identities, according to Keniston, because they are trying to "exclude from their lives the artificial, the non-genuine, the manipulative, and the hypocritical."[13] They prize the "direct, personal, I–thou encounters between two unique individuals" and reject anything that interferes with such encounters. The quality of personal relationships is "the ultimate judge of a man's life." When we consider the unlikelihood of a modern individual's spending most of his life in small, warm groups of people, we see the implicit problems. What implications for education do we find in the privatism of young radicals, in their refusal to play the culture's "game"? How can we reconcile this idea of private personal relationships with such views as John Dewey's—of the individual as a basically social organism becoming a full and responsible self as he participates more and more fully in social life? Some of the young people Keniston describes have, in effect, refused to move beyond the stage of youth; they have refused Dewey's conception of the imperative of growth. We must ask what growth has to do with a conception of the human being, what participation has to do with "being a man," what "being a man" entails.

Izell Blair, a black law student, told Robert Penn Warren at a meeting in a basement room: "Black is a symbol of evil. Everything that is white is good. If you go to heaven it's in a white gown. If you're an angel, the angel's white. This is the image I faced in growing up in American society. Everything white is pure. So you begin to wonder. You say, 'Well, what am I?' You feel you're rubbed out, as if you never existed."[14] This brings the question back to fundamentals again: a young man asks, "what am I?" And he begins to find out by dint of struggle. Another student, Robert Watson of Southern University, said: "What am I struggling for? I am struggling for the heights of a man. Regardless. I think that if I reach the heights of a man in a limited all-Negro society, I have not reached the heights of a man by world standards."[15] (And what does it mean to talk of "the heights of a man"? When, if ever, is it necessary to posit "world standards"? *Are* there "world standards"? Are there norms that determine what "being a man" should involve?)

Martin Luther King, Jr., had "manhood" constantly in mind when he spoke of his "Dream" and when he spoke of compassion or redemptive love. Stokely Carmichael, former head of the Student Non-Violent Coordinating Committee, was talking mainly about manhood when he introduced the slogan "Black Power" and shouted to student audiences that "Black is Beautiful." In his essay "What We Want," Carmichael said:

> The white man is irrelevant to blacks, except as an oppressive force. Blacks want to be in his place, yes, but not in order to terrorize and lynch and starve him. They want to be in his place because that is where a decent life can be had . . . But our vision is not merely of a society in which all black men have enough to buy the good things of life. When we urge that black money go into black pockets, we mean the communal pocket. We want to see money go back into the community and used to benefit it. . . . The society we seek to build among black people, then, is not a capitalist one. It is a society in which the spirit of community and humanistic love prevail. The word love is suspect; black expectations of what it might produce have been betrayed too often. But those were expectations of a response from the white community, which failed us. The love we seek to encourage is within the black community, the only American community where men call each other "brother" when they meet. We can build a community of love only where we have the ability and power to do so; among blacks.[16]

"Humanistic love . . ." Quite likely, Carmichael had in mind a humanism reminiscent of the Renaissance: Da Vinci's era, Michelangelo's, Pico della

Mirandola's, Erasmus's, Sir Thomas More's, Shakespeare's, the Medicis'. Like so many of his rebellious brothers, Carmichael was battling the sense of nothingness, claiming the right to stand tall in the center of the world. "I've had enough of someone else's propaganda," Malcolm X wrote in a letter to some friends, "I'm for truth, no matter who tells it. I'm for justice, no matter who it is for or against. I'm a human being first and foremost, and as such I'm for whoever and whatever benefits humanity *as a whole.*" (And, we ask again, what does "to be 'a human being first and foremost'" mean? What does "humanity" imply?)

Wherever we turn these days, we hear talk of manhood and dignity and power. Everyone who feels excluded from participation (the poor Puerto Rican family in Oscar Lewis's *La Vida,* the "invisible poor" in Michael Harrington's *The Other America*) perceives himself as someone whose essential dignity is being eroded, whose "natural rights" are being withheld. Women, too, are protesting against humiliation as well as discrimination. Their demands for equal rights and equal pay have become, in many places, demands for "liberation" on every front. Recognizing themselves as members of what Simone de Beauvoir once called "the second sex," women are rebelling against sex role stereotypes, against being demeaned as servants or adored as lovely dolls. Fundamentally—like Indians, Blacks, Chicanos, prisoners, even mental patients—they are rebelling against being treated as objects rather than as persons. They are calling for struggle, with joy in the struggle. Germaine Greer, the British commentator on women's plight, puts this notion in language which already has general application:

> Revolution is the festival of the oppressed. For a long time there may be no perceptible reward for women other than their new sense of purpose and integrity. Joy does not mean riotous glee, but it does mean the purposive employment of energy in a self-chosen enterprise. It does mean pride and confidence. It does mean communication and cooperation with others based on delight in their company and your own. To be emancipated from helplessness and need and walk freely upon the earth that is your birthright.[17]

How can a teacher evade such demands, such hope, such joy? However he perceives himself, he must at some moment confront human beings in his classroom. What does he see when he looks at a child, at a young person of any age? A spiritual creature? A social organism? A half-civilized barbarian? A potentially rational being? Does he see a case sitting before him, an instance of cultural deprivation, an IQ, an underachiever or an overachiever, a kid, a pupil, a fellow creature? What does he mean when he says someone is only human, deeply human, not even human? What does he mean when he discusses self-concept, identity, individuality? What does he mean by *man?*

One reaction might be to look up the word *man* in the dictionary. A more serious response would be to consult the sciences of man. After all, never before has so much been empirically known about the human organism and the varieties of human behavior. The biologist informs us of the DNA molecule; the psychologist presents generalizations about human development, learning behavior, responses to controlled stimuli, conditioning and feedback mechanisms, and (if he happens to be a depth psychologist) the dynamics of the unconscious, the functioning of impulses and instincts, and the patterns of sleep and dreams. The sociologist reports on the behavior of groups, the structure of institutions, the interplay of social forces within a society. The anthropologist, as we have seen, studies men in their diverse cultures and investigates values, attitudes, beliefs, and faiths. Depending on what scientist one has been reading, the human being appears as a sentient creature; a rational, projective, impulse-driven organism; a gregarious, dependent, acculturated animal; a conditioned being; or an open system for which anything is possible within the limits of the cultures now known.

Acquainted with all the empirical data (if that were conceivable), capable of adjusting one construct to another, the teacher would still have to ask, "Who am I?" and "How am I to conceive the other—that child, that colleague, that man?" It is not enough to know that the child—or the man—is a physicochemical organism charged with certain drives and energies, that he goes through a lengthy period of infantile dependence, that he is a social being with certain rights and duties, that he is equipped to conceptualize in distinctive ways at different stages of his development. The teacher encounters numerous diverse persons, young and old, in the course of his career. If he is willing to do philosophy, the teacher will ponder about what they have in common—if anything. He will examine his stubborn tendency to reach out for some notion of "essence," a shared quality to be judged precious, worthy, "endowed by his creator."

Specialization increases within each area. The social scientist, like the natural scientist today, often develops increasingly abstract formulations of his discoveries. Mathematical or other symbolic notations become extremely difficult for the layman to decipher. Even the teacher who has mastered the fundamental principles of one of these subjects has not necessarily determined all its implications for his work. For example, sociologist Talcott Parsons discusses the individual in relation to the social system and his participation in social interaction. Considering the individual as a system with values and goals, Parsons conceives two or more individuals interacting in such a way as to constitute an interdependent system. In the environment, where they face each other, there are opportunities for goal attainment, and there are sources of frustration. There is always a danger that the frustrations will increase so much that the interdependent system dissolves. For stability, says Parsons, "a common set of normative conceptions which attribute the meanings to the roles performed by individuals" must exist throughout society. He might explain powerlessness as a result of the growing frustration with respect to opportunities for goal attainment; but he would not say how to allay such powerlessness. Other sociologists—Marxists, for instance—might provide other explanations, most of which would attempt to be objective or value free. Given his students' social environments, how might the teacher reduce frustration in the classroom and provide a sense of attainable goals? If indeed society lacks a set of general agreements with respect to the meaning of individual roles, what does this signify for the teacher as he works to equip his students for participation in society as it now exists? If, as Marxists are prone to say, self-fulfillment is inconceivable under capitalism, what does this imply for a teacher eager to promote social satisfactions for the young? Sociological insights obviously help him to widen the context in which he perceives his students and their lives; but the potentially philosophic questions remain open. Is he to think of the individual as a system or as an embodiment of particular class relations and class interests? What does education mean under conditions of instability and strain? How might the teacher counteract the disintegrative forces sociologists describe where particular human beings are concerned?

The problem becomes still more interesting when, as in modern psychology, the best-known investigators in a field differ in their fundamental premises. We refer to the profound differences, for example, between behavioral psychologist B. F. Skinner and humanist psychologist Carl Rogers. When so many people are becoming enthusiasts for behavioral engineering, programmed learning, and the like, and just as many people are espousing encounter groups, sensitivity training, and nondirective therapy, no teacher can be entirely unaware of the controversy. Each point of view derives from and culminates in a particular conception of human existence and education. More often than not, the teacher—sometimes with no more than a layman's knowledge—has to decide himself which point of view to adopt.

The issue between the two schools of psychology has largely to do with the locus of control concerning productive human behavior. Skinner asserts that "people behave in ways which, as we say, conform to ethical, governmental, or religious patterns because they are reinforced for doing so." He means that they are reactive organisms, responding primarily to *external* causes and conditions, which can not only be studied and understood, but be arranged in specifiable ways so as "to *produce* behavior according to plan."[18] Rogers, on the other hand, stresses inner controls, choice, and self-actualization. "We will have to live with the realization," he writes, "that to deny the reality of the experience of responsible personal choice is as stultifying, as closed-minded, as to deny the possibility of a behavioral science."[19]

Dedicated focally to survival, Skinner argues for the deliberate application of science to human affairs. This "technology of behavior" would involve a process called operant conditioning, through which environmental stimuli are manipulated to select or elicit specifiable responses from the organism. Feedback informs the organism of the consequences of his behavior; and if the consequences are rewarding, certain responses will be reinforced. If the consequences are unpleasant, involving the use of "aversive" stimuli or the withdrawal of positive reinforcers, the responses will be extinguished. According to Skinner, education is inefficient, because teachers refuse to take the responsibility for "manipulating external variables" in this way. Instead, they make the student responsible for his learning and rely on "inner states" whose existence they cannot prove. It is as meaningless to blame ignorance on the student because of a lack of "inner wisdom" or "will to learn" as it is to define freedom in terms of feelings or states of mind. "Man's struggle for freedom," Skinner writes, "is not due to a will to be free, but to certain behavioral processes characteristic of the human organism; the chief effect is the avoidance of or escape from so-called 'aversive' features of the environment." The notion of autonomy is meaningless, as is the concept of human dignity. The only viable alternative—the only *humane* alternative— to such ideas is control by the environment. And Skinner sees wonderful possibilities for behavioral technologies:

> It is hard to imagine a world in which people live together without quarreling, maintain themselves by producing the food, shelter, and clothing they need, enjoy themselves and contribute to the enjoyment of others in art, music, literature, and games, consume only a reasonable part of the resources of the world and add as little as possible to its pollution, bear no more children than can be raised decently, continue to explore the world around them and discover better ways of dealing with it, and come to know themselves accurately and, therefore, manage themselves effectively.[20]

Skinner's philosophic novel *Walden Two* further develops this utopia vision of a world in which all are good and wise and happy. The community he describes may strike many readers as bland and overly organized. But jealousy, pride, competition, and violence are all eradicated there; and, except on premises grounded in a belief in free will, Skinner's notion of the "good life" is difficult to challenge. Perhaps strangely, his utopia has appealed to young people living in communes; and others have modeled communes after Walden Two. They may have used the language of Thoreau's *Walden* when they first rebelled against American institutional life; but once they established their communities, they could not help seeking a way of perpetuating the "personal warmth or the straightforward natural strength," which are said in Skinner's novel to be responsible for the success of Walden Two.

Frazier, who says he is a man with an "idée fixe . . . the control of human behavior," is the founder of the fictional utopia; but he admits that he is cold, conceited, and selfish. In fact, he adds, he "couldn't possibly be a member of any genuine community." The point, however, is that he is not a product of Walden Two. "Give me credit for what I've done or not, as you please," he says, "but don't look for perfection. Isn't it enough that I've made other men likable and happy and productive?"[21] Here is the crux of the philosophical problem, even for people who have come to be acutely pessimistic about the nature of man. Who has a right to *make* other human beings "likable and happy and productive"?

The issue was raised bleakly and dramatically in Anthony Burgess's *A Clockwork Orange* (written in 1962 and made into a movie nine years later). The novel deals with a future period, when a welfare state is in existence but when gangs of delinquent young men entertain themselves by engaging in "superviolence" against indiscriminately chosen victims. The narrator, Alex, is one of these young men, a vicious and antisocial gang leader. When he finally commits a murder, he is jailed. After two years, he volunteers for a program of reeducation so that he can be made into a good person and released. The program involves deliberate conditioning, undertaken (in Alex's case) to make sex and brutality so repulsive that he gets sick whenever he confronts either one. The conditioning process is successful, and the results are demonstrated to the officials. The demonstration reaches a climax when Alex literally licks the boots of a man who insults and attacks him physically; and at that moment the prison chaplain objects: "'He has no real choice, has he? Self-interest, fear of physical pain, drove him to that grotesque act of self-abasement. Its insincerity was clearly to be seen. He ceases to be a wrongdoer. He ceases also to be a creature capable of moral choice.'" And the (probably Skinnerian) psychologist responds: "'These are subtleties. . . . We are not concerned with motive, with the higher ethics. We are concerned only with cutting down crime. . . .' "[22]

More than likely, Rogers would ask the same question the chaplain asks. Rogers' priorities differ in almost every respect from Skinner's; he objects strenuously to manipulating human beings into acceptable forms of behavior—in the cause of survival, cutting down crime, even happiness. In one response to Skinner, he said:

> We can, if we wish, choose to make men submissive, conforming, docile. Or at the other end of the spectrum of choice, we can choose to use the behavioral sciences in ways which will free, not control; which will bring about constructive variability, not conformity; which will develop creativity, not contentment; which will facilitate each person in his self-directed process of becoming; which will aid individuals, groups, and even the concept of science, to become self-transcending in freshly adaptive ways of meeting life and its problems.[23]

Self-direction is at the core of Rogers' conception of the human being: warm and accepting human relationships help individuals become self-initiated learners, "more original, more self-disciplined, less anxious and other-directed." If the therapist, or administrator, or teacher can express authentic feeling and concern, can create climates that allow people to value themselves and become what they want to be, he will be facilitating both growth and mastery. He will be liberating people to actualize themselves by bringing their feelings into play and tapping the resources of their innerness. He will be granting them the responsibility for creating themselves and the *dignity* of self-determination.

Rogers' view corresponds to those protesting manipulation and conditioning. His view of the human being appears to correspond to the views of young radicals and libertarians. But it offers no guarantees for the present or the future. Rogers and his fellow humanists treat personality as an open system in an open universe of flux and novelties. They are not, as is Skinner, concerned with survival; they design no utopian societies. To release a person from anxiety and inauthenticity is enough; to liberate many persons may at least increase the chances that a good society will someday emerge.

There probably is no way of proving Skinner's claim that inner states do not exist; nor is there a way of proving Rogers' claim that persons can be freed to actualize themselves. Much depends on whether the teacher believes in free will, whether he believes that his students can effectually choose to learn or not to learn instead of requiring conditioning from without. There has been agreement throughout much of history that voluntary action is possible and that a "faculty" called the will, which philosophers have called "intermediate" between reason and desire, does indeed exist. There has also been some agreement that the will is self-determining, uncaused by outside factors. Because it is not susceptible to empirical proof, it can only be known *immediately* by the individual, especially when he asks himself whether he can will *not* to perform a particular act.

On occasion (in the classroom, in the political arena, in the corporation office) explanations for behavior, which do not depend on assumption of free choice, may be preferable. But it is difficult for many people to deny their existential experiences of being able to decide for themselves. As long as they are convinced that certain things *might* have been left undone, those existential experiences appear to be confirmed.

A great deal depends on vantage point. The teacher who conceives education intentionally or "from inside a form of life" is likely to assume a considerable degree of freedom in his classroom. He is also likely to hold his students responsible for taking the kinds of action demanded for learning how to learn. The teacher who sees himself as a technologist or a manipulator of environmental variables, such as the outside researcher who observes someone else's classroom, is far more likely to focus on behavioral responses to visible occurrences in the environment. As we shall see in the following chapter, the teacher's primary concern will have to be with the consequences of each approach to (or definition of) man for his teaching or curriculum planning or whatever else his project turns out to be. Whether he chooses a Skinnerian or a Rogerian view (or a Freudian or a Catholic view) becomes a moral rather than an analytic issue. As a practitioner, he will have to decide on the basis of actual consequences which approach is right for him.

The same response is warranted when other types of information—scientific, pseudoscientific, or nonscientific—confront the teacher. As we have already seen, some ways of structuring social reality focus on oppression, exploitation, acting out, and violence. People come to see their worlds in ways that highlight certain factors and suppress others; and frequently their perceptions affect their conceptualization of man. On some level, the teacher has to take into account awarenesses, which play as significant a role in certain individuals' lives as what is taken, on the basis of acknowledged evidence, to be verifiably true. Often, they give rise to the kinds of belief that seem to settle a range of uncertainties no exact knowledge can resolve. Like the convictions of powerlessness and nothingness, they must somehow be dealt with, because, like so many other stray currents of thought, they may well affect the teacher's preconceptions about the human beings he encounters in his everyday life.

The books of Konrad Lorenz and Robert Ardrey have attracted considerable interest; and there has been a growing tendency to make their conclusions foundational to expectation and belief. Both works involve ethological anthropology and have to do with animal aggression and such notions as territoriality. Each writer draws conclusions about human behavior from his studies of conflict in animal societies and of animal predilections for staking out and defending territories, sometimes against their species. Working with evolutionary theories and by means of analogy, the two writers treat human aggression as the natural product of biological systems rather than of cultural life. Although seriously challenged by the scientific community, ideas of this sort have penetrated official as well as popular culture. Laymen and policy makers speak of inborn aggressiveness —thus far mainly in connection with delinquents or criminals. Artists become preoccupied with violence and criminality, as if to suggest that symbolic engagement (or collaboration) with what is secretly desired can somehow purge. The widespread fascination with violence is explained by its spread through all levels of our society as well as by the recognition of violence in our history. It is explained as well by the persistence of frightful (and publicized) conflicts abroad, by the constant reminders of bombing and gassing and napalming, by the omnipresence of suffering in everyday life. Some people are resigned to violence as part of man's nature; others celebrate when it is used for good or for the people's cause. The establishment is called an embodiment of impersonal brutality. The more police helmets, clubs, and gas canisters appear, the more justifiable and "human" it seems to many to take violent action in attack or self-defense. Jean-Paul Sartre supports the view that political violence can be purgative and can restore a sense of manhood to the oppressed. He suggests that to be violent when the occasion is right is to act on one's freedom, to refuse to be a mere object.

This dimension of human existence may remind the teacher of what Herman Melville called "the power of blackness," the ambiguities below the surface of things. If he is sufficiently awakened to modern life, the teacher may respond by trying to take action against the dehumanization violence causes; he may work to move his students to rebel against the numbness too much exposure entails. But, no matter what he eventually discovers about man's animal ancestry, he ought never to act on the presumption that man's end—*any* man's end—is in his beginning.

Just as some individuals in the late nineteenth century believed that the natural laws of evolution dominated human as well as animal existence and that natural selection weeded out the fit for survival in a capitalist society, so we are tempted to attribute unacceptable behavior to genetic inheritance. The teacher need not return to a glorified vision of the angelic child to combat such pessimism. Instead he can think about the multiple untapped possibilities in each complicated organism he is trying to teach. The human creature, after all, stops being merely the victim of evolutionary determinism once he develops a mind, once he can consciously intervene in the course of events. He has the potential for creating his purposes, even for controlling the direction of social change, because the mind's "function in civilization," as sociologist Lester Ward explained at the start of this century, is "to preserve the dynamic and prevent the statical condition of the social forces."[24] By means of their cultures, their designs for living, human beings become more than "natural," whatever their origins. One of the teacher's tasks is to free those he can reach to take a hand in their own destinies—to "liberate" (as so many people are demanding) themselves.

The theories of human aggression, like the conviction that individuals can be totally subordinated to the system, implicitly challenge conceptions of dignity. Although we no longer enjoy the Renaissance confidence in man's centrality in the universe, we can still cherish the image of the free man, the political man capable of participation in the life of a polis. Recalling the Promethean vision, we can still affirm the individual's potential for living with his eyes open, consenting consciously and thoughtfully to the rule of law. To identify violence with power is to suggest that the human being can live only in a command–obedience relationship. Whether he is the tyrant or the slave, does not matter; his true power, which may be his ability to define himself as a free person and to act in concert with other men, is submerged. And, indeed, those who feel afflicted by powerlessness seem to have just this notion in mind. For the teacher, to think this way is to think of multiple possibilities. To act in the light of such possibilities is to take action against alienation and estrangement as well as against the claims that human beings are naturally aggressive and bound by their territoriality. Hopefully, it is also to act against violations of personality in the classroom and the school; for to violate means to do violence, and this is a negation of the teacher's power to free his students to be.

The teacher, then, must confront and assess more than the facts of the case. Becoming as conscious as he can of his situation, clarifying what *he* understands (and feels and imagines) human nature to be, he must decide what to take as fact, what to treat as operationally useful, and what to take as serious belief. In all the domains we have mentioned—the arts, the social sciences, ordinary human experience—the open questions multiply. They are distinctively modern questions, which the teacher can neither answer absolutely nor evade.

have already seen how many of these questions have become
ınd urgent, how they nag at persons trying to break free. We
ʾe that feelings of hollowness, doubts about decency and
thousands of people, including children. What Emile
ᴜmed *anomie* is more than ever the disease of the modern age.
are occurring so rapidly that traditional norms and rules no
hold; nor do traditional limits, now that controls are being set aside
ᴄh an extent. Desires and passions become, according to Durkheim,
ʾe exigent and out of control." Few people feel grounded in a
sustaining and meaningful reality, as paradigms shift daily and constructs
become obscured. Yet some long so desperately for stability that they
constantly verge on suicide. What Durkheim called *anomic suicide*—
whether actual or symbolic—is painful evidence of felt meaninglessness,
believed-in nothingness. Clearly, the only way to combat it is to move
people to save their lives.

Are human beings capable of saving themselves? Are their fearful
feelings justified? If they are justified, how do these feelings affect the
teacher's sense of what is possible? As we have seen, much of what is
happening to individuals has been attributed to the anonymity of life in
"the lonely crowd," especially in the megalopolis where most Americans
now live. Increasingly, people are claiming that there is something
antihuman in vast institutional structures, which keeps them from
becoming what they will. This claim, too, presumes a conception of human
nature. It presumes that the "technique," which seems to dominate so
much of life, enforces an abnormal existence, especially when it works to
absorb the individual into the mass society, making him a mass man.

Again, empirical proof is probably unattainable. But it is worth noting
the numbers of people who are coming to believe this to be the case. We
have already referred to artists and their particular subjective responses;
and we have talked somewhat about the liberation movements founded on
the same premises. In the areas of health, mental illness, retardation,
correction, and rehabilitation, for example, large institutions, challenged
for their impersonality and inhumanity, are giving way to more
individualized community services. Seldom has so much attention been
paid to individual needs and demands; seldom has so much onus been
placed on the system and the crowd.

Some of the best-known educational critics are reacting to the same
forces and the same perceived dangers. Many of them are romantic
thinkers preoccupied with the nature—and the integrity—of man. Like
Ralph Waldo Emerson a century ago, they believe that "society is
everywhere in conspiracy against the manhood of every one of its
members." The American schools, for such men as Paul Goodman, John

Holt, Edgar Z. Friedenberg, and Ivan Illich, help to reinforce that conspiracy. The issue for the teacher *in* the school is not so much whether the critics are right or wrong in their more sweeping condemnations but whether the teacher's view of himself and the individuals in his class permits him to work authentically toward the realization of possibilities. If he sees a kind of determinism within the institutional structure, an embodied violence no personal action can allay, he must choose himself as one species of teacher (either as defeated and acquiescent or as reduced to working beyond the law). If he believes that, even *within* the bounds of institutional rules, he can promote self-awareness and move young people to learn how to learn, he needs at least to be clear about his definitions of personhood and individuality, his expectations of human beings pressured and distracted by a confusing world.

Paul Goodman conceives compulsory education in America to be a universal trap; and he has communicated some of his outrage to numerous popular audiences. In the present day, he asserts, the primary function of the school is to provide "apprentice-training for corporations, government, and the teaching profession itself." Children are brainwashed by "a social machine not interested in persons, except to man and aggrandize itself." Unique, vigorous persons are transmuted into "personnel." Most appallingly, teachers too often serve the system blindly and help it render human beings into hollow, inauthentic, resigned creatures with no hope of becoming independent or free.

John Holt describes school children as subject people forced into a school that is a kind of jail. He finds the coercion by adults and the subject matters imposed to be warping; he sees children "withdrawing the most intelligent and creative parts of their minds" when they are in school. Like eighteenth century philosopher Jean Jacques Rousseau, Holt believes children are born free and are naturally spontaneous and curious until adult society puts them in chains. He presumes that true humanity is in some manner inborn and that it expresses itself most truly in the wonder of the unspoiled child. Holt's view is contrary to John Dewey's, which treats "humanness" as something learned. Although Holt does not speak of learning as a process apart from group life, he does put far less emphasis than did progressivist thinkers on the importance of participation in a vital, complex community. In fact, his later writings suggest that schools should be abolished, that the miniature communities they sometimes create are no longer conceivable.

Edgar Z. Friedenberg, describing the public school as "the instrument through which society acculturates people into consensus before they are old enough to resist it,"[25] believes that modern civilization suppresses the vital energies of young people because of adult frustration and fear. Any group with "an exuberant and expressive personal style," he writes, tends to antagonize the authoritarian and squeamish adults who administer and teach in the schools. To make matters worse, children "processed" by the system learn a "disrespect for human personality" and "a contempt for privacy," like that which characterizes their elders.

Unlike some of his fellow critics, Friedenberg does not reject the intellectual component of schooling; and he believes that competent individuals ought to be able to pursue a variety of meanings in the classroom. Competence, however, is linked to a special giftedness and vitality, traits which Friedenberg finds most frequently among children untainted by middle-class respectability and small-mindedness: the freewheeling, talented upper-class young or boys capable and courageous enough to become gang leaders in the slums. There is an elitism in this view which perplexes and alienates many teachers, even those who become stimulated by Friedenberg's work. Try as they may to identify with his point of view, they find that they are dismissed with considerable scorn when they affirm a willingness to break with the processing model that is so despised. Then, too, most teachers are indeed middle class and committed, on some level, to majority values. They cannot help being troubled by the fact that Friedenberg deliberately excludes from his image of the desirable human character so many ordinary, well-meaning people: children of the blue-collar worker; small-town adolescents who cheer for basketball teams; people who have experienced what Norman Mailer calls "the good simple funky nitty-gritty American joys."

When he began writing about the "vanishing adolescent" and such qualities as courage and loyalty, Friedenberg was mainly concerned with the ways in which an other-directed society disapproved of and tamped down the spontaneity of adolescents, black and white. He was also disturbed by the ways in which schools forced bright, knightly boys (often black boys) into lower middle-class molds. But that was when the apathy of the 1950s was just giving way to the protests of the 1960s, and many observers were lamenting the blandness that had so long prevailed, the barbecue-pit culture of suburbia, the dominance of the organization man. With the civil rights movement and campus unrest, a nationwide youth culture suddenly sprang into being, and before long a full-fledged counter-culture was in evidence. The vitality and expressiveness Friedenberg had said were so suspect now were being displayed on all sides. Quite naturally, this vitality often brought youth into direct confrontation with older people threatened by the new morality and new life styles; but spontaneity could no longer be tamped down. The rebellious young today refuse to "vanish" or to be pressed into molds; and, even when lulls in overt protest occur, styles remain visible, along with images quite different from those the school are cultivating. Are the members of the counter-culture more natural, more authentic than the repressed, resentful young people of the past? Does the majority culture indeed distort personality and make originality impossible? *Must* the teacher, as a representative of the official culture, exert his major influence on behalf of adjustment, self-discipline, and control?

Ivan Illich says that the institution of the school is, by definition, repressive. Because young people are compelled to attend, they can in no sense be considered free to initiate their learning experiences or to create themselves. The schools exist to manipulate them into a consumerism, on which capitalist society depends. Most learning takes place casually, outside of schools; "teachers, more often than not, obstruct such learning of subject matters as goes on in school." Young people, probably without exception, are naturally willing and able to learn (until their schooling stops them). With the resources of ordinary life—things, models, peers, and elders—they require no obligatory curriculum, certainly no obligatory involvement with a school. However, Illich does not allow for the possibility that some children might be indifferent, that others might be crippled by their lives. He regards every person as originally independent and outreaching. If given opportunities to study voluntarily with peers, each one would learn what he wants to learn and that would be enough. He does not talk of some subject matter as being more desirable than other subject matter, of adjusting teaching to the capacities of the child. He does not mention free citizenship or conscious transformations of reality. He talks only of deschooling, which, he believes, has the potential to transform society because it will decontrol the young.

We spoke earlier of the Promethean vision of what human beings can become when they are enabled to emerge from ignorance. It is relevant to note that Illich describes that vision as the "Promethean fallacy." He implies that something about rationality dehumanizes, tempts human beings to manipulate and control.

> Prometheus is usually thought to mean "foresight," or sometimes even "he who makes the North Star progress." He tricked the gods out of their monopoly of fire, taught men to use it in the forging of iron, became the god of technologists, and wound up in iron chains.[26]

He proposes that we reject Prometheus in favor of his brother Epimetheus, whose name means hindsight and who represents a negation of authoritarian reason. The new man—Epimethean Man—values "hope above expectation." He loves people more than products; he tends the earth; he cares. The teacher may detect a cruel either–or proposition, especially knowing that Illich believes the schools put persons "in iron chains." Yet the vision of Epimethean Man may stir his heart. Who would not be stirred by talk of privacy, love, the ability to wait on the other? The teacher may wonder if a commitment to heightened consciousness and the search for meanings excludes the securing of such values—most particularly if that commitment is acted on in a school. Is he condemned, no matter what his aspirations, to obstruct, manipulate, enchain?

A great deal depends on how the teacher adjusts his perspectives on human beings and the institutions they have made. Much also depends on how he chooses himself as a teacher, how he decides to act on what he has come to know.

Notes and References

1. Thomas Hobbes, *Leviathan,* ed. Francis B. Randall (New York: Washington Square Press, 1970), p. 85.

2. Giovanni Pico della Mirandola, "The Dignity of Man," in *The Portable Renaissance Reader,* ed. James Bruce Ross and Mary Martin McLaughlin (New York: Viking Press, 1959), p. 379.

3. Marcus G. Raskin, *Being and Doing* (New York: Random House, 1970).

4. Charles A. Reich, "The Limits of Duty," *The New Yorker,* June 19, 1971, p. 52.

5. Bertram M. Gross, "Can It Happen Here?", *The New York Times,* January 4, 1971, p. 31.

6. Philip Slater, *The Pursuit of Loneliness: American Culture at the Breaking Point* (Boston: Beacon Press, 1970), p. 27.

7. Samuel Beckett, *Waiting for Godot* (New York: Grove Press, 1954), p. 15.

8. Samuel Beckett, *Waiting for Godot,* p. 61.

9. Robert Coles, *Children of Crisis* (Boston: Atlantic Monthly Press, Little, Brown & Company, 1967), p. 47.

10. Claude Brown, *Manchild in the Promised Land* (New York: The Macmillan Company, 1965), p. 95.

11. Warren Miller, *The Cool World* (Greenwich, Conn.: Fawcett Publications, 1964), p. 88.

12. Thomas Hayden, "Student Social Action: From Liberation to Community," in *The New Student Left,* ed. Mitchell Cohen and Dennis Hale (Boston: Beacon Press, 1967), pp. 279–280.

13. Kenneth Keniston, *Young Radicals* (New York: Harcourt Brace Jovanovich, 1968), p. 279.

14. Robert Penn Warren, *Who Speaks for the Negro?* (New York: Vintage Books, 1966), p. 370.

15. Robert Penn Warren, *Who Speaks for the Negro?,* p. 364.

16. Stokely Carmichael, "What We Want," in *The New Student Left,* ed. Mitchell Cohen and Dennis Hale (Boston: Beacon Press, 1967), pp. 118–119.

17. Germaine Greer, *The Female Eunuch* (New York: McGraw-Hill Book Company, 1971), p. 328.

18. B. F. Skinner, "Freedom and the Control of Men," *The American Scholar,* vol. 25, no. 1, winter 1955–1956, excerpted in *Models of Man,* ed. Paul Nash (New York: John Wiley & Sons, 1968), p. 415.

19. Carl R. Rogers, *On Becoming a Person* (Boston: Houghton Mifflin Company, 1961), p. 400.

20. B. F. Skinner, *Beyond Freedom and Dignity* (New York: Alfred A. Knopf, 1971), p. 214.

21. B. F. Skinner, *Walden Two* (New York: The Macmillan Company, 1962), p. 249.

22. Anthony Burgess, *A Clockwork Orange* (New York: Ballantine Books, 1971), pp. 125–126.

23. Carl R. Rogers, *On Becoming a Person,* p. 400.

24. Lester Ward, quoted in Lawrence A. Cremin, *The Transformation of the School* (New York: Alfred A. Knopf, 1961), p. 65.

25. Edgar Z. Friedenberg, *Coming of Age in America* (New York: Random House, 1965), p. 170.

26. Ivan Illich, *Deschooling Society* (New York: Harper & Row, Publishers, 1971), p. 29.

Further Reading

Robert Ardrey, *The Territorial Imperative* (New York: Atheneum, 1966).

Hannah Arendt, "Reflections on Violence," *New York Review,* February 27, 1969.

Simone de Beauvoir, *The Second Sex* (New York: Alfred A. Knopf, 1957).

John Dewey, *Democracy and Education* (New York: The Macmillan Company, 1916).

Emile Durkheim, "Anomic Suicide," from *Suicide* in *Theories of Society,* vol. 2, ed. Talcott Parsons, Edward Shils, Kaspar D. Naegele, and Jesse R. Pitts (New York: The Free Press, 1961).

Ralph Waldo Emerson, "Self-Reliance," in *Emerson's Essays* (New York: Thomas Y. Crowell Company, 1951).

Edgar Z. Friedenberg, *The Vanishing Adolescent* (New York: Dell Publishing Company, 1959).

Paul Goodman, *Compulsory Mis-education* and *The Community of Scholars* (New York: Vintage Books, 1964).

——, *People or Personnel: Decentralizing and the Mixed System* (New York: Random House, 1965).

Michael Harrington, *The Other America: Poverty in the United States* (Baltimore: Penguin Books, 1963).

Martin Luther King, Jr., *Why We Can't Wait* (New York: Harper & Row, Publishers, 1964).

Oscar Lewis, *La Vida* (New York: Random House, 1966).

Konrad Lorenz, *On Aggression* (New York: Bantam Books, 1967).

Norman Mailer, *The Armies of the Night* (New York: The New American Library, 1968).

Malcolm X, *The Autobiography of Malcolm X* (New York: Grove Press, 1965).

Karl Marx, "The Material Forces and the Relations of Production," from *A Contribution to the Critique of Political Economy* in *Theories of Society,* vol. 1, ed. Talcott Parsons, Edward Shils, Kaspar D. Naegele, and Jesse R. Pitts (New York: The Free Press, 1961).

Kate Millett, *Sexual Politics* (Garden City, N.Y.: Doubleday & Company, 1970).

José Ortega y Gasset, *The Revolt of the Masses* (New York: W. W. Norton & Company, 1957).

Talcott Parsons, *Societies* (Englewood Cliffs, N.J.: Prentice-Hall, 1966).

Richard S. Peters, "Education as Initiation" (London: Evans Brothers for the University of London Institute of Education, Monograph, 1963).

Marcus G. Raskin, *Being and Doing* (New York: Random House, 1970).

David Riesman, *The Lonely Crowd* (New Haven: Yale University Press, 1952).

Jean-Paul Sartre, Preface to Frantz Fanon, *The Wretched of the Earth* (New York: Grove Press, 1963).

Henry David Thoreau, *Walden* (New York: Washington Square Press, 1963).

Chapter Four

Being and Learning

In spite of Death, the mark and seal of the parental control,
Man is yet free, during his brief years, to examine, to criticise,
to know, and in imagination to create. To him alone, in the
world with which he is acquainted, this freedom belongs; and in
this lies his superiority to the resistless forces that control his
outward life.

> Bertrand Russell
> "A Free Man's Worship,"
> *Mysticism and Logic*

Only when the individual knows the other in all his otherness
as himself, as man, and from there breaks through to the other,
has he broken through his solitude in a strict and transforming
meeting. It is obvious that such an event can only take place if
the person is stirred up as a person. In individualism the person,
in consequence of his merely imaginary mastery of his basic
situation, is attacked by the ravages of the fictitious, however
much he thinks or strives to think, that he is asserting himself
as a person in being. In collectivism the person surrenders
himself when he renounces the directness of personal decision
and responsibility. In both cases the person is incapable of
breaking through to the other: there is genuine relation only
between genuine persons.

> Martin Buber
> *I and Thou*

There are no final answers, nor are there directives to govern every
teaching situation. If he is to be effective, the teacher cannot function
automatically or according to a set of predetermined rules. Teaching is
purposeful action. It must be carried on deliberately in situations never
twice the same. The teacher must personally *intend* to bring about certain
changes in students' outlooks; he must *mean* to enable them to perform in

particular ways, to do particular tasks, to impose increasingly complex orders upon their worlds.

His intentions will inevitably be affected by the assumptions he makes regarding human nature and human possibility. Many of these assumptions are hidden; most have never been articulated. If he is to achieve clarity and full consciousness, the teacher must attempt to make such assumptions explicit; for only then can they be examined, analyzed, and understood.

Many things stand in his way, among them a reliance on slogans and abstractions, which abound in American educational talk. Slogans are unsystematic, popular ways of talking about education. They are, writes Israel Scheffler, phrases "repeated warmly or reassuringly rather than pondered gravely."[1] Some have to do with self-fulfillment and self-realization; others, with democratic citizenship and life adjustment. They suggest that the answers are already given and perform a kind of magical function for people who need to believe that the schools, by definition, promote both personal development and social adaptation. Yet all slogans, as Scheffler says, are "rallying symbols." They in no sense describe what actually exists, yet they are taken—wishfully or desperately —to be generalizations or statements of fact.

Educational slogans may have a particular appeal in the United States because of their association with the American Dream and all that it implies. Such expressions have customarily focused on the mythic individual—man in his dignity and perfectibility. The fundamental mythology of American education has in fact had to do with the ways in which the schools serve to nurture perfectibility. History is so full of world views presenting man as sinful or degraded that it has been difficult to resist the attractions of a glorified image especially contrived for the New World. Surely there is much of value in a culture's preoccupation with Man rather than with Nation, Fatherland, or Heritage. A commitment to freedom and moral equality seems implicit in this view; education finds it's sanction in the highest moral ideals.

Nevertheless, the teacher needs to recall that the traditional image of man was a function of eighteenth century experience, of an Age of Reason extending back to the classic past. The terms 'man' and 'democratic citizen' both refer to abstract qualities arbitrarily used to define the human essence. These qualities can best be described as dignity, rationality, and self-sufficiency, which are all interrelated and are probably present, at any given moment of history, in only a few individuals. The image of the individual, although purportedly capturing the defining characteristics of a universe of men, actually excludes more than it encompasses. Among other things, it excludes fallibility, ambivalence, passion, and most of instinctual life. It suggests an ideal so lofty, so civilized, that the ordinary person can scarcely aspire to it. Yet it has given rise to what has long been thought to be the proper standard of behavior, America's mythical cultural norm. We are only now beginning to realize how inequitable this image is—and how intolerable. Not only has it bred suspicions of spontaneity, enthusiasm, and expressiveness; it has made it unimaginably difficult to ascribe "humanness" to people whose life styles veer from the norm. Today, as before, some teachers assert that certain children "aren't even human." Some point to a child who cannot achieve and call him "a little animal." They could not speak this way if they did not have in mind some abstract model of what they think a human being ought to be.

It is not only the American Dream and the slogans associated with it that feed people's notions of what such terms as 'man' and 'reason' and 'education' imply. As in other domains of thought, a history of paradigms has to do with the human being and the way he ought to be reared. Since the days of the ancient civilizations, scholars and philosophers have devoted their energies to determining the most desirable patterns of behavior for their particular cultural circumstances. The identity and meaning of a culture, after all, depend on the degree to which the young internalize characteristic attitudes, beliefs, skills, and values. The person concerned with remaking the culture must necessarily think of ways to bring about changes in the dispositions and commitments of those who will continue it over time. Moreover, he must define some image of man which embodies or symbolizes his ideal. This has happened repeatedly over the course of generations—in Plato's day, Aristotle's, Locke's, Rousseau's, Kant's, Dewey's, Freud's. Each image, each definition was a function of a complex structure of knowledge and thought. It was only with the nineteenth century that a body of dependable scientific knowledge about human behavior developed; but the absence of empirical studies did not stop earlier philosophers from describing or prescribing.

Descriptions and prescriptions still dominate imagination today. The fictions they created were often compelling, as were the way they gave rise to "necessary" conceptions of educational method and aim. Because specific images were *named* and then elaborated on, they seem (even today) to have actually existed; and they remain somehow in the background of modern thought like silent presences demanding respect. To become conscious about our views of teacher and learner, we need to understand the significance of those presences. We need to know something of their origins, of the way they determined educational ideas. Our objective in recalling them is not to disclose sacred writs or immutable ideals but to consider the inventiveness with which human beings have made sense of the diverse constructs they devised for thinking about themselves and about education.

As we have suggested in the preceding chapter, there is a whole spectrum of visions, with man as animal at one end, man as paragon or god figure at the other. At each point in the spectrum, there is a distinctive approach to education, usually derived from a definition of man or a definite vision of man-in-the-world. Most of these approaches share the conviction that no matter how sacred the child or how close to the divine, something specific has to be done to enable him to become a true human being—to enculturate him. They also have in common a prejudice against stasis and inertia—the idea that the living creature must be awakened if he is to learn.

In Plato's *Apology,* Socrates compares himself as teacher with a gadfly and tells the Athenian citizens that he was "always fastening upon you, arousing and persuading and reproaching you." To remain immobile, to refuse to inquire was to be caught napping, to resist being stirred into life. But it was not enough merely to awaken: an individual had to be brought, on his own initiative, to regard virtue. He had to be stimulated to take an active role in the search for his perfection; he had to be courageous enough to turn toward the Good. Socrates has been likened to a midwife, equipped to deliver people of the illusions, the unexamined judgments, the mere opinions that kept them from recollecting what was Good and True. These two modes of teaching—questioning and eliciting—followed from a particular view of the human being. He existed in two worlds: one part of him was caught in the flow of time and imperfection; the other belonged to eternity. His very nature compelled him to want to transcend mere finitude and wish for immortality—or a return to his soul's true home. Only by loving the Good could he bring his energies and appetites under the control of Reason. Only by seeking to clarify the Forms, of which he was dimly aware, could he overcome his earthly ambitions and achieve his true humanity. Man was defined, therefore, in terms of what Plato conceived to be his perfection: to be fully human was to exist in a condition of love or pure, unalloyed rationality. Hence, education could only be a process of helping people actualize their latent power to discern the fixities in the fluid world they inhabited and, by that means, to attain recognition of the Real. No attention was devoted to the practical arts or the manipulative arts; no attention was given to understanding or valuing specific, concrete phenomena or to controlling the direction of earthly change. The fully realized person had higher, better things to do. And that person still remains in the background for teachers today. He may be fading somewhat; he may be only a blurred image. But with his lofty preoccupations and his complete intellectual purity, he is still a kind of rallying symbol. He still makes normative demands.

For Aristotle, the universe is continuous, and everything within it is forever seeking actualization of its essence, its true form. The acorn strives for the form of an oak tree; the child aspires toward the "excellent" exercise of his faculties. The human soul is endowed with certain potentials at birth; and the function of education is to enable the individual to acquire the habits and dispositions that will actualize the potentials. Man is, by definition, a rational animal with reason separating him from other animals and bringing him closer to God; hence, the highest excellence is associated with the fullest rationality. People, however, differ at birth in the kinds of realization possible. "All persons share in the different parts of the soul," wrote Aristotle, "but in different ways."[2] The slave lacks the faculty of deliberation; the woman possesses it "but in an inauthoritative form," whereas children have it only in an immature form. Contemplating this traditional differentiation, reminded of the traditional habit of arranging human beings in hierarchies, we may look again at our modes of categorizing people. Notions of upper and lower have always appealed to supporters of inequitable social arrangements, particularly when they have tried to justify those arrangements by grounding them in a conception of the "real." A contemporary reader can easily challenge such views as archaic and undemocratic, particularly when he recognizes that they originated in the context of slave civilizations. It is more difficult, however, for him to see how the paradigm persists in the background of thinking about endowments and capacities in the present day.

A modern Aristotelian, Jacques Maritain, makes especially clear how an emphasis on some true human essence may lead to a conception of methods and aims. He writes that a "philosophical–religious idea of man" deals with "the essential and intrinsic, though not visible or tangible character, and with the intelligible density of that being we call man."[3] Thus, the sciences cannot direct the course of education adequately because they ignore man's "nature and destiny" in favor of what can be measured and observed. Education must, Maritain says, be concerned with more than "animal nature"; it must involve "a respect for the soul as well as for the body of the child . . . and a sort of sacred and loving attention to his mysterious identity, which is a hidden thing that no techniques can reach." Education, then, should be devoted to promoting exercises of the will and the intelligence, which can draw the child toward the infinite realm of Truth. If the human being is regarded as a spiritual organism, in the sense that his spiritual aspirations draw him toward perfection, then education should stress character building and growth toward intelligible reality. Again, if the human being is considered to be *essentially* rational, then education should concentrate on the devices and subject matters (mathematical exercises, logical syllogisms, the Great Ideas) that will put reason to work.

On the other hand, if man is thought of as first of all a natural being, then life itself should become "the business" of the learning process. "Life is not just breathing," wrote Rousseau, "it is action, the functioning of organs, senses, faculties, every part of us that gives the consciousness of existence."[4] Learning, therefore, involves both physical and mental activity; but if that activity is to be "natural" (meaning, for Rousseau, reasonable, temperate, and healthy), it must be deliberately guided because an unguided person is likely to become "the most misshapen of creatures." This follows from Rousseau's notion that each person is born free but is put in chains by a society that corrupts him or makes him unnatural. The individual is a malleable creature, susceptible to the attractions and artificialities of social life; in consequence, his teacher must remove him from social life and place him in a benevolent, serene natural environment. Reared according to nature, the student is expected to balance his desires and his capacities, to become attuned to his "true," his natural self. All this, of course, is a function of an eighteenth century view of Nature as well as an eighteenth century rebellion against artifice and rigid authorities. We have already seen how the image of the natural man seems to haunt the imaginations of such reformers as John Holt and even Ivan Illich. To them, quite simply, the school puts children (all "born free") "in chains"; and the only way to educate humanely is to follow nature, to permit children to pursue their interests, to learn what they desire and not what society imposes on them. But, again, this idea follows from a particular definition, from a *naming* of certain human attributes. Are we to accept it as *the* definition? If not, what shall we put in its place?

There have been other, frequently conflicting paradigms. Kant, much impressed by Rousseau's having "discerned the 'real man' beneath all the distortions and concealments" society has enforced on him, acknowledged that each human being was born with the desire to be free but without the knowledge needed for freedom. Therefore, the individual requires discipline, which must consistently be imposed on him until he is old enough and rational enough to *will* what is right. As we shall see in later chapters, Kant thought that rationality entailed a knowledge of moral law and an awareness of free will. In fact, Kant would say that man's true distinctiveness lies in his ability to derive the law of his being and in his ability freely to decide the kind of man he will be. Unlike Rousseau, Kant saw the human being as achieving his inner freedom within civilization. But because that freedom depends so much on a high development of reason, children could not be taught permissively. We must prove to the child, he wrote, "that restraint is only laid upon him that he may learn in time to use his liberty aright, and that his mind is being cultivated so that one day he may be free; that is independent of the help of others."[5] Even with all the emphasis on self-determination, there is still a sense of human essence; a stern conception of what man *ought* to be, whatever the circumstances, wherever he might appear.

The development of experimental and functional psychologies in the nineteenth century presented the philosopher with new problems in defining man. Darwinism and other theories of evolutionary development were bound to make a difference, even to those who preferred to set aside "the scientific nature of man." As we have already seen, John Dewey's work is especially important to contemporary educational philosophy. Dewey was both a psychologist and a philosopher, influenced not only by Darwinian ideas about development and change but by inquiries that showed the self to be a function of society. The mind, he believed, is a mode of behavior and adaptation. It develops, he thought, by means of shared experience, mediated and communicated by language. In consequence, education should stress the provision of stimulating classroom experiences and the establishment of miniature communities in which children could learn how to be intelligent participants in social life.

Concerned as he was with the social aspect of conduct, Dewey made the development of habits or dispositions central to his prescriptions. Anticipating certain, later social behaviorists, he spoke often of the need for guidance and control within a matrix of interpersonal relationships. "Social purpose," he said, must be substituted for traditional individualism; and this required control over "teaching and discipline and materials of study" in the interests of "a more genuine development of individuality for the mass of individuals."[6] Dewey meant that with the proper guidance and the proper encouragement of inquiry and growth, individuals would be able to *achieve* mindfulness and, with it, individuality. But he always emphasized interaction between the human being and the natural and social environment. He said that "progress proceeds in two ways, and that freedom is found in that kind of interaction which maintains an environment in which human desire and choice count for something." And then:

> There are in truth forces in man as well as without him. While they are infinitely frail in comparison with exterior forces, yet they may have the support of a form-seeing and contriving intelligence. When we look at the problem as one of an adjustment to be intelligently attained, the issue shifts from within personality to an engineering issue, the establishment of arts of education and social guidance.[7]

Dewey also drew implications for his conception of education from what he thought of as the realities of human nature. Many have pointed to his neglect of personality and inwardness; and Dewey once felt "obliged to admit what [Gordon Allport] says about the absence of an adequate theory of personality." Many have also pointed to Dewey's overly "healthy-minded" emphasis, his neglect of anxiety, uncertainty, *anomie*.

Nevertheless, Dewey's view may be among the most significant approaches for the American teacher. It has had an enormous effect on conventional educational wisdom, much of which the teacher inevitably absorbs. It is operative in both the behaviorist tendency and the so-called progressivist tendency, which today is being realized in the movement for "open schools." To orient himself, to be clear about what he believes, the teacher must gain as much perspective on this view of human nature as he has on the more ancient visions. Dewey's work is closer in time; it is responsive both to the sciences and to the actualities of democratic life. But this does not warrant mere acceptance. Nor, for those disturbed by Dewey's talk of "engineering," does this warrant rejection. The teacher is only asked to bring to the fore those images in the background of his consciousness, which, often without his knowing, affect his perceptions of man. There are multiple examples of such images: Freud's view of the libido-driven human being; Jung's view of the collective unconscious; Buber's view of the "I and Thou." The struggle to find a viable definition of 'man' has been continuous. Many people have tried to *fix* human nature and then to develop a theory of education based on their notion of what the human being (so defined) ought to be. Now, with all these examples of description, desire, and aspiration behind us, we must ask whether the practicing teacher should attempt to devise his own definition. He has the sciences to which he may refer; he has the great resources of the past from which to select; he has his personal experiences, his outlook on the world. What choices must he make if he is to deal effectively, authentically, and humanely with the persons he is trying to teach? Does he need to define 'man' after all? He does not possess the special knowledge required of a scientist involved in working out theories of behavior or learning. He cannot be expected to use the esoteric language now and then associated with particular scientific specialties. When a behavioral scientist uses advanced statistical techniques, for example, or when he expresses his discoveries by means of some mathematical notation system, he is not concerned about clarifying things for the teacher or the general public. His objective is to communicate his findings to his fellow researchers, who are familiar with his symbol system and his methodology. His definitions, as well, are not necessarily justified by the way they direct or clarify clinical or teaching practice. They are justified to the extent they contribute to the adequacy of the theory he is developing, and they do not *have* to be couched in ordinary language.

Now, the teacher is not asked to build theories. Questions of definition arise in the context of his day-to-day work. They may arise, as we have said, when he tries to clarify the relationship between judgments he makes about particular children and certain definitions he may have accepted from the tradition. (Alfred North Whitehead once said that "our doctrines of education," like our sociological and political theories, "are derived from an unbroken tradition of great thinkers and practical examples from the age of Plato." It would not be surprising if the same were true about definitions.) Definitional questions may also arise in the course of discussions with colleagues, parents, or the general public; but the definitions provided need only be nonscientific or "general" ones.

According to Israel Scheffler, three kinds of general definitions exist: stipulative, descriptive, and programmatic. A stipulative definition "exhibits some term to be defined and gives notice that it is to be taken as equivalent to some other exhibited term or description, within a particular context."[8] The simplest example is the use of letter grades—S, LP, F—in place of the more familiar terms "satisfactory," "low passing," and "failing." The teacher can properly legislate a manner of speaking that will help in a discussion or make things somewhat clearer than they would be if he relied on more conventional usage. Suppose he is asked to talk about a student as a "human being." He might say something to this effect: "I am quite aware that there are many, many ways of talking about the human being, especially in this post-Freudian age. Some still speak of the student as a rational animal who fulfills himself to the degree he perfects his intellect. Some prefer to speak, as Skinner does, about observable variations in behavior and controlled changes in the environment. Others prefer to talk about man in relation to his achievements and activities. And still others focus on the human being in his relationships with the social and physical environment. *I* prefer, in the course of my discussion, to use the word *man* to refer to an existing person, subjectively aware of himself and his possibilities, free to create himself in the situations of his life, free to choose. I recognize that other philosophers of education mean different things by the word *man* and might find my view indefensible. But, for my purposes in this discussion, I am turning to the existential philosopher of education for an idea of what 'man' might be taken to mean." In this view, the teacher is *stipulating* a definition of "man" or "human being." Conscious of what he is doing in the context of a particular discussion (perhaps with a restive student, perhaps with an authoritarian supervisor), the teacher is simply declaring that he is going to use "existing person . . . free to create himself," as an equivalent for "human being." This notion is quite different from offering a scientific definition; it is also different from presenting a descriptive definition.

A descriptive definition, according to Scheffler, attempts to "explain the defined terms by giving an account of their prior usage." A dictionary provides descriptive definitions, since its purpose is largely to describe how words are and have been used in various contexts of discourse. "Man," in the Oxford Dictionary, is defined as a human being, a person, the human being regarded abstractly, the spiritual and material parts (respectively) of a human person, the spiritual condition of the unregenerate and the regenerate, and in several other ways. The word is also exhibited in a number of contexts: biblical, biological, literary. It is useful to have such descriptions of conventional usages at hand, just as it is helpful to be acquainted with how philosophers have used the term in the course of Western history.

Dictionary and historical overviews, however, only begin to suggest the range. We have seen numerous descriptive definitions of "man" or "human being," and we cannot determine which definition is "best" simply by referring to the dictionary, the philosophy book, or the textbook in behavioral sciences. Everything depends on context and the person's purpose for describing. In anthropological discussions, "man" is treated in relation to diverse cultural patterns; in biological discussions, "man" refers to a particular genus of animals; in linguistics, "man" is the language animal. We have already seen how, in psychology, "man" may refer to a reactive creature, an open system of feelings and attitudes; a neurotic, repressed creature (as in Norman Brown's phrase, "the disease called man"); a decision-making person creating himself in an interpersonal world.

The teacher, with so many definitions available, often has to choose arbitrarily among them. What is he to say when he reads a selection from Sigmund Freud and discovers that Freud believed that men are scarcely "accessible to reasonable arguments and [are] entirely governed by their instinctual wishes"? Dewey, we recall, argued for the cultivation of "good habits of thought," on the assumption that impulses then could become motivators of judgment and rationality. Freudian man, at least in this context, is different from Deweyan man. However, because Dewey and Freud selected different vantage points and different dimensions of behavior for description, the teacher cannot say one is a "true" description and one is not. But he has to decide which description he will hold in mind.

At this point, the programmatic definition becomes relevant for the practitioner. The teacher, confronting a vast variety of descriptive definitions, must indeed choose how he ought to define "man." Faced with a peculiar mix of "is" and "ought," he cannot solve his problem simply by making a stipulation ("I will call man an existential being" or "I will refer to man as X"). In this case, he does not want or need to depart from conventional usage mainly for the sake of making a point in discussion, becoming more efficient in his communication, or sharpening certain of his ideas. He is concerned with action in his classroom, with some program relating to curriculum or method. Relevant for his purposes, then, are general definitions, which, as Scheffler describes them, "are often keyed directly into social practices and habits of mind." This becomes important when the teacher is deliberately trying to choose—from among a wealth of descriptive definitions—one that will make sense in his context and seem relevant in some integral way to his vision of himself and the other human beings in his immediate world.

To treat a definition as programmatic is to be prepared to keep evaluating it, to discover its consequences for teaching and learning. The old puzzle of whether a given definition of human nature (as essentially or potentially rational, for example) logically implies that a particular curriculum (oriented to the liberal studies, for instance) can be set aside. The teacher is presumed to have more important things to do than to work out the problem of the logical implications to be drawn for action from propositions about the nature of man. He is presumed to have more important things to do than to determine what "man"—in abstract or in general—is *really* like. Nevertheless, he has to have sufficient knowledge of *how to think about* human actions so that he can make practical judgments in his teaching. He requires some familiarity with the methodology of the behavioral sciences and with the constructs they have made available. He also requires some ability to use the technique called *verstehen,* which has been called "the particular experiential form in which commonsense thinking takes cognizance of the social cultural world."[9] Using this technique, the teacher can interpret what another person intends in his action and how he perceives his situation. Although not a subjective way of knowing, *verstehen* demands the ability to imagine oneself in another person's skin. The teacher can only do so, of course, on the basis of self-understanding. "Now when we understand a person's behavior in terms of his attitudes, goals, perceptions of the situation in which he finds himself, etc.—in short, of the phenomenology of the situation—what we are doing is, so to speak, attaching the facts of the particular case to the terminals of our own response system, i.e., our own personality."[10] At once, we have to hold in mind the differences between various subjectivities and allow for the possibility of entirely alien modes of behavior, which we understand but are not capable of ourselves. This mode of awareness is important for the teacher who wishes to engage in dialogue with his students, at least to the extent of arousing them to learn. However, he will not be able to evaluate objectively different types of behavior if he is not *self*-conscious and if he has not been able to examine his preconceptions of the nature of man. His "habits of mind" must be such that he is alert to the models and paradigms affecting his vision, so that he can break through the screens of seductive abstractions when he confronts the individuals in his classroom—and takes the risk of intervening in their lives.

Herman Melville has described as "bachelors" those who took abstractions for reality, who refused to look below the glossy surfaces to the ambiguities and particularities. An example is Captain Delano in Melville's "Benito Cereno": "a person of a singularly undistrustful good nature, not liable, except on extraordinary and repeated incentives, and hardly then, to indulge in personal alarms. . . ."[11] Kindly, myopic in his self-righteous certainties, the Captain is unable to see that slaves in revolt have seized the mysterious Spanish ship he tries to rescue. He cannot see that the "faithful fellow" acting as body servant to Don Benito, the derelict ship's captain, is actually holding Don Benito captive and that the Spaniard's apparent illness is due to fear for his life. One reason for Captain Delano's failure to perceive the situation is that the reality structure he has lived by all his life excludes the possibility that men taken as slaves can rebel. He is familiar with an orderly, reasonable world: slaves remain slaves and stay in their allotted places; Spanish officers (effete and inefficient though they undoubtedly are) remain in command of their ships. Another reason he cannot see is that his stereotype of the Negro prevents him from acknowledging that black men can be anything more than sullen captives or willing servants. He cannot individualize Babo, the supposed body servant, or the royal giant Atufal, or the young woman ("naked nature, now, pure tenderness and love . . .") nursing her child. His sanguine, self-indulgent innocence almost has fatal consequences; it is not unlike the innocence of a teacher who confuses some abstract vision of man or the world with reality.

Ancient images, abstractions, and slogans too often hang like veils between the teacher and "the phenomenology of the situation." He may feel disturbed by apathy, stupidity, or lack of discipline; but he is all too likely to take refuge in all-encompassing statements about "socializing" the young, "improving" them, "Americanizing" them. He may persist in thinking that education *must,* by definition, enlighten, release, redeem. He may still regard the school as a place where young people learn to be law-abiding citizens, to be rational men, to adjust. Yet below the surface the water keeps churning; children refuse release, refuse redemption, and appear inhuman in consequence. What *are* these children? What does the idea of "man" have to do with them? Why are they so obdurately individual? Why does no scheme seem to apply?

If he chooses consciousness, if he is alert to the veil, the teacher will realize that to talk about something, to name something is not to guarantee its existence. To say that children are "learners" when they come to school or that all are provided "equal opportunity" or that "discovery" is necessarily taking place when someone is permitted to study independently is to speak logically and meaningfully enough. But the logic and meaningfulness of such statements do not imply their empirical truth. Meaning is a function of linguistic context; existence, empirical reality must be demonstrated. It is as easy to be misled by words and phrases (and elegant classical arguments) as it is to confuse a rebel leader with a body servant, or an outraged, hungry Chicano boy with "lower socioeconomic class." This notion is particularly important when we speak of "achievement" or "IQ," or even "teaching." The teacher is prevented from considering his assumptions *and* actual, everyday events if he insists on coping by means of slogans, abstractions, mere names.

Similar consequences follow when he gives way to the temptation of identifying individuals by means of the categories in which they have (hopefully, for good pedagogical reason) been placed. He may well forget that IQ score, skin color, verbal facility are particulars abstracted from complex organic wholes. Such terms as "slow learner," "the gifted," "teen-ager," and "underprivileged" refer to common denominators, specific characteristics individuals share when categorized or grouped with a particular end in view. To talk of a "slow learner" is to speak of a characteristic a single child possesses in common with other children when his achievements are measured on a scale. To refer to the "underprivileged" is to point to a particular socioeconomic predicament numbers of children share. None of these terms can fully identify a child or young person. None can do justice to or encompass his uniqueness. Yet grouping and categorizing are often necessary in classroom situations. Frequently, the teacher must be able to recognize the child with hearing problems and the child with reading difficulties. He must be able to discern the retarded child and the hyperactive one. Obviously, he cannot treat all his pupils as if they had identical capacities or could perform in identical ways. Categorizing becomes damaging, however, when the teacher perceives an individual only by means of the abstract term selected for categorizing him. It becomes damaging, too, when the teacher bases his expectations on a child's membership in a category instead of on what he has directly observed. This mode of perception is precisely what imposes invisibility on so many persons; for invisibility, in Ralph Ellison's sense, is due to a condition within the one who looks—in this context, the teacher, who needs to spend time pondering what he has taken for granted about certain human beings as well as what he believes about human existence in the world.

By confronting the feelings he experiences when he is rendered an object by someone else's gaze or when his sense of himself as a person is treated as irrelevant, the teacher may become more sensitive to the importance of encountering others as individuals. Leo Tolstoy's "The Death of Ivan Ilyich" captures these feelings with a rare poignancy and exposes them to view. Ivan Ilyich is a Russian civil servant in the nineteenth century, utterly staid and conventional, caught up in trivial concerns. He discovers that a minor injury has become a fatal cancer; and abruptly he realizes that he—Ivan Ilyich—is going to die:

> The syllogism he had learned from Kiesewetter's *Logic:*
> "Caius is a man, men are mortal, therefore Caius is mortal,"
> had always seemed to him correct as applied to Caius, but
> certainly not as applied to himself. That Caius—man in the
> abstract—was mortal, was perfectly correct, but he was not
> Caius, not an abstract man, but a creature quite, quite separate
> from all others. He had been little Vanya, with a mamma and a
> papa, with Mitya and Volodya, with the toys, a coachman and a
> nurse; afterwards with Katenka and with all the joys, griefs, and
> delights of childhood, boyhood, and youth. What did Caius
> know of the smell of that striped leather ball Vanya had been so
> fond of? Had Caius kissed his mother's hand like that, and did
> the silk of her dress rustle so for Caius? Had Caius been in love
> like that? Could Caius preside at a session as he did? Caius
> really was mortal, and it was right for him to die; but for me,
> little Vanya, Ivan Ilyich, with all my thoughts and emotions, it's
> altogether a different matter.[12]

Ivan Ilyich's doctors talk to him about the vermiform appendix and the kidney; his friends make fun of his "low spirits"; his wife sees his illness as "another of the annoyances he caused her." Naming, classifying, abstracting, none of them takes the man who once was "little Vanya" into account.

It does not require a fatal illness for the reader to understand the gap between "Caius" and Ivan Ilyich or between "the patient" and the person experiencing his own pain. Awareness of the tension may be intensified by recognition that it is often necessary to speak of "Caius," of "pupil," or "lower-class child." There is little point in a medical doctor's treating a patient as "a fellow creature" when he comes to him as "a case." There is little point in a teacher's treating a particularly gifted child, or a restless child, or a child with reading difficulties, simply as Johnny "quite, quite separate from all others." For one thing, to *talk* about individualizing is not to solve the problem of finding out (by means of intuition, dialogue, or *verstehen*) how Johnny experiences his separateness, his giftedness, or his inability to read. However the child experiences these, the teacher may find that techniques and materials tested with many "others" work for Johnny, distinctive as he is. His biography differs; his standpoint differs; his family life, his place within the family, his way of addressing himself to the everyday—all differ from other children's. But, if he is nine years old, the level of his conceptual development (which *he* certainly does not experience) is probably much akin to the level of other nine year olds; and his teacher is probably justified in building expectations on the basis of what he knows about nine year oldness as well as what he knows about Johnny. No teacher, given a group situation, can make all his plans in the light of personal encounters with individuals—each one "quite, quite separate." Nevertheless, even when he develops activities for the whole class, the teacher needs to remember that membership in that class does not define or adequately identify any person there. Each one exists and experiences himself apart from the labels and the categories; and the teacher, in some sense dependent on categories, must keep in mind that they are irrelevant to the individual's self-consciousness.

James Herndon makes this stunningly clear in his book *How to Survive in Your Native Land,* which tells of an effort to set up a school-within-a-school, in an ordinary, dreary junior high school in a California suburb. The program, called "Creative Arts," was to be entirely nonrestrictive. The category of students the initiators had in mind was a group of expressive, probably creative people bored with "studying Egypt," impatient with rules and regulations, and eager to explore on their own. They did not expect the young people who "came in wising off and horsing around, equally clearly prepared to disbelieve and test us out." They did not realize "that all the stuff we thought the kids were dying to do . . . was in fact stuff that *we* wanted them to do, that *we* invented, that interested *us*—not only that but it interested us mainly as things to be doing during periods of time when something had to be going on, when no one was supposed to be just sitting around doing nothing." When the school-within-a-school dissolved, the teachers noted some of their tacit assumptions:

> The school exists, and most everyone is going to go to it. It
> ain't going to change either, hardly. It is *absolutely irrelevant* to

the lives of children, who don't need school at all, who want to
have real work to do, who want revelation, adventure, who want
to learn what the school is designed to prevent them from
learning, who need to go up on mountains, dream, and invent
their names.[13]

They were thinking, of course, about how children experienced the school;
they were not making judgments about the *uses* of schooling to the
community. Putting down what they considered to be platitudes, they were
calling attention to something no teacher can afford to forget: each child,
each person, moves in *his* way to make sense of *his* life-world, which is in
some degree different from others' life-worlds and "quite, quite separate"
from the world of the school. Yet, in some way, the young person must
live in the intersubjective world (absolutely irrelevant though it may
appear to him); and pursue his meanings, achieve his perspectives, create
himself. And the teacher? He must live in tension, torn between
recognizing the need "to go up on mountains, dream, and invent their
names" and confronting the necessity to arouse his students to act on their
societal possibilities, to choose themselves as individuals whose futures lie
in the world.

The teacher who thinks of future possibilities will be able to abandon
traditional notions of predetermined abilities and predetermined
fulfillments ("all the stuff we thought the kids were dying to do"). He will
recognize that human beings are protean, with innumerable modes of
self-expression and various life styles. A person is never one thing and one
thing only. When the teacher chooses to conceive his students as
predominantly rational or predominantly sensual, as intuitive or emotional,
he is actually deciding to modify the expression of his students' capacities
selectively and in the light of certain consequences he prefers. This
conception is quite different from establishing the boundaries of the
concept "human nature"; it is also quite different from asserting that one
has finally found "the right definition" of the human being, finally learned
how to distinguish him from automaton and beast. It is quite different, in
other words, from concluding that students are—by definition—*essentially*
rational, sensual.

Now, the consequences the teacher prefers may signify effective
enculturation. A child may be exercising powers that do not result in what
Jerome Bruner calls "competence." He may not understand complicated
directions; he may not be able to use subordinate clauses; he may not be
able to symbolize or build mental models of the world. The teacher may
realize fully and sympathetically that the child's so-called "retardation" is

due to environmental attrition at home, to a lack of sensory stimuli and complex, formal conversation. But, when certain psychologists tell him that a child so seriously deprived is not likely to advance beyond a fifth grade reading level, the teacher is often in danger of labeling that child "inferior"; so it hardly matters whether inferiority is charged to environmental or hereditary factors. A determinism or a fatality comes into play: the child's early history (genetic or environmental) is perceived to have *forced* him into a particular mold.

Not long ago, psychologist Arthur Jensen wrote a controversial article entitled "How Much Can We Boost IQ and Scholastic Achievement?"[14] He argued that genetic more than environmental factors determined IQ and that the most significant environmental factors were prenatal ones, mainly nutritional. Thus, he maintained that the various compensatory programs developed for young children had little relevance when it came to raising the IQ of the deprived. Various psychologists either affirmed or criticized Jensen's methodology, hypotheses, and empirical findings. David Elkind, for example, responded from the standpoint of Jean Piaget's structural psychology of intelligence; working on premises differing from Jensen's, Elkind concluded that intelligence might well be developed in experience. Just as philosophers differ on their views of the nature of man, Elkind maintained that psychometric and developmental psychologists came to disparate conclusions because they were interested in "describing different facets of intelligent behavior."[15] Lee J. Cronbach, in his response, raised a question that went beyond the psychological: "Intelligence for what?", he asked, touching on matters closer to the philosophical.[16] Carl Bereiter, known for his innovations in remedial work with disadvantaged children, challenged Jensen's pessimism by saying he wanted to keep the question of whether education could "equalize effective intelligence" open. In his program, Bereiter wrote, he was not "trying to 'stimulate the growth of intelligence,' but rather to teach academic skills directly in ways that did not demand of the children abilities they demonstrably did not possess."[17]

This controversy relates to the projects of increasing numbers of teachers. Most teachers are in no position to choose among the contesting definitions of intelligence or to decide between the psychometricians and the structuralists. They are not usually equipped to evaluate such reassuring researches as Robert Rosenthal's, which point out the beneficial effects of positive expectations. "What *does* the known demand?", the teacher, following Dewey, may ask. When so much is known and when the knowledge claim is understood to be contingent on the questions that initiated the inquiry, on the hypotheses devised and the methodology used, the teacher may well say—like Ivan Karamazov—that anything is possible.

But, as we have reiterated, the teacher's obligation is to choose and to act, even in the face of uncertainty.

The uncertainty is often more tolerable than the certainty communicated when predictions are made about the continuing retardation of certain children. A low reading score in the third grade may justify a number of predictions with respect to IQ in the eighth grade—given certain hypotheses and certain conceptions of measurement. There is evidence regarding the heritability of intelligence along with social and racial class differences.[18] Some talk about the social determinants of intelligence and the hope of doing something to remedy poverty and oppression. Others talk about the effect of teachers' attitudes on learning and IQ. Others make optimistic claims for programmed learning and its remedial consequences. Still others insist that warm human encounters make all the difference. No teacher can be sure.

If he thinks about what he is doing, however, the teacher will make every effort to clarify such notions as determinism and to take a stance with respect to freedom. Despite conventional wisdom, he will remain skeptical about suggestions that imply the end is in the beginning for most young people, especially the poor. We have already spoken of B. F. Skinner's attack on "the literature of freedom" and the idea of human autonomy, and we have suggested that the teacher in some sense dissents from this view every time he presumes a student can choose to learn or not to learn. We have attempted to answer those, like Gilbert Ryle, who say that will is an illusion. "Volitions," writes Ryle, "have been postulated as special acts or operations 'in the mind', by means of which a mind gets its ideas translated into facts."[19] He finds "volition" to be an artificial, entirely unnecessary concept, largely because it appears to presume that invisible performances can take place behind the scenes, inside the mind conceived as "a spectral machine." As little concerned with inner states as is Skinner, convinced that to posit invisible events preceding action is a category mistake, Ryle would have the teacher watch behavior.

The only response, as we have said, is to consult one's existential experience of being able to exert one's will freely, of being free to choose *not* to do—as well as to do—certain things. It may be necessary to respond to skeptics as Dostoevsky's Underground Man does: "You see, gentlemen, reason is an excellent thing, there's no disputing that, but reason is nothing but reason and satisfies only the rational side of man's nature, while will is a manifestation of the whole life, that is, of the whole human life including reason and all the impulses. And although our life, in the manifestation of it, is often worthless, yet it is life and not simply extracting square roots."[20]

For the determinist, uniform laws govern all nature, including living beings. These laws are rationally connected with one another; thus, every event can be viewed as causally determined by some prior event. The person who believes in free choice is likely to argue that the very insertion of consciousness in the world opens possibilities for events which are not predictable and therefore not causally determined. The human being, involved in changing and often novel situations, may act on impulse, out of passion, by caprice; or he may be aware—or think he is aware—of some contingency he could not be expected to perceive. In such cases, the presumably orderly course of events is disturbed. The underlying "indeterminacy," of which Werner Heisenberg and others have spoken, is exposed.

Few exponents of free choice would deny that limits exist; nor would they deny the existence of causation. Whitehead has written that we cannot narrow our notions of freedom to the things men do to and for each other.

> This is a thorough mistake. The massive habits of physical nature, its iron laws, determine the scene for the sufferings of men. Birth and death, heat, cold, hunger, separation, disease, the general impracticability of purpose, all bring their quota to imprison the souls of women and of men. Our experiences do not keep step with our hopes.[21]

We have already spoken of such limits; we have spoken of necessity. Those who assert the reality of free will know that choosing takes place against the background of such "iron laws," including the law of man's mortality. Insisting that free choice is not illusory, they say that causes may well exist but do not, in every case, compel. A young man of the slums may be hungry; he may be enraged by bigotry or maltreatment; but he does not *have* to steal from "the Man." A young woman may have been reared by sensitive, understanding parents who worked with her teachers and had great respect for her talents and distinctiveness; but she does not *have* to remain in some suitable environment for the sake of self-actualization. She may, like the Underground Man, deliberately choose to live in a detrimental way. Choice, writes Dostoevsky, may be rational and appropriate, "within bounds." But often "choice is utterly and stubbornly opposed to reason ... and ... do you know that that, too, is profitable, sometimes even praiseworthy?" For all the predictions that might reasonably have been made, the girl was not *compelled* to do the proper thing when she graduated from high school. As hippie, factory worker, terrorist, pacifist, or wanderer across the country, she could demonstrate daily that she had been free not to do what she ought to have done.

Michael Scriven makes a distinction of considerable relevance for the teacher when he clarifies the difference between predictive determinism and explanatory determinism. He says that those who emphasize the significance of choosing are prone to say that choices are essentially unpredictable. Admitting the importance of choice in determining outcomes and admitting that the person who makes the choice can usually not predict it with certainty, he still says that the individual can make predictions, at least in principle.

> It is perfectly clear that in practice, predictability of most human choices not only is impossible now, but will forever be impossible. This is simply because human choices are determined by a very large number of variables, the crucial values of many of which we cannot obtain, except in a post-mortem examination or in a full-life follow-through, and even in a full-life follow-through we are not—nor will we ever be—in a position to obtain all the data that we need to cover the whole of a person's behavior.[22]

Only if the environment were severely restricted (as in *Walden Two* or in *1984*) could the efficiency of our prediction be markedly increased. More realistic, however, is explanatory determinism. Working with a particular class, a teacher might find that the behavior of the students follows a specific model at some point in time. In other words, he might be able to explain why they react to certain stimuli, by using some of Skinner's ideas. Or he might be able to explain their lack of discipline, by consulting a Freudian model and saying, for instance, that they were engaging in a generational revolt. Or he might be able to explain their progress by recalling some of John Dewey's statements about active participation in the learning process. He might not have been able to predict which model the class would follow; but once the behavior was well under way, he could properly explain what *had* happened by selecting a model with enough information to serve his purposes. No matter how many cause and effect relationships the teacher can identify, his explanation cannot eradicate his students' freedom to choose or to have chosen. His ability to explain cannot negate the fact that human beings (such as Eldridge

Cleaver, George Jackson, Franklin D. Roosevelt, Helen Keller) have the capacity to frustrate predictions, especially when they know what predictions are being made. This notion applies to poor children with low reading scores; to apparently delinquent adolescents in crowded urban high schools; to individuals purportedly fated by their genetic inheritance, for even they can be enabled to act on some possibility, to escape predicted failure, to surprise.

Conclusions about freedom and determinism depend a great deal on the vantage point taken by the one raising the questions about the future of a man or men. Looking in retrospect, most individuals see a necessity in their past lives; and often, they see a fatality. What *has* happened almost always seems necessary; because it happened, it *had* to happen, although no one may have realized it at the time. Thomas Wolfe, tracing the ancestry of Eugene Gant at the start of *Look Homeward, Angel* writes:

> Each of us is all the sums he has not counted; subtract us into nakedness and night again, and you shall see begin in Crete four thousands years ago the love that ended yesterday in Texas. The seed of our destruction will blossom in the desert, the alexin of our cure grows by a mountain rock, and our lives are haunted by a Georgia slattern, because a London cutpurse went unhung. Each moment is the fruit of forty thousand years. The minute-winning days, like flies, buzz home to death, and every moment is a window on all time.[23]

The family's life, Wolfe says, was "touched by that dark miracle of chance," but nonetheless there was a "destiny." If an Englishman named Gilbert Gaunt (who later changed his name to Gant) had not come to the United States, if his son Oliver had not been drawn southward by the sight of the Rebels going to Gettysburg, if Oliver had not lost his first wife and married Eliza Pentland, Eugene Gant would not have existed; and, for Eugene Gant, that would have been unthinkable. And yet Oliver Gant could well have stayed in Pennsylvania; he could well have ridden in another direction when he came to North Carolina and never stopped at Altamont where Eliza lived. Like every other human being, he moved in a world of contingencies; his actions were not logically necessary. Yet, for his son Eugene, all was inevitable.

The vantage point of the narrative in *Look Homeward, Angel* is Eugene Gant's, and thus a sense of the marvelous is communicated from the interweaving of necessity and chance. Other renderings of the problem are far more stark because the "omniscient" narrator is concerned with relaying "truth." For example, Émile Zola believed that determinism was experimentally proved. In the mode of nineteenth century mechanist science, Zola saw thought and passion as fixed laws in human behavior. He saw individuals as creatures of heredity and environment, victims of their social milieu. He called himself a naturalist; and his series of novels about the Rougon-Macquart family (including *L'Assommoir, Nana, Germinal*) render the family members as fixed in their frailties and their station in life. Nana, for example, is "descended from four or five generations of drunkards, and tainted in her blood by a cumulative inheritance of misery and drink." The Paris slums and pavements have shaped her; she is "rotten," a "blind power of nature"; she has no hope of escaping what she is.

Theodore Dreiser saw an inexorable conflict between man's instinctual life and social regulations. In *An American Tragedy,* Clyde Griffith, a passive victim of biological and social determinism, lacks the strength needed for self-control. He murders Roberta Alden (or permits her to drown) not out of will but out of necessity. Reading Dreiser and Zola today, the teacher will almost immediately detect the weaknesses in their views. Granting the presence of conditioning forces, he still sees no justification for conceiving the human being as a passive object, a piece of clay battered by energies over which he has no control. A human being may be susceptible to influence. He may be a function of a culture, a product of a particular inheritance; but he is also a center of energies, an organism in transaction with a changing world, a person who *selects* many of the stimuli to which he responds. He is an individual—not to be duplicated.

If this is convincingly the case with the fictional characters Clyde and Nana, why is it not the case with the Puerto Rican child or the Indian child in the classroom? Desperate for an explanation of slow learning, the teacher too frequently gives way to the temptation of a determinist answer. And then he makes the mistake of assuming not merely that a person's capacities are already set by the age of three but that those capacities determine the kinds of experiences appropriate for that person, the kinds of fulfillments he needs. If the Puerto Rican child (having to learn English as his second language) cannot reach grade level in reading or arithmetic, his teacher is likely to anticipate nothing better than a vocational high school for him. Then why enrich his "cultural" experiences or even pay too much attention to his speech? He can barely master the rudiments in elementary school; why expose him to possibilities he can never realize in his life? If, on the other hand, the white middle-class child is gifted and curious, the teacher sees every reason to diversify his experiences, familiarize him with the arts and the sciences, involve him in research and library work, expose him to the exciting parts of the world.

The teacher who thinks this way believes that what a person *is* determines what he *should* be. But we have talked about the difficulty of asserting categorically what man—or any individual—*is.* Of course, an individual's endowments and capacities have something to do with what he becomes. However, at any given moment, we cannot identify all endowments and capacities. The tools of evaluation are bound to be selective; no test taps *every* capability a human being possesses. In a sense, then, the teacher can never know the absolute range of a student's potential, which depends a great deal on his cultural milieu, the encouragement and stimulation he receives, and the choices he is enabled to make. We have mentioned that when he decides how he will think about human nature, a practicing teacher is actually determining how he will direct the expression of students' capacities. He may not fully intend to direct in this way; but he usually cannot help being aware of the limiting conditions, which include the culture, the student's backgrounds (as he understands them), the social arrangements within the school, the curriculum, the available materials, and the teacher's repertoire of skills. Within limits, he attempts to guide, modify, *move* his students from one state of being to a more desirable state. Much of the time, he can do little more.

Nevertheless, the teacher should remember that a child is capable of a great deal more than anyone can define and that different modes of explanation are needed to account for the diverse forms of behavior and personality. Determinants and limits certainly exist; but intentions, decisions, and various kinds of intervention play unexpectedly causal roles. The teacher who believes that his students can indeed develop their potential, if equipped to do so, must break with conventional thinking from time to time. He might, for example, attempt to think of his students' futures in other than vocational or professional terms. What might they imagine themselves to *be* outside their jobs and careers? What of the "quality of life" about which so many people speak today?

Although much sporadic talk has centered about "career education," teachers know that they cannot prepare the young for specific jobs. Because of rapid technological changes, no one can predict precisely what skills will be needed or how these skills will be rewarded, even in the near future. We generally assume that the rudimentary skills of literacy will be necessary. To the limit of his ability, each person ought to try to learn at least enough to make sense of what impinges on his personal life. Whatever devices are needed to help him learn ought to be put to use; because, if he cannot orient himself in his own society, he will be helpless and therefore in no way free. The teacher can work to stimulate cognitive thinking without necessarily having career goals or status or material success in mind. He may, in fact, be a more effective stimulator if he is concerned to open up diverse *human* possibilities, various modes of action to which he can spontaneously ascribe worth. There are the pleasures of looking at the faces of the world, of caring for a piece of the earth and keeping it clean. There are walls to paint, objects to make, cars to fix, odd subjects to study, streets to explore. There are opportunities for conversation and exchange of views, chances to play and improvise. There are art works to be discovered, sports to be learned, campaigns to be undertaken. And there are people to be attended to: lonely children, drug addicts, delinquents, the mentally ill, the aged. Fundamental as it is to work for a living, "real life" need not be ancillary to the job. The individual's worth need not be made dependent on status or material success.

The teacher who believes in stimulating and developing potential will be challenging, at least implicitly, the inhumanity of credentialing systems, which sort and rank people according to market demand. He will be challenging the depersonalization of a society that offers fewer and fewer opportunities for people to use their initiative, to put their vital energies to work, to find their own voices and their own skills. But the teacher cannot meet this challenge through "good feeling." He cannot accomplish it by simply deciding to let students do what they are interested in, by permitting them to be themselves.

Persons have to be aroused to action, especially in a society that continually bombards them with "messages" and exerts so many controls. They are aroused most effectively by other persons, including teachers, who themselves are attuned to risks and uncertainties in a universe they truly feel is open but offers no guarantees. Yet the serious teacher is in constant tension. On the one hand, he knows that he cannot tell his students how to invent and choose themselves. No matter how many contingencies he controls in his classroom, he cannot predict what every person will do. On the other hand, he knows he has to take deliberate action to enable diverse students to learn how to learn; and sometimes this deliberate action must take the form of engineering, or behavioral control.

There he stands, with his memories, his sedimented meanings, his biography. Like every other human being, he has an impulse life, an emotional life; he is conscious of his consciousness, of his presence in the world. He may be the stronger for what Gerald Sykes calls "bilinguality." This term means, abstractly, "knowing what you do," or more concretely, "the capacity to speak both the language of tough-mindedness and the language of tender-mindedness . . . the gentle, suggestive vulgate of poetry

and the hard, precise Latin of science . . ."[24] Lacking bilinguality, the
teacher may well be frozen in a position of either–or.

By thinking in terms of the principle of complementarity, the teacher
can avoid the either–or position. Scientist Niels Bohr, reacting to the
irreconcilable conflict in physics between the "wave" and the "particle"
theories of matter, found a way of accepting both theories as valid.
Assuming that both concepts were needed for an adequate explanation and
that they were mutually exclusive if applied simultaneously, Bohr proposed
that they be accepted in alternation, "like the two faces of an object that
never can be seen at the same time but which must be visualized in turn,
however, in order to describe the object completely." Bohr and his
colleague, Max Born, saw analogies in human affairs. As Floyd Matson
explains, the meaning of complementarity here "is that of the mutually
antagonistic but peculiarly cognate relationship between the traditional
scientific method of 'causes and mechanisms' and the traditional
humanistic method of purposes and reasons."[25] Bohr's dictum may still be
relevant for the teacher torn between the need to be humanistic and the
equally compelling need to ensure his students' achievement: "The opposite
of a correct statement," says Bohr, "is a false statement. But the opposite
of a profound truth may well be another profound truth."

Such complementarity may be necessary in working with unmotivated
children or those with cognitive deficits. Instruction may conceivably be
individualized through the use of machines. Selective reinforcements may
be carefully used; rewards, "tokens" of various kinds may even be offered
at each step of the learning enterprise. Rather than study psychological
difficulties and family problems, Kenneth B. Clark has advised that the
teacher concentrate on relevant and observable behavior, particularly
verbal behavior, and specify his behavioral objectives. Such an approach
entails an extremely selective view of the human being: only "one face" of
the student is permitted visibility; subjectivity is effectually ignored.
However, the teacher can still be aware of purposes and reasons as well as
the child's potential for ordering his life-world. We have said that the
principle of complementarity forbids the *simultaneous* application of both
descriptions of the human being. When he is engaged in teaching skills or
in attempting to compensate for some cognitive lack, the teacher should
not be diverted from what Skinner calls the "expediting of learning" or
from the variables he must manipulate if such expediting is to take place.
But the child should know that the teacher who is doing the expediting
also cares for him and addresses himself to his freedom at other moments
in the day. And the teacher ought to remain aware that the child does
indeed have another "face" to which he can attend at another time.

By this other "face" we mean the learner as a person, as subject rather than object, as consciousness rather than behaving organism. Granting variations in competence and precision, we can assume that every teacher can learn to take the behavioral view when necessary, that he can also learn to teach didactically. But we can also assume that no involved teacher can wholly escape the vantage point of subjectivity, the vantage point from which "the close presence of others" will be felt. "How," asks Maurice Merleau-Ponty, "can an action or a human thought be grasped in the mode of 'one' since, by its very nature, it is a first person operation, inseparable from an *I*?" He, too, admits that the behavior of others is understood by "analogy with my own, and through my inner experience." He realizes that the "existence of other people is a difficulty and an outrage for objective thought";[26] but he is saying that objective thought does not—and never can—embrace everything a human being experiences.

Setting aside questions of definition, then, setting aside his thoughts about the "constitution of the true object," the teacher can conceive his personal perspective on his students to be part of his "insertion into the world-as-an-individual." He can discover, at appropriate moments, what it is to meet his students' gaze and become aware of their existence as his own gaze comes in contact with theirs. An encounter of this sort—an "I-Thou" encounter—occurs always in a present moment, in a domain apart from the object-world. In such a dialogic relation, the teacher can experience being a learner; he can become, in a distinctive fashion, a learner himself. "In learning from time to time what this human being needs and does not need at the moment, the educator is led to an ever deeper recognition of what the human being needs in order to grow."[27] This is not a psychological approach to the definition of needs. According to Martin Buber, the human being needs to be freed to reach out for himself. To grow involves the ability to perceive the lacks in his experience, the insufficiencies in his life, the guilt feelings for refusing his possibilities. In other, perhaps complementary contexts, related insights might be associated with "self-concept" or the sense of efficacy which moves a person on to learn. Here, however, the focus is on the learner's breaking free to be, to search, to appropriate the concepts required for gaining perspective on his world.

The teacher, no longer relying on slogans or abstractions, will have to decide how to conceive man. He will have to decide if and when he can take the risk of dialogue while intentionally working to help students learn. But in the course of making such decisions, he will become more intensely conscious of himself as person and as teacher. Only as he acts and makes his choices, does he confront the ever open question: "What is man?"

Notes and References

1. Israel Scheffler, *The Language of Education* (Springfield, Ill.: Charles C Thomas, Publisher, 1960), pp. 36–46.

2. Aristotle, "Politics," bk. 1, ch. 5, in *Introduction to Aristotle,* ed. Richard McKeon (New York: The Modern Library, 1947), p. 561.

3. Jacques Maritain, *Education at the Crossroads* (New Haven: Yale University Press, 1961), p. 5.

4. Jean Jacques Rousseau, *Emile,* in *The Emile of Jean Jacques Rousseau,* tr. William Boyd (New York: Bureau of Publications, Teachers College, Columbia University, 1962), p. 15.

5. Immanuel Kant, *Education* (Ann Arbor, Mich.: Ann Arbor Paperbacks, 1960), pp. 4–5.

6. John Dewey, *Education and the Social Order* (New York: League for Industrial Democracy, 1934), p. 8.

7. John Dewey, *Human Nature and Conduct* (New York: The Modern Library, 1930), p. 10.

8. Israel Scheffler, *The Language of Education,* p. 13.

9. Alfred Schutz, "Concept and Theory Formation," in *The Problem of Social Reality, Collected Papers* I (The Hague: Martinus Nijhoff, 1967), p. 57.

10. Michael Scriven, "The Contribution of Philosophy of the Social Sciences to Educational Development," in *Philosophy and Education Development,* ed. George Barnett (Boston: Houghton Mifflin Company, 1966), pp. 60–61.

11. Herman Melville, "Benito Cereno," in *Selected Writings of Herman Melville* (New York: The Modern Library, 1952), p. 256.

12. Leo Tolstoy, "The Death of Ivan Ilyich," in *World Masterpieces,* vol. 2, ed. Maynard Mack (New York: W. W. Norton & Company, 1956), pp. 1964–1965.

13. James Herndon, *How to Survive in Your Native Land* (New York: Simon & Schuster, 1971), p. 129.

14. Arthur R. Jensen, "How Much Can We Boost IQ and Scholastic Achievement?", *Harvard Educational Review,* vol. 39, no. 1, winter 1969, pp. 1–123.

15. David Elkind, "Piagetian and Psychometric Conceptions of Intelligence," *Harvard Educational Review,* vol. 39, no. 2, spring 1969, p. 323.

16. Lee J. Cronbach, "Heredity, Environment, and Educational Policy," *Harvard Educational Review,* vol. 39, No. 2, p. 341.

17. Carl Bereiter, "The Future of Individual Differences," *Harvard Educational Review,* vol. 39, no. 2, p. 315.

18. Richard Herrnstein, "I.Q.", *The Atlantic,* September 1971, pp. 43–64.

19. Gilbert Ryle, *The Concept of Mind* (New York: Barnes & Noble, 1949), p. 63.

20. Fyodor Dostoevsky, "Notes from the Underground," in *The Short Novels of Dostoevsky* (New York: Dial Press, 1945), p. 147.

21. Alfred North Whitehead, *Adventures of Ideas* (New York: The Macmillan Company, 1933), p. 84.

22. Michael Scriven, "The Contribution of Philosophy of the Social Sciences to Educational Development," p. 66.

23. Thomas Wolfe, *Look Homeward, Angel* (New York: The Modern Library, 1932), p. 3.

24. Gerald Sykes, *The Hidden Remnant* (New York: Harper & Row, Publishers, 1962), p. 171.

25. Floyd Matson, *The Broken Image* (New York: George Braziller, 1964), p. 151.

26. Maurice Merleau-Ponty, *Phenomenology of Perception* (London: Routledge and Kegan Paul, 1967), p. 349.

27. Martin Buber, *Between Man and Man* (Boston: Beacon Press, 1957), p. 101.

Further Reading

Aristotle, "Nicomachean Ethics," in *Introduction to Aristotle,* ed. Richard McKeon (New York: The Modern Library, 1947).

————, "On the Soul," in *Introduction to Aristotle,* ed. Richard McKeon (New York: The Modern Library, 1947).

H. S. Broudy, "Can We Define Good Teaching?", *Teachers College Record,* vol. 70, no. 7, April 1969.

Norman O. Brown, *Life Against Death* (Middletown, Conn.: Wesleyan University Press, 1959).

————, *Love's Body* (New York: Random House, 1966).

Jerome S. Bruner, *Towards a Theory of Instruction* (Cambridge, Mass.: Harvard University Press, 1966).

Martin Buber, *I and Thou* (New York: Charles Scribner's Sons, 1970).

Ernst Cassirer, *Language and Myth,* tr. Susanne K. Langer (New York: Dover Publications, 1946).

————, *Rousseau, Kant, and Goethe,* tr. James Gutmann, Paul Oskar Kristeller, and John Herman Randall, Jr. (New York: Harper & Row, Publishers, 1963).

Kenneth B. Clark, "Alternative Public School Systems," *Harvard Educational Review,* vol. 38, no. 1, winter 1968.

Martin P. Deutsch, "The Disadvantaged Child and the Learning Process," in *Education in Depressed Areas,* ed. A. Harry Passow (New York: Bureau of Publications, Teachers College, Columbia University, 1963).

John Dewey, *Experience and Education* (New York: Collier Books, 1963).

————, "Experience, Knowledge and Value," in *The Philosophy of John Dewey,* ed. Paul Arthur Schilpp (New York: Tudor Publishing Company, 1951).

Theodore Dreiser, *An American Tragedy* (New York: Dell Publishing Co., 1959).

Joseph Featherstone, *Schools Where Children Learn* (New York: Liveright Publishing Corporation, 1971).

Sigmund Freud, *The Future of an Illusion* (New York: Liveright Publishing Corporation, 1949).

Werner Heisenberg, *Physics and Beyond* (New York: Harper & Row, Publishers, 1971).

Richard S. Peters, *Education as Initiation* (London: Evans Brothers, 1963).

Plato, "Apology," in *The Works of Plato,* tr. B. Jowett (New York: Tudor Publishing Company, n.d.).

————, "Meno," in *The Works of Plato,* tr. B. Jowett (New York: Tudor Publishing Company, n.d.).

Carl R. Rogers and B. F. Skinner, "Some Issues Concerning the Control of Human Behavior," *Science,* vol. 124, no. 3231, November 30, 1956.

Robert Rosenthal and Lenore Jacobson, *Pygmalion in the Classroom* (New York: Holt, Rinehart & Winston, 1968).

Jean Jacques Rousseau, *The Social Contract and Discourses* (New York: E. P. Dutton & Company, 1947).

B. F. Skinner, *Beyond Freedom and Dignity* (New York: Alfred A. Knopf, 1971).

Ira S. Steinberg, *Educational Myths and Realities* (Reading, Mass.: Addison-Wesley Publishing Company, 1968).

Max Weber, *The Theory of Social and Economic Organization,* tr. A. M. Henderson and Talcott Parsons, ed. Talcott Parsons (New York: The Free Press, 1947).

Émile Zola, "The Experimental Novel," in *Paths to the Present,* ed. Eugen Weber (New York: Dodd, Mead & Company, 1964).

————, *Nana* (Cleveland: World Publishing Company, 1933).

Chapter Five

Knowledge: Science and Subjectivity

Rationalists, wearing square hats,
Think, in square rooms,
Looking at the floor,
Looking at the ceiling.
They confine themselves
To right-angled triangles.
If they tried rhomboids,
Cones, waving lines, ellipses—
As, for example, the ellipse of the half-
     moon—
Rationalists would wear sombreros.

Wallace Stevens
"Six Significant Landscapes"

    No matter how the teacher conceives the human being, his primary task is to teach the young person to know. The school has traditionally been understood to be the place where knowledge is transmitted, where children are exposed to world pictures accepted by their culture, where beliefs and truths are taught. In the early nineteenth century, it was not difficult to decide what constituted the knowledge that had to be transmitted to different kinds of children. People thought in terms of elementary skills, duties, the national heritage. The important ideas and beliefs were defined by a "public philosophy," which encompassed the conventional wisdom prevailing at a particular moment of time. The ideas were *there*—funded, preexisting—for the young to master. School reformers, such as Horace Mann and Henry Barnard, came to see that children differed in capacity and in the dominance of certain "faculties"; and they knew that adjustments to difference should be made. However, they were not inclined to make adjustments in subject matter. They might extend the curriculum; they might add geography or a foreign language or music, for example, but every new subject represented a specific fund of knowledge, a collection of facts expanded over time.

And, indeed, when most people lived in small, semirural communities, this stress on fixed and funded knowledge seemed appropriate enough. Children learned their most meaningful lessons outside of schools: how to plow a field; how to grind flour; how to sell dry goods in a store; how to vote at a town meeting; how to select associates and friends. Change seemed to occur slowly enough to permit younger generations to follow inherited patterns of behavior and to survive. Relatively few struck out for the frontier, and many of these bore the familiar patterns with them. Only now and then did someone run off to sea, move away to a Walden Pond, disappear in a city, or rebel. "We teach our boys to be such men as we are," wrote Ralph Waldo Emerson regretfully. As long as this was the mission of the public schools, the "problem of knowledge" would trouble very few.

By midcentury, and particularly after the Civil War, the rate of social change began increasing. The expansion of industry, the growth of the cities, the waves of immigration began transforming the face of the land and the day-to-day lives of individuals. The inherited way, the ancestors' way became abruptly archaic. The fathers, transplanted into alien surroundings, could no longer serve as models for their young. The traditional wisdom, so long depended on to assure continuity, began to seem irrelevant. Some people tried to cope with this change and disorder by reaffirming the old structures of knowledge, the old hierarchies of authority. Others, unable to think what they were doing, continued the old rote teaching in the schools. Scattered reformers began challenging the practice of imposing ready-made knowledge on repressed, quiescent pupils denied the freedom to investigate for themselves.

In the 1890s, John Dewey began talking about the necessity to educate for a world in flux, for an industrializing and open society. If the schools continued to treat knowledge as something to be doled out, if they continued working mainly for the command of certain symbols, people would become mere appendages to the machines they operated. Children's instincts needed to be "trained in social directions, enriched by historical interpretation, controlled and illuminated by scientific methods" so they could cope effectively with change. Knowledge should no longer be conceived as an "immobile solid," solely the province of an elite; knowledge was "actively moving in all the currents of society itself." The learning process, at such a moment, should not be purely passive and abstract. It should be self-directed, dynamic, social; it should involve challenging, lifelike situations; it should build on young people's tendencies "to make, to do, to create, to produce, whether in the form of utility or of art."[1]

Dewey found his model in scientific thinking, which he believed to be human intelligence working at the peak of its efficiency:

> Science has made its way by releasing, not by suppressing, the elements of variation, of invention and innovation, of novel creation in individuals. It is as true of the history of modern science as it is of the history of painting or music that its advances have been initiated by individuals who freed themselves from the bonds of tradition and custom whenever they found the latter hampering their own powers of reflection, observation, and construction.[2]

Dewey was an optimist of scientific progress when he wrote in that vein, linking scientific method to the values of individualism and democracy. He was aware that men had been asking questions about their world and themselves since the beginnings of Western civilization. He knew that they had wondered helplessly about what "worked" and what was true but that the masses had always been deprived of opportunities to find out for themselves. They had, instead, been forced to take refuge in authorities of various kinds. The world, however, had buffeted and tantalized and perplexed. There were floods, plagues, famines; and most people were left to be innocent victims despite the assurances and the "truths."

The rise of science opened up the great vistas in the Western world. Knowledge became a powerful, beneficent magic in contrast to the black arts of the superstitious past; and, with such power available, freedom for individuals could become a reality. They could control natural forces and explore heretofore forbidden domains. But, most important, challenges were mounted by the questing intelligence of individuals, and the restraining authorities were forced to withdraw. Because of science and man's searching intelligence, the universe became "an infinitely variegated . . . world which in the old sense can hardly be called a universe at all, so multiplex and far-reaching that it cannot be summed up and grasped in any one formula."[3]

The scientific revolution was not, however, greeted with universal enthusiasm. Religious authorities were threatened by it until Francis Bacon, René Descartes, Gottfried von Leibniz, and others assured them that the realm of ultimates was not the province of the natural philosopher. Scientists would concern themselves with the material world; values were to be left to the churches, to the poets. Even so, certain nineteenth century philosophers and literary men began posing uneasy questions to the scientists: questions about the stark neutrality of the universe the physicists called real; questions about the modernization of society, which the sciences, in particular, had caused; questions about the impersonality of the natural laws. Such men as Friedrich Nietzsche protested the disinterestedness of objectivity; Fyodor Dostoevsky rebelled against "2 X 2 = 4"; but few persons denied the value of the scientific method as a means to comprehend—and control—the physical world. Stephen Crane might write:

> A man said to the Universe:
> "Sir, I exist!"
> "However," replied the universe,
> "The fact has not created in me
> "A sense of obligation."[4]

Alfred Lord Tennyson might despair at "nature red in tooth and claw." Charles Baudelaire might rage against "the iron law of industry"; Henry David Thoreau might lament "the machine in the garden." But most persons recognized the productiveness of scientific inquiry and the benefits applied science brought to the human race. In the United States, where faith in automatic progress had long persisted, advancing science and invention seemed always to hold inspiring promise of a better life.

Today as well, the teacher is likely to associate the scientific outlook with what is most advanced in thought. He sees all around him the fantastic fruits of technology, the union of science and the machine. Knowing something about cybernation, programming, systems analysis, and the rest, he is likely to believe that the new sciences can bring about any improvements men decide they want. He finds that he can no longer conceive the scientific method as a mere extension of intelligent thinking, because he knows how many methods exist and how complex some sciences have become. Despite his vague understanding of the contemporary scientific revolution, he tends to believe that the only reliable knowledge is gained through scientific discovery. He may not be pleased by such recognition; but he knows that if his students are to understand "what is," they must learn to perform, to some degree at least, like physicists or chemists or biologists. However, he does not believe that his students will necessarily develop democratic values by learning to think scientifically.

If he were living in the period preceding World War II, the teacher would be talking to his pupils about the intellectual commonwealth or the community of science. He might be stressing the free market of ideas associated with the life of science, the rational and humane commitments of working scientists, the release of novel creation in individuals. The tentativeness and open-mindedness associated with the scientific method, the insistence on results openly arrived at, the affirmation of change and risk and possibility all might suggest to him a new morality. Indeed, if he were teaching in the 1930s, he might find it extremely difficult to believe that an experimental scientist could knowingly use his expertise in an evil cause. The enemies of progress, the reactionary forces would appear, almost by definition, to be anti-intellectual and antiscientific. Science would be associated with planning, with gradual improvements, with concern for mankind.

Two great and terrible revelations came with the 1940s, however, and the beneficence of science was never to be taken for granted again. First was the news of the atomic bomb, secretly produced in the greatest cooperative intellectual commonwealth ever established. J. Robert Oppenheimer, administrator of the project, later said he thought of a line from the Bhagavad Gita at the time of the first atomic explosion: "I am become death—the shatterer of worlds."

Second was the disclosure of the Nazis' final solution of "the Jewish problem": the application of scientific knowledge to mass extermination. Later, the so-called medical experiments on prisoners were publicized, along with the willingness on the part of trained physicians to use their skills to maim, torture, and gas. Those physicians were, in fact, among those who had graduated from some of the great humanistic universities in Europe; yet they supported what George Steiner has called the "political bestiality" of our age:

> The ultimate of political barbarism grew from the core of Europe. Two centuries after Voltaire had proclaimed its end, torture again became a normal process of political action. Not only did the general dissemination of literary, cultural values prove no barrier to totalitarianism; but in notable instances the high places of humanistic learning and art actually welcomed and aided the new terror. Barbarism prevailed on the very ground of Christian humanism, of Renaissance culture and classic rationalism. We know that some of the men who devised and administered Auschwitz had been taught to read Shakespeare or Goethe, and continued to do so.[5]

Hannah Arendt has written of the "banality" of the evil done by such men as Adolf Eichmann, mere clerks, cogs in the wheel; but it has become apparent that scientists, too, once enlisted in bureaucratized organizations, can commit crimes as matters of routine.

In 1964, Max Born wrote:

> During the last decade, the belief in the possibility of a clear separation between objective knowledge and the pursuit of

knowledge has been destroyed by science itself. In the operation
of science and its ethics a change has taken place that makes it
impossible to maintain the old ideal of the pursuit of knowledge
for its own sake which my generation believed in. We were
convinced that this could never lead to any evil since the search
for truth was good in itself. That was a beautiful dream from
which we were awakened by world events.[6]

Born was not giving way to a failure of nerve; he was not turning his
back on scientific intelligence and rationality. He was, however, drawing
attention to the problematic function of science in a technological world.
He was suggesting some of the difficulties now confronting individuals
concerned with the search for truth. The teacher is bound to be affected by
such questions and such despair, especially if he has not been initiated into
the specialized protocols and languages of the modern sciences. Such a
person has developed a more or less general conception of science.
Committed though he may be to teaching respect for the scientific attitude,
he is as vulnerable as any layman to the myths, clichés, and fears to which
the very mention of science may now give rise. He may also be nagged by
uncertainties respecting the meaning of the pursuit of knowledge and the
search for truth. To what degree does the scientist work with
"experience"? To what degree, with logic and pure mathematics? What do
the scientist's abstract formulas have to do with nature, with the tangible,
physical world? What does it mean "to know," "to be sure," to hold a
confirmed belief? What does it mean to be intelligent, to use one's mind?
What of other modes of awareness: feeling, intuition, empathy? When does
an individual *know* what he knows? How does he communicate his
knowing to another?

Rarely is a teacher fluent enough in mathematics to understand
mathematical descriptions of physical and biological occurrences. In many
respects, he has to accept scientific findings "on faith." The scientists of
the past were wont to describe their discoveries in words, which—at least
to the educated—seemed to provide a distinctive means to "reflect" reality,
to bring the human consciousness in contact with what was true. "In the
beginning," after all, "was the Word." The *logos,* the rational principle
that supposedly governed the cosmos in ancient times, resembled a cosmic
mind whose contents were expressible in words. Being the speaking
animal, man had access to that mind and thus held a preeminent position
in reality. If he could use and understand language properly, any rational
man would find the universe knowable and feel at home on the earth.

The teacher is still likely to assume that most of "reality" can be
verbally expressed, that visual models can be made, that such metaphors

as "mechanism," "watch," "organism" can be used to explain. He may *know,* on some level, that this is not the case; but the old metaphors and the old faiths are difficult to shed, especially for the person who has not been rigorously trained in a scientific specialty. Alfred North Whitehead once wrote how the sciences have "practically recoloured our mentality so that modes of thought which in former times were exceptional are now broadly spread throughout the educated world." The "new tinge," he said, "is a vehement and passionate interest in the relation of general principles to irreducible and stubborn facts." Along with this interest is "a widespread, instinctive conviction in the existence of an 'Order of Things', and, in particular, an 'Order of Nature'."[7] Most people find it extremely difficult to give up the expectation that the Order can be expressed in words.

Yet this period is marked by a definite swing from metaphor to mathematics. In most fields of knowledge today, Daniel Bell says, "the dominant mode of intellectual experience is mathematical, and especially in our new 'intellectual technology' (linear programming, decision theory, simulation) we have the 'new language' of variables, parameters, models, stochastic processes, algorithms, heuristics, minimax, and other terms which are being adopted by the social sciences."[8] This vocabulary is purely formal; it does not refer to empirical events in the world, to experience, or to things. It refers only to abstract formulas in the special domain for which it has been devised.

The teacher, then, for all his involvement with language and cognition, must recognize that "the Word" has lost its primacy. "The trouble," says Hannah Arendt, "concerns the fact that the 'truths' of the modern scientific world view, though they can be demonstrated in mathematical formulas and proved technologically, will no longer lend themselves to normal expression in speech and thought.[9] When such truths are spoken of conceptually and coherently, she continues (quoting Erwin Schrödinger), the resulting statements will be "not perhaps as meaningless as a 'triangular circule,' but much more so than a 'winged lion'." For George Steiner, a universe in which reality cannot be described in words is silent. David Hawkins, a philosopher of science, writes: "To those without fluency in mathematics—still the greatest number of educated persons today—the mathematical description of nature is bare, formal, and unrewarding. Nature so rendered is icy and colorless, far from the world that we know, by a more primitive intuition, to be our home."[10]

The current tendency to mathematicize the diverse fields of knowledge is one thing. In addition (and related to it) is the growing realization that Ludwig Wittgenstein was right: language *can* cause a "bewitchment of intelligence" by making people believe whatever can be named exists. Teachers are coming to see that language is nothing more than a system of signs, from which words and sentences derive their meanings. Human beings live their lives within such systems; much of their thinking, in fact, can best be understood as an activity involving mainly the manipulation of signs. Logic and mathematics, according to this view, are also languages—sign systems; they have no more capacity to disclose reality than do ordinary words. The scientist simply communicates more precisely and rigorously by using abstract, "empty" symbols. We mentioned stipulation in the preceding chapter. Biologists, chemists, even sociologists now stipulate that certain abstruse symbols will stand for the phenomena that once were ordered, interrelated, explained by means of words.

Understanding only a few of the existing symbolic systems, the teacher confronts a secret universe. Trying to learn the secrets, he may feel like Kafka's K., attempting to telephone the Castellan so that he can apply for a permit to enter the Castle: "The receiver gave out a buzz of a kind that K. had never before heard on a telephone. It was like the hum of countless children's voices—but yet not a hum, the echo rather of voices singing at an infinite distance—blended by sheer impossibility into one high but resonant sound which vibrated on the ear as if it were trying to penetrate beyond mere hearing."[11] Or the teacher may feel like the waiter in Ernest Hemingway's "A Clean, Well-Lighted Place":

> What did he fear? It was not fear or dread. It was a nothing that he knew too well. It was all a nothing and a man was nothing too. It was only that and light was all it needed and a certain cleanness and order. Some lived in it and never felt it but he knew it all was nada y pues nada y nada y pues nada. Our nada who art in nada, nada be thy name thy kingdom nada thy will be nada in nada as it is in nada. Give us this nada our daily nada and nada us our nada as we nada our nadas and nada us not into nada but deliver us from nada; pues nada. Hail nothing full of nothing, nothing is with thee.[12]

At times, the teacher may encounter what Albert Camus calls the "muteness" of the spheres. The teacher knows that his mind wants desperately to reduce reality "to terms of thought," to make a total sense of things, to feel at home again. But when he thinks of his scientific knowledge, he cannot be sure. He cannot know the DNA molecule as he knows the feel of his desk and the taste of water. He cannot know the atmosphere of the moon as he knows the trees in the park he passes on his way home.

> ... all the knowledge on earth will give me nothing to assure
> me that the world is mine. You describe it to me and you teach
> me to classify it. You enumerate its laws and in my thirst for
> knowledge I admit that they are true. You take apart its
> mechanism and my hope increases. At the final stage you teach
> me that this wondrous and multicolored universe can be reduced
> to the atom and that the atom can be reduced to the electron.
> All this is good and I wait for you to continue. But you tell me
> of an invisible planetary system in which electrons gravitate
> around a nucleus. You explain this world to me with an image.
> I realize then that you have been reduced to poetry: I shall
> never know.[13]

Poetry or mathematics: neither can fully explain. Nor can either assuage the desire for a world that is reasonable in ordinary human terms. "The world in itself is not reasonable," Camus asserts; it does not satisfy our desires for harmony and explicability. The mathematical scientist would differ:

> An old and powerful tradition identifies the ideal of science as
> the achievement of mathematical description. This ideal has two
> aspects. One aspect is the coherence and semantic compression
> achieved by formal deductive systems, and the other is the
> language of number. But this ideal, in either aspect, is
> meaningful and realizable only on sufferance of nature. The
> mathematical style of science is not to be explained as mere
> human contrivance or convention. Nature has style as well, and
> the major developments of mathematics are major because they
> imitate a pervasive style of nature.[14]

He is saying, in effect, that—if one is capable of "speaking" advanced mathematics—the universe is perfectly harmonious.

Contemplating these two points of view, we return to Whitehead and the "vehement and passionate interest in the relation of general principles to irreducible and stubborn facts." For Camus, the great abstractions do not explain or account for the "stubborn facts," nor do they help to make them bearable. From the vantage point of the human being who cannot incorporate proliferating knowledge, the world is simply irrational. But even so, the individual yearns for clarity, order, meaningfulness. Yearning, realizing that the answers he really wants are unattainable, he experiences what Camus names "the absurd": "But what is absurd is the confrontation of this irrational and the wild longing for clarity whose call echoes in the human heart. The absurd depends as much on man as on the world."[15]

Camus does not imply that the world is objectively absurd. Insisting that absurdity determined his relationship with life, he simply means that he lived in a state of tension, refusing to give way to nihilism but quite aware that he could never know all he wanted to know. What is left for the teacher who feels this way—and who feels obligated to transmit knowledge to young people? Camus would say that rebellion is left: the conscious effort to become lucid, to impose form, to make sense.

In some respects, this brings Camus's position near to John Dewey's. According to Dewey, "completeness and finality" were out of the question where knowledge was concerned because the "nature of experience as an on-going, changing process forbids." An understanding of "generality, totality, and ultimateness" cannot be gained from the sciences, he said. They are, rather, philosophic matters because they concern attitudes toward the world, not reports on it. "Totality," for example, signifies a "consistency of mode of response in reference to the plurality of events which occur."[16] He meant that a reflective man maintains a certain continuity in his habits of thinking and acting. In this context, a philosophical disposition enables such a man to continue probing, learning, seeking connections and meanings. In fact, the disposition to find out best equips the human being to bear vicissitudes and pain.

The tension involved was associated with the "sense of problem." Originating in the indeterminacies of experience as an awareness of uneasiness or perplexity, it urged the intelligent man to define and specify what troubled him and to move on to reflective inquiry. The tension would be allayed when the problem was resolved, at least to the extent that the diverse feelings, perceptions, and ideas involved were balanced in relation to one another. When that balance occurred, a moment of equilibrium would ensue—until, once again, wondering began. Tension of this sort—and its resolution—belongs to the domain of problem solving. Presumably, the problem, once defined, would touch on many aspects of the individual's experience; and the solution would have significant consequences for his social life.

But the original unease would not be existential, as it would be for Camus. For Dewey, it might stem from some dislocation in social life, a moral dilemma, or an unanswered question in one of the sciences. Camus was speaking out of a sense of predicament that might well be alien to Dewey because it was not really susceptible to conceptualization or definition. The predicament was irremediable because of the human being's habitation in a universe that refused to be reduced to terms of thought. The dilemma had to do with man's feeling of homelessness at a moment in history (somewhat later than Dewey's) when science, by dint of mathematical description, had indeed achieved an abstract totality, although a kind of totality unassimilable by ordinary men. Hence, the predicament, as Camus saw it, cannot be equated with the Deweyan problem; it cannot be solved reflectively. Nevertheless, confronting his predicament, the individual *can* choose to adopt certain attitudes, which may well be dispositions to rationality.

Let us take as an example the assassination of John F. Kennedy and compare the responses to it. There were few people, at the time of that tragedy, who did not look for some "reason," some encompassing explanation. The murder conflicted with all humanly conceived order and with most people's conception of right. It presented great difficulties, therefore, for those who needed to believe that things made sense. They could cope with the situation by means of problem solving or rebellion. After the initial shock, the man with the philosophical disposition (in the Deweyan sense) would begin to frame hypothetical explanations and seek connections among the multiple factors involved. His habit of mind would presumably be experimental; he would confine his thinking to factors he could conceptualize and explore empirically: the degree of violence in American society; the effects of charisma on a troubled mind; the psychology of Lee Harvey Oswald; the absence of gun-control laws; the role of the Dallas press before the Kennedy visit; the climate of opinion in the South. He would expect no cosmic explanations and would look for none. He would simply try to be as consistent and intelligent as he could in his responses; striving to understand, he would ward off irrationality and despair. Moreover, with the plight of American society in mind, he would pursue certain social purposes and try to make his study useful in some way. Putting aside metaphysical questioning, he would concentrate on specific action and the possibility of control.

The irrational forces revealed through the killing would profoundly affect the man who felt he was in an "absurd" relationship with the world. He would be intensely conscious of his rage at the universe's injustice as well as his desire for an explanation that would reconcile the fact of the assassination with a conception of "justice" or "reason"; yet he would also recognize the abstractness of such words and despair of ever receiving such an explanation. Rebelling, he would refuse to be reconciled; he would refuse to tolerate violence and plague. And ("because it was merely logical"[17]) he would work to *achieve* justice and rationality. In doing so, he would be choosing himself and at once creating a sphere of human order in defiance of the irrational.

The teacher, too, must choose his disposition; but the choice will not be easy in the confusing present moment. Not only is this a period of technological domination; it is also a time increasingly characterized by a "new irrationalism." On all sides, the teacher must confront either–ors: the cognitive *or* the creative–expressive; the sciences *or* the humanities; rationalism *or* subjectivism; logic *or* experience. Mathematicians, logical empiricists, positivists argue for rigor, clarity, verifiability. Poets, painters, humanist psychologists argue for spontaneity, sensitivity, sincerity. On one side is the chill purity of form; on the other is the palpitant stuff of immediacy. The integrations such men as Dewey achieved with their concentration on experience seem hardly likely now. There is too great a disjunction in the culture between the happenings of everyday life and the rational (or mathematical) constructs used to explain.

Not long ago, Charles P. Snow said that the difficulty involved the separation of two cultures in the face of the scientific revolution. Literary men were at one pole; physical scientists, at the other. The writers were so preoccupied with the tragedy of the human condition that they expressed little, if any, social concern. The scientists, scornful as they were of literary culture, knew full well that the condition of each person was tragic but did not believe that this knowledge made social commitments meaningless. The artists were pessimists; the scientists, optimists. Understanding almost nothing of the other group's expertise, neither humanities people nor science people attempted communication; and each culture existed in a dangerously sealed world. The solution, according to Snow, was to reform the educational system: to do away with specialization; to enable every student to understand the scientific revolution; to involve the pure scientists with humanistic subjects; to provide all students with the perspective they would need to improve their society as well as other areas in an imperfect world.[18]

Since Snow wrote his book (and weathered the resulting storm raised among literary intellectuals and social scientists), the outlook, particularly in the United States, has altered considerably. Rebel students and avant-garde artists have expressed such hostility toward the "technetronic society" that they have vigorously denounced the sciences making such a society possible. They feel that the inhuman manipulations of the state have endangered the "life force," and the state, in its bureaucracy and impersonality, has become "scientific" in its orientation. This reaction is partly a consequence of the feelings of powerlessness endemic to a technological, highly centralized society. Institutionalized science no longer offers the opportunities for individual growth and effectiveness Dewey and others described. Gigantic, esoteric, almost infallible agencies, such as those engaged in space exploration, connote what Jacques Ellul had in mind when he discussed "technique." Moreover, for many individuals, government science seems somehow related to chemical warfare, riot control, bugging, and various kinds of behavioral engineering.

The teacher may not share this point of view, but he cannot remain unaffected by the polarization taking place. The authority of the sciences is countered by another kind of authority—a "life style," a "counter culture," what Lionel Trilling calls a "second environment."[19] All three give centrality to feeling and impulse, to sensuality and sexuality. All erect a norm of the "natural" in opposition to restrictive rules. All tend to give immediate awareness priority over the mediated knowledge associated with science. For the restless and rebellious, the abstractions of the sciences—particularly the social sciences—sterilize and distort reality.

We have already mentioned the tradition in Western thought, which appears to sanction the new irrationalism. As far back as the seventeenth century, when the scientific method was first being defined, mathematician Blaise Pascal talked of man's limitations:

> We sail within a vast sphere, ever drifting in uncertainty, driven from end to end. When we think to attach ourselves to any point and to fasten to it, it wavers and leaves us; and if we follow it, it eludes our grasp, slips past us, and vanishes forever. Nothing stays for us. This is our natural condition, and yet most contrary to our inclination; we burn with desire to find solid ground and an ultimate sure foundation whereon to build a tower reaching to the infinite. But our whole groundwork cracks, and the earth opens to abysses.[20]

Pascal opposed Descartes, his contemporary, because Descartes had "made too profound a study of science." Great logician though he was, Pascal knew that the forms of logic could never encompass the human condition. Others, many others, followed in the same path. They were aware of nothingness and abysses; they suspected the limitations of reason.

Poet William Blake, at the end of the eighteenth century, wrote of the way narrow rationalist and mechanist forms constrained man and kept him from becoming vitally alive. In his poem "London," he called those forms "mind-forg'd manacles" and linked them to the hypocrisy and social tyranny he discerned in a commerce-dominated London. In another poem, sometimes called "The Scoffers," Blake deliberately made comic and pathetic figures out of the critical rationalist and the romantic naturalist, both of whom believed that a single human faculty (reason *or* feeling) could encompass reality. Recalling it, we can easily see why young rebels prize Blake so highly today:

> Mock on, mock on, Voltaire, Rousseau,
>   Mock on, mock on; 'tis all in vain;

You throw the sand against the wind
And the wind blows it back again.
And every sand becomes a gem
    Reflected in the beams divine;
Blown back, they blind the mocking eye,
    But still in Israel's paths they shine.
The Atoms of Democritus
    And Newton's Particles of light
Are sands upon the Red Sea shore,
    Where Israel's tents do shine bright.[21]

The poem speaks of the mysterious and the ineffable; but it is not a traditionally religious poem. "Israel" and "the Red Sea shore" represent the great creative forces in the universe, the darkness and the radiance scientists can never describe. Rejecting the old categories used to limit or objectify for the sake of study, Blake called for a fourfold vision, with senses, intuition, feelings, and reason all given roles to play. Any single-dimensional vision, he thought, would falsify; a purely rational approach would mechanize and depersonalize at once.

This language of antirationalism was developed still further by the romantics, the symbolists and certain early realists. In the twentieth century, D. H. Lawrence wrote:

We don't exist unless we are deeply and
            sensually in touch
With that which can be touched but not known.[22]

Numerous other contemporary artists felt the same: Henry Miller, Wallace Stevens, Hermann Hesse, William Burroughs, Norman Mailer—the list is long. The continuing activity of such persons demonstrates that there are —and have been—two opposing traditions in Western thought. One emphasizes form, lucidity, intelligence; the other stresses subjectivity, sincerity, sensuality. When artists and young people began to perceive a latent violence in American culture and to relate it to the technological system, they did not have to *invent* an idiom of protest. Like the scientific ideal, like the democratic credo, antiscientism and antirationalism were present in the "great tradition." In other words: the Dionysian impulse, long suppressed by the public view, was secretly challenging the Apollonian force all the time.

Herbert Marcuse's work, Norman Brown's, along with the Living Theatre and Susan Sontag's work in criticism, are in many respects part of a new wave, which has only recently broken upon the schools. But in many respects, too, they belong to one of the major lines of Western art and thought; and they need to be taken seriously. For example, Marcuse's *One Dimensional Man* is a post-Blakean outcry against "the present technological organization of reality." The writer perceives "the scientific conquest of nature" being used for "the scientific conquest of man"; and he wants people to change their lives in such a way that they refuse to accept any longer the efficiency and mass productivity that are the consequences of rationality.[23] Only then, he says, can they achieve true consciousness and rediscover themselves. Brown wants to see "an end to analysis," the reaffirmation of the body, the destruction of all boundaries. "To return the word to the flesh," he writes. "To make knowledge carnal again; not by deduction, but immediate by perception or sense at once; the bodily senses."[24] The prophets of the Living Theatre speak similarly. "The actor must discover forms of behavior and experience that unite the physical body with the mind if he is to serve the needs of the public," says Julian Beck. "I demand *everything*—total love, an end to all forms of violence and cruelty such as money, hunger, prisons, people doing work they hate," says Judith Malina. In *Against Interpretation,* Susan Sontag objects to a preoccupation with content in art. She writes that interpretation is "largely reactionary, stifling."

> Like the fumes of the automobile and of heavy industry which befoul the urban atmosphere, the effusion of interpretations of art today poisons our sensibilities. In a culture whose already classical dilemma is the hypertrophy of the intellect at the expense of energy and sensual capability, interpretation is the revenge of the intellect upon art. Even more. It is the revenge of the intellect upon the world. To interpret is to impoverish, to deplete the world—in order to set up a shadow world of "meanings." . . . The world, our world, is depleted, impoverished enough. Away with all duplicates of it, until we again experience more immediately what we have.[25]

Radical young people are similarly hostile to formulas and rules, similarly drawn to immediacy and authenticity. Both hippies and activists have associated science with objectivization, manipulation, "depletion." Kenneth Keniston talks of the ambivalence of young radicals toward technology:

> The depersonalization of life, commercialism, bureaucratization, impersonality, regimentation, and conformity of modern society seem destructive and unnecessary to these

young men and women. Bigness, impersonality, stratification, fixed roles, and hierarchy are all rejected, as is any involvement with the furtherance of purely technological values. Efficiency, quantity, the measurement of human beings—anything that interferes with the unique personality of each man and woman— are strongly opposed. In its place, post-modern youth seeks simplicity, naturalness, individuality. . . . [26]

Others have pointed to the rebels' concern with action rather than with thought. A young radical, Christopher N. Reinier, has written about politics as art. He talks of revolution and goodness and sharing. He says: "Philosophers act in order to contemplate; political actors contemplate in order to act. Philosophers leave the cessation of their contemplation to death; men of action construct their own ending to contemplation. There lies the beginning of their art. We want to be artists."[27] Impatient with doctrine, casuistry, authority, they intend to invent their own values, to focus on the now. Deliberation and reflection are not for them, because these processes are slow and tentative, because they involve testing in terms of experience. Rebels prefer to use participatory democracy in decision making, a communal experience resembling the Quaker meeting, depending a great deal on intuitive awareness and the desire for unity. Also, they prefer to make demands, often arbitrary demands, rather than to engage in argument. Because most rebellious students are familiar with logical relationships and the concepts of certain disciplines, their explicit rejection of the scientific or the reflective method expresses a conscious anti-intellectualism.

Their dissenting elders, especially those in the university, aim their attacks more specifically at "mindless specialization and irrelevant pedantry." Theodore Roszak writes, significantly:

> There is probably not a single field of the social sciences and humanities that does not already boast a larger body of "knowledge" than could be "popularized." . . . Is more "knowledge" of this surplus kind, expertly gleaned by precise techniques, what we really require? Or, in the protracted emergency in which our civilization finds itself, should our highest priority be placed on a scholar's ability to link his special knowledge or moral insight to our social needs?[28]

Objecting to the use of scientific expertise in the interests of war and exploitation, dissenting scholars raise epistemological as well as moral and political questions. Although they demand a rational dialogue on public questions, they believe that knowledge and theory are useless as long as power is misused and thermonuclear destruction hangs over the people of the earth. The mindful teacher is bound to ask once more about tests for truth, about knowledge claims, about the difference between knowing and the known. Is knowledge worth having only when it is used for moral ends? How does belief relate to knowledge? What does it mean to talk of knowledge "as an end in itself"? What is the difference between immediate knowing, vicarious knowing; knowing how, knowing that? When is knowledge relevant, irrelevant? How does belief relate to action? How does theory relate to practice? Again, the questions swarm.

Abstract discussion about the crisis in the culture offers the human being little help in understanding. The teacher must confront the problematic role of science in the modern world, the opposition of "affective" to "cognitive," the widespread desire—not to know but to "groove." And, as he does so, he must try to think about what he is doing and what he is expected to do in the school. Whether he thinks of education as a process of initiation, self-realization, or liberation, he is certainly aware that his focal concern is with enabling young people to conceptualize, to develop perspectives on their worlds. He must, no matter how intense his doubts, help them to develop their cognitive capacities. He must help them learn how to think and discover and probe.

Notes and References

1. John Dewey, "The School and Society," in *Dewey on Education,* ed. Martin S. Dworkin (New York: Bureau of Publications, Teachers College, Columbia University, 1961), p. 47.

2. John Dewey, "Science and the Future of Society," in *Intelligence in the Modern World: John Dewey's Philosophy,* ed. Joseph Ratner (New York: The Modern Library, 1939), pp. 358–359.

3. John Dewey, *Reconstruction in Philosophy* (Boston: Beacon Press, 1948), p. 61.

4. Stephen Crane, "A Man Said to the Universe," in *The Range of Literature,* ed. Elisabeth W. Schneider, Albert L. Walker, and Herbert E. Childs (New York: American Book Company, 1960), p. 361.

5. George Steiner, *Language and Silence* (New York: Atheneum, 1967), p. 5.

6. Max Born, "What Is Left to Hope For," *Bulletin of the Atomic Scientists,* April 1964, p. 2.

7. Alfred North Whitehead, *Science and the Modern World* (New York: Pelican Mentor Books, 1948), p. 75.

8. Daniel Bell, "The Disjunction of Culture and Social Structure: Some Notes on the Meaning of Social Reality," in *Science and Culture,* ed. Gerald Holton (Boston: Beacon Press, 1967), p. 247.

9. Hannah Arendt, *The Human Condition* (Garden City, N.Y.: Doubleday Anchor Books, 1959), p. 3.

10. David Hawkins, *The Language of Nature* (Garden City, N.Y.: Doubleday Anchor Books, 1967), p. 13.

11. Franz Kafka, *The Castle*, tr. Willa Muir and Edwin Muir (New York: The Modern Library, 1969), p. 27.

12. Ernest Hemingway, "A Clean, Well-Lighted Place," in *The Short Stories of Ernest Hemingway* (New York: Charles Scribner's Sons, 1954), pp. 382–383.

13. Albert Camus, *The Myth of Sisyphus and Other Essays*, tr. Justin O'Brien (New York: Alfred A. Knopf, 1955), pp. 19–20.

14. David Hawkins, *The Language of Nature*, p. 2.

15. Albert Camus, *The Myth of Sisyphus and Other Essays*, p. 13.

16. John Dewey, *Democracy and Education* (New York: The Macmillan Company, 1916), p. 379.

17. Albert Camus, *The Plague* (New York: Alfred A. Knopf, 1968), p. 122.

18. C. P. Snow, *The Two Cultures and the Scientific Revolution* (New York: Cambridge University Press, 1964), pp. 1–22.

19. Lionel Trilling, "The Two Environments: Reflections on the Study of English," in *Beyond Culture* (New York: Viking Press, 1965), pp. 209–233.

20. Blaise Pascal, *Pascal's Pensées* (New York: E. P. Dutton & Company, 1958), pp. 19–20.

21. William Blake, "Poems from MSS," in *William Blake*, ed. J. Bronowski (Baltimore: Penguin Books, 1958), p. 67.

22. D. H. Lawrence, "Non-Existence," in *The Complete Poems of D. H. Lawrence*, ed. Vivian de Sola Pinto and F. Warren Roberts (New York: Viking Press, 1971), p. 613.

23. Herbert Marcuse, *One Dimensional Man* (Boston: Beacon Press, 1964), pp. 8–12.

24. Norman O. Brown, *Love's Body* (New York: Random House, 1966), pp. 258–259.

25. Susan Sontag, *Against Interpretation* (New York: Dell Publishing Company, 1966), p. 7.

26. Kenneth Keniston, *Young Radicals* (New York: Harcourt Brace Jovanovich, 1968), p. 282.

27. Christopher N. Reinier, "Politics as Art: The Civic Vision," in *The New Student Left*, ed. Mitchell Cohen and Dennis Hale (Boston: Beacon Press, 1967), p. 27.

28. Theodore Roszak, "On Academic Delinquency," in *The Dissenting Academy*, ed. Theodore Roszak (New York: Pantheon Press, 1968), pp. 36–37.

Further Reading

Hannah Arendt, *Eichmann in Jerusalem* (New York: Viking Press, 1963).

Zbigniew Brzezinski, "America in the Technetronic Age," *Encounter*, January 1968, pp. 16–26.

Albert Camus, *The Rebel* (New York: Alfred A. Knopf, 1954).

Arthur C. Clarke, *2001: A Space Odyssey* (New York: Signet Books, 1968).

Barry Commoner, *Science and Survival* (New York: Viking Press, 1967).

Harvey Cox, *The Secular City* (New York: The Macmillan Company, 1965).

Jacques Ellul, *The Technological Society,* tr. John Wilkinson (New York: Vintage Books, 1967).

Ralph Waldo Emerson, "Education," in *Emerson on Education,* ed. Howard Mumford Jones (New York: Bureau of Publications, Teachers College, Columbia University, 1966), pp. 204–227.

Victor C. Ferkiss, *Technological Man: The Myth and the Reality* (New York: George Braziller, 1969).

Eli Ginsberg, ed., *Technology and Social Change* (New York: Columbia University Press, 1964).

Michael Harrington, *The Accidental Century* (New York: The Macmillan Company, 1965).

Aldous Huxley, *Brave New World Revisited* (New York: Harper & Row, Publishers, 1958).

Arthur Koestler, *The Ghost in the Machine* (New York: The Macmillan Company, 1968).

Horace Mann, "Tenth Annual Report" (1846) and "Twelfth Annual Report" (1848), in *The Republic and the School: Horace Mann on the Education of Free Men,* ed. Lawrence A. Cremin (New York: Bureau of Publications, Teachers College, Columbia University, 1957).

Leo Marx, *The Machine in the Garden* (New York: Oxford University Press, 1964).

Donald N. Michael, *Cybernation: The Silent Conquest* (Santa Barbara: Center for the Study of Democratic Institutions, 1962).

Bertram Morris, *Institutions of Intelligence* (Columbus: Ohio State University Press, 1969).

Lewis Mumford, *The Myth of the Machine: The Pentagon of Power* (New York: Harcourt Brace Jovanovich, 1970).

Jack Newfield, *A Prophetic Minority* (New York: Signet Books, 1967).

Friedrich Nietzsche, *The Genealogy of Morals* (Garden City, N.Y.: Doubleday Anchor Books, 1956).

George Orwell, *1984* (New York: Harcourt Brace Jovanovich, 1949).

Aldo Rostagno, with Julian Beck and Judith Malina, *We, The Living Theatre* (New York: Ballantine Books, 1970).

Theodore Roszak, *The Making of a Counter Culture: Reflections on the Technocratic Society and Its Youthful Opposition* (Garden City, N.Y.: Doubleday Anchor Books, 1969).

Jerry Rubin, *Do It! Scenarios of the Revolution* (New York: Simon & Schuster, 1970).

Stephen Spender, *The Year of the Young Rebels* (New York: Vintage Books, 1969).

Wylie Sypher, *Literature and Technology* (New York: Random House, 1968).

Norbert Wiener, *Gods and Golem, Inc.* (Cambridge, Mass.: The M.I.T. Press, 1967).

William P. D. Wightman, *The Growth of Scientific Ideas* (New Haven, Conn.: Yale University Press, 1953).

Chapter Six

Approaches to Truth and Belief

Every life is a point of view directed upon the universe.
Strictly speaking, what one life sees no other can. Every
individual, whether person, nation, or epoch, is an organ, for
which there can be no substitute, constructed for the
apprehension of truth. This is how the latter, which is in itself
of a nature alien from historical variation acquires a vital
dimension. Without the development, the perpetual change and
the inexhaustible series of adventures which constitute life, the
universe, or absolutely valid truth, would remain unknown. The
persistent error that has hitherto been made is the supposition
that reality possesses in itself, independently of the point of view
from which it is observed, a physiognomy of its own. Such a
theory clearly implies that no view of reality relative to any one
particular standpoint would coincide with its absolute aspect,
and consequently all such views would be false. But reality
happens to be, like a landscape, possessed of an infinite number
of perspectives, all equally veracious and authentic. The sole
false perspective is that which claims to be the only one there is.

José Ortega y Gasset
"The Doctrine of the Point of View,"
The Modern Theme

To ask epistemological questions is to stimulate thinking about
knowledge, truth, meaning, and belief—all of which are, in some degree,
problematic today. To ask such questions from an educational vantage
point is to do so with particular purposes in mind. Fascinated though the
teacher might be with ancient puzzles about trees falling in forests and
sticks looking bent in the water, he soon realizes that he confronts
exigencies about which the purely speculative thinker is scarcely
concerned. Because of his involvement with teaching and learning, the
teacher should understand the actualities of knowing and truth seeking. He
should make sense of the processes associated with knowing and reasoning
not as intellectual puzzles but as modes of ongoing action. For him, they
are significant events, which in some manner become visible when teaching
is effective and individuals are stimulated to learn. When he begins dealing

with the "knowledge problem," he is interested in discovering how he can make his teaching more effective at a time when so many traditional notions have become questionable. He is also interested in articulating some of his uncertainties about what can and should be known. If he is to develop a valuable theory of teaching, he needs to clarify what knowing really means, what knowledge is dependable and what is not, what the functions of reason are, what role intuition plays, what credence can be granted to common sense.

Philosophic consideration of such matters differs from that engaged in by behavioral scientists. Psychologists and certain linguists conduct empirical investigations to arrive at theories subject to test. Theories of this sort may be thought of as end products, conclusions to distinctive ways of pursuing knowledge. They are statements that something new is demonstrably known about the workings of the human mind, learning processes, and the like. Jean Piaget, after years of empirical study with children, arrived at a theory having to do with the functions of intelligence "in building up structures by structuring reality." Doing so, he helped to explain things about the nature of intelligent thinking, which were largely unknown before he did his work. The same is true of the linguist Noam Chomsky. His studies of language and linguistic behavior led him to a theory having to do with "the interplay of initially given structures of mind, maturational processes, and interaction with the environment." His objective was to add to the available stock of knowledge, to extend the range of what was known. Whether they are validated in the long run, such theories are not the same as philosophic theories because the former come at the *end* of a particular type of scientific investigation.

The person doing educational philosophy is concerned with devising a theory of teaching; and teaching is a practical activity. A theory of a practical activity, as Paul Hirst points out, "is constructed to determine and guide the activity"; it is not "the end product of the pursuit."[1] To construct an adequate theory of teaching, an individual must consult his own values and beliefs; he must consider a range of subject matters, including the behavioral sciences and studies of the discipline to be taught. Philosophy, especially epistemology, has a part to play in this type of theory construction, if philosophy is understood to involve clarification and heightened consciousness. Questions about such terms as 'knowledge', 'belief', 'meaning', and 'truth' must be answered. Such concepts as 'structure', 'perspective', and 'subject matter' must be explicated. The special contributions of the sciences and humanities to an understanding of teaching must be explored; so must the place of behavioral and other objectives. The questions to be posed by the person who does philosophy are not specifically answerable by empirical investigators, although they may refer to matters with which the sciences also deal. The framing of philosophic questions does not lead to an increase in the substantive knowledge available. The aim of the philosophic inquirer is to make things clearer, to sharpen awareness of alternatives, to indicate relationships and connections, all in the hope of making practical judgments that will affect the teaching act.

Most twentieth century philosophers have associated knowing with a type of participant action or with deliberate engagement in problematic situations. Some stress the role of *praxis,* or the transformation of an existing reality; few conceive knowing as passive or merely contemplative. It is an active process carried on by a knower; and, each time it occurs, it culminates in something known. An individual, let us say, comes to know the location of the Mississippi River. More properly, he comes to know how to read a map in such a way as to locate the Mississippi in the southern and midwestern United States. The river's location, in this case, is the known; it represents the culmination of a type of cognitive action. The concept 'knowledge' refers to something more: understandings or information or meanings funded over time. There is, clearly, a great store of public knowledge regarding the Mississippi River; and the individual learner draws from the store as he creates his own knowledge structures in the fields of geography, economics, and history. If the information he gains is organized so that it makes logical sense, can be retrieved at will and communicated to others, the individual not only *knows* but possesses knowledge.

Many open questions remain with respect to all this. What sort of action is involved in the knowing process? How is the act of knowing recognized? How is it distinguished from other kinds of mental activity? And what of the knower, who—after all—is focal to the process? How important is his subjectivity, his stance, his particular life history? How relevant is the information he receives through his senses compared with the knowledge his reason reveals? The answers provided throughout history, like those provided today, reflect preferences and ideals. At one extreme are the orientations to ideal and necessary truths, untarnished by contingency or opinion; at the other end are the views that put personal meaning and subjective knowledge first, that make evidence and logic subordinate to moral commitment. Between the extremes are views that place differing degrees of emphasis on the subjective and the objective in the knowing process. Each has its predilections on the possibility of truth, the security of beliefs, or the importance of experiential tests. Quite naturally, the views overlap here and there, but they are distinctive in the sense that each tends to highlight dimensions of the knowing process others overlook. Pondering them, the individual is challenged, not to synthesize them into one great synoptic vision but to define his epistemological position with the help of whatever clarification he achieves.

The oldest, and probably the best known, approach is associated with philosophic rationalism. With its concentration on ideal and necessary truth, as exemplified by mathematics, it was for many generations the veritable paradigm of theories of knowledge, especially for those who saw reality in terms of hierarchies, who aspired toward the purity of immateriality and absolutely unalloyed Form. This rationalism can be found in Plato's dialogues, especially those preoccupied with the conversion of the soul. Conversion meant "turning around," in effect the turning around of the soul toward the Idea of Good. Since this was the primary aim of philosophic education, Plato would certainly search for the type of knowledge that would effect such turning around. The science of numbers, he seems to have concluded, was best suited "to convert the soul from the visible world to the world of thought."[2] Therefore, if the teacher used this science to stimulate thinking rather than for practical ends, he could rely on it to kindle the soul and to awaken or elicit reason.

Plato implies that knowledge of necessary truths is already present but the proper mode of questioning must elicit this knowledge. The famous dialogue called the *Meno* dramatizes this idea with haunting effectiveness. The dialogue involves Socrates and a young Thessalian named Meno who is accompanied by a young slave. It begins abruptly, when Meno puts a succinct question to Socrates: "Can you tell me, Socrates, whether virtue is acquired by teaching or by practice; or if neither by teaching nor by practice, then whether it comes to man by nature, or in what other way?" Meno is forced to attempt a definition of goodness; but, each time he provides one, Socrates exposes it as unsatisfactory. Socrates then raises the issue of learning as a process of reminiscence: the soul "knows" what is true but loses its knowledge when it comes into the world. It can only recover the truth by engaging in hard and steady thinking, usually stimulated by an arresting sense experience. Socrates summons Meno's slave boy, who can understand Greek but has never studied mathematics, and proceeds to demonstrate that the boy can be made to see geometrical truths once he is asked appropriate questions and shown suggestive diagrams. The boy is thereby aroused to think and, at length, to call forth inner knowledge he never knew he possessed. Once the boy agrees that "the double space is the square of the diagonal," Socrates tells Meno that "there have been always true thoughts in him, both at the time when he was and was not a man, which only need to be awakened into knowledge"[3]

Of all the disciplines, mathematics and logic are the least concerned with experiential content. Their symbolic notations cannot be exemplified; the diagrams shown to the slave boy *suggest* the truth of the theorem rather than illustrate it. The "true thoughts in him" were not thoughts about the natural world; and the "knowledge" he gained was not knowledge about that world. Instead, he came to know certain connections between self-evident truths; he saw relationships, not new experiences. As Immanuel Kant said centuries later, the principles of reason are regulative principles; they state the *conditions*—the rules—governing inquiry; they do not compose the substance of inquiry. Socrates conducted the slave boy down a path of logic; but it is difficult to believe that the boy actually "knew" more at the end of the journey than he knew at the beginning.

Nevertheless, when exploring cognitive possibility, men have repeatedly tended to perceive reason as a higher mode of apprehension than any kind of empirical awareness. We have already spoken of the old paradigms: until the seventeenth century at least, reason was associated with sunlit mountaintops, with release from the "dark wood" or the "cave." The liberal arts tradition, born in such an orientation, perpetuated these paradigms. "The 'seven liberal arts'," writes Albert William Levi, "comprising the sciences of harmony and measure as well as measurement and the 'trivial' skills of textual interpretation, linguistic persuasiveness, and analytic judgment were pointed toward the disciplining of mind in all the possible modes of its occurrence."[4] The aim of the Platonic Academy, the medieval cathedral school, and the Renaissance university was to turn the elite few toward "wisdom," toward that apprehension of the Idea of the Good.

As late as the twentieth century, such educators as Robert Maynard Hutchins were associating wisdom with a rational view of the universe, which could only be achieved through metaphysics. Proposing the teaching of grammar, rhetoric, and logic in general education, Hutchins awakens ancient echoes:

> Logic is a critical branch of the study of reasoning. It remains only to add a study which exemplifies reasoning in its clearest and most precise form. That study is, of course, mathematics, and of the mathematical studies chiefly those that use the type of exposition Euclid employed. In such studies the pure operation of reason is made manifest. The subject matter depends on the universal and necessary processes of human thought. It is not affected by differences in taste, disposition, or prejudice.[5]

The values of clarity and precision can be pursued without orienting education to the "universal and necessary" and certainly without denigrating "differences in taste, disposition, or prejudice." Epistemological views, which make absoluteness the alternative to relativism and contingency, actually obscure what has for two centuries now been conceived to be the proper role of reason. Its function, we have said, is regulative; it is the source of the rules and principles that govern intelligent inquiry. Without the ability to reason, men could not achieve self-consistency; they could not draw inferences, frame arguments, construct propositions to explain their observations. Most significant is the part that reason plays in organizing experience and making sense of a chaotic world. Teachers today are aware of the need to teach the concepts or principles fundamental to the various subject matter disciplines. They may not realize that, when they teach these principles, they are enabling their students to reason, to effect relationships, to impose order in an intrinsically inchoate world.

The process of knowing, however, involves far more than reasoning. The information provided by the senses may well be meaningless if reason does not go to work on it; but without such information and experience, concepts are empty. The presumably rational person who has lost touch with the rich and contingent world of sensation resembles Jonathan Swift's abstract Laputans in *Gulliver's Travels,* who are completely cut off from the earth. These people are "so taken up with intense Speculations, that they neither can speak, or attend to the Discourses of others" without being aroused by a "Flapper" employed to strike their mouths and the ears of those to whom they address themselves. Gulliver remarks on their utter contempt for practical geometry, their awkwardness, and their inability to give clear instructions on anything except mathematics and music. "They are," he says, "very bad Reasoners, and vehemently given to Opposition, unless they happen to be of the right Opinion, which is seldom their Case. Imagination, Fancy, and Invention, they are wholly Strangers to, nor have any Words in their Language by which those Ideas can be expressed; the whole Compass of their Thoughts and Mind, being shut up within the two fore-mentioned Sciences."[6] For Gulliver, the Laputans may be "bad Reasoners"; but in their self-absorption and sterility, they are exemplars of abstraction, of total estrangement from ordinary life.

Understandably, many philosophers have tried to clarify the knowing process by looking at the human being who is not estranged in this fashion. Breaking with the tradition of rationalism and the old hierarchies that made pure intellectuality the highest good, various empiricists have stressed sensory experiences. Like John Locke, many of them have posited a passive mind, a *tabula rasa* on which experience inscribes its messages. In contrast to Plato, who compares sensory information with mere shadows on a wall and calls the world known to the senses only an approximation of the real world, the empiricist asserts that knowing begins with sensation. The mind has the capacity to combine sensations, to effect associations, and even to generalize; but experience provides the starting point.

This position stresses the existence of a creature of sense, will, and desire in confrontation with a concrete and various world. Affirming the importance of sensations, it maintains that the individual gains knowledge on the basis of his experiences. For example, Locke said that an individual cannot perceive a plum tree in a garden if he has no previous idea of what a plum tree is. But the idea of a plum tree is not innate; it is not a "true thought" waiting to be "awakened into knowledge." It derives from certain sensations that form into clusters of images and ideas. "Knowledge, then," wrote Locke, "seems to me to be nothing but the perception of the connection and agreement, or disagreement and repugnancy of any of our ideas."[7]

The sensations with which knowing began, however, were discrete and separate. The mind could observe, analyze, associate, and combine; the mind could also associate certain ideas with pleasure and pain. Because the mind could only work with the materials to which it was exposed (and which it passively received), claims to knowledge had to be limited. Knowers might differ in the effectiveness of their mental habits; but no matter how hard he tried to comprehend the natural world, no individual could transcend experience or the particular sensations composing it. For all such limitations, empiricism has remained attractive to people troubled by excessive abstraction and the sterile environments in which so many growing children live. Students of early childhood education, from Jean Jacques Rousseau to Martin Deutsch, have tended toward empiricism particularly when they warn against the dangers of empty formalism and environmental attrition. Poets have spoken frequently of the need for vital sensory experiences in early life; some, going further, have talked of the uses of profusion and even confusion in the early years. Samuel Taylor Coleridge wrote about "the happy delirium, the healthful fever" of the growing child:

> There is indeed "method in't," but it is the method of nature
> which thus stores the mind with all the materials for after use,
> promiscuously, indeed and as it might seem without purpose,
> while she supplies a gay and motley chaos of facts, and forms,
> and thousand-form experiences, the origin of which lies beyond
> the memory.[8]

Even Coleridge, so much concerned with imagination as an active principle of mind, here treated mind as a storehouse for a chaos of disorganized particulars. We can grant the significance of experiential variety even while questioning the notion of the mind as merely acquiescent and receptive. The power to generalize might create orders of a sort, but these were always thought to reflect patterns that were present in nature. Nature, in fact, was long thought to be inherently orderly and rational; the logical structures men achieved were thought to be structures they *found*.

A kind of innocence might easily be associated with such a view. Empiricism might coexist with the romantic view that a child, a peasant, a natural man unencumbered by theoretical schemata could somehow know more than the scholar or philosopher. William Wordsworth affirms this notion in "Ode on Intimations of Immortality" and "The Prelude":

> Call ye these appearances
> Which I beheld of shepherds in my youth . . .
> A shadow, a delusion, ye who are fed
> By the dead letter, miss the spirit of things,
> Whose truth is not a motion or a shape
> Instinct with vital functions, but a Block
> Or waxen Image which yourselves have made,
> And ye adore.[9]

According to Wordsworth, a man has to be subservient to external things. Old authorities, traditional constructs are like waxen images, which obscure the particulars of the world. Taking an approach opposite to the one Plato takes in the Myth of the Cave, Wordsworth warns against neglect of the sensuous ground in which thinking ought to begin. The shepherd (like the Child and the Countryman) sees into the "spirit of things"—and knows more than the presumably wise.

But particulars that are only sensed provide no ground for knowing unless they are organized within a context of meanings. The untutored shepherd is far more likely to perceive what William James calls a "buzzing, booming confusion" than the "spirit of things." Even if he has developed good habits of observation and association, the shepherd may still lack the interpretive principles necessary for making sense of the world. And indeed, say latter-day empiricists, without some conception of organizing principles, knowing can never adequately be explained.

Modern empiricism may be exemplified by pragmatism, which finds its primary model in experimental science. Objecting vehemently to the notion of a passive mind and to disembodied reason, the pragmatist begins with a conception of transactions between an active organism and a changing environment. The human being is never passive, he is never acted on by experiences he considers external. According to Dewey, the individual exists *within* a continuum of experience, a vital matrix in which all things are interrelated—the individual and society; mind and matter; thought and the phenomena of the world. "Experience is *of* as well as *in* nature. It is not experience which experienced, but nature. . . . Things interacting in certain ways *are* experience."[10] Caught up in these relationships, man moves from one transactional situation to another as he pursues his fulfillments and tries to bring elements of his environment under human control. There are phases, rhythms in his experiences as he acts on the world: obstacles arise, along with doubts and uncertainties, and equilibrium is lost. He is continually challenged to reorient himself, to resolve his doubts, to solve the problems posed, so he can regain his equilibrium and move on to the next stage in his life process. He meets this challenge largely through thought, and the knowledge he achieves becomes "involved in the process by which life is sustained and evolved."

Reflective thinking (or inquiry) advances step by step, from belief to doubt to reflection to empirical inference. Dewey provides a simple illustration in *How We Think*. A man, trying to get home from a walk in the woods, finds a fork in the road and tries to decide intelligently which fork he will take. If he really cares about getting home before dark, he will not aimlessly or impulsively take the fork that first appeals to him. He will look at the sun; he will study the shadows; he will consult whatever knowledge he has about the woods and the terrain; he will try to anticipate the consequences of following either path. He will, in other words, make reflective use of his experience and settle his doubts as intelligently as he can. Then, having decided on which path to take, he will begin walking again; he will find out if his idea (or his hypothesis) is correct only by seeing whether that path takes him home.

Let us use Shakespeare's *Hamlet* as a more complex illustration of the pragmatic point of view. After he has encountered his father's Ghost, Hamlet begins to transform a vaguely troubling, indeterminate situation into a truly problematic one. Not altogether sure he can believe what he thinks he heard, ridden by doubts about what has happened, Hamlet sees the problem as something rotten in Denmark. Like the other characters in the tragedy, he is not sure precisely *what* is wrong. Once he confronts the perplexity, he begins to take action to solve the problem; if he does not act, he will continue to be ridden by guilt, despair, and seemingly endless grief. He hypothesizes that his uncle murdered his father; and he proceeds to put this idea to test. If he were simply to wait, he would never find out what is wrong; so he makes a plan of action: he "puts an antic disposition on"; he mocks Polonius, rejects Ophelia, puts on a play "to catch the conscience of the king." Each maneuver is a response to a particular perception of the problem confronting him; each is dictated by certain ideas he has defined as part of his response. For instance, the play-within-the-play is dictated by the notion that the dramatization of the murder of another king would be unbearable to Claudius if Claudius were guilty, impelling him to stop the play. And this is exactly what happens. Hamlet has tested his hypothesis and has found it to be true. He has learned something (the cause of the sickness in Denmark) through self-initiated inquiry. The knowing process has been an active one, with major consequences for him and, at length, for the king and queen. Because he is entirely conscious of the connection between his actions and the consequences, Hamlet has had what Dewey would call a meaningful experience; he has come to know what he did not know before.

For the pragmatist, then, knowing involves both rational and empirical thinking. It demands formal or informal experimentation and requires an attitude of tentativeness, coupled with a willingness to reexamine and revise. Whereas the older empiricisms were functions of a mathematically ordered world, this more modern empiricism is a function of an open universe in which changes are continually taking place and novelty is inescapable. Underlying this empiricism is an enormous faith in intelligence and in the capacity of intelligence to predict, control, and transform. Concerning "the recognition of the place of active and planning thought," Dewey wrote:

> ... reason is experimental intelligence, conceived after the pattern of science, and used in the creation of social arts; it has something to do. It liberates man from the bondage of the past, due to ignorance and accident hardened into custom. It projects a better future and assists man in its realization. And its operation is always subject to test in experience. The plans which are formed, the principles which man projects as guides of reconstructive action, are not dogmas. They are hypotheses to be worked out in practice, and to be rejected, corrected and expanded as they fail or succeed in giving our present experience the guidance it requires. We may call them programmes of action, but since they are to be used in making our future acts less blind, more directed, they are flexible. Intelligence is not something possessed once and for all. It is in constant process of forming, and its retention requires constant alertness in observing consequences, an open-minded will to learn, and courage in readjustment.[11]

We have already spoken of the decline of this faith in intelligence and the loss of confidence in experimental science. However, loss of confidence

does not in itself invalidate an epistemological theory any more than
optimism validates it. Questions have been raised about the presumed
resemblance between experimental intelligence and scientific method. The
natural scientist is not concerned with "giving our present experience the
guidance it requires"; and he is not involved with personal or concrete
experiences. His aim is to construct symbolic formulations with predictive
and explanatory value—formulations that will effect connections between
sets of facts. "We reserve," write Morris Cohen and Ernest Nagel, "the
term 'science' for knowledge which is general and systematic, that is in
which specific propositions are all deduced from a few general principles."
They go on to describe the method as "the persistent application of logic
as the common feature of all reasoned knowledge . . . simply the way in
which we test impressions, opinions, or surmises by examining the best
available evidence for and against them."[12] The best available evidence
has nothing to do with morality or human fulfillment. We need only recall
the testing that led to the A-bomb and the H-bomb, to extermination
camps, to nerve gas, to napalm—as well as the research that led to the
Salk vaccine, antipollution devices, and heart surgery.

"It has become generally accepted," write Solon Kimball and James
McClellan, that the theory of intelligence we have been discussing "was
erroneously labeled the 'scientific method.' The actual procedures by which
scientific discoveries are made and tested bear resemblance to Dewey's
theory of how we think only in that both methods represent ways, albeit
quite different ways, of using human intelligence."[13] Even so, emphasis on
the problematic remains significant, as does concern for the tentative,
open-minded approach to inquiry. The pragmatist, more than any previous
philosopher, shows the meaninglessness of old separations between the
rational and the empirical. Under the impact of his thought, the notion of
a passive, acquiescent mind gives way. He begins to perceive the mind as a
mode of behavior, a function of an active social organism. He considers
experience to be the individual's encompassing "reality," which becomes
significant to the degree that the organism reflects his doing and
undergoing. Reflecting, deliberating, weighing alternatives, he has the
capacity for giving his life form.

He can learn to regulate his transactions with the environment
according to what Dewey calls a "logic of inquiry"; but the protocols or
methods the individual uses in resolving his perplexities are generally not
of his making, although he has undoubtedly learned them through his
efforts. They are products of an informed consensus developed over time;
they express the cumulative funding of the meanings he reaches in the
course of repeated inquiries. The inquiring individual, then, pursues truth
and meaning in a well-lit human laboratory with windows open to the past
and the doors ajar. In touch with the world, participating in all kinds of

conversations, the intelligent individual becomes increasingly able to reconstruct his experience but in a manner others can interpret, in a language others can understand.

Pragmatism is criticized for its preoccupation with the calculative. It is challenged for its neglect of subjectivity, what takes place in the person's "underground." Even so, Dewey was not so narrowly focused as his interest in the experimental would suggest. The paradigmatic experience for him was the aesthetic experience: "*an* experience when the material experienced runs its course to fulfillment," when every trait is intensified and clarified, when consummation occurs.[14] He stressed the continuity between rhythm in nature and rhythm in experience and placed great emphasis on the forms that appear when equilibrium is achieved and a kind of coherence develops out of interacting energies. He talked of inexpressible qualities of experience, which were simply enjoyed or "had." Attuned to richness and variety, Dewey wrote: "The realm of meaning is wider than that of true-and-false meaning, it is more urgent and more fertile."[15] He was including poetic meaning and moral meaning; and his statement still holds great relevance for those concerned with diversifying their perspectives on a continuous and complicated world.

Many people respect the good sense of such a mode of thinking even though they reject it for themselves. They may reject it because they have undergone—or are undergoing—an experience Dewey scarcely touched on: the "experience of nothingness," or because they suffer ennui, a pervasive boredom of which Dewey (in his healthy mindedness) seemed to know little. They may feel somewhat like Marlow in Joseph Conrad's *Heart of Darkness,* the man who tries to explain to his fellow seamen the experience of piloting an ancient steamboat into the depths of Africa, where "the mere incidents of the surface, the reality—the reality, I tell you —fades." Like Marlow, they are aware of blankness and inscrutability; staring at their immensities, they too feel, as Conrad says, "very small, very lost." They cannot credit the purported solidity of their culture. Like Marlow, they find the pursuits of managers and other busy people to be "monkey tricks" in the face of nothingness. They find the search for objective knowledge to be a kind of game. Pragmatic approaches to knowing and problem solving seem oddly irrelevant to them. The notion that reason can help men achieve a better future seems either empty or overly optimistic for the voyages into darkness on which they have embarked. Pragmatic theories, to them, are linked to the manipulative sciences and tainted by the heartlessness they ascribe to scientific thought in general. They associate pragmatism with science; they associate both with the depersonalization that seems to cause their feelings of powerlessness. Like R. D. Laing, the British psychiatrist, they find modern society to be a Procrustean bed. They prefer immediate awarenesses to mediated knowing; they often seek mystical illuminations or drug-induced insights.

Like students who profess total disinterest in their classrooms, few alienated persons are explicitly concerned with epistemology, even when they castigate objectivists and rage against scientific naturalists for being "square," sterile, and myopic. When they talk of "expanded consciousness," "grooving," and "transcending," they are unaware that what they are saying derives from certain presuppositions respecting knowledge, knowing, and the known. Without realizing, they frequently raise phenomenological questions; they suffer from strains and tensions the phenomenologist has been describing for almost a hundred years.

The phenomenologist takes issue with both the rationalist and the empiricist for their neglect of the stream of thought in inner time. Unlike either one, he embarks on his epistemological inquiries with questions about how the phenomena of the world—"things themselves"—present themselves in inner time. Consciousness is his fundamental concept; but for the phenomenologist it is in no sense mere innerness or introspection. It thrusts *toward* the world, not away from it. The term refers to the multiple ways in which the individual comes in touch with the world: all the activities by means of which objects, events, and other human beings are presented to him. These activities include perceiving, judging, believing, remembering, imagining. It follows that all the experiences which appear in the inner stream *refer* to objects, events, or other human beings which are perceived, judged, believed, remembered, or imagined. It follows too that consciousness is characterized by intentionality: it is always *of* something—something which, when grasped, relates to the act of consciousness involved as the meaning of that act. Conrad's Marlow perceives the African river from his vantage point as the sweating captain of a steamboat always in danger of scraping bottom. Through his acts of consciousness (his watching, remembering, perceiving, listening, anticipating), the river presents itself to him as a road "back to the earliest beginnings of the world," into the "heart of darkness"; and this is the *meaning* of his watching, remembering, and the rest. His passengers are ivory hunters en route to the station up river. They believe that, if they can stand the climate, "anything can be done in this country." Through their acts of consciousness, the river and the riverbanks present themselves as conquered territory, sources of potential wealth.

Consciousness may be referred to, then, as "experienced context"; [16] and each person's life-world is his context as he experiences it. The phenomenologist makes this life-world central to his thinking and, in consequence, places great stress on each person's biographical situation, on each one's "standpoint" and the way it affects what he sees. Much of the time, of course, the individual teacher or student is not conscious of his standpoint or of his consciousness. He lives immersed in his daily life. He takes a "natural attitude": he takes for granted the commonsense reality of things. He functions habitually, conventionally; he assumes the constancy of the structures around him and the validity of the recipes by which his social group governs its life. But there are always fringes, boundaries at the edge of the familiar. There are horizons scarcely noticed and never explored. Sometimes, however, what he has taken for granted suddenly becomes questionable; there is an interference with the habitual flow. "To solve the problem, whether of a practical or theoretical nature," writes Alfred Schutz, "we have to enter into its horizons in order to explicate them."[17] Ordinary ways of perceiving have to be suspended; questions have to be posed. The individual has to be jolted into awareness of his own perceptions, into recognition of the way in which he has constituted his *own* life-world.

The rationalist, as we have seen, avoids commonsense experience and begins his inquiries with, as Hutchins has put it, the "pure operation of reason." The early empiricist begins with experience reducible to sensations that bombard the passive mind. The pragmatist begins and ends within a sociocultural matrix in which indeterminate experiences are made significant by means of the process of inquiry. The phenomenologist begins with the individual in the midst of everyday life, where he is located in terms of the various experiences he has had in the course of his existence. His situation is to some degree unique because his biography is unique. He lives, certainly, in what is accepted as *the* world; but he transmutes it into *his* world in the light of who and where he is.

Let us again consider *Hamlet,* but this time from a phenomenological rather than a pragmatic point of view. The Prince, returning from Wittenberg for his father's funeral, reenters a commonsense world, which is in many respects "given," ready-made. The castle in Elsinore contains a royal court with all the accepted ceremonies and trappings of a monarchical system. Like his countrymen, Hamlet takes much of this world for granted: there are soldiers and servants delineated by their costumes and their occupations; there are noblemen and commoners, trumpeters and pages, gravediggers and lawyers; arguments are settled by duels; suicides cannot be buried in hallowed ground. All this provides an arena for what he has done as a youth and what he intends to do now. He shares his contemporaries' interpretations of the structures at Elsinore. In other words, he takes for granted the same things the courtiers and commonmen do, he acts much of the time according to this scheme. He sees his fellowmen as fellowmen; he predicts their behavior, communicates meaningfully with certain ones, cooperates with them. If a modern man were to be swept back in time and inserted in Elsinore at Hamlet's side, he would *not* see as Hamlet does because he would not be prepared to take for granted the rituals of court life, the social hierarchies, the customs of the Danish state. His typifications would be different because reality from his vantage point is structured in another way.

Although, compared with modern man, Hamlet takes a great deal for granted through his "natural attitude," he nevertheless perceives the court from a distinctive point of view. After all, he is the son of the dead king; he was in line to inherit the throne. His peculiar biography is bound to make his interpretations somewhat different from Horatio's, say, or Laertes', or even Claudius's. These men all belong to the same cultural matrix; they participate, without much thought, in the same ceremonies. But having had different subjective experiences, each of them is in a distinctive situation and bound to interpret novel events in his particular fashion. What each one comes to "know," therefore, will have much to do with the way he locates himself and with the relevance of what is happening to his own concerns.

Hamlet is grief-stricken and despairing at the start. He is preoccupied, however, with his mother's "wicked speed" in remarrying, not with suspicions of murder. The problem of his anger can be dealt with within the scope of the conventional: "I must hold my tongue." Only when he confronts the Ghost does he perceive a problem beyond the range of the commonsense reality he shares with others. ("There are more things in heaven and earth, Horatio,/Than are dreamt of in your philosophy.") If he were convinced of the Ghost's existence, if he were sure Claudius had killed his father, if he felt free of guilt himself, he could act in what would be considered a normal manner in Elsinore: he could take revenge on Claudius and assume his rightful place on the throne. Acting in what would be a traditional fashion (for example, as Fortinbras would have acted in the same situation), Hamlet would be treating his discovery pragmatically. The "natural attitude" would suffice; the ordinary reality structures would be undisturbed.

Because of his biography, because of concrete experiences he has had (with his mother, perhaps, or with his late father), he cannot integrate this new occurrence with the everyday. There is a moment of shock, even of hysteria. He makes his friends swear "Never to speak of this that you have heard." His consciousness, the phenomenologist would say, moves from everyday reality to other spheres and other structures of meaning. ("'Sblood, there is something in this more than natural, if philosophy could find it out.") Like other human beings, Hamlet is aware that the world of which he is conscious is composed of "more than natural" spheres of reality. Consciousness is always *of* something; it grasps; it intends multiple structures of meaning. There are dreams, memories, layers of belief and perception, stocks of knowledge, fantasies. In this case, trying to cope with a problem impervious to commonsense solutions, he begins to reflect on his condition, his experiences, his perceptions. ("I have of late,—but wherefore I know not,—lost all my mirth, forgone all custom of exercises; and indeed it goes so heavily with my disposition that this goodly frame, the earth, seems to be a sterile promontory.") In reflecting, he excludes or brackets out typical and conventional interpretations. He attempts to rid himself of ordinary presuppositions, the assumptions that distract him from his stream of consciousness and force him to see in stereotyped ways. ("I am very proud, revengeful, ambitious, with more offences at my beck than I have thoughts to put them in, imagination to give them shape, or time to act them in.") He can only discover the meaning of what is happening if he engages in the kind of self-interpretation that will enable him to interpret the significance of the Other, who is Claudius, and the Other's actions in the world. He can only discover what is rotten in Denmark if he refuses to take for granted any longer the rituals that apparently legitimate the court.

The phenomenologist, then, focuses on the engaged observer when he tries to clarify the knowing process. Not only is the observer's subjectivity involved; so are the subjectivities of his contemporaries, and the intersubjective reality they mutually create. Yet reality is not necessarily dependent on the knower for its existence. The natural and social worlds exist both in space and time; orders of real phenomena and events are continually being presented to consciousness. For the phenomenologist, however, intersections, zones, and horizons are significant in the knowing process. Each person, for example, is to some degree aware of an inner time, which differs from clock time, the intersubjectively accepted time of everyday reality. The person must adapt to standard time sequences throughout his life, but these sequences are never completely syntonic with the levels of inner temporality. Similarly, each person has systems of relevances, which depend on his biographical situation, his location, his purposes. And when he sees an object—a plum tree, for example—he does not see it in isolation; he sees "a field of perceptions and cogitations with a halo, with a horizon, or to use a term of William James, with fringes relating it to other things."[18]

The difference between the pragmatist and the phenomenologist lies fundamentally in what each one takes for granted. The pragmatist is far more likely to posit a disinterested observer or inquirer whose possibilities of objective knowledge are as extensive as the range of inquiry itself. The private mind, with its sedimentations and zones, is not relevant here. Experimental and logical techniques give the observer the capacity not merely to organize his experience anew in responding to each particular problem but to surmount the limitations of private perspective in approaching verifiable truth.

The phenomenologist does not question the natural scientist's ability to overcome subjective interpretation and develop objective, or in some sense "ideal," constructs. He does question the social scientist's ability to explain a social reality without taking his biography, his temporality into account. Because of this doubt, the phenomenologist would sympathize with those who challenge the indifference of social scientists and planners who treat social situations as natural phenomena, or human beings as inanimate objects susceptible to measurement and manipulation. He would be sympathetic as well to those who feel obliterated as personalities because some Other overlooks the role of inner time. And he would understand all too well people like Joseph Conrad's Marlow, who experience the difficulty of explaining their ideas to others who take for granted what they find on the surfaces:

> "Absurd!" he cried. "This is the worst of trying to tell. . . . Here you all are, each moored with two good addresses, like a hulk with two anchors, a butcher round one corner, a policeman round another, excellent appetites, and temperature normal—you hear—normal from year's end to year's end. And you say, Absurd! Absurd be—exploded! Absurd! My dear boys, what can you expect from a man who out of sheer nervousness had just flung overboard a pair of new shoes?"[19]

Marlow is willing to break with the predefined, the stereotypical, to reflect his experience in such a way as to perceive meanings no one with a one-dimensional vision could perceive. Useless though his journey is, futile though his efforts may have been, Marlow has come to know something about the human condition, which he had never perceived the same way before.

He has gained this vision because he has penetrated more than one sphere of reality. He has been able to do so because he has broken with the presuppositions of his culture and given up the presumed necessities: a good address, a butcher, a policeman on the corner, a healthy appetite, a normal temperature. His voyage to the heart of darkness has been a voyage into himself. Risking this voyage, he has encountered structures of meaning that seem absurd to those who never examine their assumptions, who take for granted the everyday reality in which they live. Such persons resemble the manager Marlow meets, the man "who originated nothing [but] . . . could keep the routine going—that's all." He was not intelligent;

he had no organizing talents; but he kept his health. "Perhaps there was nothing within him."

Existential thinkers, much influenced by phenomenology, would describe the manager as a serious man incapable of releasing himself to his subjectivity. When they consider the problem of knowledge, they begin with the subject, the existing self. Only as a "single one," they say, can a person know who he is and discover what is fundamental in his experience. Only as a "single one" can he overcome the separation traditionally perceived between subject and object. When a gap exists between the human being as subject and the phenomena he tries to know, the subject becomes a spectator. Conrad's manager is such a spectator, sealed off from the continent around him, seeing things from a great distance. To see that way is to break the world into fragments. Experience is distorted; reality is never perceived truly, wholly; engagement becomes impossible.

The pragmatist also speaks in terms of continuities. Dewey spent much of his philosophical career challenging dualisms of all sorts and criticizing the spectator or merely contemplative stance. We have seen how Dewey treated knowledge within the context of human action and transaction, how he believed that knowing involved the effecting of changes in the world. However, the existentialist would say that the pragmatist was concerned with calculative or objective thinking and that his overriding aim was to attain objective knowledge. Like Søren Kierkegaard, the existentialist would assert that the way of objective reflection made the subject—or the knower—a mere accident and transformed existence into something it was not. Or like Friedrich Nietzsche, he might say that the pragmatist defined himself by means of a will to power, that he was preoccupied with controlling what lay beyond him. Since Kant, the existentialist would point out, we have understood that the reality available to human beings is merely a flux of appearances. Theories and explanations are only tools, helping us to cope with becoming and change; but they cannot be considered "knowledge," and they do not provide us with truths by which we can live. Personal life and existence are the important factors that must be grasped and understood.

Affirming this belief, the existentialist turns away from the traditional epistemological problems. He suggests that, in any case, the ability to know is only one feature of the self, that the self must not be identified with reason or with mind. To speak of the self is to speak of an individual's body as well as his mind, his past as well as his present; the world in which he is involved, the others with whom he is continually engaged. To grasp the idea of self, a philosophical mode of reflection, quite different from objective thinking, is required. Jean-Paul Sartre, in fact, associates "bad faith" with the kind of thinking that solidifies the self into a spurious object. The individual must be able to distinguish among self, the world, and other people if he is to gain knowledge; but these distinctions must not result in a splitting apart of consciousness from the world. Knowledge may be said to be the way a man comes in touch with his world, puts questions to it (recognizing that the questioner is always part of whatever questions he poses), transforms its component parts into signs and tools, translates his findings into words. Meanings are found in the way he relates to the world: science is one mode of relating; logic is another; philosophy is a third. Truth is a particular kind of relationship; but just as knowledge is always partial and incomplete, so is truth only an approximation, because the existentialist, like the phenomenologist, conceives the knower as a person in a concrete situation, not as "man" in the abstract or as "scientist" or as "inquirer." Each knower, each man-in-the-world responds to questions arising out of his situation, which is partly known to him and partly unknown. He sees some aspects of it as near, some as indistinct and remote, some on the horizon. He perceives, remembers, judges, believes; and, in each mode of awareness, something new presents itself to be grasped. Often, he is aware of a basic uncertainty he wishes to relieve; and he finds his consciousness leaning, stretching, reaching out to transform what is mute or apparently meaningless into a communicable reality, significant for him.

The emphasis is on self-consciousness, on self-encounter. The individual must appropriate what he has learned into his life; he must use this knowledge in making choices and in determining his future actions. He must constantly decide on the appropriate techniques for particular explorations; and each choice he makes involves a commitment, a discipline. For example, when a man chooses to do the meditative thinking demanded by philosophy, reflective thinking releases him to himself. But, in addition, calculative thinking, involves the inquirer in planning and classifying, although not in encountering subjective reality. Here, again, the pragmatist would not distinguish experimental from philosophical thinking in this manner. For the existentialist, science cannot serve as model or paradigm, largely because scientific thinking is concerned with objectification and excludes the intuitive awareness and the self-encounters required of philosophy. When the existentialist speaks of knowing, he speaks of passionately engaging and of vouching for his ideas with his life. The cool neutrality of experimental inquiry is usually alien to such a man, as is the search for consensus and something approximating objectivity.

Yet the existentialist is not an antirationalist, for all his questioning of the possibilities of knowing. We can grant his rejection of behaviorisms and universal laws, especially those used to "explain" human actions. We can grant, as well, his skepticism about objectification and his neglect of the traditional epistemological questions. The pragmatist and the language analyst may consider nonsensical his preoccupation with consciousness and the recovery of being (or wholeness or identity). The rationalist may consider irresponsible his preoccupation with groundlessness and his denigration of autonomous reason. Nevertheless, in the bulk of existential literature, there is a fundamental respect for reasoning as well as reflection, for experience as well as subjectivity. The existentialist may deny the primacy of knowledge, as Sartre does when he talks about self-consciousness and the discovery of the being of the knower; but he will also vehemently challenge (as Sartre also does) someone who becomes an anti-Semite because he is impervious to reason and experience. Since Kierkegaard, existentialists have attempted to arouse human beings to take notice of their existence, to find out for themselves. They have also attempted to make people realize that existence precedes thought, that the purpose of knowledge is to clarify and to open up a life.

Another reason for the charge that existentialism is irrationalist is the interest of certain existential thinkers in the transcendent, the encompassing—the "boundary situation." Kierkegaard, who insisted that the human being lives in his subjective decisions rather than in his reflections, wrote of the need to "plunge confidently into the absurd," and of the "paradox of faith." At times, man leaps beyond what his intelligence can grasp; like Kierkegaard's Abraham, "he accomplishes nothing for the universal but only himself is tried and examined." Such decisions are made in isolation and in terrible tension. "The knight of faith," writes Kierkegaard, "is obliged to rely upon himself alone, he feels the pain of not being able to make himself intelligible to others, but he feels no vain desire to guide others. The pain is his assurance that he is in the right way."[20] This is the uttermost boundary, the point at which a man risks everything he has. Great heroes have reached this limit; people of profound commitment have reached it—and *are* reaching it every day. But they have no rational way of justifying their actions and appraising the consequences. Marlow's listeners would call such choices utterly absurd. The pragmatic thinker, the liberal, the reformer would warn against the isolation these actions entail, the dangers in unintelligibility. They might say that if a man cannot explain what he proposes to do, if he can give no good reason for it, he is probably acting impulsively, or he is permitting himself to be driven by unconscious forces he should be able to control. For the existentialist, however, this is the culmination of the "single one." Kierkegaard's answer would be:

> He who would only be a witness thereby avows that no man, not even the lowliest, needs another man's sympathy or should be abased that another may be exalted. But since he did not win

what he won at a cheap price, neither does he sell it out at a
cheap price, he is not petty enough to take men's admiration
and give them in return his silent contempt, he knows that what
is truly great is accessible to all.[21]

The point is that, although an individual may know perfectly well what he
is doing, his knowledge of his actions is not objective. Nor is it of the sort
that should make him feel admirable. If he is a witness in Kierkegaard's
sense, he has simply been released to his subjectivity; what he has learned
in his self-consciousness he can—without explaining—teach.

What, then, does it mean to be a knower, to know, and to gain
knowledge? How are we to conceive truth and meaning as we attempt to
launch young people on their personal searches for both? Before moving
on to talk of teaching and learning per se, we must pause for a moment
and look back over the way we have come. We have conceived various
approaches to the problems of knowledge, each of which has highlighted a
particular phase of pondering and inquiry and exploration. Each one, too,
has expressed a particular ideal concerning cognition and carries with it an
implicit notion of human capacity, experience, and existence. From his
standpoint, the teacher should be somewhat more conscious of the
multidimensional character of the knowing process and of his ideal
concerning the knower. After all, his objective—or his project—is to free
himself as well as those he teaches to explore consciousness and the
life-world.

If, for a moment, he were to take several approaches as hypothetical
models, the teacher might find himself working out an enriched conception
of knowing and the known. The rationalist approach, for example, may
promote a sharper awareness of the significance of lawfulness and order.
We have spoken of the bombardments of sensation, of the chaotic
impressions requiring some kind of organization if sense is to be made.
Rationality gives rise to such organization and makes principled thinking
possible. We shall be talking of rule-governed, or norm-governed, action as
we go, of the kind of thinking that demands rational justification. The
rational life, writes Israel Scheffler, is "a life in which the critical quest for
reasons is a dominant and integrating motive."[22] On occasion, we shall ask
whether a life so motivated can be sufficiently open to experiential
ambiguities, to personal awarenesses. We shall ask if such a life allows for
the leaps of imagination existential thinkers describe, if it permits what
phenomenologists speak of as a return to things themselves. Once we
divorce the rationalist orientation from fixations on innate ideas and
preexistent forms, we cannot exclude from our conceptions of knowing
principles, reasons, and rules. Without them, there could be no "plan of

living." Without them, men could never emerge from their undergrounds. Still, to do so, they must be able to order the materials of their lives.

As we have seen, empiricist approaches place great stress on those materials. For the later empiricist, the mind is a function of the organism's multiple transactions with the environment; and the mind's growth depends to a large degree on the richness of the experience as well as on the way structures and connections are understood. (We might summon up Walt Whitman's famous lines: "A child said What is the grass? fetching it to me with full hands; How could I answer the child?"[23] The only way to answer is to help that child effect connections within his experience and see relationships between things done or undergone with respect to grass—and the consequences of those things.) Why would anyone ask questions without a recurrent perception of the problematic? Why would anyone want to know if there were no obstacles to his progress through life? The individual must learn, as he lives, to intellectualize the data of his observations and encounters. He must embody sensory input in some symbolic language if he is to achieve knowledge; he cannot simply link together or process the particulars he perceives. The career of Albert Camus's antihero Meursault in *The Stranger* provides an instance of such an inability to know. Meursault is a character who is intensely aware of the sensual delights of the world. He feels the sun, notices the brightness of day or lamplight, watches a passing streetcar light up "a girl's hair, a smile, or a silver bangle." But he draws no inferences, makes no judgments. ("All I was conscious of was our mad rush along the waterfront . . ."; "I didn't care one way or the other, but he seemed so set on it, I nodded and said, 'Yes.' "; "A moment later she asked me if I loved her. I said that sort of question had no meaning really; but I supposed I didn't.") For no reason, good *or* bad, he kills an Arab on a sun-dazzled beach; and he is tried for murder. At the end of the trial, after his counsel's final appeal, Meursault responds in this fashion:

> And then a rush of memories went through my mind—
> memories of a life which was mine no longer and had once
> provided me with the surest, humblest pleasures: warm smells of
> summer, my favorite streets, Marie's dresses and her laugh. The
> futility of what was happening here seemed to take me by the
> throat. I felt like vomiting, and I had only one idea: to get it
> over, to go back to my cell, and sleep.[24]

This moving statement is the revelation of a man unable to think cognitively about his life situation. Life, as he remembers it, is nothing but an accumulation of sensations; now, at the moment of extreme crisis, he has only one thought: to sleep. It is not that Meursault is unintelligent or cowardly. Certainly he is honest in his refusal to pretend. He simply refuses—or is incapable of—rationality. The "critical search for reasons" is wholly alien to him; and this may be partly why the jury finds no extenuating circumstances. He is sentenced to death "because he refused to cry at his mother's funeral." Facing the questions of the court and the society, he never attempted (and undoubtedly would have been unable) to say why.

Considering Meursault as a human consciousness, the phenomenologist would not blame Meursault for his lack of rationality so much as for his submission to the everyday. He takes everything for granted, at least until he shoots the Arab. The shooting is partly a consequence of his refusal to question, to look at his or Raymond's preconceptions. He even falsifies his standpoint. What, after all, were the Arabs to him? Just as the phenomenologist would insist on consciousness of one's biographical situation in the effort to know, so would the existentialist insist on the necessity for initiative and commitment. Meursault is, to an extent, a "single one"; but he never makes a choice; he never becomes passionately engaged in a struggle to know; he never appropriates what he learns into his life. For all the differences among the philosophic positions we have described, in general Meursault would be condemned for not being self-conscious, critical, or responsible. He would also be criticized for his disengagement from life, his aimlessness, his almost total inability to act. ("Nothing, nothing had the least importance, and I knew quite well why.")

Nothing could be more antithetical to the attitude of the functioning teacher than this kind of indifference. The importance of what he does must consciously be defined. He must become passionately engaged in prompting younger people to take initiatives and to act mindfully. If *they* are to become self-conscious and responsible, the teacher must continually think about what he is doing as he teaches them. And part of this thinking must have to do with what he takes "knowing" to mean and what he considers the significance of enabling others to know.

Notes and References

1. Paul Hirst, "Philosophy and Educational Theory," in *Philosophy and Education,* ed. Israel Scheffler (Boston: Allyn & Bacon, 1966), p. 89.
2. Plato, Book VII, "The Republic," in *The Works of Plato,* vol. 2, tr. B. Jowett (New York: Tudor Publishing Company, n.d.), p. 277.

3. Plato, "Meno," in *The Works of Plato,* vol. 3, tr. B. Jowett, p. 35.

4. Albert William Levi, *The Humanities Today* (Bloomington: Indiana University Press, 1970), p. 21.

5. Robert M. Hutchins, *The Higher Learning in America* (New Haven, Conn.: Yale University Press, 1962), pp. 83–84.

6. Jonathan Swift, *Gulliver's Travels* (Garden City, N.Y.: Doubleday & Company, n.d.), p. 156.

7. John Locke, *An Essay Concerning Human Understanding,* bk. 4, ch. 1 (New York: E.P. Dutton & Company, 1947), p. 252.

8. William Walsh, *The Use of Imagination: Educational Thought and the Literary Mind* (London: Chatto & Windus, 1959), p. 25.

9. William Wordsworth, "The Prelude," Book Eight, in *William Wordsworth's The Prelude with a Selection from the Shorter Poems, Sonnets, The Recluse, and The Excursion,* ed. Carlos Baker (New York: Holt, Rinehart & Winston, 1962), p. 342.

10. John Dewey, *Experience and Nature* (New York: Dover Publications, 1958), p. 4A.

11. John Dewey, *Reconstruction in Philosophy* (Boston: Beacon Press, 1948), pp. 96–97.

12. Morris R. Cohen and Ernest Nagel, *An Introduction to Logic and Scientific Method* (New York: Harcourt Brace Jovanovich, 1934), p. 192.

13. Solon T. Kimball and James E. McClellan, Jr., *Education and the New America* (New York: Random House, 1962), p. 98.

14. John Dewey, *Art as Experience* (New York: Minton, Balch & Company, 1934), p. 35.

15. John Dewey, *Experience and Nature,* p. 411.

16. Aron Gurwitsch, "Towards a Theory of Intentionality," *Philosophical and Phenomenological Research,* March 1970, vol. 30, no. 3, p. 364.

17. Alfred Schutz, "Some Structures of the Life-World," in *Studies in Phenomenological Philosophy, Collected Papers* III (The Hague: Martinus Nijhoff, 1966), p. 117.

18. Alfred Schutz, "Some Leading Concepts of Phenomenology," in *The Problem of Social Reality, Collected Papers* I (The Hague: Martinus Nijhoff, 1967), p. 108.

19. Joseph Conrad, *Heart of Darkness,* in *Heart of Darkness & the Secret Sharer* (New York: New American Library, 1950), p. 120.

20. Søren Kierkegaard, *Fear and Trembling,* tr. Walter Lowrie (Garden City, N.Y.: Doubleday & Company, 1954), p. 90.

21. Søren Kierkegaard, *Fear and Trembling,* p. 91.

22. Israel Scheffler, *Conditions of Knowledge: An Introduction to Epistemology and Education* (Chicago: Scott, Foresman & Company, 1965), p. 107.

23. Walt Whitman, "Song of Myself," in *Leaves of Grass* (New York: Aventine Press, 1931), p. 33.

24. Albert Camus, *The Stranger* (New York: Vintage Books, 1954), p. 132.

Further Reading

William Barrett, *Irrational Man: A Study in Existential Philosophy* (Garden City, N.Y.: Doubleday & Company, 1958).

John Dewey, *How We Think* (Boston: D. C. Heath, 1933).

John Dewey, *Logic: The Theory of Inquiry* (New York: Holt, Rinehart & Winston, 1938).

John Dewey and Arthur F. Bentley, *Knowing and the Known* (Boston: Beacon Press, 1949).

Martin Heidegger, *Discourse on Thinking,* tr. John M. Anderson and E. Hans Freund (New York: Harper & Row, Publishers, 1966).

Edmund Husserl, *Phenomenology and the Crisis of Philosophy,* tr. Quentin Lauer (New York: Harper & Row, Publishers, 1965).

Søren Kierkegaard, " 'The Individual': Two 'Notes' Concerning My Work as An Author," in *The Point of View for My Work as An Author,* tr. Walter Lowrie (New York: Harper & Row, Publishers, 1962).

Jean-Paul Sartre, "Bad Faith," in *Being and Nothingness,* tr. Hazel E. Barnes (New York: Philosophical Library, 1956).

Chapter Seven

"What the Known Demands ..."

I would believe teaching needs at all times to be
non-institutional; done along the streets, individually as Socrates
did it or for that matter as Jesus did; or at very most—
organized in the poverty and intensity of the mediaeval
beginnings of Universities; that any further organization and
acceptance into society suffocated learning how to try to use the
mind intensely and independently, i.e. how to become in certain
senses a "free" rather than a "bonded" man; this latter being
probably the first and maybe the only great obligation of
teaching. If or when one has got some of this
duty-of-independence, he may then much more safely go about
becoming a scholar or whatever he pleases.

> James Agee
> *Letters of James Agee to
> Father Flye*

The manners of teaching are the manners of argument. They
are the manners of civility, deliberation, and inquiry, even when
they lead to false conclusions. Thus, a society that sought to
encourage the manners of teaching would be one whose legal
institutions, whose uses of speech, whose exploitation of nature,
and whose religious institutions would seek to cultivate those
habits associated with the demands of thinking.

> Thomas F. Green
> *The Activities of Teaching*

Few teachers today are unacquainted with the work being done by
psychologists, linguists, and other specialists concerned with understanding
how human beings come to know. Never before has there been so much
interest in the problem of learning; never before have teachers found so
much relevant information at hand. Such names as Jean Piaget, Jerome
Bruner, and Noam Chomsky need only be mentioned to evoke the
diversity of inquirers into the development of conceptual abilities and

linguistic skills. Disciplinary scholars have been examining their own subject matters to determine their logical structure, or the order in which the principles that compose them are arranged. Others have been attempting to clarify the "practical arts" of devising appropriate curricula and enabling individuals to learn.

At first glance, these investigations seem to promise recipes for the practicing teacher. Once in his classroom, however, he soon realizes that he cannot simply deduce courses of action from statements about what is known. Confronting fluid, often unprecedented situations, he must continually decide on the most appropriate course of action. He must choose intentionally—sometimes on the spur of the moment, always as someone who is *there*—because he is committed to a distinctive mode of practical activity, entailing a variety of strategic as well as logical acts. If he is thoughtful about this activity, of course, he will have in mind some of what he has learned about the nature of human development. He will take into account aspects of what Dewey and Piaget call the "science of education." In fact, at times he will borrow from something Piaget or another psychologist has written; but he will only borrow what seems appropriate to his undertaking at the time. The question of the relation between empirical information and his classroom performance will remain open. When the teacher tries to work out the specific implications of empirical research for his teaching, he will be thrust into doing philosophy.

Let us take the example of Piaget's research, since it has become so influential on contemporary educational thought. The teacher is bound to be familiar with Piaget's descriptions of the ways children of different ages accommodate to and assimilate aspects of their environments. He is likely to take for granted what Piaget and his co-workers have said about the cumulative development of conceptual capacities. He may even be acting habitually on the assumption that the stages of an individual's development may be identified through the logical operations of which the individual is capable at different times. If he is dealing with young children, he may expect them to be able to classify and arrange things in order, thus indicating that they have reached the stage of concrete operations. If his pupils are a bit older, he may expect them to grasp intuitively certain elements, say, of set theory without being able to explain the theory. The teacher may be convinced that only when children reach adolescence will they begin to think systematically and begin reflecting on their own cognitive activities. This being so, he will not demand abstract conceptualizations of children too young to coordinate the forms of knowledge. He will not ask for theoretical explanations from pupils he considers incapable of doing mental experiments without recourse to concrete operations.

All this may give the teacher a sense of assurance when he makes his plans each day. Nevertheless, he ought to realize that not all psychologists agree with Piaget. Some believe that the middle-class Swiss children with whom Piaget worked are not necessarily typical of all children in all parts of the world. Jerome Bruner and others differ with Piaget on the age at which abstract thinking can be expected to begin. Many critics assert that Piaget pays too little attention to social and cultural influences upon children or that he simply assumes a certain type of social influence and the acquisition of a certain set of linguistic skills. More seriously, questions have been raised about the existence of general laws of child development. Can such laws be discovered? Is there only one path a child must follow if he is to acquire the concepts he needs for interpreting his world?

The teacher is not a psychologist and is not required to settle such questions in any general sense. He *is* required to confront individual children and do what he can to move them from where they are conceptually to new explorations and discoveries. He knows that he can do little if he is not aware of the concepts his pupils already possess and the relationships they are able to appreciate. In each case, the concepts possessed depend to an extent on the experiences the person has had, the things he has gathered together according to some principle of relevance. A child understands the concept of a tree, for example, when he recognizes that evergreens, willows, birches, and oak trees can all be gathered together under a single rubric. In other words, he has acquired the concept when he recognizes a tree *as such;* but that recognition may have emerged after a great variety of experiences and actions with respect to trees, a variety distinctive to the child's own life. One of the teacher's tasks is to help each child understand *why* it is relevant to include both evergreens and maples under the concept 'tree' and, when the time comes, how that concept relates to concepts like 'plant,' 'flower,' and 'bulb'. There are moments when it will be useful to refer to general principles of learning and growth in the effort to determine priorities. There are other moments when the teacher must focus his attention on the single child, to whom the general principles do not in every respect apply.

Because the teacher must determine priorities in dealing with children only approximately at the same stage of development, because he has to make compromises whenever he deals with a group or a class, he cannot assume that the researcher has solved all his problems. The teacher must look on the available research from his own vantage point; he must look at it critically, always from the perspective of his particular values, his experiences with individual children, his specific aims. A suggestive instance of such a critical view is that of the Cambridge Conference on School Mathematics, a group of teachers assigned to plan curriculum reforms in mathematics for British schools. Reporting on their work, they made the point that they had not taken account of recent research in cognitive psychology when they defined their goals. They wrote:

> It has been argued by Piaget and others that certain ideas and degrees of abstraction cannot be learned until certain ages. We regard this question as open, partly because there are cognitive psychologists on both sides of it, and partly because the investigations of Piaget, taken at face value, do not justify any conclusion relevant to our task. The point is that Piaget is not a teacher but an observer—he has tried to find out what it is that children understand, at a given age, when they have been taught in conventional ways. The essence of our enterprise is to alter the data which have formed, so far, the basis of his research. If teaching furnishes experiences few children now have, then in the future such observers as Piaget may observe quite different things. We therefore believe that no predictions, either positive or negative, are justified, and that the only way to find out when and how various things can be taught is to try various ways of teaching them.[1]

In a narrow frame and a shorter time span, the teacher is entitled to say the same thing. Working with his individual students, he too may "alter the data" which formed the basis of Piaget's research, by rejecting conventional teaching modes. This is not to say that he is justified in rejecting what is demonstrably known about the stages of children's conceptual growth; nor is it to suggest that the work of cognitive psychologists has been invalidated. It is simply to say that the teacher, each time he steps into his classroom, faces what amounts to an open situation. He can consider nothing to be predetermined. Confronting the future, he and his students must consider themselves free to choose.

The problem becomes more difficult, however, when cumulative deficits are discussed. Piaget has argued convincingly that capacities for cognitive mastery will not be present in an individual if he has not moved through the early stages of sensorimotor assimilation, if he has not developed the "structures of ordering and assembling that constitute a substructure for the future operations of thought." Many implications have been drawn from this notion for approaches to the education of underprivileged children, who presumably have not benefited in the early years from the rich assortment of sensory and linguistic stimuli that are foundational to future operations of thought. Deprived of such stimuli, deprived of opportunities for play and conversation, these children are said to suffer deficits that become cumulative. J. McVicker Hunt writes: "With things to play with and with room to play in highly limited, with opportunities to learn standard English—or any other standard language— markedly reduced, the youngster beyond his first year who is in the typical conditions of lower-class life has little opportunity to develop at an optimal rate in the direction demanded for later adaptation in schools and in our highly technological culture."[2]

What is the teacher to do when he is asked to teach poor children who have not been given the remedial assistance offered by Head Start and other programs devised to compensate for early deprivation? If he supposes (on the basis of what he has read about poverty) that a student's environment has been sterile and restrictive, must he conclude that the student is forever fated to a type of retardation? Again, he is confronting the problem of how to cope with the particular case in the light of findings with respect to the many. He is trying to take a stance with respect to a new type of predictive determinism, the weaknesses of which we have already discussed. As a teacher, however, he is committed to open possibilities. No matter how pessimistic the predictions, no matter how appalling the test scores, he must act *as if* his students are free agents, responsible for choosing themselves. Jean-Paul Sartre writes:

> Someone will say, "I did not ask to be born." This is a naive way of throwing greater emphasis on our facticity. I am responsible for everything, in fact, except for my very responsibility. . . . Therefore everything takes place as if I were compelled to be responsible. I am *abandoned* in the world, not in the sense that I might remain abandoned and passive in a hostile universe like a board floating on the water, but rather in the sense that I find myself suddenly alone and without help, engaged in a world for which I bear the whole responsibility without being able, whatever I do, to tear myself away from this responsibility for an instant. For I am responsible for my very desire of fleeing responsibilities. To make myself passive in the world, to refuse to act upon things and upon Others is still to choose myself.[3]

This may sound, on the face of it, as if the student is being blamed for *not* acting in such a way as to learn. This is not the case, however; for to hold an individual responsible is to hold high expectations for him. To suggest that he is not responsible, that he is a mere victim of forces he cannot conceivably control, is to acquiesce in his deprivation and thereby to acknowledge defeat.

Research indicates that self-fulfilling prophecies may be important in a school. Robert Rosenthal and Lenore Jacobson's study called *Pygmalion in the Classroom* is the best known; although it is statistically flawed, it does indicate that a teacher's prophecy of a student's intellectual performance can come to determine that student's performance. In this study, teachers in a California school were told that children were being given a test intended to identify "bloomers." A randomly chosen 20 percent of those who took the test were identified as "spurters," and their names were given to eighteen teachers in the school. A significant gain in IQ scores was reported for those called "spurters," almost all of whom were disadvantaged children; and the gain was attributed to changes in teacher expectations. A self-fulfilling prophecy presumably was at work. The teachers had not changed their methods or attempted any compensatory measures. Only their belief in the children concerned had altered: they *expected* more learning to take place than had been believed possible. How is the teacher to respond to research of this kind? The validity of the testing done has been seriously questioned; no one has been able to replicate the study; and so the reliability of all the results has been challenged.[4] Even so, it is difficult to ignore the fact that instances of expectancy (or trust or regard) have been demonstrated to stimulate learning among those considered to be hopelessly disadvantaged. The aware teacher ought to be sufficiently aroused to note the failures resulting from teacher attitudes rather than from student incapacity. He must be careful not to assume that a child, because he lives in a tenement house or because he has no father living at home, is too deprived to learn. Vast differences exist even among children who live on the same block and have been similarly battered by poverty. They are differences that exist long before the children ever set foot in a school. Robert Coles writes:

> To the teacher, the differences are a beginning, not an end. Six-year-old children are what they are, and they are quickly found out by their teachers and school psychologists and by "objective criteria"—by all those intelligence tests, each with its own twist, its own special, prideful, reasonable (or extravagant) claims. These tests are employed to separate children by "tracks": fast, medium, slow. The theory is valid; the able and gifted ones will not intimidate the fearful and slow ones, nor will the slow ones cost the fast ones their right to learn at a speed they find congenial. Yet those who score well in the tests take an interest in schoolwork and become known as first-rate students; those to whom the teachers and the work they assign are a big bore or a big fright become "the problem child," the slow-witted or stupid one—no matter how bright they may be "underneath."[5]

Teachers are just beginning to be informed of what can happen "underneath." Increasing numbers of novels, journals, and essays written by or dealing with the poor communicate the meaning of survival in American society. They reveal the things deprived children must learn about their homes, streets, welfare centers, and schools to deal with the inequitable world. Such books as *The Autobiography of Malcolm X,* James Baldwin and Margaret Mead's *A Rap on Race,* and William Grier and Price Cobbs's *Black Rage,* in which two psychiatrists present case histories of crisis-ridden black persons, can offer insights into modes of coping no test has ever measured. Robert Coles' three-volume *Children of Crisis,* Oscar Lewis's *Children of Sanchez,* Studs Terkel's *Division Street: America,* and other collections of taped interviews with ordinarily powerless individuals provide much evidence that the coping capacities rewarded in school are not the only ones that exist. Some cognitive skills, in fact, escape recognition because no means exist for testing them.

It does not follow that no incompetent or retarded young people exist. The teacher cannot deny the reality that endowments are unequally distributed. In the unlikely event that absolute equality of opportunity is achieved in this country, there will still be a great range of individual differences and of differences among social classes. Nor can the teacher deny the reality that certain of his students simply lack the capacities American society today selects as valuable. None of this should prevent him, however, from questioning the criteria used for tracking young people in his particular institution or from taking a critical approach to the standards used for determining worth.

The linguist William Labov has challenged the notion of verbal deprivation, which is one version of the theory of cumulative deficits; and, in so doing, he has demanded that attention be paid to what teachers have come to take for granted—*because* of the limited criteria normally used. Reporting on research conducted among black boys in a New York City slum neighborhood, Labov suggests that lower-class children perform poorly because their teachers have never adapted to the language and learning styles of most of those who attend inner-city schools. Nonstandard vernacular speech has been thought of as primitive, without the means for expressing logical relations. Because poor children have not mastered middle-class speech habits, they are considered incapable of thinking logically. They must be taught, it is believed, standard English if they are to develop the capacity for logical analysis, learn to read, and master arithmetic. Labov writes: "The essential fallacy of the verbal-deprivation theory lies in tracing the educational failure of the child to his personal deficiencies." He goes on to point out that nonstandard dialects are not primitive; they are highly structured systems. If these dialects are regarded and understood, the children who speak them will be found to be perfectly logical in their arguments, often succinct, often precise. The reason they are judged to be stupid is that the patterns of their logic are neither recognized nor comprehended. Labov concludes:

> Teachers are now being told to ignore the language of black children as unworthy of attention and useless for learning. They are being taught to hear every natural utterance of the child as evidence of his mental inferiority. As linguists we are unanimous in condemning this view as bad observation, bad theory, and bad practice. That educational psychology should be strongly influenced by a theory so false to the facts of language is unfortunate; but that children should be the victims of this ignorance is intolerable. If linguists can contribute some of their valuable knowledge and energy toward exposing the fallacies of the verbal deprivation theory, we will have done a great deal to justify the support that society has given to basic research in our field.[6]

Once again the teacher is reminded that he cannot seek his directives in theories which have won acceptance at a particular moment of time any more than he can seek them in conventional wisdom. He has to keep asking seriously: What does the known demand of me as a teacher? Each day of his life within the classroom, he has to choose.

Cognitive psychology and the theory of cultural deficit have, of course, led certain educators to effect deliberate reforms in the nursery and the elementary schools. Piagetian research, along with Susan Isaacs' discoveries with respect to children and certain of John Dewey's proposals, fed into the reforms recommended by the Plowden Report published in 1967 by the Central Advisory Council for Education in England. The report sanctioned deliberate encouragement of spontaneity, informality, and individual discovery in the lower schools, where traditional rigidities had been victimizing children, especially the children of the poor. Lillian Weber had been studying informal education in England between 1965 and 1966. She was followed by American journalists and teachers who came to visit the British Infant Schools; and their enthusiastic accounts soon stimulated interest in setting up domestic versions of such informal schools. "Informal," writes Weber, "refers to the setting, the arrangements, the teacher–child and child–child relationships that maintain, restimulate if necessary, and extend what is considered to be the most intense form of learning, the already existing child's way of learning through play and through the experiences he seeks out for himself."[7] This interest might not have developed so rapidly were it not for the widespread acquaintance with Piaget's work, the Head Start innovations, and the disenchantment with overly routinized and organized schools. The proponents of the open classroom, taking seriously what was being said about the stages of concept development, were going to *prevent* the cultural deficits that ensued when children's early opportunities were limited.

There is enough evidence of the preoccupation with timetables, schedules, and lesson plans in the traditional schools. There is accumulating evidence of the increased vitality and child initiative that result when schoolrooms are opened to the corridors or to the world outside. Environments are enriched; teachers are given more aid and support; communication increases; children appear to be more interested in learning. Again, however, the facts of the cases thus far reported do not tell the teacher what he should do moment-by-moment in the new-style classroom. Should he place socialization and involvement first in his priority scale? How might he adjust the need for skill mastery to the concern for permitting each child to follow his interests at his particular rate of speed? Might the teacher assume that once he has provided appropriate experiences, the necessity for learning skills will become clear to the child? What might the teacher do if he wishes to guide a child in an orderly fashion to more and more complex conceptualization in a given field? How is the teacher to know when friendly guidance gives way to imposition?

The teacher is once again charged to think about what he is doing, even in a situation where traditional restrictions are removed. The issue of self-direction and autonomy, for instance, opens questions each teacher needs to clarify. Richard S. Peters, offering a constructive critique of the Plowden Report, has said:

> On the one hand a powerful plea is being made for the value of individual autonomy, for the importance attached in a democratic society to individual choice, independence of mind, and to more recondite virtues such as creativeness and originality. . . . But three types of comment are in place. Firstly this, like any other value, must surely be asserted not absolutely but with an "other things being equal" clause. How far are we going to press the value of self-chosen activities if young people overwhelmingly reject scientific subjects in a highly industrialized society which needs increasingly a vast array of technicians and technologists? We may be moving towards such a situation—and it is no good comforting ourselves on the number of young people who seem to be "choosing" sociology in higher and further education. For we may soon be turning out too many people who can talk knowledgeably in a reformist

way about society but too few who can contribute decisively to
its economic base. If we think, too, that education is
incompatible with narrow specialization how far are we justified
in pushing young people into a variety of subjects and activities
if they would rather specialize?[8]

We know too little about how autonomy is developed, he went on; and
children have to be deliberately equipped to make effective and informed
choices. Moreover, much thinking has to be done respecting the role of the
teacher, who still has to "stand between the generations and to initiate
others into the various aspects of a culture within which the individual has
eventually to determine where he stands."

Somewhat the same problems were posed in the 1960s, during the
curriculum reform movement. Before that time, curriculum controversies
generally had to do with whether curriculum should be child-centered,
subject-centered, or geared to societal needs. Then there was a resurgence
of interest in the relationship between the logical structures of the
academic disciplines and the developing structures Piaget associated with
cognitive growth. Although most attention was paid to mathematics and
the sciences, studies were undertaken into the inherent logic of geography,
history, and other subjects as well. Materials were prepared; institutes were
organized to acquaint teachers with modes of enabling students to discover
for themselves the fundamental principles of each discipline. With the
exception of mathematics, few far-reaching changes were brought about.
The schedules, the atmospheres, the supervisory systems in the schools
remained largely as they had been before the initiation of the reforms. Few
questions were posed with respect to the relevance of particular subject
matters for different students; even fewer, with respect to the connection
between the disciplines and the purposes of American schools.

The importance of a cognitive emphasis was widely acknowledged; yet
today the teacher faces unresolved questions on how that emphasis can be
integrated with a concern for independence and creativity. Certain notions
remain influential, especially those in Jerome S. Bruner's report of the
1959 Woods Hole Conference entitled *The Process of Education.* Such
concepts as discovery, generative learning, intuition, and structure have
become familiar to almost every teacher and teacher-to-be. Since the report
leaned heavily on Piaget's studies of the stages of growth, many teachers
now interested in reforming early childhood education are attracted by
Bruner's views of curriculum. He speaks eloquently of helping children
"pass progressively from concrete thinking to the utilization of more
conceptually adequate modes of thought." He says:

> Intellectual activity is anywhere the same, whether at the
> frontier of knowledge or in a third grade classroom. . . . The
> schoolboy learning physics is a physicist, and it is easier for him
> to learn physics behaving like a physicist than doing something
> else . . . the curriculum of a subject should be determined by the
> most fundamental understanding that can be achieved of the
> underlying principles that give structure to that subject.[9]

Such talk had and still has a tonic quality; but a variety of questions
remain. Just as questions have been raised with regard to general laws of
child development, so they have been raised with regard to a general
theory of instruction.

Raising questions about the preoccupation with structure, broad
principles, and the search for theories that concern *all* subject matters,
Joseph Schwab demands a return to the practical. He asks for renewed
attention to deliberation, which "requires consideration of the widest
possible variety of alternatives if it is to be most effective." For the
teacher, consideration of alternative modes of teaching a subject requires
increasing sensitivity to the demands of the deliberative process and
increasing attention to particular students and their needs. Training for
such competence "will not only bring immediate experience of the
classroom effectively to bear on problems of curriculum but enhance the
quality of that experience, for almost every classroom episode is a stream
of situations requiring discrimination of deliberative problems and decision
thereon."[10] The question of the teacher's commitment again becomes focal,
as does his ability to experiment consciously in a real situation, to make
discriminations, and to choose.

Perceptions of individual autonomy and open situations are reinforced
by the work being done on the phenomenon of language today. Chomsky
began by taking issue with Skinner's view that language is nothing more
than a type of behavior learned by means of responses to controlled
stimuli. Chomsky maintains that such mechanistic explanations cannot
account for the creative uses of language or for the distinctively human
ability to use combinations of words and to recognize sentences never
heard before and never intentionally taught. He also points out that,
although young children can quickly go beyond what they have been
taught to say, a theory of conditioned responses does not account for this
fact. Fundamental processes, quite independent of environmental feedback,
are at work. Chomsky ascribes these processes to the existence of deep
structures or schematisms within the mind; and he conceives these to be
fundamental to all human languages. In other words, certain general

features of grammatical structures are universal, although Chomsky admits that this explanation is formal rather than empirical. However, precisely because the explanation *is* formal, the principles he defines "provide a revealing mirror of mind (if correct)."

Chomsky admits that he has returned to the Cartesian notion of innate ideas, presumably invalidated long ago. He does not believe that knowledge of language can be acquired through step-by-step inductive operations. Although agreeing that some innate equipment (such as memory span and memory capacity) is relevant to language learning, various scholars have challenged Chomsky's claim that the mind is programmed at birth to learn natural language. Charles Hockett, a well-known linguist, typically objects to the idea of working from underlying forms to spoken forms. He says that independently existing underlying forms are only convenient tools. The controversies are likely to remain unresolved; but, once again, the teacher must take a stand somewhere. He surely can take seriously Chomsky's claim that he is advancing the humanistic approach Bertrand Russell had in mind when he said that "the humanistic conception regards a child as a gardener regards a young tree, i.e., as something with a certain intrinsic nature, which will develop into an admirable form, given proper soil and air and light." We have noted some of the difficulties involved in identifying the "intrinsic nature" of man; but attention must nonetheless be paid when Chomsky quotes Russell and then goes on to say that Russell's conception is "given substance as we discover the rich systems of invariant structures and principles that underlie the most ordinary and humblest of human accomplishments." And indeed Chomsky seems to have reinforced conceptions of human autonomy and competence with his suggestions that a hidden landscape marked by structures that generate surface structures of a different kind may exist. Not surprisingly (having begun with a challenge to Skinner), Chomsky has been among those taking strong issue with Skinner's attacks on freedom and dignity. Writing that Skinner's book *Beyond Freedom and Dignity* contains no clearly formulated proposals for an effective behavioral technology, Chomsky continues:

> We can at least begin to speculate coherently about the acquisition of certain systems of knowledge and belief on the basis of experience and genetic endowment, and can outline the general nature of some device that might duplicate aspects of this achievement. But how does a person who has acquired systems of knowledge and belief then proceed to use them in his daily life? About this we are entirely in the dark, at the level of scientific inquiry. If there were some science capable of treating such matters it might well be concerned precisely with freedom

and dignity and might suggest possibilities for enhancing them.
Perhaps, as the classical literature of freedom and dignity
sometimes suggests, there is an intrinsic human inclination
toward free creative inquiry and productive work, and humans
are not merely dull mechanisms formed by a history of
reinforcement and behaving predictably with no intrinsic needs
apart from the need for physiological satiation. Then human
beings are not fit subjects for manipulation, and we will seek to
design a social order accordingly. But we cannot, at present,
turn to science for insight into these matters.[11]

Chomsky is here talking about what most directly concerns the teacher.
Knowing that science will not provide the answers *or* tell him what he
should do, and having taken the "known" gravely into account, the
teacher can only go on to do philosophy.

In the previous chapter, we talked of various ways of doing
philosophy with respect to the acquisition of certain systems of knowledge
and beliefs. These systems were developed in the contexts of differing
world views, each one a response to "queer" questions raised at a specific
moment of cultural history. We have seen that certain approaches have
had to be revised because of later empirical studies. We have also seen that
some questions (Plato's and Locke's, for instance) remain unanswerable
from an empirical point of view. The matter of preexistent forms is to
some extent unsettled; the matter of innate ideas has again been vigorously
raised. The search for meanings and the troubling issue of meaningfulness
are still in many ways unclear. In what sense, after all, is the
self-conscious use of logic and reasoning, or one of the thought structures
Piaget identifies more desirable than, say, an uninhibited engagement with
the concreteness of the world? Michael Novak writes:

For the former generation, the word "reasonable" meant that
a man was objective, calm, cognizant of the consequences of his
actions, intent on being effective rather than on "merely"
expressing his feelings. For the present generation, "reasonable"
is not entirely a coveted description of oneself. The young do
wish to be thought irrational or unreasonable, but they think it
reasonable to give priority to feelings, experiences, spontaneities,
inner connectedness, and the expression in action of inmost
convictions.[12]

Whether this is universally true is unimportant. What is important is a
recognition (increasing since the beginnings of industrial capitalism) that

pragmatic rationality and cultivation of objectivity too often have led to depersonalization. They have permitted people to quantify, to separate ends from means, to put aside their moral concerns when developing "game plans," to treat themselves mainly as managers alienated from the human world. The teacher who has these notions in mind must at least look at the preconceptions underlying proposals that make cognitive development central to education, often to the exclusion of feelings, experiences, spontaneities. He must look at the preconceptions underlying proposals that make affective learning central to education, often to the exclusion of rationality. He must look partly in the interests of his authenticity, partly for practical reasons having to do with the difficulty of helping young people to learn.

Education, according to Dewey, is fundamentally concerned with assisting the human being to adjust to his environment and to reshape it as he lives. Like Chomsky, Dewey wanted to know how the person who acquires knowledge and beliefs proceeds to use them in his daily life. Since all genuine education comes through experience, the teacher's obligation is to arrange for the kinds of experience that exact and promote thinking. More is involved than asking leading questions. More, certainly, is involved than confronting textbook materials. According to Dewey, learning takes place when students are given something to *do* rather than something to learn. What they do should be significant and worthwhile; it should relate to real life undertakings. Thus, the teacher needs to develop procedures to ensure that "the doing is of such a nature as to demand thinking, or the intentional noting of connections. . . ." Obviously, he must create conditions "which will interact with the existing capacities and needs of those taught . . ."; and he must work to help his students acquire habits and dispositions that will permit them to increase their control of the means for achieving their ends. They need guidance that will help them develop the power to transform their environments. They need to be enabled—through habituation and stimulation—to initiate inquiries. To be equipped for inquiry is to be equipped to engage in a process through which objects and events can be seen in connection with other objects and events in the experienced world.

Just as a student's classroom experience is continuous with his experience outside school, in the past and in the future, so is the process of inquiry continuous with the vague, sometimes confusing sense of being caught up in transactions with the environment. As we have seen, the individual exists *within* a continuum of experience: what he observes cannot be divorced from his observing; what he knows cannot be divorced from his knowing. Therefore, instead of talking about an individual coming face-to-face with an independent world of brute fact, Dewey stressed the situation, where individual and environment are involved in interactions.

At this point inquiry begins. First, the individual feels that he is in a situation that is either indeterminate or confused. Let us say the situation is a meeting in the school assembly hall. It is recognizable, set off from the experiential flux. Its parts—the rows of chairs, the platform, the students sitting and standing, the teachers' silhouettes, the subdued roar—are articulated sufficiently to form a context; but something may be wrong because the context is not quite the familiar one. Policemen are at the doors and in the front of the hall. The students' initial response may be uneasiness or perplexity; they may gape at one another and squirm. Then someone poses a question about the reason for the presence of the police. For those who heed, the situation becomes problematic. They begin to put their minds to work, to think about what is happening. For Dewey, the mind is "a course of action intelligently directed," and thinking is the process by which the action is carried out.

Certain students may recall—and say they recall—seeing strange adults on occasion in the halls. Someone may mention seeing a boy dozing in a corner; someone else may have seen a plasticine bag. Serious inquiry begins when the students see connections within their experiences and identify, on that basis, the facts of the case. They may develop a hypothesis: the police are here to find out who is selling drugs or who is presently taking drugs or who is carrying a plasticine bag. Vague uneasiness has given way, at least for some, to cognition. They have resolved their perplexity; they wait to see if they are right. If they are correct, if the police do indeed single out the heroin users, then these students have learned something as a result of their questioning.

If their experience is really to be fruitful, however, the teacher must try to make it feed into future experiences. Having restored balance to the disturbed situation, the students may well be in a position to refocus their attention and to pose questions relevant to a wider context. Why do some young people and not others become addicted to heroin? What is the relation between poverty and drug addiction? What accounts for the traffic in drugs? What has been done to deal with the problem of addiction? What can be done? Solving the original, more or less practical problem, the students are different from the way they were when they first noticed the policemen. A bit more self-assured, a bit more confident, they are ready to ask larger questions, larger with respect to both means and ends. They are ready to exert themselves somewhat more in seeking out answers. If the teacher arranges for experiences that pose problems different in content and quality from those posed in the past, the students (as long as they have developed the necessary powers and see the significance of the new problems) will find that they perceive more and more alternative solutions; they will deliberate more creatively and effectively; they will grow. Yet "the pursuit of knowledge must race ahead of practical problems posed and do without their aid. It must be unchained from past experience, even from the present. It must go on 'for its own sake,' for the future." However, the origin of pursuit must be found in each student's actual experience as that experience is gradually intellectualized and understood. Each person lives—and continues to live—in a series of situations, always in transaction with things and other human beings. If he is capable of growth, he uses the knowledge he has gained through the transformation of each situation as a means of coping with the exigencies of the next. In this way, even as he pursues knowledge, he begins to achieve an orderly world in which to live, a world in which parts hang together in mutual adjustment with a quality of harmonic wholeness. Having reached that point, he may become capable of more and more consummations and fulfillments. But the pursuit can never cease. "Since in reality," Dewey wrote, "there is nothing to which growth is relative save more growth, there is nothing to which education is subordinate save more education. It is a commonplace to say that education should not cease when one leaves school. The point of this commonplace is that the purpose of school education is to insure the continuance of education by organizing the powers that insure growth. The inclination to learn from life itself and to make the conditions of life such that all will learn in the process of living is the finest product of schooling."[13]

Dewey's concern for the individual is central to his thinking: the individual finds his satisfactions as he relates productively to others and responds to situations by doing what each one calls for, with learning as the result. The method of responding is always individual; the end in view (attained through continuing reconstructions of experience) is to socialize, to enlarge, to initiate the person into the larger world—into wider and more encompassing meanings, always subject to change. Innerness? Existentiality? Alienation? These were not the primary concerns of Dewey and the Progressives who followed him. Nor was consciousness in the sense in which we have been using the term.

Maurice Merleau-Ponty, equally concerned for the pursuit of meanings, talks of a primary reality, which we must take into account if we are to understand the growth of intellectual consciousness. This primary reality is a perceived life-world; and the structures of the perceptual consciousness through which a child first comes in contact with his environment underlie all the higher level structures that develop later in his life. Dewey emphasizes the power of immaturity and of plasticity, which "is the capacity to retain and carry over from prior experience factors which modify subsequent actions." However, he does not stress the persistence of any *original* world in the background of consciousness. For Merleau-Ponty, this original world is the natural and social domain in which the individual as a child was first involved corporeally and affectively. Touching, smelling, listening, crawling about his physical environment, the child became aware of his surroundings before he was capable of logical and predicative thought. He perceived what lay around him; and perceiving, he organized his world around his body, around himself.

Merleau-Ponty accepts the idea that cognitive ability develops by stages; but he differs with Piaget in important respects. Most particularly, he insists—as Piaget never would—that each person has within him an "interior silence," a primordial reality of consciousness, which is the ground of all knowledge and rationality. Piaget talks of the need for a continual decentering of the subject. He means a gradual separation of the "epistemic subject, that cognitive nucleus which is common to all subjects at the same level" from the individual subject and his lived experience. Without such decentering, the individual will not learn to generate cognitive structures that exist apart from him. Piaget is referring to the various disciplines or subject matters, each of which must be generated by means of cognitive action on the part of a learner. According to this view, cognitive structures belong to the learner's operational behavior, which must proceed apart from the "fragmentary and frequently distorting grasp of consciousness."

Merleau-Ponty asserts that no learning can be purely cognitive and speaks of a "lived decentering." For example, a child learns "to relativize the notions of the youngest and eldest." He learns to *become* the eldest in relation to a newborn child; he learns to take differing perspectives on his place in the family and to bring those perspectives into reciprocity. This learning occurs through actions undertaken within the vital order, not merely through intellectual categorization; and that order becomes part of a child's biography, his history, just as do the meanings he achieves as he grows.

As he develops, the child assimilates a language system and becomes habituated to using language as "an open system of expression" capable of expressing "an indeterminate number of cognitions or ideas to come." Multiple acts of naming and expression take place around the core of primary meaning found in "the silence of primary consciousness," the fundamental awareness of being present in the world. The point is that the world is constituted perceptually *before* the construction of cognitive structures. The child moves continually outward, into more and more diverse realms of experience in his search for meaning. When he engages with the presumably independent structures of knowledge associated with rationality, he may bracket out or exclude certain subjective awareness. But the essential awareness remains in the background; the original perceptual reality continues as the ground of rationality, the base from which he leaps to the theoretical.

Central to this idea is a conception of consciousness. Behavioral scientists tend to treat consciousness as an object to be studied or observed; or they are likely to think of it as Dewey does: a state of awareness of meanings, a "perception of actual events, whether past, contemporary or future, *in* their meanings, the having of actual ideas." Like Dewey, too, they tend to think that consciousness can be *had* but not communicated, that whatever significance it might possess is due to the system of meanings in which it occurs. Merleau-Ponty says that a scientist wishing to study consciousness inductively cannot arrive at a conception of it. Induction must be combined "with the reflective knowledge that we can obtain from ourselves as conscious objects." We can understand consciousness only "from the inside of consciousness itself."

Yet we need not resort to introspection or withdrawal from the world. Consciousness throws itself outward, *toward* the world. It is intentional; it is always *of* something: a phenomenon, another person, an object or event in the world.

> Through an act of consciousness, some "object" is presented to the experiencing subject and stands before his mind. Of that object the experiencing subject is conscious through the act. . . . Object, here meant in an all-inclusive sense, comprises not only material things perceived, as well as remembered or imagined, but also mathematical relations, musical compositions, and theoretical implications.[14]

To be aware of this idea and of the multiple perceptions required to gain a sense of the world's "reality" is to awaken to the reflective life of consciousness. Reflecting on himself as a conscious object, the individual is, therefore, confronting his relation to his surroundings, his manner of conducting himself with respect to things and other human beings, the changing perspectives through which the world presents itself to him. Merleau-Ponty talks about the need to rediscover continually "my actual presence to myself, the fact of my consciousness which is in the last resort what the word and the concept of consciousness mean." Whether teacher or student, then, the individual is asked to remain in contact with his perceptions, his history. He is asked deliberately to strive to constitute their meanings as he carries out his cognitive projects, as he makes his effort to know. To accomplish this end, he must achieve a state of "wide-awakeness . . . a plane of consciousness of highest tension originating in an attitude of full attention to life and its requirements." Writing more than a century ago, Henry David Thoreau had a similar idea:

> Why is it that men give so poor an account of their day if
> they have not been slumbering? They are not such poor
> calculators. If they had not been overcome with drowziness they
> would have performed something. The millions are awake
> enough for physical labor; but only one in a million is awake
> enough for effective intellectual exertion, only one in a hundred
> millions to a poetic or divine life. To be awake is to be alive. I
> have never yet met a man who was quite awake. How could I
> have looked him in the face?[15]

And Thoreau goes on to talk about man's ability to elevate his life by a
conscious endeavor. Like Merleau-Ponty and Alfred Schutz today, he was
identifying possibilities that may be highly suggestive for a conception of a
learner open to the world, eager—indeed *condemned*—to give meaning to
it. Whoever he is—poor child, blue-collar worker's son, suburbanite, urban
activist—the learner is impelled to make some sense of things as they
present themselves *to him*. To make sense is to liberate himself; and,
according to Paulo Freire, liberating education "consists in acts of
cognition." Given the kind of teaching intended to enable self-aware
persons to reach out for meanings in response to their crucial questions,
we assume that *every* person can be moved to cognitive action. Everyone,
no matter who he is, can learn to learn.

Is this a romantic vision? Is it excluded by what the psychologists say
about maturation and deprivation? The phenomenologist would say that
the self-aware teacher, functioning in situations known to be
dehumanizing, can give his students a sense of their possibilities as existing
persons present to themselves. If he is to motivate them, however, and free
them to learn, he must make sure that the learning they undertake is
conducted within the vital order built up by their own perceiving and
conceiving over time. The knowing in which they engage must be, as
Jean-Paul Sartre says, "a moment of praxis" opening into "what has not
yet been."[16] Praxis is a particular type of cognitive action which crucially
involves the transcending or surpassing of what is. Those who treat
knowing in this fashion refuse to take the social cultural matrix for
granted as a given. For instance, according to Freire, men engage in praxis
when their action "encompasses a critical reflection which increasingly
organizes their thinking and thus leads them to move from a purely naive
knowledge of reality to a higher level, one which enables them to perceive
the *causes* of reality." This means that they pose their relevant questions
and pursue answers with a sense of a *reality to be produced* and with the
intention to bring about the projected state of affairs.

Students are unlikely to pose questions about their social reality if they
are not enabled to reflect on their consciousness, on the world as it

presents itself to them as individuals, each with his or her own life-world. The teacher will be unable to arouse them to pursue meanings in response to their questions if he treats them as cases and studies them across a distance. He will be unable to arouse them to cognitive action if he is preoccupied with measuring their performances day by day. Considering the teaching situation from inside his consciousness, he may be caught up in praxis—thinking, as he wills his students' freedom, of what ought to be.

At best, however, the teacher will face many options; and he can never be sure. He may be so distressed by the inroads of the system, by "product-orientation" and the rest, that he may opt for a concentration on spontaneity and free-form discoveries. He may feel that the most effective way to avoid the pressures of channeling and social control is to concentrate on the cultivation of personal sensitivity, the nurture of trust, the expression of feeling—even of "ecstasy." He may be convinced that emphasis on the experiential continuum Dewey describes and on the dispositions needed for reflective thinking or for inquiry is now required if inhumane systems are to be overhauled and the environment remade. He may believe depersonalization can be overcome if emphasis is placed on perceptual awareness and being present to the self. Only then, he may conclude, will the individual commit himself fully—and on his own initiative—to cognitive learning, for the sake of ordering the stuff of his life-world and creating a new reality.

If he does choose himself as a teacher more concerned with combatting meaninglessness than enhancing sensibility or encouraging expressions of "real feeling," he is likely to find suggestive ideas in both Deweyan thought and phenomenological perspectives. He will certainly see the importance of engaging students—whether in dialogue or discussion—in posing or defining problems significant at a given moment. We have seen how the Deweyan individual thinks about the transformation of indeterminate situations into problematic ones. We have seen how certain constituent parts of a given situation become relevant as they contribute to the course of inquiry and the relation of means to ends. The relevance of thought in such a context is directly linked to the need to resolve doubts, to reorder habits and beliefs shaken by perplexity. If it were not linked to his fundamental uncertainties (or to social issues that engage him), the problem confronting the individual would not be a *live* one; and inquiry would not seem relevant. Those more interested in consciousness and the "sedimentation" of meanings over time would place more stress on what the student can be brought to perceive as thematically relevant within his experienced context, what is worth questioning from his biographical standpoint.

Let us say a student is just beginning to study nineteenth century American history. He comes upon a question having to do with the origins of the Civil War, a matter which has never particularly interested or perplexed him before. The progressive teacher, seeing situations in the present as continuous with those in the past, may well attempt to arrange conditions in the classroom so that his students will ferret out some of the current differences between North and South. He may initiate activities that dramatize such issues as segregation, school busing, migration from rural areas in the South. According to Dewey, "the function of historical subject matter, is to enrich and liberate the more direct and personal contacts of life by furnishing their context, their background and outlook."[17] Treating contemporary difficulties as consequences, in a sense, of past events, the students will be encouraged to frame questions that will indeed furnish context and background, that will require them to "do" history.

The phenomenologist, equally interested in arousing his students to generate the structures of the discipline, will try at the start to elicit expressions of what seems most relevant to particular persons on the general question of North–South relations. A student may, for example, have been involved in some civil rights actions at one time; he may have a special, nagging interest in the plight of blacks as well as in the anomalies of the struggle for equality. He may know something about (and be perplexed by) the ambivalence of nineteenth century Northerners on the slavery question, the dilemma of purportedly righteous people (his parents, perhaps) in the North as well as the South. A black student from a Mississippi town may be uncertain about his heritage. Another student may still accept the myth of "white supremacy" and feel only perplexity in the face of reform efforts. Each person, in other words, is potentially responsive to a particular theme. "What makes the theme to be a theme," writes Schutz, "is determined by motivationally relevant interest-situations and spheres of problems. The theme which thus has become relevant has now, however, become a problem to which a solution, practical, theoretical, or emotional, must be given."[18] The teacher can help each student detach from the total context under consideration the theme most clearly relevant to him: white ambivalence; the impact of the slave past on identity; the anxieties giving rise to racism. A network of related issues remains, of course, but (in each case) as an outer horizon, waiting to be explored when necessary. For the moment the thematically relevant elements are the ones students find (and have found) worth questioning; and these issues will be the focus of their attention for a while. Then, gradually, with the teacher's help, these themes will appear in the foreground, set off from the larger problem (the origins of the Civil War). Multiple strands of inquiry are there to be pursued when the time comes; such matters as the cotton trade, investments in Southern undertakings, discrepancies in economic development, slave revolts, the class system,

British cotton mills, *Uncle Tom's Cabin,* political representation, educational discrimination await investigation. But these matters now exist at the fringe of the students' attention as they begin working on what for them are the focal problems. They have, as it were, bracketed out the other issues to pay active, concentrated attention to what is thematically relevant for them.

The action each student undertakes in paying attention demands far more than library research, more than the invention and testing of hypotheses. He must tap a "background awareness," an accumulation of knowledge conditioned by certain typifications effected early in his life. When he was young, he could not articulate his experiences in terms of individual figures standing out against a background. Rather, he perceived certain typical structures in accord with the zones of relevancy existing in his consciousness. Perhaps he saw a black person or a laborer doing an especially menial job of work. He would not have perceived this person as someone he *recognized* as black or Negro or exploited or lower class. He might have been sharply aware of a weary gesture, a stooped back, shouted commands, a flashing and defiant smile; all would depend on his particular existential situation at the time. Typification would probably have taken place: he might have perceived a *type* rather than a unique individual, in this case a typical victim, slave, menial laborer, or rebellious servant. When, years later, something connected with the oppression of black people arises, and he confronts some aspect of that oppression as a thematically relevant element in a problematic situation, the teacher may elicit from the student a "recognition" of what he has come to know over the years. He may now see the situation as the sediment of previous mental processes. His reaction to the question of civil rights (or black identity or racism) and his perplexities may be traced back to primordial, prepredicative perceptions. He has then been helped to move back from what is seemingly "given" in the present, through the diverse mental and perceptual processes that constituted (for him) black people's predicaments over time. In this way, he can explore both the inner and the outer horizons of the problem, making connections within the field of his consciousness, interpreting his past as it bears on the present and on the "world" he has constituted during his life.

But he has not only been freed to reflect on his knowing. Having made connections between the element discovered to be thematically relevant and other dimensions of his experience, the student may feel ready to deal with the origins of the Civil War, a problem in the outside world. He is now in a position to move out of his inner time (in which all acts are somehow continuous and bound together) into the intersubjective world where he is expected to function as an epistemic subject. Bracketing out the subjectivity he has reflexively been considering with his teacher's help, he can engage as a theoretical inquirer into historical materials. Moving out to generate the structure of American history (to master its fundamental principles, to understand its logic), he may voluntarily become a partial self, an inquirer now, deliberately acting a scholarly role in a community of scholarly inquirers. He could not have done so with much authenticity and effectuality if he had not first synthesized the materials within his innerness and come to see how he had, up to that moment, built up a meaningful world.

This approach does break with Piaget's insistence on separating the "lived" from the generation of cognitive structures; although, as we have seen, the student *can* perform like a historian once he chooses to play that role. Most people would agree that the student must first have reached the conceptual level necessary, since no concentration on the centrality of consciousness diminishes the importance of conceptual readiness. However, the reasons for his attempt to achieve mastery are distinctive for the phenomenologist, who assumes that the individual is moved to constitute his world as meaningful within the stream of his consciousness. Lacks and gaps constantly appear in what presents itself to him; there are always boundaries, obscure horizons. Wanting to *be* someone, he continually moves outward, seeking to transcend, to break through to a new future. He makes this break best of all in the context of his life history, perceiving from his vantage point and *then* from a multiplicity of other vantage points, each with protocols, self-consistency, norms and rules.

How can the underprivileged or deprived be expected to engage with cognitive structures in such a sophisticated way? The phenomenologist, more than most other philosophers, may have an answer when he affirms that every human being has the capacity to look critically at his world if he is freed to do so through dialogue. Equipped with the necessary skills, he can deal critically with his reality, once he has become conscious of how he perceives it. Relevant to this is British sociologist Basil Bernstein's comment on how the civil rights movement in the United States brought about changes in linguistic codes:

> This movement and its various organizations is bringing about a change in the Negro's view of both his own sub-culture, his relation to the white culture and his attitude towards education. This movement has produced powerful charismatic leaders at both national and local levels, who are forcing Negroes to reassess, re-examine their structural relationship to the society. This confrontation (despite the violence) is likely to make new demands upon linguistic resources and to challenge the passivity of the old sub-culture and its system of social relationships. The language of social protest, with its challenging of assumptions,

its grasping towards new cultural forms, may play an important
role in breaking down the limitations of sub-culturally bound
restricted codes.[19]

Bernstein is describing something that resembles what Freire describes as
"conscientization," a process that does not stop "at the level of mere
subjective perception of a situation, but through action prepares men for
the struggle against the obstacles to their humanization." Humanization
signifies the attainment of wholeness, of completion. It is affirmed, says
Freire, "by the yearning of the oppressed for freedom and justice, and by
their struggle to recover their lost humanity."[20] It may indeed be possible
that the process of conscientization, making as it does "new demands upon
linguistic resources," can open the way to conceptual growth.

Again, the crucial concern is for self-awareness and critical cognitive
action for the sake of gaining perspective on personal life and remaking
the social domain. How should the teacher determine whether this should
be his focal concern? How might the differences among the philosophical
points of view affect his practical judgments? Can he not function on some
occasions as a latter-day rationalist and, on other occasions, as an
empiricist? Can he not, while functioning as a pragmatist, pay sufficient
heed to the truth of a student's being to integrate a notion of liberation
with the Deweyan conception of what is most worthwhile?

As we have seen, such questions remain unanswered; and the dilemma
will not be solved by the various inquirers into human development and
the structure of the disciplines. Yet these questions must be taken into
account along with those that are empirically answerable, especially when
the teacher is at the point of making choices. It should be clear by now
that he cannot simply draw implications for practice from statements
about epistemology or from particular philosophic responses having to do
with knowing, truth, consciousness, or meaningfulness. There are, however,
clues to be discovered as to how to carry on the difficult work of
clarification. Disquietude can be discovered by those wary of complacency,
convinced of the productiveness of certain kinds of unease.

It may be useful to think about a network of understanding, believing,
pondering, and commitment in which judgments about one's teaching are
made by an individual who may or may not be called on to give reasons
or explain what has fed into his decision. The process ordinarily begins
with a specific issue: how to make something clear to a heterogeneous or
uninterested class; how to move students to fill in gaps in their knowledge
of a subject; how to motivate a student to find a problem demanding
reflective inquiry; how to justify enlarging the place of a specific discipline
in a curriculum; how to make students care about evidence and elegance

and clarity. In none of these cases can the teacher consult a rule book. He cannot find the answers he needs by referring back to a methods class or a listing of protocols. A reading of a Piaget essay will not solve the specific problem; nor will a review of Bruner's work. A rereading of *Democracy and Education* will not provide the answers anymore than would a rereading of Locke, Kierkegaard, or William James.

Clearly, no matter what his chosen orientation, the teacher must know the subject matter he is teaching. He need not have mastered it as a specialized scholar; but he must understand the fundamental concepts involved, their organization, and the methods used to validate them. If the subject matter is history, for example, he must be familiar with the distinctive features of historical explanation, the use of evidence, and the framing of generalizations. Choosing to be more than a technician, not only must he be committed to an ideal of truth, he must be concerned about his students' taking truth as seriously as they search for being. And he must act on this concern without enforcing a particular kind of reality. He must know somehow that, too frequently, the norms of his society (or even of his academic domain) determine what is real for its members. If he does not permit his students to pose problems and constitute meanings, he is bound to run the risk of alienating them. They will feel submerged, as Freire puts it, in a "dense, enveloping reality or a tormenting blind alley" unless they are enabled to perceive it as an "objective-problematic situation"; in other words, unless they are free to intervene in their own reality.

Philip Phenix, among others, has said that education should be understood as "a guided recapitulation of the processes of inquiry which gave rise to the fruitful bodies of organized knowledge comprising the disciplines."[21] Hence, to master history, for example, the student would have to be helped to learn the procedures the historian used in coming to his conclusions on, say, the origins of the Civil War. At what point and why should the student make this effort? The phenomenologist would say that the student might be expected to try when it is important for him to break through a particular boundary in the effort to produce a more humane and a more coherent reality. The phenomenologist would agree that doing history should be self-conscious, that structures should be generated according to rules. But he would add that arbitrary categories are not sufficient fully to disclose historical understanding. Rules would have to be observed; the student would have to be given opportunities to think as a historian thinks; but motivation for such thinking would be sought in problematic situations or in the deeply relevant themes disclosed in the individual's search for himself.

Other theorists would be more likely to talk of the need to initiate young people into knowledge of prevailing public traditions or of the natural order of things. Whatever the justifications for teaching history, however (and there are many), most theorists agree that the teacher cannot communicate what historical method means if he cannot communicate what constitutes good reasons for coming to conclusions concerning the historical record. His consideration of such matters is bound to involve him in diverse types of critical and analytic thinking, even as it is bound to make him consult some of his value commitments, his views on neutrality and objectivity, his beliefs respecting the meaning of past events in the present. All these, along with his selections from the fund of historical knowledge, become part of a cognitive matrix in which his choices are eventually made. His considerations become part of the background against which he teaches; and, as he moves to promote inquiry in his classroom, some of his commitments become part of the foreground —the content that is his core concern.

Expressing this idea in somewhat different terms, we might say that the teacher presents himself to his students as someone who has chosen himself—*is* choosing himself—as a critical thinker with regard for principle, good reasons, and what he conceives to be evidence. If he believes that the world as it presents itself to him—the cultural and human world of which he is conscious—is "the sedimentation of all man's previous experiences," he may be able to communicate the personal relevance of historical sense-making. Confronting the problem of the past from his particular biographical vantage point (in many ways determined by that past), relating what he discovers to human choices and human actions, the teacher still remains free to appropriate the protocols developed in the history of history.

To generate—or to come to know—such a discipline is to order disparate materials conceptually and to do so in some sequential pattern, moving from the concrete, specific event to general tendencies, to laws. It is to categorize the particular events under rubrics derived from the subject's conceived structure. The teacher can engage students in a generation of that structure even as he stresses personal standpoint and the need to constitute a meaningful world, even as he attempts to clarify the choices of persons who lived in the past "through our own and ours through theirs," even as he works for the transformation of reality or the control of social change. These things, too, can become component parts of his "content"; these factors, too, can be taken into account as he acts to move his students to choose—on their own initiative—to learn.

Explaining, attempting to help students form belief systems, teaching them how to determine true beliefs, enabling them to *come* to know: all these are phases of the teaching activity for any subject matter. As we have seen, the teacher's project is quite different from that of the mathematician or historian or empirical scientist. Each time he attempts an explanation or constructs an educative situation, the teacher must keep in mind what he knows about the students he is trying to teach. At any given moment of his teaching day, he aims to enable them to learn to accomplish specific tasks, to perform in particular ways. It may be that what he undertakes to do on each occasion should not be called teaching at all if none of his students learns. Not only must he be aware of the conceptual capacities of individuals within his class, he must always recognize that learning is a mode of individual cognitive action. On a fundamental level, learning is self-directed, whether it culminates in mastery of a principle, reconstruction of some experience, or disclosure of an aspect of the world. It must result in some transformation of outlook, some clearing up of a clouded horizon, some effecting of relationships. It must be evidenced in the way a student deals with a complexity, an obstacle; in the way he speaks about what he has been considering; in the way he tackles successive tasks; in the way he *is.*

Having learned from Piaget and others how experience becomes intellectualized, the teacher should be able to distinguish teaching from mere training or conditioning. Conditioning presumes a malleable or reactive creature who responds predictably to external stimuli, to reinforcement, whether or not the reactor believes his response to be desirable or liberating. No intelligent choosing on the individual's part is expected; no initiative, no appraisal. The process of conditioning does little, if anything, to help an individual realize the possibilities we now know are opened up at each stage of development. And yet, if we are to believe such men as Jacques Ellul and Herbert Marcuse, our democratic society is permeated by manipulation and conditioning. The mass media alone create what Marcuse calls "false consciousness," which makes people *think* they require styles of life, consumer goods, or political candidates they are actually conditioned to accept. Marcuse also speaks of "enforced tolerance . . . enforced not by any terroristic agency but by the overwhelming, anonymous power and efficiency of the technological society. As such it permeates the general consciousness—and the consciousness of the critic." And, he would add, the consciousness of the teacher and the student. It is impossible to prove empirically that "technique" has the effects Ellul describes *or* that the media condition to the degree Marcuse claims *or* that the schools "process" in the manner romantic critics decry. It is equally impossible to demonstrate the consequences of corporate controls for thinking and for consciousness. Even so, the person who chooses himself authentically as a teacher is, in a sense, choosing himself as a rebel against attempts to condition; and it is well for him to do so openly, with full awareness of the responsibility involved as well as of the risks.

Training is to some degree related to conditioning; but Thomas Green, Gilbert Ryle, and others show that, unlike conditioning, training can be assimilated to the process of enabling people to acquire knowledge and belief. Green writes that training involves "forming models of habit and behavior." Ryle talks about the importance of "sheer habit-formation" and the ability to do "certain low-level things automatically and without thinking." Everyone begins in life—or in the experience of generating any unfamiliar structure—with diffuse, tentative outreachings. Every person obviously needs to develop habits of thought and action to serve as what Dewey described as "conditions of efficiency." The formation of habits may be conceived to be the ground of self-directed learning. We have discovered from the work of Piaget, Hunt, Bruner, and others how new dispositions can be generated through the initiative of the student, once certain foundations are laid. Teaching, in fact, may be said to begin at the point at which the student (having mastered fundamental skills) goes beyond what he has been trained to do or drilled to do. Whether the learning involves speaking one's native language, pitching a ball, driving a car, or understanding the origins of the Civil War, the teacher should realize that he is engaged in teaching (not in drilling, not in training) once the student begins making independent moves. He is teaching a child to read, for example, when the child begins figuring out the meaning of words he has never seen before. He is teaching someone to understand the origins of the Civil War when that person, applying what he has come to know about modes of historical explanation, about cause and effect relations, about types of determinism, and the like, begins to go beyond the issues of the Emancipation Proclamation, Fort Sumter, and the establishment of the Confederacy to a consideration of economic trends, population movements, agrarianism, expansionism, and proslavery rationales.

In somewhat different words: teaching happens when a person begins learning (on his own) how to do certain things. It happens when that person freely chooses to extend himself in order to find answers to questions he poses for himself, when he acts to move beyond what he has learned by rote. This is very much what Sartre has in mind when he speaks of knowing as *praxis* opening into "what has not yet been." Teaching happens when a student begins to understand what he is doing, when he becomes capable of giving reasons and seeing connections within his experience, when he recognizes the errors he or someone else is making and can propose what should be done to set things straight.

The mystery and the challenge of teaching are found, fundamentally, in the connection between words uttered by the teacher (and gestures made and activities undertaken) and the launching of learning activity by the student. The effectiveness of teaching is enormously difficult to demonstrate because of the diversity among human beings, because of the distinctiveness of each one's temporality, his situation in the world. But one way to talk about effective teaching is to find out the degree to which students freely appropriate the norms of critical inquiry when they begin consciously to structure their experiences. The various academic disciplines represent potential ways of structuring. Each discipline uses distinctive methods and protocols in the pursuit of meanings. Each one presumes a value in the perspectives it makes possible—be they perspectives on the universe, on the economic life of the nation, on the structure of poetic forms. An individual has to be brought to *care* about proceeding reflectively and purposefully if he is to achieve the widening of vision made possible through mastery of a discipline. "The only avenue towards wisdom," wrote Alfred North Whitehead, "is by freedom in the presence of knowledge. But the only avenue towards knowledge is by discipline in the acquirement of ordered fact."[22] If the accumulation of knowledge is not to be aimless, if the knowledge gained is not to be "inert," well-understood principles must be used actively. Such use signifies entry into the form of life represented by physics, economics, or literary criticism, along with the methods and structures that characterize them. On some level, it must be the fruit of the learner's free decision. Somehow he must be moved to *want* to fill in the gaps of his understanding, to move his picture of the world toward completion, to discover—as Henry James' Isabel Archer in *The Portrait of a Lady* wanted to so profoundly— "the continuity between the movements of her own soul and the agitations of the world."

The stress throughout this chapter has been on the engaged teacher's eagerness to counteract the meaninglessness in the world. We have continually returned to the possibility that such a teacher can integrate existential with disciplinary meanings, to refer "to the subjective point of view, namely, to the interpretation of the action and its settings in terms of the actor." This means that the teacher attempts to see the potential learner as an actor who initiates his explorations; but it also means that the teacher continually attempts to help that person acquire the skills needed for adequate interpretation. Merleau-Ponty, discussing the human search for the meaning of chance events, talks about the necessity to look through multiple perspectives, each with its own significance. Seeking understanding from a variety of vantage points, the individual is in no way prevented from choosing the perspectives of the disciplines, along with personal and subjective ones. At the same time, he can be encouraged to "reach the unique core of existential meaning which emerges in each perspective." To speak of existential meaning is to relate the attainment of meaning to an individual's particular project and standpoint, to conceive it in terms of concrete, human relations to others and to the world.

Phenix would agree that no single essence of meaning can be

discovered. He says that "we should speak not of meaning as such, but of meanings, or of the *realms of meaning.*" Each pattern of meaning he perceives is a function of a mode of human understanding. There are, therefore, meanings made possible by mathematics and nondiscursive symbolic forms; those made possible by the empirical sciences, the arts, "personal knowledge," ethics, and such integrative studies as history, religion, and philosophy. Each pattern is to be described "by reference to its typical methods, leading ideas, and characteristic structures." Unlike Merleau-Ponty, however, Phenix takes a realistic view of knowledge. He believes that concepts and theories "disclose the real nature of things" and that the disciplines "are at one and the same time approximations of the given orders of reality and disclosures of the paths which persons may come to realize in their own being. . . ." To a considerable degree at odds with the view taken in this chapter, Phenix asserts "the identity of the psycho-logic of teaching and learning with the logic of the disciplines. . . ." He is not concerned with taking into account the needs and the nature of learners; rather he defines the disciplines as "bodies of knowledge organized for the most effective instruction." He is not concerned, as John Dewey was, with psychologizing subject matter or with the problem "of inducing a vital and personal experiencing" within each potential learner. And, clearly, he is not concerned with proffering the disciplines as means by which individuals may constitute their life-worlds, avenues to pursue meanings important to them.

The teacher, once again, has self-consciously to choose; and it would seem that epistemological considerations are relevant to his choice. We have been talking about learning as cognitive action generated by free choice in response to question or need. On the one hand, this action stems from a response to what the psychologists have been saying; on the other hand, it derives from an epistemological position with respect to knowing and subject matters. Knowing, as we have described it, is participant and principled action undertaken in response either to problematic situations or to an "everyday reality" that must be imaginatively reconceived. Subject matter organized into disciplines is a deliberate selection of materials, which are ordered and systematized for the sake of providing perspectives on what is humanly known. There is nothing sacrosanct about them. They are human devices for clearing up obscurities, for responding to questions urgently posed at certain moments in history. As in the case of physics, economics, and history, the concepts composing them are open to revision as new things are discovered, new questions attended to. Often they are given new, more or less abstract, formulations; sometimes they are structured in alternative ways. Moreover, methods long considered typical are frequently transformed. We have only to recall the discovery of the atomic concept in modern physics and the changes it effected in the sciences. "Science," said Werner Heisenberg, "is made by men"; and he might have been talking about any of the disciplines known to us today. There is the development of mathematical physics; there is the recent interest in applying social scientific and ecological categories to history; there is the shift in the study of literature from formalism to an interest in "myth criticism" or alternatively to a resurgent concern for the literary experience and its relevance for living in the world.

If the disciplines are presented as opportunities for individual sense-making, then, if their structures are conceived as demanding no more than conditional assent, the teacher may be able to overcome resistance to norms, conceptualizations, even to rationality. If, on the other hand, he presents subject matter as a disclosure of "the real nature of things" or as a mode of initiating people into prevailing public traditions (without talk of transforming reality), the teacher will always be subject to the accusation that he is attempting to impose upon diverse persons a set of fossilized myths or rules of procedure only ostensibly open to question.

Most teachers do not want to alienate their students or to make them feel like strangers when confronted with predefined, unfamiliar structures of knowledge. It is far too easy to make curriculum seem external to the search for meaning. It is far too easy to make it into an alien and alienating edifice, a kind of "Crystal Palace" of ideas. Like Dostoevsky's Underground Man, the student is far too likely to taunt: "You believe in a palace of crystal that can never be destroyed . . . a palace at which one will not be able to put out one's tongue or make a long nose on the sly." Nevertheless, it is important to confront the notion that teaching always signifies a type of intervention into someone else's life. The teacher is not precisely in the position of Doctor Itard (as rendered in Francois Truffaut's film, *L'Enfant Sauvage*), who attempted so righteously and systematically to socialize a mute, highly sentient wolf-child into a culture that could only restrict and restrain. Nor is he in the position of "the little group of iron men" in Nathaniel Hawthorne's "The Maypole of Merrymount," who destroyed an Edenic colony in the name of Puritan idealism and for the sake of establishing "the rule of toil and psalm-singing" in New England forever. Nevertheless, the teacher must confront the ambiguities, the risks involved in attempting to socialize or enculturate or initiate, no matter how clear he is about what is worthwhile.

In some respect, he always represents the public world with its institutions, its predefined forms, its categories and disciplines. Every time he presents himself to his students, he speaks to them from a continuum that differs from and often collides with the one in which they exist. The routines he is obligated to maintain are governed by schedules and lesson plans frequently alien to his students' temporality, their "inner time." It is too much to expect that he will ever become fully cognizant of their diverse personal lives or wholly willing to permit them freely to choose themselves by means of what he provides. No matter how stimulating the environment he creates, he will necessarily have in mind dispositions that seem to him more desirable than others; and this constraint, in itself, is a limitation. Communicating what it is to know, to judge, to believe, he will necessarily be working to move his students toward states of mind *he* considers valuable, more valuable certainly than the states in which they began.

How, then, can he demonstrate he is right? How does he ground his judgments of the desirable, of the worthwhile? How does he know when he is authentic, when he is functioning in good faith? How, in a world of rapidly eroding norms, does he know what is good? How, if at all, can he justify his moral choice?

Notes and References

1. Cambridge Conference on School Mathematics, quoted in Edmund V. Sullivan, *Piaget and the School Curriculum: A Critical Appraisal* (Toronto: Ontario Institute for Studies in Education, 1967), p. 26.

2. J. McVicker Hunt, "Environment, Development, and Scholastic Achievement," in *Social Class, Race, and Psychological Development,* ed. Martin Deutsch, Irwin Katz, Arthur R. Jensen (New York: Holt, Rinehart & Winston, 1968), p. 325.

3. Jean-Paul Sartre, *Being and Nothingness* (New York: Philosophical Library, 1956), pp. 555–556.

4. Janet D. Elashoff and Richard E. Snow, eds., *Pygmalion Reconsidered: A Case Study in Statistical Inference: Reconsideration of the Rosenthal–Jacobson Data on Teacher Expectancy* (Worthington, Ohio: Charles A. Jones Publishing Company, 1971), pp. 1–18.

5. Robert Coles, "What Can You Expect," in *Pygmalion Reconsidered,* p. 76.

6. William Labov, "Academic Ignorance and Black Intelligence," *The Atlantic Monthly,* June 1972, p. 67.

7. Lillian Weber, *The English Infant School and Informal Education* (Englewood Cliffs, N.J.: Prentice-Hall, 1971), p. 11.

8. Richard S. Peters, "A Recognizable Philosophy of Education," in *Perspectives on Plowden,* ed. R. S. Peters (New York: Humanities Press, 1969), p. 10.

9. Jerome S. Bruner, *The Process of Education* (Cambridge, Mass.: Harvard University Press, 1960), p. 14.

10. Joseph J. Schwab, "The Practical: A Language for Curriculum," in *Curriculum,* ed. Martin Levit (Urbana: University of Illinois Press, 1971), p. 330.

11. Noam Chomsky, "The Case Against B. F. Skinner," *New York Review of Books,* December 30, 1971, p. 23.

12. Michael Novak, *The Experience of Nothingness* (New York: Harper & Row, Publishers, 1970), p. 92.

13. John Dewey, *Democracy and Education* (New York: The Macmillan Company, 1916), p. 60.

14. Aron Gurwitsch, "Towards a Theory of Intentionality," *Philosophical and Phenomenological Research,* March 1970, vol. 30, no. 3, p. 364.

15. Henry David Thoreau, *Walden* (New York: Washington Square Press, 1963), pp. 66–67.

16. Jean-Paul Sartre, *Search for a Method* (New York: Alfred A. Knopf, 1963), p. 92.

17. John Dewey, *Democracy and Education,* p. 247.

18. Alfred Schutz, "The Life-World," in *Studies in Phenomenological Philosophy, Collected Papers* III (The Hague: Martinus Nijhoff, 1966), p. 124.

19. Basil Bernstein, "A Socio-Linguistic Approach to Socialization with some reference to Educability," quoted in Courtney B. Cazden, "Three Sociolinguistic Views of the Language and Speech of Lower Class Children—with Special Attention to the Work of Basil Bernstein," *Developmental Medicine and Child Neurology,* vol. 10, no. 5, October 1968, p. 610.

20. Paulo Freire, *Pedagogy of the Oppressed* (New York: Herder and Herder, 1970), p. 28.

21. Philip H. Phenix, "The Uses of the Disciplines as Curriculum Content," in *Theory of Knowledge and Problems of Education,* ed. Donald Vandenberg (Urbana: University of Illinois Press, 1969), p. 195.

22. Alfred North Whitehead, *The Aims of Education* (New York: New American Library, 1949), p. 41.

Further Reading

James Baldwin and Margaret Mead, *A Rap on Race* (New York: Dell Publishing Company, 1971).

Harry S. Broudy, B. Othanel Smith, Joe R. Burnett, *Democracy and Excellence in American Secondary Education: A Study in Curriculum Theory* (Chicago: Rand McNally & Company, 1964).

Jerome S. Bruner, *Toward a Theory of Instruction* (Cambridge, Mass.: Harvard University Press, 1966).

Noam Chomsky, *Language and Mind* (New York: Harcourt Brace Jovanovich, 1972).

_____, *Problems of Knowledge and Freedom* (New York: Pantheon Books, 1971).

Robert Coles, *Children of Crisis,* vols. 1–3 (Boston: Atlantic Monthly Press, Little, Brown & Company, 1967, 1972).

John Dewey, *Experience and Nature* (New York: Dover Publications, 1958).

_____, "Progressive Education and the Science of Education," in *Dewey on Education,* ed. Martin S. Dworkin (New York: Bureau of Publications, Teachers College, Columbia University, 1961).

Fyodor Dostoevsky, "Notes from the Underground," in *Short Novels of Dostoevsky* (New York: Dial Press, 1945).

Joseph Featherstone, *Schools Where Children Learn* (New York: Liveright, 1971).

Thomas F. Green, *The Activities of Teaching* (New York: McGraw-Hill Book Company, 1971).

William H. Grier and Price M. Cobbs, *Black Rage* (New York: Bantam Books, 1969).

Aron Gurwitsch, *The Field of Consciousness* (Pittsburgh: Duquesne University Press, 1964).

Robert Heath, ed., *New Curricula* (New York: Harper & Row, Publishers, 1964).

Susan Isaacs, *Intellectual Growth in Young Children* (New York: Schocken Books, 1966).

Henry James, *Portrait of a Lady* (New York: Washington Square Press, 1969).

James L. Kuethe, *The Teaching-Learning Process* (Glenview, Ill.: Scott, Foresman & Company, 1968).

Oscar Lewis, *The Children of Sanchez: Autobiography of a Mexican Family* (New York: Random House, 1961).

Malcolm X, *The Autobiography of Malcolm X* (New York: Grove Press, 1965).

Herbert Marcuse, *Repressive Tolerance* (Boston: Beacon Press, 1969).

Ved Mehta, "John Is Easy to Please," *The New Yorker,* May 8, 1971, pp. 44–87.

Maurice Merleau-Ponty, *Phenomenology of Perception* (London: Routledge and Kegan Paul, 1962).

_____, *The Primacy of Perception,* ed. James M. Edie (Evanston, Ill.: Northwestern University Press, 1964).

Philip H. Phenix, *Realms of Meaning* (New York: McGraw-Hill Book Company, 1964).

Jean Piaget, *Science of Education and the Psychology of the Child* (New York: The Viking Press, 1971).

_____, *Structuralism* (New York: Basic Books, 1970).

Jean Piaget and Barbel Inhelder, *The Psychology of the Child* (New York: Basic Books, 1969).

Plowden Committee, Central Advisory Council for Education (England), *Children and Their Primary Schools* (London: Her Majesty's Stationery Office, 1967).

Gilbert Ryle, *The Concept of Mind* (New York: Barnes & Noble, 1949).

_____, "Teaching and Training," in *The Concept of Education,* ed. R. S. Peters (New York: Humanities Press, 1967).

Alfred Schutz, "The Problem of Rationality in the Social World," in *Studies in Social Theory, Collected Papers* II (The Hague: Martinus Nijhoff, 1964).

Studs Terkel, *Division Street: America* (New York: Pantheon Books, 1967).

Chapter Eight

Moral Dilemmas and Commitments

It is a strange thing to be an American.
It is strange to live on the high world in the stare
Of the naked sun and the stars as our bones live.

Archibald MacLeish
"American Letter," *Collected Poems*

"Yes," he thought, "between grief and nothing I will take grief."

William Faulkner
The Wild Palms

The teacher who wishes to be more than a functionary cannot escape the value problem or the difficult matter of moral choice. Confronting young people as he must, he presents himself as a representative—an agent —of what is taken to be adult culture. He is thus involved, sometimes against his will, in an enterprise more encompassing than the work he performs in his classroom: a process of perpetuating and remaking a distinctive way of life. From his vantage point, the aims he has in mind are far more specific. It would be almost meaningless for him to describe his day-to-day work as socializing or acculturating; nevertheless, when perceived in a larger historical context, his activities do contribute to the culture's effort to keep itself alive. "Through education," Ralph Barton Perry writes, "men acquire the civilization of the past, and are enabled both to take part in the civilization of the present and make the civilization of the future." If this is the case, much more is required than the transmission of skills and concepts. The identity of every civilization is in large measure a function of something cherished, a preference, a conception of the desirable which those who maintain the culture consider worth preserving.

What happens, however, in a time of historic tension, like the late twentieth century? What happens at a moment of extreme differentiation and strain? No teacher can be unaware of the disaffection and disillusion around him; nor can he take for granted the idea that "goods" and "bads" are simply given, as they were believed to be through much of the history of the public school. Horace Mann used to talk of making the rule of Right "stand out, broad, lofty, and as conspicuous as a mountain against a clear sky." To be virtuous, he was convinced, was to comply gladly and voluntarily with that rule. It was to achieve the kind of self-control that resulted in the formation of good habits: the traditional bourgeois habits of delaying gratifications, working dutifully, striving to create or to pursue new wealth. Moral values, associated with righteousness, were believed to have been enacted by divine or natural law, which supposedly sanctioned each objective sought in the school.

The teacher who deals with the most neutral subject matter today (linear algebra or elementary chemistry, for example) has, at some level, the conviction that it is better for a student to come to know the material than never to be exposed to it. He feels, at some level, that he is enabling the student to move from a less to a more desirable condition through the process of teaching. In fact, the concept *teaching* implies that something worthwhile is to be attained. Ordinarily, the aim of teaching is thought to be intelligent behavior. But *why* is it worthwhile to be intelligent in a corporate society that keeps so many people powerless? *Why* aim for intelligence more than personal sensitivity or aesthetic awareness or openness to others or the growth of feeling? Such questions, unthinkable in earlier times, have begun proliferating; and every time one is asked, the teacher is reminded that he must provide justification. He is highly unlikely to believe that bland talk about what is right or what is expected or what our nation wants is sufficient. He is even more unlikely to refer to natural law or to some unarguable sanction in the "public philosophy."

A public philosophy, in the sense of a structured, harmonious set of agreements, can scarcely be said to exist outside the few homogeneous communities that still survive in the United States. Most teachers hear a discordant clamor of voices when they turn to the public or the neighborhood or even the profession for guidance. There are the voices of parents, some demanding and ambitious for their children, some fiercely impatient with formal routines, some bitterly aware of estrangement and neglect. There are the voices of spokesmen and statesmen balancing special interests against one another, imposing limitations and requirements, arbitrarily introducing new strategies and codes. There are the voices of academicians, administrators, policy makers, teacher–educators. There are the vehement voices of militants and activists, the taunting or challenging voice of rebellious young people charging irrelevance, manipulation, various kinds of unfairness and bad faith. And there are the voices of diverse students in the classroom: the gifted, the slow, the ones proudly flaunting their emancipation from the Puritan ethic, the ones abstracted by tribal loyalties, the drug-dazed, the apathetic, the conformist, the resentful, the world-weary, the people devoid of hope.

One of the risks of "wide-awakeness" is that the sights and sounds of a culture in crisis may overwhelm. At one extreme, they may thrust the teacher back into reliance on precedent; defensively, he may become an automaton. At the other extreme, they may cause him deep disquietude. He may realize, as never before, that he is responsible for his moral choices, that—with dissonance afflicting him and no one to turn to for a resolution—he is dreadfully free. Thinking of those who might once have been his authorities, he may feel as Orestes does in Jean-Paul Sartre's *The Flies* when he addresses *his* authority, who is Zeus:

> Suddenly, out of the blue, freedom crashed down on me and swept me off my feet. Nature sprang back, my youth went with the wind, and I knew myself alone, utterly alone in the midst of this well-meaning little universe of yours. I was like a man who's lost his shadow. And there was nothing left in heaven, no right or wrong, nor anyone to give me orders . . . but I must blaze my trail.[1]

Or, more moderately, the teacher may decide to refer to the men of exact knowledge, the behavioral scientists, in the hope that their conclusions will provide him a sense of direction. Or he may decide, as Carl Bereiter has, that the school is no place for humanistic teaching or face-to-face encounters, no place for the pursuit of values, and that he will concentrate —neutrally, empirically—on teaching skills.

Since World War II, a moral unease has been developing in American culture. There were the terrible perplexities arising after the bombing of Hiroshima; the paradoxes of the Nuremberg War Crimes Trials, focusing on insoluble questions of innocence and guilt. There were the dilemmas of the McCarthy period, with its erosions of freedom and the Bill of Rights; there were the conflicts and puzzlements of the cold war, counterpointing the peculiar apathy and "togetherness" of the 1950s. And there were the incredible dislocations of the ensuing decade: the civil rights campaigns; the student rebellions; the assassinations; the Vietnamese War; police terror; riots; bombings; conspiracy charges; all shades of violent and nonviolent dissent. And in the 1970s? Jean-Francois Revel, perceiving the beginnings of a revolution in the United States, writes:

> [The United States] enjoys continuing economic prosperity
> and rate of growth, without which no revolutionary project can
> succeed; it has technological competence and a high level of
> basic research; culturally, it is oriented to the future rather than
> towards the past, and it is undergoing a revolution in behavioral
> standards and in the affirmation of individual freedom and
> equality; it rejects authoritarian control and multiplies creative
> initiative in all domains—especially in art, life-style, and sense of
> experience—and allows the coexistence of a diversity of mutually
> complementary alternative subcultures.[2]

This, of course, is an optimistic view; in a more pessimistic vein sociologist Daniel Bell takes account of the same phenomena:

> American capitalism ... has lost its traditional legitimacy
> which was based on a moral system of reward, rooted in a
> Protestant sanctification of work. It has substituted in its place a
> hedonism which promises a material ease and luxury, yet shies
> away from all the historic implications which a "voluptuary
> system"—and all its social permissiveness and libertinism—
> implies. This is joined to a more pervasive problem derived from
> the nature of industrial society. The characteristic style of an
> industrial society is based on the principles of economics and
> economizing: on efficiency, least cost, maximization,
> optimization, and functional rationality. Yet it is at this point
> that it comes into sharpest conflict with the cultural trends of
> the day, for the culture emphasizes anticognitive and
> anti-intellectual currents which are rooted in a return to
> instinctual modes. The one emphasizes functional rationality,
> technocratic decision-making, and meritocratic rewards. The
> other, apocalyptic moods and antirational modes of behavior. It
> is this disjunction which is the historic crisis of Western society.
> This cultural contradiction, in the long run, is the deepest
> challenge to the society.[3]

Numerous commentators have agreed (enthusiastically, fearfully, quietly, reprovingly) that the landscape has been changing dramatically, that the moral institutions are being transvalued, that a new moral order may be emerging or may have already emerged. In this context, we need not test such a claim or attempt to prove it. Instead, before we reach a philosophic discussion of ethics, morality, and obligation, we should identify some of the implications for education and, in consequence, for the teacher as a moral agent condemned continuously to choose.

Since the beginning of the cold war, a major problem bedeviling educators involves the promotion of cognitive excellence; but this problem, too, has serious moral implications. We have described the curriculum reform movement initiated in response to the Russians' launching of Sputnik, although we have said little about the "talent search" conducted in the interests of national policy. We may recall John Hersey's *The Child Buyer,* with its telling satire of the exploitation of high-IQ children by the United Lymphomilloid Corporation. Barry Rudd, the "specimen," was sold to the corporation for "unspecified educational and patriotic purposes," much like the children whose talents were sought to achieve foreign policy ends.

Soviet advances in space exploration created what many thought of as a national emergency; and this seemed to warrant the unprecedented stress placed on merit and excellence. The word *common,* once proudly linked to the concept of equal opportunity, was now equated with mediocrity. Responding to what was by then a familiar criticism of the schools, teachers began talking of rigorous, subject-centered approaches. For a brief period, there seemed to be a return to the Jeffersonian ideal of a natural aristocracy and to the Jeffersonian separation of the laboring from the learned. Educational statesmen, such as James B. Conant, began arguing for selective education, summoning up one of the oldest conflicts in American history: the conflict between Jeffersonianism and Jacksonianism. John Gardner articulated it in the subtitle to *Excellence*: "Can We Be Equal and Excellent Too?" He tried, however, to resolve the conflict by conceiving excellence in an Aristotelian manner. Every human activity, he wrote, had its own excellence; hence, each person, seeking his particular *virtus* or arête, should be provided an education suited to his talents. Despite his stress on vitality and the worth of diverse capacities, Gardner never came to terms with the problem of educating people to citizenship in a complex society. Also, despite his stress on self-realization, he never quite escaped the Aristotelian fixity of design or destiny. Is a man's end really in his beginning? When is his distinctive excellence to be defined?

Nevertheless, Gardner focused on an issue teachers had seldom confronted during the years when the challenge to educate the masses was more frequently met by a well-meaning emphasis on life adjustment. Richard Hofstadter, the historian, wrote that, "in the name of utility, democracy, and science," teachers had concentrated on the less educable child in the secondary school, "relegating the talented child to the sidelines." Believing that the selective principle (which led to weeding out the talented for special cultivation) was too much akin to the aristocratic tradition dominant in European school systems, American educators had proclaimed a concern for *all* American youth. True to the common school ideal as they understood it, they had placed utility and a kind of democratized value education higher in their priority scales than mental discipline or subject mastery. Not always fully aware of what they were doing, they had made what they considered to be highly moral decisions. Neither simpleminded nor innocent, they were to a degree affected by the deep-rooted anti-intellectualism of which Hofstadter and other have made so much. Aware that they were not members of the intellectual establishment or what Jacques Barzun calls the "House of Intellect," they were understandably ambivalent toward advanced and rigorous learning—which, by definition, was too difficult for the mass of men. Many academicians were contemptuous of the public schools. Like Barzun, they thought American education to be "a passion and a paradox":

> Millions want it and commend it, and are busy about it, at the same time as they are willing to degrade it by trying to get it free of charge and free of work. Education with us has managed to reconcile the contradictory extremes of being a duty and a diversion, and to elude intellectual control so completely that it can become an empty ritual without arousing protest.[4]

In the post-Sputnik period, public schoolmen and academics alike were forced into unfamiliar confrontations with a burgeoning technology and proliferating knowledge. There was much talk of a knowledge explosion; there was a gradually growing recognition of the difficulty involved in attaining mastery in more than one specialized field. The complexity of life in an urbanized, technologized society was articulated in new and unexpected ways. Slowly people were made aware of the power centers, which small groups of men representing government, big business, and the military supposedly controlled. As we have seen, this growing awareness had a significant influence on the way ordinary people structured social reality, their self-concepts, and their notions of expertise. Now and then someone talked more sanguinely about countervailing power, as David Riesman suggested a countervailing role the schools might perform. However, the messages with the greatest impact on consciousness had to do with the inhumanity of a society resistant to the ordinary man's questioning and increasingly impervious to his attempts at control. Traditional orthodoxies about the centrality of the individual were threatened. For a while "togetherness" was the watchword; "the lonely crowd" a convincing paradigm; the "organization man" an exemplary antihero. Value systems stemming from belief in personal potency seemed, in consequence, sadly archaic. Holden Caulfield, in J. D. Salinger's *The Catcher in the Rye,* roamed the city streets in search of a lost candor and simplicity; and thousands of young people identified with him because he expressed their mood so well. They, too, were awakening to the erosion of traditional ideals. They, too, were recognizing that all the dirty words could never be scrubbed off the walls of the schools, that no protection from the "phony" existed in the world. They were beginning to suspect that the presumably successful adults they were expected to imitate were leading hypocritical lives.

When the wave of disillusionment appeared about to break, John F. Kennedy was elected President; and, justifiably or not, he filled the moral vacuum with personal vibrancy and talk of a national mission. Ironically enough, his contemporary and pragmatic approach to leadership awakened hopes and dreams rooted in a far-off past. Causes seemed worth fighting for once again. The individual, especially the youthful individual, was offered an opportunity to serve, to protest, to be an agent of change. For almost a thousand memorable days, diverse citizens all over the country once again believed in possibility.

During that period, many climactic beginnings sprang up, and the consequences of certain events effected crucial value transformations. With the publication of Michael Harrington's *The Other America,* the so-called "invisible poor" began to present their unmet demands to the nation and the schools. Social reality suddenly looked different to many people when their attention was drawn to depressed areas around the country and to the depressed human beings who lived there—men and women who saw themselves as failures, rejects, leftouts. Harrington's concern was with a new poverty, unlike that of the early twentieth century immigrants:

> If a group has internal vitality, a will—if it has aspiration—it may live in dilapidated housing, it may eat an inadequate diet, and it may suffer poverty, but it is not impoverished. So it was in those ethnic slums of the immigrants that played such a dramatic role in the unfolding of the American dream. The people found themselves in slums, but they were not slum dwellers. But the new poverty is constructed so as to destroy aspiration; it is a system designed to be impervious to hope. The other America does not contain the adventurous seeking a new life and land. It is populated by the failures, by those driven from the land and bewildered by the city, by old people suddenly confronted with the torments of loneliness and poverty, and by minorities facing a wall of prejudice.[5]

Many were migrant workers; many had come out of the Appalachian hills to live at the fringe of the cities or (as middle-class families moved away) in central city slums. They were like the people Harriette Arnow describes in *The Dollmaker*: Gertie Nevels, who must give up carving her beautiful dolls and make cheap, tawdry ones for sale in Detroit; Reuben, who cannot adjust to the dreary city where he is called a hillbilly and scorned; Cassie who is crushed to death in the train yards. At one point, still trying to make sense of the city, Gertie visits her children's school for open house and tramps through the building, "a big perspiring woman in the crowd of mothers." At length she reaches Reuben's teacher, Mrs Whittle, who cannot remember the boy. Gertie tells her Reuben "ain't happy; he don't like school"; she says "back home he was . . .". The teacher snaps back:

> "Back home," Mrs Whittle said, as if she hated the words, her voice low, hissing, like a thin whip coming hard through the air, but not making much noise. "You hill—southerners who come here, don't you realize before you come that it will be a great change for your children? For the better, of course, but still a change. You bring them up here in time of war to an overcrowded part of the city and it makes for an overcrowded school. Don't you realize," she went on, looking again at Gertie, looking at her as if she alone were responsible for it all, "that until they built this wartime housing—I presume you live there —I never had more than thirty-two children in my section—and only one section." She opened her purse. "Now I have two sections—two home rooms, one in the morning with forty-three children, one in the afternoon with forty-two—many badly adjusted like your own—yet you expect me to make your child happy in spite of . . ."[6]

Among the new poor were Indians, Mexican-Americans, Puerto Ricans, Blacks, all variously afflicted by such stress factors as poor health, economic anxiety, family turmoil, isolation, and fear of the police. We have heard in recent years about their "culture of poverty," a concept first used by anthropologist Oscar Lewis in his efforts to understand poverty "as a way of life which is passed down from generation to generation along family lines." This culture (or, more technically, subculture) takes form among certain poor people who happen to live in a success-oriented capitalist society. These people do not and perhaps cannot achieve the upward mobility valued in that society and are therefore considered personally inferior or inadequate *because* of their lack of success. Lewis writes:

The culture of poverty is both an adaptation and a reaction of the poor to their marginal position in a class-stratified, highly individuated, capitalistic society. It represents an effort to cope with feelings of hopelessness and despair which develop from the realization of the improbability of achieving success in terms of the values and goals of the larger society. Indeed many of the traits of the culture of poverty can be viewed as attempts at local solutions for problems not met by existing institutions and agencies because the people are not eligible for them, cannot afford them, or are ignorant and suspicious of them.[7]

Neither Harrington nor Lewis has in mind *all* economically disadvantaged individuals, *all* welfare persons, *all* members of ethnic minority groups. Both are, however, talking about a population that is numerically significant, especially in the cities. They are bringing to our attention the plight of persons whom the schools have seldom considered seriously. They are challenging educators to reexamine some of their operative values, particularly their success values. Over the generations, schoolmen have tended to ignore individuals who have dropped out of their institutions. On occasion, John Dewey, George Counts, and other Progressives challenged the middle-class ethos, which made it so easy for teachers to blame the children for failures so often lamented. The point is frequently made today that the schools have functioned all along (and perhaps were intended to do so) as "selecting out" agencies, allowing individuals ill-equipped to meet market demands to fall by the wayside and "processing" those with the proper degree of aspiration and docility. For a long time, drop-outs could somehow be provided for through menial and unskilled jobs; but this became less and less likely as technology developed, and more and more of the new poor thronged into the cities from the southern hillsides and inland towns.

Today it is next to impossible to pretend that such people are invisible. It is also impossible to deny that a proven correlation exists between their low economic status and the level of achievement to be expected of their children. The IQ test, which (unfairly, perhaps) *does* measure the kind of intelligence relevant to the requirements of Western society, shows great variations between the privileged and the underprivileged, despite notable variations within each group. There is a bitter realism in what Lewis describes as "the realization of the improbability of achieving success in terms of the values and goals of the larger society." This realization presents serious problems to the teacher who is prone to take aspiration for granted. It presents problems, as well, to the teacher who questions the values and goals of the larger society. "People with a culture of poverty," says Lewis, "are aware of middle-class values, talk about them, and even claim some of them as their own; but on the whole they do not live by them." The teacher cannot simply admit guiltily that his values and those presumably governing his work in the classroom are middle class or establishment and proceed to accommodate (verbally and gesturally) to what he imagines to be lower class. Nor, even if he has come to believe that poor people are more spontaneous, more expressive, and less exploitative than middle-class individuals, and that their values ought to be appropriated by the larger culture, can the teacher evade the questions that the grim facts of the new poverty raise. These are not only methodological or strategic questions. To a large degree, as we shall see, they are moral questions, demanding choice and commitment, involving the teacher in a reconsideration of his basic beliefs and a reexamination of his norms.

The War Against Poverty and the Elementary and Secondary Education Act, both launched during Lyndon B. Johnson's administration, were explicit attempts to overcome feelings of powerlessness and exclusion among the poor. New opportunities were opened for people to participate in administering the programs. Vocational skills were taught; community representatives were permitted to speak for their neighborhoods; efforts were made to compensate for long years of deprivation. Often, emphasis was on the need to recognize the distinctiveness of the deprived child, to understand his cognitive style. The idea, almost without exception, was to discover ways of reaching young people for the sake of inducting them into the mainstream. This was the rationale for Head Start's concentration on compensating for environmental attrition in the early years, for such programs as Higher Horizons, Upward Bound, Double Discovery, Operation Bootstrap, and many others. Presuppositions (often unexamined) about "higher" and "lower" underlay all these programs. The poor were dealt with benevolently, generously, as if they were citizens of an underdeveloped country for the first time offered an opportunity to enter into the modern world. Questions on the value of modernization and development were held in abeyance. Questions on the assumptions buried in such terms as *deprived, culturally disadvantaged,* and *underprivileged* were only occasionally confronted. A poor child still had the right to say, if he had the appropriate language: "I am invisible, understand, simply because people refuse to see me. . . . That invisibility to which I refer occurs because of a peculiar disposition of the eyes of those with whom I come in contact. A matter of the construction of their *inner* eyes, those eyes with which they look through their physical eyes upon reality."

In the meanwhile, a storm was brewing. At the moment the "other America" became visible, the civil rights movement was erupting in the South. Almost a decade had passed since the Supreme Court had called a halt to *de jure* school segregation ("with all deliberate speed"); but buses, lunch counters, theaters, churches, as well as schools still discriminated against black people. It took Freedom Rides, bus boycotts, sit-ins, and brutality to convince the Administration and most liberal white citizens that blacks were tired of waiting for equality, that decisive steps had to be taken at long last. In the public sphere were proposals for legislation, voter registration campaigns, passage of a Civil Rights Act. As significant, however, were the effects on the moral lives of individuals, including young persons brought up in relative affluence and abruptly conscious of the staleness, the hollowness of their lives. In a sense, the doctrines of civil disobedience and nonviolence, as developed in the South, wrought a revolution in ethics and morality throughout the nation—a revolution that gave rise to the "new morals" in many spheres of life. No matter how tightly he has held to conventional notions of obligation and lawfulness and "good," the teacher is almost bound to have to confront the new morality and identify his codes of ethics with respect to what has happened.

Martin Luther King's doctrines had, of course, long roots in one of America's traditions (in many respects an adversary tradition), created by Henry David Thoreau and certain Abolitionists living in his time. ("The authority of the government," wrote Thoreau in "Civil Disobedience," "even such as I am willing to submit to—for I will cheerfully obey those who know and can do better than I, and in many things even those who neither know nor can do so well—is still an impure one: to be strictly just, it must have the sanction and consent of the governed. It can have no pure right over my person and property but what I concede to it." Incarnating that tradition, along with the writings of Leo Tolstoy and Mahatma Gandhi, King developed strategies of enormous contemporary appeal. Addressing himself to his fellow clergymen from the Birmingham jail, King wrote:

> You express a great deal of anxiety over our willingness to break laws. This is certainly a legitimate concern. Since we so diligently urge people to obey the Supreme Court's decision of 1954 outlawing segregation in the public schools, at first glance it may seem rather paradoxical for us consciously to break laws. One may well ask: "How can you advocate obeying some laws and disobeying others?" The answer lies in the fact that there are two types of laws: just and unjust. I would be the first to advocate obeying just laws. Conversely, one has a moral responsibility to disobey unjust laws. I would agree with St. Augustine that "an unjust law is no law at all." Now what is the difference between the two? How does one determine whether a law is just or unjust? A just law is a man-made code that squares with the moral law or the law of God. An unjust

> law is a code that is out of harmony with the moral law. To put
> it in the terms of St. Thomas Aquinas: An unjust law is a
> human law that is not rooted in eternal law and natural law.
> Any law that uplifts human personality is just. Any law that
> degrades human personality is unjust.[8]

King's personal heroism and self-sacrifice, like those of his co-workers and the young volunteers who came to work for freedom in the South, were awe-inspiring to many. After all, as a middle-class preacher with a fine education and great intellectual gifts, he had alternatives. Since the moment (as he put it) he was "suddenly catapulted into the leadership of the bus protest in Montgomery, Alabama," however, he never ceased his efforts "to make real the promise of democracy." He appeared a veritable exemplar of moral commitment, living proof of the function of the "ought" in human affairs. In his "I have a dream" speech, he told the "veterans of creative suffering," the civil rights workers who had been beaten and jailed repeatedly: "Continue to work with the faith that unearned suffering is redemptive." This notion of redemptive suffering, the appeal to the sheriffs and the Ku Klux Klan, and the reliance on a intuitively apprehended moral law might have been more difficult for secular youth to accept, were it not for the evocations of Thoreau marching to his drumbeat, doing (as young people later pointed out) "his own thing." One young person wrote from Mississippi to his parents: "You can't run away from a broadened awareness. . . . If you try, it follows you in your conscience, or you become a self-deceiving person who has numbed some of his humanness. I think you have to live to the fullest extent to which you have gained an awareness or you are less than the human being you are capable of being. . . . This doesn't apply just to civil rights or social consciousness but to all the experiences of life." In any case, the individuals who played an active part in the Mississippi Freedom Summer, in registration campaigns, in the Selma March, like those who participated in sit-ins or other nonviolent confrontations, internalized many values associated with civil disobedience. They found a sense of purpose, a justification in their teaching and community work, in spite of and sometimes because of the dangers.

Understandable, although shocking, was the demand for "psychological equality," which led to demands for "Black Power." Stokely Carmichael announced that only black people could "convey the revolutionary idea that black people are able to do things themselves." Then:

> I have said that most liberal whites react to "black power"
> with the question, What about me?, rather than saying: Tell me

what you want me to do and I'll see if I can do it. There are answers to the right question. One of the most disturbing things about almost all white supporters of the movement has been that they are afraid to go into their own communities—which is where the racism exists—and work to get rid of it. They want to run from Berkeley to tell us what to do in Mississippi: let them look instead at Berkeley. They admonish blacks to be nonviolent; let them preach nonviolence in the white community. They come to teach me Negro history; let them go to the suburbs and open up freedom schools for whites. Let them work to stop America's racist foreign policy; let them press this government to cease supporting the economy of South Africa.[9]

Not only did separatism and the Black Power idea grow rapidly among movement blacks; not only were white civil rights workers more and more firmly rejected; nonviolence itself was explicitly attacked. Talking to Mississippi civil rights workers in 1965, Malcolm X said:

I myself would go for nonviolence if it was consistent, if everybody was going to be nonviolent all the time. I'd say, okay, let's get with it, we'll all be nonviolent. If they make the Ku Klux Klan nonviolent, I'll be nonviolent. If they make the White Citizens Council nonviolent, I'll be nonviolent. But as long as you've got somebody else not being nonviolent, I don't think it is fair to tell our people to be nonviolent unless someone is out there making the Klan and the Citizens Council and these other groups also be nonviolent.[10]

Outbreaks of unrest and violence had already begun in northern cities—New York, Rochester, Cleveland—and in Watts, Los Angeles (where a match became a symbol of manhood and the slogan was "Burn, baby, burn!"). King deplored the riots but talked bitterly of the millions who "are in hopeless despair, and . . . feel they have no stake in society." Robert F. Kennedy said: "It was pointless to tell Negroes living in Northern slums to obey the law. To these Negroes, the law is their enemy. . . ." And, indeed, as economic and legal oppression was seen to be violent (in the sense of violating dignity and personal rights), groups such as the Black Panthers (wearing black berets, carrying guns) began to dramatize their hostility to the law, to "the Man," to "the pigs." They began describing themselves as residents in a colony overrun, as Algeria had been, by a foreign power.

Their casualties and internal conflicts were appalling, but their revolutionary rhetoric had an enormous impact. Drawn from Frantz

Fanon, Che Guevara, Mao Tse-tung, and other revolutionary leaders, honed in prison cells and libraries by men discovering powerful abilities to educate themselves, the language affected the reality constructs of young people all over the country. The militant style was being improvised at the same time that young Blacks were asserting an extravagant pride in their blackness, their "hipness," their African heritage. It did not really matter if the rhetoric made political sense. It made emotional sense to speak of a black colony in a oppressive society, to describe prisoners as "political prisoners," to salute with clenched fists, to cry "Right on!" Moreover, despite legislation against segregation, despite slowly expanding opportunities, tragic events continued to occur. The Orangeburg "massacre" in South Carolina, the killing of a Panther leader in his bed, the shooting of students at Jackson State College, the shooting of Augusta rioters in the back: all these, and similar although more ambiguous, incidents made the militant constructs seem accurate. The case of the Soledad Brothers; the shoot-out at the Marin County Courthouse; the flight and capture of the young Communist intellectual, Angela Davis; the tragic and vicious conclusion of George Jackson's existence in jails: all these raised complex moral issues respecting guilt, responsibility, and punishment.

There are words, hundred of words, to which self-conscious teachers must pay heed. For instance, Margaret Walker writes in "For My People":

> For the cramped bewildered years we went to school to learn
> to know the reasons why and the answers to and the people who
> and the places where and the days when, in memory of the
> bitter hours when we discovered we were black and poor and
> small and different and nobody cared and nobody wondered and
> nobody understood.
> For the boys and girls who grew in spite of these things to be
> man and woman, to laugh and dance and sing and play and
> drink their wine and religion and success, to marry their
> playmates and bear children and then die of consumption and
> anemia and lynching. . . .[11]

And Nikki Giovanni:

> [C]hildhood remembrances are always a drag if you're
> Black.[12]

And Claude Brown:

> A year later Miss Eileen went to jail for three years, and
> when she came out she wasn't as pretty as she used to be. As a
> result, she changed her "game" to selling drugs. For three years
> she was very successful in the "horse trade," but gave it up and
> did seven years for her troubles at the insistence of the
> Narcotics Bureau. The last time I saw her she was profitably
> engaged in one of Harlem's more legal vices: the "numbers"
> racket. These were the people I admired and wanted to be
> accepted by. People like Miss Eileen and my other teachers from
> the streets of Harlem.[13]

And Eldridge Cleaver:

> Any social science book will tell you that if you subject people
> to an unpleasant environment, you can predict they will rebel
> against it. That gives rise to a contradiction. When you have a
> social unit organized in such a way that people are moved to
> rebel against it in large numbers, how, then, do you come
> behind them and tell them that they owe a debt to society? I say
> that society owes a debt to them. And society doesn't look as
> though it wants to pay.[14]

Tom Wicker, writing in *The New York Times* after George Jackson's
death, summed up many of the issues when he spoke of the necessity to
"get at the truth of George Jackson's life":

> He was, that is, not merely a victim of racism, although he
> certainly was that. He was a victim, too, of the poverty and
> hunger and disadvantage that are not the lot of blacks alone in
> this richest country on earth. Its schools treated him with
> contempt. He was shot at age 15 by its violent lawmen. Its
> courts knew nothing better to do with him than to send him to
> its harsh prisons, where he spent a third of his life. There, and
> in his brief years on the streets of Chicago and Los Angeles—by
> his own account—he learned that the jungle is still the jungle,
> be it composed of trees or skyscrapers, and the law of the jungle
> is "bite or be bitten." A talented writer, a sensitive man, a

> potential leader and political thinker of great persuasiveness,
> George Jackson was destroyed long before he was killed at San
> Quentin. There are thousands upon thousands like him—black
> and white, brothers all—who will be or have been destroyed too.
> Until this wanton destruction of humanity in America is seen
> for what it is, it will go on, and consume us all.[15]

The educator is not obligated to clear the entire jungle; he is not endowed with the power to remake the law. His responsibility is to eradicate the contemptuous treatment of blacks and to get at the truth, as well as he can, of the socially wounded child's life. The white teacher must confront the traumatic situation of teaching individuals who (even when young) deeply distrust authority, who question the legitimacy of the school and all its ways. The black teacher must make difficult choices between his fidelity to his disaffected, overburdened brothers and his responsibility for acculturating their young.

Morally speaking, the teacher's problems have often clustered about the matter of equality of education opportunity. No longer an apparently simple matter of providing the same education for all races and social classes, equality now means more effectual compensatory measures, better facilities, increased parental participation and control. Only occasionally (and most particularly in the South) is it made contingent on integration. More important, at least in northern cities, is the question of community control. One black leader, Preston Wilcox, has written that the demand for equality "conflicts dramatically with the vested interests of boards of education, teachers' professional associations, unions, and other groups. The resultant clash has sharpened the issues, trained a whole cadre of educational activists and raised fundamental questions affecting not merely ghetto schools but all education."[16] Some of these questions have had to do with the merit system, with certifying examinations, with curriculum decisions and disciplinary issues. Neighborhood groups and activists have repeatedly moved into overt conflict with organized teachers. Strikes have occurred, schools have closed, and individual teachers have had painful choices to make between, say, two sets of loyalties, between one "good" and another. How *is* a teacher to decide between his loyalty to his professional group and his responsibility to his students? How is he to decide between what an expert considers desirable for a given group of children and what their parents or their community leaders demand? How is he to respond when a black scholar puts the onus on him for the unequal goods and benefits black children enjoy in the schools? Kenneth Clark, for example, arguing for integrated education, demands—first of all —greatly increased efficiency in the schools. He finds that racial separatism is "another formidable and insidious barrier in the way of the movement towards effective, desegregated public schools." He demands that public school teachers be held accountable for their performance in the classroom. *They* are responsible, he says, if children do not learn to read. Talk of those children's poverty, family backgrounds, and health problems is merely diversionary because, as he sees it, racism of the educators involved is the chief cause of failure—and an eradicable one. Clark also asks for the establishment of alternative forms of public education so that the monopoly of current establishments can be broken once and for all. "Specifically in America," he writes, "the goal of democratic education must be to free Americans of the blinding and atrophying shackles of racism. A fearful, passive, apologetic, and inefficient educational system cannot help in the attainment of these goals."[17]

In the meantime, Clark and others have been arranging contracts between various manufacturers of educational technologies (or programmed learning systems) and certain city school systems. The teacher becomes a monitor or supervisor and is bypassed in the significant choice of significant teaching strategies. How, then, is he to perceive himself? How is he to adjust his values on a scale of priorities that places efficiency first? This is not the first time the cult of efficiency has been central to the design of American schools. It is not the first time that a related factory metaphor has been used to explain what happens or should happen in public education. Here, too, the teacher has moral decisions to make. He must take a stance on managerial values, which have, for so long, shaped the functions of the schools. Managerial education is intended to satisfy effective or market demand, which is seldom properly distinguished from human or social need. Market demand means that in a market economy a number of potential buyers are ready to purchase a given commodity—in this case, the properly equipped graduate of a school. If schools were concerned with needs rather than with market demand, they would be devoted to restoring something that is absent, something that would, if present, contribute to "the full and unalienated development of human power. . . ." If schools were concerned with needs, they would be charged with "inefficiency," as many teachers have discovered. They would not be doing what some say they were intended to do: to provide the workers, technologists, administrators, soldiers, and so on presumably "needed" by society. Many ghetto parents, with justice, insist that their schools are inadequate primarily because these schools do *not* meet market demand; others, with equal justice, insist that their schools are inadequate because they crush individuality and reinforce powerlessness. The teacher, attempting to cope effectively with such conflicting points of view, cannot be content with conventional humanistic wisdom. He cannot simply *talk* benevolently and humanistically. Again, without reliable sanctions and without guarantees of being "right," he is required to act; he is condemned to choose.

Whatever he chooses, he will have to face the bitter fact that trust and cooperation have been eroding in this country, at least since the Kennedy assassinations and the death of Martin Luther King. For a time, as the National Commission has said, violence appeared to be "substituting force and fear for argument and accommodation." Young white people began sharing with blacks memories of riots, clubbings, gassings, personal assaults, obscene insults, punitive jailings. There were the campus uprisings and the police actions against them; there was the police riot at the 1968 Democratic Convention in Chicago; there were the deaths at Kent State University in 1970. There were also the sporadic sputterings of terrorist action: the burning of a San Diego bank, the fatal explosion of a "bomb factory" in a New York City town house, the fatal bombing of a Wisconsin Mathematics building. . . . There were deaths, senseless and brutal deaths. By 1971, building take-overs, expulsions of industrial recruiters, attacks on the ROTC, even "trashing" and destruction began to seem mild and almost playful. There came to be a kind of fearsome symbolism in the destruction of the People's Park in Berkeley: mechanized, plastic-masked representatives of law and order seemed on the rampage against the long-haired, expressive, outraged lovers of flowers and children, who saw no sense in fences and prohibitions, no legitimacy in establishment rules. Rocks and obscenities were hurled; gas swirled in the air; talk of conspiracy intensified. Young people spent hours in courthouse corridors, correction centers, jails. An undeclared war appeared to be in process: there were spies and entrapment procedures; there was "revolution for the hell of it"; there were Weathermen and days of rage. And, through it all, trust was eroded; authority was scorned.

Erik H. Erikson calls "a sense of basic trust" the fundamental prerequisite of mental vitality. "By 'trust'," he writes, "I mean an essential trustfulness of others as well as a fundamental sense of one's own trustworthiness." He also speaks of fidelity and the need for young people to have faith in some coherent, ongoing order with which they can identify as they grow. If incoherence and fragmentation define the contemporary crisis, extraordinary moral dilemmas confront the teacher who (by the nature of his project) *depends* on a degree of trust, a hope of fidelity.

These dilemmas become most apparent when the teacher comes in touch with the so-called "counter-culture," which emerged in the decade of the 1960s, before adults quite realized what was happening. Its history and its lasting import are still unsettled, partly because of the variations among the constructs through which it has been interpreted; but few people question the cataclysms it has caused in art, politics, and morality. Whether the origins are in the "adversary culture" which has been developing in literature for half a century, in political doctrines and anti-ideological movements, in discontent with the affluent society, in specific responses to the technological revolution, in a recurrence of generational revolt, in disgust with American foreign policy, or in the beginnings of a revolution of consciousness, the teacher must determine the consequences of this counter-culture and choose a stance. Simply no truth can be found on which all observers agree. Nor can the proliferating studies and polemical essays prescribe the kinds of action teachers *ought* to take.

The language of civil rights clearly seems to have affected many articulations of discontent today. We have already referred to the Port Huron Statement, which talked about loneliness and alienation and which also pointed out that young people had long been "used to moral leadership being exercised and moral dimensions being clarified" by their elders. *But* (and this, in effect, became a clarion call) "today, for us, not even the liberal and socialist preachments of the past seem adequate to the forms of the present." Later, Thomas Kahn, discussing the Freedom Rides, said: "On the strategic level, the Freedom Rides have provided the most clear-cut demonstration of the sterility of legalism that our generation has yet witnessed. By legalism I mean the view that social revolutions can be carried out in the courtrooms." Inexorably, skepticism built up, as young people moved on to poverty projects in the cities and to Free Speech movements on the campuses. Frustration, impatience, and disillusionment fired the early protests against the Vietnamese War and the universities' involvement with that war. Conscientious resistance to the draft became widespread: objecting selectively to that war on specifically humanist, conscientious grounds, hundreds of young men were imprisoned. It became clear how intensely young people were searching for values by which they could live. It became poignantly clear, as well, even when other young men fled the country to escape the draft, the lengths to which persons would go to defend their beliefs. Defying unjust laws and secular authorities who did not deserve the respect of the governed, young people refused to concede that the government had any right over their persons. Still others, carrying the "right to resist" to dramatic extremes (as in the Mayday demonstrations in Washington in the spring of 1971), pursued values and choices sanctioned sometimes by moral law, sometimes by inclination (or imagination), sometimes by affinity group consensus, sometimes by an insistent inner voice associated with conscience. As they saw it, the military–industrial complex had totally forsaken the traditional moral codes. The "body counts" in Vietnam, the defoliation, the bombings, the massacres convinced dissident young people that the system was cynically committed to a brutality at least equal to that for which Nazi war criminals were condemned. Hence, any action was justified, except the action of compliance, of being a "good German." The morality developing in sections of the "resistance" was the morality of underground fighters in an occupied country. Any disruption, any destruction that could cripple or slow up the war machine was justifiable to the more radical youth, most of them intelligent beings, gently reared. Separated from, often rejected by militant blacks, they used similar rhetoric and chose themselves as guerrillas after the model of Che Guevara and Regis Debray.

Now it is obvious that the majority of American youth are not radical dissidents in this fashion. Thousands have chosen the same life style, the same haircuts and accouterments that the media display and often sell; but beards, headbands, tie-dyed shirts, bell-bottomed jeans, and long hair do not *necessarily* indicate value positions. Citizens still loyal to traditional religious or cultural norms have assumed that "longhairs" are, by definition, enemies of respectability. In consequence, they have tended to make hippies into "niggers" and restless youth into a new, oppressed minority. This reaction has obscured the issue in many communities and put the sympathetic teacher into a defensive position.

Without doubt, the challenges to "bourgeois" habits, codes, and pieties are crucial, especially among middle-class children. The challenges may simply be a matter of "image" or "style"; they may signify a new language, a fashionable idiom rather than the "new consciousness" Charles A. Reich heralds in *The Greening of America.* He calls that consciousness "Consciousness III," thus distinguishing it from "Consciousness I," which refers to nineteenth century individualism, and "Consciousness II," which accompanies the social engineering approaches of the twentieth century. Consciousness III, Reich says, is a specific response to the depredations of technology; and it can be accomplished by every person willing to change the segment of his life in which he acts as a machine-part. "Consciousness III postulates the absolute worth of every human being—every self. Consciousness III does not believe in the antagonistic or competitive doctrine of life. . . . Consciousness III rejects the whole concept of excellence and comparative merit that is so central to Consciousness II. III refuses to evaluate people by general standards, it refuses to classify people or analyze them."[18] Consciousness III is presented as a total perception of reality, a "whole world view" finding expression in "an entire culture, including music, clothes, and drugs"; and Reich sees it as the source of a culturewide revolution. When his book was published, it aroused enthusiastic responses among those who found in it a way of combatting their sense of powerlessness and a source of new, exciting hope. Soon, however, its message was described as misleading, simplistic, nothing more than "the inoffensive anarchism of the well-to-do." What had been greeted originally as respectable social prophecy was now treated as pleasant fantasy.

Nevertheless, the teacher cannot ignore what has happened in the last decade and what is still happening to the value systems of the young. Margaret Mead's notion of the great discontinuity between the world familiar to present-day adults and the world familiar to post–World War II youth may be entirely warranted. Speaking of adults, young and old, she writes:

> They are like the immigrants who came as pioneers to a new land, lacking all knowledge of what demands the new conditions of life would make upon them. Those who came later could take their peer groups as models. But among the first comers, the young adults had as models only their own tentative adaptations and innovations. Their past, the culture that had shaped their understanding—their thoughts, their feelings, and their conceptions of the world—was no sure guide to the present. And the elders among them, bound to the past, could provide no models for the future.[19]

On the basis of her anthropological researches, Mead sees a "prefigurative culture" developing; and thus she speaks as did the writers of the Port Huron Statement. The traditional models are no longer applicable in the changed conditions of the modern world; young people must turn to their peers for guidance, and adults must begin learning from the young. Peter Marin, writing about the place of psychedelic experience in the youth culture, reinforces this idea by talking about the new tribalism and the uses of treating dissident young people as members of a friendly neighboring tribe.

In addition to unprecedented change (to which the new generation may simply be adapting better than the old), the "liberation" spirit and idiom have undeniably spread to women's groups, homosexual society, even to the high schools. The world of theater, film, literature, and visual arts has almost wholly been transformed; in fact, some persons (like Daniel Bell) find artists and their publicists to be the chief generators of the cultural revolution. On all sides, talk revolves around the "now," around consciousness and revolutionary experiences in sex, family life, travel, even religion. Old prohibitions and limitations seem wholly outmoded to those who treat sexual relationships as natural and preferably spontaneous. Old boundaries and fences seem meaningless to those who swing packs on their backs at a moment's notice and go hitchhiking across America, Europe, the Middle East. The special obligations of the nuclear family seem irrelevant to those aware of communal experiments, tribes, remote hillside settlements for young people like themselves.

Peter de Lissovoy, moving too late from the Harvard drug scene to what he hoped would be an active civil rights movement in Georgia, describes his meeting with a joyful old man named Feelgood:

Often we got high at Feelgood's house. I remember an
ordinary day with those cats, the Doctor and Cousin Yellow.
Various business could be taken care of, relating to staying alive
and continuing life. But none of it was pressing. Everything
could wait until tomorrow, or the day after. So we were
smoking and taking it easy, enjoying the sun high in the blue
sky. I think there was nothing I enjoyed more about the
company of my friends than their capacity for silence. In the
corner, cats would be getting high and rapping and chattering.
Sometimes I would hear them running their lines on each other
—I'm the baddest, I'm the hippest!—and in the tones and
rhythms of their words would be the sound of truth and
certainty, and the usual and certain unique symbolisms, and I
might be drawn into that and sound off too, or I might be silent
and inside myself I'd smile at it all. But that was a knowing
smile, remembering Feelgood's, and in no way related to the
silence of nothing when a laugh would signify joy, and might or
might not be followed with a word, which could only signify the
sun or the sky or the friendship or the silence.[20]

Don McNeill spent two years writing about the hip scene for the *Village
Voice* before his death by drowning at the age of twenty-three. He
summons up some of the darkness, the sense of impending doom so many
young dissidents appear to feel:

It was weird to be in the West Village. It was like a sneaky
Vietcong offense, taking the revolution into the City on a warm
spring night when the streets were clogged with tourists and the
cops were unsuspecting. But it wasn't sneaky; it was
spontaneous. The kids were exhilarated to be beyond the
boundaries. Now they didn't know where they were going; they
were just going ahead. They wove through the stalled traffic,
pounding on cars. They called to the tourists to "Join the
Revolution!" It was the revolution; the kids were shouting it to
convince themselves.[21]

Trips, moments of terror, communes, crash pads, police busts, illnesses,
injuries, be-ins, frisbee games, the *Whole Earth Catalog,* rock music,
festivals, sunlight, handicrafts: the fabric is complicated, densely
interwoven, a mix of joy and liberation and futility. And somehow the
teacher must comprehend it, take action with respect to it, try to reach
some of those involved without psychologizing into meaninglessness and
without trying to be "with it" in order to be loved.

Theodore Roszak, who invented the term *counter-culture,* stresses opposition to the technocratic society as an explanation of the moral conduct of young people today. Conceiving moral conduct primarily as a vocabulary people use to express their ethical sensibilities and their visions of life, Roszak finds its sources in some primordial world view or in the nonintellective aspects of the personality. Objecting to ordinary dichotomies—between the spontaneous and the deliberate, say, or between passionate impulse and rationality—he suggests moving below surface conduct to the level of vision. He is convinced that fascination with shocking or frenzied activity can interfere with authentic ethical expression as much as preoccupation with rules and principles can. His fundamental concern is with the authenticity of the person in tune with his nonintellective consciousness. His moral paradigm is found in "the gentle, tranquil, and thoroughly civilized contemplativeness" of Eastern religions.

Kenneth Keniston, who has studied many types of youthful behavior, stresses the fluidity, movement, and openness that mark the lives of young radicals and hippies, both of whom he describes as post-modern youth.

> Post-modern youth are non-dogmatic, anti-ideological, and intensely hostile to doctrines and formulas. In the New Left, the focus is on tactics rather than program; amongst hippies, on simple direct acts of love, expression, and communication. In neither group does one find hard-and-fast adherence to a fixed and unmodifiable system of beliefs. In both groups, youth seeks to preserve the capacity to change beliefs with changing circumstances; the goal is to remain responsive to a changing environment, even if it means altering apparently fundamental beliefs.[22]

These youth desire direct, personal, I–Thou encounters. They object particularly to the artificial, the hypocritical, the manipulative; and, as a result, they prize freely expressed love and sexuality unhampered by guilt or restless craving. Also, quite obviously, they object to being "kept" or "processed" in any situation that deprives them of the right to participate in policy making. They describe schools this way, as well as professional agencies, corporations, hospitals, and law firms. To combat bureaucracies and dehumanization, they insist on participatory values and self-determination. They believe individuals should be consulted on policies which affect them directly or indirectly: on matters of clothing, school discipline, curriculum requirements, ceremonial occasions, ethnic studies, publications, and the rest. The teacher who values etiquette, good order, and respectful silence is put into a difficult position; so is the well-meaning, liberal teacher who is sure he knows what is "best" for his students, who presumes to understand them better than they understand themselves.

Obviously, not all young people make such demands; nor do they all feel particularly alienated from their elders. There remain, quite naturally, the vocationally or professionally oriented students, who have no intention of being diverted from traditional goals. There are the boys and girls on what Peter Schrag has described as "Mechanic Street," disinterested in everything but "shop" in their schools, finding recreation in McDonald's hamburger shops, in outdoor movies, on the roads. They are, frequently, workingmen's children, who only occasionally think of going on to a senior college and hope for a little more security than their parents possess. There are also the status-minded, small-town children Edgar Friedenberg has portrayed: the "better operators"; the conforming; the pleasant; the cautious. There are the boys who have grown up in anticipation of going to "'Nam" to fight the "gooks"; there are Scouts and altar boys; there are 4-H Club children who compete at fairs. There are the young people Peter Berger has in mind when he writes of the "blueing of America" and the rejection of bourgeois culture by radical youth. Someone else will have to fill the positions in the economy they disdain.

> ... It will be the newly college-educated children of the lower-middle and working classes. To say this, we need not assume that they remain untouched by their contact with the youth culture during their school years. Their sexual mores, their aesthetic tastes, even their political opinions might become permanently altered as compared with those of their parents. We do assume, though, that they will, now as before, reject the anti-achievement ethos of the cultural revolution. They may take positions in intercourse that are frowned upon by Thomas Aquinas, they may continue to listen to hard rock on their hi-fi's and they may have fewer racial prejudices. But all these cultural acquisitions are, as it were, functionally irrelevant to making it in the technocracy. Very few of them will become sandal-makers or farmers on communes in Vermont. We suspect that not too many more will become humanistic sociologists.[23]

If indeed, for all its deficiencies and inequities, social mobility will be increasing upward in the United States, the aware teacher must come to terms with this idea as well. He must be as wary of romanticism and unthinking avant-gardism as he must be of the hollow pieties that blind so many educators to what is happening in their world. Again, he must identify himself and his principles; he must be clear about his values.

We have talked about one facet of the cultural revolution, which is likely to affect the teacher as a professional so directly that he cannot function effectively until he knows what it signifies for him. This is the so-called "romantic" critique of the schools, which connects at so many points with the rhetoric of dissidence and dissent. Whether the focus is on the "vanishing adolescent" whose sensuality arouses adult hostility, on expressive black children forced into a restrictive mainstream culture, on the angers of high school children forced to swallow lower middle-class banalities, the prominent values center on the need for autonomy, authenticity, and personal visibility. Jules Henry has written of "culture *against* man," expressing a rather widespread view of the inhumanity of most institutions, including the public schools. Teachers, it is said, need to affirm once more the values of freedom and spontaneity, even if these values turn out to be incompatible with the standpoint of the schools.

One consequence of the romantic critique is that for the first time a literary and intellectual audience has been created for literature about education. It is as if there are two disparate universes of discourse: the universe involving professionals and the world created by cultural critics or by young men such as Herbert Kohl, Jonathan Kozol, and James Herndon, who spent relatively brief periods in ghetto schools and made their reputations with reports from the front line. There has been, inevitably, some resentment in educational circles. Robert Havighurst finds false prophets and elitists among the critics of the schools. He writes:

> Free public schooling was invented in democratic countries to give greater opportunity to economically disadvantaged children and adults. It has succeeded in this to some extent, as is proven by the numbers of poor children who have become quite successful workers, citizens, and parents at least partly with the aid of the schools. Of course, no one who dislikes poverty and racial and economic discrimination is satisfied with the degree of opportunity in modern democratic societies. But those who try to work to improve the educational institutions as conveyors of opportunity are on a sounder course, in the judgment of this writer, than those who want to abolish the existing educational institutions.[24]

Charles Silberman communicates a sense of various schoolmen's resentment when he points to the "snobbery" of certain critics and their inability to empathize with the problems of the lower middle-class teacher, "whose passivity and fear of violence they deride as effeminate and whose humanity they seem, at times, almost to deny."

Because of an incipient sympathy with antiestablishment thinking, some teachers have fallen from the ranks to join the campaigns against the schools. Paradoxes have multiplied. Contempt for the heartless, prisonlike educational institutions has intensified with the invention of a distinctive language of student rebellion and a distinctive way of posing challenges to authority. Free schools have been modeled after the free universities which sprang up as part of the campus revolt. Images of A. S. Neill's Summerhill, John Holt's small private schools, the mini-schools described by Paul Goodman, the neighborhood school developed by George Dennison, and the alternative schools set up by youthful communes have made the ordinary public school (with its passes, rules, concrete echoing corridors) look more than ever like jails. Clearinghouses and switchboards offer information and services to those who wish in some manner to escape. Jonathan Kozol, who objects to escape to "pastoral and isolated Free Schools," nevertheless believes that it is necessary to move outside the system if black children are to be effectively taught. The crucial question facing him is spelled out as follows:

> How can the Free School achieve, at one and the same time, a sane, on-going, down-to-earth, skill-oriented, sequential, credentializing and credentialized curricular experience directly geared in to the real survival needs of colonized children in a competitive and technological society; and simultaneously evolve, maintain, nourish, and revivify the "un-credentialized," "un-authorized," "unsanctioned," "non-curricular" consciousness of pain, rage, love and revolution which first infused their school with truth and magic, exhilaration and comradeship.[25]

Questions of guilt and responsibility inevitably are raised for teachers who remain within the public schools. Are they accomplices of an immoral system? Are they, no matter what their motives, caught up in the establishment's grim efforts to process children and turn them into personnel? Are they—consciously or unconsciously—penalizing the divergent pupils in their classrooms, the irritatingly gifted? Are they refusing to see talents in minority children—Mexican-Americans, Puerto Ricans, Blacks? Worst of all, have those in power professionalized them into indifference and inhumanity? Ivan Illich writes: "The modern state has assumed the duty of enforcing the judgment of its educators through well-meant truant officers and job requirements, much as did the Spanish kings who enforced the judgments of their theologians through the Inquisition." Can the teacher avoid being a "theologian" only by departing from the school?

The teacher who takes such onslaughts seriously is almost inevitably thrust into value conflict. Troubled by the inequities of the credentials system, made uneasy about consumerism, uncertain about his ability to overcome the obligatory component in the school, he may well be caught between alternatives. Again, he will have to examine the order of his priorities, make some new decisions about the "reality" presenting itself to him, determine whether—if he continues in his career—he can remain in good faith. If he has never been inclined to think about his actions, the words of Ivan Illich will not trouble him. If he is certain about his intentions, he may be able to fend off the attacks implicit in the anti-institutional debate. But if he has opted for full consciousness, the new wave in the ongoing debate will prompt him to do philosophy with respect to what he cherishes and has long cherished, what he has chosen as his plan for living.

In a sense, certain critiques (warranted or unwarranted) function as do the contemporary arts in challenging customary ways of seeing. The arts, inevitably, have affected concepts of reality, feelings about being alive and pursuing values, even for the teacher who has not kept up with modernism, neomodernism, and the rest. With the collapse of traditional norms and shared preconceptions of many kinds, art forms and the elements of popular culture have become, for numerous people, both the sources and the determinants of what they conceived to be permissible, admirable, even valuable. Because the concept of art has become problematic, however, and because created works are no longer considered representative of an ideal, what Bell calls the "contradictions" in the culture have tended to become intensified. Novelist Saul Bellow talks about the "theory of creative equality [which] implies the death of art" and laments the "ugliness, boredom and spiritual trouble" resulting from the "revolution." Numerous others decry the relaxation of standards, the preoccupation with shock and ecstasy, the obscene or pornographic imagery and language, the assaults on audiences, the mockery of heritage and the past itself. There has been, in Bell's words, a "democratization of art," a "democratization of Dionysus." Part of this democratization has grown from earlier developments: a resurgent interest in childhood and the absurd; a celebration of lower rather than higher impulses; a fascination with hallucination and psychedelic experiences.

> Yet to all this the sensibility of the 60's also added something
> distinctly its own: a concern with violence and cruelty; a
> preoccupation with the sexually perverse; a desire to make noise;
> an anti-cognitive and anti-intellectual mood; an effort once and
> for all to erase the boundary between "art" and "life"; and a
> fusion of art and politics.[26]

The teacher who is fully engaged cannot simply shrink back in disgust or righteousness. For one thing, he has new possibilities of feeling and experience to explore for existential purposes. For another, he is likely to come in touch with young people's sensibilities through his encounters with modern art. The only way he can judge or evaluate new films, novels, plays, and the like is by engaging himself imaginatively, authentically, inwardly with them. The only way he can, in fact, become immediately aware of the new conditions of perception beginning to prevail is by acquainting himself with the forms and styles in art that respond to those conditions.

How else are we to explain the extreme self-consciousness with respect to the process of art making at a time when people are so aware of the arbitrariness of forms, the tension between aesthetic ordering and life? How else are we to explain the expressed "nausea" at the staleness of so much terminology, the meaninglessness of the platitudes with which so many people speak? How else are we to make sense of the spreading recognition that an artist does *not* disclose any ultimate or hidden reality? That, instead, he creates equivalents, analogues, alternate worlds?

Art, as Harold Rosenberg says, is indeed a free act. Including, as it presently does, ready-mades, happenings, optical tricks, comic strips, banal objects, styrofoam squares, as well as cool (inhumanist) representative paintings and abstractions and "minimal" designs, visual art can no longer be classified under ancient rubrics. There is the activity of professional art making; there is the process itself made blandly visible; there is the incessant questioning of art's function in the world, a questioning that involves the wide-awake spectator who is offered new uncertainties along with new visions of a reality never before suspected. The novel as traditionally conceived no longer exists. Supplanted by the "new novel," the "antinovel," the novel of black humor or the grotesque or the absurd, it no longer serves as pseudohistory or as a true rendering of a moment of time. Often ironic and ambiguous, creating intricate and contradictory patterns, it opens windows in the blank walls of the everyday. It offers satisfactions (yes, and terrors) never discovered in ordinary existence. In consequence, for the reader willing to bracket out the stereotypical and the ordinary, it reveals dimensions of consciousness unattainable by reason or common sense. It returns the reader to his original self, to the primordial silences, to his life-world.

To cope with the moral crisis of our time, the teacher must perceive as many facets as he can and see their thematic relevance for his personal life. Although in crisis, the arts may still contribute to the transvaluations taking place. Because they *are* in flux, they may offer unique occasions for the teacher, who is condemned to meaning and compelled to choose. We shall now move on to a philosophic discussion of values, morality, and ethics, which will mean little if abstracted from the contemporary context. They will mean little if the reader—concerned as he must be with teaching, with education—sets aside the problems of this age (or the perplexities we have merely hinted at in this chapter) and treats the discussion as if it were an intellectual game. There is no real escaping.

There are only the possibilities of becoming clear, of making sense, and of choosing authentically, in the name of one's own vitality, one's own commitment to survive.

Notes and References

1. Jean-Paul Sartre, *The Flies,* in *No Exit and Three Other Plays* (New York: Vintage Books, 1949), pp. 121–122.

2. Jean-Francois Revel, *Without Marx or Jesus: The New American Revolution Has Begun,* tr. J. F. Bernard (Garden City, N.Y.: Doubleday & Company, 1971), p. 183.

3. Daniel Bell, "The Cultural Contradictions of Capitalism," *The Public Interest,* no. 21, fall 1970, p. 43.

4. Jacques Barzun, *The House of Intellect* (New York: Harper & Row, Publishers, 1959), p. 89.

5. Michael Harrington, *The Other America: Poverty in the United States* (Baltimore: Penguin Books, 1963), p. 18.

6. Harriette Arnow, *The Dollmaker* (New York: Collier Books, 1961), p. 322.

7. Oscar Lewis, *La Vida: A Puerto Rican Family in the Culture of Poverty—San Juan and New York* (New York: Random House, 1966), p. xliv.

8. Martin Luther King, Jr., "Letter from Birmingham Jail," in *Why We Can't Wait* (New York: Harper & Row, Publishers, 1964), pp. 84–85.

9. Stokely Carmichael, "What We Want," in *The New Student Left,* ed. Mitchell Cohen and Dennis Hale (Boston: Beacon Press, 1967), pp. 117–118.

10. Malcolm X, "To Mississippi Youth," in *The Black American Experience,* ed. Frances S. Freedman (New York: Bantam Books, 1970), p. 260.

11. Margaret Walker, "To My People," in *The Black American Experience,* ed. Frances S. Freedman (New York: Bantam Books, 1970), pp. 271–272.

12. Nikki Giovanni, "Nikki-Rosa," in *The Black American Experience,* ed. Frances S. Freedman (New York: Bantam Books, 1970), p. 230.

13. Claude Brown, "Harlem, My Harlem," in *The Black American Experience,* ed. Frances S. Freedman (New York: Bantam Books, 1970), p. 173.

14. Eldridge Cleaver, "Playboy Interview with Nat Hentoff," in *Eldridge Cleaver: Post-Prison Writings and Speeches,* ed. Robert Sheer (New York: Random House, 1969), p. 179.

15. Tom Wicker, "Death of a Brother," *The New York Times,* August 24, 1971.

16. Preston R. Wilcox, "The Community-Centered School," in *The Schoolhouse in the City,* ed. Alvin Toffler (New York: Frederick A. Praeger, Publishers, 1968), p. 97.

17. Kenneth B. Clark, "Alternatives to Urban Public Schools," in *The Schoolhouse in the City,* ed. Alvin Toffler (New York: Frederick A. Praeger, Publishers, 1968), p. 142.

18. Charles A. Reich, *The Greening of America* (New York: Random House, 1970), p. 226.

19. Margaret Mead, *Culture and Commitment: A Study of the Generation Gap* (New York: Doubleday & Company, 1970), p. 72.

20. Peter de Lissovoy, *Feelgood: A Trip in Time and Out* (Boston: Houghton Mifflin Company, 1970), p. 331.

21. Don McNeill, *Moving Through Here* (New York: Lancer Books, 1970), p. 206.

22. Kenneth Keniston, *Young Radicals: Notes on Committed Youth* (New York: Harcourt Brace Jovanovich, 1968), p. 276.

23. Peter L. Berger and Brigitte Berger, "The Blueing of America," *The New Republic,* April 3, 1971, p. 22.

24. Robert J. Havighurst, "Prophets and Scientists in Education," in *Farewell to Schools?,* ed. Daniel U. Levine and Robert J. Havighurst (Worthington, Ohio: Charles A. Jones Publishing Company, 1971), p. 85.

25. Jonathan Kozol, *Free Schools* (Boston: Houghton Mifflin Company, 1972).

26. Daniel Bell, "Sensibility in the 60's," *Commentary,* June 1971, p. 63.

Further Reading

Saul Bellow, *Mr. Sammler's Planet* (New York: Viking Press, 1969).

Carl Bereiter and Siegfried Engelmann, *Teaching Disadvantaged Children in the Preschool* (Englewood Cliffs, N.J.: Prentice-Hall, 1966).

Raymond E. Callahan, *Education and the Cult of Efficiency* (Chicago: University of Chicago Press, 1964).

James B. Conant, *Thomas Jefferson and the Development of American Public Education* (Berkeley: University of California Press, 1962).

Lawrence A. Cremin, *The Transformation of the School* (New York: Alfred A. Knopf, 1961).

George Dennison, *The Lives of Children* (New York: Random House, 1969).

Erik H. Erikson, *Identity: Youth and Crisis* (New York: W. W. Norton & Company, 1968).

Edgar Z. Friedenberg, *Coming of Age in America* (New York: Random House, 1965).

_____, *The Dignity of Youth & Other Atavisms* (Boston: Beacon Press, 1965).

John W. Gardner, *Excellence* (New York: Harper & Row, Publishers, 1961).

William Glasser, *Schools Without Failure* (New York: Harper & Row, Publishers, 1969).

Paul Goodman, *Growing Up Absurd* (New York: Vintage Books, 1962).

David A. Goslin, *The School in Contemporary Society* (Glenview, Ill.: Scott, Foresman & Company, 1965).

Thomas F. Green, "Schools and Communities: A Look Forward," *Harvard Educational Review,* vol. 39, no. 2, spring 1969.

Charles V. Hamilton, "Race and Education: A Search for Legitimacy," *Harvard Educational Review,* vol. 38, no. 3, fall 1968.

Jules Henry, *Culture Against Man* (New York: Random House, 1963).

_____, *Jules Henry On Education* (New York: Vintage Books, 1972).

James Herndon, *The Way It Spozed To Be* (New York: Bantam Books, 1969).

John Hersey, *The Child Buyer* (New York: Bantam Books, 1961).

Richard Hofstadter, *Anti-Intellectualism in American Life* (New York: Alfred A. Knopf, 1963).

John Holt, *The Underachieving School* (New York: Pitman Publishing Company, 1969).

Ivan Illich, *Deschooling Society* (New York: Harper & Row, Publishers, 1971).

Seymour W. Itzkoff, *Cultural Pluralism and American Education* (Scranton, Pa.: International Textbook Company, 1969).

Thomas Kahn, "The Political Significance of the Freedom Rides," in *The New Student Left,* ed. Mitchell Cohen and Dennis Hale (Boston: Beacon Press, 1967).

Martin Luther King, Jr., "I Have a Dream," in *The Black American Experience,* ed. Frances S. Freedman (New York: Bantam Books, 1970).

Herbert Kohl, *36 Children* (New York: New American Library, 1967).

Jonathan Kozol, *Death at an Early Age* (Boston: Houghton Mifflin Company, 1967).

Horace Mann, "First Annual Report" (1837) and "Ninth Annual Report" (1845), in *The Republic and the School: Horace Mann on the Education of Free Men,* ed. Lawrence A. Cremin (New York: Bureau of Publications, Teachers College, Columbia University, 1959).

Peter Marin and Allan Y. Cohen, *Understanding Drug Use: An Adult's Guide to Drugs and the Young* (New York: Harper & Row, Publishers, 1971).

Ralph Barton Perry, "Education and the Science of Education," in *Philosophy and Education,* ed. Israel Scheffler (Boston: Allyn & Bacon, 1966), pp. 17–38.

David Riesman, *Constraint and Variety in American Education* (Garden City, N.Y.: Doubleday Anchor Books, 1958).

Frank Riessman, *The Culturally Deprived Child* (New York: Harper & Row, Publishers, 1962).

Theodore Roszak, *The Making of a Counter Culture: Reflections on the Technocratic Society and Its Useful Opposition* (Garden City, N.Y.: Doubleday Anchor Books, 1969).

J. D. Salinger, *The Catcher in the Rye* (New York: Grosset & Dunlap, 1951).

Peter Schrag, "Growing Up on Mechanic Street," *Saturday Review,* March 21, 1970, pp. 59–61, 78–79.

Charles E. Silberman, *Crisis in Black and White* (New York: Random House, 1964).

————, *Crisis in the Classroom* (New York: Random House, 1970).

Elizabeth Sutherland, ed., *Letters from Mississippi* (New York: McGraw-Hill Book Company, 1965).

Henry David Thoreau, "Civil Disobedience," in *The American Tradition in Literature,* vol. 1, ed. Sculley Bradley, Richmond Croom Beatty, E. Hudson Long (New York: W. W. Norton & Company, 1956), pp. 966–985.

William H. Whyte, Jr., *The Organization Man* (Garden City, N.Y.: Doubleday Anchor Books, 1957).

Robert Paul Wolff, *The Ideal of the University* (Boston: Beacon Press, 1969).

Chapter Nine

Choosing the Right

Many complain that the words of the wise are always merely parables and of no use in daily life, which is the only life we have. When the sage says: "Go over," he does not mean that we should cross to some actual place, which we could do anyhow if the labour were worth it; he means some fabulous yonder, something unknown to us, something too that he cannot designate more precisely, and therefore cannot help us here in the very least. All these parables really set out to say merely that the incomprehensible is incomprehensible, and we know that it is already. But the cares we have to struggle with every day: that is a different matter.

> Franz Kafka
> "On Parables," *The Great Wall of China*

What they undertook to do
They brought to pass;
All things hang like a drop of dew
Upon a blade of grass.

> William Butler Yeats
> "Gratitude to the Unknown Instructors"
> *The Collected Poems*

Up to now we have been engaging in a type of descriptive inquiry concerning moral phenomena. That is, we have been surveying various areas of experience where choices and decisions have been and are being made, where significant human interests are involved. Although we have highlighted a number of conflicts and uncertainties, we have not confronted the question of how people *know* what is right. Nor have we seriously asked ourselves what *ought* to be done in such specifically problematic cases as those involving black children, student rebels, and opponents of the schools. We have not asked ourselves what we *ought* to teach our students at a time of such dizzying change and fundamental doubt. We have not asked how our preferences are to be grounded, our choices justified; we have not looked at the problem of deciding among competing alternatives. In this chapter and the following one, we shall face such issues by engaging in normative thinking in the realms of ethics and morality.

The term *morality* refers to far more than the mores, rules, codes, and laws of society. Whenever they make choices with values and preferences in mind, people are engaging in moral behavior. *Moral,* therefore, applies to many kinds of valuing, to judgments of good and bad, right and wrong; and to the relationships between those judgments and the actions of men and women. Contrary to the way most laymen use the term, *moral* is not here equated with law-abiding, compliant, virtuous, or good. Its opposite is not what is generally taken to be immoral, unless immoral is understood to mean being totally indifferent, irresponsible, uninvolved. The opposite of moral, more accurately, is *nonmoral,* meaning the kind of behavior that demands no conscious choosing, that is wholly automatic, determined, coerced, or routine.

Moral choices are free choices, made by individuals who are aware of options, who *think* more than one possible action exists at a particular moment of stress and unease. The mother who reflexively puts her hand out to prevent her child from falling off the car seat when she stops short cannot be considered to be behaving morally, even though her action is motherly and right. A character like Frank Norris's McTeague, in the novel *McTeague,* who is determined by his heritage, cannot be called immoral or necessarily culpable when he performs violent acts under the influence of alcohol. The person who is abruptly told to demand money from a bank teller and feels a gun pressing against his back cannot be condemned as a thief. The teacher who routinely reads the attendance sheet, collects the milk money, shuffles messages from the principal's office, no matter what the degree of morning tension in his classroom, may be called ineffectual but not wicked or bad. When we discuss morality or moral action, we are presuming not only a degree of autonomy but a degree of awareness. We are taking for granted that some reference is being made (even if vaguely) to values and that the atmosphere allows at least a minimal amount of freedom. We are also taking for granted that the individual who makes a decision, no matter how conventional or prudential, knows on some level that he must make that decision and that what he decides depends on who he is and what he believes.

The individual, however, never makes his choices *in vacuo.* There is always a context: a network of socially acknowledged rules and codes; a more or less coherent structure of moral beliefs; a community, a church, a business organization, a school. In addition, there is the individual's personal history, with all the choices he has previously made, the experiences he has had, the bonds that link him to other human beings, his place or role in the world. It is often said that every man or woman, rather than being "cast into the world," as if he were on a desert island, is born *into* a moral institution. This is the system of rules and regulations, the customs that have developed over the generations, the traditions that characterize his community. The community may be a *shtetl* in old Russia or Poland; it may be a "little Italy" in a large American city; it may be a small New England town or a southern village; it may simply be an extended family with its inherited notions of what is acceptable, decent, right. A child is expected to internalize a range of regulations and rules, which help him to become "human" in the manner those responsible for rearing him recognize. He may be told that if he knows "what is good for him," he will do what is expected of him habitually, automatically, without questioning.

Stable, moderately homogeneous communities are much like families in their approach to standards and rules. The members of such communities tend to govern their desires and interests realistically. They function, without profound thought, according to general expectations of them. Their guiding principle is prudence; they act safely, with their well-being and comfort in mind. This does not, of course, exclude deviance or unacceptable, even "wicked," behavior; members of even the strictest communities are fallible. However, people who commit adultery, for example, or steal or get drunk in tradition-governed communities tend to recognize that they are indeed doing wrong. They do not question the existing moral institution, nor do they ordinarily try to change it. For a variety of reasons, they simply cannot "toe the line."

Others, of course, appear to conform while questioning the prevailing code from another internalized point of view. A corporation executive may be inwardly sceptical of the rat race and the motivations built into it; but he may nevertheless function prudentially, playing the game according to the rules. A teacher in a conservative community may, because of his education, be committed to progressive methodologies. Still, he may prudentially become a rigorous disciplinarian to please the school board and retain his job. These individuals differ from offending citizens: the executive and the teacher disagree with community norms even while they comply with them. The adulterer, the thief, and the alcoholic do not comply; but they take for granted that they, not the community codes, are wrong.

Again, all this assumes the existence of a stable, traditionbound community like those in nineteenth and early twentieth century Europe and the United States. Many discontented persons, many rebels abandoned such places: they ran off to sea; they moved off toward some "golden gate"; they went to seek their fortunes in the cities. American literature is replete with accounts of individuals unable or unwilling to abide by existing norms: Nathaniel Hawthorne's Hester Prynne in *The Scarlet Letter;* Mark Twain's Huckleberry Finn; Ernest Hemingway's Nick Henry, who made a "separate peace." The society each one defied or abandoned, however, was stable, relatively unshaken by moral crisis. Hester Prynne's adultery and intellectual emancipation apparently altered nothing in the rigid theocracy at Massachusetts Bay. Huck Finn's plunge toward freedom had no effect on the slave morality of the village he was leaving behind. Lieutenant Henry's desertion from the retreating Italian army did not prompt anyone to reform that army or to examine the values that resulted in so many inequitable deaths. When the standards governing behavior are generally perceived as unshakable "givens," individual refusals (although more interesting to talk and write about than ordinary compliances) can be absorbed or set aside. Looked at retrospectively at later periods in history, these refusals may appear prophetic; but relatively few rebels are ethical heroes or teachers, as Jesus and Socrates were. And, when such heroes appear, they are often punished for their public criticisms of what others take for granted. In a rigid or defensive or authoritarian society, the active gadfly cannot be tolerated. Socrates, in Plato's *Apology,* explains at his trial:

> For if you kill me you will not easily find another like me,
> who, if I may use such a ludicrous figure of speech, am a sort of
> gadfly, given to the state by the God; and the state is like a
> great and noble steed who is tardy in his motions owing to his
> very size, and requires to be stirred into life. I am that gadfly
> which God has given the state, and all day long and in all
> places am always fastening upon you, arousing and persuading
> and reproaching you.[1]

Society cannot accept such an explanation. On the other hand, if Socrates had kept his disagreements to himself and stayed at home with his talkative wife, or if he had simply decided to leave Athens for a society he thought more likely to regard virtue, life might have proceeded more or less peacefully. The state in its fallibility, with the inevitable unrighteousness and wrong characterizing many of its practices, was structured and stable enough to survive. Suspecting that the moral institution he had challenged would persist, Socrates, feels that he should ask a favor of his judges when he concludes his *apologia:*

> When my sons are grown up, I would ask you, O my
> friends, to punish them; and I would have you trouble them, as

I have troubled you, if they seem to care about riches, or
anything, more than virtue; or if they pretend to be something
when they are really nothing,—then reprove them, as I have
reproved you, for not caring about that for which they ought to
care, and thinking that they are something when they are really
nothing.[2]

The implication is that his sons, like most Athenians, are all too likely to
behave prudentially, to conform to conventional values without thinking
about their actions. For such people, the freedoms granted are relatively
limited, as Socrates well knew. The trouble is that, unless reproved,
individuals who willingly accede to what is taken officially to be correct
and right may never recognize how limited their freedom is. Feeling
perfectly autonomous and free, they go on making moral decisions on the
basis of values they consider unarguable or in accord with a conscience
that has internalized conventional wisdom about virtuousness and freedom.

Such people often have a strong sense of obligation; they fully
understand what *ought* means, even when they break laws. More than
likely, they reflect little on the reasons for their decisions; they may
function as good citizens—or bad citizens—with the same moral certainty.
(Why else would a thief or an adulterer feel guilty? It is unimaginable, in a
traditional society, for a thief to justify his actions as Jean Genêt now
justifies his crimes; for someone to defend violating and raping women, as
Eldridge Cleaver attempts to do; for people to affirm the right to commit
adultery, as so many others do today.) But the guilt, the certainties, the
lack of reflectiveness are all functions of continuing stability. They signify
the persistence of integrated norms. Under such conditions, people are not
aware—or choose not to be aware—that certain principles by which they
say they live are in conflict. For example, individualism in America has
often existed in a contradictory relationship to cooperation or togetherness:
professed beliefs are continually coupled with an acceptance of
coerciveness. Independence is presumably valued; but dependence and
respect are fostered without much recognition of contradiction. Individuals
who simply acquiesce or conform prudentially are unacquainted with or
prefer not to acknowledge the existence of alternative sets of sanctions,
standards, life styles, patterns of value, each with an integrity. In many
ways, these individuals are innocent; they are like the "bachelors" Herman
Melville wrote about so often: people who refuse to face ambiguity and
paradox, who live by fixed constructs that permit them to select out what
supports their beliefs. Many philosophers would say that these persons
behave as moral beings because they are so minimally conscious of the
judgments they make and the sanctions they use. Yet these individuals do
make decisions day by day; they do have certain feelings about rules and
ideals; and, especially when their commitments or their faiths are being

threatened (by hippies, for instance, by pornographers, by radical students), they are perfectly capable of articulating coherent and shared points of view.

The difficulty is that life has not supported the illusion of one standard of morality or the illusion of social stasis. Change, particularly in the United States, has advanced too rapidly, too ruthlessly. We have spoken on several occasions of the impact of technology on the lives of individuals, of the urbanization of America, of the rise of the corporate state. Repeatedly, in the last half century, mill towns and fishing villages and county seats have lost their economic or social underpinnings. Like Edwin Arlington Robinson's "Tilbury Town," they have frequently been abandoned by those who once worked there, made or lost money there, raised families, cheated their neighbors, aided the sick, got drunk like Miniver Cheevy "who sighed for what was not. ... " The few survivors are like Eben Flood, singing "Auld Lang Syne" to himself at night, because "there was nothing in the town below—/ Where strangers would have shut the many doors/ That many friends had opened long ago."[3] If the old towns have remained in existence, their mood may well be like that Robert Lowell communicates in "For the Union Dead":

> The old South Boston Aquarium stands
> in a Sahara of snow now. Its broken windows are boarded.
> The bronze weathervane cod has lost half its scales.
> The airy tanks are dry.[4]

The codes developed over time may seem as dry and empty as those tanks when the familiar landmarks and benchmarks are gone. New problems, never anticipated, arise. Values and expectations are beyond the compass of many individuals who thought they could forever conserve. Lowell writes, in the same poem:

> The ditch is nearer.
> There are no statues for the last war here;
> on Boylston Street, a commercial photograph
> shows Hiroshima boiling
>
> over a Mosler Safe, the "Rock of Ages"
> that survived the blast. Space is nearer.
> When I crouch to my television set,
> the drained faces of Negro school-children rise
> like balloons.[5]

The apocalyptic horror, the dominance of big business, the great outreach of science, the simultaneity of events made possible by the media, the inequities suddenly made visible: those few lines suggest once more the revolutionary nature of cultural change.

Many people have been forced to leave their familiar places, as so many immigrants and in-migrants have done. The rural islanders now in the cities, the black sharecroppers from the south, the Mexican-Americans in the west and southwest—all have obviously been compelled to find their way in a world of unfamiliar preferences. But they are not the only dislocated ones. As we have seen, all sorts of people—old and young, eastern liberal and middle American, Catholic and Jewish, black and white, union member and civil service worker—have been experiencing the disintegration of familiar norms. Principles that always seemed self-evident are being questioned; practices that always seemed unquestionably praiseworthy are being scorned; persons who always seemed deserving of admiration and respect are being attacked. New models, new ego ideals are being defined. We need only recall the challenges to the values associated with hard work, efficiency, and success; the altered attitudes toward sexual practices, family arrangements, parenthood; the skepticism about law, consumer goods, democratic representation, authorities. There is even a fundamental disbelief regarding values. Some individuals claim that the promises and contracts, which so many feel are the cement of society, are merely ceremonial, meaningless. Others assert that we have moved beyond morality, that the sanctions of the past are seldom regarded. With no sense of structure surrounding them, people are prone to act according to impulse or feeling and set judgment and appraisal aside. Nevertheless, all around, individuals can be seen groping for standards, trying to resolve value conflicts or to integrate discordant beliefs. Every day allegiances are affirmed and reaffirmed; hypocrisies are challenged; injustices and inequalities are condemned. Civil disobedience and "divine dissent" are pondered with increasing seriousness. Questions of guilt and responsibility are passionately discussed; indifference is castigated; people are enjoined to put themselves on the line.

When there is such a moral stirring, when there is so little general agreement on good and right, the time has come for the doing of moral philosophy. This means an examination of the lives we lead, an intensified consciousness of the choices we make. It means a thoughtful consideration of existing codes and values, dissident as well as conventional ones. It means critical thinking about the principles by which we try to live and our reasons for performing particular acts. It means a confrontation of the old and troubling questions: What is good? What is just? On what grounds do I make my choices? How do I decide what is morally right for others to do—for my students to do, for me to do? According to what principles do I judge it wrong to break promises, to defy the law, to take drugs, to act unfairly? To what degree am I responsible for my actions, for others' actions—for public policy? On what grounds can I hold others responsible —for wartime massacres, for repression, for poverty, for the commission of crimes? How do I justify teaching certain subject matter? On what grounds do I term mathematics or history valuable? How do I defend my preference for Beethoven over Bob Dylan, or for Dylan over Beethoven? How, in fact, can I justify "improving" anyone's taste, intervening in anyone's life? What, after all, constitutes a good reason for any moral decision—evading the draft, breaking up a marriage, supporting a strike or a moratorium, contributing to a cause? What does conscience signify? Standard, principle, norm?

Such questions involve us in ethical thinking, the aim of which is to become clearer about what is involved in moral decisions, to come closer to being free and autonomous beings in charge of our lives. As people concerned with education, we are inescapably caught up in pursuit of the worthwhile. Yet we can no longer determine what is worthwhile by consulting an authority or the community or some nebulous public philosophy. We can easily say that we are assigned to teach our students to learn how to think intelligently and critically, to realize their potential, to appreciate everwidening areas of experience. We can easily say that we want to help students develop desirable states of mind. But everyone who teaches knows that such general declarations have little meaning in the day-to-day life of the classroom. The teacher is concerned with specific actions, concrete decisions. Functioning intentionally with particular children in particular situations, he has to decide what to do to focus on worthwhile achievement. He has to decide how to communicate the idea that respect for evidence, clarity, and "elegance" *matters*. He has to choose, in individual cases, whether to permit free, creative activity in place of required tasks; he has to decide whether to nurture sensitivity at certain points instead of encouraging cognitive action. There is the question of how much he should allow for personal idiosyncrasy, or how he should adjust the demands of the clock or the schedule to the rhythms of a child's inner time. There are the multiple small uncertainties about whom to call on, whom to discipline, whom to reward. There are the appraisals, the evaluations, the consultations. And, if he is thinking about his actions, the teacher needs to justify his procedures, to give reasons for his decisions and recommendations, to persuade others that he is making sense, that he is "right."

Doing philosophy, the teacher must turn to the range of standards people have used to govern their choices, to the theories of obligation devised in response to the question of what is right. There are several theories, each one in some manner connected to a world view or a philosophical position, each one requiring a particular orientation, a way of feeling like a free moral agent in a perplexing, not always supportive, world. These theories are not to be confused with psychological descriptions of how people actually make moral judgments at different stages of their lives, although certain theories of justification do (as they must) take judgment into account. Nor are these theories to be confused with prescriptive statements, informing the teacher how he ought to approach the present-day moral perplexities of his profession. As we have repeatedly said, the teacher must become more highly conscious, more critical and clear. He cannot expect a study of ethical theories to provide answers to the moral questions raised within teaching situations. If this were so, the profession of teaching would depend largely on the profession of ethical philosophy. "Educationists," says Kingsley Price, "need not receive their values from philosophers. They have the alternative of being philosophers themselves."[6] Involved individuals have to make the moral choices, which are ordinarily specific. The more sensitive teachers are to the demands of the process of justification, the more explicit they are about the norms that govern their actions, the more personally engaged they are in assessing surrounding circumstances and potential consequences, the more "ethical" they will be; and we cannot ask much more.

Returning, then, to our inquiry into "oughtness" and the meaning of "good," we shall begin with one of the oldest responses to problems of justifying moral decisions. Some have described this response as "intuitionism" because it presumes an ability to intuit or to know immediately a preexistent "good." Others have described it as "deontological" because it assumes that the rightness of human actions is determined not by their accomplishments but by the degree to which they are in accord with a preexistent principle or rule. John Dewey saw this response as an aspect of the search for the immutable, of man's unending quest for certainty. It is, of course, closely allied to a number of religious approaches to obligation and justification; and, for that reason, it will sound familiar to certain readers at the start. In a sense, it seems to be an element of some original awareness, as if it underlies the sediments of meaning built up as a person matures. The sources are actually in classical philosophy, in such orientations as Socrates' to the ideally Good and the eternally True. There is, even today, an enormous appeal in the metaphor of an ascent toward the radiance in which Goodness is revealed. There is another type of appeal in Plato's conception of justice, which he defines in such a way as to make available a firm standard, a rational norm so that a rational man can appraise what is happening in his world, chart a life career and be assured that the path he has chosen is right. In the *Laws,* Plato stresses the necessity for men to hold a conception of excellence or *arête,* an ideal of character, because the goods men seek (health, strength, beauty, riches, and the like) must be subordinated to the "divine goods," which are the virtues of the soul: justice, self-control, piety, and courage. If the divine goods are properly cherished and harmonized, virtue or righteousness will appear of its own accord; but a fixed ideal is always required to keep drawing men's eyes to the Good. In the *Laws,* Plato began identifying the prototypical Good with a divine principle, with God —called the teacher of the world. Full knowledge of the unity of all good and of values in their harmony became equivalent to knowledge of God, an invisible force and supreme, the overarching Idea.

There are obvious differences between a *knowledge* of God as a divine principle and a submission to the will of God as revealed in sacred writs or embodied in a church. Nevertheless, for all the differences, the classical and religious approaches are alike in positing the existence of an essence, a quality, or a relation recognized as "goodness." They are also alike in their assumption of an eternal order in which values inhere like fixed stars. The order is conceived to be harmonious, characterized by recurrences somehow knowable to the rational human being capable of profound intuitions. Such persons are intimately aware of (or say they "know") "good" or "right." They can grasp, they can "see" the invisible quality that makes a particular action good or just or equitable. They can recognize the rightness of a principle or rule with a confidence similar to the way they would feel when faced with a mathematical proof. Certain principles, in fact, appear as self-evident to them as did the axioms with which scholars used to think mathematics began. From St. Thomas Aquinas, with his view of the will *necessarily* tending to the good, to René Descartes with his conception of clear and distinct ideas, to John Locke with his conviction that human beings are endowed by their Creator with unalienable rights to "life, liberty, and property," thoughtful men have articulated the certainty of moral knowledge. As we have seen, the mission of the American common school was defined with just such certainty. Horace Mann wrote:

> I believe in the existence of a great, immutable principle of natural law, or natural ethics—a principle antecedent to all human institutions and incapable of being abrogated by any ordinances of man—a principle of divine origin, clearly legible in the ways of Providence as those ways are manifested in the order of nature and in the history of the race,—which proves the *absolute right* of every human being that comes into the world to an education; and which, of course, proves the correlative duty of every government to see that the means of that education are provided for all.[7]

With the present impossibility of proving the rights of man or the existence of antecedent principles, why are so many people drawn to this approach to morality? Even though they may grant it to be inscrutable, unnameable, why do they turn so readily toward an a priori when asked to define the good? ("Can this be innate knowledge?" asks Samuel Beckett's narrator in *The Unnamable.* "Like that of good and evil. This seems improbable to me."[8]) Many people, obviously, are desperately in need of certainty, of what Camus calls a "point d'appui."[9] In the midst of flux and confusion, they seek structures and recurrences. As Dostoevsky's Grand Inquisitor knew so well, many would be willing to sacrifice freedom for the security of belief. In the famous chapter "Pro and Contra," in *The Brothers Karamazov,* the Inquisitor addresses himself to Jesus, who has returned to earth in human form on the day of an *auto-da-fé:*

> "Without a stable conception of the object of life, man would
> not consent to go on living, and would rather destroy himself
> than remain on earth, though he had bread in abundance. That
> is true. But what happened? Instead of taking men's freedom
> from them, Thou didst make it greater than ever! Didst Thou
> forget that man prefers peace, and even death, to freedom of
> choice in the knowledge of good and evil? Nothing is more
> seductive for man than his freedom of conscience, but nothing is
> a greater cause of suffering. And, behold, instead of giving a
> firm foundation for setting the conscience of man at rest forever,
> Thou didst choose all that is exceptional, vague and enigmatic!
> They didst choose what was utterly beyond the strength of men,
> acting as thou Thou didst not love them at all."[10]

Jesus offered men parables and riddles rather than Truth. Leaving them open questions instead of final answers, he condemned them, many felt, to a dreadful freedom. They wanted happiness and comfort more than freedom; they wanted to believe in something, together with other men, not inwardly and in solitude. This accounts for the great effectiveness of the Catholic Church and other institutions that bring men together to worship communally, to be told what is good and what is right.

Dostoevsky's fable highlights the place of inertia and dread in a manner relevant to teachers, especially those attempting to free young people to choose. Not only are we made to confront the risks that must be taken if moral autonomy is to be attained, we are made to realize that knowledge of good and evil must be achieved personally, apart from and sometimes in rebellion against the crowd. If such knowledge is immediate and intuitive, it is extremely difficult to share. It does not lend itself to recommendation or prescription; it is often incommunicable. A peculiar sort of courage and self-confidence is required of those willing to claim such awareness; it is seldom found among "ordinary" people. Individuals who do know in this fashion, who listen to what Socrates called the "daimon" within, are ethical heroes; and there have been few of them in history. However, men who call themselves resisters today exemplify elements of this approach: The Berrigan brothers; the quiet, often nameless persons who destroy draft records and remove FBI files; the raging, violent Weathermen. On occasion, Daniel Berrigan has presented himself as having the ability to grasp or to "see" the truly good. His vision, his witness has been called "pure, strong and occasionally distracted"; and numerous people, even though they are not rationally persuaded that he is right, have felt strangely guilty because they are not able to do what he has done. Psychiatrist Robert Coles, troubled by the apparent arbitrariness of his choices and by the logical resemblance between his claims and those of both the Weathermen and the Ku Klux Klan, asked Berrigan to try to justify some of his actions in the "underground." Berrigan replied that America's governmental institutions no longer had the authority to decide for the American people because of the crimes for which they were responsible, especially in Vietnam. When asked who did have the authority, he said, "we . . . that small and assailed and powerless group of people who are nonviolent in principle and who are willing to suffer for our beliefs. . . . " And later he added:

> My point is a very simple one: that we as active and concerned individuals are historically valid and useful for the future only in proportion as our lives are tasting some of the powerlessness which is the alternative to the wrong use of power today; and that's where I am.[11]

He was "at the edge," he admitted; his position was not a traditionally religious one. He explained that today "the important questions have an extraordinarily secularized kind of context. So I find myself at the side of the prophets or the martyrs, in however absurd and inferior a way, and I find no break with their tradition in what I am trying to stand for." And what does he stand for? For raising questions about inhumanity and about the ways men ought to live. He *acted* on this belief by burning draft records and fleeing (or going underground) to avoid imprisonment. At his trial, he talked much about moral passion. He told the judge: "It is our soul that brought us here, it is our soul that got us into trouble. It is our conception of man." He may have felt that he was acting in the true Jesuit tradition or in terms of the Word; but more likely, he was motivated by some intuition of the "good," a good irreducible to anything else. He certainly did not identify the "good" with the pouring of blood or the burning of papers, with self-sacrifice, or even with "tasting some of the powerlessness." He made no recommendations to others, told no one else that it would be "good" to do what he had done. He gave the impression that he did not feel required to explain logically why he was so desperately intent on doing what he *knew* was good. He may have felt that from the goodness he somehow "saw," if at all possible, he ought to bring it into being.

Berrigan's position, like that of many other draft resisters, raises troubling questions about the "good" and has, indeed, prompted many people to wonder whether "good" actually was some quality or unique characteristic or property different from anything in the natural world. Wondering in this fashion, they have returned to the position taken by British philosopher G. E. Moore, who came to believe that in the last analysis, the "good" was a nonnatural quality, fundamentally indefinable. Moore arrived at his intuitionist position after a serious attempt to develop a scientific approach to ethics. He tried to discover, among the diverse things and experiences human beings have called "good" or "desirable," some objective, common characteristic by which men could know what things and experiences are *truly* good. He found soon enough that moral concepts could not be defined empirically and that "good" could not be equated with any natural characteristic. In other words, "good" could not be defined in nonethical terms as, say, something desired or desirable, something considered conducive to future happiness or harmony. Those persons who did try to define ethical terms were, he said, guilty of a "naturalistic fallacy."[12] They were confusing the problem of the meaning of "good" with questions as to things which were in fact good. People might talk at length about such things, about peace and love and fulfillment; but no matter how long they talked, they would not have defined "good." The question would have to remain eternally open if "good" were acknowledged to be a nonnatural quality. In spirit, of course, Moore—an apostle of common sense—was different from someone like Berrigan; and, in explaining his actions, Berrigan would surely not refer to Moore. Nevertheless, the intuitionist mode of conceiving the "good" as nonnatural is both dramatized and clarified by individuals who perform acts for which they do not argue logically, acts which realize what they believe is "good."

Closely akin to this way of grasping goodness is the dependence on self-evident principle. The intuitionist does not logically derive the moral principles on which he acts from psychological statements or propositions about the universe. Just as he asserts that certain things or actions are self-evidently good, so he will say that certain arrangements or relations among human beings are self-evidently right. Unquestionably, he will assert that it is categorically right to keep a promise and wrong to break one. It is right to deal justly with one's neighbors, to avoid demeaning people or hurting them unnecessarily, to tell the truth. Can his claims to self-evidence be defended? At one time, moral knowledge seemed to many philosophers to be modeled after mathematical knowledge, which supposedly mirrored the structures of the world. Because mathematical knowledge was presumably derived from a few self-evident axioms, it seemed reasonable to believe that equally self-evident moral axioms mirrored certain objectively existent laws, which, behind the appearances of things, controlled and ordered the universe. Today, however, mathematical axioms are no longer considered self-evident. They are not founded, as Plato thought they were, in a recollection or intuitive apprehension of preexistent Forms; nor do they mirror the "really real." To discover the extent to which these axioms do fit physical reality, or account for events in the cosmos, scientists must deduce from them statements as to their implications or consequences; and these statements must, in turn, be experimentally confirmed. The mathematical model, therefore, no longer serves to build ethical systems on self-evident premises. Nevertheless, many people still cling to the notions that at least some moral principles are unarguable, that these principles need neither rational justification nor empirical confirmation.

This notion is commonly supported by the *feelings* individuals have about what is right and their strong convictions about certain ideas. We need only recall some of the responses to incidents on college campuses and in classrooms at the heyday of youthful revolt. Disruptions, obscenities, "trashing," vandalism seemed, at least at the start, categorically and unarguably wrong. They would not have seemed so if officials and faculty members did not believe that certain modes of behavior, gestures of respect, and ways of using language were self-evidently right. When students appeared on some campuses with guns in their hands, the official condemnations did not stress the illegality or the destructive consequences of the students' actions so much as the unthinkable departure from the norm. Who does *not* believe that it is absolutely wrong for young men to parade around a campus carrying guns? For people to take hostages? For students to run nude down college corridors? For kazoos to be played while a professor is lecturing? For property to be gratuitously destroyed? A. C. Ewing has written:

> It is a well-known fact that propositions, particularly in ethics,
> but also in other fields of thought, sometimes present themselves

> to a person in such a way that without having even in his own
> opinion established them by empirical observation or by
> argument he seems to himself to see them directly and clearly to
> be true. This is often expressed by saying that he has or at least
> seems to himself to have an *intuition* of their truth. It might be
> expressed without using the term *intuition* by saying simply that
> he knows or rationally believes them to be true without having
> any reasons or at least seems to himself to do so.[13]

In his book on the artist and criminal Jean Genêt, Jean-Paul Sartre
presents an interesting test for persons who doubt the potency of such
intuitions. A foundling child, Genêt stole money from his adoptive parents
and then chose himself to be a thief.

> In short, Genêt wants both to make himself evil because he
> does Evil and to do Evil because he is evil. This contradictory
> attitude is obviously the effect of his pride. People heap abuse
> upon him because he has stolen and because he is bad. He
> replies, "Yes, I'm bad and proud of it," and at the same time,
> "Yes, I've stolen. And I'll steal again."[14]

The teacher, confronted with a child already on the verge of becoming a
lifelong hoodlum, would indeed believe that stealing is categorically wrong.
Because the thief is a *child,* the teacher may find it intolerable to believe
he is proud of stealing and intends to go on committing thefts. Sartre,
anticipating his readers' reaction, entitles a concluding chapter "Please Use
Genêt Properly." "Let him cheat," Sartre writes, "above all, do not defend
yourself by adopting attitudes: you have nothing to gain by putting
yourself in a state of Christian charity, by loving him in advance and by
accepting the pus of his books with the abnegation of the Saint who kisses
the leper's lips."[15] The teacher, shocked though he might be, would
certainly understand what Sartre had in mind. He would probably refer
back to a variety of things he has taken for granted: a child will only say
he wants to be wicked if he is "sick," if he is hopelessly "deprived"; a
teacher should, on all occasions, offer charity and love; a person who is
fully human *must* feel guilty that he has stolen. Without sufficient reason,
the teacher most probably has an *intuition* that a child cannot possibly be
like young Jean Genêt. Certain phenomena are not simply absolutely
wrong; they are unthinkable.

Let us consider another case, from Eldridge Cleaver's *Soul on Ice.*
Cleaver had been in prison for some years when he began writing about

his experiences in the outside world. He neither denies nor apologizes for his crimes.

> I'm perfectly aware that I'm in prison, that I'm a Negro, that I've been a rapist, and that I have a Higher Uneducation. I never know what significance I'm supposed to attach to these factors. But I have a suspicion that, because of these aspects of my character, "free-normal-educated" people rather expect me to be more reserved, penitent, remorseful, and not too quick to shoot off my mouth on certain subjects. But I let them down, disappoint them, make them gape at me in a sort of stupor, as if they're thinking: "You've got your nerve! Don't you realize that you owe a debt to society?" My answer to all such thoughts lurking in their split-level heads, crouching behind their squinting bombardier eyes, is that the blood of Vietnamese peasants has paid off all my debts; that the Vietnamese people, afflicted with a rampant disease called Yankees, through their sufferings—as opposed to the "frustration" of fat-assed American geeks safe at home worrying over whether to have bacon, ham, or sausage with their grade-A eggs in the morning, while Vietnamese worry each morning whether the Yankees will gas them, burn them up, or blow away their humble pads in a hail of bombs—have canceled all my IOUs.[16]

Although such talk can be set aside as emotive or metaphorical, it should not be ignored. If it is taken seriously (as many critics and reviewers have taken it), the message Cleaver delivers may be resisted with the full force of what is thought to be self-evidently right. First, people do indeed assume that a criminal should be penitent and remorseful, no matter what society has done to him; and this assumption carries over to the classroom, where teachers are faced with discipline problems or "bad actors" or delinquent incorrigibles. Second, people generally assume that an individual who has done something unquestionably wrong should admit responsibility and in some manner compensate. Cleaver's use of the sins Americans committed in Vietnam as exoneration for his crimes is logically indefensible on many grounds; but many people are likely to respond intuitively: "You *can't!* No one is permitted to talk that way!" Again, something self-evident seems to have been affronted; and exploration of such a response is useful to determine the real meaning of self-evidence.

Convictions and strong feelings about a proposition do not determine its truth. Nor can a mere claim of self-evidence. Moral statements (murder is wrong; a criminal should feel remorse; private property should be respected; promises should be kept) *seem* true and self-justifying a great deal of the time. However, a belief in their self-evidence depends on a belief in some external order in which certain relations are good in and of themselves, in which certain nonnatural, indefinable properties exist. We cannot empirically demonstrate the existence of such a harmonious order above or surrounding the earth. The best we can do when we speak of moral principles as self-evident is to talk consciously in terms of fictions, in terms of a vast "as if."

Another objection to intuitionism is its arbitrariness. Once we call a particular principle self-evident, we stop seeking reasons to support it. Returning to the question of campus revolt, we may recall the intensity of the faculty members' conviction that students had no right to demonstrate without permission, to disrupt, to take over buildings. The rituals and privileges of academic life seemed "given"; the highmindedness of the university (its devotion to truth, its academic freedoms, and the rest) appeared to be absolute. But the students—impolitely, militantly, sometimes obscenely—demanded reasons. They forced their professors to argue in defense of their privileges, to justify the special status of the university. At the present time, response to student disruption is likely to be different. Faculty members certainly resist disturbance and penalize those responsible for it. But their claims are not nearly so arbitrary, because they realize that the principles they once used to ground their judgments were not self-evident. The principles had been defined in a long course of thinking and argument characterizing the life of the university; and the obligation of those who defended these assumptions now seems to be to articulate relevant arguments, to provide reasons for their beliefs.

Arbitrariness can be extremely dangerous in a purportedly free society. Some teachers still consider that a classroom made up of black and Puerto Rican children should be handled entirely differently from one made up of white middle-class children. They speak, therefore, with great assurance about the need to maintain order above all else, about the impossibility of teaching subject matter in any responsible way. They feel no need to give reasons. They are *sure.* What of the opponents of desegregation in the South? What of the black militants who are convinced that white people owe them reparations? What of the demonstrators who believe that any effort to stop the war machine is justified? What of the construction workers who believe that all students are hippies, un-American, subversive, and deserve to be beaten when they march? Once the idea of self-evidence is accepted, once arbitrary decisions are granted respect, anything becomes possible in the moral realm; and, ironically, the objectivity most intuitionists hope to establish becomes impossible.

The same is true of the "good" viewed as a nonnatural quality. Again, even in Berrigan's case, awareness of "good" is in some sense utterly private. There is no way of proving to others that the individual who "sees" is reporting on something which actually exists or on a quality which would be visible to others who could "see" in the same way. At his trial, Berrigan proposed to the judge that the tradition of law should be reinterpreted so that questions of conscience might be introduced into the courts; but he did *not* suggest that the judge was morally blind (although this idea might have followed naturally from his own belief). Also, when the mass of people in the peace movement either refused or did not care to do as the Berrigans had done, they should have been told they could not "see." How were the Berrigans to move them to grasp what they had grasped? What accounts for the commitments of the seven other members of the Catonsville Nine? The intuitionist approach to justification leaves unanswered the question of how others are to be moved (or convinced or directed) to do "right." If no persuasive argument is offered, if no good reasons are presented, only those persons somehow capable of grasping the precise qualities such people as the Berrigans have grasped are likely to act to realize the "good." The same thing would be true in a classroom. If he is convinced that the value of English literature is self-evident, requiring no argument, the teacher is likely to have a difficult time when he tries to guide his more reluctant students toward a loving study of Shakespeare's plays. The question of how he can justify his principles remains, as does the question of how mere assent to the "good" leads to moral action in the name of the "good."

Immanuel Kant had some relevant points to make in this regard. Not an intuitionist, he can still be classified as a deontologist because of his emphasis on maxims and rules. His most important contribution, however, was to make explicit the need for a morality binding on man's rational mind. Believing as he did that reason governed the human will, Kant made a serious effort to link ethics to rationality. At a time of preoccupation with feeling, sensuality, and spontaneity, a concern for consistency and deliberateness in decision making can be of great appeal. Rationality, impartiality, and justice are, after all, linked in many people's minds. Justice means equitable and impartial application of the same principles to different people. If the educational field were just, for instance, everyone would benefit equally from school services. To *act* justly and fairly requires the ability to cope rationally, calmly, and with a degree of coolness. It requires a certain clarity with respect to the principles governing one's actions and an ability to explain, at least, what those principles presuppose.

According to Kant, one consequence of being rational is an ability to know what action is right. Only a rational person can act in accord with moral law, which finds expression in a sense of "ought." Many teachers tend to assume something like this when they try to persuade their students to do what is right. They take for granted that, if a person is intelligent, he will understand his duties and obligations. Conversely, they take for granted that the person who constantly breaks the rules or behaves ungovernably is "stupid." Often, too, individuals committed to nurturing rational thought and conduct, to promoting "good habits" and the like, are convinced that their efforts will culminate in the development of moral character (or "democratic character"). It is extremely hard to give up the belief that reasonable, well-educated people are more likely to be virtuous than ignorant persons.

For Kant, one fundamental principle, one criterion determined the specific rules by which a man ought to live. He called this principle the "categorical imperative," which said: "Act only on that principle which thou canst will should become universal law."[17] An act is moral, according to Kant, only if the principle it embodies can be universalized without contradiction. The usual example is that of keeping promises. A person tempted to break a promise must consider whether such a principle as "promises are to be broken" can be universalized without contradiction. If this were so, people would be free to lie every time they made a promise; if universalized, this principle would involve an impossible contradiction: a deceitful promise is no promise at all, and promises would promptly become meaningless. The consequences of promise breaking are not taken into account. The morality of an act is not in any way dependent on consequences or on its impact on the world. One need only do his duty; and the rules of duty are exceptionless. Moreover, they are valid in every case, despite the consequences.

The choice made by Captain Vere in Herman Melville's *Billy Budd, Foretopman* may shed light on what is involved here. Billy is an innocent young sailor who has been taken from a trading ship called *The Rights of Man* to serve on a warship, *The Indomitable,* on sea duty during the Napoleonic Wars. In his ingenuousness and innocence, he is charged with plotting mutiny by the evil, jealous Claggart, the ship's master-at-arms. Shocked, prevented by a speech impediment from defending himself, Billy lashes out and hits Claggart when he hears the accusation; and, "whether intentionally or but owing to the young athlete's superior height," he strikes the man in such a way that he dies. A drumhead court is summoned; recognizing that the death was an accident, the members want to show compassion. But the Captain, conscious of the mutinies then taking place in the British shipyards, refers them to the Mutiny Act and decides that Billy shall hang. The captain criticizes them for their sentimentality and compassion, although he is clearly a compassionate man. ("But the exceptional in the matter moves the hearts within you. Even so too is mine moved. But let not warm hearts betray heads that should be cool.") He speaks (as Kant would not) of the possible effect on the crew if Billy were set free; but his main stress on the necessity to do his duty, to behave against nature—against predilection and desire:

> "But do these buttons that we wear attest our allegiance is to Nature? No, to the King. Though the ocean, which is inviolate Nature primeval, though this be the element where we move and have our being as sailors, yet as the King's officers lies our duty in a sphere correspondingly natural? So little is that true, that in receiving our commissions we in the most important regards ceased to be natural free agents. When war is declared are we the commissioned fighters previously consulted? We fight at command. If our judgments approve the war, that is but coincidence. So in other particulars. So now. For suppose condemnation to follow these present proceedings. Would it be so much we ourselves would condemn as it would be martial law operating through us? For that law and the rigor of it, we are not responsible. Our vowed responsibility is this: however pitilessly that law may operate in any instances, we nevertheless adhere to it and administer it."[18]

Conceiving martial law as an analogue of Kantian moral law, we can feel some of the rigor and purity of acting solely in accord with principle. Also, we can perceive the meaning of an approach to justification that primarily emphasizes the rule. Motivation, natural freedom, benevolence are made secondary. It matters not if Captain Vere is a kind man, agonized over the choice he had to make; nor does the crew's response matter much at all. Captain Vere freely willed—or chose—to do his duty. "We must ... distinguish between nature and freedom," Kant once wrote. "Nature" referred to the physical, the empirical self and the material world. "Freedom" referred to the "noumenal self," to the *ding an sich,* the thing in itself. The human being, thought of as noumenon, was conceived to be wholly free and undetermined, unlike the phenomenal self, which was caught up in determinisms, no matter how free it claimed to be. There was no way to prove that an undetermined noumenal self existed; but Kant said that its existence could be postulated on the basis of morality, because morality (by definition) presupposed freedom of will. Captain Vere, then, belonged to two realms; and, in the natural realm, he was not free. Turning his back on that realm (and the determinism of feeling, sentimentality, and what Melville described as "what remains primeval in our formalized humanity"), the Captain acted rationally and in freedom of will. "With mankind," he was reputed to say, "forms, measured forms, are everything. . . ." And, indeed, this statement is reminiscent of Kant and the search (still proceeding) for a rational ground.

As we have seen, forms and institutions are being disrupted all around; permissivism and relativism have become so prevalent that the teacher has increasingly more difficulty saying what is categorically right. When "Nature" is associated with the primeval, the sensuous, and the excessive, the return to freedom along with lawfulness which Kantianism makes possible appears to be extremely desirable. There are, of course, the perhaps unanswerable questions of whether universal schematisms exist in the human mind, whether members of widely differing cultures recognize a common moral law, and whether there truly are abstract standards of right and wrong to which all men can be expected to refer.

Can we tell the young Cleaver or the young Genet in the classroom that he really "knows" what is right to say and do, no matter how he behaves? Should we have expected the Germans, during the Nazi period, to hold fast to what they "knew" was right in conditions "where every moral act was illegal and every legal act was a crime"? Hannah Arendt has written, with respect to the Germans, that only an optimistic view of human nature "presupposes an independent human faculty, unsupported by law and public opinion, that judges anew in full spontaneity every deed and intent whenever the occasion arises."[19] It is even doubtful, Arendt believes, that "a *feeling* for such things" has been inbred over the centuries. There must be teaching if persons are to learn to judge.

How is the teacher to cultivate "a feeling for such things"? How can his knowledge of human behavior be put to use? What is the role of rules and principles? How important is authenticity? How *does* a person know when he is right?

Notes and References

1. Plato, "Apology," in *The Works of Plato,* vol. 3, tr. B. Jowett (New York: Tudor Publishing Company, n.d.), pp. 119–120.
2. Plato, "Apology," in *The Works of Plato,* vol. 3, pp. 133–134.
3. Edwin Arlington Robinson, "Mr. Flood's Party," in *The Oxford Book of American Verse,* ed. F. O. Matthiessen (New York: Oxford University Press, 1952), p. 507.
4. Robert Lowell, "For the Union Dead," in *For the Union Dead* (New York: Farrar, Straus & Giroux, 1964), p. 70.
5. Robert Lowell, "For the Union Dead," p. 72.

6. Kingsley Price, "Does Ethics Make a Difference?", in *Theories of Value and Problems of Education,* ed. Philip G. Smith (Urbana: University of Illinois Press, 1970), p. 73.

7. Horace Mann, "Tenth Annual Report" (1846), in *The Republic and the School: Horace Mann on the Education of Free Men,* ed. Lawrence A. Cremin (New York: Bureau of Publications, Teachers College, Columbia University, 1959), p. 63.

8. Samuel Beckett, *The Unnamable,* in *Three Novels by Samuel Beckett: Molloy, Malone Dies, The Unnamable* (New York: Grove Press, 1959), p. 410.

9. Albert Camus, *Notebooks 1942–1951,* tr. Justin O'Brien (New York: The Modern Library, 1965), p. 15.

10. Fyodor Dostoevsky, *The Brothers Karamazov,* tr. Constance Garnett (New York: Random House, 1945), p. 309.

11. Daniel Berrigan and Robert Coles, *The Geography of Faith: Conversations Between Daniel Berrigan, When Underground, and Robert Coles* (Boston: Beacon Press, 1971), p. 79.

12. G. E. Moore, "The Subject-Matter of Ethics," chapter one of *Principia Ethica,* reprinted in *Philosophy in the Twentieth Century,* vol. 2, ed. William Barrett and Henry D. Aiken (New York: Random House, 1962), p. 610.

13. Alfred C. Ewing, *Ethics* (New York: The Free Press, 1953), p. 119.

14. Jean-Paul Sartre, *Saint Genet: Actor and Martyr* (New York: George Braziller, 1963), p. 61.

15. Jean-Paul Sartre, *Saint Genet: Actor and Martyr,* p. 585.

16. Eldridge Cleaver, *Soul on Ice* (New York: McGraw-Hill Book Company, 1968), p. 18.

17. Immanuel Kant, *The Doctrine of Virtue,* p. 2 of *The Metaphysic of Morals,* tr. Mary T. Gregor (New York: Harper & Row, Publishers, 1964), p. 229.

18. Herman Melville, *Billy Budd, Foretopman,* in *Selected Writings of Herman Melville* (New York: The Modern Library, 1952), pp. 879–880.

19. Hannah Arendt, "Who Is Guilty—Man or the System?," *Current,* December 1964, p. 55.

Further Reading

St. Thomas Aquinas, *Summa Theologica,* in *Basic Writings of Saint Thomas Aquinas,* ed. Anton C. Pegis (New York: Random House, 1945).

René Descartes, *Discourse on Method and Other Writings,* tr. E. F. Sutcliffe (Baltimore: Penguin Books, 1968).

John Dewey, *The Quest for Certainty* (London: George Allen & Unwin, 1930).

William K. Frankena, *Ethics* (Englewood Cliffs, N.J.: Prentice-Hall, 1963).

Nathaniel Hawthorne, *The Scarlet Letter,* in *The Portable Hawthorne,* ed. Malcolm Cowley (New York: Viking Press, 1955).

Ernest Hemingway, *A Farewell to Arms* (New York: Charles Scribner's Sons, 1961).

John Hospers, *Human Conduct* (New York: Harcourt Brace Jovanovich, 1961).

John Locke, "Some Thoughts Concerning Education," in *John Locke on Education,* ed. Peter Gay (New York: Bureau of Publications, Teachers College, Columbia University, 1964).

Frank Norris, *McTeague* (New York: Holt, Rinehart & Winston, 1950).

Plato, "The Laws," in *The Works of Plato,* vol. 4, tr. B. Jowett (New York: Tudor Publishing Company, n.d.).

Paul Ramsey, *Nine Modern Moralists* (Englewood Cliffs, N.J.: Prentice-Hall, 1962).

Mark Twain, *The Adventures of Huckleberry Finn,* in *The Portable Mark Twain,* ed. Bernard De Voto (New York: Viking Press, 1955).

Chapter Ten

Justifying Human Actions

But here, I think, in Jeannine's questions, lies a real
Hogchoker: the reasons that people have for attributing value to
things are always ultimately arbitrary; that is, if the question
Why? is asked often enough, it will be discovered that the
ultimate end (which, remember, gives the whole chain its value)
is rationally indefensible, logically unjustifiable.

John Barth
The Floating Opera

Value is beyond being. Yet if we are not to be taken in by fine
words, we must recognize that this being which is beyond being
possesses being in some way at least. These considerations suffice
to make us admit that human reality is that by which value
arrives in the world. But the meaning of being for value is that
it is that toward which a being transcends its being; every
value-oriented act is a wrenching away from its own being
toward——.

Jean-Paul Sartre
Being and Nothingness

It is difficult to give up the hope that human beings know, intuitively
and absolutely, what is right and what is good. It is particularly difficult
for the teacher to give up the conviction that he possesses some independent faculty enabling him to know, under all circumstances, what he ought
to do. Not only is the school itself being challenged; the teacher's
legitimacy is now being questioned, along with the value of his subject
matter and the methods he has been taught to use. He is asked to defend
and justify beliefs he once could take for granted. He is asked to account
for himself to diverse groups of people. It becomes increasingly evident
that he cannot fall back on shared agreements or find his sanction in what
is understood to be the moral law.

Certain philosophers say that it is no longer necessary to look beyond the natural world to discover what is right and good. Taking a consistently naturalist approach, they declare that there now exists enough understanding of human nature to warrant drawing inferences about right action from what is empirically known. Deriving their notions of what human beings ought to do from available knowledge about what they are, the naturalists generally find their leads in the behavioral sciences and, occasionally, in biology. In our discussion of human nature, we have pointed to the multiplicity of descriptions and diagnoses competing for acceptance today. The development of anthropology and the advances in mass communication have made inescapable the recognition that almost anything is possible where human conduct and morality are concerned. Massacres of innocent people are justified by some; others would sacrifice their lives to protect one innocent. Gently reared, attractive young people make antipersonnel bombs and call the action good. Others go to jail or into exile to avoid killing on the battlefield. Parents batter little children or abandon them; others starve or steal to keep their children fed. Public officials tell untruths and are reelected; soldiers commit atrocities and are honored by their superiors; persons in many countries immolate themselves in the name of their ideals. Where is the norm? Where is the standard? Naturalistic moral philosophers still believe empirical studies hold the answers. They turn to psychological and other theories for explanations. Having found the explanations, they define what is right and what is wrong for humankind.

One instance is the use of Freudian theory. Freudianism puts great stress on the importance of repressing or sublimating a variety of natural desires and aggressions. Without rational controls, its exponents say, without an effective superego, the human being is likely to be victimized by his drives, impulses, infantile fears, and fantasies. He is always in danger of regressing to a savage state, like the choir boys in William Golding's *Lord of the Flies.* According to Freud, a continuous and conscious effort has to be made for any humane civilization to be maintained. Civilization, Freud wrote pessimistically, "is built up on renunciation of instinctual gratifications . . . the existence of civilization presupposes the non-gratification (suppression, repression, or something else?) of powerful instinctual urgencies."[1] In many respects, Golding's novel is a symbolic rendering of this view. Near the end of the story, the fire the marooned children have built to signal rescuers becomes the image of Ralph's and Piggy's expressed desire to return to the civilized world. However, much work is necessary to keep the fire going; and Ralph suddenly feels tempted by the release and relaxation savagery seems to entail. He has to force himself to remember that " 'The fire's the important thing. Without the fire we can't be rescued. I'd like to put on war-paint and be a savage. But we must keep the fire burning. The fire's the most important thing on the island because, because————'."[2] A naturalist who accepts Freud's theories and agrees that instinctual gratifications must be suppressed if society is to be maintained would stress the importance of Ralph's finishing that sentence. Like many teachers, he would assert that it is categorically right for the fire (meaning insight, enlightenment, superego, or self-control) to be kept burning, no matter what the sacrifice. The alternative (following Freud's discoveries) is chaos (irrationality, the rule of impulse, domination by the id); and such chaos cannot be tolerated. It follows that sublimation and rational self-discipline are desirable. Giving way to instinctual urgencies is bad.

Another naturalist might reject Freud's theory and develop his moral viewpoint on the basis of an alternative vision of man. Herbert Marcuse, whose intellectual roots are in Freudianism and Marxism, offers one such alternative. Linking the traditional demand for control over instincts to the repressiveness of an overly rationalized society, he identifies sublimation with stupefaction. He writes about human needs which demand liberation from an orientation to comforts and rewards. Decrying prevailing social controls, he says they "exact the overwhelming need for the production and consumption of waste; the need for stupefying work where it is no longer a real necessity; the need for modes of relaxation which soothe and prolong this stupefaction."[3]

Today every teacher is aware of persons who reason from these and similar premises and conclude that "liberation" and "acting out" are more desirable than self-discipline, sublimation, or control. "The reality is instinct," writes Norman Brown. ". . . Let there be no one to answer to."[4] He calls for affirmation of oceanic feelings, for carnal sharing in communion, for feasts and "excellent fooling." He prescribes, "Free speech; free associations; random thoughts; spontaneous movements" in place of the burdens of learning and accumulated knowledge. Can the teacher respond by telling such a man that he is factually mistaken and therefore ethically wrong? Norman Brown may choose not to use traditional behavioral science categories. He may agree with R. D. Laing's belief that social scientific description leads to "a brutalization of, a debasement of, a desecration of: namely, the true nature of human beings and animals." Laing goes on to say: "The description must be *in light* of the fact that the human beings have so brutalized themselves, have become so banal and stultified, that they are unaware of their own debasement."[5] What is the naturalist teacher or philosopher to answer? How is he to respond to Theodore Roszak when he writes on the "primordial world view" that lurks beyond "our socially certified morality"—and concludes that the highest good is to be found in "gentle, tranquil, and thoroughly civilized contemplativeness"?[6] On what grounds can the teacher call these people right? On what grounds can he call them wrong?

Claims that conceptions of the good can be derived from studies of how men live are indeed plausible. Even more plausible are the claims that conceptions of good can be derived from definitions of mental health or emotional maturity. But mental health is variously conceived. Freud thought of it as the ability to love and to work; Erik H. Erikson emphasizes ego integrity, generativity, intimacy, identity, industry, initiative, autonomy, and trust. Gordon Allport speaks of autonomous interests and the extension of self. Abraham H. Maslow focuses on self-actualization. Recently, Lawrence Kohlberg has studied the stages of moral development in a number of cultures and concluded that individuals are ethically mature when they achieve an "orientation not only to actually ordained social rules but to principles of choice involving appeal to logical universality and consistency."[7] There are numerous such generalizations, each of which may be sound in its own context; but the difficulty of reasoning from statements about mental health to statements about the good may be insuperable. What logical connections *can* be made between a generalization about the human being in sickness or health and propositions concerning what he ought to do?

Some naturalists have turned to the social sciences or to biology rather than to psychology in their efforts to ground moral judgments in empirical fact. They have sometimes attempted to demonstrate that whatever promotes survival or advances the development of the species is to be considered good, although they say little about the quality of the survival sought or the value of the development in question. Such arguments have been used in support of heart transplants and eugenics programs; they may even have been used in support of Hitler's "Final Solution" and the stringent order Mussolini imposed on Italy. Early in the century, Social Darwinist William Graham Sumner used a similar argument stemming from biological theory. Taking Charles Darwin's concept of the survival of the fittest as fact, Sumner said that the leaders of American society had survived competition and attained power because they were the fittest. Not only did he deduce from Darwinian principles a view that such men ought to dominate society. He was strongly opposed to public education, except as a means of maintaining order, because he thought selection processes should be natural ones. When the schools tried to raise the unfit in the social scale, they were interfering with natural selection; and what they accepted was therefore wrong.

The nineteenth century school reformers did not, of course, have modern behavioral sciences at hand; but they also grounded their view of morality in what they understood to be the "facts" of human nature.

Believing human beings to be malleable and thus susceptible to depravity and corruption, they conceived the public schools to be agents of social control—particularly where poor and immigrant children were concerned. Numerous teachers today also believe that the maintenance of existing social arrangements—no matter how ravaged by brutalization and violence —is *ipso facto* desirable, since the likely alternative is disorder, or the "anarchy" against which the school reformers warned. Michael Katz, discussing twentieth century educational reform, identifies the biases which give rise to such attitudes:

> The men and women concerned with altering the control of education had no higher opinion of poor city families than did their predecessors a half-century before. They shared the anti-immigrant sentiments and the racism of their class. Insofar as their reform efforts had an educational purpose, that goal again reflected one of the larger aims of municipal reform: the attempt to find new modes of social control appropriate to a dynamic and fluid urban environment. Their aim remained similar to that of earlier reformers: inculcating the poor with acceptable social attitudes.[8]

The assumption was (and often is) that the nature of poor children attending school was such as to require regulation. It followed that it **was** morally right to regiment, to indoctrinate, to impose rigid controls.

This is an example of a rather crude move from what is taken to be fact to a conception of the desirable, from an *is* to a *should*. Naturalists often make this mistake: they use generalizations about human nature as a basis for making moral judgments. When a person argues deductively, as these men often do, he is logically required to draw no conclusion which is not contained in his premises. When a teacher asserts that a child is black and on welfare and therefore *ought* to be severely disciplined when he lies, that teacher is deducing a moral judgment from a premise which does not contain a moral judgment. His argument is, in consequence, invalid.

In *The Way It Spozed to Be,* James Herndon describes an interview with the principal of a school where Herndon has been teaching and from which he has been dismissed. The principal is explaining why he finds Herndon's work unsatisfactory: the children did not begin their lessons on time; there was no attempt to inculcate good study habits; there was too much discussion of irrelevant issues; Herndon "had no control" over his pupils' actions. The fact that there had been no riot in his classroom meant that no control had been established, since children only rioted when there was control.

> It was right then that I really understood that I was being
> fired. It hadn't really occurred to me before. Grissum wanted me
> to understand that he knew I had worked hard, that I was
> serious about what I was doing, that my character, intelligence
> and "dedication" weren't in question. What was? It seemed a
> matter of ideas of order. This is a problem school, I do
> remember his saying. His job, and the job of the teachers, was
> to make it into something that was no longer a problem school.
> He was certain that was possible. It is the belief in this goal that
> counts, he told me. He used the word *belief* many times. No
> one is perfect, so a teacher may lose control once, twice, a
> hundred times, but if he believes in that control himself, that
> order, he will eventually win through.[9]

Arguing much like a naturalist, the principal is saying that the *fact* of a
problem school (a school crowded with deprived black children) implies
that order ought at all costs to be maintained. He mentions no moral
principle; he does not say why order and control are relevant considerations. His conclusion (as Herndon well knows) is not justified. But the
principal thinks he has the answer to the question of what is right to do in
a problem school. He thinks he has the answer because he is convinced he
can define the good.

Another objection to the naturalist approach to justification is that it
so frequently depends on a notion of good as definable, perhaps observable
—as hardness is, or malleability, or high polish on a piece of steel. The
teacher or the philosopher who wishes to be a "moral scientist" tries to
locate the good somewhere in experience or to demonstrate that it always
accompanies certain kinds of experience and can therefore be isolated and
known. Herndon's principal, if he were to make explicit what he believes,
would say that order exists when there is an efficient use of supplies and
class time, when a teacher is well-groomed and pleasant, and when control
is maintained. The good, in consequence, would be defined as order or
stability. If a teacher or a philosopher accepts the Freudian interpretation
of human nature, he might find good existing in certain kinds of
enlightened sublimation: devotion to a career, careful housekeeping,
mastery of a craft. Or he might say that good accompanies mental health
—the achievement of productivity and relatedness. If he accepts the
Marcusian view, he might find good in an eradication of false
consciousness and the attainment of authenticity. If he follows Gordon
Allport, he might equate good with autonomy.

The philosopher G. E. Moore would treat all these as instances of the
"naturalist fallacy."[10] We may indeed see many things that are good in the
world, he would say. We may find that a common quality seems to
characterize experiences we cherish. He would insist, nonetheless, that this

notion does not give us the right to say we have defined, once and for all, the "good." What terms would compose such a definition? To what would "good" be logically equivalent? Again, if we do decide that "good" should be identified with particular sorts of fulfillment, happiness, pleasure, or sublimation, and we assimilate it to such experiences, we are still left with questions. Something may indeed give us pleasure and make us deeply happy. Some situation in the classroom may provide us as teachers with real gratification. We may talk about our pleasure or our gratification and recommend it to other persons. Yet, listening to our happy tales, these individuals may still ask: "But is it really good?"

Moore went beyond pointing out the present impossibility of defining the "good." Like David Hume before him, he pointed out the sharp transitions required when one moves from any factual statement to a judgment of what people ought to do. Hume wrote:

> The end of all moral speculations is to teach us our duty; and, by proper representations of the deformity of vice and the beauty of virtue, beget correspondent habits, and engage us to avoid the one and embrace the other.[11]

Few people now would speak of "duty" or "the beauty of virtue"; but, even so, Hume was pointing out something significant about ethical discourse, especially in comparison with empirical description. When a teacher, for instance, enters the realm of morals or ethics, he must necessarily concern himself with feelings of obligation, with choosing, with the struggle to find out what he ought—in particular situations—to do. Also, he must concern himself with guiding behavior, his own and his students', not merely describing or analyzing it. He needs to understand, therefore, that the principal who says order is good is really recommending or prescribing that order be maintained. When the teacher tells his students that it is valuable for them to keep classroom journals, he is really recommending that they undertake a specific activity. Asserting that an activity or a state of being is good or telling people that they ought to do a particular thing is quite different from defining or describing. The teacher needs to be aware of the ways words like *good, bad, ought,* and *must* differ from words used in scientific contexts. The function of value words is to shape purposes, to create evaluational frameworks for teaching and learning, to move people to make choices on their own. Just as David Hume has suggested, to move from a factual statement to a judgment of what ought to be is to move into another realm of discourse. And this is one of the primary reasons why the problem of justification cannot be solved by drawing inferences from what is empirically known.

Some naturalists can take actualities into account when they consider moral decisions without grounding those decisions in empirical fact. Many of their theories are classified as "teleological," meaning that "the basic or ultimate criterion or standard of what is morally right, wrong, obligatory, etc., is the nonmoral value that is brought into being."[12] A nonmoral value is different, say, from a moral value, such as goodness and badness. Self-realization, pleasure, enlightenment, and the like are called nonmoral values. When any one of these values is achieved by a course of action, that action appears to be justified. Was James Herndon morally right in allowing his students a degree of freedom normally frowned on by the principal of his school? According to this view, Herndon could justify his treatment of his classes (and even the disorder that resulted) by pointing to the results. ("I admit," he writes, "9D could probably outshout the rest of The Tribe. . . . Probably there were a hundred shouted irrelevancies, threats and insults too. But the fact is this outcry was orderly in intent and in effect, for in about four or five minutes it was all over, readers were sitting down, they had books, the audience was getting ready to listen."[13])

Theories that focus on justification of consequences are also called "consequentialist," meaning that they "base the desirability of courses of action on their consequences."[14] To appreciate the point of these theories, the teacher might contrast them with some of the deontological theories discussed in the previous chapter. Kant said, it will be recalled, that the desirability of a course of action depends on the degree to which it is governed by principle or duty. Father Daniel Berrigan justifies the burning of draft records by talking in terms of what he intuits to be right. ("We could not   so help us God   do otherwise/ For we are sick at heart   our hearts/ give us no rest for thinking of the Land of Burning Children."[15]) In contrast, the teleologist or the consequentialist looks for his criterion in what is likely to follow from his action, not in what motivates or precedes.

One of the best known of the teleological approaches is that of the Utilitarians, most particularly John Stuart Mill. Reasoning from what he believed to be the facts about human nature (that all men desire happiness), Mill concluded that happiness, above all other things, is desirable. He also refined the "principle of utility," which said that the highest moral purpose for man to achieve was the greatest balance of good over evil in the situations in which he had to choose. This belief is sometimes called the pursuit of the "general happiness" or the "greatest good." A teacher who adopts the principle of utility would keep before his pupils some notion of pleasure, happiness, or release appealing to all of them. On the simplest level, he might say: "You want to go out for recess, don't you? Then stand in line and be perfectly still." Or: "You want to be promoted and be among older children, don't you? Then study as hard as you can so that you pass the end-term test." In effect, the teacher is saying that unpleasantness is worth the cost, because in the end there will be more happiness than there might have been without that modicum of pain. On a somewhat higher level, the teacher might talk about how compliance with certain rules contributes to the general happiness of the class and about why some enjoyments are preferable to others because of the contribution they may make to the general good. Many questions are left unsolved, of course. For one thing, there is the hedonistic component in an ethic geared to happiness, no matter how high-minded and benevolent that happiness is meant to be. For another, there is the unsolved problem of obligation. How and why do people feel obliged to consider the general good or to contribute to a fund of happiness instead of cultivating their own?

There is another problem too. It has to do with the viability of grounding notions of the valuable in what men appear to desire. This idea is especially familiar to teachers accustomed to thinking of pupils' desires, interests, or needs. It is not uncommon to find a teacher, particularly in an open classroom, linking his conceptions of what is worthwhile to what his pupils *want* to explore. He is not likely, of course, simply to say that collecting shells is good because the children want to collect them; but he *is* likely to move from acknowledging their desire to a discussion of the rightness of their investigating crustaceans, molluscs, fossils, and the rest. The question of the relation between desire (or interest) and rightness is seldom confronted; nor is the problem of explaining to the disinterested why something intensely desired by a few ought to be desired by all. Again we confront the question of what is generally good and why people should feel obliged to contribute to it. If they do not feel obliged to do a certain thing or share in a certain kind of activity, they will scarcely feel they *ought* to do what is asked of them. Even in the open classroon, then, the teacher may have to resort to compulsion or to some Skinnerian technique of reinforcing through rewards. If he takes one of these paths to the enlistment of his students in a shared activity, he puts aside the matter of obligation. This, clearly, is one of the limitations of a view basing rightness mainly on desire.

There is also the question of determining which desires are worthwhile at any given moment. Herbert Marcuse, for instance, distinguishes between what we are manipulated into needing and desiring and what we truly and authentically want. Desires for comforts and rewards are often misread as desires for personal fulfillment; what Marcuse calls "stupefaction" is often equated with the good. When we seriously confront consumerist and other preoccupations, when we remember the pressures and distractions that abound in the modern world, we soon realize that human beings are capable of desiring much that is harmful to themselves or to others. In addition, people are frequently haunted by conflicting desires. A child may want to feed the guinea pigs; he may also want to go out to play. A young man may want to accept the offer of a challenging job; he may also want to finish the work for his degree. It is simply not enough to define values in terms of satisfaction of desires. More remains to be said.

John Dewey, whose pragmatic theory of value may also be classified as consequentialist, was focally concerned about man's search for satisfaction. However, he said something of extreme importance, which distinguishes his approach dramatically from that of other naturalists, as well as from that of Mill: "There is no value," Dewey wrote, "except where there is satisfaction, but there have to be certain conditions fulfilled to transform a satisfaction into a value."[16] Enjoyments, pleasures, and satisfactions as they are experienced are merely "problematic goods." Reflective thinking is required to transform them into values—to determine determine whether the desired is desirable or whether the satisfying can be considered satisfactory.

Conceiving the human being to be a social organism forever caught up in dynamic relations with other people and the environment, Dewey dealt with the problem of moral choosing within complex life situations. The valuational process, as he saw it, occurs within the continuum of experience. Within that continuum there is no division between the emotive and the cognitive or between the will and the intellect. There is no qualitative difference between value judgments and other instances of intelligence at work. Still, valuation ordinarily takes place when needs are to be satisfied or conflicts among tendencies are to be resolved. Automatic fulfillments are few in human experience; when they do occur, valuation is not involved. We need only recall moments when we have plunged into cool water on hot days; instances when we have been applauded or unexpectedly praised; occasions when we have been deeply fatigued and permitted ourselves to fall asleep. These represent satisfactions, surely; but Dewey reminds us that they are not values, that they are not even good, unless deliberation has intervened.

Most often, needs are not immediately satisfied; something happens between the awakening of an impulse and the activity undertaken in response. We may be working on a hot day and feel an inclination to go swimming. Should we suddenly abandon what we are doing and drive out to the beach? What will our co-workers say if we leave the job half done? We yearn for the feel of the ocean; but we do not want to burden our co-workers. We want them to approve of us, to like us. We do not want to be thoughtless or to take advantage of them. We live by certain principles, after all: we believe in playing fair, in keeping promises, in doing jobs assigned. We can, of course, simply forget all about our desire to go to the beach and comply blankly with the ordinary rules. We can, alternatively, give way to impulse and run out the door. Or we can suggest that everyone stop work a little earlier because of the heat. We can consult our co-workers to see whether they would be willing to work longer the next day—or permit us to work longer—to compensate for time spent at the beach. Dewey would say that we begin to engage in valuation (making moral judgments) only when we begin to engage in such prospective and reflective thinking, when we begin weighing alternatives and anticipating consequences. The worth—or the goodness—of what we finally decide will depend on the quality of the deliberation in which we engaged, the factors we took into account, the interests we tried to adjust.

Because life situations are so many-faceted, the individual usually has several courses of action from which to choose. A variety of goods are potentially attainable, not only one. (In the aforementioned case, if the inclination to go swimming is not satisfied, there is the good experience of knowing commitments have been met, friendships maintained.) The problem for the individual is to try to determine the consequences of following different inclinations, undertaking different actions. He focuses on a tentative end-in-view as he pursues his inquiry; and Dewey makes clear that the quality of the original desire and of the end-in-view depends on the adequacy of that inquiry. No fixed or ultimate principles can be relied on to determine the course of action the individual ought to choose, although commitments and principles must be taken into account as the deliberation proceeds. No simple deductions can be made from the "facts" of human nature, although an assessment of the existing realities plays an important role. No image of a single, objective "good" guides the search for the best way to proceed, because the good (according to Dewey) is never twice the same. It varies with the situation. Its quality depends on the degree to which things in their interconnectedness have been considered in the course of choosing. It always, however, involves a resolution of conflict among goods and among inclinations. And it can never be achieved if there is not some transformation of the original situation, some freeing of the individual for further action and thought. The good is thus associated with some nonmoral value or values: a type of fulfillment or enjoyment; the satisfaction of certain interests; the release of tension. Values, writes Dewey, "are identical with goods that are the fruit of intelligently directed activity."[17]

Let us return for a moment to Melville's story *Billy Budd, Foretopman.* Let us imagine how Captain Vere would have resolved his predicament if he were, like Dewey, a pragmatist or experimental empiricist. The Captain existed in a social situation; and like all other human beings, he had memories of a past life, of fulfillments and enjoyments outside his officer role. He was an educated man, Melville makes clear; he had no patience with cant. He was also a compassionate man, as his dealings with Billy show. He had his duty to perform during the Napoleonic Wars, when England felt threatened not only by external forces but by internal disorders. Aware that certain members of his crew (such as Billy Budd) had been shanghaied from merchant ships, probably aware that conditions on the warship were fundamentally inhumane and unjust, he lived in dread of mutiny. When Billy killed the obviously evil Claggart, therefore, Captain Vere was caught in a conflict of inclinations. He also confronted a variety of conflicting goods: the good of being compassionate and expressing his obvious affection for Billy; the good of maintaining order on his ship; the good of being law-abiding, in the sense of complying with the Mutiny Act. Dewey would ask him to examine as many elements in the situation as he could; to consider as many impinging conditions and circumstances as came to mind. He would ask him to look back on past enjoyments to find clues for his present action. He would ask him to take a hypothetical approach both to the Mutiny Act and to the idea of duty, to hold neither one absolutely. He would ask him, too, to try to recognize that the opposition between "nature" and "freedom" was not fixed and inalterable, that it was one of many conceivable ways of interpreting man's role in the world. Dewey would draw attention to the importance of consulting *all* the interests affected by the decision: Billy's, certainly, because his life was at stake; the crew members', the officers', the ship's, the nation's. He would enjoin Captain Vere to try to satisfy as many of those interests as possible and to avoid thinking in a hierarchy of values, with "patriotism" at the pinnacle. Such deliberation is difficult in an undemocratic situation, and certainly in a time of war; and this point may shed light on the close connection between Dewey's emphasis on tentativeness, interconnectedness, deliberation and what he understood "democracy" to mean. Captain Vere *might* have arrived at the same decision he arrived at deontologically, if he followed the pragmatic model; but the dispositions brought into play, the habits of thinking, the attitude taken would have been different. And this is the crucial point: the method, for the pragmatist, is central. The value of the final decision is as contingent on the intelligence used in appraisal as it is on the activity finally chosen.

The teacher who adopts Dewey's distinctive naturalism in his approach to making value judgments will find that he cannot move from descriptions of behavior to conceptions of what he ought to do. Dewey had hopes of finding directives for moral conduct in the sciences (which, he believed, would replace "familiar and traditionally prized values" when people sought standards for decision making); but he always had scientific *method* in mind, hypothetical treatments of problems, and a willingness to test conclusions in experience. He would ask the teacher to consult relevant empirical data when confronting complex classroom situations, but not in isolation from other data. James Herndon's principal, for example, might discover that Herndon's students were reading far below their grade level. Dewey would suggest that this "fact" be examined in connection with the conditions under which the students were tested. He would ask the principal to look for additional evidences of capacity and incapacity, not the evidence of the reading test alone.

Pointing out that relations in social situations are "indefinitely wider and more complex" than those in the physical world, Dewey would ask both principal and teacher to explore as wide an area of relations and connections as possible, if they wished adequately to appraise the achievements of the students. He would remind Herndon's superiors that discussion of irrelevant issues and an atmosphere of freedom in the classroom ought not to be arbitrarily proscribed. The teacher ought to be given the opportunity to project imaginatively the effects of alternate courses of action: maintaining the control the principal demanded, allowing an amount of self-determination to the students, excluding those who disrupted class, and so forth. He ought to be given the freedom to decide eventually on which strategy will bring about the most desirable results.

The natural question with respect to this approach concerns how that final decision is made. At what point does deliberation stop? How does the teacher know that he has tested and explored sufficiently? How can he demonstrate or prove that his decision is the best of all possible alternatives at the moment? How can he persuade others that his choice is correct? He can always say, of course, that he did as well as he could, that he thought as carefully as he could, that he remained as open-minded as he could. We can scarcely ask more of a responsible individual; yet, for many people, the questions still remain unanswered. Some charge the pragmatists with creating situations that might lead to infinite regression before any decisions could be made. Others talk about an insupportable relativism; still others mock the emphasis on consequences as an emphasis on the "cash value" of particular alternatives. Such appalling examples of so-called "pragmatic" thinking as that displayed in *The Pentagon Papers* trouble many people, even those willing to admit that Deweyan pragmatism does not entail the fearful objectivity evidenced in the government's planning for war. Most telling, however, may be R. S. Peters' remark that "an ethical principle is needed to pick out the relevance of consequences."[18] How, otherwise, is a teacher like James Herndon to know *which* results, *which* consequences are to be preferred? R. M. Hare says, in fact, that the purpose of moral principles is to tell us what effects or consequences are more relevant than others. Returning to the example from Melville, how are we to know whether the possibility of a mutiny is more relevant than the possibility of satisfying the ordinary seamen (and saving Billy's life)? How are we to decide whether the chance of classroom noise and disruption is more relevant than the chance that each student may gain a sense of dignity because of the opportunity provided him to express himself?

Such perplexities have led many philosophers to emphasize the ethical principles that organize elementary moral convictions. Clearly influenced by naturalists and pragmatists, aware that most people make their moral decisions after examining a complex of moral and factual beliefs, they refuse to separate reason from ordinary human action. They refuse also to posit some prior existence of "oughtness" and right. In their fundamental naturalism, they resemble Dewey. But they move in a direction different from Dewey's when they isolate principles and rules for special attention and concern themselves with the validity of the reasons given for pronouncing an act "good" or "right."

These philosophers have a special interest in language as well as in principles and good reasons; and they are likely to emphasize the autonomy of ethics when they discuss values or the problem of the good. The claim of autonomy can best be understood in the light of the many twentieth century investigations into the "meaning of meaning"[19] and into the regulatory functions performed by value words. The roots of such investigations can be traced back to the eighteenth century and the work of David Hume and George Berkeley, both of whom challenged traditional beliefs about moral discourse. Hume made a sharp distinction between Reason and moral language: talk of values, he said, addresses itself to feelings and attitudes; it is intended to affect action, not to disclose Truth or to make things clear. Berkeley said that the function of ethical terminology is to express attitudes, formulate rules, and guide the behavior suitable for social life. The work of I. A. Richards in the 1930s drew attention most dramatically to precisely the same issue. With his associate, C. K. Ogden, Richards explained in detail how the "emotive" language of ethics differed from the "descriptive" language of science;[20] and British analytic philosophers went on from there to develop an "emotive" theory of ethics. According to this theory, value judgments communicate no information; they are in no sense verifiable, as statements of fact are verifiable. Much concerned about the semantic ambiguities and inconsistencies in the language of morals and about the confusions these reflected, the analysts decided to concentrate on illicit uses of moral terminology. Their object was to restore clarity through a study of language and its several functions.

Many of the confusions and misconceptions that troubled them are with us today, for all the rigor in their attempts to make things clear. On occasion, they went to extremes. A. J. Ayer wrote:

> We begin by admitting that the fundamental ethical concepts
> are unanalysable, inasmuch as there is no criterion by which one
> can test the validity of the judgments in which they occur. . . .
> We say that the reason why they are unanalysable is that they
> are mere pseudo-concepts. The presence of an ethical symbol in
> a proposition adds nothing to its factual content.[21]

If a teacher says to a student, "You were wrong to cheat on that exam,"
he is not (according to Ayer) saying anything different from, "You cheated
on that exam." To add that the student was wrong, Ayer would suggest, is
only to express the teacher's moral disapproval. It is as if the teacher had
said, "You cheated" in "a peculiar tone of horror, or had written it with
the addition of some special exclamation marks. The tone, or the
exclamation mark adds nothing to the literal meaning of the sentence. It
merely serves to show that the expression of it is attended by certain
feelings in the speaker."[22] This attack on what is ordinarily taken for
granted about moral statements was—and is—unpleasant for many people
to contemplate. Using a single criterion of "verifiability," Ayer and his
analytic colleagues emptied moral judgments of meaning. However, such
shock tactics may turn out to be important. We need only recall the efforts
that persist, even today, to link knowledge to virtue. Teachers, like many
others, still find it hard to accept the idea that increased psychological
understanding (about individual differences, levels of maturation, the
connection between language and thinking, unconscious motivations) has
not led to universal moral agreements on the right things to do. Moreover,
even though they do on some level realize that moral judgments and
practices are to a large degree functions of cultural prescriptions and
commendations, they find it hard to accept the idea that people from other
cultures or subcultures cannot "see" something so obviously right. Every
teacher who tries to cope with the problem of pluralism in his classroom
knows this to be the case. Everyone who has traveled in other countries
and tried to study comparative education knows it well. Moral discourse,
as discourse, is still widely misunderstood. We have not yet reached the
point at which the majority of people are aware that "good" and "right"
do not designate objective characteristics, that they do not stand for
properties or relationships in some way visible in the outer world.

Even so, classification of value statements as merely expressive or
emotive has not been as helpful as some thought it would be. To say that
they are "pseudoconcepts" and "meaningless" is to refuse to do justice to
the central role they play in social life. Also, it is to make almost
impossible a clarification of the distinctive meanings value words *do*
appear to possess. Late in his life, Ludwig Wittgenstein made this notion

accessible by rejecting the view that language has one particular function: to state facts. Although he did not pursue the implications of his conclusion (language could perform a plurality of functions) for a conception of ethical discourse, he did emphasize the need to treat language as a tool capable of a great variety of jobs. And his interest, at that moment, was in ordinary language, not artificial or formal languages. He said in *The Blue Book:* "I want you to remember that words have those meanings which we have given them; and we give them meanings by explanations."[23] This notion stimulated many philosophers in England and the United States to study moral talk as language with a specific relevance for an understanding of conduct. No longer concerned with asking what "goodness" (or "oughtness" or "duty" or "right") *was,* they became interested in finding out how such terms worked to control or guide or regulate behavior in human communities. This, in turn, enabled them to begin to speak of rule-governed action, principled action, much as Kant had done; but, unlike Kant, they did not need to bifurcate the human being or reach beyond the universe of human languages and logics to find a standard or ground. The criterion became reasonableness; some modes of justification were considered valid, others invalid. Appraisal and reflective thinking became crucial, as they did for the pragmatists; but now the primary interest was in "good reasons" for particular decisions and in a logical rather than an experimental mode of finding out what, in different situations, these might be.

Some philosophers say that, if "right" and "good" can be defined, the definition would involve a decision as to what reasons ought to be accepted in a particular case. "Ought," as we have already said, implies that there *are* good reasons for acting in one way rather than in another. A good reason is one that is relevant, and relevance is in part determined by an adopted principle or norm. "Relevance," writes A. Stafford Clayton, "is a specific kind of relationship, one in which bearing or pertinence is shown. To speak of questions of relevance in norm-making is to speak of so stating the norm that it reveals as clearly as possible what counts as worth-making."[24]

Let us suppose that a teacher is confronting a class of rebellious high school students who are demanding the right to participate in planning their school work. Let us assume that the teacher has decided to proceed according to the principle that "everyone affected by a policy should have a share in making it." This statement of norm-in-use makes clear enough that full student participation is considered valuable. If a supervisor were to ask why so much movement and free discussion are being permitted in the classroom, the teacher can say that students are unable to share their ideas if they are not allowed freely to converse. He can say that policy in this situation includes the techniques of classroom management, the handling of passes and late slips, the amount of homework assigned each night. Believing that *"everyone* affected" should participate, he can also say that time must be provided for every student to have his say. In addition to being reasons for the teacher's decision, these three remarks are explanations of what his principle entails. Treating his argument as logical, we might note that his principle serves as a major premise, his reasons as minor premises. Because his major premise includes a value statement, a "should," he can correctly conclude that it is right for his students to talk lengthily and in the manner they choose. The important thing is that the teacher is consciously deciding on principle, not necessarily a traditional or a borrowed one. On the basis of his private beliefs and values, his regard for individuals, his understanding of student attitudes, and his experiences in the school, he has *chosen* to make the principle his own; and his integrity as well as his ability to cope with an unsettled situation depend (at least for the moment) on that choice.

It is clear that the analytic philosopher resembles the pragmatist in his empirical orientation to the contexts of decision making and in his concern for the rationality of the methods used. He is more explicit than the pragmatist about the autonomy of ethics, the problem of language, and the degree of objectivity to be achieved when the language of morals is understood to be governed by recognizable rules. Certain rules of application, he says, prescribe how "ought," "good," and "right" are to be used. Because they are impersonal and functions of rationality, these rules permit claims that some ethical judgments are valid and some are not. They also make it possible to teach people, not what is right, but what constitute good reasons for action in different spheres of life. The mode of persuasion would have to be primarily rational, certainly not coercive. At once, people would have to be as willing to abandon mere prudentialism as they are to question authorities.

No matter what the degree of objectivity attained, no matter how universally acknowledged are the rules, the final decision is up to the individual. We have already made the point that ethical judgment is meaningless without a presumption that the individual is to some extent free to choose and to some extent autonomous. His attitudes, like the attitudes prevalent in his culture, will affect his decisions. (Even the rules of valid reasoning are, after all, rules accepted in a particular community.) At some level, he must *choose* to do what even he considers sensible or reasonable. Stephen Toulmin, arguing that "ethical reasoning may be able to show why we ought to do this action as opposed to that, or advocate this social practice as opposed to that, but it is no help where there can be no choice." But he goes on to say that, because ethics cannot answer the question, "Why *ought* one to do what is right?", the individual must recognize that "To show that you ought to choose certain actions is one thing: to make you want to do what you ought to do is another, and not a philosopher's task."[25] Knowledge, he is saying, is not virtue; nor does knowledge guarantee virtue. The best one can do is to offer good reasons to people or to point out the factors in the situation, which, if acted on, will bring about certain effects and not others. Ensuring the bringing about of desirable effects involves reinforcing in the way B. F. Skinner and others describe. Educating so that individuals choose self-consciously to do what is right involves teaching for the development of "norm-regarding action" —and leaving the choosing to those who have learned.

Choice, then, becomes focal, whether or not it appears to the analytic philosopher to take us beyond ethics. And choice, as we have already seen, is central to existential thinking. Like Kant, existentialists make ethics depend on human will; for them as well as for Kant, no good or evil could exist without will. When we recall the logical empiricists' emphasis on the *language* of morals and their skepticism with respect to inwardness, or that which is personal as contrasted to impersonal, we can see that (despite some incidental overlappings) a great gap exists between the empiricists and the existentialists. Existentialists break with more traditional philosophers, however, by refusing to develop systematic ethics and by neglecting the familiar normative questions: What is right? What is good? How do I justify a value judgment? Moving to existentialism from an overview of theories of obligation, the teacher is then required to change his vantage point drastically. Not only must he imagine himself within his concrete historical situation as it presents itself to *his* subjectivity; he must confront the problematic of all systems and universal charts, the limitations of "calculative" inquiry, and the insufficiency of abstract norms.

This is not to say, as too many do, that he must therefore opt for emotivism or some other sort of anticognitivism. Existentialists may be disinterested in "good reasons"; they may talk intensely about the need for a subjective appropriation of principles; they may warn against the estrangement from life, which so often accompanies "objectivity." But they are no more bound to reject cognitive action than they are to deny the centrality of calculative action in modern life. Like the pragmatists, in fact, they are much more disturbed by fixities and absolutes than they are by rationality per se. In *Anti-Semite and Jew,* Jean-Paul Sartre associates the anti-Semite's impassioned state of believing in a single idea with becoming as "massive and impenetrable" as stone. Sartre is talking about absoluteness and false reasoning, not reasoning itself. Like Dewey, he demands tentativeness, a willingness to reconstruct and revise:

> How can one choose to reason falsely? It is because of a
> longing for impenetrability. The rational man groans as he

> gropes for the truth; he knows that his reasoning is no more
> than tentative, that other considerations may supervene to cast
> doubt on it. He never sees very clearly where he is going; he is
> "open"; he may even appear to be hesitant.[26]

Openness and what Kierkegaard thought of as passionate engagement are required if the exercise of reason is not to separate the living subject from the objects of his knowing—be they the things of the world, physical surroundings, other human beings. The concern is for process and involvement. The individual, seeking completion, seeking meanings, *takes* or *chooses* certain phenomena to be good or bad, lovely or disgusting. He thereby creates values as he lives.

Existentialists begin and end with the individual and with his subjectivity. The individual is forever "in situation," writes Sartre. His self emerges in projects, in undertakings; it does not preexist. His acts are free acts; he is dreadfully free to make of himself, at every moment, something other than what he is. Fearful though it is (because "anything is possible"), the individual's freedom is finite. He may perceive multiple possibilities; but he can choose only against the background of necessity. Everyone has a past, a family, an environment; teachers, like other working people and professionals, are controlled or limited by "givens" connected with their jobs. These suggest only some of the necessities that must somehow be synthesized with possibility. The problem for the individual is to transform necessity into freedom by taking responsibility for it, acting toward the future rather than the past. In James Joyce's *A Portrait of the Artist as a Young Man,* Stephen Dedalus is terribly burdened by the determinants of family, nation, and the Catholic Church. He succeeds at last in saying "Non serviam—I will not serve"; but he can only do so in the process of exorcising his demons (the things that shaped him, placed him, made demands on him, obligated him) by naming them, making ordered sense of them—in his case, transmuting them into what might some day be works of art. Obviously, not every person is required to be an artist to break free. However, he *can* master his necessity— whether in the guise of "nationality, language, religion," the deficits caused by poverty, or middle-class "processing"—by refusing to acquiesce. He can make his own sense as he experiences the anxiety disclosing possibility. Like Dedalus, becoming desperate to "fly by the nets," a ghetto child may experience the disquietude of realizing that he may become a writer or a businessman, that he can act in a way that will change his plight. In a sense, he has two alternatives. Thinking back to the jobless men he saw around him in his childhood, to the inequities his family confronted, he can say that the system has arranged things in such a way that he has no chance of "making it" in any rewarding job. Self-convinced, he may then sit back, because he sees no point to working hard in school. Or, reaching back into his childhood, trying to determine the causes of the reality he perceives, he may choose to call the sort of existence he knows best unacceptable. In turn, this refusal may lead him to make a defiant effort to improve his writing or his arithmetic, either to understand his reality more completely or to become what he has not been before. In other words, his refusal may disclose a future heretofore unseen. Like Stephen Dedalus deciding to go into exile, he may have become sharply aware of himself at a particular moment. He may have realized the necessity to decide one way or another just at that moment, without any guarantee of success. Something—conscience, perhaps, or a sudden perception of intolerable lacks in his life situation—may have summoned him to action. Acting, making his choice without any promise of victory, he has created new values, invented a new self.

Although naturalist philosophers would emphasize that the stuff of identity derives in large part from the culture in which the person matures and that the self must be deeply affected by the "generalized other" (or the community attitudes internalized in the course of growing up), they also think of achieving—if not inventing—a self. The cultural components of the self might represent a "me"; but there is also a conscious and critical "I," responsible for shaping internalized notions. The difference between this approach and that of the existentialists lies mainly in the way social engagement is weighted and the way it affects choosing when ethical judgments are to be made.

For the existentialist, the self is devoid of character or coloration before action is undertaken. When the individual begins devising projects and purposes, he begins creating an identity. No outside factor or force, no science or set of rules or moral law, can make decisions for him. The only significant choices are those that involve him totally and project his existence into a future still unknown. The only meaningful choices are those for which he takes full responsibility. If he sits back and makes abstract judgments ("Yes, racism really should be abolished"; "Teachers are justified in joining the union"; "Classes here ought to be individualized"), he is in danger of "bad faith." His chances of authentication are diminished, because his authenticity depends on his capacity (or his courage) to cope with the anxiety of the human condition, his condition. The ability to confront the threat of nothingness, to acknowledge mortality, moves a person to act. He *knows* the only meanings that exist are the ones he achieves, the only values that exist are the ones he creates; he knows that, if he does not act, nothingness will overtake him and his world. He also knows that, because *he*—the concrete person—is going to die some day, he will not have an infinite number of opportunities for choosing. Conscious that he passes this way only once, he would have to suffer a nagging guilt if he did not or could not act. These perceptions come when an individual feels the "homelessness" Martin Buber describes when he realizes that "nausea" can afflict him at any moment, when he understands that the stagesets can collapse at any time. Such an individual, like the mass of men, may well yearn for what Nietzsche calls the temperate zone, where people live comfortably enough with a certainty that the "right" has been revealed. He may feel nostalgia for the time when mankind believed in a sustaining divine design, when even he might have had faith that something outside would provide. But he knows, deeply and primordially, that he has been thrown into an absurd universe without assurances or support; and he knows, if he is to create an essence, a humanity for himself, that he must act fully conscious of his plight. He knows, with an unmistakable anguish many would like to avoid, that he must choose without ever being able to prove the correctness of his choice.

Sartre's short story "The Wall" provides an extreme instance of this idea. The action takes place in a fascist prison cell during the Spanish Civil War on the night preceding the dawn on which three men are to be executed. Pablo Ibbieta, just after his two comrades are led away to be shot, is given one final opportunity to save his life by telling his captors the whereabouts of an anarchist who is his friend. Ibbieta has by then reached the point at which the cause of anarchism has come to seem wholly meaningless, his comrades detestable, the memory of his mistress worthless. He has no good reason left for his refusal, because nothing seems important to him any longer. Nevertheless, feeling totally alone, he will not betray his friend. The absurdity of the world in which he makes his momentous choice is dramatized when, after thinking he would rather die than betray (even though "life had no value"), he sends the officers on a wild-goose chase. His only motive was "to see them stand up, buckle their belts and give orders busily." Knowing that his friend is hiding at his cousin's house in the town, he sends the officers to the cemetery. Ironically, however, they return with Ramon, the friend. Crazily enough, because he "didn't want to owe anything to anybody," Ramon had left his relative's house and gone to hide in the cemetery. Ibbieta is released: "I laughed so hard I cried." Not only has he been unable to think of any good reasons for his decision; the universe has mocked him; neither reward nor reassurance is anywhere. Still, he has created himself as someone who insisted on dying "cleanly." He has acted on his freedom; he has been in "good faith."

Private and subjective as existential choosing is, however, it does not entail the rejection of human brotherhood. An individual can choose himself and authenticate himself (without "good reasons"), even when he is one among many, when he affirms his engagement with humanity.

André Malraux, in *Man's Fate,* also uses a revolution to symbolize the exemplary extreme situation, when a man makes his choice at the limit where the alternatives are ultimate ones. Near the end of the novel, some of the revolutionaries awaiting execution prepare to swallow the cyanide pills their leaders have given to them. Since they are to be killed by being thrust into the boiler of a locomotive, suicide seems a happy release. When a young wounded prisoner drops his cyanide in the darkness and loses it, Katov, another prisoner, passes him his cyanide. Then Katov presses his hand "on the verge of tears, held by that pitiful fraternity, without a face, almost without a real voice (all whispers resemble one another), which was being offered him in this darkness in return for the greatest gift he had ever made, and which perhaps was made in vain."[27] In a moment, the man next to him is dead, and no one will ever know what Katov has done. When he is marched away in the darkness and "all the heads, with a slight movement, followed the rhythm of his walk, with love, with dread, with resignation," it appears for a moment that Katov has acted charitably, according to traditional Christian norms (although he has been an orthodox Communist through most of his life) and that somehow there ought to be a reward. There is no reward, however; there is no victory. There is only a man who, at the last moment, created himself as a dignified and loving person; there are other condemned men who have created themselves as "humanity" in the face of their common fate, the communion of death.

We must grant that, in his ordinary life, the teacher does not confront such extreme situations. Nevertheless, given the uncertainties of the present, he is likely to be thrust increasingly into situations that put his values to the test. On many occasions, the local community may feel threatened or angered by what is happening in a school. The teacher may be forced to defend his right to assign a particular novel, to teach the theory of evolution, to deal impartially with different political systems. He may be challenged for his handling of religious observances, his support of certain causes, his membership in certain organizations. He may be faced with the painful reality of a boycott or a teachers' strike, when he must choose between his obligations to his students and his loyalty to the union. He may be asked to take a stand on a colleague's political opinions, his personal appearance, his behavior outside the school. Rarely are there clear precedents, reliable norms, or a general consensus about what is right for the individual to do. When he finally does make a choice, the teacher can never know absolutely that the choice was the best that could be made.

The teacher who is familiar with anguish and absurdity can hardly feel sanguine in his ordinary life. And the more he becomes sensitized to the inequities and the cruelties in society, to the complicity with which he may be increasingly charged, the less sanguine he is likely to be. For all the aura of righteousness traditionally granted his profession, he can only feel a special sort of nostalgia, a special sort of "homelessness." The schoolroom, once a refuge from the storms outside, a place where children could be molded in a manner their elders *knew* was "good," has become a place of risks and strange uncertainties—at least for the teacher willing to see. Jim Haskins writes about a not unusual Wednesday in his Harlem school:

> Everybody knew the principal was out of school all day for a meeting and the students went wild, while most of the teachers stood talking in the halls. Many teachers admit that the school is really controlled by the students. They call it "the snake pit" or "the ship of fools" because so many teachers appear on the edge of a mental breakdown. About four teachers who have been "released from duties" at other schools have found a home here.[28]

Having transformed his sixth grade into an open classroom for thirty-six Harlem children, Herbert Kohl writes at the end of the year:

> Yet how to discover what is right to teach, how to fight in a single classroom the monumental indifference of an entire system, how to help the thirty-six children now grown to sixty? I struggled with those questions, talked to the children of success and failure, of their strength and ability to overcome indifference and hostility. Words are so little, so temporary a solace.[29]

As is well known, none of Kohl's thirty-six children attained the success he or she gave promise of when he was teaching them. But Kohl was only in their school for one year. Given the nature of school and society, a year was simply not enough.

Many teachers have the support of the "system" today in opening their classrooms, individualizing teaching, consulting parents, and the like. In a sense, they—and their pupils—are confronted more directly than before with the difficult questions about values in education. Not only do they have to ask themselves repeatedly "What is right to teach?"; they have to ask *when* to teach and when to leave a child to his own devices. The child, in turn, has to cope with a new freedom, oftentimes a "dreadful" freedom. At the same time, there is the always troubling problem of compulsion, because even the new experiments are being undertaken in compulsory schools. The tension between necessity and possibility becomes inescapable. It becomes more and more unlikely that what Sartre called the "abstract and logical sense and significance of [their] undertakings" can be settled in advance. "Sense and significance" seem less and less likely to be *conferred* from outside activities, despite the apparent consensus among such "authorities" as Charles Silberman, Lillian Weber, and Joseph Featherstone. Hearing about the open classroom from such writers, the teacher may well have felt at the time that the value of such a classroom was somehow inherent in what could be accomplished there. However, once he begins honestly to individualize, to control himself when he is tempted to advise or direct or prescribe, the teacher can only feel uncertain much of the time. All the praise given to the British Infant Schools and to certain efforts within American schools does not ensure the significance of *his* particular undertaking. Sartre talks about "alarm clocks, signboards, tax returns, policemen" as "barriers against dread." The teacher may think of bells, chalkboards, hall passes in the same fashion. No matter what the disorder and uncertainty in the classroom, he can always look about and find the touchstones of "normality." The teacher who experiences existential unease, however, may find that because he can no longer function as he habitually did, the familiar teaching enterprise no longer exists. At such a point, he will understand what Sartre means when he says:

> ... as soon as the undertaking fails me, as soon as I am sent back to myself because I must await myself in the future, I suddenly find myself to be the one who gives its meaning to the alarm clock, who forbids himself, at the instance of a signboard, to walk on a flower-bed or a lawn, who lends its urgency to the chief's order, who decides on the interest of the book he is writing, who brings it about, finally, that values exist to determine his action by their exigencies.[30]

"Who brings it about ...": The "I," or the human actor, capable of free will brings values into existence, endows the world with meanings it otherwise does not possess.

We have noted that pragmatists and empiricists, too, deny the prior or objective existence of values. Unlike the deontologists, they see values as functions or consequences of intelligent action, of a conscious compliance with linguistic rules, of a free decision to govern behavior by proceeding

according to rational norms. The great difference between their approach
and that of the existentialists is partly defined by the existentialists'
emphasis on *will*. No other philosophers talk of creating values through
what traditionalists would call "normless" or "arbitrary" choice. If there
are norms or standards for existentialists, they are events within
consciousness; and the individual becomes aware of them when he feels
summoned or impelled to take responsible action for the sake of
wholeness, to correct lacks in concrete situations and thus alter them in
the light of some projected "ideal."

In the recent past, many personal reports on teaching situations enable
teachers to imagine themselves in concrete situations and to look upon
education from that vantage point rather than from the position of the
spectator. Kohl, Kozol, Holt, Herndon, Haskins, Dennison, and the others
who have written in this vein may conclude their accounts by referring to
a particular philosophic viewpoint. But when they write about actual day
to day experiences, they almost never talk about making decisions in
accord with overarching norms. They simply present accounts of choices
they have personally made (often in defiance of the customary), without
knowing whether their decisions would be approved or whether they
would "work" in any pragmatic sense. They have had various motives:
Some have instituted classroom changes out of pity for children; some, out
of enthusiasm for new kinds of learning; others, out of a desire to reform;
still others, out of a desire to write books. However, at some point or
other, most of these people have given evidence that despair or guilt or
boredom originally summoned them, as individuals, to action. The
existentialists would call such action ethical action. They would say that,
in the undertaking of it, each person was creating himself anew. They
would also say that, unlike theorists and "educationists" of the past and
present, these men (whether "right" or "wrong" in the last analysis) could
not be charged with "bad faith." These young teachers did not, at least,
give way to indifference, which is the greatest immorality. They did show,
for all the risks and perplexities, that they were capable of "care."

Also, to an extent, all these men were capable of breaking with what
the phenomenologist calls the natural attitude, with the everyday. We
recall the phenomenological concern with things themselves and with the
ways things and events, in their structures and relations, present
themselves to consciousness. In addition, the phenomenological concern
with values emphasizes the questioning of presuppositions, preferences, or
the presumably "objective." Edmund Husserl thought of ethics as a
normative science, however; and he differed from many existentialists in
his concern for establishing final norms to govern practical activity.
Although value agreements needed some rational ground, he said, values
could only be realized by individual subjectivities. Each person, pursuing

the best that is possible for him, acting in accord with his capacities, attains a kind of "self-satisfaction" whether he turns out to have been in error or not. Also, each person holds in his mind an ideal of totality or harmony, requiring, if realizable, rationally grounded agreements. There is always an ethical striving toward such agreements and the harmony they would produce; there is a sense of belonging to a human community, to "humanity" perceived as norm.

To realize values or to bring them into being, the individual must not allow himself to be dominated by his group or community or give up his subjective "need" for wholeness and completion. For Martin Heidegger, values seem to be fragments of Being, disintegrated through human forgetfulness. As remains or residues, they are evocative of oneness or unity; and men yearn after them, finding them to be desirable objects of choice. Fundamental to this is the notion of "care," of concern, the realization that the individual is the source of meaning and that, for all his finitude and consequent "nothingness," he is wholly responsible for introducing values in the world.

The phenomenologist, more than the existentialist, is interested in language, because language brings things into the open for the human being. Discussing the development of the child in phenomenological terms, Maurice Merleau-Ponty shows how intellectual, affective, and linguistic patterns of growth depend on one another.

> In sum, the intellectual elaboration of our experience of the world is constantly supported by the affective elaboration of our inter-human relations. The use of certain linguistic tools is mastered in the play of forces that constitute the subject's relations to his human surroundings. The linguistic usage achieved by the child depends strictly on the "position" . . . that is taken by the child at every moment in the play of forces in his family and his human environment.[31]

This discussion enriches the idea that the individual's perceived life-world is and remains the primary reality. Each person's life-world takes shape as the immediate experiences of the concrete, intersubjectively constituted world find expression through various kinds of behavior, including language. Valuing, therefore, takes place *within* a context accessible in large measure by language. Bringing "good" and "desirable" into existence the individual is always within the world, acting, undergoing, suffering; and all his expressions, like all his commitments, take on meaning only when he directs himself *toward* the world—not simply when he resolves conflicts of impulse or when he gives "good reasons" for his actions.

The teacher, painfully aware of his responsibility in a shifting world, is thrust into even greater uncertainties by an overview of value orientations. There is probably no way, even if he chooses the approach of "complementarity," for the individual to take from these diverse approaches fragments he can order into a whole. Eclecticism may be as inhibiting as total skepticism. Again, the teacher has to decide what makes sense for him. This decision is, after all, the object of "doing philosophy": to find apertures in the wall of what is taken for granted; to pierce the webs of obscurity; to see and then to choose. The teacher is not expected to take a self-consistent view like Peters' and attempt to merge it with Sartre's view or Heidegger's. The moods and stances are too different. He cannot be cool, objective, deliberate—and, at the same time, passionately *engagé*. He cannot (using existential criteria) charge someone like Peters with indifference because he focuses on the language of moral discourse, on reasons, and on rules. He cannot charge Dewey with "bad faith" because he pays (according to existential norms) insufficient attention to the inwardness of the man engaging in valuation, to the dread responsibility of the "single one." He can only attend to each philosopher on that philosopher's grounds, look through his perspective, and discover what the perspective reveals about his (the teacher's) life-world. He must think about what he is doing, take responsibility for his choices, *care* about the actions he undertakes to free his students and make himself the kind of teacher he wills himself to be.

Notes and References

1. Sigmund Freud, *Civilization and Its Discontents,* tr. Joan Riviere (London: The Hogarth Press, 1953), p. 63.

2. William Golding, *Lord of the Flies* (New York: Capricorn Books, 1959), p. 175.

3. Herbert Marcuse, *One Dimensional Man: Studies in the Ideology of Advanced Industrial Society* (Boston: Beacon Press, 1966), p. 7.

4. Norman Brown, *Love's Body* (New York: Random House, 1966), p. 243.

5. R. D. Laing, *The Politics of Experience* (New York: Ballantine Books, 1967), pp. 60–61.

6. Theodore Roszak, *The Making of a Counter Culture: Reflections on the Technocratic Society and Its Useful Opposition* (Garden City, N.Y.: Doubleday Anchor Books, 1969), pp. 80–82.

7. Lawrence Kohlberg, "Education for Justice: A Modern Statement of the Platonic View," in *Moral Education: Five Lectures* (Cambridge, Mass.: Harvard University Press, 1970), p. 72.

8. Michael B. Katz, *Class, Bureaucracy, & Schools: The Illusion of Educational Change in America* (New York: Frederick A. Praeger, Publishers, 1971), p. 116.

9. James Herndon, *The Way It Spozed to Be* (New York: Bantam Books, 1969), p. 173.

10. G. E. Moore, *Principia Ethica* (Cambridge, Eng.: Cambridge University Press, 1903), pp. 7–8.

11. David Hume, *An Enquiry Concerning the Principles of Morals,* in *Hume: Selections,* ed. Charles W. Hendel, Jr. (New York: Charles Scribner's Sons, 1927), p. 197.

12. William K. Frankena, *Ethics* (Englewood Cliffs, N.J.: Prentice-Hall, 1963), p. 95.

13. James Herndon, *The Way It Spozed to Be,* pp. 176–177.

14. Richard S. Peters, *Ethics and Education* (Glenview, Ill.: Scott, Foresman & Company, 1967), p. 27.

15. Daniel Berrigan, *The Trial of the Catonsville Nine* (New York: Bantam Books, 1970), p. 79.

16. John Dewey, "The Construction of Good," in *The Quest for Certainty* (London: George Allen & Unwin, 1930), p. 255.

17. John Dewey, "The Construction of Good," p. 272.

18. Richard S. Peters, *Ethics and Education,* p. 27.

19. C. K. Ogden and I. A. Richards, *The Meaning of Meaning: A Study of The Influence of Language upon Thought and of The Science of Symbolism* (New York: Harcourt Brace Jovanovich, 1948).

20. C. K. Ogden and I. A. Richards, *The Meaning of Meaning,* pp. 123–129.

21. Alfred Jules Ayer, *Language, Truth and Logic* (London: Victor Gollancz, 1950), p. 107.

22. Alfred Jules Ayer, *Language, Truth and Logic,* p. 107.

23. Ludwig Wittgenstein, *The Blue Book,* in *Philosophy in the Twentieth Century,* vol. 2, ed. William Barrett and Henry D. Aiken (New York: Random House, 1962), p. 733.

24. A. Stafford Clayton, "Education and Some Moves Toward a Value Methodology," in *Theory of Value and Problems of Education,* ed. Philip G. Smith (Urbana: University of Illinois Press, 1970), p. 133.

25. Stephen E. Toulmin, *An Examination of The Place of Reason in Ethics* (Cambridge, Eng.: Cambridge University Press, 1960), p. 163.

26. Jean-Paul Sartre, *Anti-Semite and Jew,* tr. George J. Becker (New York: Schocken Books, 1948), p. 18.

27. André Malraux, *Man's Fate,* tr. Haakon M. Chevalier (New York: The Modern Library, 1936), p. 327.

28. Jim Haskins, *Diary of a Harlem Schoolteacher* (New York: Grove Press, 1970), p. 79.

29. Herbert Kohl, *Thirty-Six Children* (New York: New American Library, 1967), p. 191.

30. Jean-Paul Sartre, *Being and Nothingness* (New York: Philosophical Library, 1956), p. 39.

31. Maurice Merleau-Ponty, "The Child's Relations with Others," in *The Primacy of Perception,* ed. James M. Edie (Evanston, Ill.: Northwestern University Press, 1964), pp. 112–113.

Further Reading

Hannah Arendt, "Lying in Politics" and "Civil Disobedience," in *Crises of The Republic* (New York: Harcourt Brace Jovanovich, 1972).

John L. Austin, *How to Do Things with Words,* ed. J. O. Urmson and G. J. Warnock (London: Oxford University Press, 1965).

George Berkeley, *Principles of Human Knowledge,* in *The English Philosophers from Bacon to Mill,* ed. Edwin A. Burtt (New York: The Modern Library, 1939).

Luther J. Binkley, *Contemporary Ethical Theories: An Analysis of the New Approach to Ethics by Contemporary British and American Philosophers* (New York: Philosophical Library, 1961).

Richard Brandt, *Ethical Theory* (Englewood Cliffs, N.J.: Prentice-Hall, 1959).

Martin Buber, *I and Thou,* tr. Walter Kaufmann (New York: Charles Scribner's Sons, 1970).

Richard T. De George, ed., *Ethics and Society: Original Essays on Contemporary Moral Problems* (Garden City, N.Y.: Doubleday & Company, 1966).

John Dewey, *Human Nature and Conduct* (New York: The Modern Library, 1930).

Marjorie Grene, *Dreadful Freedom: A Critique of Existentialism* (Chicago: University of Chicago Press, 1948).

Richard M. Hare, *The Language of Morals* (New York: Oxford University Press, 1964).

Martin Heidegger, "Letter on Humanism," tr. Edgar Lohner, in *Philosophy in the Twentieth Century,* vol. 3, ed., William Barrett and Henry D. Aiken (New York: Random House, 1962).

Edmund Husserl, *Phenomenology and the Crisis of Philosophy,* tr. Quentin Lauer (New York: Harper & Row, Publishers, 1965).

Karl Jaspers, *Man in the Modern Age* (Garden City, N.Y.: Doubleday & Company, 1957).

James Joyce, *A Portrait of the Artist as a Young Man,* in *The Portable James Joyce* (New York: The Viking Press, 1947).

Wolfgang Kohler, *The Place of Value in a World of Facts* (New York: Meridian Books, 1959).

Paul Kurtz, *Decision and the Condition of Man* (New York: Dell Publishing Company, 1968).

Friedrich Nietzsche, *On the Genealogy of Morals and Ecce Homo,* tr. and ed. Walter Kaufmann (New York: Vintage Books, 1967).

Paul Ramsey, *Nine Modern Moralists: Paul Tillich; Karl Marx; H. Richard Niebuhr; Fyodor Dostoevski; Reinhold Niebuhr; Jacques Maritain; Jean-Paul Sartre; Emil Brunner; Edmond Cahn* (Englewood Cliffs, N.J.: Prentice-Hall, 1962).

Jean-Paul Sartre, "The Wall," in *Intimacy and Other Stories* (New York: New Directions Publishing Corporation, 1948).

Paul Taylor, *Normative Discourse* (Englewood Cliffs, N.J.: Prentice-Hall, 1961).

Eliseo Vivas, *The Moral Life and the Ethical Life* (Chicago: Henry Regnery, 1963).

Chapter Eleven

Teacher as Stranger

... And must not an animal be a lover of learning who
determines what is or is not friendly to him by the test of
knowledge and ignorance?

Most assuredly.

And is not the love of learning the love of wisdom, which is
philosophy?

They are the same, he replied.

And may we not say confidently of man also, that he who is
likely to be gentle to his friends and acquaintances, must by
nature be a lover of wisdom and knowledge?

That we may safely affirm.

Then he who is to be a really good and noble guardian of the
State will require to unite in himself philosophy and spirit and
swiftness and strength?

Undoubtedly.

Then we have found the desired natures; and now that we
have found them, how are they to be reared and educated?

Plato
The Republic

The University! So he had passed beyond the challenge of the
sentries who had stood as guardians of his boyhood and had
sought to keep him among them that he might be subject to
them and serve their ends. Pride after satisfaction uplifted him
like long slow waves. The end he had been born to serve yet did
not see had led him to escape by an unseen path: and now it
beckoned to him once more and a new adventure was about to
be opened to him.

James Joyce
A Portrait of the Artist as a Young Man

To take a stranger's vantage point on everyday reality is to look
inquiringly and wonderingly on the world in which one lives. It is like
returning home from a long stay in some other place. The homecomer

notices details and patterns in his environment he never saw before. He finds that he has to think about local rituals and customs to make sense of them once more. For a time he feels quite separate from the person who is wholly at home in his ingroup and takes the familiar world for granted. Such a person, writes Alfred Schutz, ordinarily "accepts the ready-made standardized scheme of the cultural pattern handed down to him by ancestors, teachers, and authorities as an unquestioned and unquestionable guide in all the situations which normally occur within the social world."[1] The homecomer may have been such a person. Now, looking through new eyes, he cannot take the cultural pattern for granted. It may seem arbitrary to him or incoherent or deficient in some way. To make it meaningful again, he must interpret and reorder what he sees in the light of his changed experience. He must consciously engage in inquiry.

When thinking-as-usual becomes untenable for anyone, the individual is bound to experience a crisis of consciousness. The formerly unquestioned has become questionable; the submerged has become visible. He may become like Meursault in Albert Camus's *The Stranger,* when he looks at his own murder trial and sees an ingroup ritual:

> Just then I noticed that almost all the people in the courtroom were greeting each other, exchanging remarks and forming groups—behaving, in fact, as in a club where the company of others of one's own tastes and standing makes one feel at ease. That, no doubt, explained the odd impression I had of being *de trop* here, a sort of gate-crasher.[2]

Or he may come to resemble Hester Prynne, in Nathaniel Hawthorne's *The Scarlet Letter.* Ostracized for having committed adultery, Hester is forced to live at the edge of the wilderness, on the outskirts of the Puritan community. Because she has "a mind of native courage and activity," her "estranged point of view" enables her to look critically at institutions once taken for granted, to criticize all "with hardly more reverence than the Indian would feel for the clerical band, the judicial robe, the pillory, the gallows, the fireside, or the church."[3] Both Meursault and Hester are strangers in the sense that they do not share the conventional vision. Camus describes an entirely honest man who will not pretend to share the cultural pieties; Hawthorne describes a woman who is "emancipated." Both see more than their less conscious fellow citizens could possibly see. Both are ready to wonder and question; and it is in wonder and questioning that learning begins.

We do not ask that the teacher perceive his existence as absurd; nor do we demand that he estrange himself from his community. We simply suggest that he struggle against unthinking submergence in the social reality that prevails. If he wishes to present himself as a person actively engaged in critical thinking and authentic choosing, he cannot accept any "ready-made standardized scheme" at face value. He cannot even take for granted the value of intelligence, rationality, or education. Why, after all, *should* a human being act intelligently or rationally? How *does* a teacher justify the educational policies he is assigned to carry out within his school? If the teacher does not pose such questions to himself, he cannot expect his students to pose the kinds of questions about experience which will involve them in self-aware inquiry.

Maurice Merleau-Ponty attributes the feeling of certainty that rules out questioning to the ancient notion that each human being carries within him a *homunculus,* or "little man," who can "see" what is real and true. This *homunculus* represents what is best in the human being; and, unlike the person involved with the natural world and other people, the phantom creature inside always knows the Ideal. Merleau-Ponty writes:

> The "little man within man" is only the phantom of our successful expressive operations; and the admirable man is not this phantom but the man who—installed in his fragile body, in a language which has already done so much speaking, and in a reeling history—gathers himself together and begins to see, to understand, and to signify. There is no longer anything decorous or decorative about today's humanism. It no longer loves man in opposition to his body, mind in opposition to its language, values in opposition to facts. It no longer speaks of man and mind except in a sober way, with modesty: mind and man never are; they show through the movement by which the body becomes gesture, language an oeuvre, and coexistence truth.[4]

The teacher is frequently addressed as if he had no life of his own, no body, and no inwardness. Lecturers seem to presuppose a "man within man" when they describe a good teacher as infinitely controlled and accommodating, technically efficient, impervious to moods. They are likely to define him by the role he is *expected* to play in a classroom, with all his loose ends gathered up and all his doubts resolved. The numerous realities in which he exists as a living person are overlooked. His personal biography is overlooked; so are the many ways in which he expresses his private self in language, the horizons he perceives, the perspectives through which he looks on the world.

Our concern throughout this book has been to make that person visible to himself. If the teacher agrees to submerge himself into the system, if he consents to being defined by others' views of what he is supposed to be, he gives up his freedom "to see, to understand, and to signify" for himself. If he is immersed and impermeable, he can hardly stir others to define themselves as individuals. If, on the other hand, he is willing to take the view of the homecomer and create a new perspective on what he has habitually considered real, his teaching may become the project of a person vitally open to his students and the world. Then he will be in a position to define himself as "admirable" in Merleau-Ponty's sense. He will be continuously engaged in interpreting a reality forever new; he will feel more alive than he ever has before.

Seeking the communicative gesture and the expressive word, such a teacher will try consciously to move among and reflect together with his students. Coexisting with them, opening up perspectival possibilities along with them, he and they may journey toward some important truths as the days go on. "Sometimes one starts to dream," Merleau-Ponty writes, "about what culture, literary life, and teaching could be if all those who participate, having for once rejected idols, would give themselves up to the happiness of reflecting together."[5] The teacher in the United States, facing the adversity of his historic moment, facing violence and inequities and irrationality, may believe the dream to be impossible. Yet, at some level of his consciousness, he may insist on just this kind of happiness. In Albert Camus's *The Plague,* the doctor says he thinks it is *right* to refuse to be balked of happiness. Later, when the plague has reached its peak and he is exhausted by the hopeless battle against it, he still can smile at a young journalist who wants to break the quarantine and escape from the town; in fact, he tells the journalist to hurry "because I, too, would like to do my bit for happiness." There are no good arguments against such a desire. The teacher who feels he too is fighting plague can still nurture the dream.

In this final chapter, we shall have the dream in mind as we talk of possibility and moral choosing and the arts. There will be no closure for us; there cannot be. The questions implicit in our initial chapter remain open: the questions having to do with defining *education,* determining educational purposes, achieving democracy. Customarily, books on educational philosophy conclude with talk of the democratic character, summon up visions of a "good society," or explain the relationships between world understanding and effective public schools. There is always a tendency to drive toward completion, to finish the design, to stand back and look at an articulated whole. Recognizing that each reader must strive

toward such completion for himself, we choose to conclude in the mood
expressed by Nick Henry in Ernest Hemingway's *A Farewell to Arms:*

> I was always embarrassed by the words sacred, glorious and
> sacrifice and the expression in vain. We had heard them,
> sometimes standing in the rain almost out of earshot, so that
> only the shouted words came through, and had read them, on
> proclamations that were slapped up by billposters over other
> proclamations, now for a long time, and I had seen nothing
> sacred, and the things that were glorious had no glory and the
> sacrifices were like the stockyards at Chicago if nothing was
> done with the meat except to bury it. There were many words
> that you could not stand to hear.[6]

Of course, the teacher's experience is not identical with that of a
soldier trapped in a retreat; but most teachers know the meaning of the
slogans and pieties they hear on loudspeaker systems and the
proclamations they read on bulletin boards, reminders of the glorious
purposes pursued by the institution. What teacher has seen anything
sacred in the corridors? Do the things called "glorious" have glory?
Charles Silberman quotes a high school principal, who says: " 'Maybe the
public may think the schools are democratic. They are democratic as far
as the rights of the individual, but as far as the operation, they are not
democratic. In order to get efficiency in a school system, there has to be a
clear pattern of operation, behavior, rules and regulation. Then there's not
time for a group of people to sit down and thrash out a variety of ideas
and to come up with a quick, clear-cut and efficient policy.' "[7] Writing
about a singing lesson in an American school, Jules Henry describes how
the student must substitute the teacher's criteria for his own: "He must
learn that the proper way to sing is tunelessly and not the way *he* hears
music; that the proper way to paint is the way the teacher says, not the
way he sees it; that the proper attitude is not pleasure but competitive
horror at the success of his classmates, and so on."[8]

Names and concrete nouns are not the only words that ought to be
used in talk about education. But if the teacher can think what he is doing
in the concrete situations of his life, he must be aware of the conventions
currently used to organize reality. He must be conscious that the "fictions"
used in sense making (in the schools as well as outside the schools) are
mental constructs, man-made schemata, deserving only "conditional
assent."[9] This point is particularly important in a time like the present, an

era distinctive for the walls of images and words constantly being erected between us and actuality. We need only recall the bombardment of media images that replace the "reality" they purport to represent, that make "the 11 o'clock News" out of wartime atrocities, protest demonstrations, prison riots, political pronouncements, accidents, deformities, deaths. We need only recall the proliferating euphemisms, "waste the enemy," "protective reaction," "correctional facility," "national security," "behavioral engineering," "off the pig," "power to the people," and the rest. It has become all too easy to distance and distort what is experienced with language of that kind. It has become all too easy to cope with social relationships through the taking on and the assigning of roles.

The teacher is continually being asked (at least obliquely) to write a pious and authoritative role for himself and submissive or savage or special roles for the young people he teaches. He has to make a deliberate effort to realize that no role can fully encompass a personality, just as no slogan or abstraction or popular phrase can do justice to a human situation. Unless he is careful, the teacher may tend to oversimplify by means of language, to smooth over the rough places, to live by self-serving myths. For this reason, we are unwilling to end this book by spelling out overarching purposes or slapping still another proclamation on the schoolroom wall.

It makes little difference if the proclamation calls for the defense of the nation or personal liberation, citizenship or spontaneity. Once we spell out aims in general, we are in danger of "embarrassing" ourselves. Moreover, the teacher's feeling of responsibility may well be eroded by an implicit demand that he be the agent of an externally defined purpose, which he can only understand as a slogan or still another expression of prevailing piety. We would emphasize once more the need for self-consciousness and clarity on the part of the individual, the need to frame conditional orders. His aims, therefore, can only be specific ones, identified in concrete situations with respect to concrete tasks and subject matters, where structures and relevancies are not always clear. They must be pursued as lacks are perceived and actions undertaken. Because persons differ, achievements vary, horizons shift, perspectives alter, his aims can never be twice the same.

It must be clear by now that, no matter how carefully he deliberates, how artfully he develops alternative modes of instruction, the teacher is forever involved in constituting meanings. This act of forming applies to perspectives on the teaching act, on education viewed as intentional undertaking and as social enterprise. It applies to the perspectives through which persons are seen, knowledge structures apprehended, ethical problems resolved. Also it applies to questions touching on dissent, reform, and the transformation of cultural institutions; it applies to the methods chosen for responding to the inhumanities of the time. The teacher can not assert that the schools should or should not "dare to change the social order." He must choose the part he will play in such an effort. He must even choose how to conceive the "social order": as an oppressive, impersonal system, as a series of fluid human communities, as "the best of all possible worlds."

At a time of major tensions among groups and moral systems, no educator is in a position to impose designs for harmonizing clashing interests. In his school, for example, the teacher may *propose* resolutions when racial groups are fighting with each other; he may, in time of dire emergency, suppress conflict by force. But it appears to be immoral, at this time, to decide *for* any individual or group what is fair, decent, or humane. Expertise no longer possesses transfer value for other people's private, immediately apprehended experiences, for predicaments that must be phenomenologically understood. The educational task, in the moral domain as well as in others, is to find out how to enable individuals to choose intelligently and authentically for themselves. It involves learning how to equip them with the conceptual tools, the self-respect, and the opportunities to choose—in specific circumstances—how to do what they consider right.

This may be a troubling solution for the teacher who is committed to certain values, causes, or patterns of social change. As citizen or layman, he has the right (and perhaps the obligation) to work for the reforms in which he professes to believe. If he does not act on his beliefs, in fact, he may be said to be in "bad faith," expected to feel "shame." If he has no commitments, if he remains uninvolved, he may not be the engaged, wide-awake teacher young people appear to need. But this causes an inevitable conflict once he commits himself to arousing students to create their own values and seek their own resolutions. Impartial in some areas (when dealing with students as individuals or in their groups), he cannot be impartial or neutral on, say, the Vietnamese War, racial discrimination, drug addiction, or the many injustices that plague American life. Some philosophers, as we have seen, attach so much importance to cool rationality that they would advise the teacher to sublimate his political and social enthusiasms when he is working at school. The teacher has enough to do, they would say, to initiate young people into such activities as "science, poetry, and engineering and possibly a variety of games and pastimes. Most of these are intimately connected not only with occupations and professions but also with possible vocations and ideals of life."[10] Other philosophers would recommend the temperate use of intelligence in cooperative attempts to solve such problems. Still others would draw attention to crisis and adversity. They would insist that political and social commitments permeate an individual's life and that the teacher defines himself as much by the ends he pursues outside the school as by the values he creates within. Conceivably, the activist teacher can struggle for peace and justice for the same reasons he tries to liberate the young to choose for themselves. He knows, as well and as clearly as the analytic philosopher (although on different grounds), that it is morally indefensible to indoctrinate or to tell students categorically that only one mode of action is "right." He may feel, as Jean-Paul Sartre has said, that "in choosing myself, I choose man";[11] but his sense of the universality, even the absoluteness of his choice does not justify his willing against others' freedom. And this is precisely what he would be doing if he tried to use his position to impose his own beliefs.

To lecture against smoking marijuana is obviously questionable; and to proscribe, on moral grounds, use of heroin is futile. What of the student who refuses to attend school regularly because he thinks (as, indeed, his teacher might) that the compulsory school manipulates and imprisons, that he learns far more outside? What of the controversies over sex education? What of the books (such as Piri Thomas's *Down These Mean Streets* or George Jackson's *Soledad Brother*) some charge with being pornographic, subversive, or "inciting to violence"? What, more traditionally, of education for truth telling, decency, cooperativeness, playing fair?

We cannot presume that the teacher functions in an ordered world or a spacious society, where each person's duties in the various departments of his life are clearly set forth. Nor can we take for granted that fundamental agreements lie below the surfaces on a morality viewed as "an instrument of society as a whole for the guidance of individuals and smaller groups."[12] The assumption may be true in the few homogeneous small towns left in America; but it is not likely to be generally true. We have talked about the disintegrating norms throughout the culture, about the loss of trust, about the defiance of codes and the sometimes shocking acceptance of lawbreaking. Much has been written recently about so-called "new crimes": "trashing," pointless vandalism, shoplifting for sport. Gresham Sykes uses divorce as an example, because divorce was once considered shameful and now has little stigma attached to it. He goes on to say that "there are a number of areas of behavior labeled criminal by the law, for which this same sort of 'slipping out from morality' may be occurring for a number of people. The use of drugs, particularly in the case of marihuana, may often be of this order; similarly, certain kinds of sexual behavior, such as premarital sexual relations, seem to be losing a good deal of their moral resonance. The question of whether to engage in such behavior becomes very pragmatic; the question is whether one will be caught."[13]

Complicated problems confront any teacher who attempts "moral education." If he believes, as the positivist philosophers do, that only principles can be taught, along with the nature of good reasons, he still must determine which principles can be made meaningful to the contemporary young. He must determine what sorts of actions have "moral resonance," which do not and which should not. If he considers that guidelines are impossible to define any longer, if he is more concerned with the way people respond to appeals from "conscience" and the way they create themselves as norm-regarding beings, he will still find himself in tension as he watches individuals do violent and careless things. And indeed, no matter what his philosophical approach, the teacher cannot help recognize that human beings are always being demeaned and maltreated, that his students are capable of hatred and bigotries, that it is difficult for anyone *not* to falsify himself. Whether he tries consistently to remain "calm and cool" in the knowledge "that the way of life he prefers, all things considered, includes the moral way of life,"[14] whether he chooses to live "in unsatisfied indignation" because "too high a price is asked for harmony,"[15] he will find himself entangled in the problematic, haunted by open questions. In his capacity as teacher he is expected to know the answers, to have prescriptions at hand which tell the young how they ought to live. Unable to tolerate major personal uncertainties when he is engaged in teaching, he is likely to tell himself that he does indeed have it all worked out, that he *knows.* Camus once wrote: "There is not one human being who, above a certain elementary level of consciousness, does not exhaust himself in trying to find formulae or attitudes which will give his existence the unity it lacks. . . . It is therefore justifiable to say that man has an idea of a better world than this. But better does not mean different, it means unified."[16] This desire for unity or meaning may be the source of the impulse to reach out and to learn; but it can be extremely disquieting, especially for the self-conscious teacher. He can only engage in the movement we have spoken of, at the side of his students, making efforts to constitute meanings—caring intensely about the kind of thinking going on and the choices being made. As aware of his students' incompleteness as he must be of his own, the teacher can only strain to encounter his students without objectifying them; he can only act to help them, as autonomous beings, to choose.

   Let us take, as an example, the predicament of a teacher confronted with a Peace Moratorium, a day on which students stay away from classes in symbolic protest against a war. Like many other such situations, this gesture may provide occasion for a considerable amount of moral education if the teacher makes no arbitrary decisions and if the students are free to decide what they think is right to do. Let us suppose the teacher has been much involved with peace campaigns, has belonged to various peace organizations, and has participated in marches and demonstrations. Let us also suppose the teacher is deeply convinced that atrocrities are being committed in the current war and that they present a moral issue of consequence for every American. He may believe a widespread indifference partly accounts for the massacres that have taken place, the torture, the indiscriminate bombings, and the rest. He may be convinced the Moratorium will have positive results, so positive that they will erase the negative effects of violent protests carried on in the past. As he sees it, then, he has every reason for saying the Moratorium is worth supporting. He is eager, in fact, for his students to turn out in a body to demonstrate their support.

He has, however, other convictions too. The particular lessons he has been teaching are important to him. He does not believe learning sequences ought to be whimsically or foolishly interrupted; he thinks classroom activity, because it brings him in contact with his students, contributes measurably to their education. A lost day, as he sees it, might mean a setback for some of his pupils, missed learning opportunities for others; and, obviously, observing the Moratorium means his losing the day in that sense. He realizes, in addition, that observing it might suggest to the less motivated that there are more worthwhile things to do than studying; to others it might seem an excuse for time off to observe minor holidays, to celebrate World Series victories, and so on. Taking all this into account, he still believes it is more worthwhile to support the peace action than to do nothing at all.

Some would say that, in coming to this conclusion, the teacher should anticipate the consequences (moral and pedagogical) of each course. Others would stress that he must be clear about his own priority system. Still others would talk about the extremity of the war situation and the need, if only in the interests of decency, for each person to rebel. We have been describing a fairly deliberate and rational teacher, who is preoccupied with acting justly in and outside of school. He might well set up as a first principle the idea of justice: human beings ought to be treated with a proper concern for their interests; that they ought never to be discriminated against unless there are relevant grounds for treating them differently (as infant children, criminals, and mentally ill people are treated differently). Thinking of the war and the men, women, and children suffering because of it, the teacher can reasonably say that it is unjust for them to be deprived not only of the right to live in peace but of opportunities for education, economic security, and the kinds of fulfillment Americans take for granted. It makes good sense for him to present this idea to his students as well as to explain why commitment to such a principle makes relevant their idea that the war should be ended, that people should do whatever is in their power to see that this end is brought about.

The same principle of justice, however, may require that he provide each member in his class with the freedom to deliberate on what ought to be done in this instance: whether they should support the Moratorium. If he does not permit this kind of deliberation, he will be interfering with their freedom; and such interference would also be unjust. Personally involved with the Moratorium as he is, he can still recognize that as a teacher his primary obligation is to teach his students the principle of justice in the hope that they will be able to make future decisions, holding that principle clearly in mind. "Morality," writes R. M. Hare, "retains its vigour when ordinary people have learnt afresh to decide for themselves what principles to live by, and more especially what principles to teach their children."[17] The children, too, have to learn afresh as they make decisions of principle. Neither teacher nor parent can feel assured that the young will act as their elders would have done or even as their elders recommend. The point is that the young understand certain principles, make clear the reasons for their decisions, and revise their norms intelligently in response to the contingencies of the world. For the man of rational passion this ought to be enough. He wants the young to know, above all, what they are doing and why; he wants them to be able to explain in understandable language; he wants them to make sense.

When they do understand and make sense, the teacher we have been describing can say he has been successful as a moral educator in one specific situation. To demonstrate his success, he can ask people to listen to the talk proceeding in his classroom, to the way the students go about deliberating on the matter of the Moratorium. Perhaps they will decide not to support it; and they may make their decision cooperatively, slowly, rationally, paying attention to consequences and to the logic of what they are saying. The teacher can only feel gratified because they have achieved a type of mastery new to them. Of course, they could always have decided, with equivalent deliberateness, to support the Moratorium. Or, without much thought, they could have decided to march out of the classroom to join the action because it was so highly publicized, because their friends and their teacher were so much involved. In the latter case, the good teacher (activist or not) would have to feel he had failed.

A kind of heroism is demanded of the principled teacher eager to initiate his students into principled decision making and a rational way of life. *What* they decide is always in question. There are no guarantees that they will be "good" or humane people. The teacher must acknowledge that he can only deal justly with individuals he hopes will learn how to learn. When faced with issues more personally consequential than a Peace Moratorium or when dealing with elementary school children, he may focus on the formation of good habits or the cultivation of the dispositions required for reflective conduct. But here too there are no certainties, even if he resorts to traditional "habit training" or the use of punishments and rewards. We might consider the problem of drugs, for instance—clearly a far more complex question than whether existing laws should be obeyed. Peter Marin has written sympathetically about young people in search of a supportive community life, who "turn to drugs for all the things they cannot find without them." He describes the ways in which the drug cultures answer young people's needs for communities protected from adults, adult ambitions, and what the young see as adult hypocrisy. "They can walk the streets high or sit stoned in class and still be *inside it* (meaning, their own community)—among adults but momentarily free of them, a world *within* which one is at home."[18] Marin recommends a kind of loving detachment, dealing with these young people as if they composed a friendly neighborhood tribe. Whether he is right or wrong in a pragmatic sense, the detachment he recommends may enable the teacher at least to help them articulate the criteria governing their choices of life-style. Refusing to blame them, simply asking them to talk about how and why they live as they do, the teacher may be in a position to make them aware of their principles, which have often turned out to be much akin to "Christian" principles. Even though he may not convince them to give up marijuana, for example, the teacher may help them see the "moral resonance" of the decisions they are making day by day. Marin, of course, has marijuana in mind when he speaks so empathetically about the "stoned"; and he knows, as most teachers do, that far more serious issues are raised by the "hard" and dangerous drugs. When confronted with proselytizing addicts, the teacher can do little; nor can he be persuasive with youth who boast experiences of "expanding consciousness" they know he cannot share. Trying, sometimes in the face of chaos, to suggest alternative ways of getting through life, he can point to consequences and dangers, even as he gives reluctant credence to the delights that are claimed. The least productive road here, as in other moral domains, is the path of tyranny and suppression. Even here many teachers will opt for the values of justice, which (in Lawrence Kohlberg's words) "prohibit the imposition of beliefs of one group upon another."[19] But this does not mean the teacher will give license to the self-destructive; nor does it mean that he will do nothing to change their habits or their style. He might even call in legal authorities and still feel that he was, in Kohlberg's sense, "just." He is a teacher; and, in the case we have been discussing, a teacher with a prior commitment to rationality. His obligation, as he perceives it, is primarily to induce young people to decide in principled fashion what they *conceive* (not merely "feel" or "intuit") to be worthwhile.

How would a teacher with a more existential orientation handle the problems of moral education? There are many different problems, not all revolving around the matter of principles and guidelines. Obviously, he would put great stress on his and his students' freedom and on the need to make choices within frequently "extreme" situations. He would take seriously what the analytically inclined teacher is prone to ignore: the moods he and his student are bound to experience—anguish, boredom, guilt. For him these are anything but pathological states. They are appropriate responses to the contemporary universe with its injustice and impersonality, its underlying "absurdity." Furthermore, they create the affective and subjective context in which choices are made and values defined; doing so, they make unthinkable the predominantly cool, calculative approach to moral life. This does not mean that human beings are determined by their passions, because they can choose whether to give in to them. Nor does it mean that mere impulse or feeling governs moral choice. Sartre talks about "creating the man we want to be." Every act we perform creates an image of man as we *think* he ought to be. "To choose to be this or that is to affirm at the same time the value of what we choose, because we can never choose evil. We always choose the good, and nothing can be good for us without being good for all."[20] Our responsibility, then, is immense, especially when we consider that (for the existentialist) there are no predefined values, no moral principles which determine in advance what is good. Alone and condemned to freedom, the individual *must* choose. He experiences anxiety or anguish because he cannot even be sure that the person he chooses himself to be at one moment is the same as the one he will be at a later time. A student, for example, choosing to be a chemist, investing all his energies in what he has determined to be valuable, cannot know that the "essence" he has fashioned for himself will be the same the following year; yet, in the interim, he will have chosen *not* to do a great many things that might have been relevant to what he eventually decided to become. Anguish is the way freedom reveals itself. It is the expression of the nagging desire for completion—without any guarantee that the completion sought will be valuable when it is achieved. Boredom is the way the threat of nothingness and indifference reveal themselves to consciousness. Choices are made in the face of a "profound boredom" many times, "drifting" (as Martin Heidegger says) "hither and thither in the abysses of existence like a mute fog," drawing all things together in "a queer kind of indifference."[21] What, after all, does it matter? What is the point? These questions, too, are functions of the dreadful freedom in which the individual decides; and the existential teacher would have to take this notion seriously into account. Then there is the matter of guilt, so frequently suppressed or ignored. Guilt may be the expression of a feeling that the individual is not acting on his possibilities, not shaping his future; and yet here too the teacher can never be sure. The existential teacher would not try to assuage such feelings or to evade them. He would consciously stimulate the disquietude they entail; he would provoke to responsible action persons absolutely free to choose themselves.

Given the problem of a Peace Moratorium, such a teacher could not will against his students' freedom or enforce his commitments on them. He would, however, emphasize the evasions that lead to refusals to act. Simply to sit back and condemn a war one recognizes to be unjust and evil is to be guilty of bad faith, especially if there is the possibility of action. For this reason, the German who detested Nazism and still did nothing to demonstrate his opposition is called so ironically a "good German," someone who took no responsibility, who lived his life in bad faith. Therefore, more explicitly than the analytically inclined teacher, the existential educator would underline the inescapability of responsibility. Each person is "the author" of the situation in which he lives; *he* gives meaning to his world, but through action, through his project, not by well-meaning thought. If a student declared his opposition to a war but was not inclined to do anything about it or to be actively concerned about what was being done in his name, he could be charged with evasion and irresponsibility, even though no one would *tell* him what to do.

An article appearing in *The New Yorker* magazine soon after the My Lai massacre in Vietnam was exposed captures some of the feeling that stirs the existential thinker or teacher. The writer says that the war going on was not made by "Man" but by particular men.

> To lay the responsibility on Man or on War is to make nobody accountable, and is to move in the direction of regarding the massacre as part of a natural, acceptable course of events. ... And we are as accountable for our self-deceptions as for our deceptions. With the report of the My Lai massacre, we face a new situation. It is no longer possible for us to say that we did not know. When we look at the photographs published in *Life* and see bodies of women and children in piles, and look into the faces of an old woman and a young girl who (we are told) are about to be shot, we feel that a kind of violence is being done to our feelings, and that the massacre threatens to overpower us. To block it out, we may freeze. If we face the massacre for what it is, we are torn by almost unbearable grief, but if we turn away and let the rationalizations crowd into our minds to protect us, we are degraded.[22]

This statement is reminiscent of Camus's *The Plague* and Tarrou's conversation with Doctor Rieux on the night they go swimming:

"Have you ever seen a man shot by a firing-squad? No, of course not; the spectators are hand-picked and it's like a private party, you need an invitation. The result is that you've gleaned your ideas about it from books and pictures. A post, a blind-folded man, some soldiers in the offing. But the real thing isn't a bit like that. Do you know that the firing-squad stands only a yard and a half from the condemned man? Do you know that if the victim took two steps forward his chest would touch the rifles? Do you know that, at this short range, the soldiers concentrate their fire on the region of the heart and their big bullets make a hole into which you could thrust your fist? No, you didn't know all that; those are things that are never spoken of. For the plague-stricken their peace of mind is more important than a human life. Decent folks must be allowed to sleep easy o' nights, mustn't they? Really it would be shockingly bad taste to linger on such details, that's common knowledge. But personally I've never been able to sleep well since then."[23]

The "plague" represents evasion and indifference. We are repeatedly reminded in the course of Camus's book that enormous vigilance is necessary to combat the plague, that acts of will are required if a person is to achieve health and integrity, if he is to be pure. Significantly enough, the inhabitants of the town of Oran in Camus's novel are called either townspeople or volunteers, once the plague strikes. The townspeople are victims; they suffer and lash out at each other and find that fighting back is useless. The volunteers, like Tarrou, Rieux, and their "sanitary squads," do fight back. But there is no "good reason" because no one knows how to heal the sickness or stop the epidemic. Doctor Rieux keeps struggling because it is his job, it is only "logical," and because "a fight must be put up, in this way or that, and there must be no bowing down." He and his comrades talk of decency, happiness, love; Tarrou is committed to becoming "a saint without God." And they remain whole persons (out of "common decency"); they show compassion and refuse to become merely passive victims, at the mercy of the inhuman plague. They do not act on predetermined principle; in no way could they rationally justify a fundamentally "absurd" heroism. Yet, if they remain vigilant and take responsibility for themselves at this last point, they can move beyond victimization and survive (for however long they have to live) as men.

The existential teacher recognizes that he cannot *tell* another person how to live; nor can he demand that his students exercise their will and become, in their own way, volunteers. But he can set up classroom situations that make it difficult to maintain "peace of mind." He may use literature and the arts; he may focus on crisis situations—such as a Peace Moratorium; he may engage students in concrete questioning and confrontation; he may urge them to take stands. The task will not be easy for such a teacher, anymore than it will for his students because they are forever condemned to the freedom that requires them to create themselves over and over without a sense of comforting constraint or a priori norm.

The same idea applies to drug experiences. Confronted by students who praise psychedelic cultures, the teacher can do no more than ask them to choose for themselves, to avoid following the "crowd." Often he will find some who present an alternative ethic of hedonism, sensualism, gentleness, oceanic love. He will find others who say they cannot help what they are doing: their peers made them sample drugs, they may tell him; they could not be accepted unless they followed their peers. In the first case, the teacher can do little more than say that these youth are only hedonists if they make pleasure their primary value. They are only sensualists if they pursue the delights of the various senses and live for such pursuits. The point is that a mere expression of value means nothing; the expression must be acted on and realized. Sartre says that "man is nothing other than his project, he exists only in so far as he realizes himself, thus he is nothing other than the whole of his actions, nothing more than his life."[24] The teacher can ask the drug enthusiast who says he has an ethic what kind of person he is choosing himself to be, whether he has freely acted to open his way to the future. The teacher can scarcely do more. As for the student who says he cannot help his actions: the teacher can only tell him that he is rejecting his freedom and that his choices are dishonest. He can be charged with bad faith; he can be called "a coward or a stinker," not because he takes drugs but because he has refused responsibility. He has not exercised his will.

Because of the absoluteness of the freedom assumed, because the existentialist appears to have no grounds for saying any moral choice is wrong, his approach to choosing is sometimes considered incompatible with morality. "Any choice is as good as another," writes Alvin Plantinga; "there is no possibility of making a moral mistake. And that is fatal to morality."[25] The recognition that many existentialists have been and are concerned with *engagement* in a world of fellow creatures, an intersubjective world, does not lessen such disapproval. Sartre has said that "the protected status of the intellectual is over, that there are no more sanctuaries." This notion comes partly from a recognition that the intellectual too often leads a life of ease, which prevents him from confronting "the injustices and inhumanities in our own bailiwicks, in the very places we live," and partly from the realization that moral responsibility entails responsibility for the effects of his actions on others. This still does not suggest criteria for determining which effects are desirable and which are not; but it does imply that a commitment to one's own and to others' freedom *means* a confrontation with injustice and

inhumanity. Existentialists occasionally speak of a "conversion," which
will enable an individual to respond to the calls of his conscience. Perhaps,
after all, a converted conscience always makes an appeal for justice and
humanity, as it seems to be doing in Sartre's case. Perhaps "anything" is
not possible once a man wills himself to be free. None of this, however,
discounts the extreme difficulty a teacher experiences in stirring others to
action they know is authentic. Nothing is more difficult than to be—and to
ask others to be—in good faith. Nevertheless, a rebellion against
indifference and abstractness appears necessary at the present moment.
Perhaps, in the last analysis, only the rebel can summon the courage to
identify himself as a passionately rational man.

Every teacher is familiar with the vast looming structures of the
corporate society, which set up so many obstacles before those who strive
to be reflective and to live in good faith. Every teacher knows the
dehumanizing pressure of bureaucracies; he understands something about
the anonymity of crowds, the ease with which one can deny responsibility.
Also he knows, from encounters with his high school or college students,
how easily the aesthetic can overcome the moral, how people can simply
"groove" on what is made available instead of acting to constitute their
own worlds. Despair, boredom, a kind of indolence may be to blame. But
many young people are averse to making serious choices, "not so much,"
as Kierkegaard says, "on account of the rigorous cogitation involved in
weighing the alternatives, not on account of the multiplicity of thoughts
which attach themselves to every link in the chain, but rather because
there is danger afoot, danger that the next instant it may not be equally in
my power to choose, that something already has been lived which must be
lived over again."[26] Obscure powers in the personality, according to
Kierkegaard, are always driving ahead to new choices. Personality cannot
be kept a blank; personal life cannot be halted and started again. For this
reason, when they do finally make their choices, people so often feel "that
there is something which must be done over again, something which must
be revoked. . . ." For some this feeling results in an unending, almost
desperate search for freedom from what they have been in the past (in
their families, in their schools). For others it results in a desire simply to
live and experience without choosing or commitment. Kierkegaard calls
this feeling a desire to remain at the first "stage" on life's way, the
"aesthetic stage." The person who lives forever at this stage is like Don
Juan, the perpetual romantic lover who exists in an erotic present, a
discrete "now," which neither binds the past to the present nor anticipates
any future time. "The aesthetic choice is entirely immediate, or it loses
itself in the multifarious."[27] Actually, it is no choice at all, because it
involves neither consideration nor commitment; and it ends, more often
than not, in apathy or despair. The individual must move from the

aesthetic to the ethical stage, where significant choices are made and the "personality" is consolidated. "I should like to say," Kierkegaard writes, "that in making a choice it is not so much a question of choosing the right as of the energy, the consciousness, the pathos with which one chooses."[28]

We may now be emerging from a period in which "image," "style," and other such aesthetic concepts have been more important than creeds and codes. Lionel Trilling, writing about the generation of the early 1960s, has said many were more concerned with their relation to the "sources of life" than with moral decision. He means their relation to what they believe will yield sensual excitement, self-transcendence, and various kinds of liberation, rather than meaning or value or truth. Charles Reich, speaking on behalf of such persons, bears out what Trilling said. Reich places much stress on the appearance of those blessed with "Consciousness III." Describing what he saw as a "conversion," he writes: "What happens is simply this: in a brief space of months, a student, seemingly conventional in every way, changes his haircut, his clothes, his habits, his interests, his political attitudes, his way of relating to other people, in short, his whole way of life."[29] Reich conveys the impression that the student, treating himself as a species of art object, first alters the way he *looks* and then changes his habits and attitudes as if they too were mere accouterments. The term *life style* becomes far more appropriate than the existential term *project* because (with few exceptions) so little passionate engagement, so little difficult choice, seems to be involved. Such a person is tempted to distance himself from life as if it were a drama, to treat politics as theater, to perceive history as a vast, formless "happening" or a kind of empty dance.

Persistence in this tendency provides another argument for the existential teacher's efforts to stimulate the energy, the consciousness, the pathos involved in serious choice. In fact, most moral philosophers are likely to see this as a significant phase of moral education. Henry David Aiken, for instance, says : "Morality . . . is a form of self-discipline for moral subjects who hold themselves responsible for their actions."[30] Few would disagree that the principles we have spoken of are "first-personal," that is, principles a moral agent believes he *ought* to acknowledge (or he chooses to acknowledge) and then become binding on him. "Moral freedom," Aiken also says, "is not the freedom to do as you please, but the freedom to decide what sort of person you ought to be." The teacher and his students may need to move beyond the aesthetic stage to make meaningful such freedom to decide. Varied experience, expansion of consciousness, sensual enjoyment, expressiveness are important for development. But it is not enough for an individual to spend his life as a dilettante or wanderer, for all the vividness of perspective these roles make possible. At some point he must perceive himself as a potential person; he must experience what may be a *moral* demand to become, to create himself. Only then does freedom descend as it does on Sartre's Orestes. This moral demand is understood as a freedom to choose resolutely and without assurances, "the freedom to decide what sort of person you ought to be."

Here, of course, philosophic disagreements begin; the teacher may reach a fork in the road. Many philosophers say free, authentic choice is not necessarily better than choice which is not so free. A decision that an action is right for the individual does not, they say, *make* that action right. Iris Murdoch writes: "The ordinary person, unless corrupted by philosophy, does not believe he creates values by his choices. He thinks that some things really are better than others and that he is capable of getting it wrong. We are not usually in doubt about the direction in which Good lies."[31] An even more serious charge against existential views on choosing is that a nonpurposeful act or a decision for which no reasons can be given is not a choice at all. Rather, it appears to be a type of instinctive, impulsive, or merely whimsical behavior. If the appeal from conscience is held in mind, however, if it is remembered that the self exists in the world, in the midst of community, and that each person is held—and holds himself—morally responsible for everything he does, the approach cannot be disposed of as merely emotive. Relativism, however, does result from such an approach. Many existentialists would answer as did Friedrich Nietzsche's Zarathustra when asked about "the way". " 'This is *my* way: where is yours?' " And then: "For *the* way—that does not exist." And this response is understandable, because each person is thought to be creating his project, his life-world. A class of high school students may be confronted with the same curriculum materials, the same moral principles and rules of behavior. But each student will order his experience in his own fashion; each will transcend himself and appropriate dimensions of the culture as these dimensions are presented to *his* consciousness. He is bound to his fellow student not because of similar patterns in their life-worlds but because of the intersubjectivity of language, cumulative meanings, history. However, his perspectives, reciprocal as they may be, are his own. If he perceives his freedom and is enabled to act on it, he has his own way.

There arises, then, the question of authority, or what William Frankena calls a "transpersonal standard" or a "moral direction" transcending the individual. Analytical philosophers insist that direction can be found in a properly impersonal consideration of such principles as justice and respect for persons. These (and a few others, including freedom, impartiality, and truth telling) strike R. S. Peters, for example, as fundamental. But they are "nonarbitrary in the sense that they are presuppositions of the form of discourse in which the question 'What are there reasons for doing' is asked seriously." These principles, says Peters, are "of a procedural sort in that they do not tell us precisely what rules there should be in a society but lay down general guidance about the ways in which we should go about deciding such matters. . . ."[32] Experimentalist philosophers, well aware of precariousness and open opportunity, believe that sufficient study of the relevant facts of any situation, of the surrounding circumstances and the living interests involved, leads to decisions as free of relativism as possible. A "transpersonal standard" is implicit in creative intelligence itself. Using a standard of this kind, moral and social agreements can be made, ideal possibilities projected, and "control of the future" achieved.[33] Others (like William K. Frankena) talk of instilling a sense of a "Way" or "Tao," which finds expression in a set of rules, principles, and ideals.[34] Internalizing these, developing a sense of obligation, young people will be able to choose—both freely and knowledgeably—in the situations that confront them. They will find themselves on the road to the good life.

What should govern? An understanding of protocols, of procedures? A range of fundamental principles? Authenticity—the sense of the person one ought to be? Again, the teacher will have to decide, to take a stand. However, whatever he decides, whatever orientation makes the most sense to him, he will not *impose* values or virtues on his students; he will *pose* questions, do what he can to move them toward increasing awareness, deepening conviction. Granting them dignity, freedom, and autonomy (unless they are little children), he becomes a catalyst in the process of their self-identification, their learning how to learn. He may address himself to the task, more or less assured about "the good life" and "desirable dispositions." But, no matter who he is, he will not deliberately guide his students toward a boring, empty, dissatisfying life; he will not deliberately encourage the development of dispositions he believes to be destructive or "bad." And just as he must be convinced about the worthwhileness of what he is teaching, so he is convinced about the value of his own tastes and commitments.

At this point the tension originates for the teacher who is truly concerned to stimulate *action* rather than merely mechanical behavior on the part of each student. If he finds his norm in community standards of "good," in public traditions, or in the requirements of the academic disciplines, the tension is likely to be least. If he is concerned with cognitive action, with the formation of belief systems having specifiable characteristics, with evidence, with reasons, he obviously has to exert himself to critical questioning and thinking; but committed to clarity and analysis as he must be, he will not suffer fundamental doubts. If he is primarily interested in a "democratic" classroom, where cooperative experience and full participation in decision making take priority, he may

suffer the inevitable frustrations when "all" affected by policies have a
share in making them; but the doubts he experiences are likely to be
fruitful, leading to new definitions of problem, new possibilities of
resolution. If his commitment is to self-disclosure and free choosing, the
tension is likely to be greatest. Something like a dialectical struggle will be
under way as the teacher attempts to reconcile his commitments with his
desire for his students to choose themselves. He must guide, stimulate, and
challenge intentional ignorance wherever he perceives it; but, at the same
time, he must feel the most tender regard for each person's being—for
each person's privacy, inner time. The existential teacher, "nondirective"
as he may appear to be, cannot permit floundering, careless thinking, or
flaccidity anymore than can the most "directive" classroom authorities.
Curiosity, wonder, the sense of problem: these may be taken as starting
points here as in any other teaching situation. There must be a similar
awareness of the way rationality contributes to freedom, of the way
freedom of mind and widening perspectives enrich the life-world and
expand the scope of choice. The existential teacher is simply more attuned
than others to the implicit threat of coercion in a classroom situation. He,
far more than others, must confront his freedom along with the alien
freedoms of his students; and because he is bound to attend to so much
more than performance, speech, and observable instances of mastery, he
can never be sure of what he or they achieve.

We have already talked of B. F. Skinner's alternative and the
certainties associated with a determinist point of view. We have also said
that, even if the past is fixed and in some sense "necessary" from the
vantage point of the present, the future is not; and willing or choosing
moves forward into that future. The teacher, like his students, is concerned
with projecting and with possibilities. His prime preoccupation may be
with the tasks his students will be able to perform, with the achievements
at which they will arrive. It may be with the degrees by which they master
the principles fundamental to the disciplines or with the ways in which
they gain new perspectives on their life-worlds. Whatever the teacher's
concern, it is directed at the future, at what is not yet; and in no way can
the future be empirically tested. By each of his actions, each of his efforts
to move his students toward inquiry, he asserts his freedom; and,
implicitly, he affirms that choosing is significant for himself and for those
trying to learn. If choosing were not significant, he could scarcely justify
intervening in the endless chain of cause and effect except by saying that
he intended to ensure that what was meant to happen did indeed occur.
As every teacher knows, sometimes it is all too easy to accede to
disadvantage, to retardation, to apparent incorrigibility; and other times it
is mysteriously necessary to say "No!"

The troubling question of how much freedom to grant young people still remains open. For one thing, there is the matter of the age of the students involved. If, indeed, freedom means (as it does in the simplest sense) an absence of restraint, the teacher of preschool children must confront the issue differently than does the teacher of persons old enough to decide for themselves. Individuals who work with the very young have long prized the values of spontaneity and expressiveness. In many Head Start programs and nursery schools, where children are given diverse opportunities to play and express themselves, there is an appearance of almost total freedom. Yet we are aware that a great number of constraints exist and that these are not always explained to the children. Little children may not go home at will or run up and down the halls or interfere with each other's activity or injure others. All too frequently, they are not permitted to stand apart (in the closet, on the windowsill) and be alone. Their options, in actual fact, are limited, presumably because they are not old enough to understand why certain reasons are relevant and others are not. The result is what Peters calls the "paradox" of moral education: certain habits must be cultivated before children are old enough to know why; certain wants must be constrained; certain rules must be imposed.[35] Were it not for such a foundation, children could not move from their original egocentrism to a conception of pleasing others or doing what the community thinks is right.

Aristotle talked of the need for "good habits"; Dewey wrote of the need to develop "dispositions," attitudes "not to this and that thing nor even to the aggregate of known things, but to the considerations which govern conduct."[36] Schooling, traditionally, has focused on the cultivation of certain dispositions rather than others, depending on what the culture values at the moment and what attitudes are considered "necessary to the continuous and progressive life of [the] society."[37] As we have seen, the romantic critics of the present take issue with this approach. A. S. Neill, John Holt, Paul Goodman, and others like them believe that the deliberate cultivation of dispositions is manipulative. They talk of the "retroflected rage and shame" experienced by children compelled to go to school and "coerced" into accommodation with what is considered right. They think that intervention on the part of adults assigned to socialize prevents spontaneous learning that would take place if young pupils were left free. Neill, for example, objects to "hothousing" children. The implication is that habit training and the imposition of rules create an artificial environment. Natural growth becomes impossible. Moral education becomes a sham.

Bill Ayers, a young black radical who worked at a Michigan free school called Children's Community, expresses the romantic view in simple terms:

What we try to do is allow these groups of kids to learn from each other, to exchange things, throw things away, pick things up, without any kind of value judgments. I think that more than anything it is dangerous to consciously create models for kids to emulate.[38]

Children, says Paul Goodman, should be exposed to diverse models in and out of school. They should be brought into contact with "unlicensed" adults in their home neighborhoods. They could then choose their models and ego ideals spontaneously: a skillful bricklayer; a "nice cop"; a hard-working druggist; a humane priest; an old man good at working with his hands. The school, ideally, should be a mini-school (like George Dennison's First Street School) or a storefront school open to the life on the street. Children should be permitted to participate on an equal basis in community activities and to learn through friendly association with their elders. Under such circumstances, there would be no need for deliberate teaching of norms and rules. Civility, like literacy, would develop naturally through and by means of everyday experience. The total environment would educate; there would be no need for compulsory schools.

Certain teachers, anticipating alternative modes of education for the young, respond warmly to this imaging of what might be. Others are troubled by the implication that most teachers have no worthy roles to play. The reality confronting both groups, however, is the complex reality of the present moment when schools are inadequately supported and continually accused of ineffectuality. It may be that decentralization, community control, and local participation in policy making will overcome feelings of powerlessness and effect significant change. It may be that increased localism will intensify separatism and hostility between ethnic groups. The teacher, as citizen, will want to take positions on local control, busing, integration, voucher systems, and the rest; he may even want to play a part in supporting what he conceives to be reforms. It is likely, as we have said, that he will be a more vital teacher if he becomes involved in the public world.

Nevertheless, his fundamental project is pursued in his classroom, where he must cope with the effects of injustice and inequity on children, with the terrible discrepancies between the lives of the poor and the well-to-do. If he teaches in the slums, where models may be drug addicts or gang members or desperate and jobless men, he must confront the question of moral teaching squarely. Ought he not to acquaint his students with existing cultural norms? Ought he not to teach them principles to counteract what they learn on the streets? Are they being given an equal chance if they are not taught the rules of the game? Their parents, more often than not, will demand the kind of formal, even rigorous teaching that presumably equips the young to play the game. The teacher, no matter how committed he is to self-determination and free choice, must hold himself accountable to his pupils, to their parents, *and* to the community. This means he must take personal responsibility for the choices he makes in his classroom, for the accommodations he makes, and for the refusals his values demand.

The same is true in a suburb, in a working-class neighborhood, in a homogeneous small town, in an ordinary middle-class community. There may be groups of people who object to the discussion of controversial issues, other groups who emphasize "character education," still others who consider all extrinsic discipline to be bad. The teacher may be instructed to devote most of his energies to the gifted or to preparing certain students for the better colleges. He may be asked to put his main reliance on teaching machines, to substitute multimedia teaching for literature teaching, to discourage interest in such "frivolities" as art. Not only will he have to make decisions of principles with regard to curricular emphases; he will also have to make continual choices with respect to the norms he teaches as well as the way the local parents think their children *ought* to live.

The problems are inescapable, wherever the teacher is assigned to teach, because he is asked to function as a self-conscious, autonomous, and authentic person in a public space where the pressures multiply. Unlike an artist or a scholar or a research scientist, he cannot withdraw to studio, study, or laboratory and still remain a practitioner. He is involved with students, colleagues, school board members, and parents whenever and wherever he pursues his fundamental project; he cannot work alone. Moreover, he cannot avoid the great social structures beyond his classroom doors. There is always a sense in which he must mediate between those structures and the young people he hopes to liberate for reflection and choice. He must initiate them in certain patterns of thinking and acting; he must enable them to recognize and choose among the options presented to them. He must sensitize them to inhumanity, vulgarity, and hypocrisy; he must help them seek equivalents for violence and for war. And, at some level, he must enable them to comprehend their society's professed ideals: freedom, equality, regard for the individual. These are all fundamental to the democratic credo; they distinguish and dignify the democratic way of life. But they are norms, conceptions of what *ought* to be; and they must be created anew with each generation, by each person choosing to live a principled or norm-regarding life, if they are to become viable ideals that summon human beings to moral action in the world they know.

The teacher's responsibilities become more and more complex; and he is required every day to reinterpret, to make his own sense of modern life. Because modern life has so many aspects and dimensions, because it cannot be fully apprehended by conventional means, we turn one last time to the arts and their relevance for the teacher who is willing to take a stranger's view. The relevance is dual. In the first place, works of art have the capacity to disclose things about which (according to Ludwig Wittgenstein) philosophy must be silent. Imaginative presentations can engage individuals with the changing meanings of human existence, reality, and time in a manner mere description cannot achieve. In the second place, experiences with the arts offer possibilities for self-confrontation and self-identification to those willing to try to understand. Such experiences may be of peculiar significance for the teacher wishing to be present as a full person, as the "single one" Kierkegaard describes.

Traditionally, the arts were thought to be imitative forms, representations of universal and recurrent patterns. To apprehend them was to look through the windows of a time-bound world into a domain that was larger, purer, glowing, and serene. Even today, people afflicted by the banalities and brutalities on the visible surfaces of things long to find some countervailing force in the arts. In Herman Melville's *Billy Budd,* Captain Vere (attempting to justify his execution of the young sailor) says: "With mankind, measured forms are everything; and that is the import couched in the story of Orpheus with his lyre spellbinding the wild denizens of the wood." He means, of course, that the ambiguity and formlessness of the "primeval" have to be in some manner counteracted by human orders and human laws. There is still a desire, often frustrated in these times, for orders that will sustain. For many young people, however, nothing could be more alien than "measured forms." They perceive life as fluid, encompassing, an affair of discontinuous events to be felt, to be celebrated, to be sensed. Threatened by anonymity, conditioning, and quantification, they seek occasions for "grooving," for engagement, for acting out, for expansion of consciousness, for discovering what it is to *be.* The tension between their conception of art forms and traditional conceptions (which their teachers frequently maintain, no matter what) has heightened the problematic character of the arts. Not only is it necessary to decide among the multiple artistic offerings in every field; it becomes more and more important to decide the significance of the arts and aesthetic experiences in one's personal life. This experience ought to heighten perceptiveness and sensitivity, as it intensifies self-consciousness with respect to the arts. Authorities (scholars, critics, museum curators) are no longer in position to legislate standards for individual taste and appreciation. Connoisseurship has become questionable to many. "Art" can no longer be satisfactorily defined.

Nevertheless the nostalgia remains; and it is significant too. When a person thinks, for example, of *The Iliad,* with its heroic seekers after excellence, its speakers of words and doers of deeds, of the Greek tragedies with their imitation of the forms of human action, or of Shakespeare's plays, the magnitude of these works makes them seem truer, more intrinsically artistic than, say, Samuel Beckett's *Waiting for Godot,* Bernard Malamud's *The Fixer,* John Barth's *End of the Road,* Sylvia Plath's *Ariel,* Francois Truffaut's *Jules and Jim.* The blues and golds, the burnished surfaces of one of Raphael's Madonnas, Michelangelo's giant young David, Rembrandt's obliquely lit Saul seem to reveal a veritable ultimate to certain modern viewers, especially when they compare Pablo Picasso's *Guernica,* Francis Bacon's screaming figures in their glass boxes, Alberto Giacometti's spare and desolated images frozen in the void. Even though they feel the peculiar nostalgia induced by the great and familiar classical works, many people still recognize that they can no longer speak of universals, of enduring, luminescent truths. Some agree that none of the traditional explanations or theories of art can account for all the phenomena classified as "art" since the beginning of time—that, in effect, "art" cannot be defined. It is impossible, we are told, to discover a single element or essence (an x-quality, perhaps, or "artness") common to works as disparate as *Hamlet, A Clockwork Orange, Vanity Fair, A Farewell to Arms, Hedda Gabler, Waiting for Godot, Mona Lisa,* and *Guernica.* How can anyone state categorically that Andy Warhol's rendering of the Campbell soup can should not be included along with Claude Monet's *Waterlilies* in the art world because it cannot be construed to be art? Morris Weitz says that, instead of asking "What is art? How is it to be defined?", we should ask "What sort of concept is 'art'?"—and go on to discover the conditions under which we can correctly apply the term.[39] Weitz takes from Ludwig Wittgenstein the notion of "strands of similarity" and says that the best we can do is identify similarities between the new forms and such paradigm cases as those created by Shakespeare, Raphael, Dickens, Ibsen. Weitz believes that "art" should be treated as a concept with an open texture, meaning that the conditions of its applications should be held open for correction or revision. If a new form appears—such as a work of "earth art" (a cliff draped in sheets or a pile of stones on sand) or a novel without narrative or transitions—decisions on whether to extend the use of the concept or to invent a new one will have to be made. When a self-aware individual makes such a decision, he will likely consider his expectations of an aesthetic experience, the principles that underlie his judgments when he says something *is* a work of art, his criteria for recognizing "great" works, the kinds of recommendations he can reasonably make. He has been moved to self-questioning and perhaps to deeper enjoyments. Also, he is not prevented from talking about the art forms he cherishes and knows best.

Few would disagree (despite the lack of definitions) that a work of art does differ from a natural object and requires a different stance on the part of the beholder. Encountering a work as art, the beholder is expected to set aside his everyday modes of apprehending. *Guernica* cannot be encountered as if it were a cartoon or a distorted rendering of an actual bombing. Nicolas Poussin's *The Death of Socrates* cannot be "read" as an illustration of an actual event. Neither work is transparent; neither is a glass through which the beholder is meant to look at some historic occasion. Both are opaque, complete unto themselves, made of colors, shapes, lines in relationship to one another. Painted on canvas, those colors, shapes, and lines compose an equivalent, a secondary world: They are paintings, not photographs or reflections. The creators of both works were impelled, perhaps, to transmute rage, grief, or philosophic pondering into image. They were deliberately wrought to embody feeling in complex form, to objectify it as an independent existence in the world, a possibility for others to choose.

Sartre once said, of *Guernica*: "Does anyone think that it won a single heart to the Spanish cause? And yet something is said that can never quite be heard and that would take an infinity of words to express. . . ."[40] The meaning, more than likely, is in some manner inexplicable in words. Like a poem, a painting cannot be paraphrased. Too few people give it sufficient time or hold in mind the potential it offers for those willing to experience it. Too few people remember that a painting—like the Picasso and the Poussin, like a Cezanne still life, a De Kooning woman—is not a representation of some outer "real." They do not remember often enough that a painter, working with inherited conventions, seeking his vision, his style, creates formal equivalents of the subject matter with which his desire to paint began. It may be the legendary drinking of the hemlock, the bombing of the small town. It may be a landscape the painter has encountered somewhere, which he sees with lights glancing and shadows going black. It may be a loss or feeling of horror he has experienced; it may be the rush of steam, the sense of speed, or the clash of colors in the light. Working with his medium, the artist must transmute the idea, vision, feeling, or memory into gradations of color, arrangements of planes, "cryptograms" the beholder can translate into a private message incommunicable in words. The more his perceptiveness, the more his willingness to attend and prehend, the more the beholder will find his repertoire of feelings expanding, his emotional palette becoming enriched. He may find that his vision of his life space is sharpened because of his experiences in looking at painting. He may become sensitized to forms and colors never previously noticed; he may become participant in another dimension of the quest for clarified vision and for modes of ordering reality. The teacher who is drawn in this direction may well find continuities between his teaching effort and his effort to *see* more. Perceptively engaged, he may find that he cannot take a self-righteous or proprietary stance toward painting. He may be gaining opportunities to enable those he teaches to see as well, truly to see, not through his eyes but through their own.

Somewhat the same things may be said about film, that art form of such peculiar significance for the contemporary young. We are told that experiences with film are primarily visual, that film is an art of moving images. The member of the audience often forgets the illusionism involved in film making; and, as in the case of the painting, he too frequently perceives films as photographed "reality" and recalls them as if they were dreams. To encounter a film as a potential work of art is to keep in mind the ways in which the editing process alters and shapes, imaginatively transforming "shots" of an existing world. To prehend a film as a created thing is to be somehow familiar with its grammar, the syntax of its images, the uses of montage, flashback, and visual metaphors. Knowing what to look for, how to "aspect" a film, a viewer has a greatly increased opportunity to engage with it as art—and, in engaging, to discover or rediscover aspects of the self. Many people consider such films as *Bonnie and Clyde, Easy Rider,* and *A Clockwork Orange* to be morally questionable because viewers are given opportunities to identify only with delinquent characters. These films may or may not be works of art, may or may not be equal in impact to Ingmar Bergman's *The Seventh Seal,* Michelangelo Antonioni's *L'Avventura,* Charles Chaplin's *Modern Times,* Jean Renoir's *Grand Illusion,* and other works now taken to be masterpieces. But they deserve to be heeded, felt, reflected on, and criticized. They deserve to be presented to the young, not as photographs of actuality, but as fictions, *films* that have been deliberately crafted by artists working with a new technology. Only then will film experiences enable individuals to move within themselves, tap the fund of life within them, and look with somewhat different eyes on other persons and the concreteness of the world. Only then can the morally questionable be confronted honestly by people free to reflect on what they have imaginatively made their own.

There are connections between film and literature, as there are between film and the other arts. Literature, of course, is made of language, the same stuff used for factual statements, for ordinary conversations about everyday things. The imaginative writer, however, structures and shapes the raw material of language to exploit possibilities of ambiguity and indirection, to permit the words to function figuratively as well as denotatively, to permit them to be visible, sometimes almost palpable.

He creates, at length, a totality composed of many interrelated levels of potential meaning. Attending to the work—be it Shelley's *Ode to the West Wind,* Hemingway's "The Killers," Joyce's *A Portrait of the Artist as a Young Man*—as a formed expression of some speaker, engaging himself with the language in its permutations, the characters and their enactments, the movement of motifs, the development of theme, the reader is bound to shape his experience in the process. How else can he read—except in the light of his experience, except as he builds out of what has evoked in him an imaginary, fictive world—the illusioned world that is the book?

A book, after all, is a dead thing once it is written. It simply exists, as does Keats' Grecian urn—"a still unravish'd bride of quietness"—until someone lends it his life. And a reader can only truly lend a work of literature his life if he moves, with the aid of his imagination, into his consciousness, his inwardly apprehended world. "Raskolnikov's waiting is *my* waiting which I lend him," writes Sartre. "Without this impatience of the reader he would remain only a collection of signs. His hatred of the police magistrate who questions him is my hatred which has been solicited and wheedled out of me by signs, and the police magistrate himself would not exist without the hatred I have for him via Raskolnikov." Only at that point does Dostoevsky's *Crime and Punishment* come alive; coming alive, the book becomes an event in the reader's consciousness. In the same discussion, Sartre goes into particulars about the specific activity involved. He points out that reading is a synthesis of perception and creation, that the "object" (the novel or the poem, with its distinctive structure) is just as important as the "subject" (the reader, who discloses the work of art, brings it into being):

> In a word, the reader is conscious of disclosing in creating, of creating by disclosing. ... If he is inattentive, tired, stupid, or thoughtless, most of the relations will escape him. He will never manage to "catch on" to the object (in the sense in which we see that fire "catches" or "doesn't catch"). He will draw some phrases out of the shadow, but they will appear as random strokes. If he is at his best, he will project beyond the words a synthetic form, each phrase of which will be no more than a partial function: the "theme," the "subject," or the "meaning."[41]

Wide-awakeness is important; so is the ability to generate (out of the reader's accumulated experience) the structure of the literary work. Not only is the reader released into his subjectivity, his inner time; his imagination can—and usually will—move him beyond the artist's traces "to project beyond the words a new synthetic form," an order of meanings which is distinctively his.

This approach is neither permissive nor relativistic. Attention is continually drawn to the work and its multiple facets. Its structure and multivalent levels of meaning are slowly and carefully to be explored; "one must wait for it," Sartre says, "and observe it." But the work as such refers to the subjectivity of the reader, who journeys into his interior under the guidance of the literary artist—Robert Frost or Herman Melville, Samuel Beckett or William Shakespeare. For instance, there may have been woods and snow, horses and sleds in the experience of a person who comes to Frost's "Stopping by Woods on a Snowy Evening." He may have been reared in New England and known the winters; and somewhere in the background of his consciousness may be imprints of early perceptions of sleighbells, mysterious silences, sudden falls of darkness. Entering the poem, engaging with the images and sounds, he may well discover some of those perceptions rising to the surface, accompanied by feeling-tones and shreds of memory. The poem itself, however, is ready to impose its structure on amorphous materials; and, as he discloses that structure, the reader will find himself forming those materials as he has never done before. "The woods are lovely, dark and deep. . . ." He may feel, as never before, the dangerous seductiveness of darkness and all it represents: sleep, forgetfulness, even death. "But I have promises to keep. . . ." He may experience the tension of obligation, the risks involved in leaving village conventions behind—"without a farmhouse near." Almost certainly, he will see what he has never seen before in his stream of consciousness. And yet, even as he recognizes the newness of the perspective, he will probably feel that that is how the moment truly was— except that he never realized it before. He will have become visible to himself in a new way—discovering materials within his life-world through the patterns he has imposed on them, seeing them with opened eyes.

To respond to Frost's poem it is not necessary to have lived in New England, of course. Everyone has experienced dark places and pulls to nothingness, in inner city or on open plains. Nor is it necessary to have sailed on whaling ships to understand *Moby Dick.* What human being has not felt the temptation to look "into coffin warehouses" or to dash out into the middle of a busy street? What human being has not (feeling self-destructive and despairing) wanted to make a transition "from a schoolmaster to a sailor," to go off in search of whatever he imagines the "great whale" to be? The teacher who risks experience with such works must involve himself fully, aiming at private possession, at a discovery of his own inwardness. If he makes these works available to his students, he ought also to respect their privacy—certainly at the beginning and the end. Of course, there should be talk among them, interchange, mutual involvement. And the teacher may function like a good critic—affording "new perceptions and with them new values," as Arnold Isenberg has said.[42] The teacher will *know* that there is no final explanation of any particular experience with a work of art; he will also know that no one can bring about appreciation or enjoyment in another, that he can only help make others see. Nevertheless, he can try to make his students discern certain qualities they may have overlooked. He can articulate (without forcing) certain of his ideas about the work. The ideas may even take the form of directions for focusing in certain ways, for tracing the emergence of various patterns, for clarifying figures of speech, paradoxes, ironies. Knowing something of his inner voyages, however, the teacher will not try to persuade his students to adopt his evaluations or share his feelings. He will offer good reasons, try to elicit good reasons for the judgments his students make; but in the end, when they return to the work at hand, the students must embark on their own journeys—and no one can accompany them.

Confronting any art form, the teacher can only involve himself and bring his convictions to his class when he is done. He is not a missionary, not a museum guard; he is a human being trying to recapture some of his original perceptions, trying to identify himself, trying to see. He can only be present to his students *as a human being* engaged in searching and choosing, as someone who is willing to take the risk of new perspectives, as someone who cares.

The poet Rainer Maria Rilke, in "Torso of an Archaic Apollo," communicates the sense of what confrontation with works of art can do:

> Never will we know his fabulous head
> where the eyes' apples slowly ripened. Yet
> his torso glows: a candelabrum set
> before his gaze which is pushed back and hid,
>
> restrained and shining. Else the curving breast
> could not thus blind you, nor through the soft turn
> of the loins could this smile easily have passed
> into the bright groins where the genitals burned.
>
> Else stood this stone a fragment and defaced,
> with lucent body from the shoulders falling,
> too short, not gleaming like a lion's fell:
>
> nor would this star have shaken the shackles off,
> bursting with light, until there is no place
> that does not see you. You must change your life.[43]

Rilke is describing a torso sculptured by Auguste Rodin. It is a torso of Apollo, the god of light, knowledge, and art, who is "archaic" for so many modern men. Working with his own medium and out of his own experience, Rodin was able to transmute a form that would otherwise have been dead. Through his imagination he was able to restore to life a mere fragment of the past and create significance where there had been a void. That significance now calls out to the person willing to look through his own eyes. It makes a demand of the one who can encounter the vitality and radiance of the sculpture without a desire to run away and hide. "You must," the great work exhorts, "change your life."

The teacher can find an analogy here, since his very project involves making that demand. He is also engaged in transmuting and illuminating material to the end of helping others see afresh. If he is able to think what he is doing while he is vitally present as a person, he may arouse others to act on their own freedom. Learning to learn, some of those persons may move beyond the sheltered places until they stand by their own choice in the high wind of thought. They may experience the adventure Rilke speaks of in the poem entitled "Initiation":

> Whoever you are, go out into the evening,
> leaving your room of which you know each bit;
> your house is the last before the infinite,
> whoever you are.
> Then with your eyes that wearily
> scarce lift themselves from the worn-out door-stone
> slowly you raise a shadowy black tree
> and fix it on the sky: slender, alone.
> And you have made the world (and it shall grow
> and ripen as a word, unspoken, still).
> When you have grasped its meaning with your will,
> then tenderly your eyes will let it go. . . .[44]

The tree may represent the order, pattern, or perspective the individual creates when he learns. To grasp its meaning with one's will may signify the personal choice to integrate what has been disclosed, to put it to use in interpreting and ordering one's own life-world. The teacher, too, must raise his shadowy trees and let them ripen. Stranger and homecomer, questioner and goad to others, he can become visible to himself by doing philosophy. There are countless lives to be changed, worlds to be remade.

Notes and References

1. Alfred Schutz, "The Stranger," in *Studies in Social Theory, Collected Papers* II (The Hague: Martinus Nijhoff, 1964), p. 95.

2. Albert Camus, *The Stranger* (New York: Vintage Books, 1954), p. 104.

3. Nathaniel Hawthorne, *The Scarlet Letter,* in *The Portable Hawthorne,* ed. Malcolm Cowley (New York: Viking Press, 1955), p. 425.

4. Maurice Merleau-Ponty, "Man and Adversity," in *Signs,* tr. Richard C. McCleary (Evanston, Ill.: Northwestern University Press, 1965), p. 240.

5. Maurice Merleau-Ponty, "Man and Adversity," in *Signs,* p. 242.

6. Ernest Hemingway, *A Farewell to Arms* (London: Jonathan Cape, 1952), p. 186.

7. Charles E. Silberman, *Crisis in the Classroom* (New York: Random House, 1970), pp. 126–127.

8. Jules Henry, *Culture Against Man* (New York: Random House, 1963), p. 291.

9. Frank Kermode, *The Sense of an Ending* (New York: Oxford University Press, 1967), p. 39.

10. Richard S. Peters, "Concrete Principles and the Rational Passions," in *Moral Education: Five Lectures by James M. Gustafson, Richard S. Peters, Lawrence Kohlberg, Bruno Bettelheim and Kenneth Keniston* (Cambridge, Mass.: Harvard University Press, 1970), p. 39.

11. Jean-Paul Sartre, *Existentialism,* tr. Bernard Frechtman (New York: Philosophical Library, 1947), p. 21.

12. William K. Frankena, *Ethics* (Englewood Cliffs, N.J.: Prentice-Hall, 1963), pp. 5–6.

13. Gresham M. Sykes, "New Crimes for Old," *The American Scholar,* autumn 1971, p. 598.

14. William K. Frankena, *Ethics,* p. 98.

15. Fyodor Dostoevsky, *The Brothers Karamazov,* tr. Constance Garnett (New York: The Modern Library, 1945), p. 291.

16. Albert Camus, *The Rebel,* tr. Anthony Bower (New York: Alfred A. Knopf, 1954), p. 231.

17. Richard M. Hare, *The Language of Morals* (New York: Oxford University Press, 1964), p. 73.

18. Peter Marin and Allan Y. Cohen, *Understanding Drug Use* (New York: Harper & Row, Publishers, 1971), p. 15.

19. Lawrence Kohlberg, "Education for Justice: A Modern Statement of the Platonic View," in *Moral Education: Five Lectures by James M. Gustafson, Richard S. Peters, Lawrence Kohlberg, Bruno Bettelheim and Kenneth Keniston,* p. 70.

20. Jean-Paul Sartre, *Existentialism,* p. 20.

21. Martin Heidegger, "What Is Metaphysics?", in *Existence and Being,* tr. R. F. C. Hull and Alan Crick (Chicago: Henry Regnery Company, 1965), p. 334.

22. "Notes and Comment," *The New Yorker,* December 20, 1969, p. 28.

23. Albert Camus, *The Plague* (New York: Alfred A. Knopf, 1948), pp. 226–227.

24. Jean-Paul Sartre, *Existentialism,* pp. 37–38.

25. Alvin Plantinga, "An Existentialist's Ethics," in *Ethics,* ed. Julius R. Weinberg and Keith E. Yandell (New York: Holt, Rinehart & Winston, 1971), p. 23.

26. Søren Kierkegaard, "Either/Or," in *A Kierkegaard Anthology,* ed. Robert Bretall (Princeton, N.J.: Princeton University Press, 1947), p. 103.

27. Søren Kierkegaard, "Either/Or," in *A Kierkegaard Anthology,* p. 105.

28. Søren Kierkegaard, "Either/Or," in *A Kierkegaard Anthology,* p. 106.

29. Charles A. Reich, *The Greening of America* (New York: Random House, 1970), pp. 223–224.

30. Henry David Aiken, "Morality and Ideology," in *Ethics and Society,* ed. Richard T. De George (Garden City, N.Y.: Doubleday & Company, 1966), p. 159.

31. Iris Murdoch, *The Sovereignty of Good* (New York: Schocken Books, 1971), p. 97.

32. Richard S. Peters, "Concrete Principles and the Rational Passions," in *Moral Education,* p. 36.

33. John Dewey, "The Present and Future," in *Human Nature and Conduct* (New York: The Modern Library, 1930), p. 266.

34. William K. Frankena, "Toward A Philosophy of Moral Education," in *Philosophy and Education,* 2nd ed., ed. Israel Scheffler, (Boston: Allyn and Bacon, 1966), pp. 237–238.

35. Richard S. Peters, "Reason and Habit: The Paradox of Moral Education," in *Theories of Value and Problems of Education,* ed. Philip G. Smith (Urbana: University of Illinois Press, 1970), pp. 164–166.

36. John Dewey, *Democracy and Education* (New York: The Macmillan Company, 1916), p. 379.

37. John Dewey, *Democracy and Education,* p. 26.

38. Bill Ayers, "Traveling with Children and Traveling On," in *This Book Is About Schools,* ed. Satu Repo (New York: Pantheon Books, 1970), p. 334.

39. Morris Weitz, "The Role of Theory in Aesthetics," in *Problems in Aesthetics,* ed. Morris Weitz (New York: The Macmillan Company, 1959), pp. 149–151.

40. Jean-Paul Sartre, *Literature and Existentialism,* tr. Bernard Frechtman (New York: The Citadel Press, 1965), p. 11.

41. Jean-Paul Sartre, *Literature and Existentialism,* p. 43.

42. Arnold Isenberg, "Critical Communication," in *Contemporary Studies in Aesthetics,* ed. Francis J. Coleman (New York: McGraw-Hill Book Company, 1968), p. 154.

43. Rainer Maria Rilke, "Torso of an Archaic Apollo," in *Rilke: Selected Poems,* tr. C. F. MacIntyre (Berkeley: University of California Press, 1958), p. 93.

44. Rainer Maria Rilke, "Initiation," in *Rilke: Selected Poems,* p. 21.

Further Reading

Sylvia Ashton-Warner, *Spearpoint: Teacher in America* (New York: Alfred A. Knopf, 1972).

Richard Barnet, *Roots of War* (New York: Atheneum, 1972).

William Barrett, *Time of Need: Forms of Imagination in the Twentieth Century* (New York: Harper & Row, Publishers, 1972).

Gregory Battcock, ed., *The New American Cinema: A Critical Anthology* (New York: E. P. Dutton & Company, 1967).

Gregory Battcock, ed., *The New Art: A Critical Anthology* (New York: E. P. Dutton & Company, 1966).

Ernest Becker, *Beyond Alienation* (New York: George Braziller, 1967).

Daniel Bell, *Work and Its Discontents* (New York: League for Industrial Democracy, 1970).

Kenneth D. Benne, *A Conception of Authority: An Introduction* (New York: Russell and Russell, 1961).

Bruno Bettelheim, *The Informed Heart* (New York: The Free Press, 1960).

Kenneth Boulding, *The Meaning of the Twentieth Century* (New York: Harper & Row, Publishers, 1964).

Theodore Brameld, *The Climactic Decades: Mandate to Education* (New York: Frederick A. Praeger, 1970).

Harry S. Broudy, *The Real World of the Public Schools* (New York: Harcourt Brace Jovanovich, 1962).

Gloria Channon, *Homework! Required Reading for Teachers and Parents* (New York: Outerbridge and Dienstfrey, 1970).

George Dennison, *The Lives of Children: The Story of the First Street School* (New York: Random House, 1969).

John Dewey, *Experience and Education* (New York: Collier Books, 1963).

Elizabeth Cleaners Street School People, *Starting Your Own High School* (New York: Vintage Books, 1972).

Estelle Fuchs, *Teachers Talk: Views from Inside City Schools* (Garden City, N.Y.: Doubleday & Company, 1969).

William H. Gass, *Fiction and the Figures of Life* (New York: Alfred A. Knopf, 1970).

Paul Goodman, *The New Reformation: Notes of a Neolithic Conservative* (New York: Random House, 1970).

Thomas F. Green, *Work, Leisure, and the American Schools* (New York: Random House, 1968).

Nat Hentoff, *Our Children Are Dying* (New York: Viking Press, 1966).

John Holt, *Freedom and Beyond* (New York: E. P. Dutton & Company, 1972).

Judson Jerome, *Culture Out of Anarchy* (New York: Herder & Herder, 1970).

Herbert R. Kohl, *The Open Classroom: A Practical Guide to a New Way of Teaching* (New York: Vintage Books, 1969).

Rollo May, *Love and Will* (New York: W. W. Norton & Company, 1969).

Maurice Natanson, *The Journeying Self: A Study in Philosophy and Social Role* (Reading, Mass.: Addison-Wesley Publishing Company, 1970).

A. Harry Passow, ed., *Urban Education in the 1970s* (New York: Bureau of Publications, Teachers College, Columbia University, 1971).

Paul Ricoeur, *Fallible Man: Philosophy of the Will,* tr. Charles Kelbley (Chicago: Henry Regnery & Company, 1965).

Ross V. Speck and others, *The New Families: Youth, Communes, and The Politics of Drugs* (New York: Basic Books, 1972).

Stephen Spender, *The Struggle of the Modern* (Berkeley: University of California Press, 1965).

Paul Tillich, *The Courage To Be* (New Haven: Yale University Press, 1963).

Miriam Wasserman, *The School Fix* (New York: Outerbridge and Dienstfrey, 1970).

René Wellek and Austin Warren, *Theory of Literature* (New York: Harcourt Brace Jovanovich, 1956).

John Wilson, Norman Williams, Barry Sugarman, *Introduction to Moral Education* (Baltimore: Penguin Books, 1967).

Index

RETURN
TO ME

Books by Lynn Austin

All She Ever Wanted
All Things New
Eve's Daughters
Hidden Places
Pilgrimage
A Proper Pursuit
Though Waters Roar
Until We Reach Home
While We're Far Apart
Wings of Refuge
A Woman's Place
Wonderland Creek

REFINERS FIRE

Candle in the Darkness
Fire by Night
A Light to My Path

CHRONICLES OF THE KINGS

Gods & Kings
Song of Redemption
The Strength of His Hand
Faith of My Fathers
Among the Gods

THE RESTORATION CHRONICLES

Return to Me

The Restoration Chronicles · Book I

RETURN TO ME

LYNN AUSTIN

BETHANYHOUSE

a division of Baker Publishing Group
Minneapolis, Minnesota

© 2013 by Lynn Austin

Published by Bethany House Publishers
11400 Hampshire Avenue South
Bloomington, Minnesota 55438
www.bethanyhouse.com

Bethany House Publishers is a division of
Baker Publishing Group, Grand Rapids, Michigan

Printed in the United States of America

Library of Congress Cataloging-in-Publication Data
Austin, Lynn, N.
    Return to me / Lynn Austin.
        p.   cm. — (The Restoration Chronicles; 1)
        Summary: "After years in exile, Iddo and his grandson Zechariah follow God's leading home to Jerusalem, where they struggle to rebuild their lives and God's temple—bringing to life the biblical books of Ezra and Nehemiah"—Provided by publisher.
        ISBN 978-0-7642-1150-8 (cloth : alk. paper)
        ISBN 978-0-7642-0898-0 (pbk.)
        1. Bible. Old Testament—Fiction. 2. Exile—Fiction. 3. Obedience—Fiction. 4. Jerusalem—Fiction. 5. Babylon (Extinct city)—Fiction. I. Title.
PS3551.U839 R48 2013
813'.54—dc23   2013023290

Cover design by Jennifer Parker
Photography by Mike Habermann Photography, LLC

13 14 15 16 17 18 19   7 6 5 4 3 2 1

To my husband, Ken
and to my children:
Joshua, Vanessa, Benjamin, Maya, and Snir

"Return to me," declares the Lord Almighty,

"and I will return to you."

ZECHARIAH 1:3

A boom of thunder woke Daniel from a deep sleep. He lay in the darkness, disoriented, waiting for a flash of lightning to illuminate his room. The thunder rumbled again—but it wasn't thunder, it was pounding. Who would pound on his door in the middle of the night?

"Coming," he called as the noise continued. "I'm coming." He climbed from bed, his movements slow at age eighty-two, and wrapped his outer robe around his shoulders like a blanket. The stone floor felt cold beneath his bare feet as he groped his way in the dark. He opened the door to a blaze of blinding torchlight. "Yes? Who is it?" he asked, shielding his eyes.

"You're needed at the palace, my lord."

Daniel squinted at the bright light. Two men in blood-red tunics. The king's servants. He wondered if he was still dreaming. On another night years ago, King Nebuchadnezzar had also sent servants to bring him to the palace in the dark of night. The king had suffered a nightmare and would have executed Daniel and all the other wise men if the Almighty One hadn't shown Daniel the dream and its meaning. He had been a much younger man, back then. Nebuchadnezzar's grandson summoned him now.

Daniel rubbed his eyes, struggling to shake off his sleepiness. "The palace? Why? What's wrong?"

7

"King Belshazzar and the queen mother have called for you. They're waiting at the royal palace, my lord." The urgency in the servant's tone convinced Daniel this was no dream.

"Very well. I'll need a moment."

"Please hurry, my lord."

It was useless to ask why he was being summoned. The servants likely didn't know the reason, and besides, a summons from the palace couldn't be ignored. Daniel smoothed his sleep-rumpled hair, changed into his robes, and fastened his sandals as quickly as his age allowed. The king's servants walked briskly as they led him through the maze of streets and courtyards and hallways to the palace. Daniel had grown into manhood here in Babylon. He had served three generations of pagan Babylonian kings. Nothing these monarchs did should have surprised him, but his stomach churned with dread just the same.

The journey ended at the palace banquet hall. When the towering doors swung open, Daniel saw King Belshazzar and hundreds of guests gathered for one of the young king's lavish parties. The remains of the extravagant meal lay abandoned on all of the tables along with empty wine vessels and pitchers of strong drink. The party seemed to have halted in mid-motion as if frozen in time. Instead of drunken laughter and merriment, the guests spoke in hushed voices that rustled through the room like dead leaves. As Daniel entered, even the whispering stopped. The air stank of wine and sweat—and fear.

He glanced around as the servants urged him forward. The court musicians stood like statues, their instruments silent in their limp hands. He could tell by the guests' bleary eyes and sprawling postures that many of them were drunk, yet their expressions were unusually somber. Everyone seemed shaken, as if the earth had quaked, halting the revelry in mid-stride. Daniel saw them watching as he walked forward between the tables, approaching the royal dais where King Belshazzar and the queen mother awaited him. Gold and silver serving dishes glittered in the torchlight on the head table, and when Daniel recognized the designs on some of them he nearly lost his balance. These treasures had come from the temple, God's holy temple in Jerusalem. Like the Jewish people themselves, these sacred vessels had been torn from their rightful places to be demeaned and abused by pagan people who worshipped idols. The blasphemy of their use at the king's orgy shocked him. *"How long, O, Lord? Will you forget me forever? . . . How long will my enemy triumph over me?"*

Royal magi and enchanters in dark robes hovered around the king like a flock of crows, watching Daniel approach. Again, he remembered the night that King Nebuchadnezzar had called for all of his wise men and wondered if he was Belshazzar's last resort. Typically, these Babylonian rulers sought Daniel's advice only in a crisis. Otherwise, they preferred that he stay far away and not remind them of the Sovereign God of Israel and His laws.

Daniel halted in front of the king but didn't bow down. Belshazzar appeared ill, his face a sickly gray. His voice quavered when he spoke. "A-are you Daniel, one of the exiles my forefathers brought from Judah?"

"I am."

"I'm told that the spirit of the gods is in you." He glanced at the queen mother as if for confirmation. "They say that you have insight, intelligence, and outstanding wisdom."

Daniel didn't reply. Flattery from a man who displayed no common sense or self-control, much less reverence for God, meant nothing to him.

"I want you to look at this." The king pointed to the wall behind him. Daniel took another step closer and saw markings on it, as if streaks of light shone down on the wall from a source high above. But there was no window, no source of light. Daniel stepped onto the dais and skirted around the king's banquet table as he tried to discern what the markings were. They appeared to be letters and words, writing of some sort.

"I summoned my wise men and enchanters," Belshazzar said, gesturing to the men. "I asked them to read this writing and tell me what it meant, but they couldn't do it."

Daniel silently prayed for wisdom as he examined the wall up close, running his fingers over the rough plaster. "Where did these markings come from, Your Majesty? Who wrote them?"

When the king didn't reply, Daniel turned around to ask him again and saw terror in Belshazzar's eyes. He couldn't seem to speak. One of the men seated beside him said, "The fingers of a human hand appeared and wrote on the plaster of the wall."

Belshazzar nodded, swallowing, and finally found his voice. "It-it's true. I sat right here and watched as a . . . a hand . . . out of nowhere . . . wrote the words that you see."

Had it been a hallucination, the result of too much wine? A lifetime of strong drink led men to delirium. Daniel had heard of men who preferred death to the horrid beasts of their drunken imaginations. But everyone in the banquet hall stared at the writing, too. It couldn't be a mass hallucination. Besides, Daniel saw the writing, as well.

He turned to study the wall, reading the words out loud: *"Mene, mene, tekel, parsin."* They were three weights, three units of money. Again, he silently asked the Almighty One to show him the meaning.

"Now, I have heard," the king began, his voice shrill with fright. He cleared his throat to start again. "I've heard that you're able to give interpretations and solve difficult problems. If you can read this writing and tell me . . . tell us . . . what it means, you'll be clothed in purple and . . . and have a gold chain placed around your neck . . . and I'll make you the third highest ruler in the kingdom."

The third highest ruler. An honor indeed. Babylon's reigning monarch, King Nabonidas, had gone away for the winter months, leaving his son Belshazzar in charge as second-in-command. But Daniel wanted no part in this corrupt kingdom. He simply wanted to return home to his bed.

It was becoming very clear to him what the writing on the wall meant. He had spent more than sixty-five years as a captive in this nation and had served on the king's advisory council most of that time. But for the past few years, he had watched the Babylonian empire slowly disintegrate before his eyes. King Nebuchadnezzar's dream had foretold that this day would come and Babylon would fall. The statue's golden head would be replaced by a chest and arms of silver. Daniel's own dream of four great beasts had confirmed that the Babylonian kingdom would not last. But the demise had come much sooner than Daniel had imagined. He wondered what Babylon's downfall would mean for him and his fellow Jews, languishing in exile.

"Well? Can you tell us what the writing means?" the king asked.

"You may keep your gifts for yourself and give your rewards to someone else—"

"But I demand to know the meaning of the writing! How dare you refuse me?"

"Let me finish," Daniel said, holding up his hand. "While I don't want or need your rewards, nevertheless I will read the writing and tell you what it means." He waited until the murmuring stopped and a hush fell over the room. He would speak for God, declaring the truth, and whatever happened after that . . . his life was in God's hands, as it always had been.

"O king, the Most High God gave your forefather Nebuchadnezzar sovereignty and greatness and splendor. All nations and men of every language dreaded and feared him. Those who the king wanted to put to death, he put to death. Those he wanted to spare, he spared; those he wanted to promote he promoted. But when his heart became arrogant and hardened with pride, God deposed him from his royal throne and stripped him of his glory. He was driven away from people and given the mind of an animal. He ate grass like cattle and his body was drenched with the dew of heaven until he acknowledged that the Most High God is sovereign over the kingdoms of men."

Belshazzar gestured impatiently. "I've heard my grandfather's story. Get on with it. I want to know about the writing."

Daniel drew a breath, exhaling slowly to steady himself as he prepared to confront the king with God's judgment. "But you his heir, O Belshazzar, have not humbled yourself, though you admit that you knew about Nebuchadnezzar. Instead, you've set yourself up against the Lord of heaven. These are God's holy vessels," he said, gesturing to the banquet table. "They were consecrated for use in His temple, yet you brought them here so that you and your nobles, your wives and your concubines, could drink wine from them. You praise gods of silver and gold, which cannot see or hear or understand. But you don't honor the God who holds your life in His hand. Therefore, God has sent the hand that wrote that inscription."

The young king stared at him, waiting. Daniel could see that even after this dramatic reminder, Belshazzar's heart overflowed with fear, not repentance.

"This is what these words mean," Daniel said, his voice gathering strength. "*Mene*: God has numbered the days of your reign and brought it to an end."

Murmurs chased around the room. The drunken king lowered his head to his chest for just a moment, then lifted his chin again, defiant.

"*Tekel*," Daniel continued. "You have been weighed on the scales and found wanting." The king's wise men seemed appalled that Daniel would speak so bluntly. He didn't care. "*Peres*: Your kingdom is divided and given to the Medes and Persians."

Loud voices reverberated all over the room. Nervous laughter. Outrage. Daniel turned away from the writing, preparing to leave.

"Wait!" the king commanded.

Daniel halted. What now? He tried to draw a deep breath but couldn't.

"Clothe him in purple. Place my gold chain around his neck. Tomorrow Daniel shall sit at my right hand, the third highest ruler."

Daniel's shoulders sagged in relief. He shook his head in disgust. He didn't want the honor, but Belshazzar seemed determined to follow through on his promise. It took Daniel thirty minutes to free himself from the ongoing drama and return to his bedroom. The sun still hadn't risen, but Daniel thought he heard sounds of turmoil in the city streets below the palace. Had word of the startling events at the banquet hall spread so quickly?

Daniel didn't concern himself with such things. God had made it clear tonight that the kingdom of Babylon was finished, Belshazzar and his father, Nabonidas, were doomed. What their downfall would mean for Daniel's own life or for his people, he couldn't guess. Ever since the Babylonians had taken him captive in Jerusalem as a young man, his life had been in God's hands—the same hand that had written on the wall tonight. And so it would always be. No matter what came next, Daniel rested safely in the grip of his Sovereign God.

Part I

Babylon

By the rivers of Babylon we sat and wept

when we remembered Zion. . . .

If I forget you, O Jerusalem,

may my right hand forget its skill.

May my tongue cling to the roof of my mouth

if I do not remember you,

if I do not consider Jerusalem my highest joy.

PSALM 137:1, 5–6

Iddo awoke from the dream, gasping. The nightmare had nearly devoured him. He heard his wife's soothing voice, felt her hand resting on his chest as if trying to calm his pounding heart. "Shh . . . It was just a dream, Iddo. Just a dream . . ."

But it wasn't a dream, at least not the kind that other people had when they slept, seeing visions that made no sense in the light of day. In Iddo's dreams he relived memories, powerful memories, as real as on the day he'd lived them as a child. The images and sounds and horrors had imprinted on his soul the way a stylus presses into soft clay. The kiln of suffering had hardened them, and they could never be erased.

He drew a shaky breath, wiping his hand across his face, scrubbing tears from his eyes. "I'm sorry, Dinah," he whispered. "I'm sorry . . ."

"Are you all right?" she asked. "I'll make you something warm to drink."

He rested his hand on her arm, stopping her. "No, stay in bed. Why should we both be awake?" Iddo rose from their mat, groping in the dark for his robe. He wouldn't be able to sleep now.

During the daytime he could control the images that circled the edges of his consciousness like jackals by looking up at the cloud-swept sky or studying the perfection of his infant grandson's tiny fingers. But at night, when darkness hid the Creator's beauty, the images and sounds closed in on Iddo, scratching and clawing, refusing to be silenced. Once they pounced they would strip him of everything he had accomplished, ripping at the man he now was, reducing him to the ten-year-old child he had been when Jerusalem fell—helpless, terrified, naked, and shivering before his enemies. Forty-seven years had passed since he'd lived the real nightmare, and Iddo had spent those years here in Babylon. He had a wife, children, grandchildren—all born here. Yet the atrocities he'd seen in Jerusalem remained as vivid as the world he saw every morning. The nightmare never faded, never blurred.

He waited for his heart to slow, his breathing to ease, then shuffled to the door, opening and closing it soundlessly so he wouldn't disturb his household. Outside in his dark courtyard, he traced the familiar silhouette of the mud brick houses in his neighborhood, the spiky date palms growing along the nearby canal. He lifted his chin to watch stars disappear, then reappear behind the playful night clouds. "'When I consider your heavens,'" he whispered, "'the work of your fingers, the moon and the stars, which you have set in place, what is man that you are mindful of him?'" The psalms of King David were another weapon he used to keep the jackals of fear away.

The terror that had destroyed Jerusalem was the Almighty One's punishment. All of the prophets had said so. God no longer dwelled with His people because they'd been unfaithful to Him. His temple was destroyed, His people scattered among the nations, living among pagan gods. Iddo's only hope, his family's only hope, lay in studying God's Law, filling his heart and mind with the Torah, obeying every word of it every day of his life. If he sought the God of his fathers with all his strength, maybe the Holy One would show mercy and return to His people again.

Iddo shivered in the cool fall air, waiting for the nighttime peace to still his soul. But instead of the deep silence that he craved, he heard remnants of sounds from his nightmare: a low rumble like hundreds of marching feet, faraway screams and cries—or were they only the cries of birds? Iddo had spent many nights awake, but the sounds from his dreams had never lingered this way. Was he imagining things? He climbed the outdoor steps to his flat rooftop and looked out at the city. Lights danced in the distance like summer lightning—only it couldn't be lightning. The star-filled sky stretched from horizon to horizon in the flat landscape, the night clouds mere wisps.

A sudden movement in the street below caught his attention, and he squinted down at the shadows. His neighbor, Mattaniah, stood with his hands on his hips gazing toward the center of Babylon. Beside him stood another neighbor, Joel, who was a descendant of temple priests like Iddo. Could they hear the sounds, too?

Iddo hurried downstairs and out through the courtyard gate to the street. The two men turned at the sound of Iddo's footsteps. "Did the noise wake you, too?" Mattaniah asked.

"What is it? What's going on?"

"We don't know," Joel said. "The Babylonians are holding a festival of some sort for one of their pagan gods tonight, but my son Reuben thought it sounded more like soldiers marching."

"Yes . . . I thought so, too," Iddo said.

"We were wondering if the armies of the Medes and Persians had attacked the city," Mattaniah said.

Joel shook his head. "They'll never succeed. Babylon's gates are heavily fortified and the city walls are twenty feet thick. They're impregnable!" But Iddo remembered Jerusalem's toppled walls and shuddered. "My son went to have a look," Joel continued. "We're waiting for him to come back."

Iddo stood with his neighbors, listening to the distant sounds, talking quietly as they waited for Reuben to return. By the time the young man finally jogged home, flushed and breathless, an arc of pink light brightened the eastern horizon. "You won't believe it, Abba! I walked all the way to the plaza by the Ishtar Gate, and the streets are filled with soldiers all around the southern palace. Thousands of them!"

"Babylonian soldiers?" Iddo asked.

"No, sir. They weren't like any Babylonian soldiers I've ever seen."

"Then it is an invasion!" Mattaniah said.

"It can't be. How would the enemy get past our walls?" Joel asked.

"I think I know how," Reuben said. "I followed the river on the way home and the water was only this deep . . ." He gestured to the middle of his thigh. "The soldiers could have waded into the city beneath the walls, using the riverbed for a highway—like that story in the Torah when the waters parted for our people, remember?"

An invasion. Iddo turned without a word and hurried back to his walled courtyard, closing the wooden gate behind him, leaning against it. He must be dreaming. He hadn't awakened from his nightmare after all. Any moment now Dinah would shake him, and he would wake up. He closed his eyes as he slowly drew a breath, then opened them again. He was still in his courtyard, still aware of the distant rumble of marching feet.

If this wasn't a dream, then for the second time in Iddo's life enemy soldiers had invaded the city where he lived. His nightmare had become a reality once again. He took a few stumbling steps toward the house, stopped, and turned in a useless circle, like an animal trapped in a pit. He had to flee, had to escape with his wife, his family. Maybe it wasn't too late. Maybe they could wade out of the city and hide in the marshes beyond the walls. Maybe the Almighty One had parted the waters just for them, so they could escape. He took two steps forward and stopped again.

The Almighty One.

Would He help them? Iddo needed to pray, to ask for His wisdom and protection before fleeing. He climbed the stairs to the rooftop—barely able to manage them on trembling legs— and fell prostrate, facing west toward Jerusalem. "Blessed art thou, O Lord our God, King of the Universe—" He stopped. His father and grandfather had lain prostrate in the temple courtyard in Jerusalem with all the other priests, praying day and night for help and protection and salvation. Their prayers had gone unanswered.

"Blessed art thou, O Lord our God . . ." Iddo began again. Maybe something would be different this time, and the Almighty would hear His people's pleas for mercy. Iddo and the others had obeyed everything the prophets said: *"Marry and have sons and daughters. Seek the peace and prosperity of the city to which I have carried you into exile."* Iddo had done that. He and the other priests had not only tried to obey every letter of the Law, but they had constructed a fence of protective laws around the Torah to make sure no one even came close to breaking one of God's commandments. They honored the Sabbath day as best they could, even when their captors denied them a day of rest. They gathered for prayer three times a day as the three Patriarchs had done, and—

Iddo lifted his head. Why was he praying all alone? The other men must be awake by now. He would go to morning prayers, gather with the others, and decide together what to do. His household was stirring when he went downstairs to fetch his prayer shawl and phylacteries. Dinah knelt in front of the hearth with a fistful of straw, blowing on the coals to start the fire. His daughter, Rachel—lovely, vulnerable Rachel—hummed as she folded the bedding. Iddo heard murmuring in the other rooms,

as well, the rooms he had added onto his house for his sons
Berekiah and Hoshea and their wives and families. His newest
grandson was crying to be fed, and his helpless wail sent shivers through Iddo as he remembered the children in Jerusalem
who had been too hungry to cry. Would it be the same in this
invasion? The suffering, the starvation?

"I'm going to morning prayers," he told Dinah.

She looked up at him in surprise. "So early? You never go
this early."

"I need to talk with the others. Something has happened,
and I'm not sure—"

"What do you mean? What happened?" She rose to her feet,
studying him with dark, worried eyes. Her long hair still hung
loose and uncovered, and Iddo resisted the urge to gather the
soft weight of her curls in his hands. Not a single strand of
silver marred Dinah's dark hair, while his own hair and beard
had turned completely white ten years ago, when he was still in
his forties. "Are you all right, Iddo?" she asked.

He looked away. "Joel's son came home this morning with . . .
with some news. I need to talk with the others to understand
what it means."

"What news?"

He couldn't say it out loud, couldn't speak of an enemy invasion. "Just make sure you and the other women stay here. The
children, too. Don't let anyone leave our courtyard until I come
back. Don't go to the marketplace or the well or the ovens—"

"Iddo, you're scaring me!"

"Don't worry," he told her. Useless words. If what Reuben said
was true, they had every reason to worry. He turned to go, hesitat-
ing in the doorway for just a moment, wondering if he should ask
his sons to come with him. But no, Berekiah and Hoshea rarely
went to morning prayers—why should today be any different?
"I won't be long," he told Dinah. He had no idea if it was true.

The *Beit Knesset*, or house of assembly, was nearly full when Iddo arrived. It didn't take long to learn that the rumor was true: Foreign soldiers had invaded Babylon. One of Israel's elders—a member of The Great Assembly—had traveled all the way from the other side of the city with the news. "The Persians and Medes diverted the water of the Euphrates into a canal north of the city," he told them. "Their armies waited south of the city until the water was shallow enough to wade through and then entered beneath the walls in the middle of night."

The room went silent for the space of a heartbeat, two heart-beats. "How could this happen?" someone finally asked. "How could Babylon's king and his army be taken by surprise? Didn't they post watchmen? Didn't they see?"

"The Almighty One's hand is in this," the elder replied. "He promised that one day the Babylonian empire would fall, and last night it happened. The Babylonians were holding a festival to their idols and didn't even realize that the Medes and Persians were inside their walls until it was too late. King Belshazzar is dead. Thousands of his noblemen have been executed. Darius the Mede has taken over his kingdom."

Iddo sank onto one of the benches that lined the room's perimeter as everyone began talking at once, flooding the room with panicked questions.

"Will these Medes and Persians slaughter and pillage like the Babylonians did?"

"How can we protect our families?"

"Should we flee the city?"

"How can this be happening to us a second time?"

They were the same questions that Iddo lacked the strength to ask. The elder held up his hands for silence. "Listen . . . please . . . We're waiting to hear what Daniel the Righteous One and Judah's princes have to say, but in the meantime you should all return home. The Babylonians are staying inside their

23

houses today, and so should we. If the city is still quiet by the time of evening prayers, we'll gather here once again. Maybe we'll have more news by then."

As Iddo prepared to leave, a single question filled his thoughts: How could he protect his family? The truth was, he couldn't. While younger men hurried home to barricade their doors, preparing to protect the people they loved with kitchen knives and clubs, men like Iddo who remembered Jerusalem knew they couldn't save themselves.

Dinah had the morning meal ready when he returned. His sons and daughters-in-law and grandchildren had gathered in the large, central room of their house. "What's going on, Abba?" Berekiah asked. "Mama said you looked worried—and that you told us all to stay inside."

The room grew quiet as Iddo explained what little he knew about the invasion. Even his young grandchildren grew very still. "What will this mean for us?" his son Hoshea asked when Iddo finished.

"No one knows. But one of the elders from the Great Assembly promised to return with more news when we gather for evening prayers. We'll find out then. In the meantime, we must all stay inside like the Babylonians are doing." He looked at Dinah, and the fear he saw in her eyes made him reach for her hand. He was her protector, the patriarch of their family, and it grieved him to know that he couldn't keep her from harm.

"Can't we go to the well for water?" his daughter asked.

"No, Rachel. Nor to the market or the ovens."

"But—what will we do?"

"We'll stay here at home. Like we do on the Sabbath."

"But what if we run out of water?"

"We can manage until sundown, Rachel." His words came out sharper than he intended, but her question brought back memories of the long siege of Jerusalem, when the city had run out of food as well as water. He remembered his mouth being as dry as sand and the unending ache in his stomach. He remembered the vermin he had eaten to try to fill it, the brackish water that hadn't quenched his thirst. "We'll spend the day praying for mercy," he said, looking at his sons. "I'll be up on the roof if you'd like to join me there." He laid down his uneaten bread and went outside to climb the stairs.

Iddo's neighborhood and the distant city looked eerily still from the rooftop. The low rumbling of marching footsteps had finally ceased, and as he knelt on the sun-warmed tiles, he couldn't decide if the silence was a good sign or a bad one. On an ordinary day, he and his sons would have begun work by now, Iddo laboring as a scribe, tallying business accounts for the Babylonians, handling their correspondence, keeping track of their shipments and trading ventures spread throughout the empire. His two sons had formed a trading partnership of their own that had made steady profits—until now. Who knew what would happen now? But Iddo and his sons, like their forefathers, were born to be priests of the one true God. If they lived in Jerusalem instead of in exile, they would be offering sacrifices at His temple, just as Iddo's father and grandfather had done, all the way back to Israel's first priest, Aaron. Iddo remembered Jerusalem's temple, remembered watching the sacrifices as a boy, inhaling the aroma of roasting meat, listening to the Levite choirs and the trumpets. Now the holy temple was gone.

But Iddo was still a priest. As soon as he'd reached adulthood here in Babylon, he had begun his apprenticeship with the older priests who had been exiled with him, learning the regulations, trusting that one day the temple would be rebuilt as the prophet Ezekiel had promised. "It's a waste of time, Abba," both of his sons had said when they'd reached the age of apprenticeship. "Why learn dead rituals for a dead religion?" Were they right? Were the faith of their father Abraham and the laws given to

Moses mere relics of the past, as dead as the corpses that had filled Jerusalem's streets?

The city of Babylon remained quiet the entire day. None of Iddo's fears of death and destruction had materialized—yet. "Come with me to the house of assembly to pray," he told his sons that evening. "I want you beside me to hear whatever news there might be. Then we can decide together what to do."

"Shouldn't we wait a few more days until the dust has settled before going out?" Berekiah asked. "We don't know what our new captors will be like and—"

"No. You should set an example of faith for your children." Iddo gestured to Berekiah's oldest boy, Zechariah, who was nearly twelve years old and Iddo's favorite. He had fetched his father's prayer shawl for him and stood with it in his hands, watching them, listening. "We need to pray. Don't you realize how serious our situation is?" Iddo asked.

"Of course I do. And I am thinking of my children. What if our new Persian overlords misinterpret our gathering and think we're planning a rebellion?"

"I'm willing to take that chance. Come on, it's time to go."

"May I come, too?" Zechariah asked. Before Iddo could reply, Dinah gripped their grandson from behind and pulled him close.

"No, Zaki. Stay here. We don't know if it's safe yet."

The knowledge that he couldn't make his family feel safe fanned Iddo's anger into flames. He would fight this enemy of fear, replacing it with faith. The Holy One was with them, not their enemies. He reached for Zechariah's hand. "Yes, you may come with us. The Almighty One will keep us safe." He hoped it was true.

No one spoke as Iddo and his sons and grandson walked to the house of assembly. Hundreds of men had already jammed into the room and a tremor of excitement rippled through the gathering. "What's going on?" he asked one of his fellow priests. "What did I miss?"

"It's *Rebbe* Daniel," the priest whispered. "He's alive! He survived the invasion and came all the way from the king's palace to pray with us."

Iddo's uneasiness melted in relief. Rebbe Daniel the Righteous One was highly revered in Babylon, not only among the Jewish community, but among the Babylonians and their leaders, as well. If the Medes and Persians had let him live, then there was hope for Iddo and his fellow Jews. Iddo had only seen this legendary man twice before, and he was overjoyed to see him now, glad that his sons and grandson would hear what he had to say. The room fell quiet as the elderly man stepped onto the *bimah* to speak.

"We have nothing to fear from our new rulers," Daniel said. "Darius the Mede has asked me to serve him as I served the Babylonians."

"We're safe, then?" someone asked.

"Yes. We're all safe."

Iddo closed his eyes as the news sent murmurs of relief rippling through the hall.

"There's more," Daniel continued. "I have been praying and studying the prophets' words for some time now, and the Holy One has shown me that the years of our captivity are nearing an end. He spoke through the prophet Jeremiah, saying that we would serve the king of Babylon for seventy years, and when those seventy years were fulfilled, He would punish the Babylonians. This invasion by the Medes and Persians is the beginning of that punishment. More than three thousand of our captors have been executed, including the king and his noblemen. Our exile is coming to an end. We will soon return home to Jerusalem."

A shout went up from the gathered men. Iddo laid his hand on Zechariah's shoulder to steady himself. Home. To Jerusalem. He longed to shout praises along with the other men, but the news had stolen his breath. He was afraid to believe it, afraid to put his faith in something as impossible as returning to Jerusalem. And even if it did turn out to be true, could he bear to return to the ghost-filled ruins he had left behind as a child?

"Our captivity began when King Nebuchadnezzar brought King Jehoiakim here to Babylon in bronze shackles," Daniel continued. "I was part of that first group of exiles sixty-seven years ago. That means our seventy years of captivity are nearly over. We need to pray today and every day that the Holy One will now have mercy on us and restore us to the land He promised our father Abraham. That's what I've come here to do with all of you tonight—to pray."

"Did our new captors say that we could return?" someone asked.

"Not yet—but God promised that we would. We've endured punishment for a time, but the Holy One promised to take us back, to restore our fellowship with Him, to continue His plan to redeem all mankind through our people."

As Rebbe Daniel prepared to pray, Iddo turned with the other men to face the *Aron Ha Kodesh,* where the sacred Torah scrolls were kept. Daniel prayed aloud, lifting his hands to heaven, and the faith and conviction in the man's voice sent shivers through Iddo.

"O Lord, the great and awesome God, who keeps His covenant of love with all who love Him and obey His commands, we have sinned and done wrong. We have been wicked and have rebelled. All this disaster has come upon us, just as it was written in the Law of Moses. But now, O Lord our God, who brought your people out of Egypt with a mighty hand, hear our prayers and in keeping with your mercy, forgive us! Look with favor on your desolate sanctuary. We don't make requests of you because we are righteous, but because of your great mercy. O Lord, listen! O Lord, forgive! For your sake, O my God, don't delay because your city and your people bear your name."

The prayers went late into the evening, and by the time they ended, Iddo's legs could barely carry him home. But his worry had vanished as if lifted from his shoulders to ascend with his prayers. "See, Zechariah? The worst is over now," he said as they entered the gate to their courtyard. "But we must do as Rebbe Daniel told us and continue to pray. The Almighty has promised that if His people humble themselves and pray, then He will forgive our sin and heal our land. We will return to Jerusalem and—"

Berekiah took Iddo's arm, stopping him before he entered the house. "Abba. You don't really believe that we'll return to Jerusalem, do you?" he asked quietly.

"Of course I do! You heard what Rebbe Daniel said. The Almighty One has promised through His prophets that we will." Iddo looked down at his young grandson, eager to reassure him, but the boy's father nudged him toward the door.

"Go inside, Zechariah. Your grandfather and I will be there in a moment." Hoshea also waited behind, and Iddo saw his sons exchange worried looks.

"Listen, Abba. It's crazy to believe that we'll be allowed to return," Hoshea said. "Slaves never go free, and exiles never return to their native lands."

"The slaves went free under Moses," Iddo said. "It must have seemed just as impossible back then, too."

"And who will dare approach this new 'pharaoh' and demand that our captors set us free?" Berekiah asked.

"Maybe the Almighty One will send Rebbe Daniel to—"

"To do what? Can he perform miracles like Moses did? Will God send plagues and darkness to convince this army of conquerors to free us? You don't really believe all those tales, do you?"

Iddo couldn't reply. What had seemed so believable as he'd prayed in the house of assembly seemed absurd as he faced his sons' doubts.

"Abba, you of all people should know that prayer isn't a magic formula. The Holy One doesn't do our bidding. If He did, we would still be living in Jerusalem and offering sacrifices at the temple, not living here in Babylon."

"But the Holy One must bring us home," Iddo said. "If our people remain here, our faith will become extinct. I see it happening little by little every day. How can we survive if we stay here, surrounded by pagan people and their wicked practices? We'll become just like them."

"But our faith hasn't been extinguished, Abba, it has endured—even here."

"Then why don't you practice it? You hardly ever come with me to pray or to study the Torah."

"There's a difference between ritual and belief," Berekiah said. "Just because I don't pray three times a day with the other men doesn't mean I don't believe."

"But now that our leaders have asked us to come together and pray for our freedom, are you going to join us? Do you believe the Holy One's promises?"

When Berekiah didn't reply, Hoshea answered for both of them. "We think our leaders are wrong to raise everyone's hopes when the truth is that we'll never be allowed to return. It won't happen."

"Enough! I won't listen to another word!" Iddo yanked his arm free and climbed the stairs to the roof alone, to pray.

He knew it was his fault that his sons didn't believe. When they were boys, Iddo's own faith had been too weak to support the weight of their doubts and questions. Now they were grown men, more concerned with the world in front of their eyes than with the unseen world of faith and prayer.

But Iddo would teach his grandson Zechariah to believe. He would do everything right from now on. Maybe then the Almighty One would hear their prayers and end His people's exile.

CHAPTER
2

Dinah pulled the last round of bread from the fire and set it out to cool beside the others. The crusts had baked to a dark golden brown, filling the room with their mouth-watering aroma. "What else?" she asked, glancing around. "Is everything ready? Shabbat is nearly here." The sun dropped below the flat horizon much too soon on these short winter days and Dinah, her daughter, Rachel, and two daughters-in-law, Sarah and Naomi, needed to finish preparing all of the food before it did. "Are the lentils ready?" she asked.

"Yes, Mama."

"And you'll make sure everything else is prepared, Rachel? Before your father comes home from prayers?"

"I will, Mama."

"Good." She looked around again and saw a haze of smoke from the hearth lingering in the room. They usually prepared meals outside in the courtyard, but the rainy winter day had driven them inside. Dinah propped the door open to chase the last of the smoke away. When she was satisfied that everything was ready, she fetched the extra pot of food from the warming shelf beside the hearth. "I'm taking this next door to Miriam's

31

family. I'll be right back. Close the door if it gets too cold in here."

"Why don't you invite them to eat here with us?" Naomi asked, shifting her infant son to her other shoulder.

"I did invite them, but Mattaniah said no. He thinks the noise and activity is too much for Miriam." Dinah had to admit that her household was very lively with her extended family all living and eating together. But Dinah loved every minute of her busy life. At age fifty-four, her arms were full, her heart content.

She dashed from the house and hurried next door through the spitting rain, the pot of warm food swaddled in cloths. "I brought something for your Sabbath meal," she said when Miriam's daughter, Yael, opened the door. "How is your mother feeling today?"

"The same," Yael said with a shrug. She was ten years old and had barely known her mother to be well. But in recent months, the sharp decline in Miriam's health worried Dinah. "Come in," Yael said, opening the door wider. "Mama will be happy to see you."

"I can't stay long. Shabbat begins soon. I'll just set this by the fire to keep it warm until dinnertime." But the fire on the hearth had gone out, leaving the room as cold and damp as a cave. Dinah set down the food and bent to add fuel and rekindle the embers. "Is your father home?" she asked, hearing the murmur of voices in the next room.

"Not yet. Parthia is here to read Mama's fortune. She promised to read mine, too. Want her to do yours?"

"I don't think so, Yael. I can't stay long."

"But this new seer is always right. She told Abba that he would prosper, and the very next day someone hired him to build a storehouse."

Dinah blew on the coals until the straw caught fire, uncomfortable with Yael's news. She knew that Miriam's husband had paid for a string of Babylonian healers and astrologers, seeking signs and omens, desperate for a cure for his wife. But now Yael was becoming fascinated with the hocus-pocus, as well.

When the fire was blazing, Dinah stood, wiping soot and straw from her hands on a piece of sacking. She studied Yael's bright, eager face and saw a lovely child beneath her nearly wild exterior, a girl who was certain to grow into a beautiful woman. She needed a mother's guiding hand to prepare her for womanhood, but Miriam was too ill for the task. Yael often roamed the neighborhood by herself and played near the canal with Dinah's grandson, Zechariah. What would become of her if Miriam died? "Maybe I will peek in and see how your mother is doing," Dinah said. She couldn't resist brushing Yael's dark, untamed hair from her eyes, but the girl squirmed away from her.

"I have to fetch Mama some water. You go ahead. I'll be right there."

Dinah parted the curtain that divided the two rooms and found Miriam propped up on her sleeping mat, her thin face as pale as the plastered wall behind her. A dark-robed Babylonian woman with soot-black hair and skin like burnished pottery perched on a stool in front of her. Layers of necklaces and amulets hung around the woman's neck, and she wore an elaborate golden headpiece that dangled onto her forehead. Loops of shining bracelets encircled her dark wrists, jingling and tinkling as she ground spices together in a bowl on her lap. Strewn in front of her was an array of pots, filled with odd-looking leaves and roots. A plume of incense curled from one of the pots, making Dinah cough when it caught in her throat.

"Dinah, come in," Miriam said when she saw her. "This is Parthia, my new seer." The woman glanced up at Dinah without a word before resuming her task.

"I can only stay a moment. The sun is going to set soon. I brought some stew for your Sabbath meal."

"Dear Dinah. You're always so good to us."

"How are you feeling?"

"Much better. Parthia brought good news today. She said my stars are moving into a favorable position for healing."

Dinah couldn't reply. She stepped aside as Yael crowded into the room juggling three cups of water in her small, nail-bitten hands. She gave one to Dinah, one to her mother, and kept the third for herself. Dinah took a dutiful sip, even though she hadn't asked for a drink.

"I want to repay you for all of your help, Dinah," Miriam said. "Is there something you'd like to ask the seer while she's here?"

Dinah took another sip of water, stalling for time. She longed to ask if Rebbe Daniel's promise of a return to Jerusalem would really come true. Her husband had talked of nothing else since the evening after the invasion, and she feared Iddo's heart would break if it didn't happen. But she couldn't imagine the cata-strophic changes in her own life if it did occur. "Thank you . . . but no," Dinah finally replied. "Iddo got angry with me when I asked your last astrologer for signs."

"But why? What was the harm in seeking guidance to choose Rachel's wedding day? Doesn't he want your daughter to begin her married life under the most favorable stars?"

"Yes, of course, but . . . but Iddo says . . ." He had called it Babylonian nonsense and told Dinah she should pray for the Almighty One's blessing on Rachel instead of dabbling in pagan astrology. He had forbidden her to have any more to do with their neighbors' sorcery.

"Iddo doesn't need to know, does he?" Miriam asked with a smile. "Give Parthia your cup."

Dinah handed it to her without thinking and a moment later the seer tossed a pinch of powder from her bowl into the water. Her bracelets jingled as she swirled the contents around, muttering unintelligible words. Then the clinking stopped as she stared into the cup, studying the mixture, waiting for the water to settle.

"I see a great tearing in your life," the seer began. "Something very precious to you will be ripped away and—"

"Stop!" Dinah snatched the cup from her, spilling some of the contents onto the stone floor. "I don't want to hear any more!"

"Why not?" Miriam asked. "Don't you want to be prepared for the future?"

"I know my future will hold sorrow; everyone's does. We can never be prepared for it." Dinah thought of the suffering her parents had endured, and what Iddo had endured as a child. If they had known what was coming, could they have prepared for it? In fact they *had* known the future—Israel's prophets had warned them of the coming judgment—yet everyone had suffered just the same. "It doesn't help to know," Dinah finally said, "because we'll only worry about it ahead of time. I'll face whatever comes when it comes."

"Read mine next," Yael said, holding out her cup to the seer.

The woman glanced at Dinah with contempt in her eyes, then rose from her stool. "Not here, little one. Come. I brought the charts that I promised so you can learn how to read the stars." She carried the water and her bowl of powder to the front room with Yael scurrying behind her.

"I'm sorry," Dinah said. "I didn't mean to spoil anything."

"It doesn't matter. Mattaniah pays her well." Miriam sank back against the cushions again. The life that had animated her a moment ago seemed to escape from her the way a lump of bread dough sinks after being punched, releasing the air. "I can understand why you don't need to know your future, Dinah. Your life is already so wonderful. But if you suffered from my ill health, you'd want to know what to expect."

"But that seer can't possibly know for certain what will

happen, can she? Why waste the good days of your life worrying about something that may never come to pass?"

"If I'm going to die, I want to make preparations for my family."

Dinah crouched in front of her friend and took her hand. "Miriam, none of us knows if we'll live to see tomorrow. Why not live each day with hope?"

"But she does give me hope. She was right about the Persian invasion, you know. She said that Babylon would undergo a great upheaval, and she was right. She saw it in the stars."

Was there a difference, Dinah wondered, between this Babylonian woman with her stars and swirling water and Israel's prophets, who also claimed to see the future? Why would Iddo listen to one and not the other?

"Mattaniah told me what Daniel the Righteous One said," Miriam continued. "How our people may return to Jerusalem soon. So I asked the seer about his prophecy, and she said—"

"Wait! Don't tell me!" Dinah stood, dropping Miriam's hand. "I don't want to know."

"Are you sure?" A thin smile brightened Miriam's face.

Dinah hesitated for just a moment before saying, "I'm sure. Listen, I should go. See how dark it's getting already? *Shabbat shalom*, Miriam." She bent to kiss her friend on both cheeks.

"Shabbat shalom. And thank you again for the food."

Dinah hurried home to wash and change her clothes for the Sabbath. Her sons' wives had scrubbed their children—four boys and three girls—and gotten them ready while Rachel rolled out the rug where they would eat, placing the bread and wine at the head where Iddo would sit. Dinah had just finished lighting the Sabbath lights and reciting the blessing when her sons arrived home from work and Iddo returned from prayers in the house of assembly.

"May we soon be celebrating Shabbat in Jerusalem," Iddo

said as he kissed Dinah in greeting. She helped him out of his damp outer cloak and hung it on a peg near the hearth.

"Do you truly believe that we'll be returning?" she asked, thinking of Miriam's seer.

"Of course. We're praying for the Almighty One to work a miracle so we can go home."

But she *was* home. *This* was her home, the place where she had been born. Even if the Almighty One did work a miracle to bring about a second exodus, why would her husband want to return to the place of his nightmares? Their home was here in Babylon, not the desolate, ruined city of Jerusalem filled with skeletons and ghosts, a thousand impossible miles away.

"Is everything ready?" Iddo asked. "Call the children. Let's wash and eat."

Dinah watched with contentment as the men performed the ritual hand-washing and the children scrambled into their places on the rug.

Thirty-six years ago, two very different suitors had asked Dinah's father for her hand. Joel had been handsome and assertive, already a community leader at a young age. He had been born in Babylon, as she had been. But Dinah had been drawn to Iddo by his gentle nature, his uncompromising adherence to his religion. When he had awakened, screaming from a nightmare on the first night they shared a bed, his vulnerability had made her love him all the more. She longed to protect him, to help chase away his demons. But even on their happiest days, sadness always hovered over Iddo. He was like a mouse cowering in the shadows, waiting for the hawk to dive down and snatch him away. She slowly had discovered that the things she loved the most about him—his gentleness, his rigid legalism—were symptoms of a deep, unbearable grief, the same haunted grief she'd witnessed in her parents and in other Jews from the generation of the exile. As the years passed, what Dinah had grown to love the most about her husband was his ability to move forward in spite of that grief.

As Iddo blessed the bread and broke it, blessed the wine and poured it, the fierceness of her love for him gripped Dinah like a fist. She watched him pass around bowls of stew and lentils, olives and roasted grain, and saw a man who was old before his time. Would the Holy One tear Iddo away from her? Is that what Parthia had seen? If death was going to rip Iddo from Dinah's arms, she didn't want to know.

She began to relax after her busy day of cooking as the leisurely meal unwound, enjoying the food and the traditions, laughing and eating and singing with the others. But her deepest satisfaction came not from the rituals but from her family.

"May we soon return to Jerusalem!" Iddo said, raising his cup of wine. Dinah lifted her cup along with everyone else, but Iddo's words had created a tension in the room that he didn't seem to notice. "I can faintly recall celebrating Shabbat in Jerusalem when I was very young," he continued. "But those memories were overshadowed by the years when Jerusalem was under siege."

The room fell quiet. Iddo never spoke of those memories, and it must have surprised everyone that he did now. "We were starving near the end. There was nothing to eat for many, many days. And now . . ." His voice trailed off as he stared down at the table.

Dinah reached for his hand. "Now we've been richly blessed with abundant food," she said.

He looked up at her, puzzled, and pulled his hand free. "Now we will return to the Promised Land," he corrected.

"I hope you're right, Abba," Berekiah said, "but I worry that you may be disappointed. The world isn't the same place it was when you were a boy. The nation of Judah no longer exists."

"They wanted to cut us off from our land and our faith and

our traditions," Iddo said, "hoping we would mingle with the pagans and disappear!"

Dinah had never seen him this way at dinner before, his face flushed, his quiet voice raised. "Hasn't the Holy One been with us here, Iddo?" she asked. "What difference does it make which patch of land we live on?"

"It makes a huge difference!" He turned to their grandson, Zechariah. "Do you remember what we studied the other day about God's four promises?"

"Yes, Saba." The boy smiled as if pleased to be included in the adult conversation. He was such a bright boy, a gifted boy, yet still sweet and tender at age eleven. Since the day he was born he'd been able to make Iddo smile, bringing a light to his eyes each time he toddled into the room, helping him forget the grief that haunted him. Even if Dinah didn't have a million other reasons to love her firstborn grandchild, she would love Zechariah for that reason alone.

"He promised to give us the land," Zechariah replied, holding up one finger. "He promised that we would be as numerous as the stars in the heavens. . . ." He held up a second finger.

"It must be a pretty cloudy sky," his Uncle Hoshea muttered, "if we're the only stars that are left."

"He promised that through us all the nations of the earth would be blessed. . . ."

"All of the nations hate us," Hoshea said, speaking louder this time. "It's impossible to see how we have blessed anyone."

"Hoshea, please," Dinah murmured.

"But it's true, Mama. The only way we're a blessing to the Babylonians is as their slaves and servants."

"Tell us the fourth promise, Zaki," Dinah said.

"He promised to live among us and be our God."

"Yes! We were created to live with God," Iddo said. "And His dwelling place on earth is His temple in Jerusalem. That's why it's so important for us to return and to rebuild it. Without it, our sins will continue to separate us from Him."

"Does it have to be in Jerusalem?" Hoshea asked.

"Of course it does! Do you think He would dwell among us here, alongside pagan idols and pagan temples?"

Dinah's grandbaby fussed in his mother's arms as if sensing the unsettled atmosphere. Shabbat dinner was never this loud, with raised voices and arguments. Dinah stood and took the child from his mother. "Let me see if I can soothe him," she said. She left the room without looking back and carried the baby outside to the courtyard, gently rocking him in her arms.

The rain had stopped but the winter night was cool, and she held her grandson close to keep him warm. She brushed her cheek against his smooth, soft skin as she tried to soothe him and quiet her own worried heart. A handful of stars peeked between the clouds, and she thought again of God's promise to Abraham to make his family as numerous as the stars. But why couldn't the promise of many descendants come true here? Dinah was content with her life. Why couldn't Iddo be content, as well?

"Something very precious to you will be ripped away . . ."

Dinah gripped her grandchild tighter, humming a lullaby to push away the seer's words. Little by little, the baby stopped fussing and her own soul quieted, as well. When he was asleep, she carried him inside and tucked him into bed. But before she had time to rejoin the others who were still sitting together after the meal, a man from their community arrived at the door.

"Forgive me for disturbing your Sabbath meal," he said, "but it's time. My wife, Keziah, asked me to fetch the midwives."

"Yes, of course," Dinah said. "Babies don't wait until Shabbat is over, do they? Especially third babies. Let me get my shawl, and I'll come with you."

Dinah loved being a midwife, bringing new babies into

the world. She loved working side-by-side with her cousin Shoshanna, who was also a midwife, even when it meant that her meals were interrupted. She told her family where she was going and hurried down the street to fetch Shoshanna.

Keziah's baby was larger than the first two had been, and though the labor went smoothly, she had a difficult time delivering. Dinah soothed her as she struggled through hours of pain and endless contractions. "I can't do this anymore!" Keziah moaned.

"Think of the future," Dinah coached. "Think of holding your precious child in your arms. A brand-new life."

"I can't!"

"Yes, you can, Keziah. Find the strength inside yourself." After a hard struggle, Keziah's first son was finally born. She was exhausted but joyful as she held him close, and the look on Keziah's face brought tears to Dinah's eyes. The miracle of birth always moved her.

Long after midnight Dinah and Shoshanna returned to their homes. Dinah tried not to awaken Iddo as she crawled into bed beside him, but he was already awake. "I'm sorry if we upset you at dinner," he said as he held her, warming her after the chilly walk home.

"I hate it when you argue with each other."

"But do you agree with our sons, Dinah? Do you think they're right and that the prophets are all wrong?"

"I don't know. . . . What do I know of such things?" She closed her eyes, wanting to sleep, not talk. Why spoil the contentment she felt after the miracle of her night's work?

"Dinah, it's important to me to know how you feel about it. Do you agree with our sons?"

She sighed and rolled over onto her back, knowing Iddo wouldn't let the matter rest until she answered him. "Berekiah and Hoshea were only asking you to look around and see what you have now, here in this place, instead of longing for the past or trying to see into the future."

"But God always keeps His promises. He said as long as the sun and moon remain, Israel will remain. And what do you see shining in the sky every morning?"

"The sun—but it rises above Babylon, too, not just Jerusalem." Iddo gave an exasperated huff in reply. "I was born here, Iddo. This is the only home I've ever known. I've been happy here all my life with our family and my work. I've never experienced what you did or known your grief. . . . I just wish . . ."

"What? What do you wish?"

"I wish Rebbe Daniel and the other prophets had never offered you this hope. What if they're wrong and this turns out to be another loss in your life?"

"They won't be wrong."

Dinah brushed her fingers through his white hair, trailed them down his soft white beard. "Then from now on I will pray that the prophets are right. Now please, Iddo. Let's go to sleep." She closed her eyes again and nestled in his arms. But as she tried to sleep, Dinah still feared that if his hopes didn't come to pass, the disappointment would kill him.

"I see a great tearing in your life . . ." A shudder passed through Dinah. She wished with all her heart that she had never allowed the Babylonian woman to gaze into her cup.

CHAPTER

3

Zechariah sat hunched against the morning cold as he ate breakfast with his father and grandfather. Kindling a fire was forbidden on the Sabbath, and the air in the unheated room sent a chill through him. He felt his father watching him and looked up. "Come to work with me this morning, Zaki. I want you to see—"

"On Shabbat?" his grandfather interrupted. "It's bad enough that you choose to work on the Sabbath, but why ask your son to desecrate it?"

"It just occurred to me that he will turn twelve soon. He'll be an adult and his Torah studies will be finished. It's time he learned the trading business from Hoshea and me."

"And what if he prefers to come to the house of assembly with me?"

Zechariah stared at the floor as the argument bounced back and forth. He loved both men, but sometimes he felt as though his father was gripping one of his arms and his grandfather the other, yanking him in opposite directions, tearing him in two. He hated being trapped in the middle, but if they asked his opinion, he would rather go with Abba. Working alongside his father would be a welcome change from praying all morning—even though he hated to disappoint his grandfather.

"He's my son," Abba finally said. "It's my decision. We'll be back in time for afternoon prayers." He stood, motioning to Zechariah. "You ready?"

Zechariah tried to mask his excitement as he rose to his feet to fetch his outer robe and sandals. He couldn't meet his grandfather's gaze as Saba gathered his prayer shawl and phylacteries, then shuffled out the door to walk to the house of assembly alone.

Abba strode briskly as they left their Jewish neighborhood, but Zechariah slowed his steps to gaze all around as they walked through Babylon's strange, exotic streets. He rarely glimpsed this alien world except from the rooftop of his home. "What's that building?" he asked as they passed a magnificent pillared structure.

"That's the temple of Ishtar, one of Babylon's gods."

"Was the temple in Jerusalem like that?"

"I don't know. I never saw it. You'll have to ask Saba."

Two men were ascending the temple stairs wearing the most beautiful white robes Zechariah had ever seen, embroidered with purple and gold. "Who are those men?" he asked.

"Priests, I suppose. I don't really know much about Babylonian religion. They have at least a dozen temples to their pagan gods here in this city, not counting the great *ziggurat*."

Zaki stopped to stare until the men disappeared inside, then hurried to catch up with his father. "Saba says we'll wear white robes like that when we're priests, someday."

"You and I will never be priests, in spite of what your grandfather thinks."

"Why not?"

"Because there's no longer a temple in Jerusalem. It's gone. Destroyed."

"But Rebbe Daniel said—"

"The prophets are all dreamers, son. It's much wiser to place your hope in things you can see right in front of you. Then you won't be disappointed. That's why your uncle and I are working so hard to build this business for you and your brothers. You know I love your grandfather, but we can't all live in a dream world like he does."

"Is it true what you said this morning? That I'll get to go to work with you after my birthday instead of studying the Torah?"

"Well . . . maybe you should continue to study it some of the time. But my business will be yours someday, so it's time you learned how to run it with me." They reached a squat, low-roofed building near the canal a few minutes later and went inside through a rear door. After passing Babylon's towering buildings, Zechariah was disappointed in his father's gloomy office. The walls inside the one-room structure were lined with shelves and stuffed with even more scrolls and clay tablets than at the yeshiva Zaki attended. Abba showed him the worktable where he and Uncle Hoshea sat all day, buying and selling goods throughout the empire, keeping track of debts and sales. The work seemed no different or more exciting to Zechariah than sitting in the yeshiva all day, studying Torah scrolls.

Abba led the way to the front of the building and opened a door that overlooked the canal. "This is our slowest season of the year," he said. "The ships from Armenia won't begin to arrive until the trading season resumes in the spring."

"Ships like that one?" Zechariah asked, pointing to a tall-masted vessel similar to the ones he saw on the canal near their house.

"Some of them are. But the ones that come from Armenia are round and made from willow staves and animal skins. They sail downriver from Armenia with goods to sell—and carrying a donkey or two. Since the river can only be navigated in one direction, the traders sell their goods, dismantle their boats, and then load the staves and skins on their donkeys for the return trip. It's interesting to watch."

"I wish I could travel someplace new."

Abba rested his hand on Zaki's head for a moment. "Maybe you and I will have that chance someday. Listen, I have to go over my accounts now. Go ahead and explore while I work."

For the next two hours, Zechariah wandered along the edge of the canal outside his father's building, watching the flurry of activity on the waterfront and in the other shops and warehouses. He loved listening to the slurping, splashing sounds that the water made against the dock and dreaming of faraway places. But even though he wasn't doing any forbidden work, Zaki still felt guilty for not going to the house of assembly with Saba and the others on this Sabbath morning. When he finally turned to retrace his steps, he heard music in the distance and the persistent thumping of drums. He raced back to his father's office. "What's that music, Abba? Do you hear it?"

Abba had been hunched over his worktable, but he sat up straight, cocking his head to listen. "I don't know what that is. . . . But give me a minute to finish this, and we'll go see."

A short time later Abba closed the building, and they hurried up the street together, following the sound. "It's a royal procession," a stranger told Abba when he asked. "You'll get the best view from the top of the wall."

Abba found the nearest stairway leading to the top of Babylon's massive walls, and they puffed their way to the top. Zechariah had never been up this high in his life. The walls were as wide as The Processional Way, Babylon's main street, and wide enough for teams of horses and chariots to race each other. Tiny Persian soldiers in bright blue tunics swarmed in the street below like busy insects as they cleared a path for the procession. The music grew louder and louder, the drums banging and thumping in time with Zaki's heart. An escort of musicians paraded past first, followed by four magnificent white horses pulling a golden chariot. The man riding in the chariot wore a long, purple robe trimmed with gold, and the people lining the street bowed down to him as he passed. "Is that the new Persian king?" Zechariah whispered.

"Yes, I suppose it is. It's a good thing we're watching from up here. We only bow down to the Almighty One."

The dazzling parade slowly moved past—soldiers on horseback, noblemen in chariots, and golden images of Babylon's gods on wheeled carts, glittering in the bright sunshine. Zaki had never seen anything like this before, but Abba assured him that kings and emperors always traveled in such splendor wherever they went. "Did King David and King Solomon travel that way, too?" he asked.

"Maybe . . . That was a long time ago, son."

As Zechariah gazed out over Babylon, the city looked beautiful to him, the buildings and temples decorated with glazed bricks of blue and red and gold. His Jewish neighborhood of tightly clustered square buildings was dull in comparison, the color of mud. He made a slow turn, taking it all in, and couldn't imagine living anywhere else but Babylon. At last they descended the stairs again and headed home.

"Abba, are we really going to move back to Jerusalem like Saba said last night?"

He shook his head. "No king would ever let his slaves go free. Has anything changed since the Persians arrived?"

"No." Zaki's life had continued the same as always, with school and chores and prayers in the house of assembly. Today was the first hint that something new may be coming, and he was excited about it, even if his father's workplace had been a disappointment.

They went to prayers together, as Abba had promised.

Afterward, Zechariah walked home with his grandfather, trying to make amends. "There's a little time to study the Torah before we eat," Saba said. "Shall we go up to the roof?"

Zechariah stifled a sigh. There would be no escaping to play with his neighbor, Yael. She was his best friend, and even though she was a girl, she behaved more like a boy, exploring the canal with him whenever they had free time. He couldn't wait to tell her about all the things he'd seen today with his father. But Saba had already opened the gate to their courtyard and was heading toward the stairs to the roof. Zechariah glanced at the distant palm trees near the water's edge one last time before racing up the stairs ahead of him. He enjoyed learning with Saba—as long as the lessons didn't take forever.

From the rooftop he saw the Euphrates River gliding through the middle of the city like a thick brown snake. He could see the top of the ziggurat in the city's center, a long distance away from his Jewish neighborhood. He would love to climb that mountain of bricks someday and see what the view was like from such a glorious height.

"What are you looking at?" Saba asked when he reached the top of the stairs.

"I like the way the sun is shining on the ziggurat. Doesn't it look beautiful?"

Saba turned his back on the view without replying.

"Saba, I've been wondering: How can seventy years of exile have passed already? You aren't seventy years old, and you remember being brought here."

"Our captivity began before I was born, son. Groups of our people were forced into exile three different times in a little more than twenty years. I don't remember the first two invasions, but when Judah's last king rebelled against the Babylonians, their armies demolished everything and brought me here."

Zechariah sank down on the rug beside his grandfather, hoping he would tell him more. Saba never talked about the past or the things he remembered. But he'd offered a few hints at dinner last night, and Zechariah longed to hear more. "How old were you then? My age?"

"I was ten when the Babylonians broke through the walls and destroyed the temple. Now you and I will be among those who are blessed to return and rebuild it."

Zechariah felt pulled in two directions again. Babylon was his home, Jerusalem a distant place he knew only from the Torah. He celebrated the story of the exodus from slavery in Egypt at Passover every year, but it had always seemed like a myth to him, no different from the exaggerated stories that the Babylonians told about their gods, Marduk and Ishtar and Enlil. He thought of the temple and the priests he'd seen today and asked, "Do you remember the sacrifices at the temple?"

"Only vaguely. I was just a boy, too small to see over the heads of the taller men. I remember my mother lifting me up once, so I could see my father in his white robes, but I was too young to understand what the sacrifices were all about."

"Did the soldiers really destroy everything?"

Saba nodded, closing his eyes. "We tasted ash in our mouths for days and days. The charred land was empty, and when the wind blew, the ash went down our throats and into our eyes. The stench of death was everywhere. You couldn't escape it." Saba's voice had grown very soft. "You can't imagine our fear to find ourselves in enemy hands. They stripped us and forced us to march, and we were so terrified. . . ." He fell silent, shaking his head as he stared down at his lap. Zechariah knew about Saba's nightmares. He'd heard him screaming in the night.

"It must have taken a long time to walk here," Zechariah said after a moment.

"Yes, but we had no choice. The soldiers forced us to keep going no matter how tired we were—for miles and miles, across mountains and deserts. . . . Many people died along the way, especially the old ones and the little children who were already weak from starvation. People had to carry their loved ones' bodies until nightfall because the soldiers wouldn't let them stop to bury them, and we couldn't leave them for scavengers to feed on. So we buried them at night, with nothing to mark their graves and no chance to grieve or to pray before falling asleep and waking at dawn to march another day." He stopped again as his voice choked with emotion.

Zechariah was sorry for making his grandfather sad. He searched for something to say to cheer him but couldn't think of anything. At last Saba cleared his throat. "And now, if it pleases God, we will go back the way we came," he said. "The Almighty One will provide a new exodus from slavery and we'll return home, just as He promised through His prophets."

Zaki thought of how Abba had called the prophets a bunch of dreamers. He and Saba couldn't both be right.

When Zechariah heard voices in the street below, he stood to peer over the parapet. Yael was entering her courtyard with a Babylonian woman, draped in golden jewelry. He wanted to wave, but Yael didn't look up and he didn't dare call out to her. Saba stood and came to peer over the wall beside him. "What is that woman of wickedness doing in our neighborhood? And on the Sabbath, no less!"

"Yael's mother is sick, and she's the woman who's been reading her future in the stars. Yael says the stars and planets control our destiny and that—"

"Nonsense! The Almighty One created the heavenly bodies so we could keep track of the times and seasons. Why would He allow something as distant and impersonal as a star to decide our fate? Yael's father knows that pagan sorcery is forbidden. The Torah says a woman of wickedness like her should be stoned to death."

Zechariah couldn't imagine such a horrible death, pummeled with rocks and stones until you died.

"Promise me you won't go near that woman," Saba said.

"I promise."

"Come, let's begin." Saba turned his back on Yael's house, and they sat down in a patch of sunshine to study together.

"Will you help me practice my Torah portion, Saba? I want to read it perfectly on the day of my bar mitzvah. I want you to be proud of me."

"I already am proud of you."

They worked until it was time to eat, and Zechariah made good progress in studying the passage of Hebrew Scripture. When the meal was ready and they left the rooftop, Zechariah lagged behind so he could dash over to Yael's house and see if she wanted to go exploring after the meal.

He halted before reaching Yael's gate. The Babylonian woman stood with her back to him while Yael knelt beside the threshold. They were digging a hole—something that was forbidden on the Sabbath. Zechariah remembered his grandfather's story of how they had buried their dead loved ones along the road into exile and wondered if Yael's mother was going to die.

When Yael looked up and saw him, she motioned to him. He shook his head, remembering his promise. She hurried over, brushing dirt off her hands. "Come on, Zaki. Want to help us?"

"What are you doing?"

"The seer brought a clay demon and we're burying it under our threshold to keep the evil spirits away until Mama gets better. The stars say she will recover if nothing interferes."

"Do you really believe all that stuff? I mean, it seems . . . stupid."

Yael planted her hands on her hips, challenging him. "What if your mother was sick? What would you do?" For all her bravery, tears shone in her eyes.

"I don't know. I guess I'd try anything." He didn't want to imagine losing his mother, even though Safta Dinah and his aunts would take care of him. Yael had no one. He thought again of how Saba had lost his entire family. Why did the Holy One let things like that happen?

"Want to see the demon before we bury it?" Yael asked.

"I can't. I promised Saba that I wouldn't go near . . . her." He tilted his head toward the Babylonian woman.

"Parthia? Why not? . . . Hey, you know what Parthia said? She said I have the gift of divination. She's teaching me to tell the future like she does."

"The future?" He took a small step backwards. Saba said Parthia should be stoned to death.

"She says I can earn money telling fortunes and help pay for Mama's potions and things. It costs a lot of money for seers, you know. Here—give me your hand, and I'll tell you what I learned so far." She grabbed Zechariah's hand before he could stop her and turned it palm-side up. "This is your lifeline. . . . Hey, yours is really long! And this is your love line. See all these little lines branching off of it? You're going to have a harem full of wives."

"I am not," he said, snatching back his hand. Yael laughed at him. But she had such a happy, carefree laugh that he couldn't help smiling.

Then her laughter died away and she said, "I'm afraid to look at Mama's lifeline."

Zechariah felt sorry for her. They had lived side by side since they were born, yet Yael's life was so much harder than his was. He couldn't imagine his friend telling fortunes like the Babylonians, working to earn a few pennies, even though everyone Zechariah knew longed to see the future.

"Come back, Yael," the woman called, beckoning to her. "The hole is big enough. We must finish this."

"Are you sure you don't want to see the demon before we bury it?" Yael asked.

"No thanks. I have to eat. You want to go down to the canal with me afterward?"

"Sure. See you later, Zaki."

He hurried inside and quickly washed his hands before sitting down with his family. As he listened to his grandfather recite the blessings and break the bread and pour the wine, he wondered why his father didn't believe in tying on phylacteries every morning or resting on the Sabbath like Saba did. Were Saba's beliefs as useless as Babylonian sorcery? How was Zechariah supposed to tell the difference between superstition and faith? He felt pulled in opposite directions again, as if he sat in an oxcart with an animal tied to each end. The direction Saba pulled seemed right—but so did Abba's way. Zechariah loved both men, but how was he supposed to choose?

He remembered what Rebbe Daniel the Righteous One had said in the house of assembly and suddenly decided that if the Holy One made a way for them to return to Jerusalem, it would be a sign that the stories in the Torah were all true. If not, then Abba must be right, and the prophets were all dreamers. But it would break his grandfather's heart if Rebbe Daniel was wrong.

Yael knelt beside her mother's pallet and gently shook her shoulder. "Mama . . . Mama, please wake up." She felt bones beneath her mother's pale skin where flesh and muscle should be. Mama hadn't eaten in days. All she did was sleep. A tremor of fear shivered through Yael as she shook her again. "Please wake up and eat something, Mama. You can't get well if you don't eat."

At last Mama stirred and opened her eyes. They looked huge and dark in her thin face. "Yael . . . ?"

"I brought you some food. You need to eat so you'll get well." Mama couldn't die, she couldn't! The clay demon Parthia had buried last week was supposed to chase the evil spirit of sickness far away. Parthia had promised it would work. But Mama gazed up at Yael as if too weak to move.

"Where's your father?"

"At work." Yael lifted the bowl of food and held it near her mother's face so she could smell it. "Zaki's grandmother brought us some food. You should eat it while it's still warm."

"Dinah? . . . Is Dinah here?"

"No, she didn't want to wake you. Shall I help you sit up?"

"Go get Dinah. Ask her to come here."

"Why? I can help you."

"I know . . . just go get her, please."

Yael set the bowl of food on the floor and hurried next door, wishing she didn't feel so afraid. She found Dinah sitting outside in the courtyard with her family, enjoying the sunshine. "Mama is asking for you," she told her. "Can you come right away?"

"Of course." Dinah stood and passed the baby she'd been rocking to his mother. "How is your mother feeling today?"

"I—I don't know." Yael saw her friend Zechariah sitting with the others and said, "You come, too, Zaki." He made Yael feel brave when she went exploring with him, and she needed courage right now. She didn't want anyone to know how scared she really was.

She led the way home and then into her mother's room and saw Dinah's shock as she knelt beside the pallet. "Oh, Miriam . . . I'm here now," she said, taking Mama's hand. "What do you need, dear one? I want to help you."

Mama's voice sounded whisper soft, as if she was breathing out each word. "Dinah . . . promise me you'll take care of my Yael when I'm gone . . . treat her as if she's your very own daughter. . . ."

Yael collapsed to her knees beside her. "Mama, no! Don't talk that way!" Was she getting ready to die?

Mama didn't seem to hear her as she gripped Dinah's hand, gazing up at her. "I should be teaching Yael things . . . but I can't. . . . Promise me you'll teach her, Dinah."

"Of course, Miriam. But . . . but you'll be able to take care of Yael yourself when you're better."

Mama shook her head. "Help her find a worthy husband. . . . Promise you'll do that for me."

"Of course. But you must get well, dear one."

"Take Yael home with you. She'll be your daughter from now on."

"Mama, no! You won't die! The stars all say you'll be healed."

Mama released Dinah's hand and groped for Yael's. "They're wrong. I don't want to leave you, my sweet Yael, but I'm just so tired. I can't fight this sickness any longer."

Yael buried her head on the bed, weeping as she clung to her mother.

"Shh . . . shh . . . I'm not afraid," Mama soothed, stroking her hair. Her touch felt as soft as a breeze. "Dying is as easy as closing my eyes and falling asleep."

"Please don't leave me, Mama! Please!"

"I would stay if I could . . . but I can't hang on any longer, Yael. I'm sorry . . ."

"Zaki, go home and get your father," Yael heard Dinah saying behind her. "Tell him to find Mattaniah and bring him here right away."

The next several hours were like something from a nightmare. Abba arrived home and everyone gathered around Mama's bed, sitting with her and weeping as they said good-bye. Night fell and Mama slept, but even though Yael was exhausted, she couldn't rest. She lay curled beside her mother, listening as she drew one ragged breath after another. Eventually her breathing slowed. Then stopped.

"Mama!" Yael screamed.

"She's gone," Mattaniah said. "She's gone."

Yael flung herself into her father's arms, weeping angry tears. "Why didn't you do something? Why didn't you save her? You let her die!"

"I tried everything, Yael, every omen and potion and ritual I could find. There was nothing more I could do. I'm grieving as much as you are." She had never seen Abba cry, but he was weeping now as he held her tightly.

"What are we going to do without her?" she asked, her voice muffled against his chest.

"I don't know . . . I don't know . . ."

"How could she go away and leave us?"

"She didn't want to, Yael. She would have stayed if she could."

Mama was dead. Gone forever. Yael sat in a daze for the next few hours as the house filled with people who came to mourn with them. Dinah and her cousin Shoshanna washed Mama and anointed her with spices. The potent scent filled the room and clawed at Yael's throat. She looked at her mother's beautiful face one last time before they wrapped her in a clean shroud.

Yael clung to Abba's arm, unable to watch as they buried Mama, unable to think of her mother's soft, warm body lying in the ground the way they had buried the clay demon. She wanted to dig up the clay figurine and smash it to pieces. It hadn't done any good. Nothing had done any good.

As they walked home from the graveyard, the mourners' wailing cries seemed to echo in Yael's ears even though they walked in silence now. She realized that the cries were coming from a place deep in her heart. People tried to comfort her, but their words made her feel worse. "She suffered for so long," everyone kept saying. "You didn't want her to keep suffering, did you?" As if wanting her mother to live made her a terrible person.

The women brought food, but Yael couldn't eat. She stood in her family's courtyard, wishing everyone would go away and leave her alone. As she stared out through the open gate at a group of departing visitors, there stood Parthia, looking all around at the mourners in surprise. Rage boiled inside Yael, spilling out as she ran toward the seer. "This is all your fault!" she cried, shoving Parthia backwards. "You said Mama would get better, but she died! She died!" Yael was angry enough to claw out the seer's eyes, but Zechariah's grandfather raced up behind her and caught Yael before she could strike Parthia again. He gripped Yael so tightly she couldn't break free as he pulled her back inside the courtyard.

57

"Go away!" Iddo shouted at Parthia. "Go away and don't ever come back! You don't belong here!" He lifted Yael in his arms and carried her the last few yards to the house. "I know . . . I know," he soothed. "I know how you're suffering."

It was true. Zaki said his grandfather had lost both of his parents when he was Yael's age. She let Iddo hold her until the flames of her anger and grief had cooled, then wiggled out of his arms and went inside the house to hide.

The day seemed one hundred years long, but at last all the mourners left. Yael went outside again and stood with her arms wrapped around her father's waist as he said good-bye to Zaki's family, who were the last ones to leave.

"I'm so sorry, my friend," Iddo said, resting his hand on Abba's shoulder. "I understand your grief. But soon you'll leave all these sorrows and memories behind when we go home to Jerusalem."

"Why should I go there?" Abba asked. Yael heard the bitterness in his voice and knew he shared her anger. "I don't believe any of that stuff. Religion didn't do my wife any good."

"You mean those spells and Babylonian superstitions? That isn't true religion, Mattaniah."

"What's the difference? Aren't they all just myths and tales? The Red Sea parting? Miracles? Bah! Why would God take my wife? My child's mother?"

"I don't know, Mattaniah. I'm sorry. There's no easy answer, so I won't insult you by offering one."

Yael slid out of her father's arms. How could anyone expect them to leave their home? Mama was buried here in Babylon. They couldn't leave her here all alone. Yael hurried across the courtyard and ran out through her gate, not sure where she was going. She heard Zaki calling behind her, "Yael, wait! Where are you going?"

She ignored him and kept running, but he quickly caught up

with her. "Stop following me!" she said, shoving him with her elbow. When he stayed right beside her, she halted suddenly, turning on him. "What do you want, Zechariah?"

"I want to come with you."

"Why?"

"So you won't be all alone."

"But I want to be alone. I don't want to talk to you or anyone else."

"That's fine," he said with a shrug. "We don't have to talk."

He kept pace with her as they started walking again, heading toward the canal. Yael didn't say so out loud, but the farther they walked, the more relieved she was that Zechariah had come along. She would have been afraid by herself, especially when she saw a gang of Babylonian boys fishing along the canal. Zaki steered her to a clump of palm trees and scrub bushes farther upstream, and they sat down together in the shade. Birds wheeled overhead, calling to each other as barges and single-mast vessels floated down the canal. How could the world keep going the same as before, as if nothing had happened? It didn't seem fair.

"What happens to people after they die?" Yael asked after a while.

"The Torah says their body stays here in the ground but their spirit keeps on living in a different place."

"Where? Where does it go?"

"No one knows for sure. The Torah doesn't tell us about the afterlife because we're supposed to pay attention to how we live now, so that we'll be ready for eternal life."

"Do you believe that? About our spirits not dying?"

"My grandfather explained it this way: the Holy One told Adam and Eve that if they ate from the forbidden tree they would die. Well, they ate anyway, but they didn't drop dead as if the fruit was poison. They kept on living but in a different place, not in *Gan* Eden. This teaches us that death isn't the end. Our spirit keeps on living, but in a different place."

"So I'll see Mama again?"

He nodded. "And she won't be sick anymore."

Yael began to cry, and Zechariah wrapped his arms around her, letting her lean on him. They sat side by side for a long time until the warm sunshine and gently lapping water made Yael feel sleepy. She stood, leaning on her friend's shoulder as she struggled to her feet. "Let's go home," she said.

They were nearly there when Parthia suddenly stepped out of the shadows and into Yael's path. "I'm so sorry about your mother, little one. She was a very brave woman."

"You were wrong!" Yael lunged at her, fists tightened as she tried to strike her. "You said Mama would get better, and she didn't!"

Parthia was too quick for her this time. She caught Yael's wrists in her hands and held them tightly. "I'm sorry but the spirit of unbelief was too strong, and it hindered my efforts. It came from there," she said, indicating Zaki's house next door with a tilt of her head. "I did everything I could, but it wasn't enough. I told your mother that the spirits of unbelief were too strong here among the Jews, but she wouldn't leave and come with me."

"I didn't want her to die!"

"I know, little one. I know."

Yael finally stopped struggling, and Parthia pulled her into her arms, holding her tightly. The seer smelled wonderful, like incense and sweet perfume. And she was so beautiful with her burnished skin and fine linen robes and golden jewelry. Yael clung to her, weeping, longing to hang on to a part of her mother and what she had believed.

"You are a young woman of great faith, Yael. And you have been given the gift of deep spiritual insight. I have been waiting for all of the mourners to leave so I could talk to your father. I want to ask him to let you come and live with me. I'll teach you everything I know, everything your mother believed. You'll be like a daughter to me—"

"You need to leave here right now!" Zaki's grandmother interrupted. Yael released her hold on Parthia and looked up to see Dinah hurrying toward them, shaking her finger. Zaki was by her side. He must have gone home to get her.

"Quick, I have something for you," Parthia said. She slipped a necklace over Yael's head, letting it drop beneath her clothing. "It's the moonstone amulet I promised you. Wear it for protection. And take these star charts I made for you." She pushed a bag stuffed with scrolls beneath Yael's arm, pulling her outer robe over them to conceal them.

"You need to go back where you belong," Dinah said, "and don't come around here again. Yael, your mother asked me to take care of you, remember? I promised her that I would and—"

"The child is strong enough to decide for herself," Parthia interrupted. "It should be Yael's choice." Her bracelets jingled as she rested her hand on Yael's head. "What would you like to do, little one? You are welcome to come home and live with me."

"She isn't yours," Dinah said, pushing Parthia's hand away. "Yael is Jewish. She belongs with us. That's what your mother wanted, remember, Yael?"

Yes, she remembered. But Dinah and her God might be the reason why Parthia's spells hadn't worked. Should she leave and go live with Parthia, following Mama's beliefs?

The two women were watching her, waging a silent tug-of-war. Yael didn't know what to say. Parthia broke the silence first. "Don't worry, little one. I will talk to your father another time and explain to him about the gift of insight that you've

been given. Such a gift could earn him a great deal of money."
She turned and walked away.

Yael didn't care about money. She didn't want either woman
to take care of her, she wanted her mother back. She ran into her
house and threw down the scrolls, then collapsed on Mama's
bed, crying as if she would never stop.

CHAPTER
5

I ddo hated walking through these pagan sections of Babylon, but there was no way to avoid them. He kept his head lowered, staring at his feet to avoid glimpsing the forbidden images and idols, wishing he could move faster through the crowded streets. The Babylonians decorated their important buildings, temples, and even the city walls with images. Iddo had asked his neighbor Mattaniah to walk with him, not certain he could find his way through the sprawling city by himself.

"Any idea why the Men of the Great Assembly called this meeting?" Mattaniah asked.

"You know as much as I do—something about a proclamation from the Persian king that concerns us."

Five months had passed since the Medes and Persians had invaded Babylon, and so far Iddo's life had continued the same as always. In his experience, important news usually meant bad news, so the mysterious proclamation was a greater source of worry for him than the idolatrous sights. Iddo had entertained the fleeting fantasy that he and his fellow Jews were assembling for an audience with King Cyrus so they could tell this new pharaoh to let their people go the way Moses once had. But in truth, Iddo's sons had eroded his certainty these past few months by insisting that the prophets were foolish dreamers and that their people would never be allowed to go home.

"You haven't come to prayers lately," Iddo said. "We've missed you."

"I've been very busy at work," Mattaniah replied. "We have a commission to build a new storehouse by the river."

"So you will return when the work is finished?"

"I don't know, Iddo. What good are prayers?"

"How will our people continue in the faith if young men like you and my sons keep drifting away?"

"I have to work to pay my bills and feed my daughter."

Iddo decided to let the matter go. Dinah said he nagged too much and was too hard on people who weren't as committed to their faith as he was. Iddo walked on in silence beside Mattaniah until they finally reached the southern palace, once home to Babylon's kings and now to their new Persian overlords. Other Jewish leaders and elders were already gathering in the huge paved square in front of the palace, and he and Mattaniah found a place to stand beside their neighbor, Joel. Iddo knew it was foolish, but he always felt uneasy around Joel, the man who had also asked for Dinah's hand in marriage years ago. Of course Dinah hadn't chosen Joel—but Iddo wondered if she ever regretted her choice, especially when her cousin Shoshanna had married him instead.

"Did we miss anything?" Iddo asked him.

"Not yet. But that's Daniel the Righteous One, isn't it? Standing up there at the top of the stairs?"

Iddo shaded his eyes. "Yes. And those men with him are Judah's royal princes. I've only seen them a handful of times at important occasions, so I forget their faces. But who can forget those embroidered robes?"

"Well, this must be a very important meeting if they're here," Joel said.

Maybe Iddo's fantasies would come true after all. Maybe Judah's princes and elders really would demand their nation's freedom. "The older, gray-bearded man is Sheshbazzar, son of King Jehoiachin," Iddo told the others. "The younger one is his nephew Zerubbabel, son of Shealtiel and grandson of King Jehoiachin."

"I didn't know Judah still had a royal family," Mattaniah said. "I thought the Babylonians executed them."

"Not all of them," Iddo said. "The Holy One promised King David that he would always have an heir, and the Holy One doesn't lie. Rebbe Daniel is also descended from the royal family."

At last Daniel stepped forward and raised his hands for silence. "This is a day of great news for our people," he began, "the day that the Holy One promised us. It's only right that Prince Sheshbazzar be the one to read the royal announcement from our Persian sovereign, King Cyrus."

Iddo tensed with anticipation as Sheshbazzar unrolled the scroll he held and began to read. "Hear the words of Cyrus, king of the Persians and the Medes and of all the earth: 'The Lord, the God of heaven has given me all the kingdoms of the earth and he has appointed me to build a temple for him at Jerusalem in Judah. . . . '"

Iddo gripped Mattaniah's arm. "What did he say?"

"'Anyone of his people among you—may his God be with him, and let him go up to Jerusalem in Judah and rebuild the temple of the Lord, the God of Israel, the God who is in Jerusalem.'"

Iddo gave a cry of joy as shouts and exclamations rang through the crowd.

"' . . . And the people of any place where survivors may now be living are to provide him with silver and gold, with goods and livestock, and with freewill offerings for the temple of God in Jerusalem.'" Sheshbazzar looked out over the crowd as he rolled up the scroll again. "Rejoice, people of God! King Cyrus is allowing us to go home to Jerusalem! We're going to rebuild God's temple!"

There was a long moment of silence as the men stared at each other in disbelief. Then everyone began talking at once. "Can this really be true?" Mattaniah asked.

"I don't believe it," Joel said. "There must be a catch—some stipulation or requirements or . . . something."

"It's a miracle!" Iddo breathed. He had prayed for this, hoped for it, but even though he'd just heard the news with his own ears, he could scarcely believe it.

"King Cyrus has reversed the policies of the Assyrians and Babylonians," Sheshbazzar shouted above the astonished murmuring. "He is allowing all of the captured nations to return to their homelands and worship their gods—including us."

"We're going home," Iddo said. "We're going home!"

"The prophet Isaiah predicted this day nearly two hundred years ago," Rebbe Daniel said, stepping forward to stand beside Sheshbazzar, "and he even singled out King Cyrus by name, saying, 'He is my shepherd and will accomplish all that I please; he will say of Jerusalem, "Let it be rebuilt," and of the temple, "Let its foundations be laid."'And now it has happened. This is the mighty hand of God!"

Iddo could no longer see the platform through his tears. All around him men were hugging each other, laughing, weeping like children, unable to stop their tears. "Take this joyous news home to your families," Sheshbazzar said above the noise, "and celebrate the goodness of God. This is truly a day of rejoicing."

Iddo longed to run all the way home, shouting the good news to anyone who would listen. But he was so moved, so shaken by what he'd heard that he stumbled along in a daze, instead. "I'm glad you came with me, Mattaniah, because my family won't believe me when I tell them. They'll think I'm making it up."

"I'm not sure I believe it myself."

"Just think! Our brethren will gather from all of the places where we've been exiled, creating an exodus as great as the first one. There must be a million of us by now with our children and grandchildren, scattered throughout the empire. We'll need carts and wagons—"

"Do you really believe everyone will return?"

"Of course! Why wouldn't they?"

Mattaniah hesitated, frowning as he looked at Iddo. "Well . . . because it will mean giving up everything we've worked for here. It's not as if we've been slaving to make bricks without straw for pharaoh all these years. Many of our fellow Jews have prospered and become rich. They would have to start all over again in a land that's been desolate all these years."

"But who wouldn't be willing to sacrifice everything they have now for their children's future?"

"For some of us, the future is here," Mattaniah replied. "Like the Jew whose storehouse I'm building. He has a very comfortable life here and so do his sons."

"But didn't you hear what the proclamation said? We're not only going home, we're rebuilding the temple. God will dwell with us again. Think of it!" Iddo thought he might burst from joy as he envisioned serving as a priest with his sons. "When we celebrate Passover in a few weeks, Mattaniah, won't it be glorious to remember that first exodus now that the Almighty One has provided us with the miracle of a second one? Who would have ever believed it?"

"Yes . . . Who would have ever believed it?"

The evening meal was waiting for Iddo when he arrived home. His sons and their wives milled around the courtyard in the fading evening light, waiting to hear the reason for the gathering of elders. He saw their worried faces and could no longer hold back his tears, too overcome with joy to speak.

Dinah hurried over to him. "What is it, Iddo? What happened? What's wrong?"

"These are tears of joy, Dinah. The Persian king has set us free."

His sons quickly gathered around him, too. "What, Abba? What did the king say?"

Iddo wiped his eyes. "The Persian king announced that he is allowing our people to return home to Jerusalem and rebuild the temple."

"I don't believe it."

"It's true. We're going home after seventy years, just as the prophets said we would."

Iddo's son gripped his arm. "Are you certain you aren't mistaken?"

"Ask Mattaniah and Joel. They heard it, too. Didn't I tell you we would return home to our land?"

"This is unbelievable," Berekiah said.

"Our leaders won't waste any time. As soon as they can make the arrangements, we're leaving Babylon for good." His family didn't seem to share his joy. They looked stunned, incredulous. Maybe they needed time for the news to sink in.

"Come, Dinah. Open a skin of wine," Iddo said. "This is a night to rejoice and celebrate and praise the Almighty One for this incredible miracle."

A spontaneous celebration broke out that evening as everyone in the community gathered in the square by the house of assembly. Musicians brought out their instruments and Iddo and the other men danced and whirled in joyous circles, clapping and singing and praising God. He couldn't remember ever being this happy in his life. *"Give thanks to the Lord for He is good,"* he sang along with the others. *"His love endures forever."*

Dinah's cousin Shoshanna led a circle of dancing women, singing the song of their ancestress, Miriam: *"I will sing to the Lord, for he is highly exalted. The horse and its rider he has hurled into the sea."*

Iddo was nearly exhausted by the time the celebration ended and people drifted home, but he still felt too restless to settle down for the night. He was bursting with joy and with thoughts of the Almighty One, and who better to share them with than his grandson. "Come with me, Zechariah," he said, steering him away from the rest of his family. "I want to show you something."

"Where are you going this time of night?" Dinah fussed. "It's late." But her worry couldn't destroy Iddo's good mood. He felt giddy with joy, not wine.

"We won't be long. Go on home with the others." He led his grandson in the opposite direction, down the narrow lanes through the maze of houses.

"Where are we going, Saba?"

"I thought we would walk to the canal where you like to play."

Zechariah halted like a guilty man, forced to return to the scene of his crime. Iddo laughed out loud. "You thought I didn't know where you ran off to on Sabbath afternoons with your friend Yael?"

"Are you mad at me, Saba?"

"No, son. I'm not mad. Who can blame a young boy for preferring activity over study now and then? Come on, show me where you go."

Zechariah still looked unsure and a little worried, but he led Iddo through the dark streets where very few of the drab, mud brick homes still had lamplight shining from their windows.

"What do you think of the announcement, Zechariah?"

"Everything the prophets said came true, Saba!"

Iddo heard the wonder and awe in his grandson's voice, and

laughed. "Yes, of course! Our God is real and His word to us is real."

"Abba said that kings never let their slaves go free, but King Cyrus did! He really did, just like Pharaoh! The Torah is all true, Saba!" Iddo pulled the boy close for a hug.

They reached the wide, shimmering void of the canal a few minutes later and halted near the bank, listening to the gentle sighing of the water. Fishing boats rocked on the waves, their tall masts swaying. The air was cooler by the water, and a cluster of palm trees swished softly in the breeze. Best of all, the sky seemed to open up above their heads.

"Look up, Zaki. See all those stars? Do you remember how the Holy One created those stars and the palm trees and the birds? What does the Torah teach us?"

"It doesn't say how. God just said, 'Let there be light' and—"

"And there was light! Exactly! The Almighty One *spoke* creation into being with His words. That's why I brought you here, to talk about the importance of words. Today King Cyrus gave us a proclamation—words on a piece of paper—and do you see the power that those few words have? They will move us from Babylon to Jerusalem, from people with nothing to people with a homeland. Those words will move stones into place to build a temple for our God. Powerful words, yes?"

"Very powerful!" Zaki's dark eyes glistened in the moonlight.

"Do you know why God is allowing us to return? Because of His grace and love. He will forgive us and dwell among us again."

They gazed at the water, and it was so still that Iddo could see the moon's reflection on the shimmering surface. When Zechariah shivered and crossed his arms against the nighttime chill, Iddo turned and motioned for them to start walking back.

"We're made in the Holy One's image, so our words also have power. You tell someone they're ugly or that they're a fool, and if you repeat it often enough, you might create ugliness or foolishness in that person. You praise them for their goodness or kindness, and your words just might create even more kindness in that person. We must be careful to speak words of life."

A few minutes later they reached the gate to their house. Iddo thought of his sons, how convinced they had been that the prophets' words weren't true, convinced that their people would never return from captivity. He wondered if their words of unbelief would now have power over them. Perhaps they hadn't wanted the prophecies to be true because they didn't want to return. And as unimaginable as it was to Iddo, he wondered if his sons would fulfill their own words of unbelief and refuse to walk through the door that the Holy One had so miraculously opened.

CHAPTER

6

Dinah lifted her water jar onto her head and made her way to the community well. Time was passing much too quickly. Ever since King Cyrus made his proclamation, the weeks had raced by like fire through straw. On the surface, her life continued the same as always as she cared for her home and her family. But an undercurrent of change crackled beneath each day, slowly growing into an inferno that threatened to consume the life she knew and loved. Dread of the future robbed Dinah of the present, as if she knew the precise hour of her death and watched time speed toward that date.

Her friends and neighbors already stood laughing and gossiping around the well when she arrived. "Dinah! We've been waiting for you," her cousin Shoshanna said. "We want to hear all about your plans for returning to Jerusalem. Aren't you excited?"

Dinah lowered the rope and bucket into the well shaft, as careful with her task as with putting her feelings into words. The other women looked up to her, respected her, but the truth was, Dinah didn't want to leave Babylon. Every day she searched for a way to talk Iddo out of going. But she didn't dare admit in public that she disagreed with her husband. "Iddo is doing all the planning," she said as she drew the bucket to the surface again. "He said the journey would take at least three months. I can't imagine such a long, exhausting trip, can you? It seems impossible."

"I think it's exciting," Shoshanna said. "Joel wasn't sure he wanted to go at first, but I convinced him that we should."

"Shoshanna! Why?"

"Because this is the most important thing we could ever do. If we don't obey the Almighty One and rebuild our temple, we'll be separated from Him forever."

Dinah stared at her cousin. They had worked side by side as midwives for twenty years. How could they feel so differently? Dinah quickly finished filling her jar as Shoshanna explained to the others how Joel and Iddo had produced their genealogies to prove their ancestry as priests. The women seemed interested, but Dinah simply wanted to hurry home before Shoshanna asked more questions.

Iddo assumed that their entire family would leave Babylon together, but Dinah knew that her sons didn't want to go. What would she do if the unthinkable happened and her family split in two, some staying here, others moving to Jerusalem? The uncertainty weighed on Dinah's heart and interrupted her sleep. *"I see a great tearing in your life,"* the seer had told her. As each day passed, she tried to cling to everything she treasured, but it became more and more impossible, as if precious jewels were slipping through her fingers, lost forever.

At dinner that night Iddo turned to their sons and asked, "How many carts will you need for your families? How many oxen and donkeys? The elders have asked all of the family heads to provide them with an estimate."

Their sons exchanged looks. Berekiah finally replied for both of them. "Abba, we've . . . um . . . we've decided to wait here in Babylon."

"What?" Iddo spoke the word with quiet disbelief, not anger.

"We won't be leaving when the first group departs next month."

"I don't understand."

"Our children are too small to travel such a great distance. Maybe when they're a little older . . ."

"And Naomi and I have the baby to consider," Hoshea added. "He's too small to travel that far."

Iddo's face turned as hard and white as marble as he gazed at his sons. "You can't stay here in Babylon. The Almighty One has made a way for us to return, so we must obey Him."

"I understand, Abba. But this isn't a good time. Hoshea and I have decided to come later."

Dinah waited for her husband's response. He had gone very still, his face showing no emotion at all. Please, God, maybe he would see the wisdom in staying here as well. As the terrible silence lengthened, she dared to say, "Maybe we should all wait and go together, Iddo."

"No, no, no!" His voice grew louder with each word. "God worked a miracle for us, and you're going to refuse it? There will always be one more reason to wait, one more excuse. The Almighty One lost patience with our forefathers, and He will lose patience with us if we ignore His command."

"But this is a bad time, Abba—"

"And when will it ever be a good time? Surely there were women with babies during the first exodus. And many small children, too."

"It was a difficult decision to make," Berekiah said, "but Hoshea and I both believe it's the right one for us."

Iddo closed his eyes as if he could shut out the reality of what their sons had just told him. When he opened them again, he leaned toward both men as if to convey the seriousness of what he was about to say. "Come with me. Now! All of you!" He swept his arm to include the entire family, then rose to his feet and motioned toward the door.

"All of us?" Dinah asked as she stood and went to him. "What about dinner? And . . . and the children?"

"Dinner can wait. Bring all of the children. I want everyone to see what I'm going to show you."

Had Iddo lost his mind? They left their half-eaten meal and followed him out of their house, carrying their little ones. A few minutes later, they were walking through Babylon's darkening streets. Dinah had lived in this city all her life, but she'd never been where her husband was now leading her. She pressed close to the others in a tight little group, as if the dangers she had long been warned against lurked beyond every corner. "Where are you taking us, Iddo?" she asked. He didn't reply.

At last he halted and gestured to an enormous stone building in front of them. "This is a temple to one of Babylon's idols," he said breathlessly. "An obscene place where worshipers serve their goddess by sleeping with strangers. Young girls sit on display here like produce in the marketplace, waiting to be chosen by men they've never met before. They turn the sacred act intended by God for marriage into a vulgar, degrading ritual of blasphemy!"

"Abba, don't—" Berekiah began, but Iddo interrupted him.

"I can't imagine letting my daughters come to a place like this, can you? And these pagans have the nerve to call their orgies worship. When mankind stopped worshiping the one true God, *this* is where it led them!" Dinah looked away from where Iddo was pointing, shivering in the cool evening air.

"Listen to me," Iddo continued. "All of you were born in Babylon. You all grew up here where sights like these now seem like everyday things to you. But more and more young women from our community are being enticed by Babylonian men. More and more of our sons are being attracted to Babylonian women. In another generation or two, *this* is where our sons and daughters and grandchildren will be coming to worship. And they'll think nothing of it!"

Before any of them could reply, Iddo turned and strode away, leading them deeper into the city, farther from home. Dinah gripped her grandson Zechariah's hand, heartsick with dread and sorrow at what Iddo was forcing them to see. She heard the din of murmuring voices in the distance and a few minutes later, Iddo halted again. Dozens of diseased and disabled people sat in the city square, huddled on rugs and beneath makeshift hovels. The murmuring was the sound of their voices, pleading with the passing crowds.

"They're calling out their symptoms," Iddo said, "hoping that some stranger will share news of a potion or an amulet or a curse that will bring a cure. Their sorcery is evil, their superstition useless, but our own neighbors, Miriam and Mattaniah, turned to such omens and sorcery for a cure. You were all influenced by such things. Don't tell me you weren't impressed, Hoshea, when one of Miriam's seers correctly predicted that your last child would be a son. And you, Dinah—didn't you want to ask an astrologer to seek the best day for our Rachel's wedding?"

Dinah stared at her feet, ashamed to remember that the seer had made another prediction for her. "This is how idolatry begins," Iddo said. "With simple curiosity. Before long, we grow accustomed to seeking signs and omens, and they no longer seem like abominations. The idols seem worthy of our worship. The pagans believe they can manipulate their false gods and bribe them to do their bidding. But the Holy One cannot be bribed. Instead we bend our wills to match His. The Torah instructs us to remain separate, to be holy."

He walked on—for miles, it seemed to Dinah—leading them at last to the base of the great ziggurat at the very center of

Babylon. "This!" he shouted. "This is what's at stake! Worship of the one true God will be lost forever, swallowed up by this counterfeit religion, this tower of man's own creation, unless we obey our God! He opened a way for us to leave all of this and to return to Jerusalem and to Him. He provided the means for us to rebuild His temple. We dare not disobey. I've seen the wrath of God. I've experienced it. And I don't ever want to see it or experience it again!"

A crowd of curious Babylonians gathered around as Iddo pleaded with his family. Unlike Dinah's quiet neighborhood that grew more deserted after dark, Babylon was coming to life as night fell, like a living beast awakening from its afternoon slumber. "Please, Iddo. Let's go home," she begged.

He gazed at his family for a long moment, then turned and led them back the way they had come. Dinah breathed a sigh of relief when they reached their own familiar streets at last, but Iddo paused again in front of the house of assembly. "My children, listen to me, please. We've been studying the scroll of the prophet Jeremiah. He was right about everything—the fall of Jerusalem, the fate of our kings, our exile. And he was right about our seventy years of captivity, too. But please, please, listen to me. Jeremiah also said, 'Flee from Babylon! Run for your lives! Do not be destroyed because of her sins. It is time for the Lord's vengeance; he will pay her what she deserves.' Don't be fooled by the bloodless invasion by the Persians. God is going to punish Babylon's wickedness, and if you live here, if you're part of this city, you'll be punished, too. Please don't refuse His grace."

At last they reached home and went inside to finish their ruined meal. Dinah saw the deep pain in Iddo's eyes as he pleaded with them one last time. "The only thing that matters is doing God's work. The only thing. If you turn your back on His light, you'll worship the darkness."

CHAPTER
7

Z echariah? Are you coming to afternoon prayers with me?" Saba asked.

Zechariah shook his head, staring at the ground beside their gate. He knew that if he looked up he would see disappointment in Saba's eyes. His grandparents were leaving for Jerusalem soon, and Zechariah was running out of time to spend with Saba, but he was too restless to sit in the house of assembly and pray. In fact, he longed to burst through the courtyard gate and keep on running and never stop.

He was so confused. Rebbe Daniel's prayers had been answered, the prophets' predictions had come true—which meant that Saba had been right about the Holy One and all of His miracles, and Abba had been wrong. Yet in spite of his grandfather's impassioned pleas, in spite of the things he had shown Zechariah and his family in the streets of Babylon that sobering night, Zaki's father and all of his aunts and uncles had decided to stay in Babylon.

Zechariah waited until Saba was out of sight. Then, knowing that everyone would assume he had gone with his grandfather, he slipped through the gate and ran across the lane to his friend Yael's house. He found her kneeling alone in her cramped courtyard, stirring the lifeless coals in the hearth as if expecting flames to magically appear. She heard him come in and looked up. "I hope you came to help me start this fire because I'm not having any luck with it."

"I came to ask if you wanted to go down to the canal with me."

A spark of life returned to her eyes, and Zechariah could tell by the way she scrambled to her feet, brushing the soot from her hands, that it probably didn't matter to her where they went. "Sure. Let's go."

They walked side by side to the edge of the canal, the familiar fishy scent growing stronger, the air cooler as it fanned through the tall palm trees. Zechariah lost track of time as they explored all their usual places, poking sticks into holes, watching fishermen mend their nets, running up and down the shoreline. When they finally ran out of energy, they sank down in their usual spot to watch a crane pick its way along the opposite shore. Zechariah scooped up a handful of pebbles to toss into the water, offering some to Yael, but she shook her head. He felt sorry for her. She was still so sad, still grieving for her mother.

"Shouldn't you be studying or praying or something?" she asked after several minutes had passed.

"Probably. My birthday is soon and—"

"Your birthday is in the month of Iyyar? Then you were born under the sign of the ram."

He glanced at her, uneasy to hear her talking about pagan things, especially after his grandfather's speech. "I should be getting ready for my bar mitzvah but—"

"Why aren't you?"

"I just don't feel like it," he said with a shrug. "It's supposed to be a happy occasion, but I don't see how it can be happy when everyone in my house is arguing with each other."

"What about?" She sat with her legs tented, her arms wrapped around them, her chin resting on her knees as she listened.

"The same thing everyone else is arguing about—going back to Jerusalem. And my family is putting me in the middle of their tug-of-war. My grandfather keeps begging my father, telling him that he has to return to Jerusalem for *my* sake. As if the future of the entire priesthood depends on me. My father refuses, and they've been pulling on me, back and forth—and I'm tired of it."

"At least the fighting will end in a few more weeks. Once your grandfather leaves, what's there to argue about?"

Zechariah stared at her for a moment, surprised to realize that it was true. But instead of constant fighting, there would be silence . . . and a hole in Zechariah's life that no one but Saba could ever fill.

"Do you wish you were going, Zaki?" she asked.

He threw another stone into the water. "I wish my whole family was going." He couldn't shake his lingering fear that Abba was making a mistake. That they would all face the Holy One's wrath if they remained behind. "I hear that you and your father are going," he said. "Are you excited?"

Yael suddenly sat up straight, folding her thin, limber legs beneath her to sit cross-legged. "If I tell you a secret, will you promise not to tell anyone? No one else in the whole world knows about it. But you have to promise, first."

He had just confided in Yael, so he understood her need to share. But he wasn't sure that he wanted the added weight of a secret on his shoulders.

"Promise?" she asked again, poking his arm.

"I promise," he finally said.

"I'm not going to Jerusalem." Her voice dropped to a whisper. "I'm staying here."

"Staying? . . . Did your father change his mind? His name is on the list, and his genealogy as a Levite was approved and—"

"Abba is going but I'm not. I'm going to live with Parthia."

Zechariah stared at her to see if she was joking, but he could tell by her crossed arms and jutting chin that she wasn't. "You mean . . . that Babylonian woman? The sorceress? Why?"

"Because if I leave here, I'll lose all my memories of Mama. This is where she lived, where I remember her. She's buried here. And I know you'll hate me for saying this, but I don't want to go where they worship your God. He let my mother die."

"That's not true—"

"Besides, I heard your grandfather telling Abba that no one will be allowed to consult the stars or seek omens in Jerusalem, and my mother believed in all of those things. I want to worship the moon goddess like she did."

Zechariah fought the urge to grip his friend's thin shouders and shake some sense into her. The moon goddess? Omens? All the things that Saba said would happen to them if they remained in Babylon were already happening to Yael. She was his friend, and he cared about her—and he didn't want to lose her to idols.

"Your father agreed to this? He's letting you stay here?"

"No, of course not. I'm going to run away. Parthia already said I could live with her."

"Yael, you can't do that! My grandmother is going to take care of you, remember? I was there when your mother asked her to. It's what she wanted."

"Mama didn't know that your grandmother was leaving Babylon. She never would have wanted me to leave. No, I've made up my mind to run away and live with Parthia—but you can't tell anyone, Zaki. You promised."

He felt desperate to stop her, but he didn't know what to do or what to say to change her mind. "Yael, none of that stuff Parthia taught you is true. She can't see the future any more than the rest of us can."

"Doesn't your God have people who can tell the future? Your

grandfather said one of them predicted that we'd go back to Jerusalem."

"That's different."

"How do you know?"

"Because . . . because there's only one God, and none of the other gods are real."

"How do you know they aren't real?"

"I've been studying the Torah for my bar mitzvah and learning about the real God, the God of our ancestors. Our people are supposed to worship Him alone. We say it every morning when we pray—'Hear, O Israel: The Lord our God, the Lord is one.'"

"Girls don't pray, Zaki. Besides, I don't care about the stupid Torah." She lifted her chin even higher.

Her words and attitude shocked him. Zechariah's father may not pray all the time like Saba did, but he still believed in Israel's God. How could he convince Yael to believe? "Listen, you and your family are from the tribe of Levi and mine are priests. Our families were chosen to serve in the Almighty One's temple—"

"Then why is your father staying here instead of going back?"

"I don't know . . . but . . . but you're my best friend, Yael, and I'll miss you when you and your father move to Jerusalem, but that's what I think you should do. I can't explain it, but I get a terrible feeling inside when I think of you running away to live with that wicked woman."

"She's nice to me."

"Isn't my grandmother nice to you, too?" Yael gave an indifferent shrug. "Please don't do this, Yael. If you really want to stay here in Babylon then come live with me. I'm sure my mother and father won't mind. You can be my sister from now on. But please don't live with that Babylonian woman."

"Abba will never let me stay behind with your family. The only way I can stay is if I run away. But you can't tell anyone, Zaki." She poked his arm again, harder this time. "You promised!"

He felt trapped. He couldn't break a promise, but he couldn't let his friend run away to live with that wicked woman, either.

Yael stood, brushing sand off her clothes, and started walking back home without him. Zechariah hurried to catch up. "Listen, I can help you talk to your father about staying here and living with me and my parents."

"Your parents won't let me learn about the stars and worship the moon goddess." She broke into a run, sprinting the rest of the way home, leaving Zechariah behind.

"Do what you want, then," he shouted behind her, kicking at stones. "I don't care." But he did care. He slouched through the gate into his courtyard, weighed down with worry, and nearly collided with his grandmother.

"Where have you been, Zaki? We've been looking all over for you."

"I went for a walk with Yael."

"Well, go up to the rooftop right now. Your father and grandfather are waiting to talk with you."

"Am I in trouble?"

She shook her head. He saw tears in her eyes. "No, Zaki. You're not in trouble."

He took his time climbing the steps, afraid to face them. They were talking quietly when he arrived, but they stopped when they saw him and waited for him to sit down on the rug beside them. Zechariah saw his father's jaw tighten and his hands squeeze into fists as he waited for Saba to speak.

"Just so I'm clear, Berekiah," his grandfather began, "you said you plan to return to Jerusalem at a later time—just not with this first group?"

"I have small children to consider."

"So if you *are* coming at a later time, why not let Zechariah come with Dinah and me now?"

Zechariah's stomach plummeted as if he'd fallen down a deep

well. Go with Saba on the long journey to Jerusalem? Without his mother and father? He couldn't speak. Abba appeared stunned as well, as he groped for words. "He . . . he's my oldest son. My firstborn. He belongs here with me. His mother and I would grieve if he moved so far away from us."

"Exactly! And that's how your mother and I feel at the thought of being separated from you—our firstborn son."

"I know, I know, but—"

"And if you're coming soon," Saba continued, "you'll only have a short time to miss Zechariah. Let him be among the first to return, to be part of this new exodus. You'll be reunited with him when you come with the rest of your family, no?"

Zechariah's father groaned. He stared down at the rug, holding his head in his hands. "I know what you're trying to do, Abba, and I don't want to argue about this anymore. I'm tired of arguing." He lifted his head again as he rose to his feet. "Come on, Zaki." Zechariah stood and was about to walk away with Abba when Saba stopped them.

"Why not let Zechariah decide for himself if he wants to stay or go? He'll be an adult in one week, a Son of the Commandments. He'll be responsible for following God himself from now on, so a decision as important as this one should be his to make."

Abba reached for Zechariah and pulled him close as if he'd been about to fall off the roof and it was up to Abba to save him. "Don't put my son in the middle of this. He can't make a decision as difficult as this one."

"Why not? I allowed you to decide important matters once you became of age, remember? You decided you didn't want to come to prayers with me anymore. I tried to change your mind, but you said it was your decision to make, not mine, and so—"

"Stop it," Abba pleaded. "Just stop!"

Zechariah longed to run back to the canal and hide until all of this was over, but Abba clung to him.

"No, I won't stop," Saba said. "Is what we're telling Zechariah about his bar mitzvah true or isn't it? If he's truly of age and responsible for following God on his own, then he should be allowed to decide for himself whether he wants to return to Jerusalem or stay here in Babylon."

Abba looked down at Zechariah, ran his hand over his head, stroking his hair. Then he looked at Saba again. "Listen, I understand how hard it must be for you and Mama to leave all of us behind, I truly do. But—"

"Don't change the subject. Your son is old enough to decide for himself. Do you want him to resent you when he's older because you made this decision for him? That's the choice I had to face, you know. If I forced you and your brother to come to prayers with me every day, you would have seethed with resentment."

Zechariah watched his father's face as he struggled to reply. Then he saw defeat in Abba's eyes before he closed them and lifted his hands in surrender. "You win," he said. "Zechariah is old enough to decide if he wants to stay or go." He gave Zechariah a gentle shove toward his grandfather and walked away from both of them, hurrying down the stairs. Zechariah started to follow, but his grandfather stopped him.

"Wait, Zechariah. Listen to me." Zechariah's stomach twisted as he looked at his grandfather. "You have a calling to be a man of God. To serve as His priest. Your father and your uncle do, too. Your life will be without meaning if you don't follow that calling. Do you understand that?"

"Yes, Saba." The knowledge terrified him. The God who had worked a miracle at Passover, who was working the miracle of a second exodus, was calling Zechariah to serve Him.

"You must choose for yourself," his grandfather continued. "And you mustn't let either your father or me sway you. Do you understand?"

He couldn't reply. How did adults make up their minds? How did Saba decide it was right to go and Abba that it was right to stay? And even if Zechariah did choose, how would he know if he was making the right choice or a mistake, as Saba insisted that Abba was doing? He thought of Yael and her fortune-tellers, searching the stars, seeking omens to glimpse the future, and for a moment Zechariah thought he understood why people went to seers and used sorcery.

"I don't know how to decide," he finally said.

"Ask God for guidance. From now until the day we leave, every morning when you pray, every time you go to the house of assembly with me, ask the Holy One to show you what He wants you to do. Then listen for His voice."

"Will I hear Him talking to me?"

"He has many ways to answer us besides a voice that we can hear. Sometimes the answers come in dreams, but most often the answers we seek are found in His Word."

It seemed impossible to Zechariah. His parents and grand-parents had been deciding for him all his life. He nodded to Saba and went downstairs, wondering how he could ever make such an important decision.

CHAPTER

8

Zechariah sat cross-legged beside his study partner in the house of assembly, staring at the scroll as his partner read aloud from Genesis. Zaki heard none of it. They were supposed to be studying this weekly portion from the Torah so they could discuss it with the rebbe later today—and the rebbe was notorious for asking difficult questions. Zechariah had to be prepared. Yet he couldn't seem to concentrate. The buzz of droning voices sounded like a beehive. He looked up at the room full of yeshiva students with their faces bent over their scrolls in concentration and saw only the tops of their heads, covered by the dark circles of their *kippahs*.

He watched an older boy stroke his chin and the stubble of his newly grown beard. A younger boy played with the fringe on the corner of his garment, twirling the tassels around his finger. All of the students seemed intent on their work. None of these students, he guessed, wrestled with a decision as impossible as the one he wrestled with.

"Zechariah . . . Zechariah!" His study partner elbowed him in the ribs. How long had he been calling his name?

"Huh? . . . Sorry . . ."

"What's wrong with you today? You were a long way from here—and not even pretending to listen to this Torah passage."

"Sorry," he said again. "I haven't slept all week. I keep having these weird dreams."

"What kind of dreams?"

They were nothing like Saba's nightmares, but they still alarmed and confused Zechariah. "I don't know . . . galloping horses and Torah scrolls that fly through the air like birds. Last night I dreamed about workmen measuring the foundations of Jerusalem as they got ready to build." And one dream that he didn't want to share had been about Yael. She was lost, and he'd searched everywhere for her only to discover that the Babylonian sorceress had hidden her inside a large storage basket. He awoke from these dreams drenched with sweat, wondering what they meant. If God had sent them as signs or as an answer to his dilemma, Zechariah had no idea how to interpret them.

"Well, we'd better finish studying this passage, or the rebbe will give us both nightmares. He always seems to know when we aren't prepared."

Zechariah bent over the scroll again, forcing himself to concentrate. Every morning and evening when he'd gone to the house of assembly to pray with his grandfather, Zechariah asked the Holy One whether he should stay in Babylon or go to Jerusalem. Nothing ever happened. No voice called down to him from the clouds, no answer leapt off the page of the Torah, no burning bushes appeared. And every day as the time of departure drew closer, Zechariah felt more and more pressure to choose.

This was too hard, he decided as he looked around at the other students again. How could he concentrate on his studies? Tomorrow was his bar mitzvah. He would go up to read the Torah for the first time, and from that day forward he would be considered a man in the Almighty One's sight. He would have to make difficult decisions like this for the rest of his life. Was it always going to be this hard?

Somehow, Zechariah got through the rest of his studies that morning. Thankfully, the rebbe called on every student but him that afternoon, as if aware that Zechariah's mind was elsewhere on the day before his bar mitzvah.

"So, Zechariah. Have you decided what you will do?" his grandfather asked as they walked home from prayers later that evening. It was the first time that Saba had mentioned the decision since telling him he had a choice a week ago. Abba hadn't asked him about it either, but Zechariah had caught his parents gazing at him as they ate together as if he were a stranger.

"No," he told his grandfather. "My heart says to stay here with my parents."

"You are a man now, not a child."

"Even so . . ." Zechariah's eyes filled with tears at the thought of never feeling his mother's arms around him again or seeing Abba smile at him in pride. "How will I know for sure if the Holy One is speaking to me?"

"His answer will be unmistakable. In the meantime, you can't trust your emotions if you want to do what God is telling you to do."

They walked side by side in silence the rest of the way, but Saba stopped when they reached home, pausing just outside the gate to their courtyard. "Tomorrow will be a joyful occasion for all of us as we celebrate with you. But you must be careful not to let your parents or me or anyone else pressure you into choosing what they want you to do. It must be what the Holy One tells you to do."

Zechariah barely slept, tossing on his mat all night. He walked to the house of assembly with his family the next morning with the new prayer shawl they had given him draped around his shoulders. Abba hired musicians with flutes and cymbals and drums to accompany his procession, making music as their neighbors and friends walked with Zaki, clapping and singing. As they crowded inside the house of assembly, Zechariah suddenly felt nervous about reading the Torah for the first time, even though he had practiced and practiced. Everyone in his family, everyone in his community, would be listening.

The leader began with prayer, and while Zechariah waited to be called up to read, he prayed, just as he'd prayed every day, asking the Holy One to show him if he should go to Jerusalem or stay in Babylon with his family. God still didn't answer him.

At last the moment came. It was time for Zechariah to read. His heart beat faster as he stepped onto the bimah. He watched in a daze as the leader carefully removed the scroll from the ark and laid it out before him, opening it to today's passage. Zechariah drew a breath and exhaled slowly to calm himself. He looked down at the page, focusing on the tiny Hebrew letters. Then he cleared his throat to read from the first book of the Torah.

"'The Lord had said to Abram, "Leave your country, your people and your father's household, and . . ."'" Zechariah paused, hearing the words as if for the first time. He had read this Hebrew passage over and over during the past few months as he'd practiced it. But his daily language was Aramaic, and he had been so intent on learning to read and pronounce the unfamiliar Hebrew words that he hadn't paid any attention to the meaning of them. Now God's words to Abraham seemed to pierce him like an arrow.

Leave your father's household.

He swallowed and drew a breath to continue. "'"And go to the land I will show you. . . ."'" The room shrank until it seemed as though all of the other people had vanished. A bright light, shining like a hundred torches, illuminated the page. It was so bright it made his eyes hurt. He put the pointer under the words to keep from losing his place.

"'"I will make you into a great nation and I will bless you; I will make your name great, and you will be a blessing. . . ."'"

Could this be the answer Zechariah had prayed for? *Leave your father's household.* The assigned Torah portion for this day had been scheduled long before Zechariah was born, long before King Cyrus gave his proclamation to return to the Promised Land. Zechariah cleared his throat again.

"'So Abram left, as the Lord had told him. . . .'" As Zechariah continued to read the passage, every word, every letter shimmered on the page like sunlight rippling on the waves of the canal. This was much more than a trick of lighting or the slant of the glowing sun, because along with the light, Zechariah also sensed a Presence beside him, surrounding him, loving him. He knew without knowing how that it was the Presence of the Almighty One. And Zechariah never wanted Him to leave his side.

Somehow he kept reading. The golden warmth that filled the page and surrounded Zechariah seemed to consume him, filling him with joy. This was what it was like to be in the presence of God, the God of his ancestors. This was the Presence that had once filled the temple. And the Holy One was speaking to him— to *him*! God was calling him to leave Babylon and follow Him.

Zechariah must return to the Promised Land. And to God.

He closed the Torah scroll and looked up. Everyone in the room was looking at him, smiling at him. He should feel proud of the job he had done. He had read perfectly. But God's presence had vanished along with the light, and now he felt terrified.

Saba hugged him tightly after the service, and Zechariah could tell he was proud. "That was perfect, son. Perfect." The musicians played their joyful music again as Zechariah walked home for the celebration. But he wondered if the day really had begun or if he was still in bed, still dreaming. When his mother took his face in her hands and kissed both of his cheeks, he nearly changed his mind. How could he ever bear to kiss her good-bye? How could the Holy One expect him to? He thought of Abraham and Sarah and remembered that they had left their families behind, too.

Everyone gathered to eat the feast that his mother and grandmother had prepared, but Zechariah wandered away from the food-laden table without an appetite. He stood looking through the gate, wishing he could gallop far away on one of the horses from his dreams and never tell anyone about what had happened when he'd read from the Torah. After a few moments, he felt a hand on his shoulder.

"What's wrong?" Abba asked. "You did very well. You read every word perfectly. Why aren't you celebrating?"

What could he say? How could he describe what he had experienced in the assembly hall that morning? It would be like trying to describe a dream, and they always slipped through your grasp when you tried to put them into words.

"Zechariah, what's the matter?" Abba asked again. He lifted Zechariah's chin until he was looking up into his father's eyes.

"Saba told me to pray and ask the Holy One whether He wanted me to stay here with you and Mama or go to Jerusalem. So I did that. I've been praying and praying every day and . . ." He was afraid to say the words out loud, afraid they would sound silly. But he was even more afraid of their permanence.

"Tell me, son."

"The Holy One said, 'Leave your father's household—'"

"Wait . . . You mean the Torah passage you just read?"

Zechariah nodded. "I think . . . I think the Holy One wants me to go to Jerusalem. To the land He promised to Abraham's offspring—to us." He saw emotion twist his father's face, as if he was fighting tears. Abba gave his shoulder a hard squeeze and hurried away.

Zechariah shivered at the enormity of what had happened this morning. The God of Abraham and Moses had spoken to him through the words of the Torah. Those sacred scrolls weren't mere stories of the dusty past for old men to read, but the living Word of God. The Almighty One was real, and He was inviting Zechariah to walk with Him in faith the way Abraham had, the way Moses had.

He closed his eyes for a moment, longing to pray for strength, for guidance, longing to feel God's presence again, but he didn't know how to pray to the Almighty One outside of the house of assembly. He opened his eyes again and gazed around at the gathered crowd, eating, laughing, balancing plates of food in their hands. Some of them would be going to Jerusalem. Others had decided to stay here. He thought of Yael and realized that now, more than ever, he had to convince her not to run away with Parthia and be a seer and adopt Babylonian ways. He wanted her to go with him and follow God. They would go together.

Zechariah wove his way through the courtyard, dodging around all of the adults, searching for her. He found Yael sitting with his younger sisters and cousins, eating the sweet treats that Safta had made, giggling with them. She was just a child, he realized, like he had been yesterday. Today he was an adult, and he felt responsible for her. He reached for her hand and pulled her to her feet. "Come with me, Yael. I have to tell you something."

"Don't eat all the treats while I'm gone," she called back to the others. Zechariah led her through the crowd and out through the open gate, stopping on the other side. "Why so serious, Zaki? What's wrong?"

"The Holy One spoke to me, and now I know that He's real and that all of the stupid Babylonian gods are false. The Almighty One is . . ." How could he describe the certainty he had experienced for those few brief moments, the sense of radiant awe and joy he'd felt in His presence?

Yael was gazing back at the celebration, not at him, shifting her feet impatiently. "Is that all you wanted to tell me?"

"Did you hear the passage I read from the Torah?"

"I guess so, but what does that have to do with anything?"

"I asked God for a sign, whether He wanted me to go to Jerusalem with you and the others or stay here in Babylon."

"A sign?"

"Yes . . . You know how your father hired the seer and asked her to look at the stars so they would guide him? Well, I asked God to give me a sign—He can do that, you know, without using sorcery or the stars. And He answered me! He answered me through the words of the Torah, just like Saba said He would."

"Why are you telling me this?"

"Because I'm going to Jerusalem, Yael, and you have to come with us. You and I belong with our own people, not here in Babylon. We'll go together!"

She took a small step back, and he could see that his enthusiasm hadn't convinced her. "But my mother is buried here."

"So? That's no reason to stay."

"You'll never understand." She turned to go, but he grabbed her arm again.

"Maybe we can bring her bones with us. The Torah says that Moses carried Joseph's bones back to the Promised Land so that he could be buried there."

"Do you think Abba will do that?"

"I don't know, but you belong with the living, Yael, not with the dead. And not with the Babylonians. You have to come with us."

"Is your whole family going now? Did your father change his mind, too?"

"No. He's still staying here." Zechariah felt a new wave of misgiving. "But I've decided to go with my grandparents. And with you."

"I told you, I'm not going. I'm staying here."

She was just a slender little thing, the arm he was holding so thin he could almost encircle it with his fingers. He should let her go and be done with her. Why should he care what she did? Why did he feel the weight of her secret like a heavy stone that he had to drag everywhere with him? "Yael, your mother isn't here anymore. Her spirit doesn't live inside her body anymore—"

"Stop it! . . . Let go of me! I don't want to listen to you!"

"There's no reason for you to stay here. Please come with us, Yael. It will be the best adventure we've ever had in our lives." She finally yanked her arm free and glared at him, her arms folded across her chest, her mouth stubbornly closed.

His mother called to him from the other side of the gate, "Come on, Zechariah, you're missing the feast. And you're the one we're honoring today."

"You'd better go," she said, tilting her head toward the party. "They're waiting for you."

"Are you coming with me, Yael?" He meant to Jerusalem, but she simply shrugged in reply. "Yael, please!"

"I never should have told you my secret," she said.

He sighed and left her standing alone outside the gate, knowing she was right, wishing that she never had told him.

CHAPTER
9

Tomorrow. They were leaving Babylon tomorrow. How had the day crept up on Dinah so quickly? She wasn't ready. She would never be ready. But Iddo assured her that he had packed everything they needed for their new life. It was time to go.

Dinah's quiet Jewish community had become nearly unrecognizable, the market squares and homes overflowing as exiles from throughout the empire assembled to begin the long journey to Jerusalem. Thousands of horses and mules, camels and donkeys jammed the lanes and alleyways. But as she lay in bed, trying in vain to fall asleep, it seemed that all of the pieces of her life had been tossed haphazardly into a sack, shaken together, then dumped out again. And now, against her will, others had sifted through those pieces, deciding which ones she would be allowed to keep and which ones had to be thrown away.

Iddo lay awake beside her, neither one of them able to sleep. "What are you thinking about, Dinah?" he whispered. She couldn't reply. He sat up on one elbow to look down at her in the dark. "I wish you could have been with me yesterday to see all that gold and silver! I saw the temple treasures, Dinah, can you imagine? The Persian treasurer counted out every single item to

Prince Sheshbazzar, more than five thousand articles—so much gold that it didn't look real! The Persians are sending soldiers with us tomorrow to keep the caravan safe."

Tomorrow. The word felt like a kick in the stomach. The journey that had once been a distant worry would begin tomorrow. Staying or leaving, it was probably too late for anyone to change his mind.

Iddo lay down again. "I was very disappointed when they announced the final tally of how many people are going, though. Only a little more than forty-two thousand. Can you believe that? It should be ten times that number. Hundreds of thousands of us were exiled, Dinah—including the northern tribes, who the Assyrians carried off. They're free to return home from exile, too, but not a single one of them is going."

"That still seems like a lot of people to travel in one caravan."

"We won't all leave at the same time. We've divided them into smaller caravans, leaving a day apart from each other. You and I will be in the first one, along with the temple treasures. Even so, I just don't understand why we are so few people. . . . But I can hardly lecture the others when our own sons aren't coming."

Dinah turned over, facing away from him. The hours seemed to pass slowly and quickly at the same time as the moon made its way across the sky. Iddo rose long before Dinah did, but it was still dark outside, the stars shining in the heavens, when he came to tell her that it was time to go. She tied on her sandals and combed her hair, pinning it up beneath a scarf.

"The caravan is assembling over on the main street," Iddo said. "I've loaded all of our things, but look around and make sure we didn't forget anything."

Dinah heard his voice, but his words meant nothing to her. "What did you say, Iddo?"

He rested his hand on her shoulder, his eyes filled with pity.

"This day will be the hardest one. I promise you that it will get better from now on."

Dinah's family roused from their beds to say good-bye, standing bleary and teary-eyed in the predawn darkness. When she finally had to let go and walk out of her loved ones' embraces, it was worse than a death. People didn't choose to die, but she and Iddo could have chosen to stay. For the hundredth time she remembered the seer's words: *"I see a great tearing in your life. . . ."*

She reached for Zechariah's hand. But his father grabbed him one last time and held him so tightly that Dinah wondered if he would ever let go. She hadn't seen Berekiah weep since he was a boy, but he was weeping now.

"Don't do that to the boy," Iddo said. "He asked for God's guidance, and the Almighty One answered."

"Why is it so impossible to follow God?" Berekiah asked bitterly.

"It's hard," Iddo said. "That's why so few people do it. But it's not impossible."

Berekiah finally released his son. "You'll come later, right, Abba?" Zechariah asked tearfully.

"When we can, son. As soon as we can."

Dinah had to believe he was telling the truth, or she never could have found the strength to leave her family behind. She took Zechariah's hand, gripping it tightly in her own, and turned away. They followed Iddo through the streets, jammed with Jewish families dragging their children and possessions to the waiting caravan. The sounds of heart-wrenching sobs and lingering good-byes filled the morning air. The crowd jostled her. She had to look down to watch her footing on the dark, uneven road, her tears still blinding her, and when she finally wiped them away and looked up, Iddo stood waiting beside the two-wheeled cart that held all their possessions. A lifetime of memories crammed into a wagon that a single mule would pull—a mule that would plow land when they arrived. Iddo helped Dinah and their grandson climb onto the seat he'd made for them. He would walk in front of them, leading the mule.

The stars were beginning to fade, the sky in the east turning light when the cart finally lurched forward and began to move. The procession filled the road from one side to the other, and Dinah couldn't see the beginning or the end of it. They had traveled a very short distance and were still inside the city walls when she saw their neighbor, Mattaniah, running toward them against the flow of the caravan, weaving in and out between wagons and animals and people. He halted beside Iddo to ask breathlessly, "Is Yael with you?"

"No, I haven't seen her all morning. Have you, Dinah?"

She shook her head.

Mattaniah swayed as if his knees threatened to buckle. "She's missing, Iddo! I can't find her anywhere!" Iddo pulled the cart over to the side, motioning to the others to go around them. "I woke Yael up this morning, and we carried everything to our cart and loaded it. She said she was going to sleep in the back of it, but when I looked beneath the blanket just now, she was gone!"

Too late, Dinah remembered her promise to Miriam to take care of Yael as if she were her very own daughter. She had been too engulfed in her own grief to do what Miriam had asked.

"I thought she might be riding with you," Mattaniah continued, "but if she isn't here . . . Have you seen her, Zaki?"

Dinah saw the unmistakable look of guilt on Zechariah's face. He wouldn't meet anyone's gaze as he shrank back from Mattaniah as if wanting to hide. "Zaki? Do you know where Yael is?" Dinah asked.

"I-I promised not to tell. I can't break my promise."

"Well, I can't leave her behind!" Mattaniah shouted. "Don't you understand that? She's my daughter!"

"Tell us, son. Please," Iddo said.

"But I gave my word, Saba. How can I break my word?"

"A promise may be broken if it's a matter of life and death. Yael is just a child. She can't survive here without her father. You have to tell us what you know." But Zechariah bent forward and buried his head in his arms, sobbing. Mattaniah seemed about to leap onto the cart and shake the truth out of him, when Dinah suddenly remembered something.

"Wait! Don't torture the boy. I think I might know where Yael is. After Miriam died, I overheard that Babylonian woman telling Yael that she could live with her. She was enticing her to become a sorceress even before Miriam died."

"You're right," Mattaniah said. "She had the nerve to come to my home and ask to take Yael with her. Of course I refused but—"

"Do you know where she lives?" Iddo asked.

"In the Babylonian part of town, near the temple of Marduk."

"I'll go with you." Iddo handed the reins to Dinah. "Wait here. And we'd better ask some of the other men to come with us, Mattaniah. We may have to threaten her if she's hiding Yael."

"What if Yael isn't there?" Mattaniah asked. "Then what am I going to do?"

Zaki lifted his head and wiped his eyes. "Saba? I-I just remembered a dream I had about Yael. I dreamt that the wicked woman was hiding her in a big storage basket."

"Thank you, son." He and Mattaniah hurried away, racing back toward the city.

"What a terrible way to begin a journey," Dinah murmured.

"Yael won't like being carried away from here against her will."

"I know, Zaki. But sometimes we have no choice." Dinah wondered how many other people in this dreary caravan—wives and children too young to decide for themselves—were making this journey against their will.

Zechariah lowered his head again. "Yael's going to hate me," he said with a moan. "She's going to think I told on her."

"We'll make it very clear to her that you didn't. Besides, that woman has no right to steal one of our children away like that."

There was nothing to do now but sit and wait, watching as carts and wagons and camels and pedestrians streamed past. Dinah wondered if she and Iddo would have to stay behind in Babylon after all, and join a later caravan. But as the sun rose higher in the sky, Iddo and Mattaniah finally returned. Yael was in her father's arms, weeping inconsolably.

"Let me take her," Dinah said, reaching for her. "Yael can ride with us for a little while." They would console each other.

"It's a good thing Zechariah told us about the basket," Mattaniah said as he handed his daughter up to Dinah. "That's exactly where we found her, hiding in an empty storage basket." He thanked them again and jogged ahead to where he had tethered his own cart.

Yael gave Zaki a malevolent look as she settled onto Dinah's lap. "You broke your promise!"

"I didn't tell them your secret, I swear! I never told anyone!"

"He's telling the truth," Dinah said as the cart lurched forward again. "I was the one who guessed where you were. Zechariah didn't tell."

The steady stream of traffic hadn't stopped flowing while they'd waited, and Iddo quickly rejoined the river of vehicles moving out of Babylon. Before long, Dinah saw the massive city gates ahead, guarded by armed soldiers, the enemy who had kept her people inside all their lives, reminding them that they were slaves. She was about to pass through those gates for the first time in her life. Her people had been set free. Under any other circumstances, Dinah would have rejoiced.

She held tightly to Yael, who had cried herself to sleep in her arms. The caravan stretched in front of them and behind them on the vast plain as far as Dinah could see, enveloped in a cloud of dust like the glory cloud that had accompanied Moses and her ancestors. As the miles rolled past, she wondered if Iddo would grow tired of walking. But no, he stood taller than she had ever seen him, his back no longer bent as if carrying a heavy load. His face shone with sweat and with tears of joy in the sunlight. She closed her eyes, unsure in that moment if she loved him or hated him.

CHAPTER

10

I'm tired of riding, Abba," Yael called to her father. "May I please get down and walk?" The cart's monotonous bumping and swaying, the endless rumble of the wheels along the dusty road bored her. A choking cloud of grit hovered over the caravan like fog.

"I suppose so." He slowed the cart so she could scramble down to walk beside him. "But be careful, Yael. And stay close."

Yael would never admit it to anyone, but one month into the journey she was glad that her father had found her and forced her to come along. At first the open countryside that surrounded and dwarfed her had terrified Yael. She had clutched the moonstone amulet Parthia had given her, wishing the seer could have read her stars one last time and given her a glimpse of her future before Abba had snatched her away. But little by little as the days and nights passed, Yael had found comfort and hope in looking up at the familiar stars each night and watching the moon goddess' steady waxing and waning. Parthia had taught her well, and Yael knew that once she was able to study her star charts again, she would find advice and direction for the future on her own.

It didn't take long before Yael grew tired of trudging along at the caravan's dreary pace. She walked faster and faster through the weeds along the side of the road until she was far ahead of her father. She heard Zaki calling to her above the rumble of hooves and wheels and finally stopped to wait for him. He straggled up beside her, puffing for breath. "Your father said not to run off like that. You're going to get lost."

"How can I get lost?" she asked, spreading her arms. "You can see forever! I would stand out like a flea on a bald dog." She wished she could run through the green fields and wade through the canals on the north side of the road, exploring all the way down to the Euphrates, washing her dusty feet in the wide, murky water. The river was nearly always in sight, sometimes tantalizingly close to the road, sometimes shying away again to disappear for a while like a serpent slithering into the grass. So far, the caravan road had followed the winding Euphrates like a shadow, staying just beyond the broad swath of green farmland and date groves along the river's banks. But on the other side of the road, away from the river, the flat landscape looked desolate and lifeless.

"Let's walk together," Zechariah said, tugging her arm.

Yael wiggled out of his grasp and stayed right where she was. "No. You're no fun anymore." She watched as their two carts rumbled past and continued down the road, side-by-side as if competing in a slow-moving chariot race.

"Come on. We don't want to fall behind," Zaki pleaded.

"I know, I know! 'It's important to keep up. No dawdling or lagging behind,'" she said, imitating the nagging voice of their caravan driver. She stubbornly waited until the two carts had nearly vanished in the dust cloud then raced to catch up, reaching them before Zaki did.

"Stop running off," Abba scolded. "If you don't stay where I can see you, I'll make you ride in the cart again."

They heard shouts ahead and the irritated bray of camels.

The flow of vehicles slowed and began squeezing to the right side of the road. "Another caravan must be coming," Zaki said. "We have to get out of the way." He was right. And now their entire procession of people and carts would have to move aside to make room for the string of camels and donkeys approaching from the other direction, their drivers bellowing at their laden beasts. The delay would slow their own progress.

"Get in the cart," Abba said.

"Why? I promise I'll stay close from now on and—" But her father picked her up and set her on top of their load before she could finish.

"These traders would love to carry away a beautiful young girl like you and sell you to some rich man for his harem."

They had to move aside again to let three more caravans pass before the day ended. By the time they camped for the night, the sun had already set and the sky was growing dark, the air cool. No matter how hot the sun shone during the day, the desert air turned surprisingly cold at night.

Yael helped Safta Dinah fetch water and kindle a fire to prepare their evening meal. Abba said their leaders carefully planned each day's journey to allow them to reach a caravan stop with a source of water by nightfall. But some delays couldn't be helped, and as time passed, the group had divided into three smaller ones, a day or two apart from each other. So far, Yael and her father were still in the leading group along with Zechariah and his grandparents. They camped with each other and ate together every night, and she had begun calling Zaki's grandmother "Safta," the same as he did. Dinah had seemed pleased.

While Yael helped prepare the meal, Zechariah helped the men set up the shelters where they would sleep. Little more than a roof over their heads, the tents needed to be simple so the men could take them down quickly each morning and pack them away. The wind tried to blow out the fire as Yael and Dinah cooked, and it carried particles of dirt that blew into their food no matter how carefully they tried to shield it. They had to shake grit out of their clothes every night.

After their meal of flatbread and lentils and dates, they all sat around the fire, weary from the long day of traveling. Their neighbors from back home, Shoshanna and Joel, had camped alongside them, and they all talked together as they watched the embers die. "Our father Abraham began with a journey like this into the unknown," Zaki's grandfather said, "traveling in the desert, camping beneath the stars." He had become more talkative as they'd traveled, as if weariness and discouragement couldn't touch him.

"And his wife Sarah went everywhere with him," Shoshanna added. She reached for her husband's hand like a new bride. Safta's jolly cousin didn't seem to get sad or to miss home the way Safta did.

"Zechariah, do you know why the Almighty One chooses to take us through the desert?" Iddo asked. Zaki shook his head, enthralled with his grandfather's stories. This was exactly what Yael had meant when she'd told him he wasn't fun anymore. "It's because He wants to use the desert to strip us of our self-sufficiency," Iddo continued, "so we'll learn to trust Him and lean on Him."

"Is He going to feed us with manna?" Zaki asked. "Like in the Passover story?"

"He doesn't need to send manna this time," Iddo replied. "He already provided everything we need through our fellow Jews, the ones who aren't making the journey with us. The Persian king ordered them to pay our way."

Yael stood, feeling restless. She was tired of sitting still and didn't want to hear stories about the God who had let her mother die. But Abba grabbed her hand to stop her before she could take two steps. "Where are you going?"

"Just over there. I want to get away from the campfire so I can see the stars."

"No, Yael. You can't leave the caravan for any reason. You could easily get turned around in this trackless waste and die of thirst."

"Besides," Iddo added, "there's nothing out there except the bones of people who wouldn't listen."

Yael exhaled. "I know you think I'll run away again, but I won't. I promise. I'll just be standing right over there."

"I'll go with her." Zechariah stood and walked a few yards away from the others, motioning for Yael to follow. Abba released her and she hurried away, stopping beside Zechariah a short distance from the smoke and firelight. The sky was blacker out here than on any night in Babylon, the stars more numerous, more brilliant. Shining across the middle of the sky was a milky swath, like clouds, that Parthia said was a thick band of stars, all gathered together in a luminous ring. Yael searched the sky for the constellation of the twins and smiled to herself when she found it. She wished she could peek at the sky charts that Parthia had given her, but she didn't dare. They would have to remain hidden in her bag for now.

"Please don't be mad at me anymore," Zechariah said. "Can't we be friends again?"

"You can't keep a secret. Abba said you told him where to look."

"No, I didn't! The only thing I told him was that you might be hiding in a storage basket."

"How did you know that's where I'd be?"

"I had a dream. I know that sounds weird, but it's true. I dreamt I saw Parthia hiding you in a storage basket."

Yael stopped gazing at the stars to look at him in surprise. "You have dreams that foretell the future?" There had always been something . . . different . . . about her friend, different from the other boys in their neighborhood. Sometimes when they played together they could almost read each other's thoughts and know what the other would say before they spoke.

"I have a lot of strange dreams," he said with a shy, little shrug, "but that's the only one that ever came true."

"The gods speak to people in dreams, you know."

"Don't say *gods*, Yael. There's only one God. You need to forget all that pagan stuff from Babylon." She ignored him and looked up at the stars again. "So, can we be friends?" he asked again.

She planted her hands on her hips and gave him a stern look. "Will you promise not to tell my secrets this time?"

"Yes, I promise."

"All right. . . . In that case, I'll tell you another one of my secrets to see if you can be trusted."

"I can."

She moved closer to him and lowered her voice. "I know how to see the future in the stars. Parthia taught me. She told me I had a true gift for it."

"Why do you need to know the future?"

"Because everything in my life keeps changing—first my mother died, now my father is taking me hundreds of miles away from home. The future is like a huge, deep hole in the road up ahead, and I want to see it before it comes so I don't fall in and get swallowed up. I want to be sure there's a way to get across it to the other side. The stars can tell me all that."

"We're supposed to trust the Almighty One, Yael." She heard disapproval in his voice and knew he was frowning at her. "Abraham didn't know what was ahead of him, either, but he had faith—"

"That's the God of *your* father and grandfather. My mother believed in the moon goddess. You follow your family's beliefs, and I'll follow mine."

"Yael, your father is a Levite. You worship the same God I do. The only God."

"No, I don't—and that's another secret you can't tell." She turned away from him to walk back to the campsite.

"Yael, wait . . . Listen!"

"Don't forget," she called over her shoulder to him. "It's a secret."

Part II

Promised Land

When the Lord brought back the captives to Zion,

we were like men who dreamed.

Our mouths were filled with laughter,

our tongues with songs of joy. . . .

The Lord has done great things for us,

and we are filled with joy.

PSALM 126:1–3

CHAPTER
11

Zechariah stood behind the loaded cart and pushed as his grandfather prodded their mule up the hill. The hard work tired him, but they were nearly there, nearly to Jerusalem. Last night their caravan had camped outside the village of Bethel, agonizingly close to their goal. Zechariah had barely slept as he'd waited to make the final climb up to the city, starting just after dawn. "I never knew the Promised Land was so mountainous," he said, straining as he pushed. "It's so different from Babylon."

"It's beautiful, isn't it?" Saba asked. "I forgot just how beautiful after living in a flat, featureless land for nearly fifty years. We're almost home . . . at last."

For most of their journey, the view of endless wilderness had barely changed from day to day. Pale sand and dark rock. Lifeless. Colorless. Then they'd reached the snow-capped peaks of the Mount Hermon range and the countryside had turned greener. They had traveled through Galilee, past the shimmering lake that nestled among the hills, and Zechariah thrilled to know he was following in Abraham's footsteps, retracing the path that the patriarch had taken when he entered the Promised

Land for the first time. Like Abraham, he had obeyed God and left his father and mother to make this journey.

The cart finally reached the crest of the hill, and Saba halted by the side of the road for their first glimpse of Jerusalem. Yael and Safta stood beside them. But instead of a city, Zechariah saw a wasteland. Desolate piles of rocks and rubble, overgrown with weeds and bushes. No signs of life. "Are you sure this is the right place, Saba? Maybe Jerusalem is on the other side of that hill over there."

"No, son. That's Jerusalem down there—what's left of it."

"It doesn't even look like a city," Yael said. "Where are all the palaces and temples and big buildings like they had in Babylon?"

As Zaki shaded his eyes to study the view in front of him, he began to see traces of crumbled walls beneath the vegetation, gates and towers and charred buildings where the city had once stood. How would they ever clear out all that growth and move all those stones? Where would they begin? The task seemed overwhelming. His grandfather wiped away tears, and Zechariah wondered if they were tears of joy or sorrow. Maybe both. Beneath all the debris lay the bones of Saba's family and thousands of other people who had been massacred.

"Oh, Iddo," Safta groaned. "It will take a lifetime to rebuild all of that. How can we possibly do it with so few people?"

Saba cleared his throat. "That rubble shows us the consequences of our disobedience. It should serve as a warning to us not to fail again."

"Where was the Almighty One's temple?" Zaki asked.

Iddo pointed to an enormous pile of toppled building stones on a distant hill above the other ruins. For a moment he seemed too moved to speak. "Up there," he finally said. "It used to be right up there on Mount Moriah. And that's where we'll rebuild it."

The caravan had continued flowing past them all this time,

and the first vehicles in their group had already reached the ruins below. The collection of carts and people and livestock that had seemed so numerous along the caravan road looked tiny and insignificant against the expanse of destruction. Zechariah wondered if Safta was right, that it would take his entire lifetime to rebuild all of this.

Saba gave the reins a tug, and the cart began to move again, joining the others as they headed down the winding path into the city. "Where did you live, Saba?" Zechariah asked as they started downhill. "Are we going to rebuild the same house that you lived in before?"

"My family's home was in Anathoth, not Jerusalem—a couple of miles from here. But we took refuge inside the walls when the Babylonian army surrounded the city. See that hill, closest to us? Can you make out the circle of walls around it? That's the *Mishneh*, or Second Quarter, built during the time of King Hezekiah."

Zechariah looked where Saba was pointing and saw the faint outline of city walls. But huge sections of them, along with the gates, had been toppled. Rubble lay strewn everywhere, swallowed up by a sea of weeds and scrub brush and tangled vines.

"Hezekiah had to expand Jerusalem," Saba continued, "because so many refugees fled here to escape the Assyrians. The old city couldn't hold them all. God performed a miracle to rescue the king and his people from their enemies."

Zechariah looked up at him. "If the Almighty One could rescue Jerusalem in King Hezekiah's time, why couldn't He rescue it from the Babylonians, too?"

"Because we no longer deserved His mercy. By then our sins were too great, in part because of the long, evil reign of King Manasseh. See that valley south of the city? That's the Valley of Hinnom where Manasseh—"

"Don't say it, Iddo." Safta interrupted. "It's too horrible."

He nodded and didn't finish. But Zechariah knew from his studies that people used to sacrifice their children to Molech in that valley.

"The blood of those innocent children contributed to Jerusalem's destruction and our peoples' exile," Saba said.

The main road and city streets were so overgrown with vegetation and choked with rubble that it took the rest of the afternoon to reach the narrow Kidron Valley east of the City of David. "Our leaders have decided to camp here for now," Saba told them, "beside the Kidron Brook."

Zechariah helped pitch their tent and make camp. At dinner, he poked at his food, weary from the effort of scrambling over debris and the hard work of pushing the cart up and down Jerusalem's many slopes. But his disappointment outweighed the weariness he felt. Jerusalem no longer resembled the beautiful city that the psalmists had described. Restoring it would be challenging enough if Zaki were a grown man and an experienced builder, but he was neither. Why had the Almighty One commanded him to come here? What could he possibly do in the face of such overwhelming desolation?

He was about to say good-night to the others and try to go to sleep when he heard a single flute playing a slow, haunting melody. He listened for a moment, and the sound began to grow as other instruments joined in—more flutes, finger cymbals, drums. The tempo gradually quickened, and he heard clapping and then voices, singing a familiar song of hope and joy: *"Those who trust in the Lord are like Mount Zion, which cannot be shaken."* His family used to sing it at Passover and weddings.

"It's a celebration," Saba said. He smiled for the first time all day. "Let's join them." He led the way, with Safta, Zechariah, Yael, and Mattaniah following behind. Zaki's pulse began to beat in rhythm with the joyful music as they joined in the singing.

"As the mountains surround Jerusalem, so the Lord surrounds his people, both now and forevermore."

Before long, it seemed as though everyone in the caravan was dancing and singing in spontaneous celebration. *"I rejoiced with those who said to me, 'Let us go to the house of the Lord.' Our feet are standing in your gates, O Jerusalem."* It was true. He had sung the words of this psalm all his life, and now he was standing here, in Jerusalem. Zechariah's weariness and discouragement vanished as he danced and celebrated with his grandfather and the others until late into the night.

It was barely dawn when Saba shook him awake. "Get up, Zaki. Get dressed. There's a mob of local men coming." Zechariah tossed back the covers and scrambled to his feet, his heart pounding. While he dressed and put on his sandals, Saba roused Joel and Mattaniah. They hurried to the edge of the camp, joined by hundreds of other men from their caravan, halting near the Kidron Brook. On the other side of the narrow stream a mob of Samaritan men, several hundred strong, marched steadily toward them. Many of them carried swords. Others had bows and arrows. Some carried farm implements such as scythes and hoes and winnowing forks.

"What do they want, Saba?" he whispered. It surprised him that his grandfather had asked him to come at all, considering the danger. Maybe his grandfather no longer saw him as a boy but as one of the men.

"I imagine they've come to see what we're doing here."

"Are they Jews, like us?"

"Some of them might be. The Babylonians left the very poorest of our people behind during the exile and carried away all our leaders and craftsmen and priests. But most of those men are probably descendants of exiles from other countries who were forced to settle here the same way we were forced to go to Babylon."

Zechariah watched as Prince Sheshbazzar walked forward to speak with the mob's leader—a fearsome-looking man with a sword strapped to his side. The white-bearded prince would be no match for him. "We've come in peace," Sheshbazzar called out, holding up his hands.

"Who are you?" the leader asked. "What are you doing on our land?"

"I'm Sheshbazzar, a descendant of King David and of Judah's last king, Jehoiachin. We're all sons of Abraham, returning from exile in Babylon to reclaim our ancestral land. This is our destination—the city of Jerusalem and the land of Judah."

The mob began to shout and jeer in protest, and when their leader settled them down again he said, "This is *our* land, not yours! We've lived on it and tended it for three generations. You have no right to settle here. Take your caravan of intruders and move someplace else." There were shouts of agreement from the mob and more sword-waving, but Sheshbazzar continued to speak calmly to them.

"King Cyrus, the Persian monarch, authorized us to return and rebuild the temple of our God. I'm certain that the governor of your Trans-Euphrates Province received a copy of this proclamation from Persia. He will verify that what we're saying is true."

"We'll send envoys to him immediately, but in the meantime, take your caravan off our land and camp someplace else. This land belongs to us. If you try to occupy it or do any rebuilding, we will interpret it as an act of war."

Zechariah's pulse raced as he listened. *An act of war?* The Holy One needed to strike this enemy dead the way He once killed the Egyptians under Moses.

"Listen, we don't want any trouble," Sheshbazzar continued. "But Jerusalem has been deserted all these years, so it will make no difference to you if we settle there—and that's what we intend to do."

"You have no right!"

"When you contact the governor, you'll see that we have every right. We've been commanded by God and by the king to rebuild the Holy One's temple, and that's our most important task. There will be many of us settling here in Jerusalem in the days to come. Others from our caravan will return to the villages where their forefathers lived, to reclaim their ancestral land. They must start plowing and planting before the fall rains begin."

"They may reclaim *nothing* until we've received word that what you're saying is true!" the leader shouted, and the mob behind him responded with such a terrifying cry, waving their swords and scythes above their heads, that Zaki was certain they would surge forward and attack.

"We will not take any of your land," Sheshbazzar shouted above the noise. "Only what's rightfully ours. But we cannot wait to begin building. We must obey our God, not your threats." The angry response reached an insane pitch as the prince turned his back on the men and walked away with the elders. Zechariah wanted to run—he and Saba were unarmed! The Samaritans could easily wade across the shallow creek.

"Let's go eat our breakfast," Saba said, turning his back, as well.

"But, Saba—"

"The Almighty One is on our side. Do you believe that, Zaki?"

He didn't reply. Any faith Zechariah possessed came second-hand from stories in the Torah, not real life. He glanced over his shoulder at the shouting mob as he followed his grandfather and Mattaniah back to their tents.

"So the opposition has started already," Mattaniah said as they walked. "I wondered if it would. Do you think we should be worried? Will we have to fight them?"

"The Samaritans will find out soon enough that our claims are legitimate. In the meantime we can trust God."

"I was hoping that the local people would be friendly," Mattaniah said, "so we could work alongside them."

Saba shook his head. "We would be wise to keep our distance from them and trust no one." He halted before they reached their tent. "Let's not talk about this with the women and worry them unnecessarily."

"But our families are very vulnerable living in tents in this unprotected valley," Mattaniah said. "And the Persian guards will be heading back to Babylon soon. We'd better start building homes higher up on the ridge right away."

"The temple must come first. The very first thing that God commanded our ancestors to do after leaving Egypt was to build His sanctuary. The people camped below Mount Sinai in tents until it was finished. Building His sanctuary must be our top priority, too."

Zechariah hurried through breakfast and his morning prayers, looking over his shoulder, expecting the Samaritans to attack any minute. When they didn't, he worried that they might come at night, while everyone slept. Then, for the second time that morning, Saba surprised him when he invited him to survey the temple mount with him and the chief priests.

As usual, Saba walked too slowly. Zechariah raced up the ramp that led into Jerusalem ahead of his grandfather, then stopped to wait for him near the top. He could see the caravan sprawled out, without protection, in the valley below, and he also noticed the scattered Samaritan settlements dotting the Kidron Valley and perched on the slopes of the Mount of Olives. Workers resembled tiny ants as they tended their vines and groves on the terraced hillsides. The olives would be ready to harvest soon, the dates and figs in another month. The sight of those Samaritan villages made Zechariah uneasy.

The men had been so angry this morning, insisting that this was their land.

Saba soon caught up with him, and they continued to climb until they reached a pile of ruins below the temple mount, swarming with men and even a handful of Persian soldiers. "Why all the activity around here?" Saba asked the others. "What's going on?"

"This is where the palace once stood," the high priest replied. "Sheshbazzar and Zerubbabel were looking through the rubble and found an underground storehouse. We've decided to use it as a treasury to store the temple vessels and other supplies. Can you come back and help us, Iddo? We'll need you to record the transfer of all the silver and gold from the Persian guards."

"Yes, of course I will."

Saba and the other chief priests assembled outside the palace, then made their way to the stairs that led to the top of the mount. The ascent was harder than Zechariah had anticipated, the steps broken and slanted and clogged with stones, but he arrived on top at last, winded from the steep climb. On the wide, flat plateau that had once been the threshing floor of Aranau the Jebusite before it became the temple mount, barely a square foot of land could be found that wasn't covered with debris and weeds. The tumbled building stones were too huge to climb over, so Saba and the other men could only walk forward a short distance. Scrub trees and scraggly cedars and thorn bushes grew among the rocks.

"This can't be right," Saba said. "How could the temple mount have trees growing on it? I don't remember seeing trees."

"Nearly fifty years have passed since the temple was destroyed," his friend Joel reminded him. "Fifty years is plenty of time for saplings to sprout between the ruptured paving stones and grow into trees."

Zechariah tugged his grandfather's sleeve to get his attention.

"Saba, isn't this the place where Abraham offered to sacrifice Isaac before there was a temple?"

"Yes. That's right."

"Well, there must have been trees when Abraham was here. And bushes, too. Didn't he find a ram caught by his horns in a thicket?"

"Ah, yes. You're right." Saba smiled as he rested his hand on Zaki's shoulder. "You're a very clever boy. And you remember your Torah, that's good."

"At least there's no shortage of building stones in Jerusalem," Joel said. "But it's going to take a trememdous amount of work to clear this plateau."

"Our first task is to find the site where the bronze altar stood," Saba said. "It's where Abraham's sacrifice also took place. Once we rebuild the altar, we can offer the daily sacrifices again."

"I think we'll have to wait until the Samaritans simmer down before we rebuild anything," Joel said.

Saba turned on him. "No, Joel! We dare not wait a single day! If we want God's guidance and help, we must ask for our sins to be forgiven through the sacrifices." He strode off to work with the other priests, moving stones to make way for the altar. Zechariah had plenty of time to think as he helped pull weeds from between the cracks and clear away some of the smaller rocks. He wondered when the Almighty One would speak to him again and tell him what he was supposed to do next. The God of Abraham had won the tug-of-war between Zechariah's father and grandfather, proving that He was real by providing a second exodus from slavery. But the threat from their enemies that Zechariah had witnessed this morning and the enormous amount of rubble piled in front of him made him question his role in the Almighty One's plan.

Late that afternoon, they retraced their steps to their campsite in the valley, hot, weary, and thirsty from the day's work. Apart from a few mounds of gathered brush and some shifted stones, the temple mount looked little different from before. "Our job is going to be really hard, isn't it, Saba?"

"The Almighty One brought us back to our land, but we still have to do our part to conquer it, just like our ancestors did under Joshua. Our task is to build His temple, and the Holy One's enemies will do everything they can to try to stop us."

"Like they did this morning?"

Saba nodded. "Each obstacle we face is like an ancient Canaanite king who needs to be defeated, or a walled city like Jericho that we need to tear down. You and I and the others have already conquered the first strongholds by choosing to leave the comfort of Babylon and the pull of family ties and by turning our backs on its paganism."

Zechariah remembered Yael's entanglement with sorcery and looked away. The guilt of her secrets felt like his own. They soon reached the ruined Water Gate and headed down the ramp toward their camp.

"Will we let all these obstacles stop us?" Saba continued. "Or allow the hard work of rebuilding to discourage us?"

"No, Saba." He smiled as he imagined himself as part of Judah's army, going into battle, defeating their enemies. Or commanding teams of oxen as they hauled building stones into place for God's temple. "What's my job going to be from now on, Saba?"

"Your job is to study the Torah."

"What?" Zechariah halted. He must have misunderstood. "But . . . but that's what I did back in Babylon. I want to be a soldier and learn how to fight. And I want to help rebuild the temple."

"The way we conquer our enemies is by obeying God's Word. When Joshua obeyed, the walls of Jericho fell down. But how can we obey if we don't know what God's Word says? That's your job, Zechariah—to learn what it says."

123

Zechariah couldn't believe it. He would spend his days in this new land studying the Torah? Not learning how to use a sword or how to build, but studying? He couldn't disguise his disappointment as they started walking again. So far, his return to Jerusalem wasn't at all like he had imagined.

CHAPTER
12

The screams startled Yael awake. She sat up, clutching her blanket, her heart pounding. Should she run? Hide? Had the Samaritans attacked? The terrifying cries came from the tent right beside hers—from Zaki's grandfather. Abba leaped out of bed to go see what was wrong, and so did everyone around them, it seemed. Yael heard the mumble of voices as Iddo reassured everyone that he was fine and sent them back to their beds.

"He had a nightmare," Abba said when he returned a few minutes later. "Go back to sleep, Yael." He lay down again.

It seemed like a long time passed before Yael's heart stopped pounding. Her skin still had a funny, tingling feeling from being frightened half to death, as if ants were crawling all over her. As the camp settled down again, she could hear Iddo and Dinah talking softly. "All the way here, three long months of traveling and I never had a single nightmare," Iddo said. "I'm so ashamed . . . I-I don't understand it."

"There's no reason to feel ashamed. This is where your real nightmare happened. I'm sure the others realize that."

"I thought the dreams were gone for good."

125

"Maybe this will be the last one now that you've returned and faced what happened in the past."

"Or maybe God is punishing me with these nightmares because of all the mistakes I've made."

"Go to sleep, Iddo."

"I can't. I may as well get up."

Yael heard shuffling as he left his tent. She couldn't fall asleep, either, and she lay on her back, staring at the dark tent hovering above her head. One edge of the animal-skin covering was attached to their cart, the other to poles, with the excess hide hanging down to form sides that reached to the ground. Abba slept close to the cart, but Yael liked to sleep near the open side of the tent. She inched over to it, trying not to make too much noise, dragging her blanket with her for warmth. Maybe if she lifted the covering she would be able to see the stars.

The hide had the strong odor of animals and stank nearly as bad as the donkey that had pulled their cart. She managed to lift a flap of the heavy skin and look up at a small patch of star-flecked sky and the brilliant full moon that illuminated the roofs of the other huddled tents. Parthia had taught Yael about the phases of the moon and said that people could be "moonstruck" or even become "lunatics" during a full moon. Was that what had happened to Zaki's grandfather? He didn't believe in the moon goddess and refused to worship her, so maybe the nightmare was her punishment. Yael wondered when Iddo's birthday was. If the moon was rising in his star sign, that could cause even more trouble. Or maybe the dream was a warning to him. Parthia said the gods spoke through dreams.

Yael inched a little farther outside the tent. How beautiful the stars looked tonight! She knew how to read some of their mysteries and secrets, but she longed to know all of them. *"The heavenly bodies and celestial events all have powerful effects on what happens to us on earth,"* Parthia had said. And all of that information could be found on the star charts she had given her. Using pictures and symbols, the charts showed the lunar months and the sign of the zodiac that was dominant each month. Before Abba had decided to move to Jerusalem, Parthia had taught Yael how to locate the signs of the zodiac in the night sky. She closed her eyes for a moment, remembering the soft tinkling of Parthia's jewelry, the sweet smell of her incense.

"Once you learn to read the charts," Parthia said, *"you can warn people of trouble ahead or advise them of the best times to pursue love or financial success."*

Yael glanced over at Abba. He had rolled onto his side, facing away from her, and she could tell by his soft snoring that he had fallen asleep. She sat up, the tent roof skimming the top of her head, and reached for her bag, the one she had packed to take to Parthia's house when she'd run away to live with her. Good thing Abba hadn't looked inside it or taken it away from her when he'd dragged her here. Yael pulled the bag close and quietly rummaged inside until she found the charts. Then she felt around for something else—the little stone figurine of the moon goddess that Parthia had given her. It was small enough to fit in the palm of her hand, and it felt comforting, somehow, when she gripped the smooth, polished stone figure in her fist. *"Hold it tightly whenever you are afraid or in danger,"* Parthia had told her. *"And someday when you're giving birth to a child of your own, she will protect you."* Yael studied the little naked figurine in the dim light, then tucked it back inside the bag. It would have to stay hidden for now.

She inched toward the opening again, carrying the star charts. She lifted the tent flap to stick her head out, then pulled the moonstone amulet from beneath her dress. The smooth white stone looked as radiant and luminous as the real moon. She wished she could wear it on the outside of her clothing, but she was afraid that Iddo or Zechariah would see it and ask questions. Safta Dinah had noticed it once when Yael was bathing but Yael had lied and said that the necklace had been a gift from her mother.

The scroll made a crinkling sound as she unrolled it. Yael glanced at Abba again. He was still asleep. He probably wouldn't care what she did—after all, he had consulted Parthia and other Babylonian seers when Mama was sick. But now that he had moved back to Jerusalem, maybe he didn't believe in them anymore. Yael couldn't take that chance.

She looked down at the open chart, hoping that the moon would give enough light to read it. But the light was still too dim, the tiny figures on the scroll too small, even when she held the parchment close to her eyes or tilted it toward the moon's light. It was the month of Ab, which meant that the constellation of the lion was dominant in the sky. She heard movement in the next tent, but before she could hide the charts again, Zaki poked his head out from beneath the flap.

"Yael? . . . What are you doing?" he whispered.

"Nothing." The scrolls rustled like dry leaves as she quickly rolled them up again. Zaki moved toward her on his hands and knees.

"Are you doing sorcery or something?"

"No—I'm just looking at the stars, that's all."

"What are the scrolls for?"

She sighed, wondering if she could trust him. "They help me figure out what the stars are saying."

He moved closer and lowered his voice even more. "If they catch you doing those things here, you know what the punishment will be? Death! The Torah says to stone a sorceress to death!"

Her heart beat a little faster. Was he telling the truth? "You can't tell anyone, Zaki. You promised." She shoved the charts into her bag again and pushed it beneath the tent flap.

"You have to get rid of those scrolls before someone catches you."

"No, I don't. They're mine. I need them." She would never be able to explain how much she longed for guidance in this strange new place. Ever since Mama died, her life had felt so uncertain, like being tossed around in the back of a runaway cart with nothing solid to hang on to. The stars remained the same no matter where she traveled. "Good night, Zaki."

Yael ducked beneath her tent and lay down again, but she was still too restless to sleep. When she heard Zaki settle down in his tent, she lifted the flap and poked her head out one more time to look up. A falling star streaked across the sky and she made a wish on it, wishing for a new friend now that Zaki was so bossy.

The most important star, the one that all of the others circled around, shone brightly above her. Parthia had taught her how to find it by looking at the constellation that resembled a huge dipping gourd. The morning star was an important one, too, but it hadn't risen above the horizon yet—or else the mountains across the valley blocked it from sight. The longer Yael looked at the sky, the more stars began to appear, as if they'd been hiding behind their mother's skirts like shy children. Soon the heavens were white with them. How beautiful they were, holding secrets she longed to discover.

At last her eyes grew tired, and she rolled back inside the tent and tucked her moonstone amulet inside her tunic again. She would have to find a way to grab a few moments to herself during the day so she could study the charts without being seen. Then she could find the constellations more easily at night. Someday she would know all of the stars' secrets.

Wrapped in her blanket, Yael finally drifted off to sleep.

CHAPTER

13

Iddo didn't sleep for the rest of the night, his mind racing back and forth like a weaver's shuttle between the ghosts of his past that haunted the ruins of Jerusalem and excitement for a future he never dreamed he would see. The nightmare left him badly shaken. Why had the dreams started again after so many months without one?

At breakfast, his hands still shook, and he nearly spilled the bowl of roasted grain as he reached to take it from Dinah. "Are you sure you're all right?" she asked, steadying it for him. "Your face is as white as your beard. The circles under your eyes look like bruises."

"Thank you for that fine description. Now I have no need of a mirror."

"Iddo, no one will mind if you stay here and rest today. You've barely slept for two nights and—"

"You don't need to remind me or anyone else about my nightmares." Wasn't it bad enough that he had awakened half the campsite with his screaming last night? Why remind everyone of his weakness as they sat together, eating?

Dinah passed him the basket of figs next, watching him closely. "Will you promise not to work so hard in the hot sun today?"

He didn't reply. How could he promise such a thing when the Holy One had given him a job to do?

"May I go with you again today?" Zechariah asked.

"I'm sorry, Zaki, but I promised the other priests that I would help catalogue the temple treasures, and it will take us all day. Stay here and help Safta." He ate a few more bites of food, aware of everyone's scrutiny, then decided to leave.

Iddo hated the way his legs trembled as he climbed up the path to the city. Thankfully, he would sit all day as he recorded the treasures, making sure that everything on the long list of silver and gold items had arrived safely from Babylon.

"Prince Sheshbazzar has called for a meeting first," the others told him when he arrived at the treasury. "He wants to make an announcement."

The prince got right to the point as soon as everyone had assembled. "After time to reflect on recent events, I've decided that we need to build houses for ourselves and our families right away. Our work on the altar will have to wait a little longer."

"Wait," Iddo interrupted. "Build houses? Shouldn't rebuilding the temple be our top priority? Isn't that what the Holy One brought us back here to do?"

"Yes, and it still is a priority, Iddo. But the anger and hostility we saw in the Samaritan mob the other day is a serious concern. They see us as invaders, and there have already been some attacks. Some livestock has disappeared from our caravan during the night, and we fear these attacks will escalate. We're too vulnerable living in tents. We need to build houses, and I believe the safest place is up here on the ridge, in what used to be the old City of David." Sheshbazzar wasn't finished, but Iddo interrupted him again.

"The Almighty One didn't set us free so we could live comfortable lives in stone houses. We were comfortable and safe in Babylon."

"Yes, but I feel it's important to stake our claim to Jerusalem by building a permanent settlement here and—"

"We can stake our claim—and the Almighty One's claim—by rebuilding His temple."

"And we will do that, Iddo. This delay is only temporary. Once we're all out of the valley, we will return to our projects on the temple mount." Sheshbazzar was losing patience with him, but Iddo didn't care. He had to convince him and the others that this decision was a mistake.

"Listen," Iddo said, "if our enemies are a threat, then restoring the daily sacrifices becomes even more urgent. Without the sacrifices, what right do we have to petition the Almighty One for protection?"

Sheshbazzar stroked his white beard, his face stern. "I'm sorry, Iddo, but I didn't call this meeting to discuss the issue. I called it to announce that I'm suspending our work on the temple mount to give everyone time to move out of the Kidron Valley and into permanent homes. I ask for your patience."

"Let's hope the Almighty One will be patient." Iddo felt helpless. Sheshbazzar was a royal prince and the official governor of the new territory of Judah. His decision was final.

When the meeting ended, Iddo went to work tallying the temple treasures, taking all morning and part of the afternoon to account for every article. As he was rolling up the finished scrolls, the high priest drew him aside. "Can you stay and work a little longer? The leaders of some of our wealthier families have come forward to give freewill offerings to help rebuild God's house," he said. "We could use your help recording those donations."

The totals were staggering. Iddo counted sixty-one thousand drachmas of gold and five thousand minas of silver—all worth hundreds of years of wages. The patrons had also contributed one hundred linen garments for the priests to wear. Iddo laid aside his scrolls for a moment to examine the beautiful clothing, running his hand over the luxurious fabric. There were turbans of fine linen, headbands, and undergarments of finely twisted linen. Sashes of blue, purple, and scarlet yarn, exquisitely embroidered. As a slave in Babylon, he had never worn garments of such fine quality, but one day he would wear these. "The treasures we catalogued today need to be put to use to serve God," he told Jeshua, "not locked in a storehouse. These garments need to be worn."

"And they will, Iddo. In time. Can you come with me, please, so I can show you one more thing?" The high priest lit a small oil lamp and led Iddo into the windowless treasury. He set down the lamp inside and picked up a slender object about four feet long wrapped in a linen cloth. He carefully unwound the wrapping to reveal a straight, slender tube with a flared end, made from hammered silver. He handed it to Iddo. "According to our temple records, the men in your family once played these silver trumpets."

"Yes, I remember . . ." As Iddo ran his fingers over the cool, smooth metal, tracing the instrument's flared bell, he recalled standing in the temple courtyard as a boy, listening to the penetrating trumpet call that sounded from the pinnacle. His father had been the one blowing it.

"These trumpets will announce the appointed feasts and New Moon festivals and will be an important part of our worship. The Torah says that the sound of the trumpet shall be a memorial for us before our God. We need you and your sons to carry on the tradition of your forefathers."

Iddo handed back the instrument. "I-I'm sorry . . . but I don't know how to blow it. I was too young when . . . when the end came."

"I understand," Jeshua said, wrapping the linen cloth around the trumpet again. "I've asked around and unfortunately, none of the other priests remember how to play it, either. Even so, I would like you to take a shofar home to practice on. Someone needs to learn how to play it again." He picked up one of the long, curved ram's horns that were lying with the trumpets and handed it to Iddo. "Maybe by the time the Feast of Trumpets comes in a few months, you'll be ready."

Iddo carried the ram's horn down to his campsite in the valley when the workday ended. It didn't weigh much, but it felt heavy in his hands, weighted with responsibility. "Is that a shofar?" Zechariah asked as he ran out to meet him. "What's it for, Saba?"

"Yes, it's a shofar. The high priest asked me to learn how to play it, so I can blow the silver trumpets the way our forefathers once did. You'll play the trumpets one day, too."

"May I hold it?" Iddo handed it to Zechariah and watched him turn the horn over and over in his hands, studying it carefully before looking up at Iddo again. "You never told me that our ancestors played the shofar."

"I had forgotten all about it until today. Do you remember where the tradition of the ram's horn comes from?"

"Um . . . from when Abraham offered to sacrifice Isaac on Mount Moriah?"

"Very good. But don't make your answer sound like a question next time. Now tell me, what does the sound of the shofar remind us of?"

Zechariah thought for a moment. "God's salvation?" Iddo frowned, and Zaki quickly changed his reply from a question to a statement. "It reminds us of our salvation."

"Very good. In faith, Abraham told his son that God himself would provide the lamb for the sacrifice. And the ram that took Isaac's place and saved him was captured by its horn—like this one."

"Will you play it for me, Saba?" he asked.

"I don't remember how." He lifted the small end to his mouth and blew air into it but nothing came out except a sound like the wind. "I will have to learn how," Iddo said. But who would teach him?

That night another nightmare catapulted Iddo from his bed. He'd been so weary after two sleepless nights that he had fallen into an exhausted sleep only to be jolted out of it in terror. Once again, his screams awakened his neighbors, who came running. "I'm fine, I'm fine," he assured all of them. "I'm sorry for disturbing you again."

Iddo put on his outer robe and went outside his makeshift tent to sit on the broken block of stone that served as their table. He gazed across the valley at the Mount of Olives, afraid to close his eyes again. He would be barred from the priesthood if his nightmares were seen as a mental defect.

A moment later, Dinah came out to sit beside him. "I'm sorry for waking you," he told her. "Please go back to bed." Instead, she nudged him to move over so she could sit beside him.

"Maybe if you talked about your dreams you would get past them, back to the good memories of when you lived here."

"I can't talk about them."

"Iddo, we've been married nearly forty years, and I've never asked you to tell me about your nightmares or what those terrible memories were. But I'm asking you now, for your own good." When he didn't reply, Dinah placed her hand on his cheek and made him turn to face her. "If you tell me what your dreams are about, maybe they'll stop."

He hesitated. What if he told her the truth? Would she despise him? It was a risk he had to take. The dreams had to stop. He needed to sleep. He needed to wear that linen robe and embroidered sash to serve as a priest. He looked over his shoulder at the shofar, lying where he'd placed it just inside his tent last night. It was his family's job to play it.

"What's the earliest thing you can remember?" Dinah prompted.

"My earliest memories are in Anathoth, the village in the mountains where my family lived. I remember how green it was, and how the wind rustled as it blew through the trees. I used to listen to the birds singing at dawn every morning." He couldn't recall any birdsong in Babylon.

"Is the village far from here?"

"No, only a few miles. We would walk from there to Jerusalem in about an hour's time. My father used to carry me on his shoulders until I got too old to be carried. Then he carried my brother."

"You never told me you had a brother. What's his name?"

Iddo had never told anyone. He hadn't wanted to think about his brother or remember his last moments with him. "His name was Jacob," he said after a long pause. "He was two years younger than me. My father said it was my job to watch over him, to help take care of him. . . ." He bent forward, holding his stomach as the ache of regret gnawed at him.

Dinah rested her hand on his back, rubbing gently. "What else do you remember?"

He waited for the dull pain to ease before sitting up again. "We moved from Anathoth into the city when the Babylonian soldiers invaded our land for the final time. Everyone did. No one dared to stay outside the walls. And once we were safely inside Jerusalem, we remained there for two and a half years while the city was under siege. We had nothing left to eat in the end. I remember how thin my brother became, how his bones seemed to poke through his skin. I suppose I looked the same, but I didn't think about it at the time. . . . My mother had grown very thin, too, except for her stomach. She gave birth to another baby the final year of the siege but he was stillborn. How could he live when my mother gave all of her food to my brother and me? It was my fault—"

"No, Iddo. You know that you would do the very same thing for our children. Any parent would." He gave a small shrug, admitting the truth of her words. "Tell me about your father," she continued.

"I used to hear him crying at night after he thought we were asleep. His own father had been captured during the second exile along with a group of priests that included Rebbe Ezekiel. My father kept weeping and saying, 'We were wrong . . . we were wrong . . . and now my family will pay the price.' I didn't understand what he had done wrong. Even now I'm not sure."

When he paused, Dinah squeezed his hand. "And then . . . ?"

Iddo looked up at the sky. It was a lighter shade of black above the mountain across from them. The stars were gradually fading, and morning would soon dawn. "And then the end came," he said. "The Babylonian soldiers broke through the walls and flooded the streets. My father told us to stay hidden inside the house while he and the other chief priests went up to defend the temple. We tried to hide, my mother and Jacob and me, along with dozens of other people who crowded together in the house. It had once been a beautiful home with polished stone floors and plastered walls, much finer than our tiny home in Anathoth. But several families lived there with us—women and children and old people. I don't even know who they all were. But after the Babylonians broke through the walls, all we could do was cower there together, hoping they wouldn't find us."

Iddo realized that his shoulders had slumped forward again as if he was trying to hide, trying to make himself small so he wouldn't be seen. His voice dropped to a near whisper. "A long time passed," he finally said. "Jacob and I huddled close to my mother, her arms around us. I put my fingers in my ears to shut out the sounds from the streets outside, screams and cries and shouts. Then thick black smoke began leaking past the shuttered windows and doors and into the tiny room where we hid.

We tried so hard to be quiet, but the smoke grew thicker and thicker until we coughed and choked on it. Then part of the roof collapsed in flames, right in front of us. Our house was on fire and we had to get out! We had to run!"

Iddo stopped. He didn't want to remember any more, but Dinah gave his hand a firm squeeze, encouraging him to continue.

"We ran into the maze of streets, everyone scattering as we tried to escape the flames. Jacob and I each clung to one of Mama's hands, and I could see the terror in her eyes. She led us toward the stairs to the temple, up to where my father was, groping through the smoke. My eyes stung and watered from it. The air felt as hot as the *khamsin* winds that blow in from the desert. But we never made it to the temple. A group of soldiers appeared through the haze, marching straight toward us. Mama tried to turn around and run the other way, but there were soldiers behind us, too. Mama pushed Jacob and me to the ground, shoving us beneath something on the side of the road—a cart or a table, I don't remember what it was. But she didn't have time to hide with us. The soldiers attacked her. One of the men threw her to the ground, climbed on top of her . . ."

Iddo no longer tried to stop his tears. It was impossible. Dinah rested her head on his shoulder. "When the soldier was finished, he pulled out his knife and killed her. He slit my mother's throat in the same cold, practiced way that my father sacrificed sheep." He stopped and covered his face with his hands, unable to speak.

After a moment, he felt Dinah lean away from him. She pulled his hands down from his face and said, "Then what happened, Iddo?" He shook his head, unwilling to tell her the rest. "Please," she said softly. "Tell me."

He drew a breath. Exhaled. "Jacob and I had been clinging to each other, but my brother suddenly broke free and crawled out of our hiding place before I could stop him. He went to

Mama, calling for her. . . . And the soldier killed him, too. He lifted him up in the air by one leg and . . . and smashed his head against the stones." Iddo closed his eyes to shut out the image, but it was still there. It would always be there.

"And all that time," he said when he could speak again, "all that time as I watched them kill my family, I stayed hidden. I was a coward, Dinah, so I hid."

"No. You were a child."

He shook his head. "In all of my nightmares, I'm hiding beneath that cart again. I always tell myself to get up this time, to help my mother, to save her before the soldier kills her. I promise to hang tightly to Jacob this time and not let go. But even in my dreams I can't move. I don't help my mother, and I don't stop my brother from crawling out and going to her. Night after night I'm too cowardly to move."

"You were just a child," she said again. "How could you defend them against soldiers with swords? No one could possibly blame you for what you did."

"No one has to. I blame myself." Iddo ran his hand over his face, wiping his eyes. "Now you know why I never wanted to talk about what happened. I didn't want you to know the truth. I was too ashamed to tell you that I was a coward. And my cowardice is the reason why I lived while all the others died." He looked up at Dinah, her face clearly visible now in the dawning light. He expected to see revulsion in her eyes. She would despise him from now on, and he deserved it. Instead he saw pity. And love.

"Yes, you lived, Iddo," she said, stroking his face. "And now our nation and our people will live, too. We have three beautiful children who wouldn't be alive today if you had died. Seven grandchildren—maybe eight by now if Deborah had her baby. Think of all the generations who will live after you because you had the wisdom to stay hidden."

"It was cowardice."

She shook her head. "And where does the Almighty One fit into your story? If He thought you were a coward, why did He allow you to survive?"

"So He could punish me with exile. And He is still punishing me by sending these nightmares, forcing me to relive my shame."

"Your nightmares come from your own imagination, not from the Holy One. Thousands and thousands of our people were either killed or exiled by the Babylonians. And from what I can see, the same fate met those who believed in God and those who didn't, good people and bad people, heroes and cowards. Even Daniel the Righteous One was sent into exile, wasn't he? He certainly wasn't a coward, am I right?"

"Yes. You're right," he mumbled.

"But you said it yourself, Iddo—our punishment has ended and God is restoring us. If it was His will to destroy our people, He had plenty of chances to do it. But do you believe that He's showing mercy now?"

"He must be because we're back in Jerusalem." Where the sky was growing brighter and brighter, painting the dawning sky pink, turning all of the scattered building stones into gold.

"Then if He's showing you mercy, nothing else matters. Put the past behind you."

She was right. God's people weren't merely coming home, they were rebuilding the temple. Soon, when the altar was finished and the first sacrifices were slain, Iddo could ask God to forgive him for all his sins.

Dinah took his hand again. "Afterward, Iddo. What happened afterward?"

"What do you mean?"

"After you crawled out from your hiding place?"

"I don't know . . . I . . . I remember staying hidden for a very long time . . . until I got hungry. The soldiers finally left, and I couldn't bear to stay there any longer and see my mother and my brother, so I crawled out to search for food. I walked through streets that were black with smoke and blood and soot. Day or night? I didn't know. I had to step over countless bodies because there was no way around them. I was trying to find my way to the temple to look for my father, but none of the streets looked familiar.

"Eventually, I reached the open square at the base of the temple mount where the stairs and the empty ritual baths were. I found a group of survivors all huddled together, guarded by soldiers. But when I saw that these people had food, I didn't care about the soldiers. I was so hungry that I ran toward the survivors and grabbed a piece of bread from a woman's hand. She didn't stop me. She was half-crazed with terror and grief, and she let me have her bread. She kept calling me Gideon, thinking that I was her son. She wanted so much to believe that I was him, so I let her. I never learned her name. She took care of me all the way to Babylon, but she lost her mind from grief not long after we arrived. She had suffered so much abuse that she didn't know who she was anymore, let alone who I was. By then, the Jews who had been carried to Babylon during the first and second exiles all had homes in the city and they took care of all the women and orphans after we arrived, making sure we were fed and had places to live. You know the rest, Dinah."

"Yes, I know the rest."

Morning had come, and it was time to start the workday. Iddo heard the shuffling and murmuring of people moving around in some of the nearby tents, women grinding wheat between stones to make flour, the crackle of kindling when it caught fire. He wrapped his arm around Dinah's shoulder and pulled her close. As a lonely orphan, Iddo had never imagined that he would love another person again. Or be loved by anyone.

"All my life I've hated the Babylonian people," he said. "Hated being among them, looking at them face-to-face. I saw in each one of them the features of the man who slaughtered my family."

"I understand," she said. "And now that you've told me the very worst of it, Iddo, tell me what you remember from before the Babylonians invaded."

"When we still lived in Anathoth?"

"Yes. Tell me what you remember about the good days."

He lowered his head into his hands again. His head ached, hammering as hard as it had during those long months in Jerusalem when he was always thirsty, always hungry.

He heard Dinah's cousin Shoshanna singing as she prepared breakfast in a neighboring tent, and he remembered that his mother used to sing, too. "My mother loved Shabbat. She used to say it was her favorite day."

"Why?"

"Because she didn't have to cook or clean or wash anything for an entire day. She could rest and play with us, sing to us."

"And your father?"

Iddo reached through the open tent flap behind him and picked up the ram's horn that the priest had given him to use for practice. As he ran his fingers down the shofar's long, gentle curve, another buried memory suddenly came to him. His father had taught him to make a buzzing sound with his lips, making them vibrate against each other. Iddo imitated the sound, stiffly at first, but it became easier and easier as he continued doing it, letting his lips relax. Dinah watched him, saying nothing.

"That was how my father played the shofar. He said his lips did all the work. The horn simply made the buzzing sound louder so it would carry into the distance."

"Show me, Iddo."

"I'll wake the entire caravan."

"Do it softly, then."

He repeated the buzzing sound with his lips, then lifted the shofar and pressed the narrow end of it against his mouth. The shofar gave a short *toot*. "Abba said he used his tongue to make the calls. He would go 'tu, tu, tu' with his tongue against the mouthpiece. I remember now!" Iddo held it to his lips again and made another soft *toot*, wary of blowing too loudly and waking his neighbors—or sending the ones who were already awake into a panic. He lowered the horn to his lap. It was a start.

Dinah leaned against him, and he wrapped his arms around her, holding her tightly. Across the valley from them, the sun had risen in splendor behind the mountain, so blindingly bright he had to look away.

"What would I ever do without you, Dinah?" he murmured. "When God created the paradise of Eden, He said that everything was good except for one thing—it was not good for the man to be alone. So He created Eve to be Adam's helper. And He gave you to me when I was all alone. Do you know what that word *helper* really means?"

She pulled back to look into his eyes and shook her head.

"It means so much more than simply baking my bread and sharing my bed. Moses used the same word to describe what God does for us. 'He is your shield and helper and your glorious sword.' You're stronger than I am, Dinah. You always have been. I need you in the days ahead to help me face all of my battles. I'm so blessed to have you by my side."

CHAPTER
14

Sunlight leaked through the crack beneath the tent covering when Yael opened her eyes. She smelled smoke from the campfire, the aroma of flatbread baking, and heard the low mumble of voices outside. Her father's sleeping mat was empty. She sat up beneath the sagging roof, rubbing the sleep from her eyes, then lifted the tent flap to look outside. Safta Dinah had spread the rug on the ground for breakfast and Zaki, his grandfather, and her own father all sat around it, eating.

For a second night, Iddo's nightmares had awakened Yael, and once again she had poked her head outside the tent to study the night sky for a while. She had lain awake for so long that now she had overslept. She quickly put on her outer robe, tied the belt around her waist, then crawled outside to sit beside Abba on the rug. No sooner had she sat down when Iddo and Zaki both stood.

"Are you ready to go, Mattaniah?" Iddo asked.

"Go without me," Abba said, waving him away. "I have plans."

"What plans are more important than morning prayers?"

Abba looked away for a moment, then up at Iddo. "I'm going to walk over to the local village this morning."

144

Yael was suddenly wide awake. "May I go with you, Abba?" He didn't seem to hear her.

"What is your business in a Samaritan village, if you don't mind me asking?"

Abba looked uneasy as he ran his fingers through his beard. Yael could tell that he did mind Iddo's question. "Well . . . I went for a walk while you were gone yesterday and found a nice piece of land that I would like to farm. I've decided to talk to the village elders about leasing it or buying it from them."

"Wait. You're *buying* the land? We don't have to purchase land, Mattaniah. The Holy One gave all of it to us."

"I understand," he said, rising to his feet. "But I'm going to offer to pay for it as a gesture of goodwill. The villagers aren't happy about us 'invading' their country, as they see it, and so—"

"That's a very bad idea, Mattaniah. You're setting a bad precedent for the rest of us. The local people will expect everyone to pay for land from now on."

"Look, the patch of land I have in mind already has a small grove of olive trees and a few fig trees on it. The property is neglected and overrun with weeds, but it's close enough for me to farm and still live here in Jerusalem. It's also close to the local village, so I thought I would make friends there."

"Come to prayers with us, first. I think you should discuss this with our leaders."

"There's nothing to discuss," Abba said. "My mind is made up."

Yael tugged on his robe to get his attention. "Abba, may I please—?"

He held up his hand, warning her to wait and not interrupt. "I want this piece of land, Iddo, and I'm going to make the elders an offer."

Iddo exhaled. "Listen, aside from the issue of buying or

not buying, we need builders with your experience to help us with the temple. We have plenty of men who can farm the land already."

"I understand. But I became a builder by necessity, not by choice. Our fathers were brought to Babylon as slaves and put to work. None of us had a choice."

"I thought you liked your work as a builder. You had a good business in Babylon."

"It was work, nothing more. None of us could own land in Babylon, and I want to work the land. I've agreed to live near Jerusalem and to perform my duties as a Levite, and I'll keep that promise. But in between those duties I want to grow wheat and olives and grapes."

The two men studied each other for a long moment. Yael took advantage of the brief silence to tug on Abba's robe again. "May I come with you today? Please, Abba?"

He looked down at her in surprise, as if he had forgotten she was there. "Don't you have work to do here with Safta Dinah?"

Yael stifled a groan at the thought. How could she make him understand how she felt, confined like a sheep in a pen that was too small? She longed to explore the world the way she used to do in Babylon, to meet interesting people like Parthia and learn fascinating things instead of cooking all day. She stood and went to Safta Dinah, wrapping her arms around her for a rare hug, hoping to win her over. "You don't mind if I go with Abba, do you, Safta? Please?"

She brushed a strand of hair from Yael's eyes. "Are you sure that it's safe to go near the Samaritans, Mattaniah?"

"I'm not afraid," Yael said.

"The pagans often choose wives as young as Yael," Safta added. "And she's a lovely girl."

Abba appeared to be thinking. "Well . . ." Yael tensed, preparing to beg some more. "I guess you can come with me," he

146

finally said. "I might seem less threatening to the Samaritans if I have my little daughter along."

Yael squirmed out of Safta's arms and quickly fetched the wooden comb. She stood submissively while Dinah untangled all the snarls and braided her thick hair into a long plait that hung down her back. It was a small price to pay for a chance at freedom. A few minutes later Yael skipped along the Kidron Brook beside her father, thrilled to leave their campsite, the braid thumping against her back. They took a different path than the one the women took when they went for water and headed toward a cluster of low stone houses across the valley. The sun grew hotter and hotter as it climbed in the sky, but Yael didn't care. She felt like dancing beneath it.

As they came to the outskirts of the village, Yael spotted a small shrine similar to the ones she'd seen in Babylonian neighborhoods like Parthia's. "Look, Abba. Someone made an offering to the gods. Do they worship Marduk and Ishtar here?"

"Don't ask questions, Yael. Just stay beside me and keep quiet." He reached for her hand.

A group of men sat on a rug outside the unwalled village as if guarding the entrance. Yael paid no attention to the conversation as Abba stopped to talk with them, gazing instead down the main road into town. The stone houses sprawled in a haphazard circle with an open area in the middle, where ragged children played and chickens pecked in the dirt. Another group of squealing children chased after a goat, waving their arms as they tried to herd it back to its pen. The village looked dirtier than the Jewish community where Yael had lived in Babylon. Rubbish littered the street and the stench of manure made her want to pinch her nose closed. She turned back to her father as the sound of the men's voices grew louder, and she heard one of them say, "You must talk to Zabad, our village leader. The land belongs to him. Come. I will take you to his house."

Yael gripped Abba's hand tightly as they entered the village, crossing the open area. The children stopped to watch as they passed, staring wide-eyed as if they'd never seen strangers before. Yael smiled and wiggled her fingers in a friendly wave but none of them returned the gesture. The man led them across the plaza and down a shadowy lane. The house at the end of it was the largest one in the village and stood apart from the others. They walked through an open gate and into a broad, sunny area paved with cobblestones and bustling with activity. It reminded Yael of Zaki's house back in Babylon, with women of all ages laboring busily over their chores. One woman ground grain, another kneaded dough, a third shaped the dough into flat rounds and laid them on a hot stone to bake. An elderly woman with a face as brown and wrinkled as a raisin ran a shuttle back and forth through the long, vertical threads of a loom. Beside her, a wispy girl with dark, curly hair tried to spin a clump of wool into a strand of yarn. It seemed as though none of the women dared to look up as she and Abba halted in front of the door to the house. A boy Zaki's age stood guard.

"This is Mattaniah, one of the new Jewish settlers," their guide told the boy. "He would like to speak with Zabad."

"This way," the young man said.

Abba let go of Yael's hand. "Wait out here with the women," he said as he followed the others into the house.

Yael looked around again. The women glanced shyly at her before quickly lowering their heads. She wandered over to the girl who struggled to spin the yarn. "Slow down, Leyla," the old woman chided. "It takes patience to spin. If you go too fast the yarn will turn out lumpy and will be useless."

The girl concentrated on her work but the strand of yarn frayed and snapped. "Oh, I can't do this! It's too hard!" She dropped everything into her lap and looked up at Yael. "Do you know how to spin?" she asked.

148

"No, and I don't want to learn either, but Safta Dinah says I have to."

The girl laughed. "My name is Leyla. What's yours?"

"Yael."

Leyla laid her work aside and stood. Her pale skin was nearly transparent, the color of the moon on a bright, sunlit day. Her dark eyes looked large in her thin face, the way Mama's had before she died. Yael could see fine, blue veins beneath Leyla's skin.

"I've never seen you in our village before, and I know everyone," Leyla said. "Are you one of the people from that big caravan that's camped in our valley?"

Yael nodded. "We used to live in Babylon, a long way from here."

"How old are you?" Leyla asked.

"Ten."

Leyla smiled. "We're the same age." But she looked very small and frail to be ten years old. They talked for a while, and Leyla explained that her father had three wives and several sons but she was his only daughter. She pointed to the boy who had led Abba inside—he had emerged from the house again to stand in the doorway—and said, "That's my brother Rafi. He's going to inherit everything Abba owns someday. Rafi is the only friend I have." Yael could see the resemblance between the two. Rafi had the same beautiful wide eyes, the same head of dark, loosely curled hair. He wore it longer than Jewish boys did, and it encircled his head like a thick halo. "Abba doesn't let me play with the village girls," Leyla continued, "because he's afraid I'll get sick if I run around outside. Will you be my friend?"

"I would love to!" Yael remembered the wish she had made on a falling star and was pleased that the moon goddess had answered it so soon. "I don't have any sisters or brothers at all," Yael said. "I used to have a friend named Zaki, but he never wants to have fun anymore."

"Then I'll be your friend from now on. I think the stars must have brought us together." Yael's heart beat a little faster. The stars? Was Leyla a believer, too? She followed Leyla around to the side of the house where a little pen held a small herd of goats. Yael leaned against the fence, petting the goats that wandered over to her. Their heads felt knobby beneath their stiff, rough fur. "You and your father are Jews, aren't you?" Leyla asked after a while. Yael hesitated before finally nodding. "My father is Jewish, too," Leyla said.

"He is? I thought all of the Jews went to Babylon."

"My father's family didn't. His grandfather hid in the mountains when the soldiers came so he wouldn't get taken away. Soldiers brought my mother's family here from a different country. Mama died when I was born and so my grandmother—the one who's trying to teach me to spin—takes care of me now."

"My mama died, too," Yael told her.

"We're so much alike, aren't we? Both the same age, and we both lost our mother. We're going to be best friends, I just know it." Leyla reached for Yael's hand. "Come on, let's go back and sit in the shade. I get dizzy if I stand in the sun for too long." They walked back to Leyla's grandmother and sat on a rug beneath the overhanging roof. Vines climbed up the wooden supports and hung over the top making a cool, shady place to sit.

"Your necklaces are very pretty," Yael said, admiring the pretty stones and feathers and other objects hanging from thin leather thongs around Leyla's neck.

"They're amulets." Leyla fingered the one that looked like a small embroidered pouch. "I get pains and fevers sometimes, and my grandmother says the amulets bring good luck from the gods and keep the fever away."

"My friend Parthia gave me this moonstone for good luck." Yael pulled it out from beneath her tunic to show her.

"It's beautiful. The moon goddess is very powerful."

Yael's heart beat a little faster. "Do you worship the moon goddess?"

"Yes, my grandmother and I do." Leyla eyed her curiously. "But I didn't think Jews like you did."

"Most of the people I know don't believe in her," Yael said, "so I have to keep it a secret. But my mother worshiped her and so do I."

Leyla smiled. "You don't have to keep it a secret here. Why don't you live in our village from now on? We could be best friends."

"I don't think I can live here, but Abba wants to plant a garden near here. If I get a chance, I'll study my star charts and see what the stars say about—"

"You know about astrology?"

Yael jumped when Leyla's grandmother interrupted them. She had forgotten that the old woman was sitting right behind her. Why had she blurted it out? Zaki said Jews would kill a sorceress and Leyla's father was Jewish.

The older woman came to crouch beside her. "It's all right, Yael. We look to the stars for guidance, too."

Yael gave a sigh of relief. This was all too wonderful—finding a new friend and people she could share her beliefs with, without fear. "I'll bring my star charts the next time I come," she said. "We can study them together."

"And I'll make an offering to bribe the goddess so she'll let you come back again," Leyla said. "We'll be best friends."

Abba's voice interrupted before Yael could reply. "Time to go, Yael." He stood in the courtyard with Leyla's brother, beckoning to her.

"Can't we stay a little longer, Abba?"

He shook his head. "Come on." She gave Leyla a quick hug then rose and took Abba's hand as they left the village and started across the valley to their campsite.

"I liked that village, Abba. Can we live there? I made a new friend."

"We need to live with our own people."

"Leyla's father is Jewish like us."

"Yes, I know. He told me. I made him an offer on that piece of land I want to buy, but he says he needs a few days to consider it. But even if I buy or lease the land from him, we're still going to live with Iddo and Dinah and the others in Jerusalem."

"Will I get to play with Leyla again?"

He gave her braid a playful tug. "I have a feeling that maybe you will."

That afternoon Yael sat with Safta Dinah beneath the shade of their tent as the hot summer sun blazed above them. The air around their campsite felt like the inside of an oven. "Iddo says that we'll start building our new house tomorrow," Safta said, fanning herself with the edge of her head scarf. "A real house, not a tent." She seemed like a different woman to Yael, as if the happy, contented woman she'd known in Babylon had stayed behind with the others while a pale, unhappy shadow of that woman traveled here.

"You hate it here, don't you, Safta? You wish you were back home with your family."

Safta glanced around as if worried that someone would overhear them. "Yael, I never said . . ."

"You pretend that you're happy, and you don't let anyone see your tears, but you wish you had never left Babylon."

For a moment, Dinah's fan stilled, her gaze never leaving Yael's. "Where did you get such an idea?" she finally asked.

Yael shrugged. "Sometimes when I look at people it's like I'm looking through their skin. I can see what's on the inside and not just the outside. Parthia said I had a special gift. I can tell what people are thinking and feeling even though they don't say a single word out loud."

Dinah looked away. "It probably doesn't take a special gift to see that I miss my children and grandchildren." She stared into the distance as she slowly fanned the stifling air. "The Persian soldiers will be returning to Babylon any day, and I keep dreaming of traveling home with them."

"You would really walk all the way back there?" Yael asked. "After it took months and months to get here?"

Safta didn't reply, but Yael knew the answer was yes. She would travel twice that distance to go home. Safta didn't seem to care at all about the Jewish God the way that Iddo and Zechariah did. Yael decided to take a chance.

"If you want me to," she said carefully, "I could look at your stars and see if you ever get to go home in the future."

"What?" Dinah stared at Yael, but her expression was one of surprise, not shock or disapproval.

"I learned to read the stars when we lived in Babylon. And Parthia was right when she told you about your future once before, remember? She said you'd be torn away from home, and you were." Dinah nodded and looked away, but not before Yael saw the sheen of tears in her eyes.

"I don't need to look at the stars to know that I won't be going home." She stood and went inside to begin preparing supper.

When Yael saw Zechariah returning with Iddo later that afternoon, she left her half-finished chores and hurried to meet him, longing for someone to talk to.

"What did you do today, Zaki?"

"Nothing . . . We spent the day figuring out where to build our house and where the new house of assembly is going to be." Yael sank down on the ground in the open space in front of her tent and pulled him down beside her.

"You explored the ruins? That sounds like fun." But Zaki's expression looked as gloomy as Safta Dinah's had. He picked up a stick of kindling wood from the pile and drew marks in the dirt with it. "What's wrong, Zaki?"

"Saba is worried because we're supposed to be building the Almighty One's house, not our own."

"Oh," she said with a shrug. "Well, I went to the Samaritan village today and made a new friend. Her name is Leyla, and I can't wait to go back to see her again. You should come with me next time, Zaki. She has a brother your age named Rafi. Maybe we could all play together like you and I used to do, remember?"

"I can't. They're building the house of assembly so they can start a *yeshiva*. I'll have to go there every day to study the Torah when it's ready."

"Every day? Why?"

"Because when our ancestors stopped studying the Torah, they fell into sin."

"They fell . . . where?"

"They started doing things that the Torah forbids. Their biggest sin was worshiping false gods."

Yael rolled her eyes. He would probably call her little carved moon goddess a false one. She was about to ask him why his grandfather had moon dreams if the goddess wasn't real, but Zaki wasn't finished. "Worshiping idols was one of the reasons why Jerusalem was destroyed and our ancestors were carried to Babylon. We have to be very careful to study the Torah from now on."

"But all day?"

Zaki poked in the dirt so hard that the stick cracked in two. "I'm going to be a priest, and it's the priests' job to teach the Torah to everyone. We're supposed to dedicate ourselves to living a holy life as an example to the people. That means I have to know all the rules and everything."

"It seems to me that your God of Abraham is a very gloomy god."

"Yael! Shh! You shouldn't say such things!"

"Why not? Is He going to strike me dead on the spot or something?" She looked up at the sky, shielding her head in mock fear.

Zaki looked uneasy. "Let's talk about something else."

She leaned closer to him and whispered, "Have you had any more dreams about the future?"

"I don't know . . . I had a crazy dream the other night about a Torah scroll flying through the air like a bird."

"That's what happens when you study too much. What do you think it means?"

"What difference does it make? It's just a dream."

"Parthia said that all our dreams have meanings if you know how to interpret them."

"Listen, Yael, you need to forget all those things that wicked woman tried to teach you." He stabbed at the ground again with his broken stick as if he was mad at her.

"Zechariah?" Iddo called. "It's time to pray." He and Abba were getting ready to leave.

"You're praying *again*?" Yael asked in disbelief.

Zaki stood and dropped the stick on the ground. "I have to go."

Yael remained seated. She probably should help Safta Dinah, but she didn't want to. Instead, she looked up at the pale, daytime moon and thought of her new friend, Leyla. Maybe she was looking up at the very same moon. The thought made Yael smile.

CHAPTER

15

N o one could possibly expect Dinah to live here, could they? She looked at the jumble of toppled stones and weed-filled holes that Iddo pointed to, then up at her husband in disbelief. Was he joking?

"We chose this spot because the foundations of these houses aren't too badly damaged," he said. He was still short of breath after the uphill climb from their camp in the valley, and Dinah felt winded, too. "We can rebuild this house with a little work."

"This?" she asked, spreading her arms. "I don't see a house, Iddo. I see huge rocks that are too big for us to move and hundreds of small stones that will take a lifetime to move, and brambles growing where you say my kitchen courtyard will be, and—"

She was afraid she was going to cry, and she didn't want to lose control in front of the others. Zechariah and Mattaniah rummaged among the weeds within earshot, and Yael was making a game of balancing on the foundation walls, leaping over the gaps between them, scaling the higher walls using the ragged stones for steps. "Yael, be careful!" she scolded, venting her frustration.

"I won't fall," she called back. "Watch this!" She struck a pose on one leg, balanced on a teetering wall of rocks, then grinned and leaped across a void to another pile of stones, as graceful as a gazelle on a mountain slope. Dinah turned her back. Yael's father needed to discipline her, but he wasn't paying attention.

Dinah looked at the pile of rubble in front of her again. "I don't understand why we can't build a house down where our camp is in the Kidron Valley. Wouldn't it be easier to build near the spring or the brook?"

"Are we wiser than our ancestors?" Iddo asked. "King David built Jerusalem on this hill for protection."

"Are we in danger down there?"

"Don't put words in my mouth. I didn't say we weren't safe."

But Dinah could always tell when he was avoiding a subject by the way he played with the fringes on the corners of his garment. He was twirling them now. "Tell me the truth, Iddo. I have a right to know."

"Some of our Samaritan neighbors are a little . . . discontented," he said, lowering his voice. "They see us as invaders. Once they learn about King Cyrus' decree, things will settle down and . . ." He paused as Zechariah made his way back to them.

"Saba, are those caves over there on that hill?" he asked, pointing to a spot across the valley.

"I haven't seen them up close," Iddo said, "but I'm told they're tombs."

"Real tombs?" Yael asked. She jumped down from a nearby foundation wall with a graceful leap. "Do they have dead men's bones inside them and everything? Let's explore them sometime, Zaki. Want to?"

Iddo replied before Zechariah could. "Our families are priests and Levites, Yael. The Torah has rules about becoming ritually unclean from dead bodies."

"Oh. That's too bad," she said with a sigh. She climbed onto the low wall again, then jumped down to the other side and crouched to pick up pieces of broken pottery. "I'm finding some really big pieces, Zaki," she called. "Come see."

He went to kneel beside her, and a few minutes later Dinah heard him shouting, "Saba! Come look what I found! I think it's an arrowhead!"

Iddo climbed over the rocky foundation stones and took the metal object from Zechariah's hand. "Yes, I think it is. I imagine you'll find more of them, if you look. But listen, if you see any bones, don't touch them. They need to be handled with respect and dignity, and buried by men who aren't priests or Levites."

The talk of arrowheads and bones made Dinah shiver. "Tell me the truth about the Samaritans, Iddo," she said when he returned to her side.

"Mattaniah seems to think we can trust them. But our leaders decided that the sooner we move up here from the valley the better."

"I never felt threatened back home in Babylon," she said.

"Joel and your cousin Shoshanna are moving right next door to us. You'll have family close by again and—"

"Will this be our main room? Right here?" Dinah interrupted. She needed to stop him before he tried to tell her that it would be just like home. It wouldn't be.

"Yes. We'll build on these foundations." He traced the outline with a sweep of his hand. "One room will be enough at first, for you and me and Zechariah. As soon as we clear away these stones and repair these walls, we can put our tent covering over it for a roof and live here. I want to get settled as quickly as possible so we can start working on the temple again." He climbed over the low wall and into the space he had indicated, then held out his hand to Dinah as if inviting her into their home.

"It's very small . . ." she said, stepping over the rocks.

"I know. But it's just for now. I'll build you an outdoor hearth near that spot where Yael is digging. I found some blackened stones over there, so I think that's where a hearth used to be. This second, adjoining room will be for Mattaniah and Yael. And we'll repair this alcove back here for storage. There's even a cistern beneath the floor, chiseled out of the bedrock. Once we clean it out and re-plaster it, it'll be as good as new."

"Maybe we'll find buried treasure inside," Yael said. She wandered over to peer inside the cistern, and when she stood, Dinah smoothed her tangled hair away from her face and out of her eyes.

"You need to let me braid your hair again," she said. "You're such a pretty girl, but your hair needs to be tamed and un-tangled."

"It's fine," she said, shrugging away Dinah's hand. Dinah looked up at Iddo to see if he noticed Yael's unruliness, but he was much too engrossed with his building plans.

"Eventually, we can build a wooden roof over these rooms," Iddo continued, "and channel water into the cistern when it rains. That will spare you the long walk down to the spring every day. Once we plaster the walls and the roof . . ." *Don't say it!* But she couldn't stop him in time. "It will be just like our house in Babylon."

Dinah sighed and closed her eyes. This would never be like their house in Babylon, overflowing with children and grand-children. Why did Iddo talk as if it would?

"Good morning, Joel," Iddo called out. She looked up to see her cousin Shoshanna and her husband walking toward them.

"This view is beautiful!" Shoshanna said. "Just think—we'll get to wake up to this incredible sight every morning." She halted beside Dinah, linking her arm through hers. "And there's a nice cool breeze up here, too. Won't it be wonderful to live in a real house again, side by side? It will be just like back home."

Dinah gritted her teeth. Not Shoshanna, too!

They cleared stones and weeds all morning, piling rocks on top of the foundations to make the walls higher. The hardest things to clear away were the thick thatches of brambles with roots that seemed to go all the way to the base of the mountain. Dinah heaped the pulled weeds into a pile to dry out and use for kindling. When she lifted a medium-sized building stone, the ground beneath it squirmed and writhed with snakes. Dinah cried out and dropped the stone, nearly falling as she quickly backed away. Some of the eggs in the nest were still intact, some half-open, and some had already hatched, sending innumerable small snakes slithering over and under the rocks. Everyone came running, even Shoshanna and her husband. "What is it, Safta?" Zaki asked.

"There's a nest of snakes under that stone. Be careful!" Dinah stood at a respectful distance, but Yael crouched close to see.

"Can I pick one up?" she asked.

"No, don't!"

Iddo hefted a sizeable rock and began crushing the living snakes and the eggs. So many of them slithered around that Zaki and Yael had to help him. Dinah looked away with a shiver.

They worked all afternoon until it was time to return to their camp. "We've made good progress on our house," Iddo told her as they ate together that evening. "Tonight will be the last night we'll sleep down here beside the cart. Tomorrow we'll carry our goods up the hill and live there from now on. We'll be settled in our house in time to celebrate Shabbat in two days."

Dinah closed her eyes. She couldn't imagine celebrating the Sabbath in a pile of rubble. The caravan had rested on the Sabbath all the way here, and it had been good to stop for a day and not have to pack everything up. But as badly as she needed the day of rest, Dinah knew it wouldn't be a proper Sabbath without her family gathered around her, laughing and eating and celebrating life.

The first night she spent in their half-finished house, Dinah felt so weary and discouraged that she couldn't stop her tears. Her blistered hands were scraped and sore, her muscles so tired from moving rocks all day, that she didn't know how she would carry a water jug to the brook and back. Her body ached from bending and lifting stone after stone, and there were still so many of them left to move. Did the earth grow new ones while she slept?

The men had stretched the tent covering over the foundations to form a roof, weighing it down with rocks. Dinah had to crawl inside on her hands and knees since the walls were barely three feet high—and she couldn't forget the snakes.

She had known the splendor of Babylon, and even though her neighborhood of mud-brick houses hadn't been much, it had been home, the place where her children had been born and where they'd grown. Iddo noticed her tears as he watched her unroll their sleeping mat for the night.

"What's wrong, Dinah?"

"We gave up our home, our family, for this?"

"We're doing this for our children's sakes. We sacrificed what we had so that they can have a better future. So they can worship the Almighty One in His temple."

"But our children aren't here. And to tell you the truth, I don't think they'll ever come." She brushed away a tear and shook out their blanket. "I keep thinking of Rachel and wondering if she's expecting a baby yet. Deborah's baby must have been born by now, and Shoshanna and I weren't there to help her. I'll probably have a dozen more grandchildren someday, babies that I'll never see, never hold, children whose first steps I'll never watch—"

"Don't, Dinah." He took the blanket from her and gripped her hands in his. "You told me to forget the past, remember? Now you must do the same."

"I can't forget our children and grandchildren, Iddo! You can't ask me to forget them."

"We won't forget them. But the Almighty One told us to come here, and we chose to obey Him. Blessings come from obedience. Sarah and Abraham left their families, and didn't God bless them?"

"Sarah didn't leave children and grandchildren behind." Dinah pulled her hands free and finished spreading the blanket. Her tears still fell as she lay down to sleep.

The next morning Shoshanna greeted Dinah with a smile, as cheerful as always. "Let's prepare Shabbat together today," she said. "We'll make all the food and then eat it together. Want to?" Dinah didn't know what to say. Shoshanna walked through the opening where the courtyard gate would be and bent to admire the hearth that Iddo had made. "We should cook everything on your hearth," she said. "Yours looks much nicer than mine."

"Yes. Iddo finished it for me last evening. It . . . it will be nice to work together. Thank you, Shoshanna. It will be very nice."

"It was Iddo's idea. He came over this morning and suggested that I ask you."

Of course. Dinah turned away so Shoshanna wouldn't see her tears. Iddo was trying so hard to make her happy, offering her everything except what she wanted most—to go home.

Shoshanna slipped her arm around Dinah's shoulder. "What's wrong, Dinah? You seem so sad."

"This place will never be home. I miss my family, and I miss delivering babies, don't you?"

"The babies will come, you'll see." She smiled and rested her head on Dinah's shoulder. "And so will our families. In the meantime, we get to prepare a new home for them."

"I hope you're right." She heard a rustling sound behind her and turned to see Yael emerging from her tent. "There you are," Dinah said. "Shoshanna and Joel are going to have Shabbat with us. We're going to cook the meal together."

"Then you don't need my help." Quick as a cat, Yael jumped

up on a half-finished wall to scamper away. But Dinah was just as quick and grabbed Yael's slender arm to stop her.

"Oh no, you don't! It's going to take all three of us if we want to be finished by sundown."

She gave Yael several jobs to do—sorting lentils, grinding grain into flour, peeling cloves of garlic. Each time Yael finished a task she would ask, "Now are we done? Can I go now?" Her shoulders would sag like a weary old man's every time Dinah replied, "No, Yael, there's still more work to do."

Late that afternoon, the three of them walked down to the spring to draw extra water for tomorrow's day of rest. It was a much longer walk than the one Dinah used to make to the well in Babylon, and the trip home would be uphill, carrying the heavy jars. Yael tried to balance a jug on her head like Dinah and Shoshanna but it kept slipping off. "Careful!" Dinah chided. "You'll have more potsherds to add to your collection, and I'll have one less water jug."

"I hate doing women's work like cooking and carrying water," Yael said with a sigh.

"I promised your mother I would turn you into a proper young woman and find you a good husband—"

"I don't want a husband!"

Shoshanna laughed. "You make it sound like Dinah was offering to find you a scorpion."

"The two are just as bad." Yael's jar slipped off her head again, and she caught it moments before it hit the ground. Dinah looked away.

"You may not be thinking of a husband now," Shoshanna said, "but someday a young man will catch your eye and your heart will be drawn to him, and he'll be the only thing you can think about."

Dinah remembered feeling that way about Iddo. She had been overjoyed when their betrothal was announced, and had

163

floated on a cloud of happiness for days. She hadn't been able to stop smiling, and her sisters said she even smiled in her sleep. That happiness had never faded after all these years—until now. Now her joy seemed to die a little more each day, replaced by resentment as bitter as vinegar. Dinah was aware of what was happening, but she didn't know how to stop it.

"One day the young men will be fighting for your hand, Yael," Shoshanna continued. "Just like they fought for Dinah's. She was such a beautiful woman—and she still is. My husband Joel certainly thinks so. He wanted to marry her—did you know that? But Dinah was in love with Iddo. Only Iddo. I've always envied you, Dinah. I know I'm short and plump and that my hair is a frizzy mess—"

"But Joel loves you," Dinah said. "I can tell he does."

"Why do I have to get married at all?" Yael asked. She gave up trying to balance her jug and carried it in her arms.

"Because that's what we were created for," Shoshanna said. "When the Almighty One made the world, He saw that everything was good except for one thing. He said it was not good for the man to be alone. So he gave Adam a wife to be his helper."

"Adam just wanted someone to do all his work," Yael mumbled.

When they reached the bottom of the long, steep slope that led from the city, Dinah saw a crowd of women gathered around the spring. "Look at all the people!" Shoshanna said. "I hope it won't take too long to fill our jugs. Shabbat is coming."

"I'll run ahead and save us a place," Yael said.

"No, Yael! Wait—" She didn't listen. She took off ahead of them, running down the road like a deer.

"I apologize for Yael," Dinah told Shoshanna. "Her family let her run wild when Miriam was dying, and the girl picked up some terrible habits. I'm trying to tame her, but I hardly know where to begin."

"We all have a little too much Babylon in us. But you're doing a good job, Dinah. She'll soon settle down. Just keep loving her." But Dinah wasn't sure if she wanted to risk being a mother to Yael if it meant losing her someday the way she'd lost her other daughters.

They reached the spring and saw that a group of local women had formed a circle around the reservoir, standing with their water jars, blocking the way. Dinah and Shoshanna joined the growing crowd of Jewish women huddled off to the side looking bewildered and frightened. "What's going on?" Dinah asked one of them.

"We've been waiting for our turn, but they won't let us through. We can't get past them to draw water."

Shoshanna stepped toward the women who were blocking the way, smiling as she said, "Excuse me, please. Our families need fresh water."

"This spring is ours, not yours," one of the local women shouted back.

"I'm sure there's enough for everyone if—" But the women drowned out her words with loud cries, waving their arms as if trying to chase away a flock of birds.

Dinah's pulse began to race. "Let's go home," she told Shoshanna. "We need to get out of here." She scanned the crowd of women, searching for Yael.

"Dinah's right, we may as well leave," one of the other Jewish women said. "They're going to block the spring until the sun goes down, and it'll be too late to draw water, let alone carry it all the way up the hill."

"Where's Yael?" Dinah asked, her panic swelling. "Do you see her?"

"Maybe we should walk back to the caravan camp and draw water from the Kidron Brook," Shoshanna said.

"There isn't enough time," Dinah said. "It's too far, and we need to be home before the sun sets. . . . Yael! Yael, where are you?" she called. The local women were still shouting their fearsome cries. Dinah wanted to run.

"I'm right here," Yael said, weaving through the crowd.

Dinah sagged with relief. "Come on. We're leaving." She turned to hurry back the way she'd come, with Yael and Shoshanna and the other Jewish women following her. "It was a mistake to move back here," she said as she walked. "This land and the spring belong to the local villagers. They've been living here all their lives, and we just arrived."

"Everything will work out," Shoshanna soothed. "We're all a little frightened right now. But they'll share the water with us, you'll see."

"I hope we'll have enough to last until Shabbat ends."

"Why can't we just come back tomorrow?" Yael asked.

"Because it's the Sabbath," Shoshanna replied, "and the Almighty One is giving us a day of rest."

"He sure has a lot of rules to remember," Yael said. "Doesn't He know it's impossible to obey them all? Besides, I don't see why we need to rest for a whole day. I'm not tired."

"We don't rest because we're tired," Shoshanna said. "It's a privilege to be able to stop working whether we're finished or not—and you know our work is never finished. The Holy One gives us an entire day of freedom. Believe me, you'll be thankful for it tomorrow when we can rest and not worry about cooking food because it's already prepared."

By the time the men returned home from their prayers, Dinah and Shoshanna had the rug spread out with the food arranged in the middle of it and the Sabbath lights kindled. The courtyard was open to the sky, and as everyone sat down to eat, the first stars began to appear above them. Iddo recited the blessings over the wine and the bread, the way he had every Friday evening in Babylon. Dinah closed her eyes, remembering her family, picturing them gathered for the meal with their little ones. Were they still keeping Shabbat without them?

She told Iddo what had happened at the spring as they lay in bed together later that night. "From now on we'll send guards with you to protect you. Our women can all go to the spring together later in the morning, after the local women are finished."

"By then the day will be too hot. That's why we go early in the morning or before dusk."

"Everything will be fine, Dinah. Don't worry. God will protect us."

That wasn't what Dinah wanted to hear. She shifted on the sleeping mat, unable to get comfortable beside Iddo.

The Day of Atonement was coming in a few months, the day when Dinah was supposed to confess all her sins and ask the Holy One for forgiveness. She was supposed to reconcile with those she was angry with and ask their forgiveness. But as she looked up at the goatskin ceiling hovering a few feet above her head, it seemed to her that Iddo was the one who needed to ask for forgiveness. He was the one who had dragged her here so far from home.

CHAPTER
16

Yael thought of her friend Leyla every time she saw the pale daytime moon. "When are we going back to Leyla's village?" she asked her father again and again.

"When our new house is finished," he told her. "I'm much too busy to return now." But at breakfast one morning, Iddo had declared their house fit to live in.

"I'm going back to work on the temple mount," he told everyone.

"Now can we go down to Leyla's village, Abba?" she begged. "Please?"

"Not today. I promised to help Iddo."

Yael fingered the round lump of her moonstone, hidden beneath her dress, and closed her eyes, asking the goddess to please make a way for her to see her friend Leyla. In the meantime, she would have to help Dinah with all the tasks that she hated like cooking and carrying water.

Their group of women left late in the morning to walk down the hill to the spring, knowing that the local women would be gone by then. Two Jewish men accompanied them to act as guards. When they arrived, one local woman sat on the stone lip of the reservoir, and Yael recognized her dark, wrinkled face right away—Leyla's grandmother! She broke into a run.

"Yael, stop! Come back!" she heard Dinah yelling behind her, but she kept on running.

"You're Leyla's grandmother, aren't you?" Yael said breathlessly. "I'm her friend, Yael."

The old woman rose to her feet. "Yes, I know who you are. I've been waiting to speak to you."

"To me? Why?"

"Leyla is sick, and she's asking to see you. Will you come to the village with me?"

"I would love to!" The moon goddess had heard her prayer. Yael set her water jug on the ground, ready to leave it behind and go. But a moment later, Dinah gripped her arm.

"What are you doing, running off?" She gave Yael's arm a little shake. "Didn't you hear me calling you?"

"My friend Leyla is sick, and she's asking for me. Can I please go with her grandmother to visit her? Please?"

Dinah backed up a step, pulling Yael with her. The pressure of her fingers made Yael's arm hurt. "We have to ask your father. I'm sorry," she said, addressing Leyla's grandmother. "It's up to him to give permission."

"Tell him that Zabad has personally made this request for his daughter's sake."

"I will. If Mattaniah agrees to let her come, he'll bring her to your village." Dinah continued to step backward as she spoke, tugging Yael with her.

"Ow! You're hurting me. And what about my water jug?"

"I'm not letting go of you again, Yael. Every time I do you run off instead of obeying me." She moved forward so Yael could retrieve her jug but Leyla's grandmother was already walking away, heading down the road to her village alone.

Since Dinah refused to release Yael's arm, Shoshanna had

to fill all three jugs and hand them out. Dinah still wouldn't let go as they retraced their steps up the hill. When they reached the top, she sent one of the guards to fetch Yael's father from the temple mount.

"What's going on?" he asked breathlessly when he arrived twenty minutes later. Iddo had come with him. "Is everything all right?"

Dinah finally released Yael, and she ran to her father, flinging her arms around his waist. Her words came out in a rush of tears. "Leyla is sick, and she's asking for me. Her grandmother was waiting for me at the spring to take me there but Safta wouldn't let me go. Can I please visit Leyla? Please, Abba?"

"Who's Leyla?" Iddo asked. "The guard said the old woman was one of the local Samaritans."

"She is," Abba replied. "Leyla's father is the man I spoke with about that piece of land I want to buy. He's the village leader. I think I'd better take Yael there."

"Will she be safe?" Dinah asked. "I thought the local people hated us."

"Some of them do. But I think we can trust Zabad."

"Thank you, Abba! Thank you!" Yael hugged her father tightly, then ducked into their makeshift house to fetch her bag. Maybe she could use her star charts and the little moon goddess to help Leyla get well. "I'm ready," she told her father a moment later.

On the long walk down to the village, Yael wavered between excitement at seeing her friend and fear for her health. Leyla's brother Rafi met them at the gate to the compound, and she started to ask him a thousand questions, but Abba put his fingers over her lips to stop her. The last time she'd visited, she'd noticed that men spoke only with men and women with women.

"Thank you for bringing your daughter," Rafi said to Abba.

"I will take her inside, and you are free to go. I know my sister will be very happy to see her."

Abba laid his hand on Yael's head. He seemed reluctant to leave. "I'll come back for you in a little while, Yael. Try . . . try to remember all the things that Safta Dinah taught you."

Rafi led Yael through his courtyard and into the large central room inside the house with doorways leading off from it. Rafi opened one of those doorways and gestured to where Leyla lay sleeping on a pile of cushions. Her skin looked even paler than the last time, and a fine sheen of sweat glistened on her forehead. A flood of memories washed over Yael of how her own mother had lain ill this way for such a long time. She felt a stab of fear—and then anger at the thought of losing Leyla, too. She knelt by Leyla's side and took her hand. It felt very warm. Leyla's eyes fluttered open, and she smiled.

"Yael . . . you came back. . . ."

"How are you feeling?"

"Better now that you're here."

They talked as if no time had passed at all, as if they had known each other all their lives. But after a while, a loud argument outside the bedroom door interrupted them. Yael opened the door and saw Leyla's grandmother holding a pottery cup in her hands while Leyla's father tried to wrest it away from her.

"Leyla needs this," her grandmother insisted. "It's a special potion made with goat's milk."

"And blood! You mixed it with blood!"

"It will give her strength."

"My religion forbids us to drink blood!"

"And mine prescribes it! Do you want your daughter to get well or don't you?"

Yael went back to Leyla's bedside. "I hate it when they fight because of me," Leyla whispered. "Grandmother knows lots

171

of potions from her ancestors, but Abba doesn't like me to use them."

"When my mama was sick, my father was willing to try anything, even if our neighbors said it was forbidden." Yael didn't want to tell Leyla that nothing had worked. Or that she still blamed her Jewish neighbors and their unbelief.

The old woman eventually won the argument and brought Leyla the cup. Yael helped her sit up so she could drink it. "Don't sip it, Leyla," her grandmother said. "Drink it all at once." The potion was pale pink. Was she really drinking blood? Leyla took a sip and made a face.

"How does it taste?" Yael asked.

"It doesn't matter," the old woman said, frowning at her. "Just drink it down. It will make you well." Leyla obeyed, gulping the contents, then sank down on the cushions again as if the effort had tired her out.

"I have something to make you better, too," Yael said after the old woman left again. She lifted the moonstone necklace from around her own neck and slipped it around Leyla's. "You can borrow this. It'll help you get better."

"Thank you." Yael could tell by her voice that Leyla was growing tired.

"I brought my charts, too," she quickly continued. "The stars can tell us all kinds of things about your future. When's your birthday?"

"The tenth day of Ab. I turned eleven a month ago."

"That means you were born under the sign of the lion."

"Is that good?"

"Yes! It means you're strong and courageous like a lion."

"I think I'll sleep now."

Yael spread the charts on the floor beside the bed after Leyla drifted to sleep, trying to remember everything Parthia had taught her. She wouldn't let her friend die. Parthia had been wrong about Mama getting better, but she'd said it was because Zaki's family lived next door. Would it be the same in this village? Would Leyla's father hinder the stars' power?

"I see you brought your astrology charts." Yael whirled around when she heard the old woman's voice. Leyla's grandmother searched Yael's face as if trying to look inside her. Parthia had looked at her that way, too. "Don't worry, Yael," she finally said. "I believe in the power of the stars, too."

Yael sagged with relief. "I only know a few things. I was just learning to read these charts when we had to leave Babylon."

"May I see them?" She reached out with her wrinkled hand, and again Yael felt a moment of panic. What if the old woman was lying? What if she tossed them into the fire before Yael could stop her? But she didn't. She carried them over to the window where the light was better, to study them. "Where did you get these? They are beautifully done. I didn't think Jews like you consulted the stars."

"I knew a seer in Babylon. She gave them to me."

"I might be able to teach you a little more. But don't let Leyla's father see them."

They studied the charts as Leyla slept and discovered which heavenly bodies currently decided Leyla's fortune. "This is very good," her grandmother said. "Now that we know which gods we must influence, I'll go and prepare the proper offerings to make Leyla well." She rolled up the scrolls and handed them back to Yael, smiling.

Yael sat by Leyla's side all day, telling stories about life in Babylon when she was awake, describing how she and Zaki used to explore along the canal. Some of Yael's stories made Leyla laugh, and her grandmother said that was the best potion of all. Yael didn't want the day to end, but she could see the sun sinking lower in the sky, the shadows in the room growing longer. When she heard the door to the room open, she looked up to find Abba standing there beside Rafi.

"Time to go home, Yael."

"Oh, please let her stay. Please?" Leyla begged.

"Yes, please, Abba?"

Leyla's grandmother spoke to Yael's father without looking at him, her eyes never leaving the floor. "My lord, Leyla's father would be honored if you would allow your daughter to stay with us for a few more days until Leyla is stronger. Yael is very good medicine for her. Her stories cheer my granddaughter and help her forget her pain."

"Are you sure she's not a bother?"

"Not at all, my lord."

"Well . . . then I guess she may stay."

Leyla smiled and gave Yael's hand a squeeze. "Thank you."

"Please, wait a moment longer, my lord," her grandmother said, "while I fetch some gifts to send home to your family to show our appreciation."

"I thank you as well, my lord," Rafi said. "I sometimes stay with Leyla when she's ill, but I had to work for my father today. Thank you for letting your daughter take my place."

For the next few days, Yael spent all her time in her friend's room. At times, Leyla burned with fever and whimpered from the pain in her bones and joints. Yael told story after story to distract her friend and even sang songs to help soothe her to sleep. While Leyla slept, Yael studied the star charts with her grandmother. The old woman reminded Yael of all the things that Parthia had taught her, things she had forgotten in the months since leaving Babylon. At night, they walked outside into the open courtyard and studied the sky. "That's Leyla's sign, the lion," her grandmother said. She pointed to the sky overhead as Yael picked out the stars in the constellation. "But see the position of the moon within her constellation? And the moon's phase? What does that tell you?"

"The moon is waning! That's why Leyla is sick, isn't it!"

"Very good. You have a gift for this, Yael."

"If anyone finds my charts back home, they'll take them away from me."

"How foolish! Your own people once knew the power of the stars. David, your most famous king, wrote a psalm of praise to God about learning from the stars. He wrote, 'The heavens declare the glory of God; the skies proclaim the work of his hands. Day after day they pour forth speech; night after night they display knowledge. There is no speech or language where their voice is not heard. Their voice goes out into all the earth, their words to the ends of the world.' So, no matter where we go, no matter what age we live in, the heavens will speak to us and give us wisdom."

"I knew Parthia was right! I knew it! Wait until I tell Zaki!"

"Be careful who you share your insights with, Yael. The spirit of unbelief can be a powerful force."

"That's why my mother died. It's why Parthia's spells didn't work."

The old woman nodded sadly. "And it's why Leyla's mother died, as well. But we can use the knowledge from the heavens to protect Leyla. I'm so glad you're her friend and that you're a believer."

By the time Abba returned for Yael a few days later, Leyla was well enough to sit outside and look up at the stars with them. Her father, Zabad, was so pleased that he agreed to sell Mattaniah the parcel of land he had asked for.

"Come back and visit every chance you get," Leyla begged as they hugged each other good-bye.

"May I come back, Abba? Please?"

"Well . . . . you're supposed to help Safta Dinah with the cooking. You have to do your share of the work."

"You must let her come," Zabad insisted. "She has brought happiness to my daughter and made her well again. She is good for Leyla."

"Then of course she may visit."

Grandmother loaded Abba down with gifts: almonds and figs from their trees, vegetables from their garden, a skin of aged wine, and fresh goat cheese wrapped in grape leaves. "Bring your charts when you come again," she whispered as she kissed Yael's cheek.

"I will."

Yael hoped her father hadn't heard her mention the charts, but on the way home he asked, "What does she want you to bring when you come?"

"Nothing."

"Yael, you know we don't have much, and Leyla's father isn't giving me the land for free. By the time I pay for it with a portion of our crops, we'll barely have enough to eat ourselves. What are you promising to bring her?"

"Abba, they have plenty of food. Didn't you see how much? And their home is three times bigger than ours was in Babylon. They don't need anything like that from us. Leyla just wants to be my friend. She only has brothers, and her mother died just like Mama did, and so she wants us to be friends." Yael held her breath, hoping he wouldn't ask again.

"Just be careful what you promise. Her people are very suspicious of us as it is, and we need them if we're going to survive here in the land."

"Why can't we all be friends like Leyla and me? Why don't her people and ours get along, Abba?"

"It's complicated. I would like it if we all got along, but I guess our biggest disagreement has to do with religion. We believe our God gave this land to us, and they believe their gods gave the same land to them. Religion can cause the biggest divisions of all."

Yael remembered the argument between Leyla's father and her grandmother over the potion that Leyla drank. And she knew she had to hide the little figurine and the charts that Parthia had given her from people who didn't share her beliefs. Yael had learned a lot from Leyla's grandmother, and soon she would be able to read the future in the stars and make decisions for herself. In the meantime, she couldn't wait to return to the village and visit her friend.

Chapter 17

Zechariah held the weighted cord next to the stone wall of his house and let it dangle freely. As he had feared, the last course of stones weren't quite straight. He would have to remove them and build all over again—and his arms already ached from lifting them into place. He groaned aloud in frustration.

"What's wrong, Zaki?" Yael peered around the corner of the house from where she'd been working with his grandmother.

"My studies ended early today, and I wanted to get this part of the wall done before Saba comes home. I wanted to surprise him. Now I have to take all these stones down again."

"Why isn't your grandfather working on the house with you?"

"Because he's rebuilding the temple, and that's much more important." Zechariah lifted a stone from the top row and dropped it to the ground.

Yael came to stand beside him, one hand on her hip. "I don't understand why you have to take them down."

"Because the wall isn't straight. See?" He held up the weighted cord to show her. "If it's just a little bit off in the beginning and you don't correct it, it will get further and further off as you build higher. The entire wall could collapse." He reached up to remove another stone and set it on the ground. Yael sat down on a large rock to watch him, idly jiggling her foot. "Aren't you supposed to be helping my grandmother?" he asked her.

"She went to borrow something from Shoshanna. You and Abba got a lot done while I was visiting Leyla," she told him. "The walls in my room are higher than my head now. I can stand up under the tent covering."

Zechariah removed another block, then held up the cord again. "Saba says the Torah is like this plumb line. We can measure our lives with His word to see if we're living straight. And if we stray from the Holy One's laws just a tiny bit, pretty soon our whole life will be off course."

Yael gave a long, loud sigh. "All you ever talk about is the Torah. Don't you get tired of studying sometimes? Don't you want to do something different for a change?"

Zechariah remembered going to the canal in Babylon with Yael, watching the ships sailing past, feeling free. He remembered walking to work with his father and watching the laborers unload cargo from all over the world. Now he spent all day studying with the handful of boys his age who had come to Jerusalem with their parents.

Yes, he wanted to tell Yael. Yes, he did wish he could do something different for a change, but he didn't dare say so out loud. "Studying the Torah is very important," he said instead.

Yael exhaled again. "My friend Leyla has a brother your age, and he doesn't study all the time."

Zechariah felt a stab of jealousy, envying Yael's freedom. He turned his back on her and continued working. "What do you do when you visit your friend?" he asked.

"Well, we couldn't play the last time I was there because Leyla was too weak to get out of bed. So I told her stories about how we used to go exploring in Babylon. Remember? She wants to go with us when she's better. She gets sick a lot, so I gave her

179

my—" Yael stopped so abruptly that Zechariah glanced over his shoulder to see why. She had her hand over her mouth, a guilty expression on her face.

"You gave her your . . . what?"

"Never mind."

"No, I'm curious. What did you give her?" He stopped working and leaned against the wall, waiting.

"Just a necklace I had. She's much better now. You should come with me sometime and meet her brother Rafi."

Zechariah would never be allowed to go. He felt another stab of jealousy and wished he could do something to erase the contented smile from Yael's face. "You should stay away from that village," he said. "Those people are our enemies."

"That's not true. Abba and I made friends with them."

"They're idol worshipers, you know. They don't worship the same God we do."

"That's not true, either. Leyla's father is a son of Abraham."

Zechariah couldn't ruffle her contentment, and now he felt more irritated with her than before. He leaned close to her to whisper, "Did you get rid of your pagan stuff, yet?"

"I don't know what you're talking about," she said with a shrug.

He returned to his labor, reaching up to remove another stone from the top of the wall. "Well, instead of sitting there, why don't you gather up some of those smaller rocks to stuff between the cracks?"

She did what he asked, picking up a handful of smaller stones and carefully wedging them between the larger ones. "Don't you ever wish we could go exploring like we used to?" she asked as they worked.

"I'm not a child anymore. I'm a son of the covenant now—and I like studying. Every time I think I've learned all of the lessons from one passage in the Torah or studied all of the words in one verse, I discover that there's another layer of meaning beneath it and—"

"You're no fun anymore. Why did you come to Jerusalem, anyway? You could have studied the Torah back home." She struck her usual pose, her hand on her hip, a look of disapproval on her face.

Had he imagined that the Almighty One had spoken to him? Zechariah could barely remember the feeling of His presence on the day of his bar mitzvah. He did remember being in the tug-of-war between Saba and his father, remembered the dull pain he used to get in his stomach when they had argued about him. But God had proven that He was real, and Zechariah had obeyed His call to come. If only God would speak to him again and tell him why. What was he supposed to be doing here—besides studying? Every night he tried to remember the dreams that disturbed his sleep, hoping God would speak to him through them. The dreams seemed weighted with importance, but Zechariah could never remember them when he woke up, their content and meaning floating just beyond his grasp.

He lifted another stone from the top and dropped it to the ground. What would he be doing if he had stayed in Babylon? Would he be working with his father by now? But staying would have meant disobeying God's call. "Maybe after we finish building our house I'll have time to explore again," he told Yael. At least he hoped it was true.

"Promise? Promise that we'll do something fun when we have time?"

Zechariah hesitated, aware that he had fallen into Yael's trap before by making rash promises. But he missed her and longed to spend time with her again. Most of all, he longed to convince her to give up her sorcery. Before he could stop himself he replied, "I promise."

"Thank you!" She scampered off to finish preparing dinner

while he grabbed another rock from the last course of stones and tossed it onto the ground. Yael had reignited a longing for adventure that still nagged him as he sat through prayers at the house of assembly later that evening. The longing intensified when Mattaniah stood up after the prayers ended and addressed all of the assembled men.

"Listen, I received a message today from my new friend Zabad, the leader of one of the local villages. He asked me to extend his invitation to all of you to attend a celebration in his village tomorrow night."

"What kind of celebration?" the high priest asked.

"It's an annual festival to celebrate the olive harvest. But Zabad is also celebrating his daughter's recovery. She was very ill, and he seems to think that my daughter, Yael, contributed to her recovery somehow. That's why he's inviting all of us."

A chill went through Zechariah. What could Yael possibly have done to help her friend recover? Was it sorcery?

"Zabad has also agreed to let me farm that patch of land I wanted," Mattaniah continued. "Our neighbors are offering to make peace with us, so I think we all have a reason to celebrate."

Zechariah listened as the men discussed the invitation, and when they eventually agreed that a delegation should attend for the sake of goodwill and friendship, he longed to go with them. But the frown of disapproval on Saba's face told him that he would never be allowed to go. The restrictions Saba placed on him chafed like ill-fitting sandals, and he silently bemoaned the fact that Yael would certainly be going to the festival. Then he remembered that he did have the freedom to go. He was a man now. He could decide for himself what he would do, just as he'd made the decision to leave Babylon.

"I want to go with you tomorrow night," he told Mattaniah as they walked home.

Saba halted and pulled Zechariah to a stop beside him. "No,

son. I can't let you go. Priests of God have no business going to pagan celebrations."

"But I'm not a priest yet . . . and Zabad is a son of Abraham, and . . . and I want to go." His voice shook as he defied his grandfather for the first time. He saw Saba's surprise and disappointment, but he drew a steadying breath and said, "I'm old enough to make my own decisions now."

"You may be old enough, but you're not showing much wisdom. Did you pray and ask for guidance before deciding? I believe you should." Saba started walking again, but Zaki slowed his steps and turned to Mattaniah. His mind was made up. "I'm going with you," he told him.

The following evening as the sun was setting, Zechariah walked to the festival with Yael and Mattaniah and a dozen other Jewish men. This was the first time he had ventured away from their caravan camp and their settlement in Jerusalem, and his heart raced with excitement as they hiked across the narrow valley. The unwalled village, perched at the foot of the Mount of Olives, was little more than a cluster of plastered stone houses, but at least he was away from his studies and seeing something new, something different. A snaking path led uphill from the town, and Zechariah saw the glow of flames halfway to the top and a knot of men gathered around a stone altar. The aroma of roasting meat filled the air. A tingle of shock rippled through him. Were they worshiping at a high place?

"What are they cooking way up there?" he asked Mattaniah.

"I think they're making a sacrifice. It's an ancient tradition from the time before there was a temple—and since the temple is gone, where else can they offer sacrifices?"

A pagan image from the pages of the Torah had sprung to life right in front of Zechariah. "But the Torah says—"

"We're guests here, Zaki," he said, lowering his voice. "Let's not start preaching the Torah to our hosts."

A group of elders stood at the entrance to the village to greet them, ushering Zechariah and the other men into the open village square. Yael, the only girl in the delegation, was sent off to join the village women. A variety of rugs and woven mats had been spread out in the square, and when the sacrifice on the high place ended, the men sat down to feast. The women brought platters and trays and bowls of food and laid them before the gathered men, then disappeared again. Someone handed Zechariah a cup of wine as he sat down beside Mattaniah.

"Welcome, my esteemed guests," Zabad said, lifting his cup. "Please eat and drink your fill!"

Zechariah waited for his host to recite the traditional blessings on the bread and wine, but he never did. Zaki mumbled the blessings himself as the other men dug in, using their bread as a spoon as they ate from the common dishes. Every time one platter emptied, the women quickly set a full one in its place. Mattaniah gestured to a heaping plate of roasted meat and said, "Help yourself to some lamb, Zaki."

It smelled delicious, roasted to perfection and seasoned with fragrant rosemary. But as he reached to take a portion, he remembered the altar and the high place above the village. What if this meat had been sacrificed to idols? He had just studied the Fellowship Offering and knew that portions of that sacrifice would be offered to God while the rest would be eaten by family members and guests. He had no way of knowing if he was feasting with the Almighty One or with idols. No one had mentioned the God of Abraham or offered blessings to Him. Zaki shook his head at the mouth-watering lamb and nibbled on the eggplant and lentil dishes instead. Wine flowed as freely as the food. Mattaniah and the other Jewish men seemed to be having a good time, but Zechariah worried about the dozens of ways he was being tempted to disobey the Torah.

Toward the end of the meal, a troupe of musicians began

to play. Zaki didn't recognize any of the songs. When the men rose to allow the women to clear away the remnants of the feast, he decided to look around for Yael. "Most of the women are out there," a boy his age told him. He pointed to the village entrance. Zechariah watched from a distance and saw that Yael was surrounded by a group of women. They seemed to be coming and going, talking to Yael and an elderly woman for a few minutes, looking up at the stars together and pointing toward the heavens, then leaving again. Yael held a scroll in her hands, and when he remembered the ones she had consulted on the night of Saba's nightmare, he felt sick inside. These village women were coming to Yael to have their fortunes read in the stars.

He had to stop her. He and Mattaniah needed to leave with Yael before the other men from Jerusalem saw her practicing astrology. He hurried back to find Mattaniah, wishing with all his heart that he hadn't seen what Yael was doing.

The music and drinking had continued after the feast, and the celebration was growing very rowdy. As he searched the crowd for Yael's father, Zechariah saw several young couples lurking in the shadows away from the torchlight, their arms entwined. The thundering drumbeat and the dancing weren't like any Jewish celebration he'd ever attended. All the men sat back to watch the young women dance—and the girls were bare-armed and bare-legged. Their movements were so sensuous that Zechariah felt his face grow warm. He quickly looked away, not knowing what to do or where to turn. He remembered the story in the Torah about how the Midianites had tempted his ancestors to take part in an orgy and knew Saba had been right. Zechariah never should have come. He found Mattaniah watching the dancers and hurried over to whisper in his ear. "I don't want to stay here. I want to go home."

Mattaniah turned around to face him, his eyes bleary, his

face flushed from too much wine. "What? . . . Look, I'm sorry. I didn't realize this was how they celebrated."

Zechariah nodded. "I'm leaving. Should I take Yael with me?"

"Yael?" Mattaniah gazed into the distance toward Jerusalem for a long moment, then sighed. "No . . . No, I can't let the two of you walk home alone. . . . I'll go with you." He slowly rose to his feet as if hoping Zechariah would change his mind. He wouldn't. If anything, he was even more anxious to leave as the dancing and pounding drums continued. "Give me a minute to thank our host," Mattaniah said.

Zaki followed him as he wove through the crowd and crouched to speak in Zabad's ear. A moment later Zabad's voice boomed above the noise. "No, my friend! Must you leave so soon? The night is just beginning."

"I'm sorry, but I didn't realize the celebration would last this late. . . . Have you seen my daughter?"

Zabad gestured to the village entrance. "She and Leyla are out there with the women."

Mattaniah thanked Zabad again, clapping him on the shoulder. His steps were unsteady as he turned to go, and Zechariah took his arm as they made their way from the square. Outside, Yael and the other women were still stargazing. Maybe Mattaniah would see what she was doing and take away her scrolls. Maybe he would forbid her to ever return to this village. But Yael's father took no notice at all of the pagan charts she still held in her hands. "Time to go home, Yael," he said.

"Can't I stay? I could spend the night with Leyla."

He looked as though he might concede until Zaki pulled on his sleeve and whispered, "She needs to leave here. Now." He gestured to the revelry and Mattaniah finally seemed to understand.

"Not tonight, Yael. You need to come with us." She pouted

all the way home, but at least they had rescued her from that terrible place.

Zechariah knew he should warn Yael's father not to let her go back there, ever. But how could he do that without explaining the reason why and breaking his promises? Zechariah also knew he should tell his grandfather about the festival so they could warn the other men about being lured into temptation—but then he would have to tell Saba what he'd seen, and he was ashamed to do that.

The music faded in the distance as Zechariah walked up the hill, the path becoming harder and harder to see as he made his way into the dark night.

Two days after the festival, the lingering images still hadn't faded from Zechariah's mind. Since none of the other Jewish men reported what they'd seen and done, he decided not to say anything to his grandfather about that night. Yet his guilt and his fear for Yael wouldn't go away.

He had just drifted to sleep for a Sabbath afternoon nap like everyone else when someone shook him awake. "Zaki! Wake up!" He opened his eyes to see Yael crouching beside his mat. "Come on, let's go," she whispered.

"Huh? . . . Go where?" She tiptoed from the room without answering, as quietly and gracefully as a cat. Zechariah rubbed the sleep from his eyes and followed her out to the courtyard. "Go where?" he asked again, still groggy with sleep.

"Exploring! You promised, remember?"

He glanced around, worried that someone had overheard, but his grandparents and Yael's father were all napping. Even so, Zaki kept his voice low. "We can't go anywhere. It's Shabbat."

"So? We used to go exploring on Shabbat when we lived in Babylon, remember?"

"That was different."

"How? How was it different?" She stood with one hand on

her hip the way she always did when she argued with him. She was so sassy for a girl, but he liked her that way, even if her daredevil spirit scared him. "You promised," she said. "Are you going to break your promise again?"

The worst image from the festival that he hadn't been able to erase was of Yael telling fortunes beneath the stars. The memory made his stomach knot up. If he went with her now maybe he could convince her to stop practicing sorcery. "Well . . . I guess we could go somewhere," he said. "As long as we don't go more than a Sabbath day's walk."

"Whatever you say," she replied with a shrug. "Come on, I want to show you something." She took off at a brisk pace, and Zechariah had to hurry to keep up. They went through the destroyed Water Gate and down the ramp, then turned up the path that led across the valley, heading in the direction of Leyla's village.

"Wait. Isn't this the way we went the other night? I don't think we should go back there—"

"We're not going to the village. Quit worrying."

They kept walking—much farther than a Sabbath day's walk—but he was afraid that if he turned back now she would continue on without him. The valley was unnaturally quiet; the metallic ring of chisel against stone that could be heard up in the city on most days had been silenced for the Sabbath. Even the birds weren't stirring on this warm fall afternoon. They passed a mere stone's throw from the village, and Zechariah was relieved when they didn't enter it. He should talk to her now, but he didn't know how to begin. "Um . . . what were you and the village women doing outside at the festival the other night?"

"Just admiring the stars."

"But you had your scrolls . . . your astrology charts . . . didn't you?"

"What if I did?"

"Yael, you have to get rid of them. You can't worship idols—"

She halted in front of him, blocking his path. "Do you still want to be my friend or don't you? I didn't invite you to come with me so you could argue with me."

"Of course I want to be friends, but—"

"Then just be quiet and have fun for once in your life."

They walked on, and a few minutes later he saw a stone cliff ahead of him with carved entrances that looked like doorways leading into the rock wall. He realized where Yael was taking him and stopped.

"Wait. These are the tombs that we can see from up in Jerusalem, aren't they?"

"Yes. I've been dying to see them up close, but Abba is always too busy to bring me here."

Zechariah could tell that this graveyard had once been very beautiful. But like everything else in Jerusalem, the cemetery was overgrown with weeds and brambles and scrub trees. The Torah said he shouldn't go near a cemetery. It would make him unclean.

"Well? What do you think?" Yael stood looking at him as if eager to see his reaction. Maybe she was waiting for him to take the lead in exploring the tombs the way he had led in all their other explorations in Babylon. Zaki wanted so badly to impress her. To show her that he was fearless and brave and adventurous.

But he hesitated just a moment too long, and before he could stop her, Yael turned and pushed her way through the weeds and graves, stopping in front of the entrance to a tomb that had been carved into the face of the cliff. "Hey, come look! This one has been pried open. If we squeeze through this crack we can look inside."

"I can't go in, Yael. Saba says priests can't touch unclean things."

"You aren't a priest yet, are you?"

"Well, no . . ."

"Then what difference does it make? Come on. I'm going in." She shoved several rocks aside to make the opening larger, grunting with the effort, then dropped to her hands and knees to squeeze through the narrow opening. One minute she was moving broken stones out of the way and the next minute she had vanished.

"Yael?" he called. No answer. Other girls would never dream of doing the crazy things she did. They would be too scared of spiders and snakes and ghosts to crawl inside a burial cave. "Yael?" he called again. He felt the foolish urge to impress her and followed her into the cemetery. He crouched down to peer into the hole, but it was too dark inside to see anything. Zechariah hesitated, then got on his hands and knees and followed Yael through the opening. He bumped into her a few feet inside. The cave was damp and stale-smelling—and darker than nighttime.

"I can't see anything," Yael said as they both stood up. "It's too dark." Judging by the flat sound of her voice and the lack of an echo, the space was small, the ceiling low.

"Me either. Let's get out of here." He started to turn around, but Yael grabbed his arm.

"No, wait. Our eyes will get used to it in a minute." She clung to his arm while they waited, not because she seemed scared, but probably because she didn't want him to change his mind and leave. As Zaki's eyes adjusted, he saw that the room was rough-hewn, like a cave. Massive stone tombs the size of wagons were arranged in a semicircle around the walls. Sealed inside those boxes were the bones of several generations of families.

"See? There's nothing in here but tombs," he said. "Let's go."

She released his arm and moved forward a few more feet. "I want to look for treasures, first."

"There won't be any treasures. Someone already broke into this place before we came. If there were any treasures, I'm sure they must be long gone. That's what grave robbers do, you know."

But Yael groped her way around the tiny space for a few more minutes—just to be contrary, he was sure—brushing cobwebs out of her hair as she went. She even tried to lift the stone lid from one of the burial boxes without success. At last she sighed and said, "All right, we can go." She led the way as they ducked outside into the sunlight again.

Zechariah shaded his eyes against the brightness and bumped into Yael a second time as he stood up. She had halted directly in front of him. "Why are you stopping—?"

And then he saw why. They faced a ring of boys his age, maybe a little older. Eight of them. And they weren't wearing kippahs on their heads. Their garments had no tassels.

Samaritans.

He and Yael were in trouble.

Yael recovered from her surprise first and marched forward. "Get out of our way," she demanded.

"Who's going to make us?" One of the boys stepped in front of her, planting his hand in the middle of her chest, shoving her backward. "What are you doing down here, anyway? You're Jews, aren't you?"

"Sure they're Jews," a second boy said. "Can't you tell? Just look at his stupid little hat and the fancy fringe on his robe." He walked up to Zechariah and shoved him backward until he was up against the rock wall. The boy was taller than he was, stronger. No one would hear him if he yelled for help. And he couldn't expect the Holy One to answer his prayers after he'd broken the Sabbath laws by walking here and entering a tomb.

"You don't belong here!" the biggest boy said. "This is our valley." The circle of boys moved closer, trapping them.

"My father has land near here," Yael said. "Let us through so we can go home." She sounded defiant, not frightened. Zechariah wondered if she was really that brave or if she was as terrified as he was.

"Home? You must mean back home to Babylon. That's where you belong."

Zechariah tried to step sideways and slip past the boy who blocked his way, but he wouldn't let him. "You're part of that locust swarm that invaded our land. And you know what we do to insects that invade our land? We crush them!" He pushed Zaki backwards again, slamming him against the rocks.

"I think we need to give them a message to take home to their friends," the leader said. "Then they'll know better than to come down here again."

Two boys suddenly moved in from both sides and grabbed Zechariah, pinning his arms. He struggled as hard as he could, kicking and flailing, but they were too strong for him. A third boy reached for his kippah and yanked it off his head. "Yael, run!" Zaki shouted. She was small and nimble and as fast as a deer. She could easily get away. "Run!" he shouted again. But the three boys had crowded in so close that he couldn't see around them to see if she had escaped.

Someone grabbed Zaki's fringes, tearing them off, ripping his robe. "What do we have here?" the boy mocked. "Aren't they pretty?"

"Stop it! Leave me alone—" His words were cut off by a punch to his mouth that split his lip and smacked his head against the stone. Before he could recover, someone punched him in the gut, knocking the breath from him. He tried to double over, but they jerked him upright. A second punch to his stomach left him reeling with pain.

"Rafi, tell them to stop!" Yael yelled. Zechariah couldn't see if the others were hurting her or not as the three boys pummeled him with blows. He was desperate to free himself, to help Yael, but he couldn't draw a breath.

"Rafi, it's me," Yael said. "Tell them I'm Leyla's friend!"

"What about you?" one of the boys holding Zechariah asked. "Are you Leyla's friend, too?" They struck him again and again, punching, kicking, and laughing at his futile attempts to free himself.

"Rafi, make them stop!" Yael yelled.

"Hey! She's the seer, isn't she," one of the boys said. "The girl who reads the stars."

"Yes, I am! And you'd better let us go before I put a curse on you!"

Zaki's attacker punched him again before saying, "Come on, let's go." The boys released him and he fell to the ground, too injured to stand, humiliated that Yael had rescued him instead of the other way around. He should have protected her. One of the boys kicked him in the back, another in his side, the third one kicked his head. The pain was excruciating, his punishment for disobedience.

"We delivered our message. Let's go."

"Don't come back here again, or you'll really be sorry!"

His tormenters shuffled away, and Yael ran to him, kneeling beside him. When he saw that she was uninjured, he closed his eyes in relief. "Zaki! . . . Zaki, say something! Are you all right?"

He nodded, but it wasn't true. He lay stunned and bruised, every inch of his body in agony. "I'll go get help," she said, but he reached for her arm, stopping her.

"No, don't. I'll be okay in a minute."

"You're bleeding!" She touched his bloodied lip, then wiped blood from his eye. It came from a gash on his forehead. "Does that hurt?"

He didn't reply. He didn't want to lie, but he didn't want to admit the truth, either. Yael stood and offered her hand to help him up, but he shook his head. "I can stand by myself. I just need a minute to catch my breath."

"You better hurry in case they come back."

He crawled to his feet, leaning against the rock wall to support himself. The ground swayed beneath him. He looked down at his robes, bloody and torn, and waited for the world to stop spinning. "How am I going to explain my clothes?" he asked. He looked around for his kippah but didn't see it anywhere. "They took my head covering."

Yael bent to pick up the fringes that the boys had ripped off his garment and handed them to him. They were supposed to remind Zechariah of God's laws—and he surely must have broken several of them to deserve this. "That's why David cut the fringes off King Saul's garment," he said. "To remind Saul that he was sinning."

"What are you talking about? Are you sure you're okay, Zaki?"

He was too old to cry so he let his emotions spill over in anger. "I shouldn't have listened to you! This is all your fault!"

She took her usual, brassy stance. "That's a fine way to thank me for saving you!" She turned around and strode away.

"Yael, wait!" He took a few feeble steps, limping in pain. The bruises to his stomach and ribs made him double over. He would never make it home without her help. "Yael, I'm sorry. . . . Thank you for saving me. I'm sorry!"

She stopped and waited for him, and he saw her pity. "You can barely walk. Come on, lean on me and I'll help you." They wrapped one arm around each other and headed toward home. It seemed a hundred miles away.

"I thought they were going to kill you," Yael said, and for the first time, her voice trembled with tears.

"Well, Saba is going to kill me when he finds out what happened."

"I can help you make up a story."

"No, don't. Lying will make everything worse." He remembered how one of the boys had called her the seer, and he felt sick inside. What if his fellow Jews found out? He was scared for her and for himself because he loved her—and he knew that he shouldn't love a sorceress. He should have nothing to do with her.

"Are you sure you're fine?" she asked. "They punched you so hard."

Zechariah suddenly felt nauseated. The pain was so excruciating that he had to bend over and vomit. It was one more humiliation in front of Yael. When he was finished, he wiped his mouth on his sleeve, leaving a streak of blood from his cut lip.

"Come on, we'd better walk faster," Yael said, "in case the boys decide to come back without Rafi." He draped his arm around her shoulder again and limped home as quickly as he could manage. "Maybe everyone will still be napping," she said as they neared the spring, "and I can help you clean the blood and dirt off your clothes before they wake up. I can sew your fringes back on, too." But Zechariah knew it was hopeless. Safta was certain to notice his cut lip and the gash above his eye. He couldn't even stand up straight.

His grandmother was awake and sitting outside in their court-yard when Zechariah hobbled home. She covered her mouth in shock when she saw him. "Zaki! What happened?"

"He fell," Yael said. "We were climbing on some rocks, and they shifted and—"

"Don't," he said, silencing her. Saba came out of the house as Safta was looking him over, examining the cuts on his lip and his head, the bruises on his arms.

"I'll get some water and bandages," Safta said.

"What happened?" Saba asked.

"I know you're going to be angry with me," Zechariah said, "and you have every right to be. I shouldn't have gone there, and I'll never, ever do it again."

Safta returned before he could finish explaining, and she

made him sit down on the low stone wall. She fussed over him, washing the blood off his face, holding a compress against the gash on his forehead. "Can you move your arms and legs?" she asked. "Are any bones broken?"

"I don't think so." His eye was swelling shut, but he could still see the tears in his grandmother's eyes as she worked. When she finished, she helped him lift his torn robe over his head. His grandfather stood watching with a sad expression, waiting for Zechariah to finish explaining.

"Yael and I went down to the valley for a walk," he said. "A gang of boys from the village attacked us. . . . They attacked me, I should say. Yael is fine."

"One of the boys was Leyla's brother," Yael added. "He wouldn't let them touch me. And he told the others to stop hitting Zaki."

Zechariah looked up at his grandfather, waiting for the scolding that was certain to come. Instead, Saba beckoned to him and said, "Come. It's time for prayers."

"He can't go like this!" Safta said. "He's hurt. He needs to lie down!"

"And my kippah and fringes are gone," he said, reaching up to feel his bare head. It required a great effort not to cry.

"I have a kippah you may borrow," Saba said.

"Iddo, no!" Safta said. "Can't you see that he's injured?"

"You can wear your old robe until Safta repairs that one. Go get changed, Zechariah. We don't want to be late for prayers."

"How can you be so cruel?" Safta said. She threw Zaki's tattered robe on the ground and strode across their courtyard, hurrying through the opening where the gate would be. She kept going, walking faster and faster, weaving between the half-finished houses in their neighborhood until Zaki lost sight of her.

Saba didn't call to her or chase after her. "Change your clothes," he said. "Quickly."

Every movement caused him pain as Zechariah ducked inside his room and put on one of his old robes. He couldn't stand upright as they walked uphill to the house of assembly. The pain in his belly and ribs made him feel nauseated again. "I'm so sorry, Saba," he mumbled. "I never should have gone down there." The Day of Atonement when he would have to confess his sins was still a few weeks away, but he knew that his guilt would easily last until then.

"I planned to start teaching you how to blow the shofar tomorrow, remember?" Saba asked. "Now we'll have to wait until your lip is no longer swollen."

Zechariah walked with his head lowered, wiping the tears that slipped down his cheeks. "I'm so sorry," he said again.

"Yes. I can see that you're sorry. And the Holy One sees it, too. But true repentance, true *teshuvah*, means that we turn around and walk in a different direction from now on."

"I know, Saba. And I will."

His grandfather halted for a moment and said, "Let me ask you something. Do you believe that the Almighty One called you to follow Him? To return to Jerusalem and become a man of God?"

"Yes . . . I believe it."

"You know that following God means all or nothing, don't you? A man of God does the right thing whether it's popular with the rest of the crowd or not. He speaks the truth and isn't afraid to challenge others when they're doing wrong. Men of God don't look for power or riches or man's approval but for God's approval. Each day in a hundred different ways you must choose all over again whether you still want to follow Him or not."

"Yes, Saba . . . I understand." And that meant he couldn't listen to Yael or anyone else who enticed him to do wrong. He should have nothing more to do with her.

But that was impossible. They'd been friends forever, and he loved her . . . and he needed to find a way to win her back to God before he lost her forever. Because if the other men in their community ever discovered what Yael was doing, they would stone her to death.

CHAPTER

19

The stench hit Iddo before he and Zechariah reached the house of assembly for morning prayers. They both covered their mouths and noses with the sleeves of their robes. "What's that terrible smell, Saba?" Zechariah's face was mottled with purplish bruises, and the cuts on his lip and eye were still healing from the attack three days ago.

"Something dead. But what is it doing so close to the sacred temple area?" Iddo hurried toward the ritual baths, where a group of his fellow priests stood talking, their faces shielded, as well.

"Vandals dumped rotting animal carcasses into the *mikveh* last night," one of the men told him. "We just finished repairing and refilling it, and now it will have to be drained and purified before we can use it for our ordination."

"Another delay," Iddo said, his jaw clenched. Anger, along with the stink, nearly suffocated him. He could barely breathe.

"We sent for volunteers who aren't priests to clean it out." But the nauseating smell contaminated the nearby house of assembly as well, invading the half-finished building like an invisible enemy and making everyone's eyes water. Their prayers and the yeshiva classes would have to be cancelled for the day.

"Can I go to work with you, instead?" Zechariah asked.

"You haven't been back to the temple mount since we first arrived, have you?" The boy shook his head. Iddo knew that Zechariah's decisions to attend the festival and to explore the tombs were symptoms of a restlessness that needed to be satisfied. "All right. Come on, son. Let's hope the air is fresher up there."

They climbed the stairs to the temple mount together and thankfully the stench wasn't as strong higher up where a fresh breeze blew. Iddo paused to let Zechariah see the progress they'd made in the past few months. The site resembled a beehive of activity with hired workers lifting and moving stones. "We've finally cleared away the place where the bronze altar once stood," Iddo said. "And we'll build the new altar on the same foundations. When it's finished, it will measure thirty feet square and be fifteen feet high with a ramp leading to the top."

"Will it be ready in time for the Feast of Trumpets?"

"I pray that it will be, but the feast is barely a week away. We should have begun much sooner, but we allowed enemy opposition to delay us. Now we're running out of time."

"Have they started rebuilding the temple, Saba?"

"Not yet. We haven't even cleared away the rubble or the trees and scrub bushes. It's a much bigger job than we ever imagined." Iddo closed his eyes for a moment, remembering the façade of Solomon's temple adorned with gold; the tall bronze pillars that supported the portico; the huge Bronze Sea, fifteen feet across, where the priests would wash in living water. Looking around now, a ferocious sense of urgency gripped him. They had to complete the task God had given them. The sabotaged mikveh was the latest reminder that the Holy One's enemies didn't want them to succeed.

"If that's going to be the new altar," Zechariah said, interrupting his thoughts, "what's that other platform for?" He pointed to a stone structure near the eastern edge of the temple mount, not far from the stairs.

"That's for the musicians. When the month of Tishri begins, we'll sound the silver trumpets for the first time to announce the Feast of Trumpets."

Zechariah looked at him and smiled. "Everyone in the City of David will be able to hear you, Saba. They'll probably hear you down in the valley, too, and in all the local villages."

"Yes, that's what we're hoping." He rested his hand on Zaki's shoulder for a moment, aware that not too long ago he would have rested his hand on his head. The boy was taller than his grandmother now, nearly as tall as Iddo.

They made their way across the recently cleared plaza where the worshipers would soon stand. Every morning Iddo and his fellow priests met where Solomon's porch once stood to discuss the day's tasks with Jeshua the high priest. The chief priests and Levites used to hold meetings there before the destruction, and Iddo remembered it as an open portico supported by pillars. Of course the roof was gone, and shattered sections of carved pillars and columns lay strewn across the weedy ground. He and Zechariah sat with the others on the remnants of broken pillars.

"We must concentrate on finishing the altar in time for the fall feasts," Jeshua began. He looked weary and worried, as if required to carry one of the huge pillars on his back.

"Won't the altar have to be sanctified?" someone asked. "Will there be enough time for that?"

"Yes, it must be made holy before it can be used to atone for sin. But I assure you that we'll be ready for the sacrifices on the Day of Atonement if we have to work day and night to do it. This is the beginning of our service to the Holy One. It's what we came here to do. After the feast, the daily morning and evening sacrifices will continue from now on. The altar fire will never be allowed to go out again."

"Is there any chance that the vandals who desecrated our mikveh will be caught and punished?" a voice called out.

"That's probably impossible," Jeshua said, shaking his head. "Nor can we be certain that there won't be more acts like it. I'm posting guards on the mount day and night to make sure no one desecrates the new altar."

"I thought when the local villagers invited us to their festival they were making peace with us. What happened?"

The high priest lifted his hands in a gesture of helplessness, then let them drop. "I don't know what happened."

"It was a ruse," Iddo said. "They let us think we were at peace so we'd lower our guard. And it worked. Now we have to start all over again with the mikveh."

"I'd like to think such an act couldn't happen again," Jeshua said, "but the walls around the city and the temple mount have too many breaches. And we have only 139 gatekeepers who must be divided into shifts. They can't possibly guard the hundreds of places where vandals could sneak in. And you know all too well that there are no city gates to close. We must post more guards from now on, so I'll need everyone to volunteer for a shift."

"I can't possibly spare any of the men under my supervision," Joel said. "They still need more training before they're ready to slay the sacrifices correctly. And we're all exhausted. Every priest has been assigned at least two jobs already."

"What about your musicians, Iddo?"

"I have 128 temple musicians," Iddo said. "Most of them are already doing more than one job, but I'll ask for volunteers."

"We could ask the yeshiva students to help us," one of the priests said, gesturing to Zechariah.

Iddo jumped in before anyone else could. "It's much more important for our young men to study. Weren't our ancestors punished because they didn't know the Torah or follow it?"

"But the students are eager to help," the other priest insisted.

"We should let our young men be part of this. We won't ask them to do anything as dangerous as standing watch in the night. Besides, they'll have all winter to resume their studies."

"I disagree," Iddo said firmly. "We would be sending the wrong message. There is nothing more important than knowing the Torah. Besides, if these vandals are anything like the gang that attacked my grandson . . ." He didn't finish.

"I heard about that incident," Jeshua said. "It was near one of the local villages, wasn't it? You have recovered, I hope?" he asked Zechariah.

"Yes, sir. I'm fine."

No broken bones, thankfully. That's what had frightened Iddo the most. Any lasting damage such as a limp or a broken arm that failed to heal straight would have made Zechariah a cripple and ineligible to be a priest.

"Have you received justice from those who were responsible?" Jeshua asked.

Iddo shook his head. "The only witness was Mattaniah's daughter, and the Samaritans would never accept the testimony of such a young girl."

"We need the yeshiva students' help," the other priest argued. "These acts of terrorism emphasize the importance of celebrating the feast on time and starting the schedule of daily sacrifices. God's enemies will do anything to try to stop us."

The high priest looked from Iddo to the other priest, as if trying to make up his mind. "I'm sorry, Iddo," he finally decided, "but we need the students' help. We'll only recruit young men like your grandson who have come of age."

The decision upset Iddo. He could tell that Zechariah and some of the others were losing interest in their studies, and taking them out of the classroom now would only fuel that disinterest. But the decision had been made, and Jeshua was moving on to the next topic.

"We won't give in to fear," he said. "There's work to be done, and we'll divide it among the four divisions of priests. This altar must be finished in time for our national day of repentance."

"What about building the storehouses?" someone asked. "The Jewish families who returned with us and settled in hometowns such as Tekoa and Bethlehem will be coming to Jerusalem with their offerings. We need a place to store the tithes that belong to us and to the Levites."

"Wait," another priest interrupted. "We have to build pens for the sacrificial animals first. We'll be sacrificing a goodly number of animals throughout the eight days of the festival—bulls and rams and lambs. We need pens for these animals and—"

"And the men who'll perform these sacrifices need to be fully trained," Joel added.

"And there's another reason why we must be finished on time," Iddo said. "The feast includes a ceremony to pray for rain. The early rains should begin next month, and we need the Holy One's blessing."

"We must explain all these needs to every able-bodied man in the community," Jeshua said. "Ask for additional volunteers and recruit the yeshiva students. One last thing before you start: I'm pleased to report that the workers have moved enough debris for us to see where the temple foundations once were. Unfortunately, we won't have a chance to begin laying the new foundation until next spring when—"

"What?" Iddo interrupted. "Why not?"

"We have to wait until after the winter rains end."

"Why? Why can't we work through the winter?"

"The ground will be too muddy for one thing, and the hired laborers will never agree to work in the rain and the cold."

"How can we expect the Holy One to protect us from our enemies if we aren't doing what He sent us here to do?"

205

"The delay can't be helped, Iddo. We'll start rebuilding the temple next spring. That's all for today. We have work to do."

Iddo's temper simmered all day. As much as he enjoyed his grandson's company, he knew it was a mistake to keep the young men from their studies. It was also a mistake to delay the rebuilding during the winter months, but he was helpless to change things.

His mood hadn't improved by the time he arrived home that evening, and he could tell right away that Dinah was still angry with him. She knelt alone in their courtyard, mashing chickpeas into a smooth paste, but didn't greet him or even lift her head as Iddo came through the gate. He watched her for a moment, remembering how she had stormed away from him the day that Zechariah had been injured, furious with him for not coddling him, refusing to understand that the boy needed to face the consequences of his actions. She had remained angry with him ever since. The crack in their once-strong marriage seemed to widen every day. They used to be so close, two people who were truly one. Iddo had no idea how to repair the widening rift.

"You used to sing while you worked," he said quietly. "I've noticed that you don't sing anymore." Iddo moved into the courtyard and sat down on the low wall, facing her. She continued working without looking up. "What are you thinking about, Dinah? You look so sad."

"I miss our family."

"I miss them, too."

She finally lifted her chin and he saw reproach in her eyes. "It doesn't seem that way. You never talk about our children and grandchildren. You don't seem to notice how different our Sabbath meals are without them. It's as if . . . as if they never existed for you."

"Of course I notice the difference. But don't you understand how important this work is? We're rebuilding this temple for their sakes and for future generations so that the Almighty One will dwell in our midst again."

She huffed and bent over her work again, the grinding stone crushing harder, moving faster. Iddo lost his patience. "Don't you see that anything we put in place of God or that keeps us from serving Him with all our heart and strength is an idol? Even if it's our own children and grandchildren?"

He saw by her reaction that he had said the wrong thing. She slammed down the bowl and pestle, spilling some of the food onto the ground, and rose to her feet. "Your heart has turned to stone, Iddo." He tried to catch her arm so he could hold her, but she twisted away. "Leave me alone!" She fled into their tiny house, and if they'd had a door, she would have slammed it in his face.

He would celebrate the Day of Atonement soon. Worshipers were supposed to examine themselves and search their hearts for all the ways that they had sinned—sins against God and against other people. It was a time for repairing relationships, but Iddo had no idea where to begin with his own wife.

He walked the short distance to where Shoshanna and Joel lived and found them sitting in their outdoor courtyard. "May I please speak with you, Shoshanna?" he asked. "It's about Dinah."

Iddo couldn't talk to another man's wife alone, so Joel would have to hear this, too. Since Dinah could have married Joel instead of him, it embarrassed Iddo to admit that she was unhappy. But he had to do something to make her happy again besides taking her back to Babylon. Iddo would never do that.

"Yes, of course," Shoshanna replied. "Won't you sit down?"

Iddo shook his head. He fingered the fringes on his robe as he spoke. "I know you spend a lot of time with Dinah, and I wondered if you've noticed a change in her."

"Yes . . . I've noticed."

"She seems . . . despondent . . . and I don't know how to cheer her up."

He saw compassion in Shoshanna's eyes as she looked at him. "Dinah was a leader among the women in Babylon, dearly loved and respected. I know I'm biased because I'm her cousin, but she was strong and wise and everyone admired her. She loved her work as a midwife, and all of the young mothers depended on her. But she has nothing to do here. She barely leaves her house, barely speaks. She doesn't even join our conversations at the spring."

"Does she ever say what's wrong?"

"She used to have her children and grandchildren with her all day, and now she only has Yael—who can be difficult at times."

"What can I do, Shoshanna?"

"I don't know. I wish I did. . . . It might help if she could work as a midwife again. Maybe once she has new babies to bring into the world . . . Maybe Dinah needs a child to hold and care for."

"Won't it make it worse for her, remembering her own children?"

"I don't know. We'll have to wait and see."

Iddo had been right in guessing that Dinah was despondent, right about the cause. But what should he do? "Thank you for your time, Shoshanna." He went home, his feet heavy, his heart heavier still. Dinah knelt in the courtyard again, mashing the chickpeas. "We must talk," he told her. She nodded but didn't look up from her work. "You barely look at me anymore. Are you truly that angry with me?"

"I'm tired, Iddo. You know I haven't been sleeping very well."

"I know. I used to be the one who couldn't sleep." Now Dinah was often awake in the night, and she would climb out of bed to wander outside and stare up at the cold night sky. "What can I do to make you happy again?" he asked her.

"Nothing."

"I don't know what to say or what to do. In all the years we've been married, we never struggled like this to talk to each other. We were always close."

"I'm sorry for disappointing you."

"Dinah, please. Yell at me, get angry, whatever it takes—but tell me what I can do to help."

She finally looked up at him and the deadness he saw in her expression frightened him. "I've done everything you've asked me to do, Iddo. Followed all the rules, made the sacrifice of this move, started my life all over again. But there's no meaning in what I do. No life from it, no joy. I used to be so satisfied, so full. Now I simply do what you expect of me. Don't ask for more, because I don't have anything left to give."

Iddo struggled to comprehend her words. How could she not see the higher purpose in coming here? What about all of God's promises, the gift of freedom their people had been given? "I thought you came here to serve the Almighty One," he said.

She shook her head. "I'm your wife. I had to come. It was never my choice to leave Babylon. That's where I truly want to be."

"And so now you're simply going through the motions without love in your heart?"

"There's nothing in my heart, Iddo. My heart is still in Babylon. But I could ask you the same question. Why are you enduring all this hardship? Why do you want to perform all those rituals at the temple? Is it from love or from duty? Is it merely to appease the Almighty One because you fear more punishment if you don't?"

Iddo didn't know what to say. Was it true that he served God only out of fear? Could he say that he loved God or that he believed God loved him? He wanted Dinah to walk beside him because she loved him—was it possible that God wanted the same thing?

"You asked why I'm unhappy," she continued. "Why don't you ask Zechariah the same question? Why don't you explain to him why you treated him so harshly after he was attacked?"

"I was only doing what any father would do."

"You believe that's how God treats us. We have to follow all the rules, do everything exactly right, or He'll punish our smallest misstep. And so you made the boy limp up the hill for prayers when he was in pain, and you humiliated him in front of all the others. You used to do the same thing with our sons. You were always criticizing them, making it impossible for them to keep all your picky little rules or to have a life of their own. The moment they were old enough to think for themselves, they walked away from your religion. They certainly saw no reason to uproot their lives to serve as priests for such a harsh, unloving God."

"That's . . . that's not true, Dinah." She was allowing bitterness to cloud her memories. He started to explain that he had raised their children according to the Torah, but she interrupted.

"All you think about is appeasing your God. What about the people in your life? You accuse me of making them into idols, but you don't care about them at all. People aren't important to you. Does your God see us as His slaves who are required to wait on Him at all costs? Even at the cost of the people we love?"

"Of course we aren't slaves. But we should be willing to sacrifice everything for Him."

"Why? And why is He so cruel that He demands everything?"

"He isn't cruel. . . ." Yet Iddo found he had no explanation for the horror he'd witnessed as a boy—horror that God had allowed.

"Well, I've sacrificed everything, Iddo, and it seems as if God still isn't pleased."

Iddo knelt down in front of her. "You haven't sacrificed everything, Dinah. We still have each other. And I love you." He took the bowl from her hands and set it on the ground, then gathered her in his arms. He clung to her tightly, but her embrace felt empty and rigid in return. She was angry with him and with God for losing her family. And in his heart, Iddo knew he was still angry with God for losing his family as a child. Was he doing the same thing Dinah was doing—going through the motions out of fear instead of love, holding anger inside?

He had wanted to rebuild the temple for the sake of his family and for the future of their people, the generations that would follow. But the coldness in Dinah's embrace made him wonder if he would lose his family all over again.

CHAPTER

20

Iddo left his house before dawn the next morning to take his turn as a guard near the Sheep Gate on the temple mount. "It's been a quiet night," the man from the last watch told him.

"That's the best kind," Iddo said. They exchanged a few words before the guard shuffled away to catch a few hours' sleep. Iddo didn't mind standing watch. The hours alone before dawn gave him a chance to pray about Dinah's unhappiness and the accusations she had made. He needed to pray for Zechariah, too. Iddo wished he knew for certain that it was merely youthful curiosity that had led him to go to the village festival with Mattaniah and to explore the tombs with Yael. The boy was wrestling with the call of God on his life, and like the enemy opposition his community faced, Zechariah faced testing, as well.

"Why can't I learn to shoot a bow and arrow," he had asked Iddo yesterday, "or fight with a sword? I want to help defend Jerusalem."

"Because it's a priest's job to intercede for the people in the temple. If we're obedient to Him, He'll fight all our battles. If we're not, then it won't matter if you're the most valiant swordsman in the world." But had that been the right answer? With all of the troubles they faced, maybe the young men Zaki's age should learn to fight.

A narrow rim of light had just appeared above the Mount of Olives when Iddo heard sheep bleating. He stood in the opening where the collapsed gate once hung and gazed down the darkened road. A man approached, walking like a drunkard with a swaying, limping step. A handful of bedraggled sheep followed him. What were they doing here? The shepherds weren't supposed to bring the sheep for the sacrifices until next week. The pens weren't even finished yet. Iddo watched warily as the odd little band drew closer, the sheep bleating piteously. Then he recognized the man. He was indeed one of the temple shepherds, and he wasn't drunk. He had been savagely beaten, his clothes torn and streaked with blood. Iddo rushed forward to help him.

"Are you all right? What happened?" He wrapped his arm around the man to support him as he helped him sit down on a large stone inside the toppled walls. "What happened?" he asked again.

"Hanan and I were guarding the temple flocks last night when we were attacked."

The man clearly needed help before being interrogated further. He looked ready to faint. Iddo remembered Dinah's accusation that he had a heart of stone, and he took pity on the man. "What's your name?"

"Besai."

"Stay here, Besai, and catch your breath. I'll go get help." The sheep seemed content to graze on the grass that still grew between the paving stones. Iddo left them and jogged as fast he could over the rough terrain until he reached the guard at the next breach in the wall. "Go wake the high priest," Iddo told him. "Our shepherds have been attacked. Gather some of the others and meet me back at the Sheep Gate. . . . And fetch some food and water and bandages for the poor man."

Besai was sitting on the ground when Iddo returned, his back propped against the stone, his eyes closed. Iddo let him rest until Jeshua and the others arrived.

"Tell us what happened, Besai," Jeshua said, after giving him something to drink and bandaging the worst of his cuts.

"We herded the sheep inside the stone pen for the night, as we always do, and we were taking turns keeping watch. Hanan stood guard first, so I lay down to sleep in front of the door to the enclosure. Our attackers came out of nowhere. Hanan barely had time to cry out before they jumped him and beat him. I woke up when he yelled, but before I could help him, two more men attacked me. They stole most of the sheep and left Hanan and me for dead. These are all that's left of the flock." He gestured to the handful he had brought with him. "They were too frightened to follow the strangers."

The sky was fully light now, and Iddo could see how badly Besai had been beaten, his face swollen and still oozing blood. He sat hunched over as if his stomach and ribs ached. One of his ankles had swollen to twice its size and was turning purple. "What about the other shepherd, Hanan?"

Besai shook his head. "They beat him worse than me. He was still unconscious when I left to get help. I hated to leave him, but I didn't know what else to do."

"And you walked all the way here in your condition?" Jeshua asked. "Don't the temple flocks graze on the other side of the mountain, at least three miles from here?"

Besai nodded. "There was no other place I could go for help. I didn't trust the people in the nearest village. They might have been the ones who attacked us."

"Don't worry. We'll send some men back to help Hanan," Jeshua said.

"You'll need a litter," Besai said. "He'll have to be carried."

"Where should we bring him? Do you know where he lives?"

214

"He and his family are still in the tent city in the valley. We both arrived with the very last caravan, and we've been too busy tending the flocks for the feasts to build proper houses."

"You can bring both men to my house," Iddo said. "My wife will know how to care for them. She and her cousin Shoshanna work as midwives."

Someone quickly fetched a tanned hide to use for a litter, and Iddo left with three other men to help the injured shepherd. The walk down through the valley seemed peaceful in spite of the violence Besai had just described. Birdsong filled the air as the sun dawned in the pale pink sky. Any other day, Iddo would have enjoyed the walk and the tranquility, aware that the pace at the temple would accelerate once the fall feasts began. But his concern for the injured shepherds and stolen sheep overshadowed the beautiful morning. What if there weren't enough sheep left for the sacrifices?

They reached the grazing lands on the other side of the mountain and found Hanan still lying unconscious, savagely beaten. The large flock of sheep he and Besai had tended had vanished. Iddo helped lift him onto the litter and carried him the three miles back to the city. By the time they arrived, Dinah and Shoshanna had cleaned and bandaged Besai's wounds, and he was resting inside Iddo's house. They laid Hanan's litter in the courtyard and both women knelt over him. "He has a very bad head injury," Dinah said. "It isn't good that he's still unconscious."

"Does he have a wife and family?" Shoshanna asked. "If so, we should send for them right away. And for Besai's family, as well."

"I'll go for them," Iddo said. "Besai told me that they're still living in tents down in the valley." It was time for morning prayers, and Zechariah was dressed and waiting to go. Dinah's criticism still worried Iddo—she'd said that the people in his life weren't important to him, that he'd been too strict as a father. Would it hurt the boy to miss prayers this one time? Didn't a priest need to learn compassion as well as laws and statutes? "Come with me, Zechariah," Iddo said at last. "I may need your help."

It took a great deal of searching, but they finally found the tents where the shepherds' families lived side by side among the hundreds of people still camped in the valley. Both of the men had young wives and small children—and they were astoundingly poor. None of the returning exiles had much, but at least Iddo had a roof over his head and something resembling a real house to sleep in at night. Dinah had a proper hearth where she could cook instead of a crude campfire.

The two shepherds' wives reacted with shock and tears when Iddo told them the bad news. They didn't seem to know what to do or which way to turn. "Do you have families here who can help you through this?" he asked.

"We left our families behind in Babylon."

Iddo's heart broke for these women and for the sacrifice they had made. "Gather your children and anything else you might need," he told them. "You can stay with us and be close to your husbands. We'll carry your household goods up to the city later."

Besai's wife wrapped a small baby in a sling and tied him to her chest so she could hold her little boy's hand. Zaki lifted Hanan's little girl and carried her for Hanan's wife, who was round with child. Iddo shouldered the few necessities they had gathered, and they all set off up the hill.

When they finally arrived, Dinah pulled Iddo aside to whisper, "Hanan is still unconscious. That's not a good sign."

"I was afraid of that. Listen, I'm sorry for making more work for you, Dinah—"

"No, it's the least I can do for these poor souls." She coaxed the frightened children to sit on the rug so Yael could give them

216

something to eat. When they were settled, she concentrated on soothing the frightened wives.

By now Iddo and Zechariah had missed morning prayers. "The high priest will be waiting for news about the shepherds," he told Zechariah. "Come with me." They walked up to the temple mount together and found Jeshua conferring with several others about the stolen sheep.

"We don't have the manpower or the authority to find the thieves," he was saying. "Our stolen sheep are likely grazing in the Negev by now. We'll simply have to purchase more if we want to have enough for the Feast of Tabernacles. And this time we'll guard them well."

The injustice angered Iddo. So did his helplessness. "Listen, we owe it to those two shepherds to help them and their families. It's the least we can do. The rainy season is coming, and the very poorest of our people are still living in tents in the valley."

"I share your concern," Jeshua replied, "but what can we do? We barely have enough time or workers to finish everything at the temple."

"I know, and I've been thinking about that problem on the way up here. My grandson, here, helped me build our house. He knows the basics and how to use a plumb line."

"I thought you were against taking them from their studies," the high priest said.

"Learning compassion is also part of their studies. Yes, the altar and the sacrifices are our top priority. But it's also important to take care of the people in our community."

CHAPTER
21

Zechariah couldn't understand it. He stood on the temple mount on the tenth day of Tishri, jammed among thousands of pilgrims who had gathered for the Day of Atonement, his mind whirling with questions. Last night the young shepherd, Hanan, had died of his injuries. Why had the Almighty One allowed it? Why bring Hanan and his family hundreds of miles from their home in Babylon to have his life end in violence? Wasn't the Holy One supposed to save His people from their enemies? And why wouldn't their leaders, Sheshbazzar or Zerubbabel, go after the murderers and punish them? Hanan's killers would go free, just as the boys who attacked him had. It didn't make sense.

The courtyard was too crowded, Zechariah too far away from the altar to see the high priest conducting the ritual in his embroidered robes. He could only catch glimpses of movement and smell the occasional aroma of the sacrifices as they blew toward him on the breeze. But he knew from his studies that on this holy day, the Almighty One would forgive his sins and the sins of his nation if they repented. The sacrificial animals would die in his place. After nearly seventy years without an altar, without a way to cancel their sins, he and all of God's people would finally find forgiveness.

Had Hanan failed to repent? Had a terrible sin in his life led to his death? Or maybe they had all sinned by failing to build the temple right away. Or by compromising with pagans at the village festival. Maybe it was because Yael—and who knew how many others—still practiced sorcery.

If that was true, then Zechariah deserved to die, too. He was guilty of attending the village festival. He had broken the Sabbath by walking down to the tombs. The psalmist's words had echoed in his mind as he had fasted and prayed in preparation for this somber day: *"Blessed is the man who does not walk in the counsel of the wicked or stand in the way of sinners or sit in the seat of mockers."* Zechariah had made all of those mistakes. *"But his delight is in the law of the Lord, and on his law he meditates day and night."* He confessed that he hadn't delighted in his Torah studies in the past, craving adventure instead. And now his studies had halted. The elders had closed the yeshiva as Zechariah worked alongside the other Torah students in a dreary, gray rain, helping to build sturdier housing in the City of David for all of the people still camped in the valley. He and Saba added a room onto their own house for Hanan's widow and her two children, and another room for the surviving shepherd, Besai, and his family. But Zechariah now vowed to return to his studies with a different attitude when the week-long feast ended. Today's sacrifices would restore his standing with God.

He watched and waited throughout the lengthy ceremony, but nothing miraculous happened. No blinding light appeared to him, no sense of the Holy One's nearness overwhelmed him. Had he really heard God speaking to him back in Babylon? Why couldn't he feel His presence now that the altar had been consecrated and the sacrifices restored? The high priest was supposed to take the blood of the sacrifice into the holiest place on the Day of Atonement and sprinkle it on God's mercy seat, but there was no temple, no mercy seat.

The long ceremony dragged on and on, and Zechariah grew tired of standing. When it finally ended, his disappointment felt like a dull ache in his stomach, the same ache he'd felt after being punched and kicked. Their long journey from Babylon to Jerusalem, their hard work and anticipation, had ended with a crowded square, the sound of distant music, and the aroma of smoke and roasting meat. That's all. God's presence hadn't returned in a pillar of fire or a cloud of glory. If Zechariah's sins were truly forgiven, he felt no reassurance. He wondered if the other worshipers felt differently or if it was just him, if his sin still stood between him and the Almighty One like the huge stone blocks that littered the temple site. But who could he ask about it? Certainly not Saba.

The morning after the sacrifice, a nightmare jolted Zechariah from sleep. He sat up in bed, his heart racing. It had been the same dream he'd had in Babylon, the one that had come true. The Babylonian woman with her long, black robes and dangling jewelry had been pushing Yael into a large storage basket so she could hide. But in this dream, Zechariah had been helping them. The images had been so vivid that it took him a moment to realize that he was in his room in Jerusalem. There was no basket, no Babylonian woman.

He knew what the dream meant. By keeping Yael's secret he was helping her continue to sin. But what if he told on her and the elders stoned her to death? He didn't want Yael to die. Every time Mattaniah went down to the valley to work his land, Yael went to the Samaritan village to see her friend. And each evening when she returned she brought home gifts—a bag of pistachios, fresh goat cheese wrapped in grape leaves, a bouquet of rosemary—payment for predicting people's futures in the stars. He had to stop her, but how?

The sun had dawned. He heard voices outside in the courtyard and the sound of the women grinding grain. Zechariah tossed the covers aside and quickly dressed to join them. He glanced anxiously around the courtyard but didn't see Yael. Safta and the other women were baking bread and feeding the little children. Mattaniah sat on the rug finishing his breakfast. Zechariah hurried over to sit down beside him, keeping his voice low. "Are you taking Yael down to the village again today?"

"Yes, she asked to go. Why?"

How could he reply without telling a lie or betraying a secret? "Um . . . maybe Safta could use her help."

"She hasn't said anything to me about it."

"Well . . . but . . . Yael is gone so much of the time. She's hardly ever home."

"Her friend is the chieftan's daughter, Zaki. The villagers have asked her to come, and we need good relations with these people." He rose from his place, and a moment later Zechariah heard him calling to Yael, asking if she was ready.

He scrambled to his feet and went to the hearth where his grandmother baked flatbread on the hot stone. "Safta . . . I think Yael should stay home today and help you."

Safta made a huffing sound. "Yael does more complaining and sighing than she ever does helping. And she's not much help with the little ones, either."

"Well . . . I don't think you should let her go down to the village so often. They're not nice people. Remember how they beat me up?"

"If it was up to me, I wouldn't let her go," Safta said. "But it isn't up to me."

Zaki turned to his grandfather next. Iddo had just retrieved his prayer shawl from his room and was preparing to leave.

"Saba, don't you think it's dangerous for Yael to keep going down to that village all the time? What if that gang of boys—"

"Mattaniah assured me that she's safe. She's his daughter."

Dinah rose from her place by the hearth and said, "Mattaniah doesn't have sense enough to realize how beautiful his daughter is. Or the foresight to see what a village full of heathen boys might do to her."

"Dinah, please . . ." Saba murmured. "Don't talk of such things." He glanced at Zaki with a worried look. But Zechariah knew what his grandmother meant. He had read the story in the Torah of how a Gentile man had raped Jacob's daughter when she visited the local village. "Mattaniah wants to keep Zabad happy so he can plow and plant his land without worrying," Saba said.

"Is his land more important to him than his daughter?" Safta asked.

"Of course not. But it's none of our business, Dinah. Let the matter go. You have other women to help you now. You don't need Yael."

Zechariah could only watch helplessly as once again, Yael left with her father for the day.

On the fifteenth day of Tishri, Zechariah and his new extended family sat beneath the *sukkah* he had helped Saba build out of leafy branches for the Feast of Tabernacles. They would eat their meals and sleep outside in this booth throughout the week to remember their ancestors' long desert wanderings. "It's a blessing to eat and sleep outside," Saba said as he raised his cup of wine in a toast the first evening.

"How is it a blessing?" Safta asked. "Didn't we live in tents all the way here? Was that a blessing?" Everyone at the table seemed to freeze at her unexpected question. Every day, Safta's unhappiness became more apparent to Zechariah and tonight her demanding tone highlighted it. "Why eat in this flimsy sukkah when we just worked so hard to get out of our tents and build a proper house?"

"The booths remind us of how temporary our lives are," Saba replied. "How we are strangers and sojourners in this world. And they remind us how very much we depend on the Almighty One for all of our needs. It was too easy to forget Him when we were settled in Babylon living comfortable lives."

"Can't we be reminded some other way?" she argued, "without having to wave branches in the air and sleep outside?"

Zaki waited for his grandfather's reaction. Safta had never argued with him or questioned the Torah's commands when they'd lived in Babylon. His grandfather replied patiently. "Our rituals are what bind us together and sustain us as a people. They aren't meaningless, Dinah. They give hope to everyone in the community. And the sacrifices reconcile us with God. Each step we take brings us closer to the day that all the prophets saw, the day when we will have a restored kingdom with a son of David on the throne who will give us victory over all our enemies."

At the mention of enemies, Zechariah could no longer keep quiet. He glanced at Hanan's widow, still in mourning, and asked, "Do we have to wait until the Messiah comes before we fight back? Didn't the Almighty One tell our ancestors to fight against our enemies and drive them from our land?"

He thought it was a valid question, but Saba studied him for a long moment before asking, "Are you still thinking about the boys who attacked you? That happened weeks ago. You must let it go, Zechariah."

"But it isn't fair! They should be punished for what they did! And what about the men who attacked Hanan and Besai? Why can't we demand justice?"

Saba closed his eyes for a moment as if the memory pained

him. "We've been over this, Zechariah. That attack took place at night. If Besai can't identify the men who did it, how can we get justice?"

"Won't there be more attacks if these evil men keep getting away with it?"

"The prophet Isaiah wrote, 'The Lord has a day of vengeance, a year of retribution to uphold Zion's cause.' We need to leave revenge in the Almighty One's hands."

Zechariah had been told to let it go. He was causing pain to his grandfather and to Hanan's widow, seated beside Safta. But he couldn't drop it. "Why can't we ask the Persians to send their soldiers back to keep us safe? I'll bet they could find our stolen sheep."

"The Persian soldiers are not ours to command. Prince Shesh-bazzar sent a report to Persia, but it will take many weeks to get a reply."

Saba's patience only fueled Zechariah's anger. "Then we need to form our own army in the meantime and defend ourselves."

"We're priests and farmers and shepherds, not warriors."

"King David was a shepherd, and he fought God's enemies."

"Let it go, Zechariah," Saba said again. "Didn't the Almighty One avenge the destruction of Jerusalem for us? He judged the Babylonians for what they did and sent the Persians to conquer them. And now He has brought us back to our land. We're going to rebuild His temple when spring comes. Let's just do the work He has given us, and in His good time our enemies will be avenged."

Zechariah was too angry to let it go. And he knew that the real source of his frustration was his failure to stop Yael from sinning and worshiping idols. The fresh figs on the platter in front of him were one of the many "gifts" she had brought home with her. If only he and the others could conquer that stupid village and raze it to the ground in revenge, then she couldn't go there anymore. He excused himself and went to sit alone outside the sukkah where he could see the night sky. The clouds had blown away and thousands of stars had taken their place. *"The heavens declare the glory of God,"* King David had written. *"The skies proclaim the work of his hands."* King David had talked to the Holy One beneath these same heavens and written his psalms of praise. He had worshipped the one true God, not the moon and the stars.

Zaki heard someone approaching and was afraid to look up, worried that it was Saba. It was Yael. She sat down on a stone beside him. "I heard what you and your grandfather were arguing about, and I don't blame you for wanting justice. See those stars up there?" She pointed to the sky. "The constellation Libra—the balance scales—is above us during the month of Tishri. If you want to see the scales of justice balanced, this is the time to do it, while Libra is high in the sky."

"Please, Yael, you've got to stop worshiping the stars," he said with a groan. "You're going to get into terrible trouble with all that nonsense."

"It isn't nonsense. The heavens can tell us the best times to do things, like when to plant our crops or choose a wife or get revenge on our enemies. And everyone wants to know the future, don't they? It gives us hope to see what's ahead."

"It's idolatry, Yael. And it's wrong. There's only one God— the God of our father Abraham. Only He knows the future."

She made a sound of contempt. "The moon goddess had a beautiful temple in Babylon. Why is your God's temple a pile of ruins?"

Her questions stirred his fear for her the way a stick stirs coals into flames. "It's in ruins because our ancestors stopped worshiping God and turned to idols, just like you're doing. The prophet Ezekiel watched the Holy One's presence leave the temple before it was destroyed. But all of God's promises about returning from exile and rebuilding the temple are coming true. That's why we're here."

"There. You said it. Your prophets are able to foretell the future, too. How do you know they didn't see it in the stars? Leyla's grandmother said that King David knew how to read the stars."

"No, he didn't."

"He wrote in one of his songs that the heavens give us knowledge at night."

Zechariah felt a chill run through him. Hadn't he just been thinking of that psalm? "'The heavens declare the glory of God . . .'" he quoted. "'Night after night they display knowledge.'"

"Yes! That's the one! King David wrote those words, didn't he?"

"Yes, but he must have meant something else because the Torah clearly says that sorcery and astrology are wrong."

"You can believe whatever you want," she said with a shrug, "but I can see things in the heavens, and what I see always comes true."

"Shh! Don't say things like that where people can hear you!" He sat very still, waiting to see if Saba or Joel or one of the other men had overheard. But the soft murmur of laughter and voices from inside the sukkah reassured him that they hadn't.

He struggled to think of a way to convince Yael that she was wrong, and he remembered that the prophet Ezekiel had also seen the Almighty One's glory and presence returning to the temple. The temple was still a pile of ruins of course, where no one was allowed to go. But what if Zechariah could sneak up there some night and find the place among the ruins where the Holy of Holies had been? Yael could go with him to help him avoid the guards and maybe they both would feel His presence. If only she could experience what he had on the day of his bar mitzvah, maybe she would finally give up her idolatry and sorcery. His heart raced as he made up his mind.

"Do you want to go exploring with me in secret?" He leaned close to ask.

"You're not going down to Leyla's village for revenge, are you?"

"No. Not there." His cheeks grew warm at the memory of how he had been beaten and humiliated in front of Yael. "I should warn you that it's dangerous to go where I want to go. We'll be in trouble if we get caught."

A wide grin spread across Yael's face. "I don't care. I'll go with you."

He shook his head at her daring. The threat of danger or trouble didn't faze her in the least. She had smiled! "You have to promise not to tell anyone," he warned.

"*I* can keep a secret," she said, emphasizing her words. "When do you want to go?"

His heart thumped faster. "How about tonight? After everyone is asleep." Before he lost his nerve.

"Sure. Where are we going?"

"Up to the temple mount."

She had been alert with excitement at the prospect of adventure but her shoulders sagged at his words. "That's not dangerous. You go there all the time for the sacrifices."

"The altar is on the eastern side of the mount. I want to explore the middle part, where the temple used to be. We're not supposed to go there, and they have guards who patrol all night. . . . You don't have to come if you're afraid," he challenged.

"I'm not afraid. If they ask me what I'm doing there, I'll say I'm looking for my father. He's been on night watch a couple of times."

"It's never a good idea to lie, Yael."

Her hands went to her hips. "Do you want me to come with you or not?"

Yes. He did. But how *would* he explain what they were doing if they got caught?

The hardest part was remaining awake until everyone else was asleep, and then being careful not to disturb one of the small children who seemed to awaken at every little sound. Yael had promised to keep the door to the room she shared with her father open a crack, and when Zechariah peered inside he saw her sitting up. He motioned to her to follow him.

"Let me lead the way. I'm better at this than you are," she whispered after they'd gone a short way. She was right. His nervousness made Zechariah clumsy, tripping over rocks and sending stones skittering downhill. Yael was as quiet and agile as a deer. She obviously enjoyed sneaking around in the dark and seemed to think that eluding the guards was a game. Meanwhile, Zaki's heart thudded as loudly as his feet. His stomach felt like he'd eaten snakes for dinner. But he hadn't changed his mind.

They crept between the clustered houses, moving up through the center of the settlement and staying away from the walls where guards watched over the breeches and fallen gates. They spotted one of the guards near the stairs to the mount where the ritual baths were, and waited until his back was turned. As soon as he walked in the opposite direction, Yael led the way to the bottom of the stairs, crouching low. Thankfully the clouds had returned, hiding the moon's light and making the shadows dark and deep. The darkness also made it hard to see where he was going. He and Yael climbed the newly-repaired stairs without being seen, feeling their way, but she held up her hand to stop him before they reached the top.

"Let me look around, first," she whispered. Zaki sat down on a step to wait until Yael returned a few minutes later. "The guard went toward the altar so the coast is clear."

"There's more than one guard—"

"I *know*!" He heard her impatience, even if it was too dark to see her roll her eyes.

Zechariah crawled to the top of the stairs and saw the altar looming ahead of them, illuminated by the soft, red glow of smoldering coals. A thin plume of smoke curled into the sky above it. He could smell the aroma of roasting meat, left to burn throughout the night. He pointed to the mound of rubble beyond the altar and they made a short, crouching sprint to Solomon's porch. Yael chose a good place to hide among the fallen pillars and Zechariah sank down to catch his breath. His breathlessness wasn't from running but from fear and anticipation. Then they crept along the western edge of the mount, staying in the shadows until they finally reached the point where piles of fallen building stones blocked their way. They sat down again to catch their breath, hidden among the enormous stones.

"The guards can't see us here," she said, her voice quickened with excitement. "Now, tell me why you wanted to sneak up here in the middle of the night. Is there buried treasure here?"

"No, nothing like that. This is a sacred place. The temple that stood here was like a map, showing us how to get back what we lost when Adam sinned."

"How can a building be a map? And what did we lose?"

"We lost the right to have the Almighty One living and walking with us. But if we rebuild the temple and follow all the steps that He showed us—offering the right sacrifices, and the incense, lighting the golden lamp, and laying out the bread of His presence, then the Holy One will dwell here with us."

Her sigh and shrug told him she was unimpressed. "So why did you want to come here?"

"I wanted you to see that the Almighty One is the only true God—and that your idols aren't."

"I don't see anything but broken stones."

"Not here. We need to go a little farther." He bent over and led the way as they scurried the last few yards into the rubble. The stones were difficult to climb over and nearly impossible to skirt around, especially in the dark. But eventually they reached an area where some of the stones had been cleared and the square outline of the former foundations had been exposed. Zechariah drew a deep breath for courage and climbed over the crumbled foundation to step into the sacred area. He was there! Inside the holy space. Standing where Solomon's temple once stood.

"This is as far as we dare to go," he whispered. "If we accidentally step on holy ground, the Holy One might strike us dead."

"You're making that up."

"No, I'm not. A Levite named Uzzah was struck dead just for steadying the Holy Ark when the oxen stumbled and the cart shifted. This is where I wanted to come. I want to pray here." He sat cross-legged on the ground and closed his eyes as Yael sat down beside him. He longed to bask in the warmth of the Holy One's presence again, and longed for Yael to feel it, too.

Where are you, Lord? he prayed silently in the darkness. *Why can't I feel your presence anymore? Why did you ask me to leave my family and come here? What do you want from me? . . . And why won't you tell me?*

Zechariah waited. Then waited some more, praying that the Holy One would draw close to them. The night was so still that he could hear the sacrificial animals stirring in their pens, the occasional bleating of sheep. Time passed.

If you won't come to me, he prayed, *then please come to Yael so she'll believe in you.* He waited a few more minutes but nothing happened. God's presence wouldn't return to a heap of broken stones. They would have to rebuild His temple first. Maybe then Yael would find Him—and so would he.

Zechariah opened his eyes. Yael had her head tilted back as

she gazed up at the stars peeking from between the filmy clouds. "That's the central star," she said, pointing to a bright one above their heads. "All the other stars circle around it."

He felt tears welling up. He couldn't let himself cry in front of her. "Let's go home," he said.

The almond trees blossomed first, a sign of hope. Iddo breathed in the cool, scented air, excited to see winter end and spring arrive. At last, they would begin rebuilding the temple. Today was the eve of Passover, the anniversary of their deliverance from slavery in Egypt, and as Iddo watched Dinah and the two young mothers preparing breakfast, his wife seemed more content than she had for many months. Once again, she had children to care for, babies to hold in her arms.

Hanan's widow, Tikvah, had given birth to a baby boy, the first child that Dinah had delivered since coming to Jerusalem. "This travail is what our nation must go through," he'd told Dinah after the long hours of Tikvah's labor and delivery had ended. "It's always a struggle to give birth to new life. But our sorrows will be quickly forgotten when we can worship in the Holy One's presence again."

Now, as joy filled him at the prospect of their first Passover celebration in Jerusalem, he dared to catch Dinah's hand as she rose from tending the hearth and say, "Isn't the Promised Land beautiful in the springtime? The trees are in bloom, the poppies and wildflowers are flourishing among the ruins. Doesn't it make you feel . . . hopeful?"

"Yes, Iddo. It's lovely." She smiled her beautiful smile before shooing him out of the courtyard. "Now, go. We have a thousand things to do before tonight."

Iddo worked all day at the temple, helping the other priests slay the Passover lambs, one for every household. Each of the thousands of lambs had to be inspected to make sure it was free from blemishes, each one slain the proper way. The priests had been forced to purchase them from the local people at inflated prices to make certain they had enough for the feast. Pilgrims from all the scattered towns and villages in Judah were making the trip to Jerusalem as the Torah commanded. Shoshanna and Joel would join his family for the *seder* at sundown.

Dinah looked tired but content when they finally sat down together for the meal that evening. The people seated around her and Iddo weren't related to him by blood, but they had become family just the same. Mattaniah and Yael. The shepherd, Besai, and his wife, Rachel, and their children. Hanan's widow, Tikvah, and her children, who were learning the Passover traditions for the first time. Shoshanna and Joel. All the traditional elements of the meal were in place—wine and unleavened bread, roasted lamb, bitter herbs and salt water for tears, *haroset* to remember making bricks in Egypt. Iddo retold the exodus story, reminding everyone of the significance of this celebration and their deliverance from slavery in Egypt.

This time last year they had celebrated Passover in Babylon with their children and grandchildren, and it had been a somber meal. Everyone had been aware of the coming separation, and Iddo had worried about the long journey ahead. But Dinah showed no signs of sadness now as she played hostess for this meal and surrogate grandmother to all of the children.

Long before the lengthy meal ended, the children grew restless and were put to bed. But as the adults lingered at the table, Iddo learned that Dinah had been thinking about their children after all. She turned to Joel and asked, "Have any of the others heard news from home? Do you think our families will be coming from Babylon soon?"

"No one has heard any news since we left," he replied. "I wish we had a way to communicate with our families, but we don't."

"They would be leaving now, in the springtime like we did, wouldn't they?" she asked.

"We can only wait and pray," Shoshanna said. She and Joel were waiting for their grown children to arrive, too, but Iddo feared they would all be disappointed. If his sons had felt any longing at all to return to the Promised Land and rebuild the temple, they would have let nothing stop them from coming with the first group of returning exiles. Instead, they had recited a litany of excuses. Iddo doubted that they would ever come.

"Whether or not our families join us," he told the group, "we have many reasons to be excited about the months ahead. The construction of the temple will move forward at last. The high priest plans to begin next month, the same month that Solomon began building the first temple."

"I noticed a construction crane on the temple mount when I went to the sacrifice yesterday," Shoshanna said. "I wondered if it was the start of something."

"It is," Iddo said. "It took quite an effort to build a crane sturdy enough to lift and move those huge stones. Our workers went to great effort to cut timber from Israel's central forests and haul it up here to Jerusalem. They used the teams of oxen that were part of our caravan. Mattaniah can tell you how the crane works."

"It's a system of ropes and pulleys," Mattaniah said. "I learned to use a crane on construction projects back in Babylon." But Iddo could tell by the way Mattaniah looked down at his lap, avoiding everyone's gaze, that he would prefer to work his land rather than build. He had told Iddo once before that laboring with bricks and stones was a slave's job—a reminder that they had labored as slaves in Egypt and Babylon. Free men worked their own land and enjoyed the fruits of their labor.

"We've already hired masons and carpenters," Iddo continued, "and sent food and wine and oil to the people of Sidon and Tyre so they'll ship cedar logs to us by sea from Lebanon to Joppa. All the plans that King Cyrus of Persia authorized and funded are moving forward."

"The new foundations will be laid in the same location as the first temple's foundations," Joel said. "We're planning a celebration once the new foundation is finished."

Iddo reached for Dinah's hand, hoping she felt the contagious excitement in the room. "Rebuilding the temple is what we came here to do," he said. "And praise God, we're doing it at last!"

The work proceeded quickly in the days that followed the Passover feast. Iddo was overjoyed when the workers completed the new foundation in a few short months. Sheshbazzar, son of King Jehoiachin, who served as the official governor of the new territory, presided over the dedication ceremony dressed in his royal robes. It seemed to Iddo that all of the thousands of people who had been part of the original caravan from Babylon had returned to Jerusalem to celebrate the foundation's dedication. Perched on his platform where he played the silver trumpet, Iddo saw people jamming every inch of cleared space on the temple mount. Tears streamed down his face as the high priest in his embroidered robes and ephod gave the signal, and all of the people gave a great shout of praise to the Lord. Iddo didn't know if his tears were from joy or grief—maybe both. He had seen Solomon's temple as a child, and like many of the older priests and Levites, he knew that the new temple would have none of the splendor of the first one. The building stones would be much simpler and unadorned. No one had the skill or craftsmanship of those first artisans, and so the temple would be little more than a large boxlike structure. They also lacked the funds to adorn the structure with gold and bronze like the first one. King Solomon had been the richest man in the world, and the temple he'd built reflected his wealth. And so the older men like Iddo wept aloud when they saw the foundations of its humble replacement.

But at the same time, Iddo couldn't help shouting for joy, so loudly that his throat grew hoarse. The Almighty One had kept His promise. He had forgiven them and restored them. Iddo would worship and serve God at this temple for the rest of his life when it was finished. He had witnessed the horror of the first temple's destruction as a child, never dreaming that he would live to see this day. With the sound of deafening praise enveloping him, Iddo stood on the platform sounding his shofar, certain that the noise could be heard far, far away.

The lingering joy that Iddo experienced at the dedication was still with him the following day when a messenger summoned all the priests to an urgent meeting at Governor Sheshbazzar's residence. Along with living quarters for the two princes, workers had built a throne room where Sheshbazzar and his young nephew Zerubbabel held court and conducted business. The high priest and most of the chief priests and elders already had crowded into the simple, unadorned hall when Iddo arrived. He and Mattaniah found a place to stand alongside one of the cedar support pillars. Worry lines creased Governor Sheshbazzar's forehead as he opened the meeting from his modest throne at the head of the long, narrow room.

"I received a message from Shimshai, secretary to Rehum, the provincial governor of Trans-Euphrates. He requests a meeting with our leaders and priests, and with a delegation of Samaritan elders from the surrounding communities."

"Did they give a reason for the meeting?" the high priest asked.

"No. The last time we communicated was when I sent a formal complaint to Rehum after our shepherd was murdered. I provided details of our neighbors' terrorist actions, the thefts and beatings. If this meeting is in response to that report, it is very much overdue."

"If he's inviting the leaders of the local villages," Joshua said, "maybe he's trying to smooth things over between us."

"Let's hope so," Sheshbazzar said. "Protocol would dictate that I respond to this request by inviting them to meet here in Jerusalem. Rehum once controlled all of Trans-Euphrates Province, and he wasn't pleased when I was made governor over this city and the territory of Judah. Prince Zerubbabel and I met with him in Samaria when we first arrived. We've lived here a year now, and this will be his first reciprocal visit. And so the question I ask you to consider is, where should we receive them? My governor's residence is still incomplete, this hall too small. And besides, we don't want them to see our treasury—or even suspect that we have one."

"We can't meet with them on the temple mount," Joshua said. "It's out of the question. It's a holy place. The barriers that will separate the Court of the Gentiles from the sacred areas haven't been completed yet."

"How about down in the valley where the caravans first camped," someone suggested. "That area is vacant now that everyone has either moved to their ancestral villages or built houses in Jerusalem."

Mattaniah moved forward to speak. "I'm acquainted with one of the local village leaders, and he would view it as an insult if we met in the valley. He would think we were deliberately keeping him out of the city."

Iddo knew Mattaniah was right, but the idea of allowing the heathen governor or hostile local leaders inside Jerusalem worried him. "When we held the Feast of Tabernacles last fall,"

Iddo said, "we built a communal booth near the Water Gate. Why not erect another pavilion like that one, with a roof for shade, and offer to hold a feast for the leaders there? It would still be inside Jerusalem."

"Iddo has a point," Jeshua said. "An open-air pavilion would demonstrate the truth to them that we aren't wealthy and don't have much that's worth stealing."

"But won't they also see how vulnerable we are?" someone asked. "They'll see that our city has no walls or gates."

"Our neighbors already know it," Iddo said. "They were able to sneak in at night and sabotage our mikveh, weren't they?"

"Very well," Sheshbazzar decided. "We'll build a temporary pavilion as Iddo has suggested and prepare a small banquet to show our hospitality. As the leaders of our community, you priests and elders should all be there. One week should give us enough time to prepare, don't you think?"

Workers quickly erected the pavilion and outfitted the space with carpets and raised daises for Rehum and Shimshai at one end and Judah's most important dignitaries at the other. The Samaritans arrived in great splendor—and with a small escort of their own soldiers as if to emphasize their military superiority. Iddo sat with the other priests and listened impatiently to all the formalities as Prince Sheshbazzar and the governor of Trans-Euphrates exchanged lavish and insincere compliments. Mattaniah pointed out Zabad to Iddo, the leader of the local village.

"I apologize for the simplicity of our banquet hall," Sheshbazzar said. "Our foremost construction project is to rebuild the Holy One's temple, so we still aren't up to the standards that you're accustomed to in Samaria, even after living here nearly a year."

Governor Rehum lifted his chin as if a reply was beneath him. He was a short, swarthy man with the black, tightly curled hair and dusky complexion of Iddo's enemies, the Babylonians and Assyrians. His secretary, Shimshai, spoke for him. "Lord Rehum would be most interested in a tour of the city to see your progress. As you know, Jerusalem and the territory of Judah were under his jurisdiction for many years before you arrived."

"Yes, I am aware of that," Sheshbazzar replied. But Iddo was relieved when the prince made no offer of a tour. He remained cordial yet firm, and after more posturing and flattery and empty formalities, Governor Rehum finally got to the point of his visit.

"A year ago I received a copy of the proclamation from King Cyrus announcing the return of Jewish exiles from Babylon. Your intention, so it was stated, was to rebuild King Solomon's temple. I am aware of the recent flurry of commercial activity in my province as building materials have been ordered and shipped through my territory from Sidon and Tyre and Lebanon. And so I have come with my fellow officials from Samaria and with many of the local leaders to offer our assistance. Together we will all rebuild the temple that our sovereign, King Cyrus, has authorized."

Iddo's stomach made a sickening drop as if he had just stepped off the edge of a high wall. He gazed around at his fellow priests and knew that the look of shock on their faces probably mirrored his own. None of them had seen this coming.

"Like you," Rehum continued, "we also seek your God and have been sacrificing to Him ever since the time of Esarhaddon, king of Assyria. He brought our ancestors here and sent some of your priests to instruct us in God's ways. Now we're offering our manpower and our resources as we work alongside you."

Sheshbazzar stroked his beard for a long moment. He seemed to choose his words carefully as he replied. "Your offer is very generous, Governor Rehum, but unnecessary. King Cyrus has already made certain that we are well provided for. As his proclamation states, it's in his best interests to see that the Almighty

One is properly worshiped, and so he has provided everything we need."

Rehum's smile seemed stiff. "Nevertheless, since we'll be worshiping the same God as you, side by side with you once the temple is completed, we believe it's only fair that we help you build it."

His words were met with stunned silence. *No*, Iddo thought. *No.* The high priest couldn't possibly allow the half-pagan Samaritans and local people to worship alongside them, much less rebuild with them. It was unthinkable. Governor Rehum must have no place, no power, in God's holy temple. And that's what this really was, a blatant grab for power. When neither the high priest nor the prince replied, Rehum continued.

"We are willing and eager to work with you, sharing the costs and the labor. We have architects and expert craftsmen, experienced men, who will gladly work out all of the details with you."

Jeshua the high priest stood to reply, his voice so soft that Rehum had to lean forward to hear it. "We'll need time to consider your offer, Governor Rehum."

"To consider it!" Rehum looked as though he'd been slapped. "What do you need to consider? King Cyrus has decreed that we must all live together, and so we're simply following his majesty's wishes and offering to work together, as well. We've generously shared our land with you, as the king has requested. But I think you'll agree that the temple mount belongs to all of us."

Iddo began shaking his head. No. The temple mount belonged to the Almighty One, and He entrusted the Jews to rebuild His temple. But the high priest answered before Iddo could speak.

"I understand," Jeshua said. "But we don't make any decisions of importance without first consulting the Torah."

"We have the same Torah that you do," Shimshai responded. It was clear from the way that Rehum had slumped back in his seat with his arms crossed that he had been insulted and would no longer speak. His secretary would speak for him from now on.

"Even so," Prince Sheshbazzar said, "please allow our chief priests and scholars the time they need to consult God's Word. We would be honored if you would accept our hospitality at a second banquet tomorrow when we will give you their answer."

All work was suspended for the remainder of the day. Jeshua sent the Torah students home so he and the chief priests and Levites could meet in the house of assembly to formulate their reply. Iddo sent word home with Zechariah that the meeting would likely last the entire night. As the gathering convened, Iddo knew that the others recognized him as one of the leading Torah scholars. But he was astounded to learn that a handful of his fellow priests didn't see the Samaritans' offer the same way that he did—including his good friends Joel and Mattaniah.

"I know you must all share my great relief," Mattaniah began, "to learn that they're extending a hand of friendship to us. We won't have to worry and watch our backs as the construction continues. Or posts guards the way we did when the altar was being built."

"Yes. Let's come to a consensus quickly," Joel added, "before we insult them further with more delays."

"Wait," Iddo said. "I believe there's more to this 'friendly' offer than what we can see. Jeshua is right to proceed with caution. We need to pray and ask the Almighty One for guidance before we agree to compromise with them. Remember the trouble that Joshua and our ancestors got into when they made an alliance with the Gibeonites without consulting the Holy One? We don't know what these men's true motives are."

"Governor Rehum already told us his motives," Mattaniah said. "The Samaritans worship the same God we do and follow our Torah. Why not let them help us?"

"Anyone with eyes can see that we need their help," Joel

added. "Why build a second-rate temple for the Holy One when it can be as spectacular as King Solomon's temple with a little more help? I know that many of you share my disappointment with what we've built so far. If the Samaritans are willing to contribute money and manpower and skilled craftsmen, I say we should let them."

"It would be completed in much less time," Mattaniah said. "And wasn't that our goal in coming here? To complete the temple?"

Iddo hated to argue with his two friends, but he couldn't allow them to sway the others. All of the sacred scrolls were right here in front of him, and he quickly found the one that contained Israel's history, unrolling it as he spoke. "The Samaritans are a mixed race and their religion is also a mixture. According to these writings, when the Assyrians first exiled our people and settled outsiders here, wild animals attacked them because the people didn't know what the God of Israel required of them. So they asked the king of Assyria to send some of Israel's captive priests back to our land with the Torah to guide them."

"And like Governor Rehum said, the priests brought back our Torah," Joel said. "End of story."

"No, those priests from the northern kingdom had already fallen away from God, which is why the northern kingdom was punished first. I can show you here in Scripture how they worshipped golden calves in Bethel and Dan and built temples to Baal and Asherah. Their worship had turned corrupt long before the exile, and their priests were no longer descendants of Aaron. Yes, the Assyrians sent priests to them, but the Samaritans mixed the worship of our God with their pagan worship. You've all seen their shrines on the high places around here. The local people still have pagan ways."

"Why not teach them the right way?" Joel said. "Their young

men can study the Torah alongside ours so that the next generation will know what's right."

Iddo grabbed the fifth Torah scroll, appalled at the thought of Zechariah studying alongside the brutish boys who had beaten and mocked him. "It says right here, when Moses gave us instructions before reaching the Promised Land, 'Make no treaty with them, and show them no mercy.' We can't be deceived the way Joshua was."

"My friend Zabad traces his ancestry to the Jews who were left behind during the exile," Mattaniah said. "The Babylonians left some of the poorest people here to work the land, remember? Zabad is a son of Abraham just like we are, and he has a right to help us build and to worship God with us."

"Is he a pure son? Are his wives Jews or pagans? Are all of his ancestors pure?"

The exchange quickly became heated, and Iddo was grateful when the high priest entered the discussion, taking his side. "If Zabad can show us his genealogy and prove that his family hasn't intermarried with the Samaritans, then yes, he and men like him may worship with us. But not men of mixed race. They must remain in the Court of the Gentiles. And I'm sorry to say that includes Governor Rehum."

"Fine," Mattaniah said. "But I still don't see the harm in accepting their help and allowing them to work with us. Heaven knows we could use it. We don't have experienced architects and craftsmen, and they do."

"If we let them build with us, they can claim that the temple is rightfully theirs just as much as ours," Iddo said. "What if they want to introduce something foreign to our worship? Or change the way that the Almighty One has said to do things?"

"We can't allow it," Jeshua said.

"The Almighty One hates a mixture," Iddo said, waving one of the scrolls for proof. "We'll end up in the same mess that caused our exile in the first place. If their sons study with ours, they could become a bad influence on our sons instead of the other way around. We don't have very many young people among us as it is."

"Yes, and they still have a lot of Babylon's ways in them," Jeshua said. "We can't risk losing the younger generation to idols."

"Fine," Mattaniah said again. "Then their sons can study in their own schools. But we still should accept their help."

"And what if they want to install their own priests?" Iddo asked. "The Torah says only descendants of Aaron can be priests. The Samaritan priests aren't Aaron's descendants and haven't been for centuries."

"Then we'll make it clear from the start that we cannot allow them to serve," Joel said. "Only men who can trace their lineage to Aaron."

"But if the Samaritans have contributed money and experts to help us build, won't they claim they have just as much right as we do to make those kinds of decisions? Won't they expect their own priests to serve in worship?"

"Iddo makes good points," Jeshua said.

"And what about their women?" Iddo continued. "If we're worshiping side by side with Samaritans, won't our young men be attracted to their daughters and want them for their wives? How will we answer them? If we've compromised and worked together in other ways, our young men will see no reason not to compromise in marriage. Since these Samaritan women have been part of their life all along, why not marry them, they'll ask. I can show you right here," Iddo said, shuffling through the scrolls again, "where it says, 'Do not intermarry with them. Do not give your daughters to their sons or take their daughters for your sons, for they will turn your sons away from following me to serve other gods, and the Lord's anger will burn against you.'"

More and more priests joined the discussion, and Iddo was relieved to see that he had swayed nearly all of them with his arguments. Late that night, when they finally reached the decision to refuse all help from the Samaritan governor and the local people, only Joel and Mattaniah still disagreed.

"I will talk to Prince Sheshbazzar myself," Jeshua said, "and give him our reasons for refusing Governor Rehum's offer." Iddo thought the discussion was finished, but Joel and Mattaniah were still clearly upset.

"How will the prince dare to refuse the governor?" Joel asked. "Rehum controls the entire Trans-Euphrates district. He could cut off our supply routes, sabotage our caravans. You're going to be very sorry if you refuse." Iddo heard the anger in Joel's tone and wondered if he had lost a friend.

"Our authority comes from King Cyrus," Jeshua said. "Governor Rehum has no right to stop us. He will be welcome to worship with us in the Court of the Gentiles, but he will have no part in rebuilding."

"You're making a huge mistake," Mattaniah said. "We need the Samaritans and the local people in order to survive. What if they refuse to sell us their produce and livestock?"

"The Holy One will provide for our needs," Iddo said.

"He already has been providing for us through the Samaritans!" Mattaniah shouted. "Who do you think we've been buying oil and grain and livestock from? Do you want our families to starve?"

"Mattaniah is right," Joel said. "What if the local people turn against us in full force? There are more of them than us, especially now that we're spread out across Judah in dozens of struggling villages. None of our settlements have walls for protection."

"Should we allow fear to rule us? Is that how we make our decisions?" Iddo asked.

"No, but we need to be practical. We don't have weapons—and they do."

"Why did the Holy One send us into exile?" Iddo asked. "Wasn't it because of our idolatry? We now have a chance to start all over again, and the first thing you're asking us to do is compromise with idolaters? Any one of our Torah students can tell you the story of how our forefathers failed to drive all the Canaanites from the land, and how the next generation adopted Canaanite ways and Canaanite gods, just as Moses warned they would. We don't have the authority to drive the Samaritans out of our land, but we must remain separate from them."

"It isn't practical to remain separate. We are too few. We need them."

"We can't afford to need them, Mattaniah." The long discussion had made Iddo's head ache. He found the third book of Moses among the scrolls and handed it to Joel. "Read this yourself. You'll find that God says, 'You are to be holy to me because I, the Lord, am holy, and I have set you apart from the nations to be my own.' We must remain separate."

Iddo stayed behind in the house of assembly after Jeshua dismissed the meeting. It was after midnight, but he knew he wouldn't sleep. He lit an oil lamp and continued to study the Scriptures until dawn, praying that he was right, praying that when Sheshbazzar refused Governor Rehum's offer tomorrow that their tiny, vulnerable community of Jews was doing the right thing.

The following afternoon, Iddo sat in the banquet pavilion again, nervously awaiting the outcome. Prince Sheshbazzar was tactful in his refusal, assuring Governor Rehum that the priests had all the help and resources they needed to rebuild the temple. "We are very grateful for your offer, but we must refuse it." As everyone feared, the governor and his officials stormed away in anger. Amid the outrage and recriminations, the local leader, Zabad, stood up to shake his fist at Sheshbazzar.

"You want nothing to do with us?" he asked. "Very well! If we aren't good enough for you, then neither is our wheat or our wine or our olive oil!"

"I told you so," Mattaniah said glumly after the delegation left.

The high priest laid his hand on Mattaniah's shoulder. "I know. You did warn us, but we had no choice. Now I want to ask a favor of you, if I may. You've been friendly with these villagers. Would you go to them and tell them the truth about how you disagreed with us? Try to keep the lines of communication open. Be our eyes and ears in their villages."

"You're asking me to be a spy?"

"I'm asking you to keep us informed so we'll know if there's an imminent threat."

"You want me to pretend I'm still their friend to get information. That's being a spy."

"Moses sent spies into the Promised Land, and Joshua sent spies into Jericho. We would be wise to follow their example. You said you were concerned for our safety, didn't you?"

"You're backing me into a corner, Jeshua. I need time to think about this."

Iddo returned home after the disastrous banquet to tell his family what had happened. He wasn't surprised when Mattaniah didn't return home with him. Dinah met Iddo in the courtyard with a worried look on her face. "What's going on, Iddo? Shoshanna and I were standing here talking when Joel burst in and grabbed her by the arm and hauled her home with no explanation whatsoever."

Before Iddo could reply, Yael came out of the house and asked, "Where's my father? Why didn't he come home with you?"

Iddo closed his eyes at the enormity of the rift he had created.

What if Mattaniah moved out and took Yael with him? What if Joel wouldn't let their wives be friends anymore? Either move would break Dinah's heart—just when she was almost happy again, enjoying the female companionship she'd had in Babylon. "Sit down, Dinah," he said gently, gesturing to a small wooden stool.

"Why?" She remained standing as if bracing for a strong wind. Zechariah and the two shepherds' wives all gathered around to hear, as well. Feeling weary, Iddo sank down on the stool he had offered Dinah.

"You all know about the delegation of Samaritans and local elders who asked to meet with us. Well, they came to offer their help in rebuilding the temple, alongside us. The chief priests and Levites met last night, and we decided to advise Sheshbazzar to refuse their offer. I won't go into all of our reasons, but we used God's Law for guidance. Joel and Mattaniah both disagreed with our decision. Now they're upset."

"Where did my father go?" Yael asked.

"I think he went down to talk to the local leaders. The Samaritans were angry with our decision, too. He's worried there might be trouble."

"But we can't get mad at them!" Yael said. "Leyla is my friend!"

"Wait, I don't understand," Dinah said. "Why did Joel make Shoshanna leave our house?"

"Because I was the one who led the opposition. And I convinced all the others to reach this decision."

"Oh, Iddo," Dinah breathed. "What have you done? Just when things were going so well here."

"We must live according to God's Word and trust Him to protect us. Our leaders made the right decision. Mattaniah and Joel will eventually see the wisdom of it."

But Iddo couldn't deny that he was afraid. He had witnessed

the wrath of godless pagans as a child. Hanan's widow was a constant reminder of the local people's brutality.

The last thing Iddo had advised the high priest and the prince to do before leaving them was to be careful—and to double the number of guards.

CHAPTER

23

This wasn't what Zechariah had wished for. He may have longed to do something more besides study all day, but he never wished for his studies to stop altogether. But the day after Prince Sheshbazzar turned down the Samaritans' offer to help rebuild the temple, the elders decided to close the yeshiva. Not only was there no way to safeguard the Torah and the other sacred scrolls except to lock them away in the treasury, there weren't enough rabbis left to teach the students. The prince had conscripted every able-bodied man in Jerusalem to serve as a guard. The building supplies for the temple needed to be guarded day and night. The breeches in the walls and even the city streets needed to be guarded, and there simply weren't enough men to go around.

The elders put Zechariah and the older boys to work as watchmen during the day. His post, overlooking the Sheep Gate on the north side of the temple mount, had a view of the distant Judean hills. Zechariah sat atop a partially toppled watchtower with a small shofar in his hand. He was supposed to blow it at the first sign of danger.

He perched on his pile of rocks all day, swatting flies and wilting beneath the dizzying sun. He easily stayed alert and vigilant at first, energized with the excitement he used to feel when he went exploring. Along with the excitement, he also felt an undercurrent of fear. Mobs of angry Samaritans might converge on Jerusalem at any moment, and he was responsible for sounding the warning. But neither the excitement nor his heroic daydreams lasted long as boredom and the sun's heat wore him down. By the third day, he found himself wishing he was back in the house of assembly, exploring the Torah's many mysteries beneath a shady roof. When his replacement arrived at the end of the third day, he handed over the shofar and hurried to meet up with his grandfather for the evening sacrifice. Their prayers were needed now more than ever.

Afterward, he and Saba stayed to hear the troubling news that continued to pour in. "Reports of property damage, thefts, and threats are coming in from all over the district," the prince said. "It's no longer safe to go anywhere alone. In some places, food is becoming scarce after the local villages closed their markets to Jews."

"Our work of rebuilding the temple has been forced to halt before it barely got started," the high priest said.

"Halted! Why?" Saba asked.

"All of our supply lines have been cut off, our caravans are being attacked, our building materials stolen before they reach us. We can't continue to build without supplies."

"Or workers," one of the chief Levites added. "We relied on local workers for our manual labor, and they've all quit. And where is Mattaniah?"

Yael's father still hadn't returned home, and Saba's friend Joel refused to serve with the other priests or speak to Saba. The three men had been such good friends and co-workers, and now this.

One of the elders from Tekoa had come to complain about vandalism and sabotaged crops. "Our families are being forced to live in fear," the elder shouted. "What are we supposed to do?"

"Come back and live in the city for now," the prince urged.

"Then who will grow wheat for us or raise our flocks or tend our grapes? Why did you have to antagonize our neighbors?" And although Saba and the other priests explained their reasons once again, Zechariah saw that the unity of their tiny community had begun to fracture. The Almighty One had performed so many miracles during the first exodus. Why wasn't He helping them this time?

"I'm sorry for all this trouble," Prince Zerubbabel soothed. "We're all praying that tempers will cool and things will return to normal. The local people will soon realize that it's in their best interests to trade with us and work for us."

"Saba, there's something I don't understand," Zechariah said as they walked home afterward. "Didn't the Almighty One promise Abraham that all the people on earth would be blessed through him?"

"Yes, that was the promise."

"Then how can we be a blessing if we shut everyone out and refuse to let them worship with us?"

"They may worship with us, but they have to do it the way God prescribed, following His Law."

"I thought that's what the Samaritans were offering to do."

Saba shook his head. "We had no guarantee that they would give up their pagan ways and serve only God. If we allowed the Samaritans to help us rebuild, we would have to allow them to make decisions with us, and we couldn't take that risk."

"But . . . when I was reading through the scrolls of the prophets, they said that someday all nations would worship with us. How will that ever happen if we keep turning them away?"

They had reached home, and before Saba could reply, Safta came out to meet them. "There you are!" she said. "Dinner is waiting." Zaki saw his grandmother's relief each time he and Saba returned home safe and sound at the end of the day.

"There must be an answer to your question, Zechariah," Saba said as they washed their hands before the meal, "but I don't know what it is, yet. As soon as this trouble blows over, I promise we'll search the Scriptures together for the answer."

They sat down to eat, but the atmosphere around the table seemed tense. "Where's Rachel tonight?" Saba asked, looking all around. The shepherd's wife wasn't eating with them or working in the courtyard.

Safta leaned close to him and said, "You need to talk to her, Iddo. She's so worried about Besai that she can barely perform the simplest household chores."

"We sent as many men as we could spare out to the grazing lands to safeguard Besai and our temple flocks," Saba told her. "But he can't return to Jerusalem until all the ewes give birth and the new spring lambs gain strength."

"I hate being surrounded by so much fear and hostility," Safta said as she pushed away her plate. The worry crease on her forehead seemed to be permanent. "Armed guards came with us to the spring again today, but we're forced to wait until late in the day once again, until the local women are gone. We have to haul water up the hill at noon, in the heat of the day." Zechariah knew all about the sun's brutal heat—and he wasn't required to carry a heavy water jar like Safta. "Your decision has divided our community, Iddo, and we need each other now more than ever."

"I'm not happy about it, either. But when we do the right thing and obey God, we can expect opposition from the world. It's always easier to compromise. There's a difference between the easy way and the right way."

They were still eating when Mattaniah finally returned home for the first time in three days. Yael jumped up from her place and ran to him, clinging to him. "I didn't know where you were, Abba, or what happened to you!" Her words sounded muffled against his chest. She had been afraid for him all this time, Zaki realized, and hadn't let her fear or worry show.

"I'm fine, Yael. I'm fine."

"Have something to eat," Safta offered as she rose to wait on him. "There's plenty."

"No, thank you, Dinah. I can't stay. I only came back for some of my things. I need to leave again before dark." He disappeared into his room, and Zechariah could hear him shuffling around as he packed his belongings. No one seemed hungry anymore. Saba stood to talk with Mattaniah when he came out again.

"I hate this rift between us. Please stay. We've come to think of you as a son, your daughter as our granddaughter."

"I'm not leaving because I'm angry. My friend Zabad has agreed to keep renting the land to me. He even sold me a couple of goats so we'll have milk for the little ones from now on, and Dinah can make cheese. But I need to show good faith by living down there instead of here in Jerusalem. I'm building a house." He paused, looking down at his feet for a moment before continuing. "I've decided to do what Jeshua asked and be your eyes and ears. Not because I like the idea—I don't. But for our families' sakes."

Yael had disappeared into the room she shared with Mattaniah while he and Saba talked. She reappeared with her bag packed and her bedroll tied, and handed them to her father. "What's all this, Yael?"

"I gathered my things, like you said, so I can go with you."

"Not this time. Everything is too unsettled. You have to stay here with Dinah and Iddo for now."

"But I don't want to stay here. I want to be with you!"

"I'll be back and forth whenever I can. You'll see me."

"I haven't visited Leyla all week. When can I see her again?"

"Not anytime soon, I'm afraid. Wait until tempers cool." Mattaniah tried to hand back her things, but Yael let them drop to the floor, then stalked off to her room. Zaki thought he heard her crying. He felt enormous relief. The only good thing to come out of this mess was that Yael could no longer go to the village and read fortunes.

Zechariah was still in bed the next morning when his grand-mother's shout awakened him. "Iddo! Iddo, come quick! Yael's gone! She's gone!" Zaki leaped out of bed and went to see. "I came in to wake her up," Safta said, "and look! Her room is empty. Her bag and bedroll are missing." This was much worse than when Yael had run away in Babylon. This time it was dangerous for anyone to go off by themselves, even grown men.

"Don't worry," Saba soothed. "She couldn't have gone far. We have guards all over the city to keep intruders out. She couldn't have gotten past them."

Zechariah knew better. Yael would make a game of sneaking past the guards. She was stubborn and fearless—and too young and naïve to know what a gang of village boys would do to her if Leyla's brother wasn't with them.

"We have to find her!" Safta insisted.

"We will, Dinah. As soon as I get back from the morning sacrifice."

"How can you go up to the temple when she's missing?"

"It's barely dawn. She couldn't have gone far. She would never leave in the dark. One of the guards has probably found her by now."

Zechariah needed to tell them that Yael wasn't afraid of the dark and that she knew how to evade the guards. But they would ask how he knew, and then he would incriminate himself. He remembered the beating he had suffered at the hands of the Samaritans and fear for his friend tied his stomach in a knot. For Safta's sake—and for Yael's—he had to say something.

"Saba? Yael is small and wiry. She loves to climb around on

rocks and things. I think she could easily sneak past the guards if she wanted to. I'll bet she went to be with her father."

"You have to go look for her!" Safta said. "Didn't Mattaniah tell us it was dangerous down there? Don't you remember the gang of boys who attacked Zechariah?"

"And haven't you been telling me how strong-willed Yael is? Perhaps suffering the consequences of her rebellion will teach her a lesson."

"Iddo! How can you say such a terrible thing?" The color seemed to drain from Safta's face. "How can you walk away when Yael might be in danger and say that she deserves it? She's a child! And we're responsible for her!"

Saba was maddeningly calm. "When I get back from prayers, I'll go look for her."

"No! You need to go look for her *now*, not mumble useless prayers!"

"Enough, Dinah. My mind is made up."

Zechariah accompanied Saba to the temple, but he couldn't concentrate on the sacrifice or his prayers. He wished the priests would hurry. Safta was right to be worried. Yael was too strong-willed, too fearless, for her own good. And Saba was wrong to waste time at the sacrifice when they should be searching for her. Again, Zechariah remembered his own brutal beating and felt sick inside. By the time the service ended, he had made up his mind to go down to the valley and search for his friend himself. "I want to help you find Yael," he told his grandfather.

"Absolutely not. If she did manage to leave the city to look for her father, I don't want you down there. Especially now, with all the trouble."

"I'm not afraid." He sounded braver than he felt.

"Zechariah—"

"I'm an adult now. I can make my own decisions."

"Yes, but this is a terrible one."

"Maybe so, but it's mine to make. If you don't let me come, I'll go search by myself after you leave—but I'd rather go with you."

Saba lifted the kippah off his head and ran his hand through his white hair before replacing his cap again with a sigh. "If you're determined to defy me, then I'd rather you come with me than go off alone." They returned home to tell Safta they were going to search for Yael, but they didn't mention that they were leaving the city.

Zechariah didn't realize how trapped and confined he had felt being cooped up in Jerusalem until he passed the guards at the checkpoint and walked down the road from the city. As the lush Kidron Valley spread out before him, he didn't blame Yael for wanting to escape. If danger lurked here, he didn't see it. He longed to run down the path in the bright sunshine, leaping like a calf set free from its stall. Much too soon they reached Mattaniah's patch of land, his sprouting crops laid out neatly in rock-bordered plots. Two goats grazed near the hut he had built, and he was already at work, bending over his grove of grape vines. If Yael was here with him, Zechariah didn't see her. Mattaniah stopped working when he saw them and stood up straight, wiping sweat from his brow.

"Is Yael with you?" Saba called out as they drew near.

Mattaniah froze for a moment before hurrying toward them. "What do you mean? No, she's not with me. I left her with you and Dinah."

Saba's shoulders sagged and for the first time, Zechariah glimpsed his worry. "Yael is missing," he said. "When Dinah went in to wake her up this morning she was gone. So were her bedding and her bag. We thought she might have followed you here."

Mattaniah appeared stricken. He glanced all around as if he needed to sit down somewhere. "I . . . I don't see how she could have left the city. I had to pass the guards myself when I came up to the city last night and when I left again."

"Zaki seems to think she could sneak past them."

Mattaniah lifted his arms, then dropped them again, help-lessly. "The only other place I can think of where she might be is with her friend, Leyla. She hasn't been able to visit her and . . ."

"Do you want us to come with you, Mattaniah?"

"Not if you're going to be hostile toward them—especially if they have my daughter!"

"I can be calm," Saba said quietly. "They wouldn't hurt her, I don't think. The gang of boys left her alone the last time, didn't they?"

"Zabad's family has always treated her well. But what if she isn't there?" He looked as though he was about to panic.

"One step at a time," Saba soothed. "We'll find her. But I think we should send Zechariah back to the city first."

"No! I want to come with you!" He wanted to show the boys who had beaten him that he wasn't afraid, that he wouldn't cower in fear. And if they had laid a single hand on Yael, he wanted to be there to exact revenge.

"What do you think?" Saba asked Mattaniah. "Is it safe for him to come with us?"

"It doesn't matter. Let's just go!"

Mattaniah set a brisk pace as they walked across the narrow valley to the village.

The elders sitting at the entrance took them straight to Zabad's house. His son Rafi met them at the gate to the compound, and although Zechariah recognized him as one of the gang members, he wasn't one of the boys who had attacked him. Rafi led them into the house and into a dark, shadowy room where Zabad sat on a raised dais like a king on his throne.

"Mattaniah, my friend," he said, gesturing for him to approach. "I think I know why you're here. We were very surprised when your daughter came to visit Leyla without you." Zechariah felt his knees go weak with relief.

Mattaniah exhaled. "Then she's here. Thank you, my lord, for taking her in."

"Yes, she's here." Zabad smiled, a grin of superiority that held no warmth. "Unlike your people, we're careful to keep a close watch over our young girls, for their own safety."

"What Yael did was inexcusable, my lord. She was upset about the rift between our people and yours. We're all concerned about it—isn't that right, Iddo?"

Saba took a small step forward and gave a slight bow of his head. "Yes. There have been too many misunderstandings in the past, and what has happened most recently has all of my fellow Jews unhappy. Our leaders never meant to imply that you weren't welcome to worship with us. We would be happy to discuss it further—whenever you're ready to speak with us, of course."

Zabad took a sip from his cup without replying. He had offered none of the usual courtesies of hospitality.

"We won't take any more of your time," Saba said. "My wife is very concerned about Yael since she disappeared without telling anyone. I know it would be a great relief to her if we brought Yael home."

"Thank you, my lord, for taking care of her for me," Mattaniah added.

Rafi escorted them from the room again and back out to the courtyard. Yael was waiting for them there, bag and bedroll in hand. She looked defiant, but at a gesture from her father she remained quiet until they were well down the road away from the village.

"I don't want to go back to the city, Abba. I want to stay with you."

"That's out of the question."

"Why can't—?"

"Be quiet! You shamed me today! Zabad thinks that I don't

259

care enough about you to watch over you. He believes that our people don't value our women."

"But—"

"But nothing! You got away with too much in Babylon because your mother was ill, but that needs to change. You can't do whatever you want to here. And you can never, ever go off alone again. Do you understand?"

"When can I visit Leyla?"

"Not until I say so. That's your punishment. And if you run away again, I'll have you beaten for your own good."

Zechariah glanced at Yael, expecting to see tears. Instead, she was dry-eyed, her chin held high in defiance. What catastrophe would it take, he wondered, before her stubbornness was finally broken?

CHAPTER 24

Dinah was on her way to the spring late in the morning with Yael and the other women when she heard someone calling her. "Dinah, wait!" She turned to see her cousin Shoshanna hurrying to catch up. Dinah pulled her into her arms for a long embrace. "I've missed you so much," she murmured.

"I know. I've missed you, too. We may not be able to cook or eat meals together, but no one can stop us from walking to the spring together." They linked arms as they continued down the ramp toward the spring, balancing their jars on their heads. "We've been friends all our lives, Dinah, and that will never change."

"Of course it won't. But do you think this disagreement between our husbands will ever mend?"

"Joel is still furious with Iddo. He's convinced that the council made the wrong decision."

"Iddo told me about it, and I want you to know that I think Joel is right. Why refuse an honest offer to work together? Look at all the trouble Iddo's stubbornness has caused. Life here was hard enough without making it nearly impossible."

"I wish there was some way we could talk to the Samaritans'

wives," Shoshanna said. "Woman to woman. We have much more in common with them than our husbands have with their husbands. We're all mothers with families—we can better understand the Almighty One's love. We should be telling our neighbors about His grace, not turning them away in anger."

"The only thing Iddo ever talks about is God's wrath and punishment. And look where that's gotten us."

The women walking in front of them suddenly slowed. "Listen!" one of them said. "What's that sound?"

At first Dinah mistook the distant chattering for a flock of birds. But as she and the others rounded the bend she saw a mob of local women, faces shielded with veils, blocking the path to the spring. Dinah halted with the others, gripping Yael's arm to make her stop. One of the Jewish guards stepped forward to shout above the chattering, "Please! Move aside and let our women draw water!" The village women drowned out his plea with shouts and high-pitched cries.

"Why don't the guards just push them out of the way?" Yael asked.

"They don't dare," Dinah said. "If our men even got close to those women, there would be war." The mob had guards of their own—a gang of young boys Zaki's age who hovered in the background behind them.

The two Jewish men continued to walk forward, testing the local women's reactions, asking them kindly to move aside. When they were still several yards from the spring, the ring of women pelted them with rocks that showered down like hailstones. Dinah tightened her grip on Yael's arm as the men backed away.

"I can't imagine all this hostility over water," Shoshanna said.

"Let's go back to the city," Dinah said. "Come on. Iddo and the other men will just have to find another source of water for us. We shouldn't have to do battle this way."

"No," Shoshanna said. "I want these women to know that we aren't their enemies." She set her water jar on the ground and began walking forward. Dinah reached out to stop her.

"Shoshanna, wait! What are you doing?"

"Somebody has to be a peacemaker."

"No, don't! Stop!" But Shoshanna avoided Dinah's grasp and continued to stride forward, skirting around the two guards who now stood out of range of the stones. Shoshanna lifted her arms and spread her empty hands as if in surrender.

"We aren't your enemies," she shouted above the din. "We're wives and mothers just like you. Please, can't we—?" Her words were cut off by a hail of stones. Dinah saw a fist-sized rock smash into Shoshanna's head. A second well-aimed stone struck her face. Shoshanna toppled to the ground from the impact.

"No!" Dinah screamed. Her instinct was to run to Shoshanna's side, but Yael blocked her way, holding her back. All around them, the other women screamed and fled back toward the city as a barrage of stones rained down on them. Dinah heard the thudding rocks fall all around her but she was too grief-stricken to care. *"No! Shoshanna, no!"* she sobbed. "Somebody help her!" The two guards braved the barrage and ran to Shoshanna. Dinah would have run with them, but Yael was surprisingly strong.

"Stay here, Safta. Stay here," she begged. She was crying, too.

"Let me go, Yael!"

"The men will help her. You aren't strong enough to carry her, Safta." Dinah watched helplessly as the men reached Shoshanna and one of them lifted her in his arms. Stones pelted both men as they sprinted back toward Dinah and Yael, but thankfully neither man took a direct hit in the head as Shoshanna had.

"Safta! We have to run!" Yael suddenly cried. "The women are chasing us!" Through a haze of tears, Dinah saw that she was right. The rocks had stopped falling and now the local women surged forward, chasing them with angry shouts. Dinah was too stunned to move.

"Wh-where's my water jar?" She had no idea what had happened to it.

"Never mind, Safta. We need to run!" Somehow Yael got Dinah turned around and pulled her back to the city as fast as they could go. The two guards caught up with them, carrying Shoshanna, and Dinah saw her friend's lifeless face, streaked with blood. So much blood! It soaked Shoshanna's curly hair and ran into her eyes. The guard's tunic was stained with it.

"Bring her to my house," Dinah said when they reached the city. "It isn't far." The men carried Shoshanna into Dinah's courtyard and laid her down. She hadn't made a sound or opened her eyes in all that time. Dinah pressed her shaking fingers to Shoshanna's neck to feel for her heartbeat. It was weak, but she was alive. For her friend's sake, Dinah knew she had to pull herself together, to lay aside her shock and fear for a moment and tend to Shoshanna's wounds. *Please, God, let them be superficial. Please, when the bleeding stops and she wakes up again, let her be fine.*

"Her husband's name is Joel. He's a priest," Dinah told the two guards. Both men were bruised and bleeding from being struck by rocks, but they weren't hurt as seriously as Shoshanna. "Find him and tell him he needs to come right away."

"Do you know where he is?"

"No. He could be anywhere. The priests all work extra hours doing guard duty. Start at the house of assembly. Maybe someone there will know. But go! Hurry!"

Yael knelt down beside Dinah and wordlessly handed her a damp cloth. She cleaned the blood from Shoshanna's face and saw that her skin was badly scraped and her cheekbone probably broken. The larger wound above her eye, near her temple, was the one that worried Dinah. She gently dabbed away the blood, then probed the wound with her fingers. She felt the fist-sized dent in her friend's skull from the impact of the stone, felt sharp edges of fractured bone, and her stomach turned inside out. *No. Oh, God, no.* Shoshanna's skull was smashed in. There was nothing Dinah could do.

She bent forward, wrapping her arms around her friend, lowering her face to Shoshanna's chest. *Please don't take Shoshanna. She loved you, God. She wanted to come here so badly! How could you let this happen?*

Dinah was still weeping when the men returned with Joel. Shoshanna was alive, but she hadn't regained consciousness and probably never would. Dinah didn't know how to tell her husband. As the news spread and more people gathered in Dinah's home, Joel's grief turned to anger. He interrogated the two guards again and again, as well as the women who had witnessed the attack, including Dinah and Yael. Over and over they told him how Shoshanna had moved forward, trying to make peace. They were able to explain to him what had happened, but no one was able to tell him why it had.

"Don't just stand there," he told all the men who had come. "Go find the people who did this to her! Bring them to justice."

"It was a huge crowd of women and young boys," one of the guards said. "There's no way to know who threw that stone."

When Iddo arrived home, Joel lunged at him, his rage overflowing. "This is your fault! This never would have happened if it weren't for you!" It took three men to hold him back and keep him from striking Iddo. When Joel finally regained control, he lifted Shoshanna in his arms and carried her home. Dinah wept helplessly, understanding Joel's anger and grief, his need to blame someone. As far as she was concerned, Joel was right. Iddo was to blame.

"I heard that our women were attacked," Iddo said, moving toward her through the knot of people. "I was so worried about you, Dinah." He reached to take her in his arms, but she backed away from him.

"No. You started all this trouble by refusing to see anyone's point of view but your own. What kind of a hateful, unloving God do you serve?" She fled out of their courtyard and ran the short distance to Joel's house. She found him sitting on the ground with his wife in his arms, clinging to her as if his tears, his embrace, could make her well.

"Is she going to be all right, Dinah? Will she wake up soon?"

"I don't know . . . I don't know . . ." She sank down beside him and closed her eyes, weeping and pleading with the Almighty One to spare her friend. This couldn't be happening. They couldn't lose Shoshanna.

All day people quietly came and went, bringing food, offering their help, their prayers. "Just find the person who did this," Joel repeated. "That's the only help I need." Hours later, when night fell, he sent Dinah home. "I want to be alone with my wife."

Dinah did what he asked, but she dreaded facing Iddo. He was to blame for this as surely as if he had thrown that stone. When she arrived, she found Yael sitting outside their house with her back against the courtyard wall, looking up at the starry sky. Yael scrambled to her feet when she saw Dinah. "Is Shoshanna going to live, Safta?"

"I don't know . . . I wish I did." She wasn't ready to talk to Iddo, so she remained outside the gate with Yael as they both looked up at the stars.

"What month was Shoshanna born?" Yael asked softly.

"What difference does it make? Why is that important now?" But then she realized why Yael was asking. She knew how to see the future by studying the stars. The Babylonian woman had once seen Dinah's future, and maybe Yael could see Shoshanna's. "Can the stars tell us what will happen to her, Yael?"

"I'm not sure. I might be able to tell if . . ." She gave a little shrug.

"She was born in the month of Nisan, the same as me." Yael nodded and walked through the courtyard to her room. Dread filled Dinah as she waited. When she could no longer stand waiting, she followed Yael inside. She had lit a small oil lamp and knelt on the floor of her room to study a scroll unrolled before her, each corner weighted with a stone. When Yael looked up and saw Dinah, a look of guilt washed over her face—or maybe it was fear. "I won't tell anyone, Yael. What do you see?"

"All of the stars . . ." she said softly, " and even the moon . . ." She shook her head, and Dinah saw Yael wipe a tear. "They're all lined up against her, Safta."

Dinah closed her eyes as her tears began to fall again. Yael had only confirmed what Dinah had known all along. The rock had fractured Shoshanna's skull, shattering the bone, sending shards into her brain. She couldn't live.

When Dinah returned to Joel's house early the next morning, he was still holding his wife in his arms. But Shoshanna's body was cold and lifeless. "Joel . . . she's gone," Dinah whispered.

He couldn't be comforted. Dinah tried, but her own grief was inconsolable. She sobbed as she helped the other women prepare Shoshanna's body for burial. They held the funeral right away. Mourners gathered outside of Shoshanna's house afterward, bringing food and condolences, but Joel refused to let anyone inside. At last Dinah went home to confront Iddo, angry with him and his God. This was the second death among the returnees, and both Shoshanna and Hanan had died violently, attacked by their neighbors.

"Wasn't our people's punishment supposed to be over?" she asked. "We've been serving God, offering all the proper sacrifices. Why did He let this happen?"

"I don't know what to say," Iddo answered softly. His eyes were red with grief, but Dinah couldn't stop her angry words.

"Are you going to seek justice and punish the murderers this time? Shoshanna was trying to make peace with those people! We were all witnesses! They killed her for no reason!"

"Did you see who threw the stone, Dinah? Can you identify any of the veiled women? Did you see the boys' faces?" She didn't reply. Iddo already knew the answers. "Even the two guards couldn't identify her murderer."

"So you refuse to get justice?"

"No. I'm not refusing anything. I'm as outraged as you are. Our leaders will go to all of the local villages and confront their leaders. We'll do everything we can to get justice."

Dinah wasn't listening. "Why is God taking away everyone I love?"

"Dinah . . ." Iddo tried to hold her and console her, but she pushed him away.

"I blame you for this. You're the one who put that stone in the killer's hand!" Iddo turned and walked away.

As the days passed, Joel remained barricaded in his house, pushing everyone away. He refused to leave, refused to have anything to do with the other priests. "Please see if you can talk to him, Dinah," Iddo urged. "We're all worried about him."

She was worried, too. After breakfast one morning, she wrapped up a portion of food that she was too grief-stricken to eat and brought it to Joel. He sat alone in his inner room with all the shutters closed, his robes torn, his hair and beard disheveled. He looked up and saw her in the doorway, then looked down again. "Go away, Dinah."

Instead, she stepped into the room. "I know you hate Iddo, but please don't hate me. Shoshanna was much more than my cousin, she was my dearest friend. We brought hundreds of babies into the world together, and for as long as I can remember, she . . ." Dinah couldn't finish as she began to weep. "I miss her so much!"

"I know," he said hoarsely. "She loved you like a sister."

Dinah went all the way into the room and knelt down in front of Joel, laying the plate of food on the floor. "You were right, and Iddo was wrong. He never should have angered the Samaritans that way. I don't understand why he's so unbending, and I don't understand the God he worships."

"Shoshanna's death is so meaningless. She was so excited to come here, wanting me to be a priest and serve God. She's the one who convinced me to come. And look where it got her." When he covered his face and sobbed, Dinah wrapped her arms around him, weeping on his shoulder. She didn't care if the Law forbid her to hold him or to be here alone with him. They needed each other's comfort.

"Thank you, Dinah," he said when their tears finally ran out.

"I'll leave this food for you. Please try to eat something."

Every day that week Dinah put aside extra food for Joel and brought it to him after Iddo left for the day. Sometimes she talked with him for a few hours, reliving her memories of Shoshanna. Sometimes she simply held him and wept in silence. More than anything else, Dinah needed someone to hold on to and grieve with. Her sorrow required the warmth of another caring person no matter what the Law said. Joel didn't eat very much, and Dinah could see his handsome face growing gaunt. She was with him one morning when a group of priests came to his door.

"This never would have happened if you had listened to me instead of Iddo!" he shouted as he threw them out. "It should've been one of your wives who died, not mine! You're the ones who murdered her! You're all responsible!" Dinah tried to soothe him after they left, but he paced the small room, too angry to sit. "I'm leaving here, Dinah. I'm going home to Babylon."

She didn't believe he meant it at first, but she couldn't stop thinking about his words after she returned home and resumed her work with the other women. Joel was right; it could have been anyone's wife who had died. Surely no sensible man would want to stay here now, even Iddo. The local people would never make peace with them. Work on the temple had halted for lack of supplies and workers. No one would sell food to the Jews. Why not admit defeat and go back to Babylon? The Almighty One was clearly against them.

Thinking about Babylon quickly became an antidote to Dinah's grief. When she saw Yael standing outside their courtyard gate one evening, looking up at the stars, she went out to stand beside her. Yael seemed subdued since Shoshanna's murder, as if her death had killed Yael's usually lively spirit. Dinah looked up at the sky with her and said, "I know you can see things up there, and I need to know . . . I need hope . . . Am I ever going home?" Yael looked down at her feet, biting her lip. "You won't get into trouble, Yael, I swear. Your sorceress in Babylon was right about my heart tearing in two, and you were right about Shoshanna. If you know what the stars say about my future, please tell me. Are they against me like they were against Shoshanna?"

Yael reached to hold Dinah tightly. "Yes," she whispered. "Your stars are the same as Shoshanna's, since you were born in Nisan, and right now they're against you. But they'll change in time."

Dinah pushed free from Yael's embrace. "How much time?" Yael looked down at her feet again, but Dinah lifted her chin and made her look at her. "Will you tell me when the time is right? When I can go home?"

Yael nodded. "Yes. I'll tell you."

Two weeks after Shoshanna's funeral, Iddo tried reaching out to Dinah again as they lay side by side in bed one night, unable to sleep. She pushed him away. "Can you tell me why God took Shoshanna?"

"I don't know why. We can never fully understand the Almighty One—"

"Then why try? Why force Zechariah to study the Torah, and why go through all this effort to try to please Him, leaving our home and building a temple and sacrificing countless animals? Will He ever be satisfied? Why is He still punishing us, killing good people like Shoshanna?"

"Who are we to question the Almighty One?"

Dinah's temper flared. "Will you still defend Him after all this?"

"I'm sorry, Dinah. What I meant to say was . . . I-I can't answer your questions."

"You're supposed to be His priest. If you don't know the answers, then who does?"

Dinah spent more and more of her time with Joel, slowly coaxing him to eat and to come out of his room and sit in the sunshine. They talked for hours, sharing memories of Shoshanna and their life in Babylon, airing their dissatisfaction with life in Jerusalem. Joel's kindness and gentleness as they comforted each other made Dinah wonder what her life might have been like if she had married him instead of Iddo. Before long, she was spending all of her time with Joel, leaving home every morning, letting the other women do her daily work.

A month after his wife died, Joel finally seemed to find his way out of his grief. "Thank you for all your help," he said when Dinah brought him his breakfast one morning. He had changed out of his torn robes and trimmed his dark hair and beard. "I needed you and—"

"We needed each other. We helped each other."

"Yes, that's true. That's why I want you to be the first to know that I've made plans to go back to Babylon." Dinah's heart seemed to halt at his words, then speed up. "I have no reason to stay here anymore," he continued. "So I'm going back to warn my children not to come. God demands too great a sacrifice. If He would take a good woman like Shoshanna, then why serve Him?"

"Are you going alone? How will you get there?"

"I'm not the only one who's leaving. Several other families have decided to return, too. We're all fed up with the hardship here, the constant danger. It was a huge mistake to come. The temple will never be rebuilt now."

Dinah's heart beat so rapidly she could barely speak. "When are you leaving?"

"I've learned that the governor of Trans-Euphrates periodically sends caravans with tax revenue to the Persian capital. If I go to Samaria, I can travel with them for a fee."

Dinah flew into his arms, clinging to him, comfortable in his embrace after so many weeks, so many tears. "Take me with you, Joel! Please!"

"You aren't serious."

"Yes, I am! I never wanted to come to this godforsaken place to begin with. I never wanted to leave my family. I only came because I had to, because of Iddo. But after everything that's happened, I don't love him anymore. This is all his fault! I want to take my grandson back to Babylon before something terrible happens to him. I want to go home, Joel. Please take me with you. Please!"

He held her tightly and let her cry. "Of course, Dinah. Don't cry . . . Of course you can come with me. It will be justice, in a sense. I lost my wife because of Iddo, and now he can see how it feels to lose his wife."

Dinah wept with relief. She would start a new life with the man she should have married in the first place, back home with her children, her grandchildren. She and Joel were still holding each other when she heard footsteps. Dinah looked up.

Iddo stood in the doorway of Joel's house.

CHAPTER
25

Iddo stared at his wife, his friend. Surely this wasn't what it looked like. It couldn't be.

"What are you doing in my house?" Joel shouted. He released Dinah and strode toward Iddo, his fists clenched. "Get out!"

Iddo couldn't speak, couldn't breathe. *Dinah and Joel? Embracing?*

He had come to talk to his friend, to ask his forgiveness. To tell him that Prince Sheshbazzar was determined to meet with the local leaders and get justice for Shoshanna's death. Iddo came to urge Joel to go with them. He had never dreamed that he would find Dinah here alone with him, much less find her in Joel's arms.

"Joel is going back to Babylon," Dinah said. She walked forward to stand beside Joel, linking her arm through his. "I'm going with him."

Her words struck Iddo like a blow. *Dinah and Joel.* Iddo couldn't think, couldn't imagine . . . He turned and stumbled away, unable to say a word.

His heart felt like a dead thing inside him, a stone that grew heavier and heavier as he hurried away. He didn't know what to do, where to go, but he found himself trudging uphill toward the temple, then climbing the stairs to the top. One of his fellow priests spotted him and walked over. "You're not on duty today, are you Iddo?"

He shook his head. "I . . . I need to pray. Excuse me . . ." He couldn't find release with tears. Shock and rage had stranded him in an arid wilderness where his mouth, his tongue, his tears, had turned to dry sand. He hadn't wept as a child, either, even after all the horror he had witnessed. And he couldn't cry now. The deadness that he'd felt inside as a boy had crept through him again, overwhelming him, turning him to stone. *Don't think. Don't feel. Don't remember.* Once again, the people he loved were lost to him.

He skirted around the worship area and the altar, passing the abandoned crane and construction site until he reached the north side of the mount and the ruins of Solomon's temple. He sank down on a sun-warmed block of stone and hunched forward in grief, covering his face with his hands.

Dinah had told him months ago that she was merely going through the motions as his wife with no love in her heart, but he hadn't wanted to believe her. Now he'd seen the truth for himself. She didn't love him. She loved someone else. But what should he do about it? His heart and mind were so shattered by what he'd seen that he could barely think—he didn't want to think. But he would force himself to sit here and talk to the Almighty One until he came up with a solution.

If he refused to divorce Dinah, if he forced her to stay, she would hate him even more than she already did. Iddo would have to let her go. Back to Babylon. With Joel.

The realization doubled him over with grief. How could he live without Dinah? He loved her. Even now, even after what he'd just seen, even though jealous rage threatened to consume him, Iddo loved her.

But what should he do? Iddo's mind whirled in turmoil. The law clearly said that Dinah and Joel should both be stoned to death for committing adultery. And when he remembered seeing them in each other's arms, his rage screamed at him to do it. To condemn them both to a violent, painful death. As a priest, Iddo not only taught the Law, but was required to set an example in keeping it. Yet he couldn't kill Dinah. He couldn't inflict that horrible punishment on the woman he loved.

His fellow priests would tell him that God's justice must be served. She must be punished for breaking her marriage covenant, just as justice demanded that the person who had murdered Shoshanna must die. But Iddo had witnessed too many deaths, seen too much evidence of God's punishment in his lifetime. He couldn't bear any more.

Maybe Dinah was right. Maybe the Almighty One was cruel and unfeeling. Why else would He command such a law? Why else would His people suffer so much trouble? Where was the God of miracles who had parted the Red Sea and destroyed their enemies during the first exodus? Iddo had come to Jerusalem to be a priest, to serve God. He had wanted to undo the mistakes of his forefathers and rebuild the temple, teach the laws of the Torah. Instead, his sacrifice had cost him his children and now his wife. Why would God snatch his family away from him a second time?

The sun felt merciless as it beat down on Iddo's head. It would only grow hotter here among the shadeless ruins as the day progressed. *What do you want me to do, God?* He posed the question to the unfeeling skies, to a cold and distant God, never expecting an answer. But Iddo heard His reply, as clearly as if God had spoken the words to him face-to-face.

Forgive her.

Was his mind playing tricks on him? Forgive her? Even after she committed adultery? How could he forgive her? Wasn't he required to uphold the Law? And what about God's justice?

He thought back to the day when he first realized that Dinah's love for him was slowly dying. She had asked him whether he served the Almighty One from love or from fear. *"You believe we have to follow all the rules, do everything exactly right, or He'll punish our smallest misstep."* And her words had helped Iddo understand that God wanted his love, wanted a relationship with him, not mere obedience to the law.

Iddo stood, too agitated to remain seated, and paced the small area among the ruins. The huge blocks hemmed him in, frustrating him, and he felt like kicking them. But that would be wrong. These were the building stones of the Almighty One's temple.

He remembered where he was—in Jerusalem. He was here with thousands of other Jews because the Almighty One had forgiven him and offered him a second chance. No one could keep all 613 of the Torah's laws perfectly. No one. Especially Iddo. He had tried and tried, and yet measured against the plumb line of the Torah, he always fell short. That's why he bowed before God every year on Yom Kippur and confessed his sins. That's why the priests offered sacrifices twice a day. Iddo didn't deserve God's mercy and grace, but He offered it to Iddo just the same. What did God want him to do in return? Offer more sheep? More calves and lambs and grain offerings?

Forgive her.

Iddo sank down again. He remained seated on the broken limestone building block all afternoon, wiping the sweat from his face and neck, as the sun pressed down on him. He couldn't move, trapped between law and grace, afraid to take a step and make a mistake. How could the Almighty One give two conflicting commands?

As the sun finally began to sink in the west, Iddo heard the distant sound of music. The evening sacrifice. Was it that late already? He should leave. Zechariah must be waiting for him.

They had to attend the sacrifice and pray together. But Iddo couldn't move.

He recognized the words of the psalm that the Levite choir was singing: *"Give thanks to the Lord, for he is good . . ."* And the crowd of worshipers echoed the refrain, *"His love endures forever."* In verse after verse, God's wonders and miracles were retold and the refrain repeated, pounding into Iddo's heart like a hammer chiseling stone: *His love endures forever . . . His love endures forever . . . His love endures forever . . .* God hadn't left them in their sins in Babylon, separated from Him. They were here in Jerusalem because of His grace—with a job to do, a temple to rebuild.

At last the music stopped. And once more, in the silence that followed, Iddo heard God speak.

Forgive her.

Forgive Dinah.

When he was certain that the evening sacrifice had ended, he stood again, needing to walk, needing to escape the cramped confines of the temple's ruins. But he couldn't go home. He didn't want to go home. He made his way across the temple mount, down the stairs, down the hill to the house of assembly. He would search the Scriptures for answers.

Every evening the priests brought the sacred scrolls out of the treasury so any man who wanted to could study them for a few hours. Iddo wasn't the only one in the study hall. Jeshua the high priest already had several of the Torah scrolls unrolled in front of him, bending over them, reading them. Iddo randomly picked up one of the remaining scrolls and sat down to unroll it, not even sure he would be able to concentrate on it.

"The word of the Lord that came to Hosea son of Beeri . . ."

Iddo closed his eyes. He didn't want to read the book of Hosea's prophecies. He already knew the story of how God had told the prophet to marry a prostitute and then, after she was unfaithful to him, to take her back and love her again. God's message through Hosea was that God would take Israel back, even though His people had betrayed Him with idols. And here they were, back in Jerusalem.

Forgive her.

Iddo remained in the house of assembly all night, long after the other men left and the priests returned the scrolls to the treasury. He didn't need to read the other scrolls to know that they would all tell him the same thing. God's love was the theme of the psalms that he and his fellow musicians sang every day: *"He does not treat us as our sins deserve . . . For as high as the heavens are above the earth, so great is his love for those who fear him . . . You, O Lord, are a compassionate and gracious God, slow to anger, abounding in love and faithfulness . . . His love endures forever."*

Was God's law more important than His love? Did Iddo want justice for his shattered marriage or did he want Dinah's love?

He wanted her love. He still loved her and always would, in spite of everything. In understanding his own heart, Iddo began to understand God's heart. And he knew what he needed to do.

At dawn, Iddo finally went home. Dinah was awake, as he knew she would be, kindling a fire to prepare breakfast. She looked frightened when she looked up and saw him, as if she expected to be dragged before the chief priest and stoned to death. Her fear broke his heart. Iddo wished she could see how much he loved her, even in his anger. How much God loved her. But how could she believe in God's love when all Iddo had ever emphasized was His Law?

"Come with me, please," he said, gesturing to her. "You don't need to be afraid."

He saw Dinah's hands shaking as she set down the handful of kindling. Iddo led her the short distance to Joel's house. He was awake as well, and when he saw Iddo he shouted loudly enough to wake the entire neighborhood. "How dare you come back here? Get out of my house!"

For a moment, Iddo's resolve weakened when he remembered what he had seen yesterday. He was the one who should be shouting in anger, condemning Joel and Dinah for adultery. Iddo's face grew warm as rage boiled through him again. But God's command to him had been clear. *Forgive her.*

"Just give me a moment to speak, Joel. Then I'll go." Iddo turned to Dinah first, who cowered behind him. "When you return to our community in Babylon with Joel, you will be shunned and labeled a *sotah*. Our children will be put in a difficult place if they receive you back while you're still married to me. And so I want you to know that I'm offering you a divorce. You and Joel can marry—"

"Whoa!" Joel said, holding up both hands. "I never said I wanted to marry Dinah. My wife just died! You think I would replace Shoshanna?"

Dinah moved from behind Iddo and slowly walked toward Joel. "But . . . but you said you would take me back to Babylon with you."

"And I will. But not as my wife! Look, I needed comfort and you offered it. And deep inside, I also wanted to get even with Iddo. Until the day I die, I'll always blame him for Shoshanna's death."

"You used me?" Dinah asked, her voice hushed with disbelief.

"We used each other. Admit it, Dinah. You were as angry with Iddo as I was."

She stared up at Joel as if too stunned to speak, then turned and fled, brushing past Iddo as she ran out of the courtyard. He longed to run after her, but he didn't know if he should, if she would want him to.

"Get out of my house," Joel said again. "And don't ever come back!"

Iddo followed Dinah home and found her in their room, curled in grief, sobbing. He waved away the other women when they came to comfort her and closed the door. He knelt beside Dinah, asking God what he should do.

Forgive her.

He needed to forgive Dinah and take her back the same way God had forgiven His people after their unfaithfulness to Him. He needed to show his love to her. And that meant not only giving up his right to condemn her, but giving her what she longed for the most. Iddo would take her back to Babylon himself. He would prove his love by leaving Jerusalem a second time. That meant giving up his work as a priest, never worshiping in the temple, or having a part in rebuilding it. Did he love Dinah that much?

Yes.

A single tear slid down his face and into his beard. This was what God wanted him to do. Iddo waited until Dinah's sobbing tapered off, praying for the right words to say.

"I know you don't love me anymore, Dinah. But I've never stopped loving you. If you want to go back to Babylon, you don't need Joel to take you. I'll take you there myself."

She looked up at him after a moment, her beautiful face ravaged by sorrow. "Why, Iddo? Why would you do that for me?"

"Because I've made too many mistakes. You were right, I was too hard on our sons, and I want to make things right with them and with you. . . . And because it's what the Almighty One did, forgiving our people even after we went after other gods. I understand His love now, how deep and wide and everlasting it is. If He binds us tightly with laws and rules, it's for the same reason that we hold our children tightly in our grasp, to keep them from hurting themselves or being hurt. But God also gives us the freedom to leave His embrace and go our own way. He won't force His love on us, and I won't force mine on you. I'll take you back to Babylon, not so you'll forgive me, but so you'll forgive God. So you'll understand the truth about His grace."

"You would do that? After I turned away from you?"

"Yes." Another tear slipped down Iddo's cheek. He wiped it away.

Dinah stared at him as if waiting for him to say more. But he had spoken from his heart and said everything that he knew to say. He stood.

"I'll find out when the next caravan is leaving."

CHAPTER

26

The knowledge that she was finally going home to her family should have cheered Dinah, but it didn't. She sat by the hearth late in the afternoon, chopping garlic and leeks for their dinner and wondering how she had messed up so badly. How had she failed to see that what she felt for Joel was one-sided? He didn't love her. Their emotional attachment was bound by their grief for Shoshanna. He had used her to hurt Iddo, to get even with him. And she had done the same.

She pulled another garlic clove from the head to peel it. Iddo said he forgave her. He still loved her. He would take her home to Babylon. She was afraid to believe it, afraid it was a dream or that he would change his mind. For the past two days she had gone about her usual chores barely knowing what she was doing, her mind a confused mixture of thoughts and feelings. Even now she burned the vegetables and scorched the pot and had to begin all over again.

"What about Zaki?" she whispered to Iddo when he returned with Zechariah from the sacrifice that evening. "Does he know we're going home? Did you tell him?"

"Not yet. I thought we would tell him together. It was his decision to come here, so he must decide whether or not to return."

Of course Zechariah would return with them. Why would he stay here? "What about Yael?" Dinah asked.

"She'll do whatever her father says. I doubt if Mattaniah will want to return with us. Where is he, by the way?" Iddo asked, looking around. "He wasn't at the sacrifice."

"When Mattaniah came this morning to bring us some goats' milk, Yael talked him into letting her visit Leyla for the day. They should be home soon. Before dark, he said." Dinah had waited all day for a chance to ask Yael to consult the stars for her, to learn the best time to leave.

She and Iddo went through the motions of washing their hands, sitting down to eat together, and praying the blessing, but the others could surely see the strain between them. Their house was too small, the family too close not to notice the emotional upheaval. Halfway through the meal, Yael burst into the courtyard, upset and breathless, with Mattaniah trailing behind her. She went straight to Dinah and knelt in front of her.

"Safta, please! We need your help! Please, please come to Leyla's village with me. Please!"

"What's wrong?"

"Raisa is having trouble giving birth. I told Leyla's grandmother that you were a midwife and would know how to help her. Won't you please come, Safta?"

Dinah pulled her hands free from Yael's. "Why should we help them? These might be the same women who killed Shoshanna."

"Besides," Iddo added, "I'm not convinced that it's safe for either one of you to go down there after what happened."

"But maybe this is what we all need," Mattaniah said. "We could demonstrate our goodwill to them."

"But what if this woman or her baby dies?" Iddo asked. "Then what? They'll blame Dinah and say she did it for revenge."

"No, they won't," Yael insisted. "Leyla and her grandmother aren't like that. Please let Safta come. She knows what to do."

Dinah listened as the men continued to argue, her own thoughts turning one way and then the other. She pictured Shoshanna, bravely stepping forward to say, *"Somebody has to be a peacemaker,"* and knew that if she were alive, she wouldn't hesitate for a moment to go and help this mother. And Dinah also knew that if Iddo could forgive her, then she needed to forgive these village women, as well.

"Don't I have anything to say about this decision?" Dinah asked at last.

"Of course," Iddo said. "But for the good of our community we need to consider this carefully. I think I should consult Prince Sheshbazzar and see what he says."

"No. This mother needs me now. Delivering babies is what I do. I think I should help her."

Iddo stood and paced a few steps, crossing his arms then uncrossing them again, his turmoil apparent as he struggled to decide. "I'll come with you," he finally said.

"And do what, Iddo? Haven't I been a midwife for more than thirty years without your help? Mattaniah will take me there. He knows these people."

"May I come?" Yael asked. Dinah hesitated. There was an unspoken rule that girls Yael's age shouldn't witness childbirth or fear would overwhelm them when their own time came. But nothing seemed to frighten Yael.

"Yes, you may come if you'd like."

Dinah left the remains of her dinner and gathered up the things she would need. A few minutes later she was hurrying down to the village with Yael and Mattaniah. Dinah hadn't left Jerusalem in more than a month—since the disastrous day when Shoshanna had been killed. In all their years together as midwives, she and Shoshanna had rarely delivered a baby without each other, and Dinah mourned for her friend all over again as she walked. But remembering Shoshanna also brought a stab of guilt for the way she and Joel had behaved. Maybe going to this village and helping the people responsible for Shoshanna's death could help her earn forgiveness. Shoshanna would have forgiven everyone, even the person who threw the stone.

Night had fallen by the time they reached the village. For the last half mile, Dinah barely had been able to see where she was going in the dark. But oil lamps blazed in Leyla's courtyard and in several of the inner rooms when they arrived. Leyla and her grandmother led them to a room off the main courtyard where two women sat vigil beside a young girl, lying on a bed of cushions. Dinah stared at the white-faced girl, who was weak with exhaustion. She looked younger than Yael! "Is she Leyla's sister?" Dinah whispered to Yael.

"No, she's Leyla's stepmother."

"Stepmother . . . ?"

"Zabad has three wives. He married Raisa a year ago."

Dinah struggled to disguise her shock. How could any man marry a child who was young enough to be his daughter? But she couldn't think about that now. Raisa began writhing in pain, screaming as another strong contraction overwhelmed her. "How long has she been in labor?" Dinah asked.

"Since this time yesterday," Leyla's grandmother replied. She carried a cup of steaming liquid to the bedside.

Since yesterday. "You probably know that it's very bad for the baby as well as the mother when a birth takes this long," Dinah said. "I can't promise a good outcome, but I'll do everything I can."

"No one will blame you," the older woman said. "The stars foresee death for both mother and child."

Her words startled Dinah. The *stars*? Was everyone giving up because of the stars? Yet Dinah recalled consulting them when Shoshanna lay dying. They hadn't foretold anything that Dinah hadn't seen with her own eyes, but now her heart told her that as long as Raisa breathed, there was hope. Dinah would do everything in her power to save this mother and her baby, to prove that the indifferent stars were wrong.

"May I examine her?" Dinah didn't wait for a reply but knelt by Raisa's side and lifted the sheet that covered her. The contraction had subsided and she lay limp against the cushions again. Her pelvis was very narrow, and although Raisa was ready to give birth, the baby was positioned with its buttocks first instead of its head. There simply wasn't enough room for the child to be born.

"Am I going to die?" Raisa moaned. "I don't want to die. . . ."

The old woman knelt on the other side of her with the warm red liquid. "Help me lift her head so she can drink this," she told Dinah.

"What is it?" When the old woman didn't reply, Dinah rose to her feet and beckoned for Yael. "What is she giving her?" she whispered. "Raisa is in no condition to swallow anything. She could choke. And what's that burning smell?" Someone had lit a brass burner of incense and the acrid odor slowly filled the room. "They need to get that smoke out of here, Yael." Another woman draped two more amulets around Raisa's neck after helping Leyla's grandmother feed her the potion. Dinah recalled Yael's mother, and how all of the Babylonian rituals had been worthless. Her anger seethed. "Can't we chase everyone out of the room?"

"We'd better let them do these things," Yael whispered. "If Raisa dies, they'll say it was our fault."

She was right. And Dinah knew what she needed to do. "I'll need your help, Yael. I know a procedure that may or may not work, but it's our best chance of saving Raisa and her baby." She waited for the old woman to move away, then knelt beside the bed again. "Your baby is facing the wrong way, Raisa, and we're going to try to turn it around. I know you're tired and

I'm sorry for causing you more discomfort, but if it works, your baby will be born soon. Will you let me try?"

"I don't want to die. . . ."

"And I don't want you to die. Yael and I are going to help you change positions, rolling you over and turning you. We'll take it step by step, and maybe the baby will turn as well."

Raisa screamed through each of the maneuvers as her contractions continued. Each time Dinah moved the girl, she checked the baby, feeling hopeful each time there was a small change. Dinah had never done this without Shoshanna's help, and she missed having a second pair of eyes and hands. "We're almost there, Raisa . . . almost there . . ." Suddenly Raisa gave a blood-curdling scream that made Yael leap backward in fright. "She's all right, Yael. Just a hard contraction." It took more than an hour of maneuvering, but at last Dinah saw the baby's head starting to crown. "Everything's good, Raisa. Now, push . . . push!"

"I can't . . . I'm so tired. . . ."

"You can do it, honey. You're almost there." Dinah lost track of time as she worked to help Raisa, coaxing her, encouraging her, pleading with her. She wanted this mother to live, her baby to live.

At last she saw the baby's head emerging. But something was wrong—the umbilical cord was wrapped around the child's neck, choking it. "Wait, Raisa . . . Stop pushing, honey . . . wait . . . wait . . ." Dinah gently eased the cord out of the way and after one final push, Raisa's daughter was born into Dinah's waiting hands. The infant was a sickly, grayish-blue color—and she wasn't breathing. Dinah cleaned the mucus from her mouth. Slapped the baby's back. Slapped her again, harder. This child was not going to die now!

"Come on, little one. Breathe . . . breathe!" The baby finally gave a weak cry, and Dinah could breathe again, too. She laid the baby down for a moment and waited for the umbilical cord to stop pulsing, then tied it off and severed it. It was time to turn her attention back to the mother. Raisa couldn't afford to lose too much blood. The newborn gave another weak cry, and as Dinah picked her up to give her to the other women to care for, she saw that the baby's left leg was twisted at an odd angle, her foot pointing inward. Before Dinah could react, Leyla's grandmother grabbed the child from her.

"I'll take care of her now."

Dinah turned to concentrate on Raisa again. She was still moaning and writhing in pain, her last reserves of strength nearly gone. "Just a little more, Raisa. Can you push one last time for me?"

"It she having twins?" Yael whispered.

Dinah managed a smile. "No, she has to deliver the afterbirth. Then you can rest, Raisa. I promise. Did you hear your baby crying? It's a little girl." Dinah watched to make sure Raisa's blood clotted, then waited until her color slowly returned and she stopped trembling. Raisa would live, God willing, but she was about to faint with exhaustion. She needed to sleep.

"Where's my baby?" she asked. "Can I hold her?"

"Of course. I'll bring her to you." Every mother deserved the reward of holding her new child after hours of hard labor. But when Dinah turned around, the old woman and the baby were gone. "Where is she?" she asked Yael. "Where did they go?" Yael shrugged.

Dinah felt a chill, remembering the deformed foot. She hurried from the room and found Leyla's grandmother in the courtyard. She no longer carried the child. "Where's the baby? Raisa is asking to see her."

"The child died."

"No. I don't believe you. She was breathing fine. Where is she? Let me see her."

"It's too late to do anything for her. Besides, the father has rejected her."

"What do you mean?"

"Zabad saw his child, saw that she was a girl and that she was crippled, and he refused her. Even if he hadn't refused her, the baby was too weak to survive."

A cold fury rushed through Dinah. She grabbed the old woman's shoulders, shaking her. "What did you do with that baby? Give her to me!"

"The child will never be worthy of a dowry because she will never walk. It's better to let her die now. Better that Raisa grieves now than for her entire life."

"Raisa's baby is alive! She wants to see her child!"

"No. If she does, she will face an impossible choice. Her husband will divorce her if she keeps her child. Then neither one of them will survive."

"You cannot let that child die! Where is she?"

"We're grateful that Raisa will live, but now you need to leave us alone. This is our way. Our village. You have no right to tell us what to do." The old woman struggled to free herself, but Dinah wouldn't let go.

"Never! Give her to me!" Dinah was still wrestling with the old woman when she heard a faint cry. She released her and ran toward the sound. Dinah found the baby outside in the cold, stuffed in a basket and covered with a wet, suffocating blanket. She lifted the tiny, naked girl out of the basket and pulled off her own head covering to wrap her in. She held the child close, warming her, soothing her. "Don't cry, little one . . . don't cry."

There were many things that Dinah didn't understand about God, but she knew from her years of experience as a midwife that each life was precious to Him. Shoshanna had told her so repeatedly. If a child was born with a defect, Shoshanna would insist that the Almighty One had a reason for it—that a wonderful blessing would come from loving that child. She had often said that we became better people when we defended the weakest ones among us, the ones God entrusted to our care. Dinah remembered seeing tears in Shoshanna's eyes each time they saved a child's or a mother's life, as Dinah had done tonight. *"When we save one life, it's as if we've saved the entire world."*

Dinah looked up through her tears and saw the old woman standing in the doorway. "I'm leaving now," she said. "And I'm taking this baby with me."

"She will only die."

"Not if I can help it."

Yael and Mattaniah met Dinah outside in the street. She refused to go back inside the house. No one spoke as they followed the road up through the valley, up to Jerusalem, the baby whimpering softly in Dinah's arms. The sun was just dawning and the light reflected off the buildings, gilding the stones and making the destroyed city shine like gold.

"Were they really going to let the baby die?" Yael asked when they finally reached the top of the hill. Dinah could only nod. "How are we going to feed her without Raisa?"

"Hanan's wife is still nursing her son. I'm sure she'll be happy to be the baby's wet nurse."

"I can't believe they would have let her die," Yael murmured.

"I know." And Dinah realized in that moment that Shoshanna's death wasn't Iddo's fault, nor had God taken her life. The Samaritans had killed her, just as they would have killed this child. There was a difference between her people and the Samaritans and Babylonians, between their gods and her God—the God of Abraham. Iddo had been trying to tell her this all along, even when they'd lived in Babylon. She looked down at the tiny baby and understood for the first time why they had to leave Babylon and return to the Promised Land.

"We'll name her *Hodaya*," Dinah said. *God be praised.*

Iddo looked relieved when they all returned home safely—and shocked when he saw Dinah carrying a baby. "They were going to let her die," she told him. "I couldn't let her die." Tikvah offered to feed Hodaya, as Dinah hoped she would. She laid the baby in Tikvah's arms, then looked around for Yael. She found her standing all alone on the eastern side of their courtyard, gazing out at the sunrise above the Mount of Olives. Dinah had rarely seen Yael so quiet and subdued, as if she had been the mother who'd labored all those long hours instead of Raisa. Was she tired from being awake all night? Shocked after witnessing a birth for the first time? Dinah moved up beside her and slid her arm around Yael's waist.

"Thank you for helping me tonight. I'm not sure I could have saved either one of them without your help." Yael nodded but didn't reply. "What's wrong, Yael? Why so quiet?"

"I don't understand it," she said. "According to the stars, Raisa and her baby were both supposed to die. I read them myself."

Dinah saw the damage she had done by asking Yael to consult the stars for her. She never should have encouraged her belief in astrology. "God is more powerful than the stars, Yael. He's the one who gets to decide such things."

"What about Shoshanna? Did God want her to die?"

"No. God didn't decide to kill her, the Samaritans did. Just like they decided to kill this baby. They don't see the preciousness of life the way we do, or the way our God does. Maybe it's because they believe that their fate is in the hands of capricious gods and indifferent stars, and so they've become indifferent, too." She paused, wondering how to say what she was thinking. "Yael . . . I'm not going to ask you to consult the stars for me ever again. I don't believe in their power. I hope . . . I hope you'll see the truth one day, too." Dinah waited, wondering if she would respond. When she finally did, her words surprised Dinah.

"May I help you deliver babies again the next time? It was so . . . amazing."

"I hope it didn't frighten you. Most deliveries aren't as difficult as Raisa's was."

"I was afraid she was going to die—and I like Raisa. But I liked helping you, too. I think I'd like to be a midwife someday."

Dinah gave Yael a squeeze before letting go. "I would be happy to train you. You were a great help to me tonight. And now, maybe you should sleep for a few hours. We've both been up all night."

"May I hold Hodaya for a few minutes, first?"

Dinah watched Yael take the baby from Tikvah, surprised by how gentle she was. Iddo came to stand beside Dinah, watching Yael, too. "Did they reject the child because of her foot?" he asked.

"Yes. Her father rejected her, and so the women left her to die."

"But she'll thrive in your hands, Dinah, and she'll grow to live up to her name."

Iddo would accept this child as his own, love her. Dinah had never doubted for a moment that he would. She took his arm and pulled him outside the courtyard where they could talk alone. "Iddo . . ." she began. She was afraid to look up at him, afraid to face him, but she knew she had to. Her throat swelled with emotion as she spoke. "Iddo, I know you saw Joel embracing me, but I want you to know that we never committed adultery . . . not in a physical way." He closed his eyes for a moment and she saw his relief, his pain. "But I was still wrong to be with him, to turn to him for comfort instead of to you. And Joel and I were both wrong to blame you for what happened to Shoshanna. Can you ever forgive me?"

"I already have."

"And . . . and can God ever forgive me?"

"That's why we have an altar and daily sacrifices, so we'll have a way to come to the Holy One and ask for forgiveness. That's why our word for sacrifice also means to come near—to have a close relationship with someone. It's a lesson I'm just beginning to learn." Again, she saw lines of pain creasing his eyes and knew how very much she had hurt him.

"Iddo, I'm so sorry. Will you show me what I need to do to make things right? And . . . and will you make the offering for me?"

"I'll be the priest on duty in two days."

When that morning came, Dinah stood in the women's court-yard and watched Iddo take his place in front of the altar, his hair and beard as white as the turban and robe he wore. A scarlet sash was tied around his waist, and like the other priests, he worked barefooted. The daily morning sacrifice was a lamb, and Dinah watched Iddo expertly slit the animal's throat, watched the life, the blood, drain out of it. So much blood. She realized how close the two were—life and death. And knew she had come close to throwing something priceless away, just as the Samaritans had with Raisa's child.

Two priests assisted Iddo as he quickly removed the lamb's skin and inner parts.

Afterward, he walked up the ramp to the top of the altar and laid the offering on the fire. A cry of joy went up from the as-sembled men as smoke and fire ascended toward heaven. Dinah closed her eyes and wept as she prayed for forgiveness.

Iddo returned home much later than she did, after he'd com-pleted his duties and changed out of his priestly robes. He came to where Dinah was kneeling, tending the fire, and crouched beside her, staring at the ground. She saw tiny crimson flecks of blood on his forehead that he had missed when he'd washed after the sacrifice.

"Has God forgiven me?" she asked.

"Yes. We're both free to start all over again."

This was the Holy One's way, substituting a life for a life, with priests like Iddo acting as His servants. There had been no sacrifices for forgiveness in Babylon.

"And you, Iddo? Can you forgive me?" She needed to hear him say it again to believe it was really true. She saw tears spring to his eyes.

"Of course, Dinah. I love you."

"And I love you," she whispered. She wanted to say she was sorry over and over again, to hold him, kiss him, but she feared that she had forfeited the right.

Iddo cleared his throat. "I was talking to some of the other men today, and I found out that we can take the main road north to Samaria and Damascus, then make our way to Babylon by joining up with local caravans each leg of the way. It might mean staying in one town for a few days while we wait for a trader who has room for us. But the road from Damascus to Babylon is a major trade route, so we'll get there eventually." He looked up as if to see if she was listening before continuing. "I have the names of reliable merchants and traders who can be trusted. Our return journey may take longer than three months, but we'll get there. Before winter, certainly."

Dinah thought of little Hodaya's birth and of the many births she had witnessed over the years. When mothers like Raisa struggled in pain, especially during the last hours of labor when the exhaustion and agony were unbearable, many of them wanted to give up. She always urged them to persevere because the most difficult and painful times were in the last moments just before birth. What if their struggles here in Jerusalem were the same? What if their tiny nation was just moments from being reborn? She and her people couldn't turn back now. They couldn't go back to the gods of Babylon. Not when the sacrifices were finally being offered again. Not when men like Iddo had just begun to serve the Almighty One in worship. Not before the temple was rebuilt and God could dwell among them again. If she returned to Babylon, she would soon make her family into idols all over again. She would find her joy and purpose in them instead of in God.

"Iddo," she said softly. "Iddo, we're not going back to Babylon."

He looked at her in disbelief. "What?"

She touched his cheek, stroked his white beard. "I don't want to go back. I want to stay here and serve our God."

Yael sat in the courtyard in a patch of morning sunlight, rocking Hodaya in her arms. This tiny baby who had entered the world so dramatically two weeks ago had shaken Yael's world. She felt a fierce protectiveness and love for Hodaya that she'd never experienced before. Safta Dinah and Iddo had taken Hodaya to the mikveh and adopted her as their own daughter, but Yael loved her as much as they did.

"There, now . . . go to sleep, little one," she soothed, shifting Hodaya from her arms to her shoulder, patting her warm, narrow back.

"You're very good with that baby," Zaki said. "You always get her to sleep when nobody else can." He was about to leave for guard duty but she gestured for him to sit down on the low wall beside her for a moment.

"I watched her come into the world. It was so amazing. . . ." The memory still brought tears to Yael's eyes.

"Safta said that the Samaritans were going to kill her?"

"It's true. I was there." She hugged Hodaya a little tighter. "They told Raisa that her baby was dead, and they put Hodaya outside in a basket to suffocate."

"Because she was born with a crooked foot?"

Yael nodded and kissed her dark hair. "I don't know how anyone could kill a defenseless baby."

"Pagan people do it all the time, Yael. They sacrifice their children in the fire to idols. When our people began doing it, too—and even our kings did it—the Holy One punished us and sent us into exile."

"I wouldn't have believed it if I hadn't been there," Yael said. "I would have thought Safta was making it up."

"I never wanted to believe those stories in the Torah, either. How could people do such terrible things? But the stories aren't made up. And these Samaritans are our neighbors."

Hodaya's eyes were closed. She was asleep. Yael should lay her down and help Safta with the work, but she loved holding her, loved feeling the baby's warmth and life. "Hodaya has the same father as my friend Leyla," she said. "Yet Leyla didn't fight for her sister's life. I keep hoping it was because she didn't know about it. She was asleep when Hodaya was born. But Leyla's grandmother knew. She was the one who tried to suffocate her. I don't think I can ever face her again."

"Is that why you don't go to visit Leyla anymore?"

"No . . . I don't know . . . I mean, Leyla isn't cruel and she could never kill anyone, but she just accepts the way her people do things—like her father marrying a girl as young as Raisa. Leyla doesn't know any better."

"But we do. We know better. I'm starting to see why our people could never partner with the Samaritans to build the temple."

Yael didn't care about the temple. She simply was trying to understand her friend's family, people she cared for. "Leyla has been sickly ever since she was a child, but they didn't throw her away. Why was this baby different?"

"Maybe because Hodaya's defect is visible?" Zaki replied with a shrug. "I don't know, but Saba is always saying that we're different from the Gentiles. That we have the Torah to teach us right from wrong. And the Torah says that life is precious, every life, because we're made in God's image. Does your moon goddess say that you're made in her image?"

"Don't start preaching to me, Zaki."

"I'm worried about you, Yael. You need to worship the Almighty One, not the stars."

Yael no longer had her star charts. She had left them at Leyla's house the night Hodaya was born. She had felt lost without them at first, and longed to use them to look into Hodaya's future. She knew the day and hour of her birth and wished she knew which heavenly bodies had influence over her. And yet she didn't want to know. Part of her wasn't sure she still believed in the stars.

Yael heard footsteps and looked up, surprised to see Abba hurrying through the gate. He had just left for his farm a short while ago and now he was back. "Did you forget something, Abba?" she asked.

He shook his head, wiping sweat from his brow. "Leyla's brother just came to see me. His sister is sick and he asked you to come."

Yael shot to her feet, waking the baby. "Don't go," Zaki said, grabbing her arm. "Please."

"I have to. Leyla is still my friend. I'd never forgive myself if something happened to her and I didn't go to see her." She carried the baby inside and gave her to Safta, explaining where she was going.

"You can't go back there, Yael!" Dinah said.

"I need to face them. And I need to see Leyla." She turned away before anyone else tried to stop her and told her father she was ready. He took another long swig of water, and they left.

A mixture of emotions swirled inside Yael as she hurried down to the valley. Anger at Zabad and his village, at their heartlessness. Dread at the thought of facing Leyla's grandmother. But mostly fear for her friend who was ill enough to ask her to come. The moon hovered above the mountain, reminding her of Zaki's haunting question: *"Does your moon goddess say that you're made in her image?"*

Abba walked with Yael as far as the village entrance, and Rafi brought her the rest of the way to the house. All of her misgivings vanished as she knelt beside Leyla's bed and her friend looked up at her and smiled. "I was afraid you weren't my friend anymore."

"Of course I am. We're best friends."

"Why did you stop coming?"

So. Leyla didn't know about the baby. She wasn't to blame for her family's cruelty. "It was hard to get away. . . ." Yael said vaguely. "There's trouble between our people and yours."

"The last time I saw you was the night that Raisa nearly died. It was so sad that her baby died, wasn't it?"

Yael couldn't reply. The memory of the child's warmth and softness, her sweet smell, was still fresh. She longed to tell Leyla that her baby sister was alive, but she didn't dare. Instead, she changed the subject, and they talked as they always had until Leyla grew tired and drifted to sleep. Yael touched Leyla's burning forehead, gazed at her pale, blue-white skin, and wished she could pour some of her own life and vitality into her friend.

She heard someone come into the room. Leyla's grandmother. Yael's anger sprang to life. She looked away, refusing to face her, hoping she would leave. "I can see that Leyla already is better now that you're here," the old woman said. She fussed around the bed for a few minutes, plumping pillows and tucking covers before asking, "Are you hungry, Yael? Would you like something to eat?"

She shook her head, determined not to speak to her. But her rage finally got the best of her and she said, "Aren't you even going to ask about Raisa's baby?"

"I already know about her," she replied, unruffled. "She died at birth. It was very unfortunate."

"She didn't die! She's alive and thriving. Her name is Hodaya."

"Raisa mourned for her daughter, of course," she continued in a soft, sad voice. "We all did. Now Raisa is asking the moon goddess for another child. Raisa is strong and well again, thanks to your friend. We will always be grateful to her—and to you for bringing her here."

"Hodaya is a beautiful, healthy baby," Yael said stubbornly, "with dark hair and the most amazing brown eyes—" Tears choked her words. She couldn't finish. Leyla's grandmother turned away, and Yael hoped she would leave. Instead, she opened a little chest at the foot of Leyla's bed and took something out. Yael's star charts.

"These are yours, Yael. You left them here the last time you came."

Yael crossed her arms, refusing to reach for them. "They're worthless," she said. "They predicted that Raisa and her baby would both die. You and I read their stars together that night."

The old woman smiled. "My dear child, sometimes the stars show only what might happen if we fail to intervene. I offered sacrifices that night on Raisa's behalf once you showed us which heavenly bodies needed to be influenced. That's why she lived. Why are you upset over an answer to prayer?"

Yael stared at her. Could that be true? She knew the gods could be influenced, but Yael had never seen it happen so dramatically. Mother and child had both lived. If the people back in Babylon had this much faith, maybe Mama would have lived, too.

"I would be very grateful if you would look at Leyla's stars with me now," the old woman continued. "As you can see, she is very ill. I believe I know which powers are holding her in bed, but I would like your opinion." She held the scrolls out to Yael.

300

"And there are others in the village who are waiting for you, too. We have missed our seer these past few weeks."

Yael couldn't let Leyla die any more than she could have let Hodaya die. Zaki was right; every life was precious. She took the scrolls from the old woman and carried them to the window where the light was better, then slowly unrolled them.

CHAPTER
28

From his post on the watchtower, Zechariah saw the soldiers marching up the road to Jerusalem. The dark forms of men on horseback had emerged from a cloud of dust, their swords glinting in the sunlight. They carried the colorful banners of the governor of Trans-Euphrates Province. He counted at least a dozen men.

Zechariah had stood watch on this crumbling tower for so long, seeing nothing unusual on the roads day after day, that now he could scarcely believe his eyes. But as a chorus of shofars began to blow, he knew that the other sentries saw them, too.

His first impulse was to climb down and join the men in challenging these invaders. If only he had a sword. If only he knew how to fight. But his community had been warned of their arrival, and now his job was to stay here and continue watching for more trouble, or for a threat from another direction. He worried about the soldiers all day as he sat at his lonely post, and when someone came to relieve him from watch duty, he begged for news about the armed strangers.

"I was told that the delegation came from the provincial capital, from the governor of Trans-Euphrates," his replacement said. "The foreigners were escorted to the governor's residence to meet with Prince Sheshbazzar. That's all I know."

Zechariah ran all the way across the temple mount and found his grandfather waiting for him to watch the evening sacrifice. "What are those Samaritans doing here, Saba? Do you know why they've come?" he asked, still panting.

"I have no idea. They met with the prince in a closed meeting. Let's hope they're coming to help us get justice for Shoshanna and to restore peace."

When the sacrifice ended, the younger prince, Zerubbabel, came forward to speak to the congregation. "Governor Sheshbazzar and I are calling for a convocation here on the temple mount in two days' time, immediately after the morning sacrifice. We're sending messengers to our brethren in all the surrounding villages, asking them to come, as well. I know you've all seen the emissaries and are wondering what's going on, but the Samaritan governor has requested that we wait until everyone has assembled before making the announcement, so that rumors won't spread and cause even more trouble." He paused, and Zechariah saw him glance at the soldiers standing outside the courtyard. "The request comes at Governor Rehum's insistence."

"What do you suppose it's about?" Zechariah asked again as they walked home.

"Believe me, I wish I knew," Saba said. "It must be serious if they're asking men to leave their land and their crops and come to Jerusalem at this time of year, so close to the grape harvest. Two days will be a long time to wait."

A huge crowd filled the temple courtyards two days later, as large as on one of the feast days. Men from all over Judah stood beneath the burning sun, waiting to hear the provincial governor's announcement. The Samaritan emissaries and soldiers watched from the Court of the Gentiles as if standing guard. Zechariah stood with his grandmother and the other women while Saba stood with the chief priests to listen. "Depending on what the announcement is," Saba had told Zechariah, "I may need to meet with the priests afterwards. I need you to make sure the women get home safely."

The crowd quieted as Judah's two princes climbed onto the platform where Saba usually stood to blow the trumpet. Prince Zerubbabel stepped forward to act as spokesman. The elderly Sheshbazzar looked too weary and defeated for the task, which could only mean that the news must be bad. Zechariah remembered the night in Babylon when Saba had talked about the power of words and wondered what power these words would unleash.

"Thank you for coming," Zerubbabel began. "Governor Rehum of Samaria has asked me to read a copy of the letter he sent to King Artaxerxes in Persia. I've been told that Artaxerxes is the son of King Cyrus and as of a few months ago he now reigns as co-regent with his father." He paused to look across the plaza at the leader of the Samaritan delegation, and Zechariah saw the controlled fury on Zerubbabel's face, heard it in his voice. "Rehum shrewdly chose not to address his letter to King Cyrus himself but to his young son—for reasons that will soon become obvious. This is what Rehum's letter said:

"'To King Artaxerxes, from your servants, the men of Trans-Euphrates:

The king should know that the Jews who have moved here from Babylon are rebuilding the rebellious and wicked city of Jerusalem. They are restoring the walls and repairing the foundations. Furthermore, the king should know that if this city is built and its walls are restored, no more taxes, tribute or duty will be paid and the royal revenue will suffer. Now, since we are under obligation to the palace and it is not proper for us to see the king dishonored, we are sending this message to inform the king, so that a search may be made in the archives of your predecessors. In these records you will find that Jerusalem is a rebellious city, troublesome to kings and a place of rebellion from ancient times. That is why this city was destroyed. We inform the king that if Jerusalem is rebuilt and its walls are restored, you will be left with nothing in Trans-Euphrates.'"

Zerubbabel lowered the letter and faced the assembled people, his anger poorly concealed. "You'll notice that Rehum said nothing in his letter about the Holy Temple, which was the true reason that King Cyrus commissioned us to return. If Rehum had mentioned the temple, then the original proclamation could have easily been found. Instead, the governor deliberately misled the new king. Now I'll read King Artaxerxes' reply, which Rehum has just received." He unrolled a second scroll and began to read, his tone edged with bitterness.

"'Greetings. The letter you sent us has been read and translated in my presence. I issued an order and a search was made, and it was found that Jerusalem has a long history of revolt against kings and has been a place of rebellion and sedition. The city has had powerful kings ruling over the whole of Trans-Euphrates in the past, and they demanded that taxes, tribute and duty be paid to them. Now issue an order to these men to stop work—'"

"No!" The outcry raced through the crowd at his words. Stop working? They had just begun! The prince waited for the cries to die away.

"' . . . Issue an order to these men to stop work so that Jerusalem will not be rebuilt until I so order. Be careful not to neglect this matter. Why let this threat grow, to the detriment of the royal interests?'"

The crowd's outrage overflowed as the prince rolled up the letter. He finally held up his hand so he could continue. "Governor

Rehum and Shimshai his secretary and their associates are now compelling us to stop working through threat of force—you've all seen their *enforcers* among us." Once again, he glared at the Samaritan leader and the soldiers standing guard beside him. "It grieves me to tell you that their order includes all work on the temple." The loud cry came from the priests this time. Zechariah craned his neck to catch a glimpse of his grandfather and saw that he had covered his face with his hands.

"And since we can no longer build our city," the prince continued, shouting to be heard above the murmuring, "it also means that new immigrants will not be allowed to come."

At this, the crowd stilled. Zechariah caught his breath. His parents wouldn't be allowed to come? He might never see them again? He looked at his grandmother and saw her standing with her eyes closed, her hands covering her mouth as if to hold back her grief.

"Rehum has assured us that once we stop building the temple and stop repairing the city walls and gates, our neighbors will make peace with us," the prince continued. "The threats and the violence will end. The local people will trade with us again."

It wasn't a fair exchange. Zechariah knew they could survive without Samaritan food, but not without God's presence. Their lives would have no meaning at all without Him. Once again Zerubbabel had to hold up his hands to quiet the people, who seemed to grow angrier every minute, like a hive of bees that had been disturbed. This time Prince Sheshbazzar stepped forward to speak.

"We all know that King Cyrus has commissioned us to build the temple. Rehum knows it, as well. Once the king's original proclamation is found among the Persian documents, it will confirm our right to be here and to build here. I'm sending emissaries of my own to Persia immediately. This matter will be settled in our favor. Unfortunately, it will take time to get the justice that we deserve, and in the meantime, I'm sorry to say that all construction on the temple must cease."

"No . . ." Zechariah murmured. He repeated it, louder, joining the chorus of protests. "No! No! We can't stop building!" He felt his grandmother's hand on his shoulder and looked at her tear-streaked face. "Why won't the Holy One help us?" he asked. "He could do miracles!" Safta could only shake her head in reply.

Once again, Zerubbabel gestured for silence. The high priest had joined the other two men on the platform, waiting to speak. "The daily sacrifices and annual feasts will continue," Jeshua said. "No one can prevent us from worshiping God as we wait for the original proclamation to be found. In the meantime, we have much to pray about."

There was nothing that anyone could do. The courtyards slowly emptied. Zechariah walked home with his grandmother and the other women, staying with them all day as Saba had asked him to instead of going to the watchtower. Why keep watch when the enemy was already in Jerusalem, defeating them?

The sun went down and the stars came out, but Saba still didn't return home. Zechariah pushed food around on his plate at dinnertime, unable to eat as bitter questions churned inside him. He waited for his grandfather outside the gate to their courtyard, watching for him, and when he finally trudged down the street toward home, alone, Saba resembled a plant that had withered in the summer's heat. Zechariah ran out to meet him.

"I don't understand why the Holy One allowed this to happen, Saba!"

"Our enemies are very shrewd, Zaki. But they won't be able to stand in God's way for long."

He blocked Saba's path, needing answers before his grandfather talked to the others. "Why doesn't He help us? The Holy

One drowned all the Egyptians and their chariots. He struck their firstborn dead and—"

"The Holy One has a purpose in this. Maybe this time of waiting will be good for us."

"How can it be good for us? We should fight back instead of giving in to our enemies."

"I've been arguing about this all day, Zaki," he said, and his voice did sound hoarse. "I told them that we should obey God, who commanded us to rebuild the temple, and not the men who told us to stop. But Prince Sheshbazzar has the final authority, and he fears that because the Persians have labeled Jerusalem a rebellious city, they will retaliate with force if we disobey. He has decided to send emissaries to Persia and go through the proper diplomatic channels and wait for a reply. He wants to protect our people."

"But . . . but the Almighty One could protect us!"

Saba laid his hand on Zechariah's shoulder. "You and I are among the very few who believe that, I'm afraid. No one listened to me today. The last time the priests took my advice, our enemies attacked us and killed Shoshanna. Now our leaders are afraid."

Zechariah turned to slouch away, but Saba stopped him before he could open the gate. "Listen, every man among us—including you and me—has to settle this matter in his heart: Did God command us to rebuild the temple or did King Cyrus? If it was King Cyrus, then construction may stop for good. But if it was God, then this setback by our enemies is only temporary."

Zechariah rubbed his eyes, fighting tears. "I heard the prince say that new immigrants won't be allowed to come."

Saba put his arm around his shoulder and pulled him close. "You're worried about your parents, aren't you?"

"Abba said that he and Mama would come later, and now they can't."

"Your father made the mistake of waiting when he should have acted. And he wasn't the only one. When we hear God's call, we need to respond to it immediately. Now all of those people who stayed behind in Babylon will have to obey the Persian authorities because they chose not to obey God."

This wasn't what Zechariah wanted to hear. He tried to escape his grandfather's grasp, but Saba wouldn't let go. "Are you doubting that the Almighty One spoke to you, Zechariah?" He didn't reply. "Listen, son. Do you remember how God tested Israel in the wilderness? How He wanted to see what was in the people's hearts—fear or faith? God already knows what's in our hearts, of course, but He tests us so we'll see it for ourselves. Our forefathers should have used their time in the wilderness to learn about God, to learn that He would lead them and provide for them and fight for them. But they didn't. As soon as the bad spies gave their report, the people were ready to turn back to Egypt. Only Joshua and Caleb had faith. Do you remember what they told the others?"

"Don't be afraid of the people of the land," he said woodenly. "God is with Israel."

"That's what you and I need to be saying to all of the others now, while we wait for justice."

"How long will we have to wait?" Zechariah asked. He had been calculating in his head all afternoon and not liking the results. It would take at least three months for Prince Sheshbazzar's emissaries to travel to Persia. Weeks or maybe months longer to go through the proper diplomatic channels and get an audience with the king. More time would be spent waiting while the king's officials searched the archives for King Cyrus' original proclamation. And even if the king issued a favorable ruling, it would take another three months for the emissaries to travel back to Jerusalem with the news.

"How long?" Saba repeated. "I suppose it depends on how long it takes us to learn the lessons of faith."

"It's not fair! We just started building the temple!"

"Life is seldom fair, Zechariah. But we can use this time to nurture our faith or to nurture doubt. That's what these times of testing are all about. How long did David have to wait before becoming our king while his enemy, Saul, chased him around the wilderness? Was that fair? During those long years of waiting, David nurtured his faith, and now the words of his psalms can strengthen ours. 'Wait for the Lord; be strong and take heart and wait for the Lord.'"

"Why can't I learn to fight while we're waiting? We could make weapons and—"

"This is the Almighty One's battle, not ours. Your job is to study the Torah."

"What? . . . No!" This wasn't what Zechariah wanted to hear.

"We've decided to reopen the yeshiva tomorrow since Governor Rehum assures us that there's no need for guards as long as we obey the king's edict." Again Zechariah tried to leave, but his grandfather stopped him. "If you really want to fight for God, then find out what He is saying to us. Study His Word and learn about God's faithfulness in the past so you'll have the faith to trust Him now. Help me speak His truth to those who have no faith. Help me convince them that the temple must be rebuilt no matter who tries to stop us. Can you do that, son?"

Zechariah nodded. He may have to wait, but he wouldn't have to like it.

Part III

Jerusalem

You showed favor to your land, O Lord;

you restored the fortunes of Jacob.

You forgave the iniquity of your people . . .

Restore us again, O God our Savior,

and put away your displeasure toward us.

Will you be angry with us forever?

PSALM 85:1, 4–5

CHAPTER
29

TEN YEARS LATER

There was so much to learn. Zechariah stood on the temple mount with his class of future priests, watching an older priest named Jakin demonstrate how to prepare a ram for the burnt offering. Jakin gripped the animal in a firm hold, subduing it, and tilted the animal's head, exposing its neck. "It's very important to place the knife in the proper position. The animal must not suffer unnecessarily."

Zechariah now spent part of each day in the yeshiva studying the Torah and the history of his people and the writings of Israel's prophets, and the remainder of his time on the temple mount receiving hands-on instruction from the older priests.

"Put the tip of the knife here and draw it back . . . like this."

His mind wandered as Jakin showed how to collect the sacrificial blood in a bowl. Beyond the altar, the temple ruins and the abandoned construction site looked the same as on the night Zechariah had snuck up here with Yael ten years ago, searching for God's presence. She had gazed up at the stars that night, pointing to them, because there was no temple to look to for meaning in life.

"When the blood has been drained and set aside, we . . ."

Everything was still in place. The crane stood ready to lift the building blocks onto the temple's new foundation, although the ropes had begun to rot. So had the piles of rain-soaked timber. Weeds and scrub brush had slowly crept back over the site, knee-high around the new foundation they had laid.

"Zechariah? Are you paying attention?"

"Yes, sir . . . I'm sorry."

Zechariah had to learn how to slaughter the sacrifices, how to skin the animals and remove their entrails, how to prepare the meat and the fat for the offerings. He had to know the differences between daily offerings, burnt offerings, fellowship offerings, and guilt offerings. Then there were the intricacies of the annual feasts to learn and the special rituals required for each one. And because Zechariah descended from a family of priestly musicians, he also had to learn the proper trumpet calls for the New Moon festivals, the yearly feasts, and most important of all, for the annual Feast of Trumpets. After his ordination in a few years, the rhythm of his ministry at God's altar would determine the shape of his days and years for the remainder of his life.

He glanced over at the ruins again, wondering if he could find the place where he had sat with Yael and prayed. He had told her that the temple was like a map, a way to find God's presence. But there was no temple, no map, and he feared that his lifelong friend was walking deeper into darkness with each passing year. And she was just one of the many people in Judah who needed to find their way back to God.

"Zechariah . . ." Jakin was staring at him, and so were all the others. "Would you stay behind for a moment, please? The rest of you are dismissed."

Zechariah could feel the heat from the great altar several yards away as he waited for Jakin to speak. "What's wrong, son? You're one of our best students. You have a brilliant mind for Torah study. But lately you've been distracted. Are we losing you like the others?"

"No, sir. You're not losing me." Three of Zechariah's fellow Torah students had recently quit, and in the past few months he'd heard of two more Jewish families who had decided to return to Babylon.

"Can you tell me what's wrong, then?"

He was about to say that he didn't know. But when he pictured Yael sitting among the huge, abandoned building stones, he suddenly realized what was wrong. "I'm fed up with all of this!" He swung his arms in a wide circle to take in the entire temple mount. "The more I learn what the Torah says the more frustrated I get because no one seems to believe any of it. They're just words on a page."

Jakin's shoulders stiffened. "Of course we believe it."

"No, you don't. The prophets Jeremiah, Ezekiel, and even Daniel the Righteous One all told us that God wanted us to come back and rebuild the temple—but we stopped building. If we truly believed these men spoke God's word—if we believed in a God of power and miracles—there would be a temple standing over there instead of rubble."

"That's not fair. Our leaders have been trying to get the king's edict reversed, but there have been setbacks. The Persian courts—"

"I know all about how our enemies in the Persian courts have sabotaged our requests. I've heard all the announcements about political intrigues and palace insiders in the Persian government working against us—the schemes and plots and important messages that were intercepted and stolen. Meanwhile, our work on the temple has been abandoned for ten years. Ten years!"

"Stop shouting, Zechariah. This is a sacred place."

He drew a breath to calm himself, inhaling the aroma of roasting meat. When work on the temple had first halted, Zechariah

315

had worried that he'd be forced to wait for a year—an outrageously long time. No one, including his grandfather, had ever imagined that ten years would pass.

"We've waited long enough," Zechariah said. "Do we believe the Torah or don't we? Moses said not to look at our enemies and tremble in fear but to remember what the Almighty One did to Pharoah and his armies. We're supposed to remember His miraculous signs and wonders and God's mighty hand."

"The exodus from Egypt was a special time when—"

"See? Even you don't believe it."

"That's not true! I resent that!"

"I've heard Jeshua and some of the other priests saying that a restored altar is enough for now—"

"And it is, Zechariah. It has been."

"You can't tell me that God asked us to leave Babylon and travel all this way just to build an altar. If so, He played a cruel joke on us. The Almighty One promised to dwell among us and be our God, but how can He dwell here without a temple? If we really heard from Him all those years ago, then we need to finish what we came here to do."

"We had no choice. The Persian authorities ordered us to stop building."

"What about the words that we pray every morning: 'Some trust in chariots and some in horses, but we trust in the name of the Lord our God.' We have it memorized, but we don't believe it."

Jakin took a step back. "This is so unlike you, Zechariah. You need to talk to the high priest. Your anger and your . . . your accusations are unbecoming to a candidate for the priesthood."

"You're right. I'll do that. Right now."

Zechariah strode across the courtyard and down the stairs, knowing he would find Jeshua in the house of assembly this time of day. He felt a growing sense of urgency with each step he took, as if they were all inside a burning building, yet no one would listen to him and stop the flames. He wanted to shout at everyone, even the high priest. At the same time, he was angry enough to simply walk away and let them all perish in the fire.

The house of assembly was empty, the students dismissed for the day, but he heard Jeshua's voice coming from the room that he used to meet privately with people. Zechariah stood aside, waiting for him to finish. He didn't mean to eavesdrop but their voices were raised, and he realized that the high priest was talking to his son, Eliezer.

"I want your blessing, Abba. Why won't you give it to me?"

"I can't give it to you if you marry a foreign woman. You and your brothers are the next generation of priests. You'll be the Holy One's intermediaries after my generation is gone. But only if you remain pure."

"What difference does it make whom I marry? All we're doing is performing empty rituals. It's not real worship. If God isn't interested in what we're doing or answering our endless prayers, why not marry whomever I want?"

"A child from a foreign wife can never worship with us. Your sons can never be priests."

"It doesn't matter, Abba! We're just pretending to be priests for a God who doesn't even care about us. I want to find a little happiness for once in my life. I'm tired of all your laws and rules—there's no use at all in following them."

Zechariah hurried away, embarrassed for hearing as much as he had. If Eliezer had drifted away from the Almighty One just like Yael and so many others had, it was too late to sound the alarm. Flames already engulfed the building.

Zechariah's anger had a chance to cool as he walked home, replaced by sadness. When he entered his courtyard, his grandmother and the other women bustled around, finishing the preparations for the evening meal. He hardly knew where to stand so he wouldn't be in their way. The simple rooms that he had helped build when they'd first arrived had doubled and then tripled in size. More rooms had been added for Besai and his wife, Rachel, and their growing family, for Tikvah and her children, and for Yael and Hodaya. As the years passed, they had plastered over the building stones, inside and out; added a sturdy roof with steps up to the top, like they'd had in Babylon. They had expanded the outdoor courtyard where they lived and worked to include a larger hearth, an oven, and two more cisterns to capture rainwater.

"Where's Yael?" he asked Hodaya. The girl was a constant shadow at Yael's side and looked lost without her.

"She's visiting her friend in the village. They're having a festival."

He stifled a groan, remembering the pagan festival he'd attended ten years ago. Yael would eat forbidden things, watch the men worship on the high places, and be drawn even further away from the Holy One. She was already lost to him.

"Zaki! There you are," Safta said, pulling him aside. "Your grandfather is upset. Please, go see if you can talk to him."

"Where is he?"

She gestured to the roof. "Up there. I'll join you in a minute."

Zechariah would have known something was wrong with Saba even if his grandmother hadn't told him. Saba stood near the parapet on the eastern side of the roof, looking out at the darkening sky above the Mount of Olives, the worry lines etched deeply into his face. "What's wrong, Saba?"

"The Almighty One is testing us—and we're failing the test."

Zechariah had heard this refrain for ten years now. "Is there some new test I'm not aware of?" he asked.

"I may as well tell you. You'll hear about it soon enough. The high priest's son, Eliezer, has decided to marry a local woman. He was one of my Torah students back in Babylon. I've tried to change his mind, but he won't listen to me."

"I know. I overheard Eliezer talking to his father. He wouldn't listen to Jeshua, either."

"I've begged him to consider what he's doing to the priest-hood—and to our people. We're such a tiny remnant as it is, and we'll disappear entirely if we intermarry with Gentiles. We only have four priestly family lines left, and we'll need every eligible man to serve once the temple is finished."

If it ever is finished. Zechariah didn't have the heart to say the words out loud and discourage Saba even further. The sky clouded over again, adding to the darkness and gloom. "Did Eliezer say when he wants to get married?" Zechariah asked.

Before Saba could reply, Safta joined them, breathless from climbing the stairs. "I came to tell you that dinner is ready. . . . And who did you say is getting married?"

"The high priest's son, Eliezer. He—"

"That's wonderful! Do I know the bride, Iddo?"

"No. She isn't one of our women. She's a Samaritan."

"Oh. No wonder you're upset." She turned to Zechariah as if desperate for him to do something about it. When he didn't, she resorted to one of her own familiar refrains. "Speaking of marriage, don't you think it's time for Zaki to find a good wife? He's already older than we were when we married."

Zaki wrapped his arm around her shoulder. "I'm waiting to meet a wife who is as perfect as you, Safta. I haven't found one yet."

"Why do you resist all my efforts?" she asked. "There are so many lovely young women in our community."

"And yet the high priest's son went looking outside our community," Saba said gloomily.

Safta gave him a worried glance before turning back to Zecha-riah. "Don't you want to get married and have children, Zaki? A good priest should be married, you know. You'll be ordained in just a few more years."

Several of the women Safta had found for him had been attractive, but none as beautiful as Yael. They shared a lifelong friendship and countless memories—but he could never marry her. A priest of God could never marry a sorceress. He couldn't explain this to his grandmother, especially with Saba feeling so discouraged, so he decided to make light of the subject. "When you find me someone as beautiful as you are, Safta, then I'll marry her."

She frowned at him. "There are other qualities to consider besides beauty. 'Charm is deceptive, and beauty is fleeting—'"

"'—but a woman who fears the Lord is to be praised.' I know what the proverb says, Safta. But can you find me a woman who can cook as well as the women in our house? I'm used to good food, you know."

"Why can't you take me seriously, Zaki?"

"Why pick on me? What about Yael? She's well past the age that most girls marry."

"I know. Can't you help me with her, Zaki? Invite some of the young men you know to come home and meet her. Or invite this Eliezer, the high priest's son, to meet her. If he saw how beautiful she is, he wouldn't be looking at foreign women."

"It's too late," Saba said, shaking his head. "Eliezer is determined to marry the Samaritan."

Zechariah had raised the topic of Yael to deflect attention from himself, and now he was sorry. He searched for a way out. "We all love Yael, Safta, but we also know that she's too independent to settle down and be a good wife. You see how she flits from our house to Mattaniah's house in the valley and then to her friend Leyla's house. Can you picture her staying home and cooking for a husband and children all day? Hodaya is only ten years old, and she's already a better cook than Yael."

"I know," Safta said with a sigh. "I suppose it's my fault for not controlling her when she was young."

"How can you control the wind?" Zechariah asked. "When she finally decides to settle down, believe me, Safta, the men will line up to marry her." But he recognized the jealous longing in his heart whenever he thought about Yael with another man. And as he went downstairs to dinner, he worried that Yael sat inside that burning building at this very moment. And it was probably too late to save her.

CHAPTER
30

Yael knelt in her room combing her hair and plaiting it into a long braid. The spring rain clouds had blown away during the night and the sun shone brightly this morning, making Yael eager to get out of the stuffy house. Abba said to meet him below the steps to the temple mount right after the morning sacrifice.

She heard the familiar thump and scrape of a crutch on the cobblestones as Hodaya came to stand in the doorway. "Are you going to see your friend Leyla today?" she asked.

"Yes, I am. It's been much too long since I've visited her."

"May I go with you?"

Yael searched for a kind way to refuse as she stood and went to Hodaya. "It's too far to walk, little one," she said, smoothing Hodaya's dark curls away from her face. "You would be exhausted before we were even halfway there."

"We could borrow your father's donkey . . . I could ride."

"That old donkey is too stubborn and grumpy to ride. He might get it into his head to throw you off, and I don't ever want anything bad to happen to you." She gave Hodaya a hug and felt her slender arms wrap around her in return.

Hodaya had grown into a strong, happy ten-year-old who

walked with her crutch nearly as well as Yael walked on two good feet. Her laughter and bright smile made everyone in the community love her. But Yael could never take her adopted sister back to the village where she was born. Leyla's family would know who she was the moment they saw her, not only because of her crippled foot, but because of her strong resemblance to her half sister Leyla and half brother Rafi. They all had the same thick curly hair and large dark eyes. Hodaya might see the resemblance herself, and Yael didn't want her to learn the truth about her birth. She belonged to this family now.

"Hodaya?" Safta called. "Where are you? I need your help."

"Why doesn't Yael ever help?" she asked as she turned to limp away. "How come she gets to run all over?"

Yael didn't wait to hear Safta's explanation. She tousled Hodaya's hair as she hurried past her saying, "See you later, little one."

Abba talked on and on about his barley crop as they walked to the Samaritan village together, describing how the plentiful spring rains had made it flourish. Yael listened patiently, smiling to herself, knowing how much her father loved his land. It had prospered under his hands these past ten years, and the land easily fed their extended family with enough food left over to sell.

Yael's father sat down with Zabad and the elders at the entrance to the village when they arrived, but Yael couldn't look at Zabad, hating him for ordering his infant daughter to be put to death. She hurried into the village as he and Abba talked, but her progress was soon slowed by the abundance of greetings from all the women and children who gathered around her. Yael's stature as a respected seer was well established, and people from other local villages now sought her advice, as well.

When she finally reached Leyla's house a few minutes later, she found her friend propped up in bed, looking pale and weak. But her face lit up with happiness the moment she saw her.

"Yael! I have wonderful news! And now I have my best friend to share it with."

Yael smiled as she walked to Leyla's bedside. They'd been best friends for more than ten years. "Tell me your wonderful news."

"I'm betrothed! I'm going to be married!" Yael could only stare in disbelief as her friend chattered on. "Abba made all the arrangements and settled on my dowry, and now I'm officially betrothed to my new husband."

"Who is he? Have I ever met him?" Foolish questions. The women in Leyla's village never socialized with the men. The fact that her brother Rafi sometimes came into Leyla's room to visit with her was highly unusual. Yael searched for something to say to disguise her shock and surprise. "Is he young and handsome?"

Leyla laughed. "If you mean as young and handsome as Rafi—no. But that doesn't matter. My husband is nearly as rich as Abba, and our marriage will seal their business partnership. I was lucky that Basam accepted me since I'm past the age when most women in my village marry."

"I see." Yael tried to smile and be happy for her friend, but she wasn't. How could her father use beloved Leyla to seal a business deal, in spite of her poor health? Yet Leyla seemed to think this was fine. At least her father hadn't married her off years earlier when she was barely grown.

"Promise me you'll come to my wedding, Yael. I want you to be my attendant."

"Of course I'll come. I would be honored." She was about to sit down beside the bed when the door opened and Rafi strode into the room.

"Leyla, I—" He stopped short in surprise. "Well, hello, Yael. I didn't realize you were here. Did my sister tell you her good news?" His smile made Yael's heart beat a little faster. She still thought of him as Leyla's brother and as a friend, the same way she thought of Zechariah as her friend. But Leyla was right; he had grown into a very handsome man. He wore his dark, loosely curled hair longer than Jewish men did and his dark beard was a little longer, too, framing his magnificent smile.

"Yes, we were just talking about it," Yael said. "I'm so happy for her."

"What I don't understand," he said, stroking his beard, "is why a beautiful woman like you isn't betrothed yet? Doesn't your father know he could ask a king's ransom for your dowry? Or is that the problem? Are the Jews in your community too stingy to pay what you're worth?" There was something about the way he looked at her today that seemed different—or was she imagining it?

"Believe me, Safta Dinah has tried to marry me off several times. She promised my mother she would find me a good husband but I told Abba that I don't want to get married yet."

Rafi's brows lifted. "Really? The fathers in our village would never allow our daughters to boss us around and tell us what to do."

The insult stung. She lifted her chin. "Besides, I'm too busy to think about a husband."

"Is it your work as a seer that keeps you so busy?"

"That's part of the reason. I'm also learning to be a midwife."

He grinned. "Ah, now I see what has you frightened of marriage—watching babies being born."

"Not at all!" His teasing made her heart race. She couldn't tell if it was annoyance or something else. She planted her hands on her hips and decided to tease him back. "And by the way, why aren't you married, Rafi?"

"I haven't met anyone I want, yet."

"Oh, so you get to choose who you'll marry and Leyla doesn't?"

"Of course. She's a woman, and I'm a man. That's the way God created it to be. The Torah clearly says that the husband shall rule over his wife."

"The Torah?" She would have to ask Zaki about that when she got home. He studied the Torah all the time. But somehow it didn't seem fair to be ruled over. "Are the men in your village ever allowed to marry for love?" she asked.

"We marry for a variety of reasons. Love is sometimes one of them." The way he looked at her was disconcerting, his dark eyes fixed on her as if memorizing her face. She needed to change the subject.

"Have you met Leyla's husband? Is he a good man? Worthy of my dear friend?" She had seen Rafi's love for his sister over the years, and knew how tender and protective he was. She had often wondered if he would have protected his other sister, Hodaya, if he had known about her. She couldn't imagine either Rafi or Leyla letting their baby sister die.

"I don't know Leyla's husband very well," Rafi said, turning away. "He's from another village. I should go. I'm keeping you ladies from your wedding plans."

"No, you're not," Leyla said. "Can't you stay?"

"Not today."

Leyla looked up at Yael and gave a sigh after he was gone. "I've always wished that you and Rafi would get married. Then we really would be sisters."

Yael couldn't speak. Why did the idea make her feel so funny inside?

"I've been waiting for you to come so you could read my stars," Leyla rattled on. "I need to find the best day for my wedding."

"Yes, of course." Yael fetched her charts from the little trunk at the foot of Leyla's bed and spread them out to get a look at Leyla's future. Zaki had warned her of the consequences if she got caught with her scrolls in Jerusalem, and so she kept them at Leyla's house most of the time. What she read in Leyla's stars today surprised her.

"I see so much happiness! It's . . . it's almost overwhelming! The moon, the stars, all of the heavenly bodies—they all line up to give favor and blessing. You will have a prosperous new life, Leyla, and many, many sons." Leyla's grandmother joined them and they bent over the charts together, choosing a favorable date for the wedding two months from now.

"There! It's settled," Leyla said happily when they were alone again.

"I still can't believe that you, my dear friend, will soon be married. Tell me more about your husband."

"I barely know him," Leyla said with a laugh. "His name is Basam. He already has one wife but she has only given him daughters. When I give him a son, he will be Basam's heir, and I'll become his primary wife. In time, we may even grow to love each other."

Yael couldn't imagine being married to a man she didn't know or love. The Jewish couples she knew all loved each other—her father and mother had. Iddo loved Dinah, Besai loved Rachel. She didn't know what to say to her friend without revealing her doubt—or her fear. "So, you don't mind that your father chose Basam for you?"

"Not at all. Rafi is right, you know. Women should never choose for themselves. Our fathers and husbands know what's best for us. They're wiser about these matters, so it's good that they should decide. We're wise to obey them." Sweet Leyla was so compliant and easy to lead—and so different from Yael. "You know what's the best part of all?" Leyla asked. "I'll have babies! I've always wanted to have lots of babies."

"Oh, Leyla . . ."

"What's wrong?"

Yael couldn't reply. She knew from helping Safta Dinah deliver babies that labor and delivery exhausted healthy women, much less one as fragile as Leyla. She also knew how much blood women sometimes lost. Leyla should never get pregnant, never have babies. Yael searched for something to say. "I'm going to give you my moon goddess for a wedding present. She'll bring you good luck and keep you strong and safe in childbirth."

"Don't you want her? Aren't you ever going to get married and have children?"

"Of course I am . . . someday. Then you can give her back to me."

As soon as she got home that evening, Yael pulled Safta Dinah aside to talk about her friend. "Leyla is betrothed to a man she barely knows. She wants to have a baby, but I'm so scared for her, Safta. You know how sickly Leyla has always been. Do you think she'll be strong enough to deliver a baby?"

"I don't know. She may never be able to get pregnant at all if she's that ill."

"It still bothers me that she didn't have a choice in the matter. Her brother Rafi and the other men in her village get to choose who they'll marry."

Rafi. He had been on Yael's mind all day like a melody that kept repeating. She thought of his smile, his halo of dark curls, his beautiful eyes. And most of all, the intensity of his gaze as he'd looked at her.

"You should be thinking about it, too," Safta said, interrupting her thoughts.

"Hmm? Thinking about what?"

"Marriage! Isn't that what we're talking about? As the daughter of a Levite, you could have the honor of marrying a Levite or a priest. I promised your mother—"

"I know, I know," Yael laughed, drawing Safta close for a hug. That was the easiest way to change the subject with Safta Dinah. "I promise I'll start thinking about marriage soon."

Rafi was still on Yael's mind as she helped the other women prepare for the evening meal. She couldn't stop thinking about what he'd said, that the husband was supposed to rule over his wife. She decided to ask Zaki about it when he arrived home from the yeshiva. She approached him as he prepared to wash his hands.

"Do you have a minute?" she asked. "I have a question for you."

"Yes, of course. What is it?" Sweet, responsible Zechariah, always so serious compared to Rafi, who didn't seem to have a care in the world. Zaki was a little taller than Rafi, but not as muscular, with the trim build of a scholar. He wore his dark hair cut shorter, his beard neatly trimmed, and his kippah slightly askew on his head no matter how many times he straightened it. He would be a priest in a few more years, but to Yael he would always be the solemn boy she had grown up with, the friend she had known all her life.

"Does the Torah really say that a husband should rule over his wife?" she asked.

"Yes, it does. The Almighty One told Eve, 'Your desire will be for your husband, and he will rule over you.'"

"But why? That doesn't seem fair."

"Well, because Eve tempted her husband to sin."

"I thought the serpent tempted them."

"The serpent tempted Eve and then *she* tempted Adam. But the Almighty One also said that Eve was created from her husband's side to be his partner. They're supposed to work together in love, two people becoming one."

"How can they do that if they don't know each other or love each other?"

"Why all these questions?" Zaki gave a slow, easy grin, and Yael saw the boy she'd long known behind the serious scholar. But concern for Leyla kept her from returning his smile.

"My friend Leyla is betrothed to an older man, chosen by her father. She doesn't even know him, but she says she has to obey him from now on. That doesn't seem right, does it?"

Zechariah grew serious again. "No. It isn't right. That's another difference between us and the Samaritans—one of thousands of differences. You already know they don't value human life, and they don't value their women, either. They see their wives as property, not as helpmates. I wish you wouldn't spend so much time there, Yael. Can't you make friends with some of our own women?"

"I asked a simple question," she said, growing angry. "I don't need a lecture on who to make friends with."

"We were friends once, weren't we?" he asked softly. "What happened?"

"We still are." She said it lightly, but it wasn't entirely true. Yael knew Zaki didn't approve of her astrology. The more renowned she became as a seer—and the closer Zaki came to becoming a priest—the more she distanced herself from him. He had once told her that the penalty for sorcery if she was caught was death by stoning.

Yael studied the married couples that evening as they gathered around to eat together, and their affection for each other was obvious in their looks and gestures. She wanted that sweet closeness for her friend—and for herself someday. She wanted Leyla to be happy. And healthy. She kept glancing at Hodaya with her dark curls and beautiful eyes and thought of Leyla.

And Rafi.

Yael stood at Leyla's bedside, her worry and frustration
leaving her too tense to sit. "Can't the wedding be post-
poned?" she asked Leyla's grandmother. Her friend had
fainted a few minutes after Yael arrived to help with the final
wedding preparations.

"I'm fine," Leyla insisted. "Just a little dizzy." But Yael made
her lie down, just to be sure, and now her fever was rising. She
moaned from the pain in every joint in her body.

"It's too late to postpone the wedding," her grandmother
said. "Her father would be shamed. The food is being prepared,
the guests are coming in three days. It can't be changed now."

"Never mind his shame—what about Leyla's health?"

"I want to get married," Leyla said. "The stars are all favorable, remember?" It was true. Yael had consulted her charts
again, and the stars showed no indication of illness.

Leyla spent the next three days in bed, drinking her grandmother's potions of blood and goat's milk, but she still wasn't
completely well on the day of her wedding. A veil hid her pale
face and bruised-looking eyes, but nothing could disguise the
fact that she was too weak to walk unaided. Yael sat beside her

as they waited for the groom's procession to arrive, trying to calm Leyla's nerves with empty chatter.

"Will I still be able to visit you?" Yael asked. "I don't even know where your new husband lives."

"In another village, only a short walk over the mountain from here. I promise that as soon as my marriage week ends, I'll send servants to bring you there for a visit."

"Have you seen your new home?"

"Not yet. Not until after the wedding. My father said that Basam added a beautiful new room just for me."

At last Leyla's groom arrived with an escort of musicians and singers and dozens of relatives and guests. Leyla was too weak for the traditional procession through the village and had to be carried on a chair decked with flowers. They proceeded to the village square for the formalities, followed by the marriage feast.

Basam was a portly, unsmiling man, older than his bride by at least fifteen years. Sitting side by side, they seemed opposite in every respect: Basam dark, and sturdy as an oak tree; Leyla pale, and frail as a willow branch. Yael remembered how fragile Mama had looked during her last months of life, and she felt a terrible foreboding for her friend. She turned to Leyla's grandmother, seated beside her and whispered, "How could her father agree to this? She's too ill to be married."

"The stars and omens have all been favorable, Yael. Remember?" Yes. It was true.

The huge feast lasted late into the night with roasted lamb and wine, followed by singing and dancing by torchlight. Yael's father had also been invited, and he sat with the men while Yael sat with the women from Leyla's household, including her young stepmother, Raisa. All three of Raisa's little children resembled Hodaya. As time passed, Yael watched her dear friend shrivel and droop like a tender shoot beneath a desert sun, but she could do nothing to help her. When Leyla's new husband escorted her to their bridal chamber, Yael packed up her star charts and left her friend's house for the last time, walking home with her father.

Yael waited a full month after the wedding, worrying about her friend, wondering how she was doing, but the promised servants never arrived with an invitation to visit. She waited a second month, then a third. By now the early fall rains had begun. Yael told herself that the bad weather was making travel difficult. But when the weather cleared and the almond trees blossomed and she still hadn't heard from Leyla, Yael decided to walk to her village one morning and ask about her friend. She saw Rafi sitting among the elders at the entrance to the village and greeted him as she would any longtime friend.

"Rafi! How—?"

"Hush!" one of the elders shouted. "Do not speak!"

Rafi quickly rose from his place, shaking his head at her as if she had committed a terrible sin. The other men glared at her in disapproval. Rafi looked very uncomfortable as he motioned for her to walk a short distance away from the others to talk.

"What's wrong?" she asked.

"Women don't address the elders at the gate. And why did you come here all alone? Where's your father? Don't you know it isn't safe or proper for a woman to travel unescorted?"

"That's silly. You can see my father's land right over there across the valley. He was too busy to come, and besides, it only takes a few minutes to walk here." She didn't understand why he was making such a fuss. "Listen, I've come to ask about Leyla. How is she? I miss her."

"My family hasn't heard from her since the wedding."

"What? That was months ago!"

"Leyla's husband hasn't invited any of us to his home or allowed her to visit us."

Yael swallowed a lump of fear. "Is she . . . do you know if she's well? Does your grandmother visit her?"

He paused before replying. "Our grandmother died two months ago. We sent word for Leyla to come, but Basam wouldn't allow it."

"That's horrible! Poor Leyla!" This was worse than Yael had feared. Leyla had not only been cut off from her and Rafi but from her beloved grandmother. "I thought Basam and your father were business partners. Surely he's heard something."

"The partnership has ended. It's a husband's right to make decisions that concern his wife," Rafi said. "There's nothing we can do." But Yael could see Rafi battling to control his emotions, his concern even greater than her own. Basam held Leyla prisoner. But why had all the stars predicted that they would have a wonderful marriage?

"When you do see Leyla, please tell her that I was asking about her. I would love to visit her. I miss her." She felt powerless—and furious—as she turned to start walking home.

"Yael, wait. Don't walk back alone. I'll come with you." Rafi hurried to catch up with her.

"Won't they think that's even more scandalous?" she asked bitterly, gesturing to the elders with a tilt of her head. She was angry with them for being men and for their stupid, controlling rules that separated her from her friend.

"It isn't a question of scandal. I mean it, Yael. Don't ever walk alone again. Ever! Your safety is the issue." He tried to take her arm as they continued down the road away from the village, but she shrugged him off.

"My safety? I thought our people were at peace. There hasn't been any trouble in ten years."

"Yes, we're at peace. But that's not the point. Not all of the young men in the local villages have the same moral traditions that you do. And the truth is, many of your young men don't, either."

"What do you mean? All the men I know in Jerusalem follow the Torah."

"You may think so, but they don't. No one talks about it, so it's a dirty little secret, but our villages have certain . . . celebrations. Especially now, in the springtime. And many of your saintly Jewish men like to join us for the festivities. In fact, that's how one of your priests fell in love with a village woman. There will be more of these affairs in the months to come, I'm certain."

"I know all about the high priest's son. Everyone gossiped about him and the Samaritan woman he married."

"The marriage was a mere formality. He had already taken her as his concubine."

Yael felt her face grow warm. "What does that have to do with me walking home alone?"

"I guess I'll have to be blunt. There's a widespread belief among my people that an unaccompanied woman must be looking for . . . a partner. The local men believe they have the right to claim her. And a beautiful woman like you . . . ?" He shook his head without finishing.

"I never heard of such a thing." Nor could she imagine Zechariah and his fellow Torah students doing something so outrageous.

"Well, it's true. The Torah says that once a man 'takes' a woman, he's obliged to marry her or pay the bride price for her stolen virtue. But if the men don't follow the Torah . . . well, she may spend the rest of her life as a prostitute." Yael's cheeks burned from such candid talk. She didn't know how to reply.

Rafi halted suddenly and drew her to a stop beside him, resting his warm hands on her shoulders. "Now that you know, Yael, promise me you won't take chances again." He smiled at her for the first time since she'd greeted him back in his village, and the warmth from his hands seemed to spread all through her. He was such a handsome man. She had to resist the urge to brush his dark curls off his forehead the way she brushed Hodaya's.

"All right. I promise." Abba's land was just ahead. Yael could see the door to his stone house standing open and hear his goats bleating in their pen. "Thanks for walking me home," she said, then turned and ran toward the house without looking back. She needed to get away from him. The way her heart raced when she looked at him frightened her. Yael remembered a morning long ago, when Safta's cousin Shoshanna had told her, *"Someday a young man will catch your eye and your heart will be drawn to him, and he'll be the only thing you can think about. . . ."*

And a week after Yael went to Rafi's village, she still thought about him. She thought of him while she worked and when she walked to the spring for water and when she lay in bed at night. She was thinking of him as she sat with Safta Dinah and Hodaya and the others after the evening meal one night—and when she looked up, there he was, magically appearing at their courtyard gate as if she had conjured him with a spell. He asked to speak with her father, not to her, but she overheard their conversation.

"I need your help, my lord. My sister Leyla is very ill. She's asking to see your daughter, Yael. May she please come? I wouldn't dream of bothering you if it wasn't urgent, my lord."

Rafi hadn't addressed Yael or even looked at her, but she leaped up from where she'd been sitting. "Let me go with him, Abba. Please! You know I've been worried about Leyla."

"Of course," Abba said. "I'll go, too."

It seemed to take forever for Abba to get ready. Yael tucked her star charts in her bag and begged him to hurry, wanting to run all the way to her friend's house. The situation must be serious if Rafi came all the way to Jerusalem looking for her. How had he even found her house? She waited until they were outside the city walls and walking down the ramp before blurting out, "What's wrong with her, Rafi? Is she sick? Please tell me! I'm so afraid for her!"

"She's gravely ill," he said quietly. "You've taken care of her during her illnesses before, and she's asking for you. She wants you to read her stars and tell her which god to petition."

"Read . . . what?" Abba said. "What are you talking about?"

"It's nothing, Abba. Leyla has always been a little superstitious."

The night had grown dark by the time they reached Basam's house. It had been a tiring climb up a winding road that took them over the top of the Mount of Olives. No one offered any introductions when they entered the house, nor did Yael see Leyla's husband. Her heart hammered with fear as she left Abba and Rafi and followed one of the women into Leyla's bedchamber. Tears sprang to her eyes the moment she saw her friend lying on a bed of blood-soaked cushions. Her skin was as white as linen. Yael ran to her side and knelt down. "I'm here, Leyla. It's me, Yael." She was alive but only half-conscious. She didn't respond. Yael looked at the bloody mattress, the piles of bloody cloths, and asked, "What's wrong with her? What happened? This isn't one of her usual weak spells."

"I'm a midwife," an elderly woman said. "She is expecting a child, but yesterday she began to bleed."

Yael's anger exploded. "Leyla is much too frail to have a baby! Something has been wrong with her blood all her life. She never should have gotten married! Never should have gotten pregnant!"

"Can you help her?" one of the other women asked. "She wants this baby." Yael saw the amount of blood and knew the truth.

"The baby is gone. Your midwife can see that as clearly as I can. Leyla already lost the baby, and now she's losing too much blood. We have to stop the bleeding."

"We tried. Her blood won't thicken and clot."

"Did you give her yarrow to drink? Pack her womb with clean cloths?"

"We did everything we could. She was asking for you to come and consult the stars."

Yael ordered more lamps and spread out her charts. She even went outside to study the night sky. She couldn't believe what she saw. The stars and the other heavenly bodies all lined up favorably. Leyla's illness didn't even appear among the omens.

"Can you tell us which gods we must appease?" one of the women asked when Yael came inside again.

"I-I don't know. Appeal to all of them!"

She sank down by Leyla's side and took her pale hand in both of hers. Leyla held the little moon goddess that Yael had given her in her limp hand. "I'm here, Leyla . . . I'm here," she said over and over. Her helplessness felt like a deep ache inside her. Leyla was dying, just like Mama had, even though there were no unbelieving neighbors this time. Yael could do nothing but watch her friend bleed to death. Hours later, Yael was still holding her hand when Leyla took her last breath.

Yael covered her face and wept for a long time. Leyla's death was so senseless. How could the stars be so wrong? Dazed with grief, she slowly became aware of the other women gathering around Leyla's body, making preparations to wash her and anoint her with spices for burial. One of them held a long, white shroud in her hands. "Wait," Yael said. "Let her brother Rafi come in to see her. He'll want to say good-bye. And where is her husband? And her father?"

"That's not the way we do things," the midwife said. She helped Yael to her feet. "She is unclean from the blood. The men won't want to become defiled. You should leave now. There's nothing more for you to do."

The little statue of the moon goddess had fallen from Leyla's hand. Yael left it lying on the floor. She took one last look at her friend and fled from the room, carrying her useless charts, longing to run and run and never look back. She found her father waiting outside in the courtyard, watching the sky turn light. Rafi was gone. She linked her arm through Abba's, pulling him toward the gate. "We can go now. It's over."

The farther they walked, the more Yael's grief and anger soared. Anger at Leyla's father for forcing her to marry. Anger at Basam for not caring enough to stay by her side during her final hours. Anger at the stars for not speaking the truth to her. "I don't want to go home to Jerusalem yet," she said as they neared the city. "Can I stay at your farmhouse for a few days? I need some time alone to grieve."

"Why grieve alone? Why not let Dinah and Hodaya and the others comfort you?"

"I can't, Abba. . . . Hodaya looks too much like Leyla, and I just can't . . ."

He squeezed her arm. "I understand. We'll go to the farm. I'm on duty at the altar during the day, but I'll come back to stay with you at night."

Yael slept and cried for most of the morning after Abba left, then ate a little bread and wept some more. She couldn't understand why the moon goddess hadn't revealed the truth to her in the stars. Why had all the signs led her to believe that Leyla would be happy, that she would live? All these years Yael had been angry with Zaki's God for Mama's death, and now her own deity had let her down.

She was lying on her mat, staring up at the rough, wooden ceiling, when she heard a man's voice from outside calling, "Anyone home?"

She sat up, her heart racing. She decided to peek out to see who it was, then remain hidden if it was a stranger. She crept to the window, staying in the shadows.

Rafi.

"Is anyone here?" he called again. Yael wiped her face and smoothed her hair, then walked to the doorway, shading her eyes in the bright sunlight, fighting the urge to run into his arms for comfort. He looked relieved to see her. "Yael. I was hoping you were here."

She nodded, wiping fresh tears as they rolled down her face. She walked outside to stand near him and saw that his eyes were red-rimmed with grief. He suddenly pulled her into his arms, and she clung to him in return. Embracing him felt as natural as embracing Leyla.

"I needed to hold someone," Rafi said, his voice breaking. "I knew you would understand." Yael felt his body shake with silent sobs as she held him tightly, felt his tears in her hair as she wept against his chest. She didn't know how long they remained that way, but finally he released her. "Thank you," he whispered.

Yael took his hand and sat down with him on the low stone wall surrounding the courtyard. She stared down at her feet, too angry to look up and see Leyla's village across the valley, too frightened of her own emotions to look at Rafi. "I miss my sister," he said hoarsely. "She was my friend ever since we were small—and she was yours, too. Thank you for being so good to her. Leyla loved you. She wanted you to be with her in the end because she knew that I couldn't be."

"I wish I knew if she'd been happy these past few months."

"Basam will pay."

"Rafi, all the money in the world won't bring her back."

"A life for a life. He let my sister die. It's my duty to avenge her death."

Yael froze, chilled by his words and by the ice in his voice. He wouldn't really kill Basam, would he? This was anger and grief talking. "I miss her so much," Yael murmured.

"I know. Me too." He squeezed her hand a little tighter before letting go. Then he stood. "I'm glad I found you here. If it's okay, I'd like to come back tomorrow. The men in my village . . . we aren't supposed to show our grief."

"I'll be here for a few more days," she said.

"Thank you."

Yael remained sitting as she watched him walk away, following his progress across the valley.

He returned the next day and the next. When she shared her confusion about what the stars had said, she learned that Rafi didn't believe in anything. "We make our own destiny," he told her, "through our own power and strength. I don't believe in gods or stars or religion."

Yael didn't care what he believed. They talked and laughed and wept for Leyla, and by the end of the week, when he kissed her for the first time, she already knew that she was in love with him. She had thought her first kiss would be on her wedding night, but after Rafi kissed her that first, tender time, she knew she wanted his lips on hers, his strong arms around her, for the rest of her life. Rafi loved her. And she loved him. In spite of her overwhelming grief, Yael was happier than she'd ever been in her life. All around her the world turned green, the wildflowers sprouted, the sun warmed the land, and she felt like she was awakening, as well. Dizzy and breathless with excitement, she could barely wait for Abba to leave every morning and for Rafi to come. She knew that Leyla smiled down on them, laughing along with them at their unabashed joy.

"Do you want to know when I first fell in love with you?" Rafi asked. They sat beneath her father's fig tree on a rug she'd spread on the ground against the chill of the damp earth.

"When?"

"That day when you were at the tombs and I was with that gang of boys. You ordered them to get out of your way, and you didn't look one bit afraid. You stood with one hand on your hip

341

and your jaw jutting out like this, and you said, 'Let us through!' You were formidable—and beautiful."

Yael laughed at his pantomime. "I didn't look like that!"

"Yes, you did."

"I may have acted brave, but I was terrified. They were hurting my friend. I never thanked you for helping us."

"I had never seen a girl stand up to a gang of boys like that. I remember thinking that no man could ever capture such a spirited woman's love, much less possess her for his own. It would be like trying to capture a flame."

"I'm yours now," she said, moving closer to him. "I love you, Rafi."

"And I'm the richest man in the world. I want you for my wife."

"Then let's tell our families. My father will be home before sunset. Let's tell him together. "

"That's not the way it's done in my village. I will tell my father that I've found a wife, and if he agrees, he'll go to your father and ask for a marriage contract. Do you think your father will accept?"

"Of course! I'll tell him he has to accept. I want to marry you."

Rafi left before Abba returned, but he promised to speak with his own father as soon as he could. Yael couldn't bear to wait through such a long, tedious process. She prepared a nice meal for Abba, and as soon as he sat down to eat it, she told him about Rafi. "I have wonderful news, Abba . . . I'm in love!" Her words bubbled out in a rush of excitement. "When Rafi's father asks you for my hand, please, please say yes!"

"Wait—you're in love? . . . With *Rafi*?"

"Yes, Leyla's brother Rafi. He wants to marry me! You know his father, Zabad."

"Yes. I know him." Abba had stopped eating. He set down his bowl and bread with a worried look. "When did all this happen?"

"I've known Rafi for years, Abba, and he's a good man. We've been friends, just like Zaki and I are friends."

"I don't think it's a very good idea to marry a Samaritan."

"Why not? I love him!"

"I need to talk this over with Dinah and Iddo."

His words outraged her. "You don't need their permission. You're my father!"

"I'm sorry, but I won't give you an answer until I've talked this over with them. You're their daughter as much as you are mine."

Yael knew what their reaction would be. Iddo and Dinah hated Samaritans. She waited until Abba fell asleep and got out her charts to study the stars, desperate to read what the future held for her and Rafi. She could make offerings to influence the heavens in her favor, if she had to. When the stars all told her that she and Rafi would be together, that they would be happy, she read them a second time and then a third, just to be sure. The stars had been wrong about Leyla's future. . . . Yael lay awake for a long time, doubting what she'd just read, questioning her ability as a seer—a seer who could no longer see.

She and Abba walked up to the city the next morning, and Yael was forced to wait with the other women all day until Abba and Iddo returned home. "Why are you so fidgety?" Safta Dinah asked. "What's the matter with you?" Yael didn't want to tell her until that evening when the four of them sat down together after the meal. Yael would find a way to be with Rafi no matter what anyone said. She had seen it in the stars.

"Yael thinks she's in love," Abba began.

"I *am* in love!" she interrupted. "With Leyla's brother Rafi. And he loves me. His father is going to ask Abba if he can marry me."

"And I told Yael that we needed to talk it over with both of you first," Abba said.

"You can't let her do this," Safta said, the first to object. "I

343

promised Miriam I would find her a suitable husband, a Jewish husband—"

"Rafi is Jewish!" Yael tried to stay calm, but she wanted to stamp her foot in frustration.

"Our heritage comes through our mother's line," Iddo said, "not our father's. If Rafi's mother is a Gentile, then so is he. God gave our people a second chance after they strayed into idolatry, and now His enemies are trying to tempt us away from Him again."

"How could you possibly live with people who kill their own children?" Safta asked.

"Rafi isn't like that." But Yael couldn't forget his cold, stony face when he'd talked of making Basam pay for his sister's death.

"How do you know he isn't like them?" Safta asked. "Once you're married to him, he might turn out to be just like his father and all of the other men in his village. It's all he knows, Yael."

"Rafi is the oldest son, isn't he?" Iddo asked. "The heir? Someday, as village elder, Rafi will marry other wives for political alliances and prestige and as a display of his wealth. Why would you endure such humiliation?"

"He wouldn't do that. He loves me." But again Yael felt uneasy when she remembered how the women remained separate from the men in Rafi's household.

"What if he forbids you to come home and see your family," Safta continued, "like Leyla's husband did? Hodaya would be heartbroken. We all would be. Remember how you felt when Leyla's husband cut you off from her? And you know Hodaya would never be allowed to visit you."

"Rafi will let me come home. Our families are at peace." Yet Yael knew that Safta was right about one thing: Hodaya could never visit his village. And she would wonder why.

"What about your work as a midwife? You would need his permission to continue, you know."

LYNN AUSTIN

"I'm sure he won't mind. The women in his village need midwives, too."

"But they don't share our values, Yael. You know that. You only have to look at Hodaya to remember what they're like. Do you really want to live with such people?"

Yael didn't want to think about all these things. She and Rafi loved each other. That was all that mattered. "We'll figure out a way to make it work."

"Yael, I'm saying this because I love you," Safta said. "You've always been stubborn and independent, but for once in your life, please listen to our advice. After the first rush of love fades, you'll be trapped in a village that's completely different from ours, living among people who aren't your family, people who think and believe differently than we do. And you'll have to obey your husband without fail for the rest of your life."

"But—"

"Dinah is right," Abba said. "I know how the men in that village think. You've always gone your own way, but not this time. I can't let you marry Rafi. It would be a mistake. I've known Zabad for more than ten years. I know how he lives and . . . and I can't let you live that way."

"Abba, no! Don't listen to Safta!" Yael's tears began to fall as she scrambled to her feet. "You can't refuse us, you can't! What will you tell Zabad when he asks for my hand? That his son isn't good enough for me? That our marriage would be a mistake? You'll start another war! Remember what happened when you said the Samaritans weren't good enough to worship with us?"

"My mind is made up, Yael. I won't listen to any more arguments."

She ran to her room where she could cry in private, hoping that Safta or Abba wouldn't follow her. But a few minutes later, Hodaya came in to comfort her.

"Why were they talking about me, Yael?"

345

"They weren't, little one, they were talking about me. They're trying to stop me from marrying the man I love, but I won't let them. Nothing can stop Rafi and me from being together."

"But they *were* talking about me. I heard them say, 'Look at Hodaya and remember.' Remember what?"

"Don't worry about it," Yael said as she pulled her close. But Hodaya wiggled out of her embrace.

"It has to do with my real parents, doesn't it? Why won't anyone ever talk to me about them?"

"This isn't the time. Everyone is upset about Rafi and me. Wait until all this blows over."

"When you move away with Rafi, can I go with you?"

Yael closed her eyes. It was impossible. Yet how could she walk away from Hodaya, whom she loved like a sister? She would miss her every time she looked at her husband and saw the resemblance. But it would destroy Hodaya if she ever learned the truth. Her father had rejected her. He had ordered her to be smothered to death beneath a soaked blanket. *Rafi's father.*

"There has to be an answer to all this," she said with a sigh. "I'll figure something out, I promise."

Late that night when everyone was asleep, Yael took her star charts and a lamp outside to the courtyard to see, once again, what the heavens had to say. But before she had a chance to study them, she heard the familiar thump and scrape of Hodaya's crutch on the cobblestones and quickly rolled them up. "Why are you up so late, Hodaya? Go back to bed."

"I can't sleep. I'm worried that you're going to leave me."

"I won't leave you." But Yael knew that she wouldn't be making that decision, Rafi would. Hodaya limped closer.

"What are you doing? What are those scrolls?"

"Nothing," she said. "Let's go back to bed."

For now, her future with Rafi would have to remain unknown.

CHAPTER
32

I n living quarters as close as theirs, Zechariah could easily hear everything that was going on. Yael was in love with a Samaritan and determined to marry him. He heard all of his family's well-intentioned pleas and arguments, and he knew that his free-spirited friend would do whatever she wanted to in the end. Zechariah had tried for years to lure her away from the Samaritans and their astrology, but he had failed. Once she married Rafi and moved to his village, no one would ever see her again. He would never win her back to God. She would die with the pagans.

The morning after Yael arrived home with the news, a familiar dream jolted Zechariah awake just before dawn. But it had a different ending this time. The storage basket with Yael hidden inside was tightly bound with ropes so she couldn't escape. In the dream Zechariah cut through the ropes with one of the sacrificial knives he was learning to use and set her free.

He lay awake in the dark, staring at the ceiling, wondering what it meant. As the sky grew lighter, he heard his grandparents talking outside in the courtyard. "Iddo, we have to do something! You know what those Samaritans are like. It makes me sick to think of Yael living with them. They'll destroy her. She's like my own daughter, and I can't bear to lose her. We can't let her marry him."

"Don't worry, Dinah. Mattaniah assured me that he's going to refuse Zabad's offer."

"She'll run away with him—I know she will. We haven't convinced her that she's making a mistake."

"Mattaniah asked us to watch her and make sure she stays here. We can't let her go to the farm."

"She ran away from here once before, remember? She went all the way to the village to see Leyla. She's fearless."

"I know. But Mattaniah needs time to figure out an honorable way to decline Zabad's proposal. Yael was right when she said that a flat refusal will start another war. We can't risk insulting him and causing more trouble."

Zechariah climbed out of bed and hurried outside as the solution to the dilemma suddenly came to him. The dream had shown him the answer, and it seemed so obvious, so inevitable, that he wondered why he hadn't thought of it sooner. "Saba, I know of an honorable way for Mattaniah to decline Zabad's proposal. He can say that Rafi's proposal has come too late. That he already chose a husband for Yael and settled on a dowry. He can show him a signed marriage contract. Then if Rafi runs away with Yael, he would bring shame to his family. He would be stealing another man's wife."

"I cannot advise Mattaniah to lie."

"He won't have to lie. Mattaniah can sign a contract with me. I'll marry Yael."

"No, Zaki," Saba said. "You should marry a wife who loves you—and who loves God."

"Yael is a Levite's daughter and—"

"Do you have proof that she's a suitable wife for a priest? Is she devoted to the Almighty One?"

Zechariah turned away, hoping Saba wouldn't read the truth

in his expression. Should he tell them about the dream he'd just had? Would they believe him?

"Yael's family dabbled in astrology and sorcery in Babylon," Saba continued, "and she's been mingling with the Samaritans all these years."

"I know. But the same is true of our entire nation, Saba. Our ancestors all drifted from the Holy One, didn't they? Yet He forgave us and offered us a second chance. Isn't Yael still a daughter of Israel? Doesn't she deserve a second chance?"

"But what kind of a marriage will you have," Safta asked, "if she loves someone else and not you?"

Zaki couldn't think about that right now. This was the answer, he was certain of it. "You both have to admit that this is the best solution to the problem. Everyone knows that Yael and I have been friends since childhood. We might have been promised to each other years ago."

"Let's not rush into this," Saba said, holding up his hands. "There must be a better solution. Once our emotions have calmed down, maybe we'll see it."

Zechariah drew a deep breath, his mind made up. "I'm my own man, Saba. The decision is mine to make. I'm going to offer Mattaniah my proposal so he can turn down Zabad's. If Yael and Rafi run off together, there's nothing we can do about it, but at least we tried."

"If they decide to run off, Yael would become his concubine, not his wife," Saba said. "I tried to explain that to her last night, but I don't think she was listening."

"I promised her mother—"

"I know, Safta." Zechariah rested his hand on his grandmother's shoulder. He was taller than her now by more than a head. "And I'm going to help you keep that promise."

"Wait," Saba said. "You need to pray about this some more and ask the Almighty One what to do."

"I already know what His answer will be," he said, remembering his dream. "The Torah forbids mixed marriages with Gentiles because we'll end up adopting their ways, worshiping their gods. Wasn't that why we were exiled? But He allowed us to return to the land to rebuild our nation. To marry and to have children—"

"Zechariah, listen to me—"

"I'm sorry, Saba, but it makes sense that I marry her. I love Yael, and I want to save her from making a huge mistake. I'm going to do this."

Zechariah returned to his room before his grandparents could argue further. He could see how upset Saba was, but Zechariah was surprised to discover that his confession was true. He did love Yael. He always had. He would do what he'd tried to do all his life and save her, even though it would cost him the priesthood. That's what the sacrificial knife had meant in his dream. He could never be a priest, never stand before the Almighty One and serve Him knowing that his own wife worshiped idols.

CHAPTER

33

Yael grabbed the front of her father's robe as she pleaded with him. "Abba, no! Please don't make me marry Zaki! I don't love him, I love Rafi!"

"It's done, Yael. I told Zabad I was sorry, but you were already spoken for, that you've known Zechariah your entire life. I showed him the betrothal agreement. He understands that it's a father's right to decide for his daughter."

"Was Rafi there? He would have fought for me, I know he would have."

"No, Rafi wasn't there. He had nothing to do with this proposal. In his village, the fathers arrange these matters."

The walls of the tiny room seemed to close in on Yael. Abba stood in front of the door, leaving no escape. How could this be happening? "Please don't do this to me, Abba! Please!"

"I'm sorry, Yael, but I honestly believe that this is what's best for you. Zechariah is a good man, and he'll treat you well. I can't say the same for Zabad's son. The Samaritans aren't like us, especially the way they treat women. How can I allow my only daughter to marry a man who sees nothing wrong with polygamy or with marrying a twelve-year-old child?"

"Rafi would never do that. He loves me."

"I know the men in his village, Yael. It's a sign of prestige to have more than one wife—and several concubines, too."

She clutched the front of Abba's robe tighter, trying to shake sense into him, but he was unmovable. "Abba, please don't do this!"

"It's done."

She remained in her room the rest of the day, refusing to speak to anyone, even Hodaya. She would figure out a way to be with Rafi. She would! Everyone watched her closely, making sure she didn't run away. Abba slept right outside her door that night, blocking her path. But just before dawn, when everyone slept, she managed to pry off the wooden shutters and squeeze through the tiny window in her room. She knew the way to her father's farm, even in the dark, and she waited there until it was light enough to walk to Rafi's village. Yael had promised him that she wouldn't walk across the valley all alone, but she had to. From now on they would be together.

Rafi wasn't sitting outside with the village elders as she had hoped. Yael lifted her chin, intending to walk past them without speaking but one of the young men who attended the elders stopped her. "What is your business in our village?" he asked. The way he and the others looked at her made her shiver, as if undressing her with their eyes. Jewish men would never gaze at a woman so directly, so disrespectfully.

"You know me," she told them. "I've been coming here with my father for years to visit with Leyla."

"Leyla no longer lives here."

"I know. But her family does." She turned and strode past them into the village, hoping they wouldn't stop her. Rafi said that her fearlessness had surprised him, and it must have surprised the elders, too, because they let her go. She hurried toward Rafi's house, her progress slowed by all the village women who rushed forward to greet her, touching her and begging her to stop and give them advice from the stars. "I-I'm sorry but I didn't bring my charts with me . . . maybe another time . . ." They followed her all the way to Rafi's house as if worshiping her.

Zabad's wives were working outside in the courtyard, their children playing in the dirt when Yael entered the family compound. They all looked up at her, then quickly looked away again as if afraid. She strode over to Raisa, who stood at the loom, working the shuttle through the threads, and said, "Good morning, Raisa. Is Rafi here?" When she didn't reply, Yael took the shuttle from her, halting her weaving. "Raisa, I helped save your life when your first baby was born, remember? Please. Send a message to Rafi that I'm here. That I need to speak with him." The women had all stopped working and even the children were still. Everyone seemed to hold their breath as they waited, watching her. Finally, Raisa summoned one of her sons.

"Go ask your brother Rafi to come here."

His brother. Yael felt the shock all over again at the reminder that this woman, ten years younger than Rafi, was his stepmother.

At last Rafi strode out into the courtyard. Yael had to resist the urge to run into his arms. She saw love in his eyes when he first saw her, then a look of pain. Then anger replaced all of his other emotions. "What are you doing here, Yael? You shouldn't have come!" Before she could reply, he glanced around at all the women and children who watched and listened, and made a sweeping gesture with his arm. "Leave us!" The courtyard emptied.

"Rafi, I love you. I came so we could run away together. Remember what you told me about claiming a wife? That if I was all alone it meant that—"

"No!" The anger in his eyes intensified. "No, Yael. That would bring shame on my family. My father is the village leader. Men of our standing pay a dowry for a suitable bride. They don't marry a sotah who throws herself at a man. And they don't steal a woman who is already betrothed."

"My betrothal is a sham."

"It doesn't matter. If I took you, you would become my concubine, not my wife. I need to marry a wife first. My heir can never come from a concubine."

"Do you love me, Rafi?"

For a moment his eyes glistened with unshed tears. "With all my soul," he said quietly. Then his face turned hard again. "Go home, Yael. Marry your Jewish friend."

"But you and I are free people. If you love me and I love you, we can defy our fathers. No one can stop us from being together."

"I would never defy my father. It would cost me my inheritance."

"Not even to marry me?"

He hesitated for a very long moment. "No. Not even for you."

Yael turned and fled—out of the compound, through the village streets toward home. Rafi didn't follow her. She felt real terror as she ran past the elders and the knot of young men surrounding them, remembering how they had looked at her, remembering Rafi's warning. Yael could barely breathe, barely see through her tears as she raced across the narrow valley, her legs pumping as fast as she could go. When she finally dared to look over her shoulder, she was horrified to see that three of the young men from the village were following her.

"Oh, God, no . . . please!"

Their steps were unhurried. They would easily catch her once she tired. She couldn't possibly make it all the way up the hill to Jerusalem, to safety. Even if she made it to her father's farm, Abba wasn't there to protect her. No one was. She heard the men's laughter behind her as they came closer.

"Oh, God, please help me!" She had no idea who she was pleading with.

She was nearly to her father's house when she saw a man burst out of Abba's front door, running toward her. "No!" she screamed. One of them must have left the village ahead of her, and now she was trapped. She veered away from the man, no longer knowing which way to run.

"Yael!" She heard the man calling to her. "Yael, wait!" She looked over her shoulder and saw through her tears that it was Zechariah. "Yael, run this way! Run to me!"

She did what he said, whirling around and staggering toward him as he closed the gap between them, falling into his arms. "You're safe now," he soothed. "I won't let them hurt you." But there were three Samaritans, and Zaki was outnumbered. She clung tightly to him, trembling with fear, as the men came within a dozen yards of them and halted.

"Yael is my wife," Zaki told them. "We're betrothed. Even you aren't low enough to rape a man's wife right in front of him, are you?" He turned Yael around, turned his own back on the men, and slowly walked with her the rest of the way to her father's house, still holding her tightly. He never looked over his shoulder.

When they reached the house, Yael stumbled inside and sank down on the floor, weeping. Zaki stood in the open doorway, gazing out, saying nothing. A long time later, she finally dried her eyes.

"You followed me," she said softly. "Why?"

"To save your life. It's what I've been trying to do all these years. That's why I've kept your secret for so long, so no one would know about your sorcery."

She couldn't comprehend it. "Thank you," she whispered.

He looked at her for a long moment, then came to crouch beside her. "Are you all right?"

"I begged Rafi to run away with me, but . . ." A long, slow tear traveled down her cheek. She brushed it away. "He refused.

He cares more about his inheritance than he does about me. He could have defied his father if he really loved me."

Zaki exhaled. "I'm so sorry, Yael. I don't know what else to say."

"We'd better go home. Everyone will be worried." She stood and they left her father's house to walk up the road to Jerusalem. She would do what Abba wanted and marry Zechariah.

Rafi didn't love her.

CHAPTER
34

Dozens of people filled the courtyard of Zechariah's house for his wedding—priests and Levites, his fellow Torah students, people who had made the long journey with him and Yael from Babylon. There was lively music and joyful dancing and a feast of food and wine, yet Yael's father looked worried and Zechariah's grandparents looked unhappy. Zechariah had misgivings himself, wondering if Rafi and his gang of ruffians would burst into their home to disrupt the celebration and steal Yael away. But the day passed peacefully. Rafi didn't come. Zechariah sat close enough to Yael to see the sorrow and pain on her face beneath her veil.

Late in the evening, he escorted her to their bridal suite—a new room added onto their house just for them. His chest ached as he closed the door behind them and set the oil lamp in its niche on the wall. Yael yanked off her veil and unpinned her hair. She was such a beautiful woman. No wonder the Samaritan had wanted her. But instead of moving toward her, Zechariah crossed to the other side of the room and sat down on the floor, leaning against the wall. "What are you waiting for?" she asked. "Just go ahead and get it over with."

He shook his head. "I know you don't love me. In fact, you

357

probably resent me for taking Rafi's place. It's supposed to be an act of love," he said, gesturing to their marriage bed. "Not a conquest."

"An act of love?" she repeated, and he heard the scorn in her voice. "Do you love me, Zaki?"

"I've always loved you. Ever since we were children. I love your spirit, your sense of adventure, your zeal for life, and I didn't want the Samaritans to destroy all those things. And they would have, you know. That's why I asked your father for your hand."

Yael stared at him for a moment, her defiant expression still in place. Then she closed her eyes, and he saw her defiance transform into grief as she sank down on their bed. "I loved Rafi . . . I really did." Her tears began to fall. Zaki longed to go to her and comfort her, but he stayed where he was.

"I believe you. But a few years from now, after the passion faded, your life with the Samaritans would have become a living hell. And you could never undo it or change your mind and come home. I know you don't see it right now, but I rescued you from a terrible life." She didn't look at him, didn't reply. "If you don't want to be married to me, if you still want to run away, I won't stop you."

Yael finally stopped crying. She wiped her tears and lifted her chin to look at him. "They're waiting for us to show them the sheets, the proof. No one believes that I'm a virgin. They think Rafi and I have already been together, but it isn't true."

"I believe you. But I won't seal our marriage until you're ready."

"Until I'm ready? You're my husband. Doesn't the Torah give you the right to rule over me? Why aren't you claiming your rights?"

"Because I'm guessing that the only way you can endure our marriage bed is by pretending that I'm Rafi. And I want you to be glad that I'm your husband. I hope you'll love me someday.

In the meantime, I saved a little bit of blood from one of the goats we slaughtered for the wedding feast. We'll put it on the sheets to fool them."

Yael lowered her face into her hands, weeping again. Her grief broke Zechariah's heart. He stood and went to sit beside her on the bed, wrapping his arms around her, comforting her the way he had after her mother died when they were children.

"Without love, we won't have a true marriage," he told her. "I see my grandparents, the love they share, and I want the same thing. Safta is devoted to Saba. And he couldn't survive without her. I know their marriage hasn't always been perfect, yet they stay together, work together, through the good years and the bad." He waited until Yael stopped crying, then stood again, pulling one of the coverings from the bed. He carried it back to his place in the corner and removed his outer robe. "I'll give you time to decide what you want to do, Yael. We're not married until you decide that we are." Then he lay down on the floor to try to sleep, exhausted from the strain of this long, emotional day.

With the lamp still lit, he watched Yael's shadow on the wall as she rose from the bed and crouched beside the bags that held all her belongings. Safta had moved Yael's things into their room earlier in the day, but now Zechariah was certain that Yael would gather them up and leave. Instead, he heard a rustling sound, and when he sat up on one elbow, he saw her sitting on the floor, bending over an open scroll. "What is that? What are you doing?" he asked.

"I need to see what the stars say about my future . . . I don't know how else to decide what to do."

He lay down again, disgusted. There was no point in telling her that the Torah forbade it—much less in a priest's house. Yael knew. He had told her many times before. Saba had warned him that he shouldn't marry her, that she still had idolatry in her heart, and here was the proof. He would resign from the priesthood as soon as his marriage week ended. He sighed and closed his eyes. "Good night, Yael."

Yael bent over her star charts, searching for answers. She'd seen things so clearly when she'd studied the charts in the past, but tonight she couldn't make sense of all the signs. They seemed to contradict each other. Maybe she was too close to the situation to read them clearly. After all, these were her stars, her future. Maybe what she wanted them to say was getting confused with what they really did say. But Leyla's grandmother was dead, and Yael didn't know anyone else who could help her interpret them.

Frustrated, she left the lamp burning in the room and went outside to the courtyard. Maybe if she looked up at the real heavens, the answer would become clear to her. The cool night was beautiful, the sky sparkling and cloudless as if scrubbed clean, the moon so bright she could read her star charts without an oil lamp. More and more stars appeared as Yael gazed up, as if coming out of hiding to talk to her. And sweeping across the center of the sky was a sparkling white river of stars.

The heavenly bodies all said that the love she shared with Rafi was real. They had predicted a happy life together, forever. But the stars had been wrong, just as they'd been wrong about Leyla's marriage. How could she have been so mistaken? What was she doing wrong? Why wouldn't they give her guidance? Her future seemed unknowable.

She was still looking up at the stunning heavens when she heard a rustling sound near the gate. She turned, startled to see a man standing there. For a moment she froze, her heart quickening. Then she recognized him—his height, his stance, his beautiful curly hair. *Rafi!* Yael ran to him, throwing her arms around him, weeping tears of joy. "Rafi! You're here! You came for me!"

"Yes. I'm here," he said. But his voice sounded strange. And he didn't return her embrace. His arms hung stiffly at his sides. Yael released him and looked up at him.

"Rafi, what's wrong?"

"Where's your new husband?" The cold expression on his face made her shiver. He seemed different tonight, not the Rafi she knew.

"Zechariah isn't my husband yet," she told him. "We haven't consummated the marriage."

"I don't believe you." Again, that strange, icy voice. She embraced him again as if her love and the warmth of her arms could thaw his coldness.

"I love you, Rafi. Zechariah knows that. He said I could run away with you if I wanted to, and he wouldn't stop us. I came out here to consult the stars for answers, but now that you're here, I don't have to. Come on, let's leave." She tried pulling him toward the gate, but he was as immoveable as a pillar.

"He and your father signed a marriage contract, didn't they?"

"Yes, but—"

"Does your husband love you?"

"That's not important, Rafi. Please—"

"You didn't answer my question. That must mean that he does love you."

"I would have run away with you before the wedding. I told you that. Why didn't you come for me sooner?"

"I didn't come for you now, Yael."

"What? . . . What do you mean?" In reply, he grabbed her upper arm, holding it so tightly he would leave fingerprint bruises on her arm. This man was a stranger, not the gentle, loving man she knew. "Rafi, let go. You're hurting me."

He yanked her toward the door to her room, the door she had left open with a lamp burning inside. "You belong to me, Yael. You're mine."

"Yes, I already told you that. Why are you acting this way? You're hurting me."

"I don't like losing someone I love. Basam had to pay for Leyla, and now it's your husband's turn to pay." They reached the door, and he kicked it wide open. Zechariah sat up, startled. "Is that your husband?" Rafi asked her.

"I told you, it isn't a real marriage. Tell him, Zaki—"

But in one swift, strong move, Rafi pulled Yael against his chest, pinning her arms to her sides. Something cold and sharp pressed against her throat. A knife. "Neither of you make a sound," Rafi said, "or I'll slit her throat right now."

Fear washed through Yael, draining her strength. If Rafi hadn't been holding her, she would have collapsed. Her body trembled so violently she might have been standing naked in a snowstorm. As tears blurred her vision, she couldn't see Zechariah's expression in the dim lamplight as he slowly rose to his feet.

"Wait! Put the knife away, Rafi. Don't hurt her." He raised his arms in surrender.

"I should have let my friends beat you to death years ago. Of all people, I had to lose Yael to you. To *you*!" He spat out the words like bitter gall. "The suffering you caused me—it was like watching Yael die, knowing I could never have her. Now you'll have the agony of watching her die. It will be the last thing you'll ever see before I kill you, too."

"She loves *you*," Zechariah said calmly, "not me. She wanted to marry you. Why would you kill someone who loves you? Kill me if you want to, but why kill Yael?"

"Because you stole her from me. And because you love her. I want you to suffer the way I have."

Yael felt his grip tighten. The knife blade pressed against her flesh. She was going to die. "No, Rafi, don't!" she begged.

Iddo awoke from the dream, gasping.

"Shh . . . It was just a dream, Iddo," Dinah soothed. "Go back to sleep." He sat up, his clothing drenched with sweat. The nightmare had been so real that it took Iddo a moment to figure out where he was. In his bed. Beside Dinah. In Jerusalem. But why have a nightmare now, after all these years without one?

"Did I cry out and awaken everyone?" he asked.

"No one heard you but me. . . . Was it the same dream, Iddo?"

"Yes." He had crouched beneath the wagon as Jerusalem burned. The soldier was attacking Mama, and his brother had crawled out to help her. Iddo had tried to leave his hiding place and save the people he loved. He had tried to move, to crawl out and rescue them—but the dream had jolted him awake before he could move. He tossed the covers aside and climbed out of bed.

"Where are you going?" Dinah asked.

"Outside for some air. I'm sorry for waking you." Iddo left the room but even the canopy of glimmering stars couldn't erase the nightmare from his mind. Fear and dread lingered like a sour taste that couldn't be washed away. What could have triggered the dream? Yesterday had been a joyous occasion—Zechariah's marriage to Yael. True, Iddo hadn't wanted him to marry her, but even so, he marveled that he had lived to see such a day. Soon there would be children, reversing the curse of death and bringing renewed life. *"Look up at the heavens and count the stars—if indeed you can count them. . . . So shall your offspring be."*

But Iddo couldn't concentrate on the night sky. The lingering horror from the dream had left behind an aura of evil. He tiptoed around the courtyard, searching for—he didn't even know what he searched for. But he recalled the nest of vipers they'd found when building the foundation of this house, and like rooting out those snakes, he felt an urgent need to find the source of evil and destroy it.

He heard a sound. Voices. They came from the new room added on for Zechariah and Yael. He inched toward the sound and saw the open door and a light burning inside. A man stood silhouetted in the doorway. Not Zaki . . . he was shorter than Zaki. Not anyone from Iddo's household.

"Now you can watch her die," the man said.

Rafi. The Samaritan.

He was holding Yael against his chest. Iddo saw the glint of a knife.

"Don't hurt her, Rafi." Zechariah's voice. "Take your revenge on me, but don't hurt Yael. She loves you."

For a moment Iddo couldn't move, frozen in horror just as he'd always been in his dream. He had to save his family! Then he forced himself to move, glancing around the courtyard for a weapon. Dinah's heavy clay water jar stood near his feet. He picked it up and crept to the opened door, then smashed it into the back of Rafi's head with all his strength. Rafi tottered but didn't fall, momentarily stunned. And in that instant, Zechariah lunged toward Yael and snatched her from Rafi's grasp. Zaki stood in front of her, shielding her as she screamed and screamed.

Rafi whirled to attack Iddo, a short, double-edged knife in his hand. He was young and strong, but Iddo was strong, too. He had killed and skinned hundreds of bulls and rams for the sacrifices. Now he wrestled for his life and for Zechariah and Yael's lives—gripping Rafi's arms to keep away the knife.

"Stay back, Zaki," Iddo shouted. "He'll kill you." But Zaki attacked Rafi from behind, punching and beating him, then wrapping one arm around Rafi's throat as he tried to pull him away.

Yael continued to scream for help as the three men struggled, loudly enough to awaken the others. Besai and Mattaniah came to help, but they moved too slowly, still groggy with sleep and with wine from the wedding. In one swift, deadly strike, Rafi managed to free one hand and stab Iddo in the stomach. Iddo felt the force of the thrust, the warm, wet rush of blood. Iddo staggered backward as Rafi pulled out the knife and whirled to attack Zechariah, the knife raised.

"No!" Iddo roared. He fought for balance and hurled himself at Rafi, pushing him sideways with all his strength, away from his grandson. The other men piled on Rafi then, knocking him to the ground, kicking the knife from his hand. Iddo snatched up the dagger and plunged it into Rafi's chest. A moment later, Rafi went still.

Iddo had used up all his strength. A fire burned in his gut where he'd been stabbed. He leaned against the wall, then slowly slid to the ground.

"Iddo's hurt! He's bleeding!" someone shouted.

They helped him lie down, and Dinah bent over him, tearing open his robe to tend to his wound. The room whirled, dream-like. It was hard to breathe. "Lie still, Iddo," she begged. "Please don't move . . . Please be all right. . . ."

"I'm fine, Dinah. Don't worry. It was just a dream . . . But I saved them this time. . . . I killed the Babylonian soldier . . . and I saved them. . . ."

Iddo closed his eyes and let the darkness take him.

CHAPTER 35

Zechariah ran home from the evening sacrifice, desperate to be with his grandfather, unwilling to miss a single moment with him, knowing each one might be his last. Three long, agonizing days had passed since Rafi had stabbed Saba, and no one was able to say if he would survive or not. Zechariah raced into the courtyard, then into his grandfather's room and saw Safta sitting beside his bed. "He's asleep," she whispered. "There's been no change." She was trying so hard to be brave, staying by Saba's side, encouraging him to get well, never letting anyone see her cry. Zechariah had also remained beside his bed all night and had heard her murmuring to Saba in the darkness, "I love you, Iddo. . . . You must get well. . . . You must."

"I'll stay with him for a while," he said as he sat down beside the bed.

"Do you want something to eat, Zaki?"

"Maybe later." Worry had stolen his appetite.

Safta nodded and released Saba's hand as she stood. "I'll warm some broth in case he's hungry when he wakes up."

Zechariah closed his eyes after she left, silently pleading with

366

the Almighty One to spare his grandfather's life. Why should Saba pay the price for Zechariah's decision to marry Yael?

As time passed, his mind began to wander, circling back to the events of that terrible night. No one in his household could comprehend the violence and hatred that had entered their gate. Rafi had tried to kill Yael. And him. And Saba. Who knew how many others he would have killed if Saba hadn't stopped him?

But Rafi was dead. At dawn, Mattaniah had sent for the elders from Rafi's village, asking them to come and see for themselves what Rafi had tried to do. The elders had carried his body home. And now all of Jerusalem held its breath, waiting to see if more blood vengeance and killing would follow.

In all the grief and confusion, Zechariah had barely spoken with Yael—his wife. Hodaya had been much better at comforting her than he was. What a terrible way to begin their marriage. If it ever truly would be a marriage.

Zechariah opened his eyes again when he heard his grandfather stirring. "Is the sacrifice finished, Zaki?" he asked in his whispery-soft voice.

"Yes. And everyone prayed for you. All of the priests and the people . . . How are you feeling?"

"Like I'm still dreaming. Like I'm half in this world and half in the next."

Lines of pain creased Saba's face. The wound had been deep, and so much blood had drained from his body that he was as weak as an infant, as pale and cold as snow. But Zechariah refused to allow his grandfather to give in to the pain and die. "Please stay in this world a little longer, Saba. We need you."

"That's up to the Holy One, not me. . . . In the meantime, tell me about today's Torah portion."

Zechariah swallowed his grief. "It's one of your favorites, the passage where the Holy One says to Abraham, 'Look up at the heavens and count the stars—if indeed you can count them. So shall your offspring be.'"

"Tell me—" He began to cough and Zechariah tensed, fearing the exertion would reopen his wound.

"Just rest, Saba. Don't try to talk until you're stronger. It takes too much of your strength."

"You know how we become stronger?" he asked, smiling faintly. "By studying the Torah."

Zechariah bit his lip. He longed to hear just one more of his grandfather's Torah lessons. Why hadn't he appreciated the wealth of wisdom and knowledge that Saba possessed? Who could ever take the place of this man of God when he was gone? Zechariah couldn't bear to think about it. "Then we'll study this passage together so you'll grow strong." He sat up straight, waiting for his grandfather to begin with a question. The room grew dimmer now that the sun had set, but Zechariah didn't want to light a lamp.

Saba drew a shallow breath. "What is the plain meaning of the passage?"

"The Holy One is telling Abraham that one day his descendants will be so numerous that we'll be like the stars in the heavens. Too many to count."

"And He always keeps His promises. . . . Don't let our tiny population fool you. Or our disobedience in failing to finish His temple. God keeps His promises even when we don't keep ours." He paused for a moment, then asked, "Do you see a deeper meaning?"

Zechariah smiled. Of course. There was always a deeper meaning. Saba had taught him this passage years before and was checking to see if he remembered. "The Holy One was not only telling Abraham that his offspring would be numerous, but also that we would shine like the stars. We would be a source of light in the darkness. The Holy One entrusted us with His

Word, and the world is enlightened by the Torah's wisdom and moral teachings when we live in obedience to it."

"Good. . . . Is there still another meaning?"

Zechariah thought for a moment but none came to mind. "If so, I'm certain that you know what it is, Saba." He bent closer as his grandfather cleared his throat.

"The Holy One asked Abraham to count the stars. An impossible task. But He knew that if Abraham attempted the impossible, his offspring would follow his example. We would also attempt the impossible if God asked us to. Because with His help, nothing is impossible. Do you believe that, Zaki?"

"Yes. Of course." This wasn't the time to share his doubts with his grandfather.

"We all believed it when we first came here," Saba continued. "We were going to rebuild Jerusalem and the temple and our nation even if the rubble and the weeds and the hatred of our enemies made it seem impossible. We started off so well and now . . . now for the past decade we've decided it was impossible. There were too many obstacles in our way, too many stars to count."

"The obstacles aren't imagined, Saba. We had to stop building, remember? The Persian king reversed his decree."

"Did the Almighty One reverse His decree?"

"No, but our enemies came with soldiers and threats and ordered us to stop. We had no choice." Zechariah tried to be gentle and not argue, even though he had once agreed with Saba when he'd argued with the priest, Jakin. "We're still under Persian control. We have to obey the king."

"Is he mightier than God?"

Before Zechariah could reply, Safta came into the room with a bowl of warm broth. "Are you tiring him, Zaki? He needs to eat something and then rest."

Zechariah stood to give her his place beside the bed. "I'll come back in a little while."

"No, Zechariah . . . wait . . . I'm not finished." Iddo motioned for him to kneel beside the bed again. "Nothing is impossible with God," he said. "Do you believe that or don't you?"

"I believe it." But he had wrestled with doubt and fear for so long that they had exhausted his certainty, just like they had exhausted the high priest and their nation's leaders and so many other people.

"Try to eat some broth," Safta said.

Saba shook his head. "God has His hand on you, Zechariah, for a very special task. I've always known that was true. . . . Tell me why you decided to come here."

"Because I felt God's presence. I heard Him telling me to come. I thought . . . I thought if we rebuilt the temple, then God's presence would dwell with us all the time, but then . . ."

"You haven't found Him?"

"No. Not yet." It shamed Zechariah to admit it.

"Are you certain about that? I think you've been searching for God in the wrong place when all this time He has been as close to you as I am."

"How? . . . Where?"

"We all want to meet God in a dramatic way like you did on the day of your bar mitzvah. But instead, the Almighty One quietly reveals himself to us in His Word. As you study it every day, you hear His voice and you see Him. You learn to know Him."

"Saba, I—"

"Don't wait for a new temple to be built or for another mystical experience like the first one. Listen to God now, son. Pay attention to His voice in the Scriptures." Saba closed his eyes. "And then when He tells you to do the impossible, go do it."

Zechariah left the room and went outside to the courtyard as his emotions overwhelmed him. Do the impossible? The others had sat down to eat the evening meal and they invited him to join them, but he wasn't hungry. Could Saba be right? Was God's presence truly as close as the pages of the Torah, the writings of the prophets? Zechariah's pain was so raw, his dread so great, that he could scarcely think, barely function. He fled to his new room—his marriage chamber—as he tried to pull his fraying emotions back together. He was still sitting there on the floor in the dark with his back against the wall when he heard the door open. He looked up. Yael came inside with a lamp and closed the door behind her. He waited while she set the lamp in its niche, not trusting himself to speak.

"We haven't had a chance to talk since that night," she said. "Since your grandfather . . ." He saw her swallow. "But I need to tell you how sorry I am for everything that happened. Can you ever forgive me?"

"For what? For loving the wrong person?" he asked with a shrug. "You couldn't have known what Rafi would do."

"I should have known. I ignored the signs because I didn't want to see them. Rafi would have killed both of us. And anyone else who tried to interfere." She walked forward a few more steps as if afraid to approach him. "Zaki, I know that what happened to your grandfather was my fault."

"It wasn't. I don't blame you. I shouldn't have interfered with your life by offering to marry you."

She moved closer and knelt in front of him. Tears streamed down her beautiful face. "If you hadn't interfered, I would have foolishly married Rafi. I would have married a man capable of murdering me. I should have listened to you and to everyone else. Please, please forgive me."

"Of course, Yael. Of course I forgive you." She was so distraught that he reached for her and pulled her into his arms, letting her sit beside him and weep against his shoulder. But in spite of his assurances, part of him did blame her for what had happened. And if his grandfather died . . . Zechariah wasn't sure he could ever look at Yael without thinking that she was partly to blame.

"I burned up my star charts . . . I threw them all on the hearth and watched them burn." Her voice sounded muffled against his robe. "I'll never look at the stars for guidance again. I'll worship your God from now on."

He didn't reply. She had spoken the words he'd waited to hear all these years. But at what price? His grandfather's life?

"Will you give me a second chance, Zaki?" she whispered.

"Of course."

Yael released him and leaned away to look at him. She took his face in her hands, touching his beard, stroking his hair. "When Rafi said he was going to kill you, he was a man I didn't know. A stranger. I could never have loved a man who would kill you. But in that terrible moment, I saw you, I knew you. You were Zaki, my friend. The man I've shared a lifetime with, the man I know so well. I love you, and I can't imagine a future without you. I'm so sorry for what I've put your family through. For what happened to your grandfather—"

"Shh . . . shh . . . Don't cry, Yael." He pulled her close again, desperate to stop her flow of words. He had promised to forgive her, the same way he had assured Saba that he believed in a God who could do the impossible—and Zechariah wasn't sure if any of it was true. He didn't know what he believed or if he could ever forgive. He needed to get away somewhere alone so he could think.

"I want to truly be your wife," she said, "if you haven't changed your mind."

"You are my wife, Yael. We're already married. I won't change my mind." But his heart, not his mind, needed to change. Especially if his grandfather died.

Her arms tightened around him. "I'm yours, Zaki. From now on. I'm yours."

"Yael, right now I . . . I need to go pray for Saba." He unwrapped her arms from around him and struggled to his feet. "I'll be back in a little while."

He left the house and walked through the dark streets, dodging the rubble still piled everywhere after so many years. Dim lamplight lit a few of the scattered houses, but not many. The inhabitants of Jerusalem were too poor to waste precious oil. Wanting to avoid the temple mount, he walked downhill to the reservoir that held the runoff from the Gihon Spring. The pool used to be inside the city walls, but they had all been destroyed by the Babylonians. Zechariah climbed onto a half-broken section of wall and sat down.

Across the valley, thin plumes of gray smoke curled into the night sky from Rafi's village. Zaki turned away from that view and gazed up the hill at the cluster of houses where he and the other settlers lived. Farther up the slope was the house of assembly and Governor Sheshbazzar's residence, and on the highest point above this mound of land where King David's city had once stood, Zechariah could see smoke rising from the Holy One's altar. It was the mountain where the temple should be.

He closed his eyes, lowering his face in his hands so he could think. Yael had given up her idolatry. She was ready to be his wife. But he knew she acted out of guilt and obligation and fear, knowing Saba might die. Zaki wanted her love. It had taken the crisis of nearly losing her, seeing that knife pressed to her throat, for him to realize how much he did love her. He had offered to trade his life for hers. As he opened his eyes again and gazed up at the place where the temple should be, he wondered if living with a wife without her love was like serving as God's priest without loving Him. Was this how God felt about Zechariah's halfhearted faith? Did He also want all or nothing, a relationship of mutual love, not mere guilt or obligation?

All or nothing. That's what his grandfather was trying to teach him. Did Zechariah believe all of the stories in the Torah, all of the impossible deeds that the Almighty One had done in the past, or didn't he?

He realized that he did. Because Saba was right—he had learned to know God through studying the Scriptures. What he saw was a God of love and miracles and laws, and he knew that a life without Him wasn't worth living. He would be no better than the dumb beasts of the earth. No better than the Samaritans.

Zechariah truly had experienced God's presence back in Babylon. The Almighty One had commanded him to return to Jerusalem and to Him. Zechariah had been longing for His presence ever since, searching for Him, waiting for God to tell him why he was here and what He wanted him to do. And as Zechariah gazed up the sloping hill, at the ruins, at the half-built city, at the empty place on the top of the hill where Abraham had offered up Isaac, the place where the temple should be, he suddenly knew exactly what God wanted him to do.

The impossible.

He jumped down off the wall and ran up the hill, hurrying through the narrow lanes as fast as he could in the dark. He raced through the gate into his house, passing the others still sitting in the courtyard, and went straight into Saba's room. His grandfather opened his eyes and looked up at him as Zechariah knelt beside the bed.

"We need to rebuild the temple," he said, still breathless from the climb. "Not because King Cyrus told us to, but because we long to meet with God. Because we love Him and are incomplete without Him. It's just like you said, Saba—God has been testing us with all these difficulties to see how important the temple is to us. Will we allow ourselves to be discouraged, or will we trust Him and do the impossible?"

A slow, gentle smile lit Saba's pale face.

"The Almighty One wants our love, Saba, not guilty obedience. That's what's been missing in my life—love. Instead of waiting for God's presence to come to me again, He wanted me

374

to pursue Him the way the Torah says to do, with all my heart and soul and strength. Following rules and offering sacrifices is meaningless without love. Am I making any sense?"

Saba nodded, still smiling.

"We need to rebuild the temple. We need to trust the God of the impossible. It's so clear to me, so obvious—but how do I get the others to believe it?"

"You'll have to convince them."

"And you'll have to help me!" Zechariah gripped his grandfather's icy hand in both of his. "You have to fight to get well and to live so that we can do this together. It was your dream, and now it's mine for us to minister together in the Holy One's temple."

He felt the gentle pressure of Saba's hand in return. "I'll do my best."

And Zechariah would do his best, too, from now on. He would build his marriage with Yael and his faith in God—day by day, one loving, impossible step at a time. And then he would rebuild God's temple.

Part IV

The Temple

"Not by might nor by power, but
by my Spirit," says the Lord Almighty.

Zechariah 4:6

SIX YEARS LATER

The relentless sun left Zechariah parched and thirsty as he made the six-mile trek home from the grazing pastures outside Bethlehem. The report that he and the others had just heard from the chief shepherd, Besai, had discouraged all of them. "Let's stop for a minute," Rebbe Jakin said. "I need to rest." Sweat rolled down his face, which was red with exertion from the uphill climb. Zechariah and the two other young priests-in-training halted in the stingy shade of a cedar tree, grateful for the rest.

"If it's this hot in the springtime, what will summer be like?" Zechariah asked the others. He took a drink from his dwindling waterskin, not expecting a reply.

Jakin gestured to the straw-colored landscape all around them. "The Judean hills look nearly as desolate as the wilderness by the Dead Sea. Have any of you ever seen the Judean wilderness?"

"No," Zechariah replied. "But I've walked this route before in the springtime and these *wadis* usually gush with water. It was a challenge to wade across some of them. Now they're all dry. Even the Kidron Brook has dried up."

The spring rains that usually filled the dry riverbeds to over-flowing hadn't come. Neither had the winter rains or the early rains last fall. Drought baked the Promised Land's fertile soil, leaving it dry as ashes.

"Jeshua won't be pleased with our report," Jakin said. "The daily offerings will need to be scaled back yet again."

"And what about the Passover sacrifices? And the ones for my ordination?" Zechariah asked. No one knew the answer. He mopped the sweat from his brow, and they set off again for the last leg of their climb over the Mount of Olives. "I'm finally going to be ordained in a few weeks," he said to the others, "and now there may not be any lambs for me to offer."

When they arrived in Jerusalem, they went straight to the house of assembly to give their report. From inside the high priest's stifling room, Zechariah heard the young yeshiva boys' voices droning like a beehive as they studied, their heads bent over their scrolls. Rebbe Jakin told Jeshua about the effects of the drought and how so many of the ewes from the temple flocks had miscarried. "If large crowds come for the Passover Feast, Besai fears that we may not have enough lambs to go around," Jakin finished. "Let alone enough for the daily sacrifices."

The high priest closed his eyes for a long moment, the strain evident on his face. "I checked our storehouses this morning and our supplies of grain and oil are critically low. Those daily offerings may have to be halted as well, for the first time since we rebuilt the altar."

"The Almighty One won't get His portion and neither will we," Jakin said. "How will our families survive? We depend on the peoples' tithes, and ten percent of nothing is nothing."

"I don't understand why this is happening," Jeshua murmured, fanning himself with a dried palm frond.

Both Jeshua and Rebbe Jakin had seniority over Zechariah, and he knew better than to lecture his elders, but he could no longer keep still. "Ask the Lord for rain in the springtime; it is the Lord who makes the storm clouds. He gives showers of rain to men, and plants of the field to everyone." The men stared at him as if trying to place the Scripture he had just quoted. Where *had* it come from? The words had sprung to Zechariah's mind, but he couldn't place the verse, either. He scrambled to think of another one that he could quote. "I was reading and praying about the drought the other day, and I found a passage about it in the Torah. May I read it to you?"

"Yes, of course."

Zechariah hurried into the yeshiva, interrupting the lessons as he borrowed the scroll of the fifth book of Moses. He searched for the verse as he returned to the high priest's room, and although it wasn't the one he had just quoted, he read it aloud to the others. "'If you faithfully obey the commands I am giving you today—to love the Lord your God and to serve him with all your heart and with all your soul—then I will send the rain on your land in its season, both autumn and spring rains, so that you may gather your grain, new wine and oil. I will provide grass in the fields for your cattle, and you will eat and be satisfied.'"

"We're all familiar with that promise," Jakin said, his irritation apparent.

"Yes, that's why I've asked all our priests and students to examine their lives for sin," Jeshua added. "Can you say that any of us don't love Him or serve Him, Zechariah? How are we failing to obey God?"

Zechariah drew a slow breath as he gathered his courage. He had been trying to get someone's attention and say these words for the past six years as he'd served his apprenticeship for the priesthood. Maybe it was finally time. "With all due respect . . . I believe that we're failing because we haven't obeyed the Almighty One's command to rebuild the temple. I think He sent this drought to get our attention."

The high priest's fan stilled. He leaned back in his seat, studying Zechariah for a moment. Zechariah's heart began to race.
Maybe the others would finally listen to him. But when Jeshua
spoke, his words were disappointing. "Prince Zerubbabel and I
met recently to discuss the temple, and we both agreed that the
time hasn't come for the Lord's house to be built."

"I disagree! The time to build was nearly twenty years ago
when we first arrived. We're disobeying God and—"

"Zechariah!" Jakin interrupted, his voice sharp. "You're an
outstanding Torah scholar, and you're going to make a fine
priest. But I think you're forgetting that it was an edict from
the Persian king that forced us to stop in the first place. Neither
Jeshua nor Zerubbabel dares to come against the might and
power of the king."

And Zechariah shouldn't come against his elders, but he
couldn't stop the flow of words as another Scripture verse came
to him: "It's not by might nor by power, but by my Spirit, says
the Lord Almighty."

The men stared at him as if he had spoken another language.
Where had *that* verse come from? One of the prophets? Zechariah couldn't recall. He had studied the Scriptures diligently, had
memorized large portions of it, and it upset him that he couldn't
recall where he had read this verse, imprinted so strongly on
his mind. He was still trying to figure it out when Jeshua said,
"The prince is concerned about the safety of our people. He's
responsible for us. He doesn't want to risk retaliation from the
king or from our enemies. We stopped rebuilding for the sake
of peace."

"But we haven't made peace, we've simply compromised with
our enemies," Zechariah said. "We're not fulfilling our purpose
for being here in the land. We're supposed to glorify the Holy
One among the nations. He wants to fulfill His promise to Abraham that through his offspring all nations would be blessed!"

"What does that have to do with rebuilding the temple?" Jakin asked.

"It has everything to do with it! Our worship at the temple demonstrates the way to find fellowship with God. He promised to dwell here among us. The rebuilt temple isn't just for us, it's so that the whole world can know the Almighty One. We're meant to bring life and hope to the world the same way we brought life from the rubble. The Babylonians and Samaritans have no hope because they don't know God. That's why they cling to superstition and try to see the future in the stars."

"If they wanted to find God," Jakin said, "they wouldn't have opposed us when we began to rebuild."

"No, I know some of those stargazers, and they're searching for Him whether they realize it or not. Listen, during the first exodus from Egypt, the Almighty One commanded our ancestors to utterly destroy all the inhabitants of the land. This time He didn't say that. I believe God wants us to live in such a way that we'll draw all men to Him. So they'll give up their idolatry and find the living God." The way Yael had, after all these years.

Zechariah got the impression that only Jeshua, out of all the men in the room, was truly listening and trying to understand what he was desperate to say. "We're supposed to remain separate from the other nations," Jeshua said.

"I know. But we haven't remained separate. In the name of peace we've gone to their pagan festivals, and we've eaten food sacrificed to their idols and followed their customs instead of showing them the right way to live and how to worship properly. My grandmother gave one of the bravest examples of how we're to conduct ourselves among unbelievers when she saved a newborn baby that the Samaritans tried to kill. She could have reasoned that killing the child was just their custom and she shouldn't interfere, but she didn't. She told them that human life is precious to our God, and she adopted the child as her own."

"We all admire her for her brave example," Jeshua said.

"We *all* need to become examples," Zechariah continued. "This is what the Lord Almighty says: 'Men from all languages and nations will take firm hold of one Jew by the hem of his robe and say, "Let us go with you, because we have heard that God is with you."'"

"Where is that written?" Jakin asked. "I'm not familiar with that verse."

Once again, Zechariah couldn't remember. Where had it come from? "I-I'm not certain . . . but God showed the prophet Isaiah a time when foreigners would seek Him. He said, 'My house will be called a house of prayer for all nations.' We need to rebuild His house! This drought is His way of getting our attention. The fact that we barely have enough offerings for the sacrifices should tell us that He isn't pleased with our worship."

"You've certainly given me much to think about," Jeshua said. But then he sighed and laid down his fan, and Zechariah could see that he was dismissing the topic. They were all hot and tired. Jeshua had other work to do. "Right now I need to figure out how to hold the Passover feast with this shortage of lambs," he said. "If the drought continues after the holiday, Prince Zerubbabel and I will call for a day of prayer to seek the Almighty One's will. Thank you all for your report."

Zechariah had been dismissed. But instead of going up to the temple mount with the others, he remained behind in the yeshiva to study the scrolls of the prophets, determined not to leave until he found the prophecies that had imprinted so strongly on his heart. He would prove the truth of God's Word to Jeshua and Zerubbabel. *"It's not by might nor by power, but by my Spirit, says the Lord Almighty."*

CHAPTER
37

Dinah rooted through the storage room, opening baskets and clay storage jars to see how much food was left. What she found—or rather, what she failed to find— dismayed her. "Look at this," she said to Yael, who had followed her inside. "Every jar is nearly empty. I wanted to prepare an enormous meal for this joyous occasion but how can it be a feast with so little food?"

"Zechariah understands, Safta. He doesn't expect a huge feast in the middle of a drought." Yael stood with one hand on her pregnant belly, the other pressed against her aching back. Dinah could see that the baby had dropped into position. It would be born any day.

"But we have guests coming," Dinah said. "We have to feed them."

"Besai and Rachel said they would bring what they could," Yael said. The couple would travel from Bethlehem where Besai cared for the sacrificial flocks, bringing Hanan's widow, who had remarried, with them. "And Abba will bring what he has from his farm. They're coming to watch Zechariah become a priest, not to dine like kings."

Dinah lifted a nearly empty jar of grain in one arm, a

dwindling basket of figs in the other. "Let me help you with those," Yael said.

"No, dear. I can manage. You need to rest and stay off your feet."

"Rest? With two little ones to chase after?" Yael asked, laughing. "That isn't likely to happen." Dinah smiled, knowing she was right. The two daughters who had been born to Yael and Zechariah—five-year-old Abigail and three-year-old Sarah—were every bit as lively and mischievous as Yael had been as a young girl, exhausting their mother, their Aunt Hodaya, and everyone else in the household.

Dinah carried the supplies out to her courtyard kitchen and set them beside the hearth. She would begin cooking for tonight's feast as soon as she returned from the morning sacrifice. Today Zechariah would minister as a priest for the first time, serving at both sacrifices. "Iddo says the Almighty One is trying to get our attention with this drought but that we're not listening."

"Well, so far we've had enough food to feed our family," Yael said, grabbing little Sarah who had escaped from Hodaya's grasp, and lifting her into her arms. "I'm sure there will be enough for this celebration, too. We didn't have very much for Passover this year but it was still a joyous occasion, wasn't it?"

"Abba said that sharing a meal with the people you love is what makes it a feast," Hodaya said. She had pulled Abigail onto her lap so she could comb the tangles from her hair.

"Yes, Iddo did say that," Dinah replied. "He said it wasn't the amount of food *on* the table that mattered but the amount of love *around* the table."

"In that case," Yael said, "tonight we will dine like kings."

"When did Besai and Rachel say they would arrive?" Hodaya asked.

Yael laughed and gave Hodaya's braid an affectionate tug.

"Why are you asking, little sister? Are you wondering about the lamb they're bringing or their handsome son, Aaron?"

Dinah watched Hodaya's cheeks turn bright red and wondered if she had missed something. Was there a budding romance between sixteen-year-old Hodaya and the shepherd's eighteen-year-old son? But Dinah couldn't worry about that right now. If she didn't hurry, they would be late for the morning sacrifice. Zechariah and Iddo had already left before dawn.

She quickly checked to see how much water was in the jars and sighed when she saw they were nearly empty. There hadn't been rain for such a long time that the cisterns beneath everyone's homes had dried up, forcing the women in Jerusalem to walk all the way to the spring for water. Hodaya couldn't hobble that far and Yael could no longer go in her condition, which meant that Dinah had to do it alone every day. Everyone told her it was too much for a woman her age to fetch water, but Dinah didn't feel old. "It might take me longer to get there and back," she had told her family, "and I may have to carry a smaller jug, but I'm still mistress of this household, thank you very much." Typically, Yael hadn't listened to Dinah and had recuited several neighbors to each carry an extra supply for them. Dinah knew that by the time she returned from the morning sacrifice, the jars would be mysteriously full.

"Is everyone ready?" she asked. "We should leave very soon if we want to get a place up front where we can see Zechariah." She turned to Yael and saw her gripping her stomach, a look of surprise on her face. "Yael? Are you in labor?"

"No, it's nothing. Just one of those false pains. And not a very strong one. This baby wouldn't dare to arrive on his father's big day."

Dinah coralled her two great-granddaughters and they all set out for the uphill walk to the temple mount. They would have to walk slowly for Hodaya's sake, and for Yael's, who stopped often to rest. "I can't believe Zechariah turns thirty years old today," Dinah said the first time they paused. "A grown man, already."

"Remember the day of his bar mitzvah in Babylon?" Yael asked—and then caught herself. "I'm so sorry. I know you don't like to talk about Babylon."

"Never mind, dear. It's okay. And yes, I do remember that day. We had a big celebration for him. Naomi and Sarah and I cooked for a week. I only wish we could do the same for this birthday."

Abigail tugged on Dinah's arm. "Come on, Safta. I want to see Abba." They started walking again.

"I still wonder about my family in Babylon," Dinah said, "but I've learned that children are only loaned to us for a short time. A husband, especially the right one, is given by God for a lifetime. Yes, it was hard to leave my family, and I grieved for a long time. But even if Iddo and I had stayed in Babylon, there were no guarantees that we wouldn't suffer sorrow and loss. I'm glad we came to Jerusalem."

"You are?" Yael asked.

"Yes. Don't look so surprised. If Iddo and I hadn't come, Zechariah wouldn't be serving as a priest today." She took Hodaya's hand for a moment and added, "And Hodaya wouldn't have come into our lives."

Dinah's adopted daughter was growing into a lovely woman with beautiful dark eyes and thick, curly hair that was the envy of the other girls her age. She could maneuver so well around their house with her crutch that no one dared to call her crippled. Hodaya knew she was adopted, but she didn't know the terrible details of her birth. So far, Dinah had been able to evade her daughter's questions with vague replies.

The women rested again at the bottom of the stairs leading to the temple mount, then began the ascent. Dinah's anticipation grew with each step. She never thought she would live to see this day. Iddo was well past the age of retirement, but the other priests had invited him to put on priestly robes today and assist his grandson with the sacrifice.

At last they reached the Court of Women and walked all the way to the front so they could see over the barrier to where the sacrifice would take place. They arrived just in time to see Zechariah emerge from the robing room and stride across the courtyard to stand beside the altar. His linen robe and turban looked dazzling white against his black hair and beard. A red sash encircled his waist. Iddo walked forward behind him, his hair and beard as white as his robe, his shoulders a little stooped. He had never regained all the weight he'd lost after being stabbed six years ago, but by the grace of God he had survived. Dinah watched them perform the sacrifice together with tears in her eyes, her heart so full she feared it might burst. Zechariah climbed the ramp and laid the offering on the altar and the crowd gave a shout of joy as the smoke and fire ascended. But Yael gave a sharp gasp and doubled over. "You're in labor," Dinah said. "We need to get you home."

"I'll be fine. Let's watch for just a few more minutes."

They did, but as soon as the sacrifice came to an end, Dinah made everyone start for home. She kept a close eye on Yael as they walked, the journey easier downhill.

"I can't go into labor today," Yael said. "I don't want to miss the evening sacrifice or ruin the celebration tonight. Besides, you need my help with the preparations and—"

"I'll have plenty of help. Hodaya is a better cook than all of us put together."

Yael's face was flushed and beaded with perspiration by the time they reached home. Dinah sent her into her room to check for spotting, but she knew the truth even before Yael returned. Her labor had begun. She insisted on helping Dinah with a few simple cooking chores, but by noontime, Yael had to give in and lie down in her room.

"Hodaya, I'm putting you in charge of the children while I go fetch the midwife." Dinah had trained another woman as well as Yael, and rarely delivered babies anymore. But she was thrilled to help deliver this one.

Yael's third child arrived faster than her first two babies had, but her labor still took all day. At the hour that Zechariah slew the evening sacrifice, his first son entered the world. Dinah delivered him with her own hands, her third great-grandchild. How could she be so blessed? "He's a beautiful, healthy boy," she told Yael as she laid him down beside her.

"I hope he's not going to be a troublemaker," Yael said with a smile. "He already made us miss his father's big day."

"I don't think Zechariah will mind in the least once he sees why."

Dinah's neighbors helped her finish preparing the meal, and by the time everyone arrived home from the evening sacrifice, the feast was ready. Dinah ran to embrace her grandson. "I'm so proud of you, Zechariah! So proud!"

"Thanks, Safta." He looked all around the crowded courtyard and asked, "Where's Yael?"

"In your room. She has a surprise for you." Dinah followed Zaki into the room, wishing she could see his face when he saw Yael lying in bed with their baby beside her.

"You have a son, Zaki," Yael told him. "And he has the same birthday as you do."

Dinah turned away to give them privacy as Zaki fell to his knees beside the bed to hold his wife in his arms.

Yael was dozing later that night when Zechariah finally said good-night to his family and guests and came to bed. When she opened her eyes he was sitting beside their bed, gazing at her. "Why are you staring at me?" she asked.

"Do you have any idea how beautiful you look, lying here?" He bent to kiss her.

"You're just saying that because I gave you a son."

"No, I'm saying it because it's true. I love you so much, Yael. How are you feeling?"

"Tired. At least my labor was quick this time. Just as grueling, but faster than the other two. I'm sorry I missed the evening sacrifice."

"You had a good excuse. And you'll have a lifetime to watch me offer sacrifices."

"How was your first day on your new job?"

"I can't even begin to describe my joy! All the long years of apprenticeship are over, and it's like I'm beginning a brand-new life. How many times do we get to begin new lives?"

"I can think of a few. When we arrived in Jerusalem . . . when you and I got married . . . when we became parents—"

"You're right, you're right," he said, laughing. "And now I'm beginning my ministry for God. Saba says priests stand as peacemakers between the Almighty One and His people. I didn't think my joy could be any more complete while I was working today, but then I came home to you . . . and our son."

"You should have seen Safta trying to prepare a meal and deliver a baby at the same time," she said, smiling.

"I told her what a wonderful feast it was—and in the middle of a famine, no less." He bent to kiss her again, then asked softly, "Are you happy, Yael?"

"Can't you tell? I can't stop smiling!"

"I don't mean right now but every day. Do you ever feel . . . trapped?"

"Zaki! Why would you ask such a question?" When he didn't reply, she nudged him. "We've been married for six years. Why are you asking me if I'm happy?"

"I used to feel trapped when we first arrived in Jerusalem and

I had to study all day. I envied your freedom. You didn't seem to want a life like my grandmother's or the other women's. Safta despaired of ever getting you to settle down. And now that you have, I sometimes wonder if . . . if you ever regret it. Do you long for more than this life we have? Tell me the truth, Yael."

"I didn't feel 'free' at the time, I felt like I was always running and never getting anywhere. Like I was missing out on something, so I had to keep looking for it. My life felt so uncertain after my mother died that it was like being tossed around in the back of a runaway cart. I couldn't find anything solid to hang on to. I tried to control my future because I didn't know God or trust that He had me in His care." She reached to take his hand. "And now I've finally found something solid."

"Are you sure you don't long for an adventure or two?" He was typical Zaki—so serious as he asked the question.

Yael smiled. "Marriage has been an adventure, don't you think? And raising children certainly has been!"

"But you never seemed to want this life, and now . . . here you are."

Yael studied him for a moment in the dim moonlight, wishing she knew why he was asking her these things. Was he thinking about Rafi after all this time? "I love you, Zaki. I know you must wonder if I still think about Rafi." She saw his surprise and added, "I can read your mind, you know."

"I thought you gave up your Babylonian sorcery." At last he smiled.

"I don't need to be a sorceress. I know you very well. You always think too much, worry too much. When good things happen you always question them, waiting for something bad to happen to balance them out. Your grandfather is the same way. You have such a brilliant mind that you over-analyze everything. Just enjoy the moment, Zaki, enjoy this day. Isn't that what the Almighty One tells us to do?"

"Yes, but you're my wife. I need to be certain that you're happy."

She gazed down at their son, running her fingers over his soft, downy head, then back at her husband. "You want to know why I was so restless and wild, exploring the tombs and getting mixed up with all that Babylonian stuff? I think I was testing the limits, wanting to be stopped. Because we're not free when there are no boundaries—we're in great danger. I see that so clearly with our children. If I allowed Sarah and Abigail to run wild without limits, they would end up getting hurt. But once I learned what the Almighty One was really like and why He sets boundaries, I saw that His way is the best way to live. Without Him, we'd be just like the murderous Samaritans." She waited for Zaki to speak, and when he didn't she said, "Now tell me what's really prompting all these questions."

He looked up at her, tears shining in his eyes. "I'm just so incredibly happy today, and I want you to be as happy as I am."

"But today was an exceptional day, Zaki. Do *you* ever feel trapped?"

"Just the opposite. I feel like my life is on the brink of breaking through into something huge . . . something enormous. I've been holding my breath, expecting a miracle or a sign, and I think our son is that sign. Especially because he was born today, at the beginning of my new ministry."

Yael wasn't sure she followed him, but his words flowed out faster than he could stop them. He needed both hands to speak. "I understand why Saba wanted my father and uncle to come with us to Jerusalem. Why he was so happy when I decided to come. The God of the universe condescends to have His dwelling place here, in the temple we're supposed to be building. And it's my calling—our son's calling—to serve as His priests. Every time I see that empty foundation where the temple should be

I want to stand up and shout at everyone to wake up! It's time to do what God told us to do!"

"Shh! Zaki! You really will wake everyone up."

"But do you understand what I'm trying to say? I don't think I'm saying it very well."

"Yes, I understand. You've found joy because you're doing God's work. And I'm trying to tell you that I've found joy, too. Because if we obey God, then our lives do have meaning, even if all He asks us to do is cook lentils and raise children."

He looked down at their son. "Today we brought another priest into the world," he said, holding the baby's tiny hand. "He's another star in the sky that our father Abraham saw."

Yael reached up to stroke his cheek. "I love you, Zaki. I never dreamed I could be this happy. And every day I thank God that you're my husband and not Rafi."

CHAPTER
38

Zechariah held his grandfather's arm, steadying him as they made their way to the priests' room to change into their white linen robes. Drenched with sweat from the relentless heat, Zechariah didn't know how they would manage to peel off their damp street clothing. But Prince Zerubbabel and the high priest had asked every able-bodied priest to minister at the evening sacrifice and to pray. Saba would sing with the Levite musicians.

Since Zechariah's ordination four months ago, the drought had continued its devastation. Khamsin winds had blown in from the desert, creating dust storms of gritty sand and scorching hot air. No hope remained for their withered crops, but the leaders had asked the nation to pray for God's mercy, for an end to the wind and the drought and the famine.

Zechariah bent to untie his sandals. The priests ministered with bare feet according to God's instructions, but today he worried that the overheated cobblestones would burn their feet. "This heat, these winds—they're the Almighty One's judgment, aren't they?" he asked his grandfather.

"The Torah says that drought and famine are curses for our disobedience."

"And we're disobeying by not completing the temple. Why can't our leaders see that?" Iddo didn't reply as he struggled to pull the white robe over his head. Zechariah helped him with it, then tied his red sash for him. "I wish I could do something to wake everyone up," he continued, "but I don't know what to do. You told me to wait until I finished my training as a priest. Will I have to keep waiting until I work my way up through the ranks and earn the respect of the other priests and leaders? Why can't they see that we're disobeying Him by not completing His temple?"

Saba picked up a linen towel and wiped his face and brow before fastening on his turban. "You need to pray the way you did as a boy and ask God to give you the answer. Ask Him to tell you what you should do."

Zechariah finished dressing and helped his grandfather walk to the platform where the musicians would stand. Thankfully, someone had laid down a layer of straw to protect their feet from the burning pavement. "I'll meet you here after the service ends, Saba." He crossed to where the other priests stood, his chest tight with anger as he glimpsed the gaping, weed-filled hole beyond the altar where the temple should be. The elderly Prince Sheshbazzar had died without completing his task. His nephew Zerubbabel had taken his place as governor. A new emperor sat on the Persian throne, a new provincial governor ruled the Trans-Euphrates Province in Samaria. Why couldn't Zechariah's fellow Jews see that the time had come to do the impossible, to trust God and start building?

While he waited, a verse of Scripture sprang to mind, as clearly as if he'd read it from a scroll or watched it happen:

The seed will grow well, the vine will yield its fruit, the ground will produce its crops, and the heavens will drop their dew. I will give these things as an inheritance to the remnant of this people.

As you have been an object of cursing among the nations, O Judah and Israel, so will I save you, and you will be a blessing. Do not be afraid, but let your hands be strong.

What a beautiful promise. But which prophet had spoken those words? He would search for it after the sacrifice and share it with the others—if he could find it. There had been so many other promises and warnings that he'd longed to share but he hadn't been able to locate the verses.

The high priest performed the sacrifice himself, leading the congregation in prayer, asking God to renew His favor and blessing on His people. The Levite choir sang, *"Restore us again, O God our Savior, and put away your displeasure toward us. . . . Show us your unfailing love, O Lord, and grant us your salvation."*

Zechariah bowed his head and did what his grandfather advised, asking the Almighty One to speak to him the way He had in Babylon. *Show me what to do, Lord.* Were he and Saba the only ones who believed that they must rebuild?

By the time the service ended, the sky blazed with a crimson sunset. The motionless air radiated with heat, as fiery hot as the altar coals. The congregation would return home to their sweltering houses and bare storerooms and meager dinners. But before Zechariah or any of the other priests had a chance to move from their places, a man stepped forward from the crowd. Nothing in his appearance made him stand out. Middle-aged, no taller than the other men in the crowd, wearing simple robes, he could be anyone's brother or father or uncle.

"Listen!" the man shouted. "Listen, Zerubbabel and Jeshua. The Lord Almighty has something to say." The courtyard went so still that Zechariah could hear the doves cooing in the treetops. The man took another step forward. "Why do you keep saying that the time hasn't come for the Lord's house to be built? Is it time for you to be living in your paneled houses, while His house remains a ruin?"

Zechariah wondered if the heat had made him hallucinate. This stranger spoke the words of his own heart. He might look like an ordinary man, but his words carried power and authority. "Now this is what the Lord Almighty says," the man continued. "'Give careful thought to your ways. You've planted much, but have harvested little. You eat, but you never have your fill. You put on clothes in the winter, but you're never warm. You earn wages but you may as well put them in a purse full of holes.'"

The awareness of God's holy presence slowly filled Zechariah, just as it had when he was a boy. But instead of warmth this time, it seemed as though a rain cloud had burst open, pouring life-giving water over him, water that could turn the dry riverbeds into rushing streams. Zechariah glanced around and saw that the others seemed just as spellbound by the force of the man's words. He was more than a man—he was a prophet! Was this what it was like to hear Isaiah or Jeremiah preach? Zechariah scarcely dared to breathe as the prophet continued to speak for the Holy One.

"'Give careful thought to your ways. Go up into the mountains and bring down timber and build my house, so that I may take pleasure in it and be honored,' says the Lord. 'You expected much, but see? It turned out to be little. What you brought home, I blew away. Why?' declares the Lord Almighty. 'Because of my house which remains a ruin, while each of you is busy with his own house. Therefore, because of you the heavens have withheld their dew and the earth its crops. I called for drought on the fields and the mountains, on the grain, the new wine, the oil and whatever the ground produces, on men and cattle, and on the labor of your hands,' says the Lord."

As abruptly as he had appeared, the man turned to leave. The awareness of God's presence vanished with his final words. Zechariah raced across the searing courtyard, the first of the priests to move, calling to the man to wait. He caught up with him before he disappeared into the crowd. "Please, we want to hear more. Come back and speak with us and with our leaders." He took the man's arm and led him to Prince Zerubbabel's platform. The prophet's entire body trembled as he crossed the pavement, but Zechariah didn't think it was from fear. The man's prophecy clearly had exhausted him, as if he'd expended a day's worth of effort in the past few moments.

The other priests gathered around the prophet, as well. Zechariah wondered if they were as deeply moved by his words as he was, or if they were angry at his rebuke, upset that their ceremony had been disrupted. "What's your name?" Prince Zerubbabel asked the man.

"Haggai."

"You spoke God's word to us today, Haggai."

"Yes, my lord. He told me to say, 'I am with you,' declares the Lord."

Zechariah felt a shiver go through him. *I am*—the name God used when He spoke with Moses.

"You are a prophet," Jeshua said. But it didn't seem to be a question. Haggai clearly was, the first prophet anointed by God since the exile. God was with them once again, speaking to them. Zechariah could no longer keep quiet.

"We need to do what the Holy One said! Our fathers didn't listen to the prophets, but we need to listen to Haggai! The Holy One has been waiting for us to get desperate enough to seek Him—and today we finally did. He answered through Haggai, His messenger." Zechariah was the newest priest to be ordained, yet he was shouting at the others, shouting at the prince! No one silenced him.

"You say that God wants us to resume building the temple?" Zerubbabel asked.

"Yes," Haggai replied. "You don't need the Persian king's

sanction. You have the Almighty One's sanction. '*I am with you.*' That's what He's telling us."

"But what if it brings renewed attacks by our enemies?" one of the priests asked.

"We can't give in to fear!" Zechariah replied. He wanted to say more, but everyone began talking and arguing at once. Zerubbabel held up his hands for silence.

"Listen," he said. "I'm allowed to govern Judah and Jerusalem, but I'm under Persian authority. All building projects require their approval. If we resume building without it, they could interpret our actions as a rebellion. I don't want to risk another invasion and exile."

"If we don't obey, the drought will continue," Haggai said. "We'll slowly starve to death. Shall we submit to Persian authority or to God's?"

Once again, Zechariah couldn't resist speaking. "The governor of Samaria who made us halt the construction is dead. So is the emperor who issued the order. God is telling us to rebuild, and He's promising to be with us. What more do we need? Let our enemies try to stop us! 'It's not by might nor by power, but by my Spirit,' says the Lord Almighty."

"I need time to think about this," Zerubbabel said. He turned to leave, obviously wishing to postpone the decision, but Zechariah couldn't let that happen.

"Wait! Do you believe the Holy One has spoken through Haggai today, my lord?" He didn't know where his sudden boldness came from, but he couldn't keep quiet. "We came together here to pray about the drought—so do you believe this was God's answer to us or not, my lord?"

It took the prince a long time to reply but he finally said, "Yes. The Holy One spoke through Haggai today. . . . And I admit that I'm afraid to disobey Him—but I'm also afraid of the consequences if I do obey Him."

"Why not trust God—who brought us out of captivity in Babylon by His mighty hand—and begin building?" Haggai asked. "Yes, our enemies will send a report to the emperor, telling him what we're doing. But let them wait for the slow movements of justice this time. Meanwhile, we'll keep building—and we won't let our enemies stop us again."

"Put me in charge of it," Iddo said. "I've been waiting for this day for nearly twenty years."

Zechariah wasn't surprised when several of the other priests began to argue against the idea, joined by many of the laymen who had come to Jerusalem to pray for the drought. But most of the people seemed to be siding with him and with Haggai, urging the prince to trust the Almighty One. The arguments grew louder and angrier until at last the prince held up his hands for silence once again.

"The decision is mine alone to make, and I'll bear the responsibility for it. Your arguments for and against won't sway me. I need to discern the word of the Lord for myself." He paused, and Zechariah sent up a silent prayer as he waited in suspense. "Today I believe that I have heard from Him," the prince finally said. "It's time to rebuild the temple."

The gathered men were silent for a long moment as if trying to comprehend the importance of what the prince had just said. Zechariah didn't wait for anyone else's response. He sank down on his knees on the scorching pavement and praised God.

Iddo presided over the first meeting to discuss rebuilding the temple. He assigned workers to assess construction needs, delegated specific tasks to engineers and laborers. And the next day, the terrible khamsin winds died away.

Restless to begin, he made it his goal to have constuction under way before the Feast of Tabernacles in less than a month.

But he knew that the real labor couldn't begin until new materials arrived and new timbers were brought up from the forests. They had to repair the crane after letting it sit idle for so many years, and hundreds of building stones had to be cut and shaped. Iddo kept a record of costs and expenditures and noted in his log that work on the house of the Lord began on the twenty-fourth day of the sixth month. On that day he went to the yeshiva and recruited all of the Torah students to pull weeds and chop away the growth that had accumulated around the temple's foundation. Iddo led the work himself.

"We're not going to hire laborers to do this," he told the young men and boys, "because we need to do it ourselves as penance for allowing the work to stop and these weeds to grow so huge. Sin is like these weeds, with roots that go down very deep and require great effort to uproot. And it will require renewed diligence on our part to keep the weeds of unbelief and apathy from taking over our lives again the way these have. And vigilance! We may think we've eliminated sin, but if even a very small seed of it remains, it quickly takes over our lives."

As Iddo and his students paused for lunch a few hours later, the first rain clouds appeared on the western horizon, rising from the Mediterrean Sea. The students pointed to them, whispering with excitement. The clouds continued to thicken and soon concealed the sun, darkening the sky above Jerusalem. But the weeding and Iddo's Torah lessons continued. "The rain never came last year, remember?" he asked. "Just a few spitting drops from clouds that had no substance, no life-giving water. That's what we must seem like to the Holy One. We've been all talk and hot air when it comes to our faith and to rebuilding His temple, but with no life-producing results."

They managed to clear away a good portion of the undergrowth by the time the first raindrops began to fall. Neither Iddo nor his students stopped working. The rain felt refreshing after the long, hot summer. "Why does the Holy One need this temple?" Iddo asked the group. "What does Scripture tell us?"

He listened with satisfaction to the lively buzz of voices as his students discussed the question for a while, offering Scripture verses that supported their arguments. One of the brightest boys replied that the Almighty One didn't need it, quoting from King Solomon's prayer during the dedication for the first temple: "'The heavens, even the highest heavens, cannot contain you. How much less this temple I have built!'"

Another student shouted out, "It says in the psalms to 'Exalt the Lord our God and worship at his footstool; he is holy.'"

"So, if the Almighty One's temple is in the heavens and if earth is His footstool," Iddo challenged, "why does He need us to rebuild the temple?"

The discussion continued, the students' voices loud at times as they argued and quoted Scripture. At last, one of the young men summarized their collective conclusion: "Because we're the ones who need it, not Him. It's a place where our sins can be forgiven so we can approach the Holy One. A place where we can meet with Him and recover the fellowship we lost in Eden."

"It's a privilege and a blessing to have the Holy One dwelling among us," another added. "He promised Abraham that He would be with him and his descendants always."

"Very good. But do we really want the Holy One to be with us?" Iddo asked. "Do we want Him badly enough to work with all our strength in spite of persecution or threats from our enemies? Is our longing for Him so great that we're willing to defy an emperor's decree?"

Every young man and boy agreed that obeying God at all costs was more important than giving in to fear. The rain was falling harder now, but no one wanted to stop the discussion or the work. If the winter rains truly had begun, Iddo was determined to build throughout the entire rainy season.

"Now comes the hardest question," he told his students. "This temple was destroyed because our ancestors stopped obeying God's Law. They became just like the Gentiles—promiscuous, filled with hatred and greed, worshiping false gods. Are we willing to live in such a way that the Holy One will remain with us this time? Will we make sure He won't turn His back on us in wrath again? Each one of you needs to answer that question in his heart and then decide if you want to come back and work here again tomorrow—and the next day, and the next. Will you come back when our enemies attack us and try to discourage us?" The rain poured down now. Everyone was getting soaked. But so was the land. They continued working until time for the evening sacrifice, singing psalms of praise as they did.

Dinah reprimanded Iddo when he returned home that evening. "You'll make yourself ill! You're too old to be standing outside in the rain and getting soaked."

"It isn't rain, Dinah, it's God's blessings. We obeyed Him, and He heard our prayers."

"But look at you! You're drenched to the skin."

"And it feels glorious!" Iddo went to bed that night knowing that if he was the only man who showed up tomorrow, he would pull weeds and prepare to build all by himself.

He awoke the next morning to the sound of rain pattering on the roof. In spite of the weather, an enormous crowd assembled for the morning sacrifice, not caring that they were getting wet. The clouds still poured when the sacrifice ended and Iddo walked back to the temple's foundation to resume clearing weeds. He stared in astonishment. Not only his yeshiva students, but young men of all ages filled the site. And they already had begun to work, filling baskets with weeds that pulled easily from the rain-softened earth.

CHAPTER

39

On the first day of the seventh month, Zechariah stood in the rain on a special platform and blew the silver trumpet to announce the Feast of Trumpets for the first time in his life. As the sound echoed off the distant mountains, the Holy One's presence filled him, just as it had back in Babylon. He closed his eyes and thanked God for the rain and for speaking through His prophet, Haggai. Work on the temple had resumed. The first course of cut stones would soon be ready to place on the foundation.

Zechariah had waited all these silent years, wondering why God wouldn't speak to him again, and now he understood. The Holy One hadn't been silent—He simply hadn't changed His mind. He had told Zechariah to leave Babylon and rebuild His temple, and those instructions hadn't changed. Today Zechariah sounded the trumpet with all his might, praying that it would awaken God's people from their spiritual slumber, praying that they would believe He was the God of the impossible.

On the twenty-second day of Tishri, the last day of the Feast of Ingathering, Zechariah stood on the temple mount again for the sacred assembly. The festival celebrated a harvest that had never come, and instead of slaying multiple sacrifices, the high priest offered a single male goat for a sin offering. Yet Zechariah and the others praised the Almighty One, joining with the Levite choir and musical instruments in singing, *"Give thanks to the Lord, for he is good. His love endures forever."*

Zechariah hated for the service to end, but when it finally did and the last strains of music died away, Haggai stepped forward from the crowd once again. Zechariah's heart sped up. The milling worshipers who had been preparing to leave fell silent.

"Who of you is left who saw God's house in its former glory?" Haggai asked, gesturing to the newly cleared foundation beyond the altar. "How does it look to you now? Doesn't it seem like nothing to you? 'But now be strong, O Zerubbabel,' declares the Lord. 'Be strong, Jeshua son of Jehozadak, the high priest. Be strong, all you people of the land,' declares the Lord, 'and work. For I am with you,' declares the Lord Almighty. 'This is what I covenanted with you when you came out of Egypt. And my Spirit remains among you. Do not fear.'"

Zechariah saw determination and renewed hope in the faces of the priests and the people in the courtyards. Haggai gazed solemnly at the temple's foundation as if seeing into the future as he continued to speak. "This is what the Lord Almighty says: 'In a little while I will once more shake the heavens and the earth, the sea and the dry land. I will shake all nations, and the desired of all nations will come. I will fill this house with glory,' says the Lord Almighty. 'The silver is mine and the gold is mine,' declares the Lord Almighty. 'The glory of this present house will be greater than the glory of the former house. And in this place I will grant peace.'"

It was what Zechariah hoped for, longed for. Not only would God's presence return, but the Messiah would come to this temple. And unlike the kingdoms of the world that God was about to shake from their places, His kingdom would never end.

Haggai turned to walk back into the crowd, and once again

Zechariah chased after him. "Haggai, wait! May I speak with you, my lord?" The prophet looked exhausted as he shivered in the cold, autumn rain. "Let's go someplace dry," Zechariah said. "The yeshiva is vacant today because of the holiday. We can go there and talk. Will you give me a few minutes to change out of my robes and meet you there?" Haggai agreed and a short time later they sat together at one of the yeshiva's study tables.

"I know you're a prophet because your words carry the anointing of God," Zechariah said. "It isn't you we hear speaking, but the Almighty One. Did you notice that we've obeyed God's word and resumed the construction?"

"Yes, I did notice. Clearly, God has stirred men's hearts."

"But even before you spoke that first time, I felt something . . . unusual . . . going on in my life. When I was a boy back in Babylon, I once felt the Holy One's presence in a very dramatic and powerful way. The experience made me decide to come here and help rebuild the temple so I could worship in His presence again and again. I've been searching for Him all my life, and ever since I discovered that I could know Him through the Scriptures, I've been reading and studying them with renewed diligence. Whenever I open the pages to read, He is there. Not quite in the way I experienced Him as a boy, but I hear Him speaking to me, teaching me, just the same."

Zechariah paused, afraid to ask if he was making sense. But Haggai nodded and said, "I understand. Go on."

"And now, even when I'm not reading but ministering as a priest—especially then—I hear His voice clearly and forcefully. It's like I'm hearing Scripture verses that I've memorized . . . 'Thus saith the Lord' . . . But the words I hear aren't found anywhere. I've searched all the prophets and the writings." Zechariah gestured to the Aron Ha Kodesh, where the Torah and the other sacred scrolls were kept. "I keep looking for the words I've heard to no avail. I'm beginning to think that maybe

I've studied too much and I'm losing my mind. But along with the words in my head I felt an urgency to start rebuilding the temple, even before you spoke to us. An urgency to tell the others that we need to return to God. To seek Him with all our heart and soul and mind."

"You're hearing the same message from God that I'm hearing."

"I know! When you spoke that first time I wanted to shout along with you. We should be dissatisfied with the stale, routine way we've been worshiping and seek His presence. We should build the temple and build a relationship with Him that's genuine and real."

"Yes. Exactly." Haggai listened intently, leaning toward him. His dark eyes seemed to read Zechariah's heart. "Go on."

"I thought this . . . this craziness I've been experiencing would end once we started building, once the others decided to listen to you and obey God. But if anything, it's becoming more intense. The words surge through my mind like . . . like a pot boiling over on the hearth. I can hardly stop them from coming, let alone ignore them. And God's presence and warmth always come with them, the same way I experienced Him as a child. And so I wanted to ask if . . . if you can help me figure out what's going on. Am I losing my mind?"

"No, Zechariah. Far from it! From what you've described, I believe the Holy One wants to speak through you the same way He speaks through me. He's calling you to be His prophet."

"His . . . His *prophet*?" Zechariah shook his head, unable to grasp it. "That's impossible. I'm not old enough or mature enough . . . Certainly not righteous enough!"

"None of that matters. You said yourself that you've learned to know God and to understand what He wants from us. Now you need to open your mouth and allow His words to flow through you."

"Is . . . is what I described . . . is that what happens to you?"

"Not exactly, but it's similar enough."

Zechariah hesitated, wanting to pepper Haggai with questions, yet he was afraid of exposing his own shallow faith. "May I ask . . . how did you know it was the right time to come forward? Where did you get the courage to speak?"

"You're afraid that people will ridicule you," Haggai said.

"No, I'm not afraid of ridicule, exactly. . . . My concern is that everyone knows me. They've watched me grow from a boy of twelve into a man, watched me become a priest, watched me make mistakes. Many of these men are the rabbis who taught me the Torah. Prince Zerubbabel and the high priest are both older than I am, and have far more wisdom and maturity and experience. How dare I come along, saying outrageous things, daring to speak for God? You came as a stranger to nearly all of these men. Your anonymity gave you a measure of credibility. They listened to you."

"It's the Spirit of the Almighty One speaking through me that gives me credibility. Speak His words, Zechariah. People may laugh, they may refuse to listen, but every prophet of God has faced those reactions."

Zechariah had read the stories of Jeremiah and Isaiah and Ezekiel. He knew Haggai was right.

"But if God wants to speak through you," Haggai continued, "how can you keep silent? Trust His Spirit. Be faithful to the message He puts in your heart and on your lips. After that, every man who hears you is accountable to God for heeding His word or for ignoring it. If they judge the message by the messenger, that's to their shame, not yours."

"May I share with you what I hear God saying? To confirm that I've truly heard?"

"Certainly."

Zechariah inhaled. "I believe the Almighty One is saying,

'Return to me!' We've slowly drifted away from Him and become distracted by things in our lives that just aren't important. We've allowed fear of our enemies and our own lack of faith to distance us from Him. We've been enticed away from Him by the temptations of the surrounding nations, first in Babylon and now here. God says 'Return to me.' He's waiting to bless us when we do."

A slow smile spread across Haggai's face. "Yes. You've heard from God. I see His Spirit in you. We'll accomplish His work together, my friend. The Almighty One now has two witnesses to speak for Him." He stood and embraced Zechariah as he prepared to leave.

"Wait . . . I have one more question. How will I know when it's time to speak?"

"You'll know. The Holy One will tell you."

Haggai's words both encouraged Zechariah and terrified him at the same time. Was it truly possible that he, Zechariah son of Berekiah, son of Iddo, was called to be God's prophet? It seemed impossible, like counting the stars. He told no one about his conversation with Haggai—not his grandfather, not even his wife. But he continued to pray, asking for God's will, offering himself as His servant.

Work on the temple site resumed after the feast, and Zechariah met his grandfather there at the end of each day so they could walk home together. The noisy site bustled with activity, and he could see the rapid progress they'd made, the piles of stones that had been cut and shaped, the newly repaired crane ready to lift them into place, the support timbers sized and waiting. Today, like many days, Zechariah had difficulty getting Saba to quit and come home. As they descended the stairs from the temple mount, Saba asked him, "Will you come with me to the house of assembly tomorrow morning? Jeshua and Zerubbabel called for a meeting after the morning sacrifice, and

I'm dreading it. I'm too old to waste my remaining years and dwindling strength arguing with dolts."

Zechariah couldn't suppress a smile. "Which dolts is the high priest meeting with?"

"Jeshua described them as 'concerned citizens' from several Jewish villages. He suspects that their concern is that we've angered the Samaritans by rebuilding."

"I'll be happy to come," Zechariah replied, and he felt a strange stirring rustle through him, the same restless anticipation he'd felt on the night before his ordination and on the morning that he'd sounded the silver trumpet for the first time. The odd feeling continued to distract him after he reached home and washed his hands and gathered with the others to eat. Yael called his name three times before he heard her.

"What's the matter with you, Zaki?" she asked. "You're a million miles away."

The people he loved sat gathered around him—his grandparents, his wife and children, young Hodaya—and he didn't know what to say to them. They had readily accepted Haggai as God's prophet, believing that he spoke the Almighty One's words. But what would they think if he told them he might be called to be a prophet, too? He could scarcely believe it himself—why should they?

"Nothing's wrong," he finally said. "I just have too many things on my mind." He smiled and joined the conversation. But he awoke before dawn the next morning and went out to sit alone in the courtyard to pray. He felt the same unease as when the weather was about to change and a thunderstorm was about to rumble through. He ate breakfast without tasting a bite of it, kissed his wife and children, and left with his grandfather.

The visiting men who gathered to meet in the house of assembly with the prince and the high priest later that morning revealed their concern in their restlessness and angry voices.

Their spokesman, a portly man named Adin from the village of Lod, began without preamble. "Why weren't all the family heads and local leaders consulted before the rebuilding began? You've put all of us in danger—our wives, our children. The construction must stop immediately until we receive proper authorization from the Persian emperor."

"Were any of you here when we sought the Holy One in prayer for the drought?" Prince Zerubbabel asked. "Or for the Feast of Ingathering? Did you hear God's prophet, Haggai, speak?"

"No, but we heard reports about him. Even if this man is a prophet, your decision to immediately resume building was foolhardy and premature. Samaritan settlements surround all of our villages," he said, gesturing to the other men. "We've lived in peace with them these past few years because you obeyed the emperor's edict and stopped building. But now that word of your violation has spread, we're back to living on a knife's edge!"

Iddo slowly stood to address the men, and Zechariah could see his barely controlled fury. "Why did you gentlemen return to this land with your families?" he asked.

"Because the land belongs to us," Adin said. "The Almighty One gave it to our forefathers."

"Were you afraid of the Samaritans when we first arrived and began to build?"

"Not at first. We had permission from King Cyrus to be here. Then you foolishly refused the Samaritans' offer to help and unleashed a firestorm of trouble."

"Did the Samaritans also cause the drought and the famine we've been experiencing?" Iddo asked.

"Of course not!"

"Then why do you suppose we've been suffering? Why have our crops and our harvests failed?"

"I don't know! Why are you asking these foolish questions? Are you going to listen to our concerns or aren't you?"

"I'm asking," Iddo said, "because I'm trying to determine what the Holy One's promises mean to you and what part you believe He plays in all of this. Did you return to the land because you wanted to walk with God the way our father Abraham did or because you were tired of living in Babylon? Because you thought you'd have a comfortable life here?"

His words were met by a storm of angry shouts and protests from the other men. When Jeshua finally calmed them down, Iddo continued. "I was an eyewitness to God's wrath and the destruction of Jerusalem. And also an eyewitness to His miracle that allowed us to return. If the Almighty One brought us here, and if we walk in obedience to Him, then He promises to give us victory over our enemies and send rain in due season. But for the past few years we've wanted peace with our enemies more than we've wanted God."

"How dare you!"

Iddo ignored Adin's outrage. "God spoke through His prophet Haggai and told us it was time to rebuild. We obeyed, and the rain we desperately needed began to fall. Was that a coincidence?"

"I have no idea, but—"

"Those of us who heard Haggai believe he spoke a message from the Almighty One, and so we obeyed Him. Were we wrong to do that? What would you have done?"

"Of course we would obey if we heard God speaking to us, but we haven't heard Him and—"

Without thinking, Zechariah shot from his seat, knocking the chair backward with a crash. "Then hear the word of the Lord Almighty!" It was his voice, and yet it wasn't. He couldn't have stopped the words from coming any more than he could have stopped a thunderstorm. "The Lord was very angry with our forefathers. He told me to tell you and all the people, 'Return to me,' declares the Lord Almighty, 'and I will return to you,'

413

says the Lord Almighty. 'Don't be like your forefathers who heard the prophets proclaim: "Turn from your evil ways and your evil practices," but they wouldn't listen or pay attention to me,' declares the Lord. 'Where are your forefathers now? And the prophets, do they live forever? But didn't everything my prophets warned about overtake your forefathers? Then they repented and said, "The Lord Almighty has done to us what our ways and practices deserve, just as he determined to do."'"

Zechariah paused to catch his breath and saw a stunned look on everyone's face. Everyone except his grandfather. Saba's eyes were closed, his head bowed, his face wet with tears. Zechariah drew another breath. "'Don't be like your forefathers,' declares the Lord Almighty. 'Return to me, and I will return to you!' says the Lord Almighty."

He groped behind him for his chair, turned it upright again, and sank onto it, exhausted. Minutes passed, but no one stirred or spoke. Then the prince slowly rose to his feet. "We've heard the word of the Lord from *two* of His prophets. I believe that's all that needs to be said, gentlemen."

CHAPTER

40

Zechariah shivered on a cold winter morning as he stood beside his grandfather to inspect the progress on the temple. "You left for work awfully early this morning, Saba. The sun wasn't up and neither was anyone else."

"I wanted to get a head start on the work before the morning sacrifice. Today we'll finish laying the first course of stones. The work will go faster as we become surer of ourselves, and as more people join us. Mattaniah finished planting his winter crops last week and has been an enormous help to us."

"It looks amazing, Saba. It's hard to believe you started building only three months ago." He took his grandfather's arm and gestured toward the altar, where the morning sacrifice was about to begin. "I'm not on duty as a priest today. I thought we could watch it together." They walked across the mount and found a place to stand in the men's court. Zechariah was aware of the shy whispers and turned heads as he passed.

He had spoken his first prophecy more than a month ago, and had worried at first that the older men he knew and respected wouldn't take him seriously. But as the news spread throughout the community that the Holy One had anointed Zechariah son of Berekiah, son of Iddo to be His prophet, the opposite had been true. The other men looked at him with respect and even deference. Unaccustomed to such treatment, he found their reaction unsettling.

"I feel a growing distance between the other priests and me," he told Saba as they waited. "As if they're afraid of me or something."

"They're in awe of you."

"They should be in awe of the Almighty One, not me."

"But He has made you His spokesman. They recognize that. Our forefathers refused to listen to the prophets that He sent us, remember? And they were punished for it. These men don't want to make the same mistake."

"Even Yael seems . . . well, shy with me. So does Safta. And you've acted a little differently around me, too."

"We're all amazed by you, Zechariah. You became a man of God when we weren't looking. And a man of His Word. That's why He chose you. We were all too close to you to notice the gradual change in you, but we recognize it now, and we're amazed."

As the priests performed the morning sacrifice, Zechariah looked around the courtyard and noticed Haggai standing with the other men. He watched the prophet closely, and his heart surged with anticipation when the service ended and Haggai stepped forward to speak. Everyone quieted to listen.

"This is what the Lord Almighty says: 'Now give careful thought to this and consider how things were before you began rebuilding the Lord's temple. When you looked for a heap of twenty measures there were only ten. When you went to your wine vat to draw fifty measures, there were only twenty. I struck all the work of your hands with blight, mildew and hail,' declares the Lord, 'yet you did not turn to me. But, from this day on, from this twenty-fourth day of the ninth month, give careful thought to the day when the foundation of the Lord's temple was laid.

Give careful thought: Is there yet any seed left in the barn? Until now, the vine and the fig tree, the pomegranate and the olive tree have not borne fruit. But from this day on I will bless you.'"

"That was a warning to us not to quit again," Saba whispered.

"He must have heard about our meeting with Adin and the other village leaders."

"Oh, I'm certain he has."

Once again, the worshipers turned to leave the temple mount and begin the day's work. But a procession of men ascending the stairs to the mount hindered their progress, forcing everyone to move aside to allow them to pass. The delegation of government officials carried the standards of the Persian emperor and were escorted by a small cadre of Persian soldiers. They approached the governor's platform where Zerubbabel had been preparing to leave. Zechariah and his grandfather followed them, arriving in time to hear the regal-looking man in a richly embroidered robe being introduced as Governor Tattenai of the Trans-Euphrates Province, along with Shethar-Bozenai and their associates.

"We knew opposition was coming the moment we ordered supplies and timber," Saba said. "The new governor was certain to hear about it—and here he is."

"Nothing is done in secret," Zechariah said. "The question is, will Prince Zerubbabel stand strong, considering all that he and his family could lose? Will he believe the Almighty One's promise that his ancestor, King David, will always have an heir on the throne?"

"The eye of our God is watching over us," Saba whispered.

Tattenai stepped forward, addressing Zerubbabel. "Are you the official in charge?"

"Yes, I'm Zerubbabel, Governor of Judea and Jerusalem."

"I was recently made aware that a large-scale construction project was taking place here. Since I hadn't been informed of any building permits being issued, I decided to come and see

417

for myself." Tattenai gestured to the sprawling site, the piles of materials. "This is no ordinary structure you're building."

"That's right. We're rebuilding the temple that King Solomon built here many years ago. A temple to the one true God, whom we serve."

"I see. Well, on behalf of Emperor Darius, I demand to know who authorized you to rebuild this temple and restore this structure?"

"The God of heaven and earth did. We're His servants."

"*God* did?" Tattenai asked, his tone scornful. The two men stood face-to-face, as if neither was willing to give an inch or acknowledge the other's superiority. They reminded Zechariah of two dogs circling each other, hackles raised, waiting for the other to either pounce or yield in submission.

"Our fathers angered the God of heaven," Prince Zerubbabel continued, "and so He handed them over to King Nebuchadnezzar of Babylon, who destroyed this temple and deported our people. However, King Cyrus issued a decree in the first year of his reign permitting us to rebuild this house of God. He even gave us the gold and silver treasures that Nebuchadnezzar had taken from God's temple and entrusted them to my predecessor, Sheshbazzar. Cyrus appointed him governor, and told him to return the articles to Jerusalem and rebuild the temple on its site. So Sheshbazzar obeyed and laid the foundations of the house of God. From that day to the present it has been under construction but isn't yet finished."

"King Cyrus is dead. Darius is king now."

"So we've heard."

"You need authorization from King Darius." When the prince didn't reply, Tattenai said, "I'll need the names of all the men who are constructing this building."

"My name is Zerubbabel. Shall I spell it for your secretary?"

"And my name is Iddo." Zechariah's grandfather stepped

forward. "I'm overseeing construction and recording the costs and expenditures."

"I'm Jeshua, son of Jehozadak, high priest of the Almighty One." More and more men stepped forward, priests and laborers alike, telling the Samaritan secretary their names. Others too far back in the crowd to approach began shouting out their names, as well.

Tattenai held up his hands, clearly frustrated. "Wait. Don't all talk at once. My secretary can't record all these names."

"He's going to need many hours and dozens of scrolls to record all of our names," Zerubbabel said. "More than forty-two thousand of us returned to our land from Babylon, and we're building this temple together, as one man."

Tanttenai gestured to his secretary to stop. He locked gazes with Zerubbabel, his forehead creased with a frown. "My men will inspect the project now, as part of my report."

"They will have to do it from a distance," Jeshua said. "This is a holy site."

Zechariah saw Tattenai's chest heave with anger. He seemed reluctant to object, reluctant to tread on holy ground. "I'll be sending a report to King Darius immediately," he finally said. "You'll receive a copy of it, as well, Governor Zerubbabel. In the meantime, all construction must halt until you receive official authorization."

Zerubbabel shook his head. "With all due respect, Governor Tattenai, we intend to continue working. We already have authorization from King Cyrus and from our God. We must obey Him."

"Well done," Iddo whispered as Tattenai stalked away with his retinue.

"I had no idea our prince was so courageous," Zechariah said. "He just took an enormous risk."

"I know. If his actions are interpreted as a rebellion against the Persian emperor, he and his family will be hauled back to Persia in chains and executed as traitors."

"And so will you, Saba . . . And yet you don't seem at all afraid," he added with a grin.

"The eye of our God is watching over us."

The show was over, and the people prepared to leave for a second time. But the prophet Haggai surprised everyone when he stepped forward once again. "The Lord Almighty spoke to me again and said, 'Tell Zerubbabel governor of Judah that I will shake the heavens and the earth. I will overturn royal thrones and shatter the power of the foreign kingdoms. I will overthrow chariots and their drivers; horses and their riders will fall, each by the sword of his brother.' And because of your courage and your willingness to obey God, the Lord Almighty declares, 'I will take you, my servant Zerubbabel, son of Shealtiel, and I will make you like my signet ring, for I have chosen you,' declares the Lord Almighty."

"Praise God," Zechariah whispered. "The Almighty One has reversed His curse!"

"Is that what Haggai's prophecy means?" Iddo asked.

"Yes. I've been reading the prophecies of Jeremiah, and the Holy One told our last king, Jehoiachin, that even if he was a signet ring on God's right hand He would still pull him off and hand him over to his enemies. God said Jehoiachin would be recorded as childless and none of his descendants would sit on the throne of David."

"Ah, yes. I remember."

"But now the Holy One has made Zerubbabel His signet ring. It's His pledge that someday the Messiah will come, a descendant of King David. An heir will once again sit on his throne."

"What a day this has been," Saba said with a sigh. "But now I have work to do. Do you have time to help me, Zaki?"

"Give me a job to do, Saba. I'm ready."

CHAPTER
41

It was one of those rare, peaceful moments for Yael when dinner simmered on the hearth and both of her daughters napped. She sat down to rest in her room as well, nursing her son and thinking about her husband. Ever since prophesying, Zechariah had become a man of standing in their community, a man everyone looked up to. Yael was proud to be his wife but also a little awed by him. Imagine, the God of heaven and earth speaking through her husband!

She was still marveling over it when she heard a knock on her door. A moment later, Hodaya peeked inside. "Can I ask you something, Yael? I'm not disturbing you, am I?"

"Not at all. Come sit beside me. I have plenty of time to talk while this little glutton fills his belly." Hodaya limped into the room and sat down on a cushion beside Yael, propping her crutch against the wall. She paused for such a long time that Yael finally asked, "What is it, Hodaya? What's wrong?"

"I want to know who I am," she said, her pretty face creased with determination. "I want to know who my parents are and how I came to live here with all of you."

Yael closed her eyes for a moment, searching for an escape. She and Safta Dinah had become experts over the years at changing the subject and avoiding Hodaya's questions by assuring her that she was dearly loved and part of this family now. But judging by Hodaya's determined look, she wasn't going to be content with vague assurances this time. "Why are you asking, Hodaya? Haven't we told you countless times how much we love you? That you belong to us?"

"Yes, but this time I need to know the truth. It's important."

"Can you tell me why?" Yael asked, still stalling.

Hodaya met Yael's gaze, her beautiful dark eyes shining. "Because I'm in love with Aaron son of Besai. And he loves me."

Yael's mouth fell open as she stared at Hodaya. How had the tiny baby she and Safta carried home from the Samaritan village grown up so quickly? Sixteen years old already, and in love with Besai and Rachel's son, Aaron, who was eighteen. He lived near Bethlehem now and worked with his father as a shepherd, but Hodaya had known him all her life. They had grown up together and now saw each other during holidays and celebrations. Yael had noticed their tender glances and shy conversations, but she wasn't prepared to have Hodaya fall in love and marry and move to a home of her own.

"Aaron thinks I'm pretty," Hodaya said when Yael didn't reply. "He doesn't even care about . . . you know . . . my crooked foot."

"You are pretty. And none of us cares about your foot. Everyone of us has things about us that aren't perfect—it's just that yours is a little more noticeable than ours."

"I don't look like any of you," Hodaya said.

"What difference does that make?" Yael said with a shrug. "My daughters don't look like me either, and—"

"That's not what I mean! I know who I *do* look like, and I want to know the truth!"

"Who do you think you look like?" Yael waited, dread making her skin prickle.

"Remember that night when Iddo was stabbed? I saw the man

who did it. The man who died. I saw his face when he was lying on the ground, before they covered him up. I peeked out of my room—and he looked like me! His hair looked just like mine!"

Yael floundered for words.

"Am I related to him? Am I a Samaritan, too?"

"None of that matters," she managed to say. "Why are you so concerned about who you look like?"

"Because the man who died was Rafi, the man you wanted to marry, wasn't he? But they wouldn't let you marry him because he wasn't Jewish. If I'm related to him . . . if I'm not Jewish . . . then they won't let Aaron marry me, either."

"Oh, Hodaya . . . of course you're Jewish. Iddo and Dinah adopted you. They took you to the mikveh and made you ours. Of course Aaron can marry you."

"The Almighty One won't accept me if I'm not Jewish."

"Hodaya, you worship in the Jewish Court of Women with us all the time. You know God accepts you."

"Aaron told me that the Samaritans aren't allowed to worship with us. He said that was why they made us stop building the temple. And why they're trying to stop us again. I heard all about it, Yael."

"Listen, we'll ask Zaki about it when he comes home, but I guarantee that he'll say you're allowed to worship with us and that the Almighty One accepts you." She hoped that would end the matter and put a stop to these questions, but Hodaya gave a huff of frustration.

"I want to know the truth about my parents and why I was adopted. I have a right to know, and so does Aaron. Why won't you tell me?"

Hodaya had raised her voice, and the baby stirred. Yael propped him against her shoulder and rubbed his back to soothe him to sleep. "We never wanted to tell you because we were afraid you would be hurt. And none of us ever wants to hurt you."

Hodaya struggled to her feet. "Then I'll find out the truth some other way if you won't tell me. Aaron and I will walk down to that Samaritan village and ask them why I look like Rafi."

"No, Hodaya! Don't ever do that! You and Aaron need to stay far away from that village. Sit down again, please. . . . I'll tell you the truth." Hodaya sank down on the cushion again.

Yael wondered if she should send for Safta Dinah, if maybe they should tell Hodaya the truth together. Safta had long worried that this day would come. "Let me get Safta, first—" she began, but Hodaya interrupted her.

"No. I want you to tell me."

Where to start? Yael took a moment to decide, praying for the right words. "Remember my good friend Leyla? The Samaritan girl I used to visit all the time? You're her half sister. You both have the same father. That means that Rafi, the man I wanted to marry, was your half brother. That's why you noticed a resemblance. I loved both of them, Hodaya. They were good friends of mine for many years until Leyla died and everything went wrong with Rafi."

"Who is my mother? Did she die, too?"

It would be less hurtful to say yes, that she had died giving birth, but it would be a lie. And Yael knew that lies always ended in grief. "Your mother's name is Raisa, and she nearly died giving birth to you. Both of you would have certainly died if Safta Dinah hadn't gone to the village that night to help. Your mother was very young when she married your father—younger than you are right now. Too young to be giving birth. You were her first child."

"Did she give me away because of my foot?"

Yael realized the truth for the first time. "No. Your mother didn't give you away at all. In fact, she loved you and asked to hold you. But Leyla's grandmother—who is no relation to you—believed that you were too weak to live. She told your mother

424

that you had died to spare her the pain of loving you and then losing you. No one expected either you or Raisa to live."

"What about my father?"

Yael sighed. "His name is Zabad, and he's the village leader. He's mostly Jewish, a descendant of the people who stayed here in the land when everyone else was carried off to Babylon."

"But my mother is a Samaritan?"

"I presume so, but I don't really know. I never asked her." Again, Yael hoped this would be the end of Hodaya's questions. It wasn't.

"Why did my father let you take me?"

Yael sighed again. "He wanted a son."

"And I was a girl—with a crooked foot?"

Yael nodded and laid the baby down on the bed. She took Hodaya's hands in hers. "Everyone thought you would die that night. But Safta Dinah said she would make sure you lived if it was the last thing she ever did. And so we brought you home. . . . I was there when you were born, Hodaya. Watching you come into the world was the most amazing experience I'd ever had. I fell in love with you that instant. We all fell in love with you." Tears sprang to Yael's eyes. "And now, if we have to give you away again, I can't imagine a more wonderful, worthy man to give you to than Aaron son of Besai."

From his foreman's shelter on the temple mount, Iddo watched a team of workers raise a huge building block with the crane, the ropes creaking and groaning beneath the strain. It twisted in the air for a moment before the men steadied it and lowered it into place on the wall of the sanctuary. The satisfaction Iddo felt was as enormous as the block. Across the valley on the Mount of Olives, clouds of white almond blossoms sprouted on the trees, announcing that winter would soon yield to spring. The days would grow warmer and longer, providing more hours of daylight in which Iddo and his teams could work. Fields of barley and flax ripened in the distant fields thanks to the plentiful winter rains, signaling God's grace and goodness, His pleasure in their obedience.

Iddo was about to turn back to his lists of supplies and expenditures when he saw Zechariah striding across the courtyard toward him. "If you're coming to inspect our progress," Iddo said, smiling, "we just laid another stone in place." He pointed to where the workers maneuvered the limestone block.

Zaki shook his head, his expression serious. "That's not why I'm here. Prince Zerubbabel received a dispatch from Samaria this morning. It's a copy of the letter Governor Tattenai sent to the Persian emperor about us. I thought you might want to come with me and hear what it says."

Iddo slowly rose to his feet. "Tattenai certainly didn't waste any time sending his report, did he?"

"No. As the proverb says of evildoers, 'their feet rush into sin.'" Zaki took Iddo's arm as they walked across the plaza, then descended the stairs from the mount. It frustrated Iddo to have grown so frail and in need of an arm to cling to for balance. He could accomplish so much more if he were as young and fit as his grandson.

"I'm sure it will take a few months for Tattenai's message to get to the emperor," Zaki said as they paused at the bottom of the steps to rest. "Then a few more months to receive his reply. How much progress do you think we can make during that time?"

Iddo wasn't optimistic. "Even if it takes a year to hear back from the Persians, that still won't give us enough time to finish. My best guess is that it will take three or four years to complete the entire temple."

They walked the short distance to the throne room in the governor's residence where Zerubbabel conducted business. The high priest and most of the chief priests and elders had crowded into the long, narrow hall already. Zechariah found a place for them to stand alongside one of the support pillars. "In the end, it won't matter what Tattenai's letter contains," Iddo said. "I'm going to continue building no matter what."

Zerubbabel stood to quiet the men. "As you've heard, this morning I received a copy of the letter that Governor Tattenai sent to King Darius. When I finish reading it to you, we can consider what our response, if any, should be." The prince unrolled the letter and began to read.

"To King Darius:
    Cordial Greetings.

The king should know that we went to the district of Judah, to the temple of the great God. The people are building it with large stones and placing timbers in the walls. The work is being carried on with diligence and is making rapid progress under their direction."

Iddo leaned close to whisper to Zechariah. "I consider that a high compliment."

"We questioned the elders and asked them, 'Who authorized you to rebuild this temple and restore this structure?' We also asked them their names, so that we could compile a list of their leaders for your information. This is the answer they gave us . . .'"

Zerubbabel looked up from the letter and said, "Tattenai gives a fairly accurate account of our reply, saying that we're building this temple for our God and that we have authorization from King Cyrus. The letter continues:

"Now if it pleases the king, let a search be made of the royal archives of Babylon to see if King Cyrus did in fact issue a decree to rebuild this house of God in Jerusalem. Then let the king send us his decision in this matter."

"Good," Iddo said, loudly enough for those around him to hear. "If they search, they'll find the proclamation. And he'll also see that exiles from other nations were allowed to return and rebuild, not just us."

"Are there any questions?" the prince asked as he rolled up the scroll again.

The captain of the temple guards asked to speak first. "What if the Samaritan governor sends soldiers to force us to stop? We don't have the manpower or the strength to fight them."

"True," Zerubbabel replied. "And you can be sure they noted

our lack of defenses when they came to inspect the building project. But for now, the province of Judah is still my territory, and the Samaritan governor has no right to send troops unless the Persian emperor orders him to."

Iddo lifted his hand to be recognized. "We should not—we *will* not—stop building while we wait for the emperor's reply."

"My concern is also for your safety, Prince Zerubbabel," the captain continued. "As the legitimate heir to the throne, you could be executed or carried back into exile if your actions are seen as rebellious."

"Thank you for your concern, but I'm trusting the Almighty One's promise that David's throne will endure forever."

"Have there been any reports of trouble with our Samaritan neighbors?" someone else asked.

"Dozens of them, just like before. They're waging a war of terrorism, using fear as a weapon. I've asked for volunteers to guard the temple mount again. But I believe that the Almighty One has commanded us to build, and we need to fear Him more than our neighbors."

Iddo returned to the temple mount after the meeting, but work ended an hour early that afternoon so the workers would have time to prepare for the Sabbath. He arrived home to find Dinah, Yael, and Hodaya scurrying around as they put the finishing touches on the Sabbath meal. But Dinah pulled Iddo aside for a moment, still holding a loaf of fresh bread in her hands. "We heard about the letter from the Samaritan governor," she said. "Some of the women are afraid there will be trouble again."

"Our cisterns are full from all the rain, aren't they?" he asked.

"Yes. Thankfully we won't need to go to the spring for water, but—"

"Let's eat in peace, Dinah. I've prepared something to say to everyone at the end of our meal." Iddo had thought about Tattenai's letter all afternoon. His family's safety was his responsibility, yet he knew he was helpless to protect them. Over and over, he had prayed to let go of his worry and fear and to trust their safety to God's hands—a prayer he would likely pray for the rest of his life.

They broke bread, sipped wine, and feasted by lamplight. Singing the traditional songs of his ancestors filled Iddo with hope and courage. Afterward, the children quieted to hear him talk about the weekly Torah portion, his custom on Shabbat. "Our portion this week is very fitting for this time in our nation's life," he told them. "In this passage, the Holy One has brought Moses and our ancestors out of Egypt, just as He brought us out of Babylon. Then the Holy One says, 'Then have them make a sanctuary for me, and I will dwell among them.' He revealed to them exactly how to build this sanctuary and the people obeyed, freely offering their treasures of gold and silver and precious stones, fine linen and wood and spices. Today we're again obeying the Lord's command to build His sanctuary, even as our enemies try to stop us. Tonight I want to ask each of you: Do you trust God? Are you willing to obey Him, no matter the cost? Because this time the Holy One's dwelling place may cost not only our gold and silver but our lives, as it did with Shoshanna. Will you offer up your fear and let Him replace it with faith?"

Dinah replied first. She sat beside Iddo, holding a very sleepy Sarah in her lap. "When the Holy One asked me to sacrifice my family and leave them behind in Babylon, I admit I wasn't willing. But that's because I didn't understand why we had to come here. Now I do, Iddo. We would have become just like all the other nations if we had stayed in Babylon. I'm willing to obey now. And I won't let fear stop me."

"I agree with Safta," Yael said. She held the baby against her shoulder, gently rubbing his back. "I used to study the stars because I wanted to know the future, while all that time, the Holy One was leading us into our future. The prophets said

He would restore our people, and here we are in our land. He said we would be as numerous as the stars, and He has blessed Zaki and me with three children. I know that God is with us, not with our enemies, and so I'm not afraid, either. That's why we named our son Joshua, because the Lord saves."

"What about you, Hodaya?" Iddo asked. She looked away, and he saw her eyes fill with tears. "Are you afraid? There's no shame in admitting it if you are."

"It's not that," she said, shaking her head. Iddo waited until she finally looked up at him again. "Yael told me about my real parents. I know I'm not Jewish. I know I'm a Samaritan, which means I'm one of your enemies. I'm not allowed to help you build the temple."

Yael handed the baby to Zechariah and tried to pull Hodaya into her arms. "You aren't our enemy! You're one of us! Tell her, Zaki. I can't explain it to her the right way."

"I know the story from the Torah," Hodaya said, pushing Yael away. "When Israel came into this land after leaving Egypt, the Holy One told them to kill every man, woman, and child. He said not to marry anyone who wasn't Jewish."

"This is my fault," Yael said. "I didn't explain it to her very well. I'm so sorry."

"Hodaya, look at me," Iddo said. He waited until she did. "The Holy One told us to totally destroy those nations for the same reason that Jerusalem was destroyed and the Jewish people taken into exile—because we had all become corrupt, worshiping false gods, doing immoral things, sacrificing our children to idols. But it has always been the Holy One's plan to bless all the people on earth through our nation. He made that promise to Abraham and repeated it to Isaac and Jacob. In the past, I didn't want to see that prophecy fulfilled because I hated the Babylonians for what they did to my family and to this city. But then you came into our lives, and the Holy One began to show me how much He loves all people, not just the sons of Abraham. You became one of us, worshiping our God and obeying His Torah. And in the future, that's what will happen with all the people on earth—they will all worship our God and obey Him."

He paused, looking at Hodaya's beautiful face in the flickering lamplight, realizing how much he had grown to love her as his daughter. "Are you listening, Hodaya? Do you understand what I'm saying? The reason we couldn't let the Samaritans help us rebuild was because they still practiced a mixture of religions. But any Samaritan who turns wholeheartedly to God is always welcome to worship with us. You're Jewish because you belong to us. But even if you weren't ours, you would be welcome to worship with us and marry our sons because you serve our God."

"Yes, Saba is right," Zechariah said. He leaned close to Hodaya and took her hand. "The prophet Isaiah wrote that in the last days the mountain of the Lord's temple will be established as chief among the mountains, and all nations will stream to it. He said that foreigners who serve and worship the Lord and keep His covenant will be accepted by Him, and His temple will be called a house of prayer for *all* nations."

"That's why we're working so hard to finish it," Iddo said. "And why our enemies want to stop us. They're rebelling against God. But you, Hodaya—you are the firstfruits of God's promise. His prophecies are being fulfilled in you."

Hodaya looked around at all of them and smiled faintly as she wiped her tears. "So . . . does that mean . . . you'll let me marry Aaron when his father asks you for my hand?"

"Yes!" Iddo said, laughing. "Yes, my dear girl. I'll dance with joy at your wedding."

"But not for another year or two," Dinah added with a worried look. "You're still much too young."

Everyone at the table laughed, and Hodaya's face was flushed with happiness.

CHAPTER 43

That night Zechariah's son awakened him from a restless sleep, crying to be fed. "Stay in bed," he told Yael, who snuggled beneath the covers on this cold, late-winter night. "I'll fetch him for you." The stone floor felt icy beneath his feet, the room chilly as he lifted Joshua from his basket and laid him beside Yael. But instead of returning to bed, Zechariah put on his outer robe and slipped his sandals onto his feet. He felt wide awake for some reason, even though dawn was still a long way off, judging by the lightless sky outside his window.

A multitude of thoughts had tumbled through his mind all day, everything from the letter that Governor Tattenai had sent to the Persians, to Hodaya's concerns about God's love for the Gentiles. He would pray about all of these things, he decided. And rather than pace the floor of his room and keep Yael from sleeping, he closed the door behind him and tiptoed outside to the courtyard.

And there stood a man.

Zechariah backed up a step, startled, remembering the night that Rafi had come. But without moving or saying a word, the man conveyed peace to Zechariah as if he had poured it from a pitcher, saturating him with it. Zaki walked slowly toward him, his legs a little shaky. And as he stepped into the open courtyard and glanced around, it was as if a curtain had been drawn back and instead of seeing the houses and streets of his neighborhood, Zechariah stood in a ravine among myrtle trees. He saw a man riding a red horse, and behind him were red, brown, and white horses. He knew he wasn't dreaming because he could feel the stone floor beneath his sandals, the night breeze ruffling his hair. But the vision in front of him was as real and vivid as the cobblestones. He heard the pounding hooves of the horses, smelled their scent. The wind rustling his hair rustled the leaves of the myrtle trees, as well.

He turned to the man in the courtyard and knew he was an angel without knowing how or why. Zechariah gestured to the horses and asked in a hushed voice, "What are these, my lord?"

"The Lord has sent these to go throughout the earth." The power of God filled the angel's voice, and Zechariah's entire body resonated in tune with it the same way his body vibrated when he blew the silver trumpet. "I asked the Almighty One how long He would withhold mercy from Jerusalem and the towns of Judah," the angel continued, "and He said, 'I will return to Jerusalem with mercy, and there my house will be rebuilt. My towns will again overflow with prosperity, and the Lord will again comfort Zion and choose Jerusalem.'"

Zechariah's heart raced with excitement. He wanted to run into his grandfather's room and awaken him with this good news, but he heard a sudden noise above him and when he looked up, he saw four horns, emblems of political power and might. "What are these?" he asked the angel.

"These are the horns that scattered Judah, Israel, and Jerusalem so that no one could raise his head. But now the nations that destroyed you are about to be destroyed."

Another sound got Zechariah's attention, and when he looked in that direction the scene had changed. He saw a man with a measuring line in his hand as if preparing to build. Zechariah felt a prickle of excitement, remembering all the building they had done when they'd first arrived, and how Jerusalem had risen from the ashes. He had learned to use a measuring line like the one this man held, and a plumb line to make sure the walls were straight. But then their enemies had brought the construction to a halt. "Where is that man going?" he asked the angel.

"To measure Jerusalem, to find out how wide and how long it is. Jerusalem will be a city without walls because of the great number of men and livestock in it. 'And I myself will be a wall of fire around it,' declares the Lord, 'and I will be its glory within.'"

Did this mean that more exiles would be allowed to return? Zechariah was about to ask, but it was as if the angel had read his thoughts. "'Come! Come! Flee from the land of the north,'" he shouted. "'Escape, you who live in Babylon. I will surely raise my hand against the nations that have plundered you,' declares the Lord, 'for whoever touches you touches the apple of my eye.'"

Zechariah wanted to shout along with the angel at God's comforting words, but the vision hadn't ended. "'Shout and be glad, O Daughter of Zion. For I am coming, and I will live among you,' declares the Lord. 'Many nations will be joined with the Lord in that day and will become my people. I will live among you and you will know that the Lord Almighty has sent me to you. Be still before the Lord, all mankind, because he has roused himself from his holy dwelling.'"

Zechariah sank down on the courtyard wall, overcome with emotion. He had left his home and his parents to seek the Lord's presence, and now He was promising to live among them. Even more, as if in answer to Hodaya's concerns, God promised that the people of many nations would become His, as well. Zechariah sat on the wall for a long moment, his eyes closed as he silently praised God.

When he opened them again, the angel beckoned to him.

"Come with me." They walked only a few steps—and there was Jeshua, the high priest. Zechariah wanted to touch him to see if he was real, but the scene had changed to that of a courtroom. The Accuser stood at Jeshua's right side as they stood before the angel of the Lord. Zechariah felt the cold chill of evil in the Accuser's presence. "The Lord rebuke you, Satan!" the Lord's angel said. "The Lord, who has chosen Jerusalem, rebuke you! Is not this man a burning stick snatched from the fire?"

The high priest wore filthy clothes as he stood before the angel and his fellow priests, robes that only the lowest beggar would wear. But the angel of the Lord ordered those standing near him to take off his filthy clothes. He said to Jeshua, "See, I have taken away your sin." And as Zechariah watched, Jeshua was clothed in a clean white robe. A spotless turban was placed on his head. "This is what the Lord Almighty says," the angel told Jeshua. "'If you will walk in my ways and keep my require-ments, then you will govern my house and have charge of my courts, and I will give you a place among these standing here. Listen, Jeshua and your associates—you are symbolic of things to come: I am going to bring my servant, the Branch. And I will remove the sin of this land in a single day.'"

Zechariah's heart beat so rapidly he feared it might burst. The angel spoke of the promised Messiah, the seed of the woman who would crush the serpent's head. Before Zechariah could react, the images faded into the night as if dissolving into a pool of dark water. When they had all disappeared, Zechariah stood in his familiar courtyard again, surrounded by the homes and streets of his neighborhood. It seemed as though days had passed, but the night sky was still black, the mountains to the east still cloaked in darkness. Exhausted, he sank down in the courtyard with his back against the wall and closed his eyes. The next thing he knew someone was shaking him. He looked up and saw the angel.

"What do you see?" the angel asked.

Zechariah scrambled to his feet. "I see a solid gold lampstand with a bowl and seven lights. And two olive trees, one on the right and one on the left of the lampstand."

"This is the word of the Lord to Zerubbabel," the angel said. "'Not by might nor by power, but by my Spirit,' says the Lord Almighty. 'What are you, O mighty mountain? Before Zerubbabel you will become level ground. Then he will bring out the temple's capstone to shouts of "God bless it!" The hands of Zerubbabel have laid the foundation of this temple and his hands will also complete it.'"

Zechariah could scarcely wait to see Saba's joy when he told him this news. But the lampstand and olive trees still puzzled him. "What are these two olive branches?" he asked the angel.

"These are the two who are anointed to serve the Lord of all the earth." The king and the high priest. God's anointed servants.

Suddenly Zechariah heard a noise like flapping wings or rattling parchment, and when he looked up he saw a huge scroll, fifteen feet wide and thirty feet long, flying through the air above him. He recalled dreaming of this as a boy. "What is that?" he asked the angel.

"This is the curse that's going out over the entire land. It will enter the house of every thief and everyone who swears falsely, and whatever they attempt to build will be destroyed, left with nothing but timbers and stones. Now look there, Zechariah."

He looked where the angel pointed and nearly laughed out loud at what he saw. It was a measuring basket, and when the cover of lead was lifted, there sat the sorceress from Babylon who used to visit Yael's house next door. She was dressed in black, and Zechariah heard the soft jingling of her bracelets and amulets. "This is wickedness," the angel said as he pushed the lead cover back into place over the woman. Zechariah watched in amazement as two women with wings like storks lifted the basket and flew away with it.

"Where are they taking her?" he asked.

"Back to Babylon where she belongs. God will remove wickedness from this land."

Zechariah watched until the winged women were out of sight, and when he turned back to the angel, the scene had changed again. Four chariots rode out from between two mountains of bronze, each chariot pulled by a team of differently colored horses—red, black, white, and dappled. He could hear the horses snorting, their hooves thundering, the chariot wheels creaking and rumbling as they raced forward. "What are these, my lord?" he asked.

"These are the four spirits of heaven, going out from standing in the presence of the Lord, going throughout the earth. Look, those going toward the north country have given God's Spirit rest in the land of the north."

Once again, Zechariah felt the Holy One's peace wash through him. This was a sign to him and to His people that whatever happened—today, tomorrow, or the next day—the Almighty One was in control, working for the good of His people and not for harm.

The sound of the chariots faded in the distance and once again the vision dissolved into blackness. Zechariah found a place to sit down, leaning against the courtyard wall so he could watch the sunrise above the Mount of Olives when it finally came. The next thing he knew, someone was calling his name, shaking him awake.

"Zechariah . . . Zechariah . . ." His grandfather, not an angel. A flesh-and-blood man, not a vision. "Are you all right?" Saba asked. "Why are you sleeping out here in the cold?"

Zechariah slowly pulled himself to his feet. "I wanted to pray, so I got up and came out here. But then . . ." He had no words to describe what he'd seen last night but he knew he had to try. "The Holy One sent an angel who spoke with me, Saba. He showed me things in visions that were so real that I could smell them and touch them. I need to get parchment and some ink so I can write them down and tell everyone." But Zechariah knew that God had etched the visions on his heart as if on stone. He would never forget what he'd seen and heard. He ran his hands through his hair as Saba stared at him in amazement.

"What you and I are doing here in Jerusalem is so much bigger than we can ever dream, Saba. I saw time pulled back like a curtain last night, and I glimpsed eternity. The things the angel showed me . . . it was like . . . like I could finally make sense of everything that's happened to you and to me and to our people. And God reassured me that we *will* finish building His temple. Zerubbabel will lay the capstone himself. Our enemies can't stop us. The Lord Almighty said, 'Not by might nor by power, but by my Spirit.' I need to tell Jeshua and the others that the defilement of the past is gone—washed away! The Accuser of men has nothing to say to us now that the Holy One has cleansed us and forgiven us."

"Praise God," Saba murmured.

The women joined them in the courtyard as Zechariah spoke. He looked at his beautiful wife and smiled to himself when he recalled the vision of the Babylonian woman who had nearly enticed Yael away. Now the woman of wickedness was gone. Their land was being purified. He gestured to Hodaya to come to him and rested his hand on her shoulder. "The Lord promises that many nations will be joined with Him," he told her. "They will become His people. You are His, Hodaya. You belong to Him." She wrapped her arms around him and hugged him tightly.

"Zechariah?" Yael asked. "What . . . how . . . ?"

"The Holy One opened eternity and showed me visions to encourage us, Yael. We shouldn't be disappointed if the work

439

we do seems small in our eyes. The future will be so much more than this temple we're building. The Holy One is coming! He is coming and will live among us!"

It was all Zechariah could say. The enormity of it—*God with us*—took his breath away.

Iddo watched his team of carpenters shape a cedar tree into a massive beam for the temple, their planes and adzes producing mounds of fragrant shavings. If only they could work faster. If only he had more expert craftsmen like these. Iddo sighed, resisting the urge to rush his workers, telling himself to be patient. The work was going well, considering their limitations and the summer's heat. The temple was slowly rising from the ashes of Jerusalem, the workers encouraged by the prophecies of Haggai and Zechariah. Iddo's grandson had just returned from traveling to other Judean towns and villages, calming people's fears with the messages he'd received from the Holy One, telling them of the glorious future that awaited them. Their salvation from exile had been a mere taste of God's worldwide salvation to come. The restoration of the temple and the nation was a picture of the restoration that the Messiah would bring one day.

Imagine! Zechariah, his own grandson, a prophet of God. Iddo wondered if his son Berekiah would hear the news someday. Would he be proud of his son and glad that Zechariah had obeyed the Almighty One and returned to Jerusalem? Did Berekiah and Hoshea ever regret their decision to remain in Babylon? Iddo sighed again, knowing he shouldn't dwell on the past when the future continued to unfurl before him like a magnificent carpet rolled out before a king. Iddo turned his attention back to the cedar beam that was taking shape and saw in it a symbol of the Holy One's work as He slowly cut and shaped Iddo's life to fit His purposes. The cutting had been painful at times, but how else could he be made to fit into the place God had for him?

When Iddo looked up again, he saw Zechariah weaving his way across the work site, coming to fetch him.

"I know, I know," Iddo said as Zaki approached. "I'm late. And I'm in trouble, aren't I?"

Zechariah grinned, holding his hands up as if in surrender. "Don't ask me, I'm just the messenger. Safta sent me to tell you—and these are her exact words—that you will still be building the temple tomorrow and the next day, but this is the only day that Hodaya will ever get married."

"But not until this evening. There's still plenty of time."

"Do you really want to risk Safta's wrath?" Zaki asked. "I certainly don't, and I'm under orders not to come home without you."

Iddo gripped Zaki's arm for support as they began the long walk across the plaza. Hodaya was getting married. Unbelievable. She had turned seventeen this spring, and Dinah had run out of excuses to make her and Aaron wait any longer.

As he and Zaki descended the stairs from the mountaintop, Iddo caught sight of a small caravan approaching the city from the northwest with horses and chariots and banners waving. "Look at that," he said, stopping to catch his breath. "That's not something you see every day."

Zechariah shaded his eyes. "Those are the banners of the Samaritan governor. Maybe he finally received a response from the Persian emperor. It's been nearly eight months since Tattenai sent his letter."

Iddo's stomach suddenly felt hollow. "I've been dreading this day. And it's not a good sign that the governor himself is bringing the news. If the Persian king has ruled against us, Tattenai probably came in person to gloat and to force us to comply."

"He can't stop us, Saba. The Almighty One assured us that Zerubbabel himself will complete the temple."

"We need to go to the palace and hear the news. Dinah will have to wait a little longer for us."

"I agree. But no matter what happens, Saba, we can't let the news spoil Hodaya's wedding."

"I know, I know." They turned up the street to walk the short distance to the governor's residence, meeting other priests and city leaders along the way. News of the caravan had traveled quickly, and Zerubbabel didn't need to call for a meeting as the chief priests and elders stopped working and streamed to the reception hall. Governor Tattenai hadn't come after all, but had sent his administrator to read the Persian king's letter. Zerubbabel wasted no time on formalities with his Samaritan visitors but called the secretary up to the platform to read the letter aloud. The hall quieted. Iddo held his breath, gripping Zaki's arm.

"In response to Governor Tattenai's letter," the secretary read, "King Darius ordered that the archives stored in the treasury in Babylon be searched. In them, a scroll was found from the first year of King Cyrus concerning the temple of God in Jerusalem. King Cyrus' proclamation said: 'Let the temple be rebuilt as a place to present sacrifices—'"

Iddo exhaled and leaned against his grandson. "So. They found the original decree after all."

"'It is to be ninety feet high and ninety feet wide, with three courses of large stones and one of timbers. The costs are to be paid by the royal treasury. Also, the gold and silver articles carried to Babylon by King Nebuchadnezzar are to be returned.'

443

"After finding the original proclamation," the secretary continued, "King Darius then took the matter under consideration and sent this letter to Governor Tattenai, stating the Persian king's decision: 'Now then, Tattenai, governor of Trans-Euphrates, you and your fellow provincial officers, stay away from there. Do not interfere with the work on God's temple.'"

A great shout went up from the assembled men, drowning out his words. Iddo couldn't stop his tears. They could continue to build! The Persian king himself had said so. Eventually the hall quieted again when they saw that the secretary was waiting to read more:

"'Let the governor of the Jews and the Jewish elders rebuild this house of God on its site. Moreover, I hereby decree that the expenses of these men are to be fully paid out of the royal treasury, from the revenues of Trans-Euphrates, so that the work will not stop. Whatever is needed for their offerings to the God of heaven must be given them daily, without fail, so they may offer sacrifices and pray for the well-being of the king and his sons.'"

Another cry of joy filled the hall. Some men hugged each other, others shook their heads in disbelief. "Did you hear that, Saba?" Zechariah asked above the noise. "Not only does Tattenai have to let us build, he has to help us pay for it with tax revenue!" Again, the clapping and cheering quieted when they saw that the secretary still wasn't finished:

"'Furthermore, I decree that if anyone changes this edict, a beam is to be pulled from his house and he is to be impaled on it. And for this crime, his house is to be made a pile of rubble. May God, who has caused his Name to dwell in Jerusalem, overthrow any king or people who lifts a hand to change this decree or to destroy this temple in Jerusalem. I Darius have decreed it. Let it be carried out with diligence.'"

Deafening cheers rang in Iddo's ears. This final portion of King Darius' decree meant that the work could proceed without fear of reprisals or terrorist acts from their enemies. "This is more than I dared to hope for," Iddo murmured as Zechariah hugged him tightly. "God is with us . . . He is with us."

"Yes! And since Governor Tattenai has to share his tax revenue with us, you can hire more laborers, Saba. The work will go faster."

"Spread the news!" Prince Zerubbabel shouted. "Tell everyone in the city and in all the villages and towns. We must celebrate this good news!"

"We need to go back up to the temple, Zaki. I need to tell all my workers that—" But Zechariah didn't seem to be listening as he released Iddo again. Without a word, he pushed his way to the front of the hall, weaving between the cheering men before leaping onto the platform beside the prince.

"This is what the Lord Almighty says," he shouted, and the hall quickly grew quiet. "'I am burning with jealousy for Jerusalem! I will return to her and dwell in Jerusalem, and the mountain of the Lord will be called the Holy Mountain. Once again men and women of ripe old age will sit in the streets of Jerusalem, each with a cane in hand because of his age. The city streets will be filled with boys and girls playing there. I will save my people from the countries of the east and west and bring them back here to live; they will be my people, and I will be faithful and righteous to them as their God.'"

He paused, and Iddo could see tears on Zechariah's face as he took another deep breath to continue. "'You who were there when the foundation was laid for the house of God, let your hands be strong so that the temple may be built,' declares the Lord Almighty. 'Before that time, no one could go about his business safely because of his enemy, for I had turned every man against his neighbor. But now I will not deal with the remnant of this people as I did in the past. The seed will grow well, the vine will yield its fruit, the ground will produce its crops, and the heavens will drop their dew. I will give these things as an inheritance to the remnant of this people. As you have been an object of cursing among the nations, O Judah and Israel, so will I save you, and you will be a blessing. Do not be afraid, but let your hands be strong.'"

Iddo's joy and pride welled up as he watched the prince and the other leaders come forward to embrace Zechariah, talking with him, rejoicing together. At last Zechariah stepped down from the platform and made his way back through the crowd to where Iddo waited.

"Come with me to the temple mount," Iddo said again. "I need to tell—"

"The wedding!" Zechariah interrupted. "We forgot all about Hodaya's wedding! Safta must be wondering where we are!"

"I know, I know, but let's go up to the temple first—"

"Not on your life," Zaki said, laughing. "I'd rather face a den of hungry lions than Safta when she's mad at me."

Iddo felt as though he was floating as they made their way home. Dinah not only forgave them when she heard why they were late, she wept with joy on Iddo's shoulder. Then she quickly dried her eyes again and gave Iddo a list of things to do to prepare for the wedding. "I should put you in charge of rebuilding the temple," he told Dinah. "It would be finished in no time."

Hodaya looked radiant as she sat in her flower-adorned chair later that evening, waiting for her groom. They could hear the shofars, flutes, cymbals, and drums of the groom's procession long before it arrived at the house, making its way up the ramp to the city, winding through the lanes and streets. The music swelled as Iddo's friends and neighbors and fellow priests joined in the parade to his home, singing of brides and unquenchable love. The feast would be held in Iddo's courtyard since Hodaya wasn't able to walk in a procession all the way to Aaron's home in Bethlehem. And what a feast it was! Dinah and Yael and the other women had outdone themselves, loading the tables with food and wine.

Iddo watched Aaron lift Hodaya's veil and claim his beautiful bride, and saw a picture of the Holy One's love for His people, His bride. Aaron didn't care about Hodaya's twisted foot or the fact that she was adopted from the Samaritans. He loved her and accepted her and took her to himself, so they would become one. And even though the Holy One had punished Iddo and His people with exile for a season, they were still His beloved, betrothed to Him once again.

Late into the night, Iddo danced with joy beneath a canopy of stars too innumerable to count.

CHAPTER

45

THREE YEARS LATER

Zechariah lay in the darkness beside Yael, staring up at the ceiling beams. The temple was finished. Complete. Rebuilt from the ashes seventy years after the Babylonians destroyed it. He thought back to all of the events that had led to this day and could scarcely believe that more than twenty years had passed since King Cyrus allowed him and the other Jews to return to Jerusalem. They'd made such a promising start before the work stalled for sixteen years. Zechariah remembered his long search for God's presence, and how their lives had become as dry and barren as the drought-scorched earth. Then the Almighty One sent Haggai to them like a cloud bursting with rain, bringing renewed life and purpose. The construction had resumed in spite of danger and threats, and now the temple was finished. They would celebrate its dedication today.

Today the golden lampstand would be lit in the Holy Place for the first time and left to burn continually before God. Today the priests would light the incense on the altar and the fragrance would ascend to heaven along with the prayers of the people. The bread of God's Presence, one loaf for each tribe, would be set on the table in the Holy Place today, replenished each week for as long as this temple endured. Zechariah would play the shofar as the priests offered sacrifices and prayers. Joy and anticipation made it impossible for him to sleep.

He rolled over to climb out of bed, trying not to awaken Yael or their newest son, Johanan, born eighteen months after Joshua. But Yael stirred and opened her eyes. "Where are you going?"

"I've been lying here thinking of everything I need to do and worrying that I've forgotten something, so I figured I may as well get up."

"I'm so excited for you, Zaki. And for Saba. You longed for an adventure when we were young, remember? Is this adventure grand enough for you?"

"I could never have imagined a thrill greater than this." He bent to kiss her and said, "Go back to sleep, love. You don't need to get up yet."

He dressed in the dark and felt his way out to the courtyard, shivering in the chill of early springtime. He wasn't surprised to see that his grandfather was awake, as well, gazing at the dark outline of the mountain to the east as if willing the sun to rise from behind it so the day could begin. "Hard to sleep, isn't it, Saba?"

"I've been standing here praising God that I've lived to see this day."

"I know." Zechariah stood beside Saba in the silent darkness, wondering what it was like for his grandfather to have come full circle. To have seen Jerusalem and the temple destroyed, their people slaughtered in an outpouring of God's judgment— and then to feel the cleansing of His grace, to see the city and temple rebuilt, his family reborn. Even as they watched, the sky gradually grew lighter, the familiar outlines of their courtyard became clearer.

"Well, there's no sense in standing around here," Saba said. "We may as well go up to the temple and get an early start."

"Not without something to eat, you won't." Zechariah turned at the sound of Safta's voice, surprised to see that she was awake and dressed, too. She yawned as she bent to rekindle the fire. "Just give me a moment."

"Safta, you don't have to cook—"

"Of course I do! Do you think I would let you leave home on such an important day without food in your stomachs?" She frowned as if to say the question was too absurd to deserve an answer.

Zechariah crouched beside her. "You've played a part in re-building the temple, too, you know. All the meals you faithfully provided day after day were just as important as the work of shaping stones and lowering them into place."

She brushed away his praise with a wave of her hand. "I've done nothing at all compared to you and Iddo."

Zechariah was grateful for the simple meal she prepared, and by the time they finished eating, it was light enough to make their way up to the temple mount. When they reached the top of the stairs and saw the enormous structure in front of them, Saba paused. "Look at that," he breathed. "It's beautiful, isn't it?"

"It truly is." Tears sprang to Zechariah's eyes. The dawning sun had turned the temple's creamy-beige stones into gold and filled its courtyards with light.

"God's house could never be built anywhere else but Jerusalem, on this mountain where Abraham offered his son," Saba said.

Compared to the temples Zechariah had seen in Babylon, this one wasn't lavish. They had built it in half the time it took to build Solomon's temple and with a fraction of the laborers. But it stood in the same place and was the same size as his, constructed from the same local limestone and Lebanese cedar. "But no gold," Zechariah said aloud. "King Solomon used thousands of shekels of gold to adorn his temple."

"Never mind," Saba said. "Don't even try to compare the two. Besides, the Holy One wants our devotion, not our gold."

As they walked across the courtyard together to the priests' robing room, Zechariah heard the distant bleating and lowing of the sacrificial animals as they stirred in their pens outside the Sheep Gate. Today the priests would offer up one hundred bulls, two hundred rams, four hundred male lambs, and then twelve male goats for a sin offering, one animal for each of the tribes of Israel. The number of sacrifices was small compared with the thousands of animals offered at the dedication of Solomon's temple. But the remnant of God's people would gather here today in the newly cleared courtyards and feast on the fellowship offerings after the service. They would celebrate their restored communion with God.

God with us.

The thought continued to astound Zechariah.

"I see we aren't the only early risers," Saba said as they crowded into the robing room. Dozens of priests were already preparing for the day's work as the Levite choir and musicians warmed up on their instruments.

"This is a once-in-a-lifetime event, Iddo," the high priest said. "How can anyone remain asleep?" He looked resplendent in his ephod, breastplate, and embroidered robe, the white turban and golden headband on his head.

With so much to do, the two hours it took for Zechariah and the other priests to prepare passed quickly. He was grateful that he'd gotten an early start. Outside, he and Saba washed in the bronze lavers filled with living water. People were already assembling in the courtyards, and Zechariah could feel the excitement building, his heartbeat accelerating. He hoped that Safta, Yael, and the children arrived early enough to find a good place to stand. He searched for them in the crowd as he made his way to the musicians' platform but didn't see them.

He quickly reviewed the order of service for the celebration with the other musicians. It was nearly time for Prince Zerubbabel's procession to arrive, announced by a fanfare of shofars. As Zechariah crowded onto the platform and prepared to play, he overheard one of the Levite musicans say, "It isn't right that our prince can't be properly acknowledged as royalty. He's our king, from the royal line of King David."

"You're right," another man said. "He should be escorted here in splendor the way the Babylonian kings always were. Remember their processions?"

Zechariah remembered. He had once climbed to the top of Babylon's walls with his father to watch a royal procession. The king had traveled in a golden chariot pulled by white horses, and his entourage included soldiers on horseback, noblemen in chariots, and Babylon's glittering idols pulled on golden carts. The people lining the street had bowed down in homage, but Abba said he would never bow to pagan kings or gods, only to the Almighty One.

A few minutes later, Zechariah saw Prince Zerubbabel and his noblemen entering the temple courtyard. He drew a breath and sounded a fanfare on the shofar as the assembled people cheered. Someday, a descendant of David would reign on his throne and the whole world would bow before him. Zechariah closed his eyes as the future peeled open before him and God's word resounded in his heart like a trumpet blast:

Rejoice greatly, O Daughter of Zion! Shout, Daughter of Jerusalem! See, your king comes to you, righteous and having salvation, gentle and riding on a donkey, on a colt, the foal of a donkey. He will proclaim peace to the nations, and His rule will extend from sea to sea and from the River to the ends of the earth. . . . On that day a fountain will be opened to the house of David and the inhabitants of Jerusalem, to cleanse them from sin and impurity. . . . The Lord will be king over the whole earth. There will be one Lord, and his name the only name.

When Zechariah lowered the ram's horn and opened his eyes he was in Jerusalem again. This celebration was a mere foretaste of that day when the whole earth would proclaim the Messiah as its king—a descendant of King David and of Prince Zerubbabel. Now the prince stood with lifted hands before the waiting crowd.

"Praise be to the Lord, the God of Israel," Zerubbabel shouted, "who with His hands has fulfilled what He promised! As we gather here today to worship Him, He is with us! He is with us! And our ancient enemies are no more. The might of the Assyrians and Babylonians and Egyptians is broken. And yet we have survived. We, the sons of Abraham, are still a people blessed by Him as He has promised. We will continue to live and to serve Him as long as day and night endure, as numerous as the stars in the heavens. Praise His holy name!"

Zechariah sounded the shofar again and the people gave a great shout that echoed off the surrounding hills and resounded in the valley below. When the praise finally died away, the high priest began to pray. Zechariah recognized his words as King Solomon's prayer for the first temple's dedication.

"'O Lord, God of Israel, there is no God like you in heaven above or on earth below—you who keep your covenant of love with your servants who continue wholeheartedly in your way. . . . But will God really dwell on earth? The heavens, even the highest heavens, cannot contain you. How much less this temple we have built! Yet give attention to your servant's prayer and his plea for mercy, O Lord my God. Hear the cry and the prayer that your servant is praying in your presence. May your eyes be open toward this temple day and night, this place of which you said you would put your Name. . . . Hear from heaven, your dwelling place, and when you hear, forgive.'"

The priests began offering the sacrifices, sprinkling the blood around the altar and laying the portions on the altar grate. Smoke and fire ascended into the sky. All the while, antiphonal choirs of Levites sang the psalms of David accompanied by trumpets, cymbals, harps, and lyres. The people knelt on the ground, bowing in reverent worship as the deep voices of the Levites praised the Holy One.

When the sacrifices ended, another great shout of joy went up. Then all of the assembled people joined the choir in anthems of praise: *"Give thanks to the Lord for He is good. His love endures forever!"* The glorious sound surrounded Zechariah, enveloping him, until it seemed as though the heavens had opened and the angelic hosts had joined them in worship. The Almighty One, Creator of the universe, was worthy to be praised! His mercy and grace would never end! And that was the true source of Zechariah's joy, and of all true joy—knowing the love of God.

The sun gleamed from the high priest's headband and golden ephod as he stood before the people and lifted his hands to give the priestly blessing. "'The Lord bless you and keep you; the Lord make His face shine upon you and be gracious to you; the Lord turn His face toward you and give you peace.'"

Zechariah closed his eyes as the Holy One's face shone on him, filling him, consuming him. The temple courtyards fell silent as a sweet breeze rustled about them along with God's overwhelming presence and peace. Then the word of the Lord began swelling inside Zechariah, and he stepped forward to speak it with joy: "'Shout and be glad, O Daughter of Zion. For I am coming, and I will live among you,' declares the Lord. 'Many nations will be joined with the Lord in that day and will become my people. I will live among you, and you will know that the Lord Almighty has sent me to you. . . . ' Be still before the Lord, all mankind, because He has roused himself from His holy dwelling."

The dedication ceremony had ended. The great feast of celebration would begin. But Zechariah knew that this wasn't the end.

It was only the beginning.

Glossary

Abba—Father, Daddy.

Aron Ha Kodesh—The sacred ark in the Jewish house of worship where the Torah and other sacred scrolls are kept.

Bar Mitzvah—Son of the commandments—The ceremony at age twelve or thirteen at which a Jewish boy is considered a man and can read Scripture in the synagogue.

Beit Knesset—House of Assembly, later called a synagogue in Greek.

Bimah—The raised platform in a Jewish house of worship where Scripture is read.

Gan Eden—the Garden of Eden.

Haroset—A mixture of chopped apples, nuts, etc., eaten at Passover to remember the mortar used by slaves when building in Egypt.

Kippah—A small headcovering worn by Jewish men.

Levite—A descendant of the tribe of Levi, one of Jacob's twelve sons, who later became temple assistants.

Mikveh / Mikvoth (pl)—A bath used for ritual cleansing and purity.

457

Mishneh—The "second quarter" of Jerusalem, built during King Hezekiah's time.

Negev—The South, referring to the southern region of Israel.

Phylacteries—Small boxes containing Scripture that Jewish men attach to their foreheads and arms while praying. (See Deuteronomy 6:8).

Rebbe—Rabbi, teacher.

Saba—Grandfather.

Safta—Grandmother.

Seder—The Passover meal and celebration.

Shabbat—The Sabbath, a Jewish day of rest. It begins at sundown on Friday and lasts until sundown on Saturday.

Shalom—Peace. A greeting that can mean hello or good-bye.

Shalom bayit—Peace in the home.

Shofar—A musical instrument made from a ram's horn.

Simchat Torah—A holiday celebrating God's gift of the Torah at Mount Sinai.

Sotah—An adulteress.

Teshuvah—Repentance, turning from evil, changing directions in life.

Torah—The first five books of the Bible, which contain God's Law.

Yeshiva—A Jewish school where Scripture is studied.

Ziggurat—A stepped pyramid used for worshiping pagan gods, like the Tower of Babel.

A Note to the Reader

Careful study of Scripture and commentaries support the fictionalization of this story. To create authentic speech, the author has paraphrased the words of biblical figures such as Zechariah and Haggai. However, the New International Version has been directly quoted when characters are reading, singing, or reciting Scripture passages.

Interested readers are encouraged to research the full accounts of these events in the Bible as they enjoy the RESTORATION CHRONICLES.

Scripture references for *Return to Me:*

2 Kings 17:24–40
2 Kings 25:1–21
Ezra 1–6
Haggai 1–2
Zechariah 1–14
Daniel 5, 9

More From Bestselling Author Lynn Austin

To learn more about Lynn and her books, visit lynnaustin.org.

For the first time, beloved author Lynn Austin offers a glimpse into her private life as she shares the inspiring, deeply personal story of her search for spiritual renewal in the Holy Land. With gripping honesty, Lynn seamlessly weaves personal events with insights from Scripture as she finds hope, renewed faith, and a new sense of direction in her journey throughout Israel.

Pilgrimage

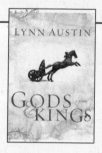

Experience the history and promises of the Old Testament in these dramatic stories of struggle and triumph. When invading armies, idol worship, and infidelity plague the life and legacy of King Hezekiah, can his faith survive the ultimate test?

CHRONICLES OF THE KINGS
Gods and Kings, Song of Redemption, The Strength of His Hand, Faith of My Fathers, Among the Gods